Adventure Guide

Belize

Adventure Guide

Belize

6th Edition

Vivien Lougheed

HUNTER

HUNTER PUBLISHING, INC,
130 Campus Drive, Edison, NJ 08818
732-225-1900; 800-255-0343; fax 732-417-1744
www.hunterpublishing.com

Ulysses Travel Publications
4176 Saint-Denis, Montréal, Québec
Canada H2W 2M5
514-843-9882, ext. 2232; fax 514-843-9448

Windsor Books
The Boundary, Wheatley Road, Garsington
Oxford, OX44 9EJ England
01865-361122; fax 01865-361133

ISBN-10: 1-58843-590-3
ISBN-13: 978-1-58843-590-3

*This and other Hunter travel guides are also
available as e-books through Netlibrary.com,
EBSCO, Amazon.com and other partners.
For details, e-mail us at comments@hunterpublishing.com*

This guide focuses on recreational activities. As all such activities
contain elements of risk, the publisher, author, affiliated individuals and companies disclaim responsibility for any injury, harm, or
illness that may occur to anyone through, or by use of, the information in this book. Every effort was made to insure the accuracy
of information in this book, but the publisher and author do not
assume, and hereby disclaim, liability for any loss or damage
caused by errors, omissions, misleading information or potential
travel problems caused by this guide, even if such errors or omissions result from negligence, accident or any other cause.

Cover photo: Yellow tube sponge & scuba diver above reef, Belize
© Brandon Cole/Alamy

Index by: Nancy Wolff

Maps by Kim André © 2007 Hunter Publishing, Inc.

1   2   3   4

www.hunterpublishing.com

Hunter's full range of guides to all corners of the globe is featured on our exciting website. You'll find guidebooks to suit every type of traveler, no matter what their budget, lifestyle, or idea of fun.

Adventure Guides – There are now over 40 titles in this series, covering destinations from Costa Rica and the Yucatán to Tampa Bay & Florida's West Coast, Vietnam, Laos & Cambodia and the Alaska Highway. Complete with information on what to do, as well as where to stay and eat, *Adventure Guides* are tailor-made for the active traveler, with all the practical travel information you need, as well as details of the best places for hiking, biking, canoeing, horseback riding, trekking, skiing, watersports, and all other kinds of fun. Cultural adventures might include dance lessons, cooking classes with local chefs, language courses and homestay programs.

Alive Guides – This ever-popular line of books takes a unique look at the best each destination offers: fine dining, jazz clubs, first-class hotels and resorts. In-margin icons direct the reader at a glance. Top-sellers include *St. Martin & St. Barts*, *The US Virgin Islands* and *Aruba, Bonaire & Curaçao*.

One-of-a-kind travel books available from Hunter include *Best Dives of the Caribbean; A Traveler's Guide to the Galapagos; Cruising Alaska* and many more.

Full descriptions are given for each book online at www.hunterpublishing.com, along with reviewers' comments and a cover image. You can also view pages and the table of contents. Books may be purchased on-line via our secure transaction facility.

Photo Credits

We are grateful to the following companies and organizations who allowed use of their photos in this book.

Slickrock Adventures: Pages 77, 61, 88, 136, 389, 403, 445, 507, 519, 521.

Island Expeditions: Pages 43, 46, 49, 59, 65, 89, 141, 194, 216, 237, 238, 239, 281, 355, 378, 422, 423, 436, 438, 439, 443, 457, 514, 529.

Belize Tourism Board/Naturalight Productions/RFCP: Pages 4, 7, 19, 22, 26, 27, 33, 52, 55, 56, 62, 124, 125, 195, 248, 252, 259, 260, 261, 269, 301, 306, 340, 352, 357, 365, 366, 367, 368, 377, 369, 375, 392 (Singing Sands), 393, 395 (Mariposa Resort), 397, 416, 419, 420, 421, 423, 428 (Circle C), 431, 447, 450, 451, 458, 468, 469 (Lily's), 483, 484, 493, 495, 496, 506, 515, 520.

GAP Adventures: Page 90, 463.

Journeys International: Pages 51, 91, 300, 495.

The Author, Vivien Lougheed: Pages 111, 114, 117, 166, 173, 180, 191, 198, 200, 217, 230, 247, 266, 270, 290, 295, 397, 308, 337, 348, 351, 359, 372, 383, 384, 404, 415, 424, 524.

All other images credit as shown.

ACKNOWLEDGMENTS

My first appreciation goes to John Harris for sticking with me even when he is lost in some foreign country or in one of my manuscripts. His dedication to me makes all my writing possible (and readable).

My second appreciation goes to Kim André. I've never before worked so closely with an editor and had so much fun.

Paige Pedersen, whose favorite country is Belize, is a major inspiration for me in my incessant travels. Her enthusiasm, along with Kelsey MacDonald's, helped me over many rough spots.

I thank Marsha-Jo Lomont for keeping in touch with me since I wrote Chickenbus in the early 1990s and for assisting me with my research in Belize. I'd like to thank her daughter Becky, too, for food, information, guiding services and patience.

Matthew Barnes I thank for his expert information about butterfly migrations, and Susan and Wil Lala for putting me onto the migrations to begin with. Thanks to Julian Sherrard for sharing information about canoeing in Belize, and to fellow Canadian Allie Ifield for supporting the women who take up the sport. Nadine Gray shared her extensive knowledge about archeology. More important, she told me where to eat.

I thank Linda Searl for looking up phone numbers and checking out bars or restaurants for me in the Belize City area. I also thank Leif Sverre and Lucy Wallingford for their advice on where to start my research and how to proceed once I found something of value. I thank Patricia Sturman for the big, cool glass of rum punch that she gave me when I needed it the most. Along with the rum came invaluable information. Thanks to Jonathan Lohr for his information about the Cayo district and to his mother Janice for her kindness in sharing her home.

I thank Knud Rasmussen for his dedication to Birdingpals and his help in promoting the idea in Belize. Thanks to Sam Tillett for recommending businesses in his area, some of whom are his competition. Thanks to Heather from Tsunami Tours, for all details she sent me about the Cayes, especially the information on food.

When we went to the Blue Creek Cave together, Luciano Logan shared his information about herbs and plants. Dennis Bruce was our patient driver. Steve Roberts was an eager source of information about the Rio Blanco area. Jessie Benner in Caye Caulker gave me the hints for picking a hotel from the Internet. Karen Pasquariello helps anyone visiting Belize. Thanks to Annie Heredia and those at the Green Reef Society for their information about sanctuaries around the Cayes. Thanks to Luis Ruiz and his brother David for their willingness to share information about Poustinia, and to Dr. Aranda for his information about the Garifuna. Golda Tillett from the Tourist Office worked on the weather charts, and Mrs. Young shared information about the Baboon Sanctuary. Thanks to Lan Sluder for looking up numerous things for me, and Placencia Tourism for their dedicated work in promoting the area.

Others who shared information about more than their respective businesses include those at Mayaland Tours, unBELIZEable Adventures, Roaring River Lodge, Global Travel in England, Five Sisters Lodge, Pook's Hill, Jaguar Creek, Kingfisher Adventures, CG Tours and Pine Ridge Lodge.

I'm sure there are many more I have forgotten. I thank everyone who helped build my archive of notes and my collection of over 2,000 e-mails gathered since I started these books.

PRAISE FOR THIS BOOK:

"... Thanks for a great guide book." Thomas Ven der Hout

"A 'must' for any destination traveler who wants to experience the outdoors of the country." *Midwest Book Review*

"Bursting with relevant and exciting information... " *Booklist*

"[Adventure Guides] aim to deliver content... Moderately-priced and truly user-friendly, they are packed with information that other series rarely cover." *Library Journal*

Contents

THE NORTH

■ MAPS

DEDICATION

I dedicate this book to my grandpar-
ents, Adam and Pauline Kwizak who, in
my youth, encouraged me to be adven-
turesome.

Introduction

In mid-winter, when gales off the plains of Siberia blow outside my window in northern Canada, I often close my eyes and visualize Belize. I see sun, sand and sea. I see white beaches, blue skies and clear waters. My memory, like a television camera, shifts to the largest coral reef in the Americas, a world brimming with exotic life: eels, jellyfish, sharks and fish striped in green and red, or dotted in purple.

This vision is what draws most people to Belize. They arrive from harsh climates and head for the islands to snorkel, swim, dive, fish, sail and hang out in the sun. They play golf, eat spicy foods, read books and drink beer. Most of all, they relax.

But if you take the time, you will find that there is more to Belize than a blissful rest in paradise. For archeology buffs there are numerous ancient Maya ruins to explore at will and an additional few that can be visited after a permit is obtained. Wildlife enthusiasts can visit the animal preserves and maybe catch a glimpse of a mountain cow (tapir) or jaguar, an osprey or toucan. There are over 200 species of birds to identify at any time of the year and an equal number of different types of orchids. Those interested in herbal medicines will find delight in a jungle full of potions to cure almost anything from a love-struck heart to a parasitic infection. For the photographer, there are an endless number of exotic images to capture and seldom a cloudy sky to dull the photograph. Belize is visually stunning.

The country also has an intriguing modern history involving pirates and buccaneers, wrecked ships and the horrors of the slave trade. Throughout the country, remnants of this history remain. If you take the time to listen, you can always find someone willing to tell you their own version of these historical events. Belizeans are proud of their exotic past and of the fact that their varied cultures live together peacefully, a big contrast to most of Central America.

Belize offers every type of accommodation imaginable, from the romantic grass hut on a secluded island to the luxurious five-star hotel complete with doorman. Restaurants can be as simple as someone's kitchen in the country or as dazzling as the dining room at Versailles. There are adventure specialists ready to give you a custom tour. If you're an independent traveler, head out on your own using this book or start walking and see where the road takes you.

The best time to come to Belize is during their summer, between November and May. This is the dry season, when clouds are seldom seen and the winds never rise above a few miles an hour. Winter, or wet season, is between May and November. This is when the waters can be a bit murky and the winds can increase to hurricane levels. However, winter offers its own splendor. The jungle becomes lush, the flowers abundant, and the skies dramatic. Archeological sites are less visited.

Regardless of the time of year you arrive, your interests or the style of travel you choose, one thing is certain: you will have a grand time in Belize and leaving will be difficult.

AUTHOR'S CHOICE OF MUST DO'S

- Look for birds in the gardens at Sittee River Lodge.
- Have dinner at Capricorn's on Ambergris Caye, then take the moonlight boat trip home.
- Take a boat tour to see manatee.
- Try overnight caving at Caves Branch River.
- Listen to the tree frogs at night at Aguada Inn.
- Listen to howler monkeys at the Community Baboon Sanctuary.

HISTORY

Anywhere I go, I want to know who was there before me. I want to know their stories. I've been traveling in Latin America for about 25 years now, so it is easy for me to get caught up in pre-Columbian history.

The history of Belize is part of the history of the greatest of all ancient American civilizations. During the Classic Period of the Maya, Belize was the heart of the empire, with an estimated population of one million people.

But even before the Maya, who?

PALEO-INDIANS

 The main pattern of Paleo-Indian settlement in the Americas (20000-7000 BC approx.) is generally agreed upon, though dates and details keep changing and infighting among anthropologists and archeologists is intense. By about 20000 BC, the last ice age was into a long decline. The ice pack that covered most of Canada and the northeastern United States retreated, creating a corridor from Beringia (connecting Asia and North America) down into ice-free southern Alberta. From there the rest of the Americas was wide open, but migrants kept moving south down the mountain chains. They stuck to the highlands because these areas supported the large herbivores that people ate: mammoth, mastodon, caribou, bison, horse, giant armadillo, giant sloth, guanaco, llama and vicuña.

The dating of sites in the Americas shows the progression, first north to south, then out to the sides. These dates also show how long the process took. Sites like Monte Verde in southern Chile have been reliably dated to about 12000-10000 BC. Estimates are that in Mesoamerica, the occupied parts of pre-Columbian Mexico and Central America, the highlands may have been populated as early as 18000 BC.

Archeologists also learn from the sites how the Paleo-Indians lived. In Monte Verde wood and skin huts contained brazier pits. Mastodon and other large herbivore bones have been found, along with the remains of seeds, nuts, berries and roots. Tools included stone hand axes, choppers and scrapers; some of these tools may have had wooden handles. The weapons were wooden lances and stones chosen or shaped so that they could be hurled by slings.

Once the Americas were occupied from top to bottom, population pressure and global warming resulted in movement into the lowlands, along the coastlines (which were further out to sea, then), and onto the Caribbean islands. The rising temperatures changed the highlands in particular, leaving them less habitable. In Mesoamerica, grasslands turned to deserts and large herbivores disappeared, leaving smaller game like rabbit and deer.

Along the Gulf of Mexico and the Caribbean, grasslands turned into forests. Since Mesoamerica was, and still is, rich in edible plants, like mesquite, cactus and agave, people ate more grains, fruits and vegetables and less meat, though ducks and dogs were being domesticated as a meat supply. By 11000 BC, people were eating wild corn, onions, amaranth (an herb with a showy flower), avocado, acorns, piñon nuts, chili peppers, maguey (used for making an alcoholic beverage), and prickly pear. By 8000 BC, the

Paleo-Indian period of Mesoamerica was coming to an end. Chasing game was giving way to clearing land, cultivating domestic plants and raising domestic animals.

By 7000 BC, the nomadic hunters were growing crops, especially squash, avocado and chili pepper. By 5000 BC, maize – a small, wheat-like ancestor of corn – was being grown in the Tehuacan Valley of Southern Mexico. By 3000 BC, pit house settlements were popular. A pit house was a tent-like wood, wattle and daubed-mud structure erected over a hole dug into the ground. By 2300 BC, pottery replaced stone jars and bowls, village life was the norm and population growth was exploding.

Pottery is evidence of early cave dwellers.

■ ARAWAK & CARIB INDIANS

There are no remains of Paleo-Indian settlements in Belize, though certainly such settlements did exist. Nor have anthropologists and linguists distinguished the shifting territories of the tribes, language groups or cultures that might first have settled in various parts of Mesoamerica. In Belize, the ancestors of the Maya might have come first. Other likely candidates are the Arawak and Carib Indians. Their settlements in Venezuela and the Guyanas date back to about 2000 BC. Eventually, they occupied much of the Caribbean shoreline and most of the islands. When Columbus first landed in America, he met the Arawak.

Both tribes have been traced to the upper Amazon River, the Arawak from around the junction of the Amazon and Rio Negro (where Manaus is now), and the Carib from further downriver. In the Amazon Basin, Arawak farming settlements have been traced back to about 7000 BC. The story of the Arawak and the Carib has become a kind of myth, a Cain and Abel story wherein the warlike, meat-eating (and cannibalistic) Carib chase the peaceful, vegetarian Arawak from the Amazon into the Orinoco, around the Caribbean shoreline and out onto the islands, and then back to the Orinoco again.

By the end of the 1500s, the Arawak had completely disappeared from the islands. Most of them (about 30,000 are left, due to the Caribs and European exploitation and disease) live in Venezuela and the Guyanas. The Carib are still found throughout the Caribbean islands.

Both tribes probably settled at various times in Belize, though the only real sign of them is the Carib blood that lives on in the Garifuna, Garinago, or "Black Carib" of Roatan and Bonacca, Honduras and Belize.

■ MAYA INDIANS

 The origins of the Maya in Paleo-Indian America have not yet been traced. Their language, it has recently been discovered, is similar to Uru and Chipaya in the highlands of Bolivia, so their migration pattern could be as complex as that of the Arawak and Carib.

The archeological record dates Maya sites in Southern Mexico, Guatemala, northern Honduras, El Salvador and Belize back to 2000 BC. The earliest known Maya settlement in Belize is Cuello in the Orange Walk District. It existed 2,600 years ago. Some archeologists think that the Maya could have spread from the coast into the interior.

In the Classic Period of Maya civilization (AD 250-1000), the biggest centers were in Guatemala, Chiapas, Campeche and Tobasco in Mexico, and in Honduras, El Salvador and the Yucatán. The major civic centers in Belize were Altun Ha, Lubaantun, El Pilar, Xunantunich, and Caracol.

The details of Maya civilization are gradually falling into place, though big pieces of the story are missing, like why the civilization began to decline shortly before the Europeans arrived. By that time, the big cities had been abandoned, and the center of Maya power was shifting north to the Yucatán. Overpopulation and depletion of land is the usual explanation. An overly rigid social structure – that favored inherited rank and knowledge over ability – is another. Many years of drought is the most recent explanation.

Maya civilization, along with the sister Mesoamerican civilizations like the Zapotec and Mixtec around Oaxaca and the Olmecs on the Gulf of Mexico, started to flourish around 500 BC. This development was a result of improved agricultural techniques. There was more time for consolidation and improvement. Textiles replaced hides, ceramics replaced worked stone, bricks replaced wattle. More and more plant types were domesticated (seeds selected, sorted and planted); Mesoamerica, particularly the Guatemalan highlands, was for a time one of the world centers of plant domestication. After harvests, fields were burned and seeds were planted with a pointed, fire-hardened digging stick; the same slash-and-burn method is still used today.

Governance, too, became more technical. The extended family units of the Paleo-Indians gave way to village clusters, and leadership became more bureaucratic – though the Maya city-states were never part of a monolithic empire as was the case with the Incas and Aztecs. During the Classic Period, Maya society was divided into ranks and classes. The supreme rulers inherited their positions, and were combined secular/religious leaders or priest-nobles. Artisans, merchants and farmers were also separate classes and inherited their specialties.

While Europe seemed to be stagnating during and after the decline of Roman power, Mesoamerican civilizations flourished.

The Maya **language** was written using a set of pictorial symbols from the Olmec. The symbols were like Chinese ideograms: a single picture represented a word, idea or number. Some glyphs are phonetic syllables that spell out words. Decoding is still in progress. Unfortunately, Spanish priests destroyed as much of this writing as they could. Almost everything written on parchment and bark and bound into books was burned. The Catholic church considered the writing heretical. But giant, carved-stone stone stelae, that seem to record important events and astronomical calculations have survived.

The Maya also developed a **numerology** that they used effectively, especially in their calculations of time. Their number system was based on 20, with the numbers 1 to 19 indicated by dots and dashes and the zero by a shell. This was much more efficient than the Roman numeral system being used in Europe at the time. The fact that the Maya had conceived of a zero put them ahead of European mathematicians. They were able to calculate numbers to over one million. Using their number system and astronomical observations, they calculated the year at 365.2425 days, long before Europeans arrived at their estimation of 365.2422 days. The Maya lunar calendar used a system of 18 months, each with 20 days, to equal 360 days. A final five "unlucky" days were at the end of the year. After calculating the orbit of Venus to within a few seconds, they even devised a Venusian calendar a full 1,000 years before Europeans were able to achieve this, and the Maya knew that Venus passed between the earth and the sun every 584 days. Modern calculations put it at 583.92 days.

These calculations, too, were carved on stone stellae, not as part of the calculation process, but to teach the calculations to the public. No one knows why the Maya were so interested in time. Macro-time, that is; they don't seem to have paid much attention to counting hours and minutes.

In **engineering**, the Maya were like the Egyptians as to the size of their projects. They built clay-lined reservoirs in places where water was scarce, and causeways to direct the flow of water or move it from place to place. They terraced hills – necessary when you

Maya ruins like this one are scattered throughout Belize.

live in mountains and depend on agriculture. They put swamps into production (mostly growing maize and cacao) with a system of "raised fields," dredging out soil and piling it at set intervals to create intersecting ridges. From the air, these raised fields look like small islands connected by dykes. They are being studied, in northern Belize, at the Pulltrouser Swamp, and their use between 150 BC and AD 850 has been conclusively documented.

 Pick up a copy of ***Pulltrouser Swamp: Ancient Maya Habitat, Agriculture and Settlement in Northern Belize***, produced by the University of Texas Press, 1983.

Finally, the Maya built incredible **ceremonial centers** in their cities. They did this without metal tools, the wheel (though they had toys with wheels) and the arch. Basically, they backpacked in rubble, dumped it, shaped it level by level (if a pyramid was being constructed), and then faced it with limestone blocks held together by mortar. Plazas were sloped to let water run off; in dry areas, they sloped into reservoirs or lined trenches that led to reservoirs. Roads connecting the plazas were made of rubble topped with limestone chips and packed with giant stones.

Temples were built on the tops of the pyramids, and roof combs topped the temples, making the structures very high. The main structure at Xunantunich is the second-highest Maya structure in Belize, measuring over 127 feet (38 meters).

The Maya never developed the arch. Instead, they put sapodilla wood or heavy stone lintels over doorways and used the corbel vault for chambers in adjoining palaces and temples. With the vault, the stones in a wall were inched inward until the two sides met at the top. The result was claustrophobic compared to an arch, and it made for narrow doors when it was used instead of a lintel.

Commerce and trade flourished among the Maya. They were not into refining metals, it seems, and imported **gold** came from southern Central America. **Salt** was being harvested along the coasts by 300 BC or earlier. Sea salt was eaten with food and used to preserve meat and fish for storage and transportation. Products from coastal areas – like salt and shells used in tools and jewelry – were transported far inland and traded for food and jade. This was all done using backpacks (the Maya didn't make use of pack animals). However, for accessing islands like the Turneffes, (18 miles offshore, past the Barrier Reef) and the cayes along the reef, the Maya built dugouts capable of holding up to 50 people and some freight. Cacao beans were used as currency. Cacao was the Maya's favorite drink; the beans were roasted, ground and mixed with maize and water.

The Maya had drugs too. Their alcohol was a fermented honey and bark drink called **balche**. It may have been used only for ceremonial purposes, though it would take a lot of evidence to convince me of that. The Maya were into visions as a part of their religious rituals, hallucinations created mainly by bloodletting, but also by the use of balche and wild tobacco which is much more potent than our tobacco. And for sports, there were ballparks, always located in the cities' ceremonial centers. The game, called Pok-A-Tok, featured a five-pound rubber ball and was a combination of basketball, football and soccer. Protective clothing made of wicker or leather was worn.

A GAME TO DIE FOR

The captains of the losing teams of the ballgames were all sacrificed to **Ek Chuah**, the Maya god of war and human sacrifice. The idea was to extract the victim's heart, while it was still pumping. This was usually done by plunging a dull knife into the chest of the captain. The blood from the heart was smeared on the stone image of Ek Chuah. If the sacrifice took place in a temple on top of a pyramid, the priests tossed the body to the pyramid's base, where it was skinned. The head priest then put on the skin and danced. Players, who earned less respect, were sometimes shot with bows and arrows rather than cut up with a knife.

THE SPANISH

 The Spanish had trouble colonizing Maya territory. Compared to the Maya, the Aztecs were pushovers and even the Incas were fairly easy. After a couple of defeats, **Cortéz**, conqueror of Mexico and founder of New Spain, pillaged the Maya island of Cozumel in present day Mexico, but still could not get a foothold on the Yucatán mainland. Spanish colonizers sailed the Honduran and Belize coastlines, but found the area uninviting – swamp and jungle inhabited by the unfriendly Maya.

Cortéz sailed north to Vera Cruz and in two years defeated the Aztecs. The Spanish then conquered territory from Panama to Peru, defeating smaller cultures like the Toltecs, Quiche and Cakchiquel in Guatemala, Nicaragua, El Salvador and Honduras. The Guatemala Maya were gradually driven towards the Yucatán.

There, **Francisco de Montego**, father and son, carried on the bloody 20-year conquest of the Maya, between 1527 and 1547. These were by far the biggest and bloodiest battles fought by the Spaniards in their New World, and they were fought for an area that had no gold or silver. The Spanish succeeded only because the Maya were at the same time involved in a civil war and smallpox had spread among them.

Even so, the struggle never really ended, and rebellions continue in Guatemala and Mexico, as the recent uprising in the Mexican state of Chiapas shows. The Maya are still the single greatest force of resistance to central (and often US-backed) authority in Central America and Mexico.

All this bloodshed is largely over the ownership of land. As the Spanish asserted control in the Yucatán and Guatemala, they set up a kind of feudal system, handing large estates (haciendas) out to their soldiers and bureaucrats. The Maya and other Indians (*peones*) working on these haciendas were exploited mercilessly – they still are, by the descendants of the original landed aristocracy. But regularly the Maya rose in revolt.

Belize is not a part of this sad history. Though the little country had its own problems, they were minor compared with those of Spanish Central America. This was partly because the Spanish had no obvious use for the area, and partly because Maya resistance in Belize and the Yucatán was so strong that it managed to hold the Spanish off long enough to allow other colonizers to establish themselves. These colonizers were the **English**. After the defeat of the Spanish Armada in 1588, the English began, along with the French and the Dutch, to colonize the Caribbean islands as well as parts of the Belize coastline.

■ THE BRITISH

 In 1631, Puritan settlers, colleagues of America's Pilgrim Fathers, came from Providence Island, off Nicaragua, and set up trading posts along the coast. The Spanish chased them off in 1641, capturing some of the 400 settlers and sending the rest running for the jungle. At the same time, colonies of log cutters, called Baymen, were beginning to establish themselves along the Mosquito Coast of Honduras and in Belize. Logwood was a valuable commodity, used for textile dyes. A little later, mahogany too became important to European furniture makers like Chippendale. The log cutters settled in for what turned out to be a long stay, with their black slaves, who soon outnumbered them. The settlers and slaves were the beginning of the Creole race that is now dominant in Belize.

Alongside these settlers and their slaves were **privateers**, who loved the sheltered coves and the maze of reefs and cayes off the Belize coast. From their bases here, they could attack the Spanish shipping lanes with near impunity.

The privateers were not desperate outcasts or criminals; they were venture capitalists. As likely as not, their leaders were English nobles, men of substance. Privateering was an important part of English foreign policy at the time. Armed with a letter of marque from the monarch, an ambitious or adventurous nobleman could raise money for the purchase and outfitting of a ship, and the hiring and arming of a crew. Huge profits were made by some of these adventurers, their investors and the crews they hired. Of course, some of the ships were never seen again. These venture capitalists had to keep track of the complex treaties that the monarchs of England and Spain were always signing. If they raided Spanish settlements and attacked Spanish ships when the Queen or King wanted peace, they ended up in the tower or dead.

> **DID YOU KNOW?** *Sir Walter Raleigh lost his head in 1618, two years after some of his ships and men attacked Los Castillos on the Orinoco River. At the time of the attack, King James was trying to make peace with Spain.*

Fighting between the Baymen and the Spanish carried on for a century, with the British government sometimes cooperating with the Spanish and sometimes with the Baymen (depending on what could be gained elsewhere in exchange for selling out the Baymen). In 1798, the Spanish made a final effort to clear the British from the mainland of Central America. They attacked St. George's Caye, the original capital of Belize until 1784 and the home of the original pirates and loggers. On September 10, in the **Battle of St. George's Caye**, 32 Spanish ships and 2,500 troops were routed by 240 Baymen. That day is now a national holiday.

With the invention of synthetic dyes the logwood industry suddenly collapsed, but the market grew for mahogany, so logging became even more important than before. In 1821, the threat from the Spanish navy disappeared when Spain was kicked out of the Americas, and Belize became the conduit for British goods, now in big demand by the new republics of Central America, which lacked ports on the Caribbean.

In 1838, Britain abolished slavery. This seemed to make little difference to the blacks, who continued logging. But it resulted in more immigrants; ill-treated slaves from elsewhere began slipping into Belize.

Spain's withdrawal did not end the bickering over Belize's borders, as both Guatemala and Mexico claimed "successor status" in regard to treaties made between Britain and Spain. Britain rejected these claims, and finally, in 1862 and at the request of the inhabitants, made Belize into an official British colony with the name British Honduras. In 1871, the British took over administration of the colony. To compensate Guatemala, which was most persistent in its claims, Britain promised to build a road from Belize to Guatemala City. Since this road was never built, the Guatemalans still claim Belize. Needless to say, no one in Belize wants to be a part of Guatemala. In fact, many Guatemalan Maya have settled in Belize.

■ INDEPENDENCE

 The logging boom collapsed in the middle of the 19th century, but still Belize remained a good place to live. Sugar and citrus fruit industries began to develop, in the north and south respectively, but it was essentially the subsidies from Britain that kept the economy afloat.

Compared to life in most other countries nearby, living in Belize seemed attractive. Belize received (and still receives) refugees and immigrants from places around the world like Canada and the United States, but particularly from Mexico and the Central American republics.

The **Garifuna** came in 1802 and, like the Arawaks, the Caribs and maybe the Maya, they took an unusual route. They hail from the eastern Caribbean. In 1675 a slave ship ran aground on the little island of Bequia, near St. Vincent. The island was populated by Caribs, who didn't eat the liberated slaves but mated with them. The Garifuna spread to other islands and were moved by the British to the islands of Roatan and Bonacca. From there, they spread to the mainland. About 30,000 Garifuna live in Belize and speak Carib. After Creole English and Spanish, Carib speakers are the next largest language group in Belize.

Between 1848 and 1858, the Caste War took place in the Yucatán. Maya peasants fought the central authority in Mexico and the local Mestizos who backed Mexico. First to arrive in Belize were the **Mestizos**, who were being slaughtered by the Maya, and then the **Maya**, who came when the Mexicans sent in the army. The Belize City merchants responded to the Caste War in their usual thoughtful way, by running guns into the Yucatán. Five thousand refugees entered Belize at this time. They took up farming in the empty north of the country. **Kekchi** and **Mopan Indians** fled slavery on the haciendas of Guatemala and settled in the south and west. Southerners, fleeing from the USA after the Civil War, settled in Toledo. Finally, from 1958 on, large numbers of German-speaking **Mennonites** entered from Canada and the USA. They took up tracts of land in the north and became Belize's great farmers.

But the economy remained stagnant. The locals wanted more independence, perhaps thinking that they could manage things better, and Britain was happy to comply. The Legislative Council, originally set up in 1871 to advise the Governor, was given more power and independence. In the 1930s and '40s, a two-party system evolved; it still exists in the form of **PUP** (People's United Party - slightly left) and **UDP** (United Democratic Party - slightly right). The Assembly gradually came to run everything but foreign affairs, defense and internal security. In 1982 a new constitution was drawn up and Belize became fully independent and a full member of the **British Commonwealth of Nations**.

In the course of this, and especially at independence, there were a number of threats from Guatemala that required the presence of the British armed forces, but through the 1970s Latin American countries switched from backing Guatemala to backing an independent Belize. In 1980 the UN passed a resolution demanding the secure independence of Belize. No country voted against this; Guatemala abstained.

In sum, Belize remains a poor country, but a proud and independent one – proud especially of avoiding the ongoing horrors that occur in the rest of Central America. There's no great gap between rich and poor, and the mix of ethnic groups is easy. Britain still subsidizes the economy, and the US is the major source of investment dollars. The main objective of government now is to make the country self-sufficient in food; about a fourth of what Belize eats is imported. Through the first half of the 20th century, it had nothing much to sell but sugar, which provided about a third of the country's export income, but the sugar markets fell in the 1980s. Still, the country has the smallest foreign debt in Central America, and most of that debt is owed to international organizations and foreign governments rather than to private banks with high interest rates. Recently, too, a lot of foreign capital (mainly US) has gone into citrus, cocoa, seafood, tourism and non-traditional agriculture. The benefits are coming in. Citrus fruits and tourism are booming.

 For an entertaining, readable history of Belize, pick up Alan Twigg's **Understanding Belize; A Historical Guide**, by Harbour Publishing, British Columbia, 2006. It sells for $25 Cd and can be ordered online direct from the publisher.

GOVERNMENT

Belize is a constitutional monarchy, one of those kinds of governments that the British left around the world when they pulled out of the Empire business. The monarch is the British King or Queen, but the constitution gives the monarch – or the monarch's representative, the Governor General – a titular or ceremonial status only. Proponents of the monarchy in British Commonwealth countries argue that in times of constitutional crisis, when something happens to incapacitate the government, the Governor General can take over and maintain stability. The monarchy doesn't cost Belizeans a cent. However, they get the pleasure of participating in the royal family gossip as part of the family, rooting for favorites. Generally, the Queen is popular in Belize. Prince Charles is another matter; people are divided. Diana was loved.

The **Constitution** of 1981 defines the structure of government, enforces universal suffrage (starting at age 18), defines certain rights and freedoms, and requires a general election every five years at least. Legislative power is in the 29-member **House of Representatives**, and executive power in the **Cabinet**, which is appointed by the Prime Minister, the leader of the party that got the most seats in the House. The Prime Minister chooses Cabinet members from both the House and the Senate. They are usually members of his own party. The Cabinet makes policy for the government. Its deliberations are secret; there is open debate in the Cabinet, but Cabinet members must keep that debate confidential.

In effect, the Prime Minister has near-dictatorial powers for five years, assuming that his majority in the House is solid. This is the major difference between the British (Westminster) and the republican (i.e., US) systems.

The system is stable if there are only two parties; one is certain to get a majority. But losing a vote means loss of confidence in the executive; a general election must be called. This can happen, too, on controversial issues where members of the ruling party might break rank and "cross the floor" to vote against their Prime Minister.

There is no proportional representation; this also tends to make for a clear majority for one party. The country is divided into 29 constituencies; whoever wins in each one, goes into the House. Though a third of Belizeans live in Belize City, their representatives cannot dominate the Assembly.

There is a second house, the Senate. It has eight appointed members: five by the Prime Minister, two by the leader of the opposition, and one by a council that advises the Governor General. The Senate studies legislation and makes recommendations, but it cannot pass legislation.

CIVIL SERVICE

For the Civil Service, there are six administrative districts run by government functionaries: Belize, Cayo, Corozal, Orange Walk, Stann Creek and Toledo. Each district has a town board that runs the main city. However, Cayo has two boards; one for San Ignacio and the other for Benque Viejo. Belize is the only district that has a city council.

The slightly left-wing **People's United Party** (PUP) generally forms the government in Belize. This was the case before independence too. For many years, **George Cadle Price** was its leader and the Prime Minister of the country. The UDP, an amalgam of three earlier parties, is the slightly right-of-center party, usually but not always in opposition.

In its foreign policy, Belize tends to side with the US on international affairs and supports a moderate free enterprise line. However, it has been careful to keep its distance from US policies as applied to Central America, not wanting to be drawn into conflicts like those that occurred in Panama, Nicaragua and El Salvador, and that are ongoing in Guatemala. Belize feels closer ties to the Commonwealth Caribbean states than to the Central American ones. But those ties, formalized in CARICOM (created from the words, Caribbean Community), can bring only limited economic benefits.

The **Belizean Defense Forces** (BDF), which include an army of about 600 (including a few female platoons), a navy of some half-dozen patrol boats and 60 sailors, and an air force comprising a couple of transport planes and the people that fly them, gets aid and training from Britain, Canada and the US. There is an officer training arrangement with Britain, involving on-loan officers from the British armed forces. The BDF's main base is near the international airport. Alongside British troops that have been based in Belize since independence and due to the tensions between Belize and Guatemala, the BDF watches the country's borders.

The **Belize Police Force** (BPF) is about the same size as the BDF and is the civilian police. There are also 32 members of the **Tourist Police Force**, most of whom are in Belize City, patrolling the popular tourist areas. However, since Godfrey Smith has been appointed as the Minister of Tourism, he has promised tourist police to be present in Cayo, Stann Creek, Placencia, Cay Caulker and San Pedro. To date, BC, Cay Caulker and San Pedro have tourist police.

ECONOMY

Belize is mostly an agrarian society, so more than half of its export income is from the production of sugar cane, citrus, bananas and vegetables. Half of this production is exported to the United States.

Historically, Belize has been an exploited colony where the people worked for low wages, lived in poor housing, suffered malnutrition and had almost no health care. In 1950, the People's United Party was formed; their main aim was to gain political and economic independence for the people of Belize. Their leader was **George Price** and in 1981, when independence from Britain was finally gained, he became the first Prime Minister.

The fight for a better life for the people was a long one. National strikes were countered when the large-farm owners employed scab labor (non-union workers) and the government protected the scabs with armed police guards. The struggle continued over wages and reforms. Finally, between 1971 and 1975, 525,000 acres of land was taken out of the hands of the few and redistributed.

George Price was the country's first Prime Minister.

US DOLLAR & THE IMF

 Following land redistribution was the collapse of the Belize dollar. In order to keep the economy fairly stable, the government in 1976 pegged the currency to the American dollar at a fixed rate of two to one.

However, the plummeting value of sugar crops in the 1980s resulted in Belize taking out IMF loans that, in turn, put more stress on the economy. Because their export market is always below the import requirements (in 1994, it fell short by $226.6 million) Belize seems to be always in the red.

ADD UP THE FIGURES

Figures from the 2003 Index of Economic Freedom.
EXPORT INCOME: 532.7 million in 2003
    66% came from sugar, bananas, citrus & vegetables; 22% from textiles; 8% from seafood; 3% from lumber.
    42% is traded with the US; 33% with Great Britain; 14% with the European Union; 6% with the Caribbean community; 1% with Canada.
BELIZE IMPORTS: $669 million
    41.4% is from the US; 12.2% from Mexico; 5.9% from the UK; 5.5% from Cuba; and 5.5% from Japan.

■ NEW PROMISE

 Mining is beginning to show promise. The Toledo district has enough dolomite (used in fertilizer) to support a viable extraction and processing industry, but so far not enough has been processed to make a huge difference in attracting foreign dollars.

Tourism is a big factor. There is a belief that the low-budget travelers who patronize local businesses, rather than the big resorts, benefit the people most. Some believe that the resorts take a lot of the profit out of the country. Bookings are arranged and paid for elsewhere and profits go to foreign banks. On the other hand, the larger resorts employ 25% of the working population, albeit at minimum wage and with no extra benefits like paid health care.

The cruise ship industry, once thought to be a great boon for Belize, has proven to be exactly the opposite. Cruise ship visitors, known locally as "the flushers," benefit only the select few. The impact on the land is immense and those working in the industry feel that this is a new form of exploitation.

Exports and tourism pay for some of Belize's food imports, but not all. Attempts to increase manufacturing are stymied by the high cost of electricity. This is also what keeps foreign investment out.

■ UNIONS, OR LACK THEREOF

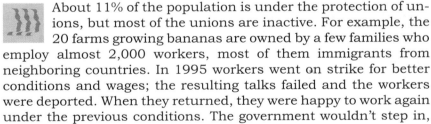 About 11% of the population is under the protection of unions, but most of the unions are inactive. For example, the 20 farms growing bananas are owned by a few families who employ almost 2,000 workers, most of them immigrants from neighboring countries. In 1995 workers went on strike for better conditions and wages; the resulting talks failed and the workers were deported. When they returned, they were happy to work again under the previous conditions. The government wouldn't step in, saying that the workers must negotiate with each individual farm owner rather than the industry in its entirety. With workers unable to form a united front, they have little power.

But there is progress. Fyffles PLC of Ireland is the fourth-largest fruit and vegetable company in the world. It is fairly prominent in Belize, and has a decent reputation for fair play. When it became public information that aerial spraying of crops was practiced in Belize and housing conditions were poor, the company actually stopped spraying from the air, reduced chemical pollution and built some new houses for the workers.

The lack of union power shows in wages. Women are paid an average of one third to one quarter less than men doing the same job. A field worker makes US $10 a day ($1.13 per hour minimum wage). The 5,000 workers in the tourist industry make even less.

Domestic workers and shop attendants (mostly women) earn 87¢ an hour and they are required to work six days a week for a total of 45 hours. Construction workers fare a bit better; a carpenter makes about $17-$20 a day, and a foreman makes even more.

With these types of wages, few people own cars or have air conditioning for their homes. But most have food and shelter, their children go to school to age 14 and, as long as they are not buying heavily taxed imported items, their life is not deplorably poor.

On the upside, taxes paid on earnings (including corporate earnings) never rise above 25% and every worker gets 13 paid public holidays, two weeks vacation with pay and up to 16 days a year in sick leave. These are all conditions imposed by the government.

PEOPLE & CULTURE

Seven major languages are used by the people who live in Belize.

- **BELIZE CREOLE ENGLISH:** 55,051 first-language speakers, plus about 103,000 second-language users, for a total of 158,000. Nearly everyone in Belize uses Creole. There are 15 Creole dialects in the Caribbean, 10 in Africa and 10 in the rest of the world. Belize Creole English is a heavily accented and bastardized form of English with loads of Misquiti, Spanish, Maya and African words thrown in for fun. An example: "Wat wi di du" means, What are we doing?

- **ENGLISH:** 60,000 speakers, although most use it as a second language. English is the national language, used in education, government and business.

- **SPANISH AND SPANISH CREOLE:** There are about 60,000 first- and second-language speakers, and that number is increasing as Maya and Mestizo refugees come to the country from Guatemala and El Salvador.

- **GARIFUNA OR CARIB:** 12,274 first-language speakers.

- **KEKCHI, MOPAN & YUCATECAN DIALECTS:** 16,000 first-language speakers.

- **MENNONITE GERMAN:** 5,763 first-language speakers.

CULTURAL GROUPS

GARIFUNA

Garifuna number over 55,000, most of whom live in villages along the Caribbean coast from Belize to Nicaragua. Honduras has the largest Garifuna population.

Garifunas are a mixture of black African slaves and the Indians of the Lesser Antilles who migrated from Guyana and the Orinoco River area of Venezuela to St. Vincent Island. During a storm in 1635, two sailing ships capsized near St. Vincent, freeing the slaves. Some made it to shore. The interbreeding between the blacks and the original Indian settlers resulted in this unique cultural group.

FASCINATING FACT: *In the Arawak language, Garifuna means "cassava-eating people."*

By 1700, the black-Indian mix had become the dominant group on St. Vincent, living in the mountains where they became good at guerrilla warfare. They actually controlled one end of the island, much to the disgruntlement of the British, who in turn treated the Garifuna harshly.

As conflicts continued, the Garifuna attempted to drive out the English, but were quickly defeated. In 1797, fearing more problems, the English decided to have the Garifuna shipped to Jamaica and then to Roatan Island in Honduras. The Garifuna were not satisfied with their new island and soon turned it over to the Spanish. They headed for the mainland of Central America and settled along the coast of Belize and Honduras.

The first to arrive in Belize came on November 19th, 1823. Nine years later there were settlements at Stann Creek, Seine Bight, Punta Gorda and Barranca.

AUTHOR'S NOTE: *Name calling, swearing and even gossiping are considered aggressive acts and are highly frowned upon by the Garifuna.*

The Garifuna have their own unique language and maintain customs and traditions that reflect the mixing of the two cultures. The

Garifuna are Catholic, but continue to tie many of the Afro-Indian rituals into church ceremonies. All religious practices include a philosophy of balance and harmony of the spirit. There are two types of holy men in the Garifuna tradition. The **curandero** is a healer of physical problems who uses herbs and natural products. A **buyei** is a spiritual healer, chosen by the spirit world. A curandero and a buyei may be a man or a woman. Once selected, the buyei accepts the role of spiritual leader and lives in a hut for 15 days to meditate on the new life. He or she sees only one woman during that time, and she prepares anything the new buyei might need.

After the initiation ritual is over, the buyei becomes the link between this earth and the next. Occasionally, the visitation of a spirit to the buyei results in a great party where drinking, music and dancing occurs for many hours. The Garifuna believe that freeing the spirit is important and this is done with a special celebration.

Traditional Garifuna music is usually of the call-and-response nature, while drums beat in the background. The accompanying dances can be sexually segregated or sexually seductive, depending on the celebration. The songs often originate as working songs, the rhythm designed to make the chore easier.

Garifuna almost always live near the sea and believe that there is magic where the land and sea meet. Inside their houses, a clay-brick dome oven is often found. I have tasted breads and meat cooked in such ovens and the flavor can't be beaten. A pestle and mortar is usually used for food and herb preparation. Woven palm leaves are used to strain and refine cassava.

MESTIZOS

Mestizos (a mix of Spanish and Indian) came as refugees escaping the Caste War in the Yucatán. The rest came from Guatemala and El Salvador. They speak English with outsiders, but usually speak Spanish in the home. Those living in the north speak with a Mexican accent, while those in the south generally have a Guatemalan accent.

Mestizo towns are traditionally Spanish in design, with a central town square bordered on one side by a Catholic church. Their food is also traditional Spanish-American and fairly boring. They serve beans and rice or rice and beans (for variety). This is interspersed with handmade tortillas (a flat corn bread) or tamales, a corn paste with a piece of spiced meat in the center. The tamale is rolled into a banana leaf and cooked.

MENNONITES

The Mennonite church was founded in Zurich, Switzerland in 1525. These anti-Catholics were originally called Anabaptists because they insisted on the rebaptism of adults rather than infant baptism.

The church was named after Menno Simons, the Dutch leader who encouraged his followers to move into Holland. During the early years, the Mennonites recruited followers from the Catholic, Lutheran and Reformed groups but, due to religious persecution, their numbers soon decreased.

Mennonites believe that they belong to the true Reformation of the Christian faith. They also believe that the state should be run separately from the church and they practice a loose form of communal living. This lifestyle has often been misunderstood and classified as communism.

Mennonites are a peaceful people who reject all violence and war. This pacifism caused some hard feelings during World War II when they became 40% of all conscientious objectors in the US and 80% of those in Canada.

As they searched for religious freedom, Mennonites moved across Europe, Russia and the Americas. By the end of World War I, they had migrated as far south as Mexico and, by the early 1950s, were looking at Belize.

The acclaimed author, Emory King helped persuade the Mennonites to settle in Belize. They readily did this, and worked hard to make the land into productive farms.

Mennonites can be seen around the country in their distinct clothing; the women wear ankle-length dresses and head coverings in the form of a straw hat or a kerchief and the men have bibbed overalls, cleaned and ironed to perfection. Their farms are efficiently run and you'll often see Mennonites in towns selling their produce. They operate their own schools, banks and churches. Much to the chagrin of some Belizians, they are also exempt from property taxes and do not serve in the military.

There is a division of belief within the Mennonites. Some believe in having modern facilities like tractors and electricity, while others want to stay with the old ways. The latter use horses and carts to come to town, pump water manually from their wells and reject the use of electricity.

Regardless of their differences, Mennonites are an asset to the Belizean economy. Just purchase some vegetables or fruit from them some time and you will agree.

Kids in any Latin American country seem happy.
These Belizeans are no exception.

MAYA INDIANS

The Maya Indians of Belize include the **Kekchi**, the **Mopan** and **Yucatán** Maya. Each of these distinct groups has its own language. Many of the Guatemalan Maya refuse to speak Spanish, the language of their oppressors.

For the most part the Maya are farmers who grow corn, rice and wheat. They live in traditional villages with thatched-roof houses. Their religion is Catholic, with Maya rituals included in the ceremonies and Maya gods personifying some of the saints. They use herbal medicines rather than Western chemical medicine.

EAST INDIANS

This group arrived in Belize after the emancipation of black slaves in 1838. They came as indentured servants, meaning they were just like slaves. An indentured servant must work for his master for an agreed-upon number of years before he is free to work for himself. However, this indenture was often extended for long periods of time and the Indians found it difficult to start their own lives. The original East Indians kept up some of their cultural traditions.

Recently, a new wave of East Indians is migrating to Belize, and the people seem to be assimilating into the Mestizo society.

CHINESE

Chinese immigrated to many countries, including Belize, in the mid-1800s. They came as laborers and kept a close community of their own. When the Japanese invaded China just before World War II, another influx of Chinese immigrants came to Belize. The third and final group came in the 1970s from Hong Kong and Taiwan.

Presently, there is a solid community throughout Belize. They have integrated well with the other groups. Freedom of religion is tolerated in Belize, and some Chinese still practice Buddhism.

GEOGRAPHY

■ HOW THE LAND WAS FORMED

 Belize and the Mexican states of Yucatán, Quintana Roo and Campeche, as well as parts of Tabasco and Chiapas, make up an 85,000 square-mile limestone platform that emerged from under the ocean about 80 million years ago.

Because of tectonic movements and climatic changes, water covered and drained from the land many times. This affected the limestone. As the seeping water eroded the rock, caverns, caves and underground tunnels were formed. Probably the largest cave system in North and South America underlies the Maya Mountains near the Guatemala border in western Belize. It's known as the **Chiquibul** complex.

Due to the water and plate movements, ripples from the old seabed form valleys with low ridges. The valleys flow north to south and fill with water. These formations are clearly visible since the forests have been cleared, especially in Northern Belize.

 MYSTERIOUS MAYA: *The ancient Maya believed that the land on which they lived sat on the back of a turtle that floated in the sea.*

While the North American plate moved in a westerly direction, it collided with the Caribbean plate that was heading east. This activity caused the land to lift, forming the **Maya Mountains** of southern Belize. These are dated from between 65 and 34 million years ago and occupy almost half the land mass of Belize. They run from the Guatemalan border for 70 miles in a northeasterly direction. The mountains include limestone, dolomite and granite. **Mount Victoria**, standing at 3,680 feet (1,122 meters), has until recently

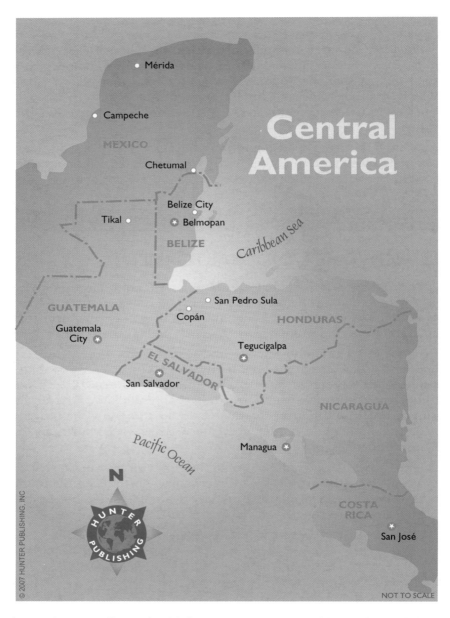

been given credit as the highest mountain in Belize. In fact, Doyles Delight in the Cockscomb Range stands at 3,688 feet (1,124 meters) above sea level. The cave system lying under these mountains has caverns that run from three to nine miles in length; one of the caves, the Chiquibul complex, is the largest in the Western Hemisphere.

ENVIRONMENTS

 Moving from the Maya Mountains to the south and east towards the ocean, the land falls quickly; within 15 miles you're at sea level. The terrain along the edge of the sea is mostly **swamp** and **mangrove**, but the land between the higher peaks and the swamps is **rainforest**, with a dense cover of palms, ferns, lianas and tropical cedar. It rains most of the year in the south; annual precipitation can total 150 inches (960 cm) or more. The north gets less than 60 inches (387 cm) and is dry from November to May.

The land falling to the west of the Maya Mountains is the "pine ridge," a **wet savanna** that has poor, sandy soil and grows little but pine trees. These lower hills, which are crossed by logging roads, cover hundreds of square miles.

The central and northern region is **savanna**. The river valleys that drain the mountains from the south have spread a thin layer of soil into the southern part of this savanna and in this soil grows some of the richest hardwoods in the world. **Hardwoods** cover about 70% of the entire savanna. Much to the credit of Belize, 44% of this hardwood forest is virgin.

The low-lying savanna in the north is spotted with swamp areas and large lagoons, which are drained by rivers flowing into the Caribbean. Again, its depressions run north and south.

Along the Caribbean Sea, Belize's coastline is rimmed with **mangrove swamp**. Not good for human habitation, but rich ecologically, it houses hundreds of bird and fish species.

OFFSHORE

 Beyond the coast is a 150-mile **barrier reef**, the longest unbroken barrier reef in the hemisphere, and second in size only to Australia's Great Barrier Reef.

The coral that is part of the barrier reef has been forming for millions of years. As the coral reef develops, the number and types of animals in and around the reef are constantly changing.

Coral is a small polyp that, for survival, requires saline water of a temperature between 70°F (21°C) and 86°F (30°C). Their life starts at about 125 feet (38 meters) below the surface, where they consume minute organisms and dissolved gasses. They form group colonies, attaching themselves to rocky coasts and other coral to

Belize's many underwater treasures, such as this coral, attract thousands of divers to the region.

build up skeletons. The cup-like cavities you may see in mature coral crustaceans were once occupied by the living polyps.

The skeletons that form the crustaceans are made of calcium carbonate and take three forms: **fringing reefs, barrier reefs** and **atolls**. Some of these formations descend to 5,000 feet (1,500 meters) below sea level. Since coral can't form that deep, scientists have proposed rising sea levels due to the melting of Pleistocene ice caused these deep formations. Also, the settling of landforms caused the build-up of reefs in successive platforms.

- Fringing reefs extend outward from the shore of a mainland or island like a shelf. The outer edge occasionally rises like the edge of a saucer, forming a rim that is cut through by channels.

- Barrier reefs are characterized by a shallow channel or lagoon between reef and shore.

- Atolls are ring- or horseshoe-shaped reefs that surround lagoons. They may have breaks in them through which the tide rushes. A number of small atolls may form rings that surround larger lagoons. Some atolls originally surrounded volcanic islands that subsided below the surface, leaving the encircling coral reef. Coral islands are atolls with volcanic rock close to the surface. Wave action pushes up coral sand over the reef. This makes for poor soil, although palm trees and other salt-resistant plants can germinate in it.

Belize's famous Blue Hole is a classic atoll.

As the most recent glaciers melted, the sea rose and the Caribbean Coral Reef ecological system became what it is today; a marine biological museum protected from the ravages of a raging sea by the coral walls. It houses millions of fish.

> **DID YOU KNOW?** *Black coral, now protected, grows one millimeter every hundred years.*

For today's traveler, Belize offers a diverse landscape of cool pine forests, sauna-like jungle, palm-dotted islands, parched brown savanna, majestic mountains both above and below sea level, and flat, muddy swamp.

PARKS

There are eight protected areas in Belize that are managed by the **Belize Audubon Society**. Mandated by the government in 1984, the Audubon Society has worked hard toward the "sustainable use and preservation of natural resources." The society is a non-profit organization that is not affiliated with any political party.

At present, the eight areas under the society's care cover about 162,000 acres of land and include two natural monuments, three wildlife sanctuaries, two national parks and one nature reserve.

To assist the society in protecting, administrating, researching and managing these areas, I encourage you to visit the parks, pay the foreigners' entrance fee and, if you can, leave the society an added donation. The Audubon Society is doing a good job in Belize, so I

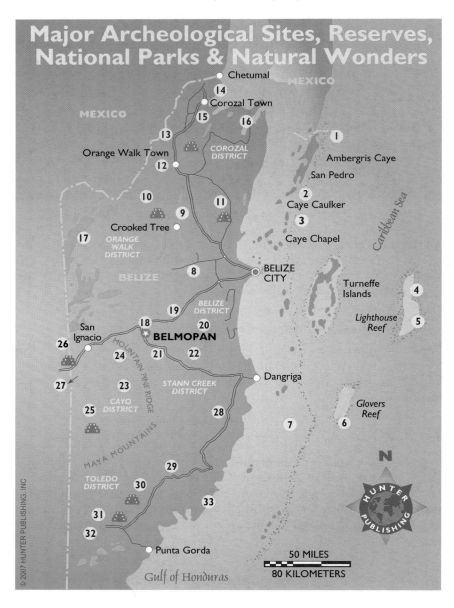

Major Archeological Sites, Reserves, National Parks & Natural Wonders

suggest you forget the irritation of paying extra as a foreigner and contribute. Your children will benefit.

AUDUBON SOCIETY-MANAGED AREAS

At present the following places are under the management of the Audubon Society:

- Guanacaste National Park
- Blue Hole National Park
- Victoria Peak Natural Monument
- Cockscomb Basin Wildlife Sanctuary
- Crooked Tree Wildlife Sanctuary
- Tapir Mountain Nature Reserve
- Half Moon Caye Natural Monument
- Blue Hole Natural Monument

The Audubon Society on Fort Street in Belize City has a nice shop across from the Tourist Village (see page 116) selling souvenirs and t-shirts. The proceeds from these items go toward the society's operation. For more information about the society, please visit their website at www.belizeaudubon.org.

KEY

The Cayes

1. Bacalar Chico Marine Park
2. Hol Chan Reserve
3. Caye Caulker Forest Reserve
4. Great Blue Hole
5. Half Moon Caye National Monument
6. Glovers Reef Reserve
7. South Water Caye/ Tobacco Caye Reserve; Laughingbird Caye National Park

The North

8. The Bermudian Landing Community Baboon Sanctuary
9. Crooked Tree Wildlife Sanctuary/Chau Hix ruins
10. Lamanai Archaeological Reserve
11. Altun Ha ruins
12. Cuello ruins
13. Nohmul ruins
14. Santa Rita ruins
15. Cerros ruins
16. Shipstern Wildlife Reserve
17. Rio Bravo Conservation Area/ La Milpa ruins

The West

18. Guanacaste Park
19. Belize Zoo
20. Monkey Bay Wildlife Sanctuary
21. Blue Hole/St. Herman's Cave
22. Five Blues Lake National Park
23. Mountain Pine Ridge Forest Reserve/ Slate Creek Preserve
24. Hidden Valley Falls
25. Caracol ruins/Chiquibul Forest Reserve
26. Xunantunich ruins
27. To Melchor, Tikal, Flores (Guatemala)

The South

28. Cockscomb Jaguar Reserve
29. Bladen Branch Nature Reserve
30. Nim Li Punit ruins
31. Lubaantun ruins
32. Uxbenka ruins
33. Monkey River Wildlife Sanctuary

EARTH'S TIME

490-443 MILLION YEARS AGO. Oceans cover North America and then drain. Corals and clams evolve.

443-417 MILLION YEARS AGO. The earth floods and the seas recede leaving salt deposits. Sea life is dominated by corals and arthropods. Fish develop jaws!

417-354 MILLION YEARS AGO. Appalachian Mountains form in North America. South America takes on its present position. This is the age of fish, when armored fish, lung fish and sharks develop. Ozone layer forms around the earth

354-290 MILLION YEARS AGO. The continents collide and the climate cools. Cockroaches emerge. The first reptiles emerge. Trees, club mosses and ferns evolve.

290-248 MILLION YEARS AGO. Glaciations occur and huge deserts abound; some corals become extinct. Herbivores and carnivores, terrestrial and aquatic divisions develop.

248-144 MILLION YEARS AGO. Continents separate and the climate warms; 75% of the earth's reptiles and amphibians die. Atlantic Ocean forms and the western mountains on the American continent form. Many dinosaurs disappear. Frogs, toads and salamanders appear. Small mammals develop.

144-65 MILLION YEARS AGO. Continents take their present shape. More mountains form and the climate warms; the remaining dinosaurs disappear.

65-34 MILLION YEARS AGO. Continental plates shift and the Maya Mountains in Belize form. Horse, rhino and camel can be found. Whales and dolphins develop.

34-5 MILLION YEARS AGO. Oceans become established. Early primates develop. Whales and walruses are now present, as are herons, ducks, eagles, hawks and crows.

5-1.8 MILLION YEARS AGO. Isthmus of Panama changes the ocean's circulation. Plates keep shifting. Primates evolve.

1.8 MILLION-10,000 YEARS AGO. Thirty percent of the earth is covered in ice. Moose, elephant, musk ox, saber-tooth cats and sloth are now present.

10,000 YEARS TO PRESENT. Glaciers recede. Tourists evolve and roam the earth.

CLIMATE

Generally speaking, Belize has a sub-tropical climate tempered by trade winds. The dry season runs from November to May. Temperatures range from 50°F (10°C) to 97°F (35.6°C), although the inland range is much greater.

Annual rainfall can be anywhere from five inches (12.5 cm) in the north to 300 inches (760 cm) in the south. But as you travel in Belize, you'll notice that few days go by without at least a little sunshine and, even during the height of rainy season, there are days without rain. It is the humidity of the country that makes the heat seem so oppressive. All year, the humidity can run from 85% to 90% and occasionally it will go higher.

MAUGER WEEK

Mauger season in August is when the trade winds stop and the mosquitoes start. Temperatures go up and rum supplies in stores throughout the country go down. The drinking is an attempt to nullify the discomfort felt from the season. It lasts about a week.

■ FORCES OF NATURE

There are two climatic disturbances that can affect the general patterns in Belize. One is the northern wet air mass that is pushed south from Canada and the US. This **arctic front** usually forces itself down the continent between November and February, bringing colder temperatures and widespread heavy rains. It causes choppy seas and forces small fishing vessels to hide in the mangrove swamps. But hiking in the rainforests is made more pleasant with the cooler temperatures.

> AUTHOR NOTE: *Huracon is the Carib God of Evil. Once winds hit 156 mph/250 kmh, the storm is categorized as class 5 and considered a hurricane.*

Hurricanes are the second type of disturbance that affects Belize. A hurricane is created when an area of low pressure forms in the upper atmosphere and the tropical waters of the Atlantic warm to over 80°F (26°C) to a depth of 200 feet (60 meters). The heat of the water causes circulation of the winds to accelerate. When the winds are less than 40 mph, it's called a tropical depression, but with stronger winds, it's called a hurricane.

Hurricane season starts on June 1; most hurricanes hit Belize between mid-August and mid-October. However, only 5% of the hurricanes that form in the western mid-Atlantic ever reach this little country.

HURRICANE FACT: *The Hurricane of 1780 blew through the Caribbean and killed 22,000 people.*

Because the reefs protect waters closest to the mainland, usually the ocean tides and waves are not noticed. However, during a hurricane there can be waves as high as 16 feet (five meters). During hurricane conditions, the swing bridge in Belize City opens before its scheduled time so boats can go up the Belize River to relative safety.

There are times when hurricanes blowing 200 miles away from Belize still cause destructive wave action along the shores. On the bright side, a good emergency evacuation plan is in place and many of the resort owners on the cayes keep in contact with the hurricane center in Miami so that they can evacuate their patrons before the storm arrives.

HURRICANES OF BELIZE

- 1931 - An unnamed hurricane killed 1,000 people.
- 1945 - Two unnamed hurricanes.
- 1954 - Gilda.
- 1955 - Janet destroyed the town of Corozal and left in its wake 681 dead.
- 1960 - Abby.
- 1961 - Hattie had winds up to 186 mph and four-meter (13-foot) tides. The storm killed 275 people.
- 1969 - Francella barely touched the southern tip of Belize.
- 1971 - Chloe, Edith and Laura.
- 1974 - Fifi and Carmen. Fifi was a Class 1 storm (mildest on Saffer Simpson Scale), but it killed 8,000-10,000 people in Honduras and did a large amount of damage in Belize.
- 1977 - Freida.
- 1978 - Greta left five dead and 6,000 lives affected.
- 1980 - Hermine.
- 1993 - Bert.
- 2000 - Keith hit around Ambergris Caye causing over $500 million worth of damage.
- 2001 - Iris almost obliterated Placencia and killed 20 people when their boat tipped over.

PLANT LIFE

With its diverse landscapes, Belize presents a whole world of trees, flowers, shrubs, grasses and bromeliads. Those are the natural plants. There are also a number of domesticated plants, like corn, sugar cane and beans. It is impossible to describe all 4,000 plants and 700 trees, but this general overview covers the most dominant plants and animals you will encounter.

FASCINATING FACT: *Of the 3,000 plants found in the rainforest, about 2,000 are known and used by indigenous peoples. Modern medical science has tested about 1% of these plants for medicinal purposes.*

THE RAINFOREST

 Rainforests are defined as areas that receive 160-400 inches (405-1,015 cm) of rain annually and have little temperature change throughout the year. The temperature in Belize's rainforests almost never falls below 16°C (60°F); when it does, the "cold" lasts only for a brief period. This consistent environment supports an ecosystem of plants, animals and insects that struggle against each other for survival.

All rainforests are found between the Tropic of Cancer and the Tropic of Capricorn and they are on land that has never been glaciated. This long period of consistency may be the reason the rain forests play host to such a huge number of different species.

Typically trees in the rainforest grow over 150 feet tall (45 meters) and their branches spread out, forming a lush canopy over the creatures living below. This canopy prevents most

Buttressed tree towers over a hiker in Belize's rainforest.

of the sunlight from reaching the forest floor, leaving the ground with few nutrients. Since the root systems of these trees must compete for the small amount of available nutrients, roots spread out sideways, rather than heading deep down into the ground. This type of growth leaves trees somewhat unstable. To counter this instability many trees, like the Ceiba, have developed buttresses at the base of their trunks that act like stabilizing arms.

Long woody vines called **lianas** often climb up trees in the rainforest and add to the dense canopy at the top. The many leaves in the rainforest produce a tremendous amount of oxygen, which is soon consumed in the decomposition process occurring on the forest floor.

Orchids are so very beautiful, although most are actually parasitic and grow on a host plant. However, there are some that grow in the ground. Depending on which source you use, Belize is believed to have 70 to 250 species of orchids natural to the country, 80% of which live on host plants.

Orchids are members of the most highly evolved plant groups on the planet. There are about 25,000 species worldwide. Their evolution has resulted in thick leaves that hold moisture for the plant. Some of the flowers are highly perfumed, thus attracting more creatures for pollination.

FASCINATING FACT: *The South and Central American Indians used vanilla, obtained from a highly perfumed orchid, as a drink flavoring long before Columbus came to the continent.*

Similar in appearance to the orchids are the **bromeliads**, or air plants. Unique to the Americas, bromeliads grow in any elevation up to 8,000 feet (2,500 meters) and in any terrain from rainforest to desert. They are also like orchids in the way they gather nutrients and moisture in their leaves; their roots are only for anchoring, not for gathering food. Some bromeliads may be as small as one inch across, while others grow to three feet (one meter).

The pineapple is the most commonly known bromeliad. It originated in Brazil and Paraguay and was spread by the local Indians before Columbus arrived. He took the plant to Europe, where it was planted and taken on to other countries. This perennial bromeliad grows up to five feet (1.5 meters) in height and its pointed leaves can be as long as 72 inches (185 cm). The edges of the leaves have sharp needles. Normally, each plant produces only one fruit.

Introduction

AUTHOR TIP: *To determine if a pineapple is good to eat, snap your finger against it. If you hear a solid dull sound, then it is good to eat. If the sound is hollow, the fruit is of poor quality.*

PINEAPPLE HOSPITALITY

Over the years, the pineapple has become a symbol of hospitality. Legend says that it got its reputation from a sea captain who was living in the Caribbean. Whenever the captain returned from sea, he would stop at his friend's place and impale a fruit onto the fence. This would be taken as an invitation for the friend to visit. The symbol was later incorporated by innkeepers who had the pineapple added to their logos and even carved onto bedposts.

MANGROVES

 Mangrove forests are found along the coast of Belize and on some of the cayes. Each species plays an important, slightly different, part in the ecological system.

Mangroves are often found parallel to coral reefs. It is believed that because the plants like brackish, nutrient-rich water, they clarify it for the coral that likes clear, nutrient-poor water.

Red mangroves, found closest to or in the water, trap silt and rotting leaves around their roots. As the debris turns into soil, the red mangrove dies (after sending seeds to other parts of the area) and the white mangrove moves in.

White mangroves are very salt-tolerant and have a unique root system that grows above high-water levels. Seed pods develop on the ends of these non-immersed roots and, after they ripen, fall into the ground and grow. The roots above the water also facilitate the exchange of gases.

Some mangroves are able to filter the salt water through their root system, while others release the salt through the pores of their leaves.

Besides being a protecting environment for hundreds of fish, mangroves are home to both birds and land animals. If birding is your thing, the mangrove swamp is where you will be happiest.

But mangroves help humans too. They keep soil erosion to a minimum and they absorb some of the harsh wave action caused by hurricanes and storms. The wood from the trees is used to make traps and nets and it can also be burned for fuel.

Since 1989, clearance of mangroves in Belize is illegal. Unfortunately, as pressure for more tourist facilities increases, the enforcement of this regulation decreases. In Placencia (a large tourist haunt), local environmentalists fought to keep the lagoon's mangroves, rather than see them destroyed for development. Although they did win part of the battle, it is obvious along the northern end of the peninsula that the mangroves are being cut down and the land filled with sand so development can continue.

HELICONIAS

Heliconias are a small group of plants found in the tropics that are characterized by their large leaves and striking flowers. Native to Central and South America, they grow in humid regions, usually at elevations below 1,500 feet (450 meters). Some of the more recognizable heliconias are the banana, the bird of paradise, ginger and the prayer plant.

Banana trees (not trees, but heliconias) are abundant in Belize. The fruits of different species vary. Some are tiny, some large, some sweet, some bitter. You'll see banana stalks wrapped in blue plastic bags on the trees, which protect the fruit from insects.

After the fruit stalk is removed from a tree, the top of the tree is chopped off and the base is left as fertilizer. New shoots grow and eight months later a new stalk of bananas is growing on the new tree.

TREES

The **hardwood forests** of Belize were what drew many entrepreneurs to the country in the first place. It was **mahogany** and **ziricote** (or zericote) that put dollars into their pockets. But try as they might, they never stripped this little country completely of its forests. Today, about 44% of the original trees are still standing, an impressive statistic when compared to similar countries like El Salvador, which has less than 2% of virgin forest left.

The **bull horn acacia** has large spines on its body and will grow up to 12 feet high (3.5 meters). The shrub's spines are home to the Acacia ant; each tree can hold 10,000 to 100,000 ants. The tree and the ants have formed an interdependency that seems to work. The tree provides a home and food (the sweet nectar produced at the base of its leaves) and the ant in turn bites or stings anyone who comes near the tree. The shrub's violet-scented flowers are used in France's perfume industry.

Cacao, grown throughout the tropics, gives the world over one million tons of chocolate powder every year. This evergreen grows to 25 feet (7.5 meters). It likes a warm humid climate without much rain. The tree produces an oblong fruit, up to 12 inches (30 cm) long that, when ripe, may be yellow, red, purple or green. The fruit, which is usually harvested after the wet season, has between 20 and 60 seeds that grow in five even rows. The five-petaled cacao flower is pink and has five smaller yellow petals inside. It opens in the morning and lives for only one day. However, the plant produces flowers all year long.

Cacao beans in a pod.

The cacao tree likes shade and starts to produce fruit at three or four years of age. An adult grove, one acre in size, can produce between 300 and 1,000 pounds (136-450 kg) of cacao per year for up to 50 years.

Once the cacao pods are picked, they are left to ferment, which reduces the bitterness. The pods are then dried, roasted and shelled. The seed inside is ground, sugar is added, and finally chocolate as we know it is ready.

Calabash trees can be identified by their white tubular flowers or gourd-shaped fruits that grow from their trunks. Up to 100 flowers or gourds can grow on one tree at any one time. It takes seven months after pollination for the fruit to ripen and fall from the tree. The people of Belize pick the gourds and, after they dry, paint colorful scenes on them. These souvenirs can be picked up in shops around the country.

The **ceiba tree** is another deciduous giant of the forest and can be identified by its gray, fan-tailed trunk. The tree reaches 150 feet (50 meters) in height and is home not only to birds and animals, but also to many aerial plants. The tree sheds its leaves during dry season and seedpods can be seen dangling from branches.

It is the seed pods, filled with a cotton-like fluff called kapok, for which the tree was once valued. Kapok is buoyant and water resistant, so until it was replaced with modern Styrofoam in the 1950s, it was used to stuff life preservers. Kapok was also used as stuffing for upholstered automobile seats.

 MYSTERIOUS MAYA: *The Maya consider the ceiba tree sacred. They believed it connected the center of the earth to the heavens. The only time the tree is used by the Maya is when a dug-out canoe is needed.*

Fruit trees grow abundantly in the tropics of Belize. There are limes, oranges, grapefruit, apple, papaya, avocado and – my favorite – the **cashew**. Although I like the nut, it is the fruit with its tart pulp that makes my mouth water. Do taste it if you are there during its season, which is early May.

Formed like a pepper, the fruit can be yellow, green or red and it has a kidney-shaped nut hanging from its bottom. Inside this hard nut is the cashew meat, surrounded by a liquid that burns at the touch. No wonder this delicacy that we prize so much is expensive. In Belize, the meat is usually exported and the fruit is used to make jams and a very sweet wine.

The **guanacaste tree** is a fast-growing tree that reaches a height of 130 feet (40 meters), a significant portion of which is trunk. Gunacaste trunks often have a diameter of over six feet (1.8 meters). The seed pods are broad and flat, about three or four inches across, and curled into a tight circle so they resemble a human ear.

Because the wood is not attacked by the pinworm that lives in saltwater, the tree is used to make dugout boats called dories. The largest known tree of this kind in Belize is at Guanacaste Park, just outside Belmopan.

The **gumbo limbo tree** is also called the tourist tree because it has a red bark that peels, much like the pale skin of tourists. It grows well in shade and is often found in the jungle or on an island that has not been cleared. The Maya used its bark to treat rashes caused by the poisonwood tree.

The **palm tree** is everywhere in Belize and comes in a number of varieties such as the cahune, banana, palmetto, silver thatch, queen and royal palm. Since lethal yellow (a palm tree bacteria) has invaded and killed many of the trees, some land owners are re-planting with the dwarf palm, a species that is supposed to be resistant to bacteria.

Palms like to live near the coast, although they can be seen at elevations of up to 2,000 feet (600 meters). They grow to 100 feet (30 meters) and have feather-like fronds that reach out 35 feet (10 meters). Their seeds are the coconuts that, once opened, produce a sweet drinkable nectar and a pulpy fruit that lines the shell. Cooking oil can be extracted from the nut and laundry soap can also be made from it. The fronds of the trees are traditionally used for thatch on houses and the heart of young trees is considered a survival food. To get to the heart, cut down a tree (one that is about 10 years old) four feet (1.2 meters) from the ground. The best part is the section between the fronds and the cut level. Once the bark is cut away, the sweet meat from one tree will feed from 15 to 20 people.

COCONUT SAVVY

To open a coconut, pick one up from the ground and shake it to hear if there is water inside. If there is, smash the outside hide off with a machete or on a sharp spike to release the nut inside. Place the nut, eyes down, on the palm of your hand; with your other hand, use a rock or piece of coral to tap all around the rim about an inch from the top. The lid will fall off, leaving you with a cup of milk to drink.

The **mahogany tree** is the national tree of Belize, a magnificent deciduous giant. A mature tree stands well over 75 feet tall (25 meters) and the foliage offers a great amount of shade. The trunk has a red, scaly bark and there are four to eight leathery leaves on each branch. Tiny white flowers appear in clusters and bear a pear-shaped fruit that has noticeable grooves along its length. The fruit produces wing-shaped seeds.

Mahogany's hard wood is used for cabinets, expensive household furnishings, caskets and musical instruments, as well as a veneer.

The **pine tree** grows most abundantly in the Mountain Pine Ridge area. Unlike its northern relative, this softwood evergreen has long flowing needles that appear soft and attractive. The bark of one species is thick and rough and more fire-resistant than the bark of a second type that grows on the ridge. Some pine trees in Belize have been invaded by the pine beetle. This little beetle, barely 1/8th of an inch long, is the most aggressive of the five known species. A mating pair will produce up to 160 kids. While in the larvae stage, these kids feed off the inner bark. Then, as they mature, they devour the outer bark. In the Mountain Pine Ridge area, you'll see skeleton trunks like giant toothpicks sticking out of the forest ground. There is some reforestation occurring, so the damage may be rectified.

The **poisonwood tree** is a species you should be able to identify and avoid. The alkaloid sap from this tree causes a skin irritation. The poisonwood is related to poison ivy, only a poisonwood infection is more severe. The tree grows to about 25 feet (seven meters) and has a short trunk, stout limbs and drooping branches. The bark is reddish-brown and covered with thin oily patches of sap. The leaves cluster in groups of five, all about six to 10 inches long (15 to 25 cm). They are smooth and glossy on top, but dull and pale underneath. If you can recognize poison ivy, you should be able to recognize this plant.

The leaves of the poisonwood are broad at the base and thin to rounded at the ends. They may be blotched with irregular black spots. The fruit looks like a yellowish berry and grows on the stem. There is almost always a gumbo limbo tree growing near a poisonwood. This is convenient as the gumbo limbo tree's sap is the antidote to the poisonwood's infection.

The **sapodilla** or **chicozapote tree** is the source of our chewing gum. The story goes that in 1866 General Santa Ana brought from South America a substance that he gave to a New York dentist, Dr. Tom Adams. Adams worked with the substance and one year later came up with the product we now know as chewing gum.

This tree, which produces a cream-colored latex, grows in northern Belize to heights of about 150 feet (45 meters). The latex makes the wood of the tree rot-resistant. The Maya knew this and used the wood for door lintels at some of their temples. Because of its resistance to decomposition, these lintels are still in good condition. The trunks of the sapodilla trees are quite pliable, so they bend in the wind and do not suffer the damage other trees do when hit by hurricanes.

The **strangler fig** is actually a parasite that chokes other living trees. Its seed is usually deposited on the host tree by a bird or insect, and a tiny root starts to twist its way down the trunk of the host while tiny branches and leaves begin to sprout. As the root moves down, it develops leaves and branches and more roots, that eventually wind around the host. The fig lives off the host plant until its nutritional value has been devoured.

The beautiful **tamarind tree**, with feathered foliage and tiny red and yellow flowers, is seen everywhere in Belize. It produces a brown fuzzy pea pod from which a paste is made. From the paste, a refreshing drink called tamarindo, is produced. If the fruit is soaked in water for a while, the water can be used as a laxative.

The **ziricote tree** is also known as ironwood because it is so dense that it actually sinks in water. Ziricote grow up to 100 feet (30 meters) in height. They are found in the drier areas of the tropics. Their bright orange flowers, shaped like a forget-me-not, make them easily recognizable. Most of the carvings in Belize are made from ziricote or mahogany.

ANIMAL LIFE

Belize has become conscious of preserving its wildlife and the habitat in which it lives. Although this consciousness may be stimulated by the desire for tourism, the results are good. There are almost as many sanctuaries, parks and reserves offering protection to everything – from animals to butterflies to snakes to orchids – as there are missionaries trying to preserve the souls of the people.

Although there are numerous preserves and parks, the money needed to maintain them is sparse. I heard time after time that wardens have applied for help to prevent poaching or destruction of plants, but get no money from the government. They try to work in their areas without radio equipment, machinery or guns for protection and so are helpless against those with other interests.

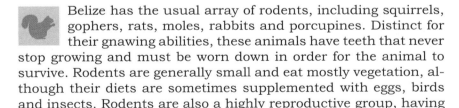

AUTHOR TIP: *The rain forests play host to a huge number of birds and animals, many of which are active at night, when it is cooler. Be aware of this when taking a tour. If someone promises to show you a tapir (a night-time hunter), for example, be sure to take an early morning or late evening tour, as the animals are never seen at midday.*

RODENTS

Belize has the usual array of rodents, including squirrels, gophers, rats, moles, rabbits and porcupines. Distinct for their gnawing abilities, these animals have teeth that never stop growing and must be worn down in order for the animal to survive. Rodents are generally small and eat mostly vegetation, although their diets are sometimes supplemented with eggs, birds and insects. Rodents are also a highly reproductive group, having at least one, and sometimes numerous, litters every year.

AMPHIBIANS

Amphibians include frogs, toads, newts, salamanders, sirenians (sea cows) and caecilians (creatures that look like earthworms). Although amphibians have lungs, they also do some air exchange through their skin. They are found world wide, except on the poles and in extreme deserts.

Amphibians are hatched from eggs and usually go through a tadpole or larvae stage where breathing is done through gills. They metamorphose and in their new form they breath with lungs. Their skins are moist, glandular and pigmented, although if living away from light, pigmentation is minimal. Some, like the salamander, are able to rejuvenate lost body parts (for some reason, the back end of the creature is quicker to respond to re-growth than are the front limbs). The most endearing feature of the amphibian is its ability to consume large amounts of insects, especially mosquitoes.

REPTILES

 Reptiles are prominent in Belize, and it would be a rare visit if you didn't see at least one iguana, snake, turtle, gecko or toad while there. Reptiles control their temperature by moving in their environment. If it is too hot in the sun, they move to the shade. They all have a tough dry skin that is used primarily to preserve body moisture. Reptiles are the first creatures along the evolutionary ladder to have developed lungs.

Reptiles have evolved a number of protection devices. Some have hard shells or scales, while others inflict a poisonous venom on enemies. Yet others just change color so they blend into their environments and can't be seen.

Reptiles always live in vegetated areas and prefer warm climates. There are more reptiles living on land than in fresh water and more in fresh water than in salt water.

TURTLES

The **hawksbill turtle** is endangered due to the commercial value of its shell, meat and eggs. In recent years, this turtle's presence has drastically declined in the Caribbean Sea and Atlantic Ocean. The hawksbill is different than other turtles in that it has a beak-like mouth and two claws on each flipper. It generally grows to around 34 inches (87 cm) and weighs 175 pounds (80 kg). However, the biggest ever found weighed in at 280 pounds (127 kg).

FASCINATING FACT: *The turtle's shell makes its ribs immoveable. In order to breath, turtles either swallow air or they kick their legs and pump the air into their lungs.*

The hawksbill can nest over a span of six months, between July and October. During this period the female nests four or five times, allowing a 14-day interval between each nesting. She lays around 140 eggs each time and the eggs hatch about 60 days later. At birth, each hatchling weighs 12-20 grams (less than an ounce).

Generally, hawksbills eat sponge from around a reef and they use the ledges of the reef for resting spots. However, garbage like plastic and Styrofoam have been found in the stomachs of these creatures. This decreases the amount of nutrition they can absorb and weakens them.

BEKKO

Bekko is a Japanese word meaning shell. For centuries, bekko has been used for making jewelry and decorating things like cabinets, door posts and mirrors. The shell of the hawksbill is considered the most beautiful, with scales colored orange, gold and dark brown.

The **loggerhead turtle** can grow up to three feet (one meter) and weigh up to 250 pounds (115 kg). Loggerheads are named for their large heads and short necks. They can be found in the coastal bays and estuaries of the Atlantic, Pacific and Indian Oceans. In the Western hemisphere, they can be found from the east and west coasts of Canada down to the tip of Argentina. They are carnivores and like shellfish; the turtle's powerful jaws can easily crush the shells of clams and shrimp.

Female loggerheads nest every two or three years. Each season they may nest four or five times and lay 100-125 eggs. The eggs incubate for about 60 days. This period, along with the sex of the turtle, is dependent on the temperature.

The **green turtle** is so named because of the color of its fat. This slow grower does not reach sexual maturity until at least 20 years of age and some are believed to wait for 50 years. The green turtle will grow to about 39 inches (one meter) and weigh about 330 pounds (150 kg). However, in the recent past these creatures would grow to twice that size. Today, we harvest them so rapidly that they no longer have time to grow.

The green turtle is vegetarian and likes to graze on meadows of sea grass that grow in warm ocean waters. However, immature green turtles are known to eat a bit of meat. The females nest once every two to four years. Each nesting season results in two or three breeding sessions, about 14 days apart. The female lays around 100 eggs each time and the youngsters hatch about 60 days later.

SNAKES

The **fer-de-lance** is responsible for most of the fatal snake bites in Central America and is the one nocturnal viper you must be aware of. It is also the only aggressive snake in Belize; most others shy away from trouble.

The fer-de-lance is not only aggressive but it is pervasive; it can be found in a tree, on the jungle floor, in the grass or out in the open. Its markings are not distinct so it is hard to identify. It has an arrow-shaped head holding two retractable fangs that appear too big for the snake's head. The fer-de-lance comes in many colors, from dark brown to gray to red, and has a row of dark-edged diamonds along its sides.

> **WARNING:** If you are attacked by one of these snakes, you must get to a doctor immediately. Twenty-four hours is too long to wait and some people say you have only 20 minutes to receive treatment before you die.

The **coral snake** is also nocturnal, but far less aggressive than the fer-de-lance. However, the coral's venom is highly toxic and every bit as dangerous as that of the fer-de-lance. Coral snakes are hard to find as they like to hide in ground vegetation. They also prefer eating other snakes, rather than sharpening their teeth on you. If you step on one and are bitten, get to a doctor immediately.

BATS

Bats are the only mammals that fly. In Central America bat wingspans range in size from a tiny three inches (seven cm) to six feet (two meters). There are over 1,000 types of bats in the world and Belize has about 85 types as residents.

The wing of the bat is like a webbed hand, with a thumb and four fingers. Also like a hand, the bat's wing can scoop up food, cradle its young or hug itself for warmth. Bats like their own homes and live an average lifespan of 30 years in the same cave, near the same hanging spot. All bats in a cave are related, except for one reproducing male who always comes from another family and area. The females give birth to one baby a year, but the infant mortality rate is high – up to 60%. During the first year of life, mothers leave their babies only when hunting for food. When they return to the cave, they call to their young, who recognize their parent's sound and answer. Following the sound, the mother joins her youngster.

Bats can eat up to 3,000 insects in one sitting and up to 1,000 mosquitoes in an hour. I don't know who does the counting but, if the figures are correct, I really like bats.

The **vampire bat** doesn't suck blood. Instead, it exudes an anti-coagulating saliva that keeps the blood of its victim flowing (rather than clotting) from the spot where the bat has bitten. It then laps the blood up with its tongue, taking in as much as its body weight during one feeding.

> ### THE FAMOUS BACARDI BAT
>
> Bacardi Rum has, since 1862, had a fruit bat on its label. Chinese believe the bat is a symbol of luck and they claim it is the bat on the label, not the flavor of the alcohol, that has made Bacardi Rum the number one bestseller world wide.

CATS

Jaguars are the largest and most powerful cats in the Americas. Often referred to as *el tigre*, the jaguar stands around 20-30 inches (51-76 cm) at the shoulder and has an overall length of six to eight feet (two to three meters). The jaguar's slender but strong body can weigh 250 pounds (115 kg).

The jaguar is built to hunt, with strong shoulders, sharp teeth, good eyesight and hearing, and claws that can rip the hamstring of a deer with one powerful swipe. The jaguar's short fur is usually yellow with black spots, or black circles with a yellow dot in the center. Some jaguars, however, are black in color, which makes their dots almost invisible.

There is no specific breeding season for the jaguar. The kittens are cared for by both parents for about one year after birth. Then everyone splits and fends for themselves. With good luck and lots of food, a jaguar lives about 20 years.

Food is usually obtained at night and the meat-eating jaguar will eat large animals like deer, peccaries and tapirs. It also likes birds,

To see a jaguar in the wild is a rare treat.

monkeys, foxes and turtles. It is a great swimmer, can kill a sleeping alligator, and loves to fish. As for eating man, this is a myth. There are stories of jaguars following humans for miles through the jungle, but the fact is that the jaguar likes to escort man out of its territory rather than attack him.

The red tiger or **puma** is also called the mountain lion, cougar or panther. Just a bit smaller than the jaguar, this animal can be found throughout North and South America wherever deer, its main source of food, is found. The puma is comparable in strength to the jaguar, and has been known to haul an animal five times its size for a considerable distance. When hunting, it strikes with lightening speed and can spring forward 25 feet (7.5 meters) in one leap or jump down 60 feet (18 meters).

Like the jaguar, the puma can mate at any time of year and both parents help look after the young. However, the puma's life expectancy is only 15 years.

The **coati** is a tree-climbing mammal related to the raccoon. It has a long snout (tipped white) and an even longer tail that is usually the same length as its body. It keeps its striped tail high and, as it walks, the tail swings from side to side. Coatis are sociable animals and the females often travel with their young in groups of up to 20. When a group of these animals attacks a fruit tree, it can devour the entire crop in a few minutes. A full grown male stands about 10 inches (25 cm) at the shoulder and will grow to about two feet (half a meter) in length. This omnivore hunts both in the day and at night and eats just about anything, so your chances of seeing one moving along in tall grass or along rocky hillsides are good.

Margay and **ocelots** are cats. An ocelot may weigh in at 35 pounds (16 kg), while the margay is not much bigger than a domestic cat. Both have black spots or rings and broken stripes on their fur. These cats hunt rabbits, rats, monkeys, birds, snakes and deer.

ANIMAL RESCUE

Should you come in contact with an injured, orphaned or troublesome animal, please call the wildlife hotline at ☎ 614-3043. This service is funded by the Woodland Park Zoological Gardens.

OTHER MAMMALS

Skunks in Belize are sometimes incorrectly referred to as polecats. However, a polecat is native only to Europe and Asia. Skunks, on the other hand, are found anywhere from northern Canada down to Patagonia. They are related to weasels, and their reputation for defense (spraying a horrid perfume up to 12 feet/3.5 meters), is well known. The skunk actually aims for the eyes of its enemy, and the liquid it emits produces temporary blindness.

Another night hunter, the skunk comes out of its den when the temperatures cool. It forages for insects, larvae, mice and fallen fruit. Skunks mate in spring and have litters of up to five or six young that are ready to look after themselves after about two months. The life span of a skunk is around 10 years.

The **red deer** is the most common of all deer. It stands four feet (1.2 meters) at the shoulder and may weigh up to 300 pounds (135 kg). This deer always has a white rump patch around its short tail. A five-year-old stag is full-grown and has antlers with six points on each side. The stag usually grows one point every year until he reaches this six-point stage and then point growth is arbitrary.

Once a year female red deer give birth to one fawn that can stand within an hour of life. Mothers hide their fawns in thickets and visit only during feeding times. The red deer is a sociable animal and can be found in large herds dominated by one reproducing female. This female is also responsible for sounding a warning to danger; the entire herd follows her lead.

The **peccary** is a small pig-like creature that has been around for 40 million years (according to fossil finds). It weighs about 65 pounds (30 kg) and travels in herds of a few individuals to as many as 300.

The peccary has two distinct features. One is the smell it exudes from a musk gland on its back when irritated. The second is its amazing nose, the tip of which is flat and reinforced with a cartilaginous disk that can lift logs and dig underground for roots and insects. A true omnivore, the peccary will eat anything from poisonous snakes to cactus.

There is no fixed mating season for the peccary and the female usually gives birth to one or two young that are about the size of full-grown rabbits. By the time the young are two days old they are ready to take their place in the herd.

The ant bear or **great anteater** is known for its lack of teeth. Instead, its elongated head has a small hole about the size of a pen from which a tongue, that can extend up to 19 inches (48 cm), whips out and snatches up termites and other insects. Its front toes and claws curl under, so it seems to be walking on its knuckles. It stands about two feet (60 cm) at the shoulder and is (including tail) about 6.5 feet (two meters) long.

The female gives birth to one baby that stays with her for an entire year. The infant is often seen riding on its mother's back. The anteater is inoffensive and usually runs (and swims) away from perceived danger.

The **armadillo**, also known as the dilly, is an insect-eating mammal that has a bony-plated shell encasing its back. This shell is the animal's protection. Although of the same family as the anteater, the armadillo has teeth that are simple rootless pegs in the back of its mouth. Because of these teeth, the armadillo is able to eat snakes, chickens, fruit and eggs. It also likes to munch on the odd scorpion.

The female gives birth to a litter of young that are all the same sex; the theory is that they develop from the same egg. The young are born with shells that remain soft until the animal is almost a year old. This is when it leaves its mother.

MYSTERIOUS MAYA: *The Maya believe that the black-headed vulture, rather than dying, becomes an armadillo when it gets old.*

The **tapir** or mountain cow is related to the horse and rhinoceros, but it is unique in the fact that it is the last surviving ungulate with an odd number of toes and it bears its weight on the middle toe. The animal's name was derived from the Brazilian Indian word meaning thick, which refers to its thick hide. This short-haired cow stands about four feet (1.2 meters) at the shoulder and when fully grown weighs in at around 600 pounds (275 kg). It has a trunk-like snout that it uses to grabs leaves from aquatic plants or forest foliage for food.

A mother tapir and its young feed on aquatic plants.

The tapir is an excellent swimmer and can stay underwater for long periods, especially when hiding from its worst enemies, the jaguar and puma.

MONKEYS

The **spider monkey** is not as common as the howler, nor is it as noisy. Spider monkeys have grasping hands that have no functional thumbs and a grasping tail that is hairless at the end. These five "hands" make the spider monkey very maneuverable. They travel in bands of 20 to 30 and will attack threatening invaders. They use fruits and branches as weapons, and some are known to urinate on enemies walking below (signs in Manuel Antonio Park, Costa Rica, warn tourists of this possibility).

The baboon or **black howler monkey** makes a horrid howling, growling sound that, if heard when you are walking alone through the jungle, will spook the hell out of you. And that is what it is meant to do. This leaf-eating primate has little facial hair, except on its chin. Like the spider, the howler has a long grasping tail. Its skin is black and its jawbone protrudes to accommodate the bladder-like resonating chamber found in the throat. It is this chamber that allows the monkey to make the frightening racket it does.

Howlers live in troops of no more than 10 and have one dominant male leader. Once a troop is formed, they eat, sleep and travel together. Howlers weigh up to 25 pounds (11 kg) and mothers nurse their young for about 18 months. Some believe the howler makes noise only at dawn and dusk, while others believe it howls when there is impending rain or danger. I think it howls because it likes to. If I could make all that noise with little effort, I'd do it too.

■ SPIDERS & MORE

 Insects and arachnids are everywhere and play an important part in the cycle of tropical life. You will not visit Belize without encountering some critters from this group. Included are mosquitoes and cockroaches, botflies and butterflies, houseflies and fireflies, fire ants and leaf cutter ants, termites and scorpions. Some bite and others don't. Some are good to eat (chocolate-covered ants) and some (such as fireflies) are not even wanted by birds, toads or frogs. I can't begin to name all the members of one family, never mind its distant relatives.

Scorpions should be avoided as they do bite; when in the jungle, shake out shoes and clothes before putting them on. Apparently, the smaller the scorpion, the more lethal the bite. These anthropods are characterized by a long body and a segmented tail. Death from a sting results in heart or respiratory failure some hours after the bite.

For the most part, **ants** work in the service industry, cleaning up garbage left around the jungle floors (and your room if you are careless). Their highly organized colonies can be many feet across and equally as high. A colony of **leaf cutter ants** (also called wee wee ants) can strip a full-grown jungle tree within a day. The ants chew and swallow the leaves, which they regurgitate. From that vomit, a fungus grows. They eat the fungus. The excretion from these ants helps fertilize the jungle floors.

A colony of leaf cutter ants consists only of females and the queen is the size of a small mouse. Her job in life is to lay eggs while her workers clean and feed her. It doesn't matter where you walk in the jungle, you will probably see a trail made by leaf cutter ants.

Other insects are everywhere. Those huge blobs of gunk that cling to trees are the homes of **termites**. If you sleep under a thatch roof, be aware of **chagus**, the insect that sucks your blood and replaces it with its own excretion. Lethal cysts can develop if the infected area is not treated immediately. Everyone should avoid **mosquitoes** (use something with DEET) and if you ever step on a **fire ant's** mound, you'll be really sorry.

Belize has interesting **moth** and **butterfly** farms. Seven hundred kinds of butterflies and moths call Belize home and their colors and designs are fascinating. Some have eye markings at their tail end (to fool predators as to the direction they will be going), while others are so bright they attract the attention of all. Butterflies and moths have no jaws so they don't bite. Instead, they suck up nutrients in liquid form. For protection from rain, high winds and extreme heat, they sit on the undersides of leaves.

The iridescent Blue Morpho butterfly (Morpho menelaus)
lives in rainforests.

■ BIRDS

 Birds are plentiful and varied. Some are common while others are rare. Not many people, whether layperson or scientist, will fail to be thrilled by the sight of a toucan with its huge bill or a colorful parrot with its loud call.

Along with the indigenous birds of the country, Belize lies in a migratory path and thus has many visiting birds during spring and fall. It also has varied environments (islands in the Caribbean, rainforests, drier savannas and grasslands, swamps and lagoons), so it attracts birds needing those habitats.

The endangered Jaribu stork.

The **jabiru stork** is the largest bird in the western hemisphere, with a wing span of nine-12 feet (three-four meters). The stork has a large bill that is good for scooping up fish and frogs. The jabiru is found in Belize only from November to June. Its most popular place to stay during that time is the Crooked Tree Wildlife Sanctuary, where a total of 24 have been seen together at one time.

The **frigate bird** or iwa can soar for hours over the sea, although it seldom goes more than 50 miles away from its home island. Because it does not lift off from water very well, the frigate steals from other birds or swoops down and catches fish swimming near the surface. It is big, black and beautiful. You will see many.

> *Sometimes the frigate bird*
> *robs them of their fish*
> *whereupon the booby*
> *is wont to say "friggit"*
> *and catches some more.*

By Al Purdy from his poem *Bird Watching at the Equator*

If you have more than a passing interest in birds, bring your favorite bird identifying book and binoculars and plan on going to some of the sanctuaries, like the Crooked Tree Wildlife Sanctuary.

 The most comprehensive tome available is the **Field Guide to the Birds of Mexico and North Central America** by Steve Howell and Sophie Wedd, published by Oxford Illustrated Press. It has both color plates and black and white drawings that cover 750 species. The book is 1,010 pages and heavy to carry.

Another guide to look for is the **Field Guide to Birds of Mexico and Adjacent Areas: Belize, Guatemala and El Salvador** by E.P. Edwards and E.M. Butler, published by University of Texas Press. This book is a mere 209 pages and much better for carrying.

A more practical and general guide to the wildlife in Belize is **Belize and Northern Guatemala: Ecotraveller's Wildlife Guide** by Les D. Beletsky. It's published by Harcourt Brace and endorsed by the Wildlife Conservation Society. It has 80 pages on birds alone, but covers everything from environmental concerns to animals.

Birds of Belize by Lee Jones, illustrated by Dana Gardener, University of Texas Press, is by far the best book I have seen. The paperback version can be purchased on the web for US $25 directly from the publisher. Otherwise, the cost is $60 for a hardcover. This book has 445 pages, 56 color plates and the illustrations make identification a breeze.

If you are here to spot birds and add to your life list, you won't go home disappointed.

UNDERWATER LIFE

After you've been in Belize for a short time, some form of underwater life will have crossed your path. There is coral or sponge that has broken off from the reef and washed up onto the shore. The sand itself is ground coral and sea shells. Walking along the beach, you may come upon tiny fish trapped in a tide pool. Most restaurants have shrimp, lobster or conch listed on their menus and there are few hotels that don't have a bowl of shells decorating the hall or stairway. Souvenir shops are inundated with shell crafts and most of the tourist industry revolves around snorkeling, fishing and deep-sea diving.

CURIOUSLY CORAL

Coral reefs, formed millions of years ago, lie a few miles off the mainland. Composed of organic skeletal deposits from both plants and animals, this land of calcium carbonate (limestone) is fascinating to explore.

- **Stony corals** such as the brain coral and star coral, the main builders of reefs and atolls, are found exclusively in warm waters no deeper than 80 feet (25 meters). Stony corals are arranged in multiples of six polyps to each tentacle.

- **Horny corals**, with eight polyps to each tentacle, include organisms like sea fans and elkhorn corals. These corals have a supporting spine and can have over a million polyps. There are thousands of types of horny corals in the waters around Belize, and just being able to identify the stony from the horny is a good start.

- **Soft corals** do not deposit or contribute to the construction of a barrier reef as they totally disintegrate after death.

- There are also **false corals**, such as the prized black coral used for making ebony-colored jewelry.

Within the coral reef are underwater plants and grasses, some that flower and all with roots. Some have thick leaves, while others

Opposite: A snorkeler looking at brain coral.

seem to be threads. Living in this environment are barnacles and conch, crabs and lobster, and fish of every color, size and shape.

The **manatee**, or sea cow, is a favorite attraction for tourists. This gentle aquatic animal weights about 400 pounds (180 kg) and is around seven feet (2.1 meters) long, although some large males have been known to grow up to 1,500 pounds (680 kg) and reach 15 feet (4.5 meters). The manatee has a torpedo-like body with a long flat tail that is used for propulsion. Its two forepaws are like paddles with tiny claws on the ends. Its upper lip is cleft and dotted with a few whiskers.

FASCINATING FACT: *The 11 teeth growing on the manatee's bottom jaw rotate. As the front two wear out, they drop off and the entire row moves forward. In the space where the very back molars were located, a new set develops.*

The manatee is a bottom feeder, eating up to 100 pounds (45 kg) of seaweed and grasses a day. Females give birth to a single young, underwater. Directly after birth the mother takes her young up to the surface to breath. After that, both parents take equal responsibility for the raising of their offspring.

Now protected, the manatee was hunted as food for centuries. Apparently, its meat is deep red and quite rich. Christians used to consider this a fish, so it was eaten on Fridays and during Lent. That belief has since been dispelled.

Dolphins are plentiful in the waters of Belize. Playful and intelligent, dolphins mature between five and 12 years and a female gives birth to one calf every second or third year. The life span of a dolphin is up to 48 years.

Dolphins travel in pods and it is suspected that each member of a pod is related. They like to stay near their home waters for their entire lives. They hunt for fish using an echo-location method similar to bats. A dolphin will eat up to 150 pounds (68 kg) of fish a day.

Groupers are one of the most common fish you will see in the waters around the atolls. Groupers are meat eaters. They have a heavy body, usually about three feet (one meter) in length, a large head and blubbery lips. Groupers are generally brown in color, with lighter brown vertical stripes.

Angelfish abound; there are 74 species of angelfish and most of them get 95% of their food from sponges. They have developed teeth that secrete a mucus around the sponge that, in turn, allows the fish to ingest the sponge. Some species of angelfish mate for life, while others may change their sex and become males if there aren't enough reproducing studs around.

Whale sharks can be seen during the snapper moon, the full moons of March, April and May. At that time, snapper and grouper are spawning and whale sharks like the taste of those newly fertilized eggs.

A whale shark is the largest fish known. It may grow to 50 feet (15 meters) and weigh 20 tons. That is a lot of animal.

NATIONAL EMBLEMS

Belize has a plethora of official national emblems and a story that intertwines each emblem with the history of the people.

National Anthem

Land of the Free
O Land of the free, by the Carib Sea,
Our manhood we pledge to thy liberty,
No tyrants here linger, despots must flee,
This tranquil haven of democracy.
The blood of our sires which hallows the sod,
Brought freedom from slavery oppression's rod,
By the might of truth and the grace of God,
No longer shall we be hewers of wood.
Arise! Ye sons of the Baymen's clan,
Put on your armours, clear the land.
Drive back the tyrants, let despots flee,
Land of the free, by the Carib Sea.
Nature has blessed thee with wealth untold,
O'er mountains and valleys where prairies roll,
Our fathers, the Baymen, valiant and bold,
Drove back the invader; this heritage bold,
From proud Rio Hondo to old Sarstoon,
Through coral isle, over blue lagoon,
Keep watch with the angels, the stars and moon,
For freedom comes tomorrow's noon.

COAT OF ARMS

The Belizean Coat of Arms, first designed in 1907, is a circle representing a shield, divided into three sections by an inverted Y. Two woodcutters hold the shield. The man on the left is a Mestizo and he is holding an axe; the man on the right is a black, and he is holding a paddle. In the lower third of the inverted Y is a ship in full

sail with a red flag waving. It could represent the British flag. The two upper sections of the inverted Y contain tools used in the timber trade. There is an axe on the right and a saw on the left. Behind the men is a mahogany tree and below them is the national motto. The entire design is circled with a wreath of green leaves.

NATIONAL FLAG

The national flag of Belize is royal blue with a horizontal red stripe at the top and bottom. The Coat of Arms sits in a white circle in the center. The flag was first adopted in 1950 when Belize, then called British Honduras, decided to move toward independence from Britain. At its inauguration, the flag was royal blue with the coat of arms in the center. When Belize finally obtained her independence in 1981, a red stripe was added to the top and bottom of the flag.

NATIONAL PRAYER

Almighty and Eternal God,
who through Jesus Christ has revealed Your Glory to all nations,
please protect and preserve Belize, our beloved country.

God of might, wisdom and justice,
please assist our Belizean government and people
with Your Holy Spirit of counsel and fortitude.

Let the light of Your divine wisdom direct their plans and
endeavors so that with Your help we may attain our just objectives.
With Your guidance, may all our endeavors tend to peace,
social justice, liberty, national happiness, the increase of industry,
sobriety and useful knowledge.

We pray, O God of Mercy,
for all of us that we may be blessed in the knowledge and
sanctified in the observance of Your most holy law,
that we may be preserved in Union and in Peace which the world
itself cannot give. And, after enjoying the blessings of this life,
please admit us, dear Lord, to that eternal reward that You have
prepared for those who love You.
Amen.

NATIONAL MOTTO

Sub Umbra Florero is Latin and means "under the shade I flourish." The shade is assumed to be that of the giant mahogany tree, but it is also metaphorical for "quiet or cool" political times.

NATIONAL FLOWER

The **black orchid** grows in damp areas and flowers all year. This orchid has greenish-yellow petals, except for the one prominent petal at the top, which is shaped like a clam shell and is such a deep purple that it appears to be black. The black orchid is a short flower, growing in clusters not much higher than six inches.

NATIONAL BIRD

The sociable **keel-billed toucan** has a canoe-shaped bill and bright yellow cheeks and it loudly croaks its presence from large trees in the lowland rainforests. The bird's serrated beak looks heavy but in fact is remarkably light. Toucans use the serrated edges of their beaks to cut fruit, their main diet. To supplement the fruit, they eat insects, lizards, snakes and the eggs of smaller birds.

The toucan nests in the hollows of trees and the female lays anywhere from two to four eggs. Both parents take turns sitting on the eggs for a period of six or seven weeks.

Found in forests from southern Mexico to northern Columbia, this poor flier grows to about 20 inches (50 cm), not counting his bill. If you happen to hear a croaking sound while walking in the jungle, try to spot this jolly flyer on a limb above you.

■ NATIONAL TREE

The **mahogany** is undoubtedly one of the most magnificent deciduous trees on earth. In spring, red buds appear, causing the hills to glow as if on fire. They soon turn into clusters of white flowers that in turn produce a pear-shaped fruit. By summer, the fruit ripens and splits open, releasing winged seeds that are carried by the autumn winds. Finally, when the rains end, leathery leaves appear, usually six or eight to a cluster. The foliage offers a great amount of shade before the leaves die and the cycle starts again.

A mature tree will stand well over 75 feet tall (25 meters), its trunk covered in a reddish, scaly bark. Mahogany is a durable wood that is soft enough to be worked with ease. The distinct grains of the wood enhance the appearance of cabinets and expensive household furnishings.

■ NATIONAL ANIMAL

The **tapir** or mountain cow is a cute animal with a fat body, short legs, a long snout and white-tipped ears. Despite its name, the tapir is more closely related to the horse and rhinoceros than the cow. It is the largest land mammal found in Central America, weighing as much as 875 pounds (400 kg). This poor-sighted herbivore has excellent hearing and smell.

The word tapir comes from a Brazilian Indian word meaning "thick," which refers to the animal's hide (rather than its stature or brains). The hide is covered with short black/brown hair and a full-grown male will stand just over four feet (1.2 meters) at the shoulder and six feet (two meters) in length. The tapir is an odd-toed ungulate; the front hooves have four toes and the back legs have three. One large toe in the middle of each hoof carries most of the animal's weight.

To get away from enemies, like the jaguar, the tapir will run (sometimes blindly) toward water. However, even without dangers, the tapir loves to wallow in mud and, like most travelers, has a bath every day. He is a strong swimmer and can stay underwater for long periods of time, especially when threatened.

The tapir is shy, hunts at night, and is rarely seen in groups larger than three or four. It breeds all year. The cows carry a calf from 390 to 400 days after mating; twins are rare. When born the calf has a brown coat lined with longitudinal white stripes and spots that start to fade when the calf is about six months old. Full maturity is reached at one year and the life span of this animal is about 30 years.

Long ago the tapir was hunted with dogs for its delicious meat. Because it is not a fast runner, dogs easily cornered the animal, but pulling it down was another matter. The tapir is known to put up a fierce battle when cornered, using its razor teeth as a defense. It was believed that the nails of the tapir, ground into powder and ingested, would cure epilepsy.

Travel Information

FACTS AT YOUR FINGERTIPS

CAPITAL: Belmopan.

HEAD OF STATE: Queen Elizabeth II of England. She has been in office since February 6, 1952.

GOVERNOR GENERAL: Sir Colville Young. He was appointed by the monarch and has been in office since November 17, 1993. He is the Queen's representative in Belize.

PRIME MINISTER: Said Musa, leader of the PUP since 1997. He is the nation's third Prime Minister and was elected in 2003 for a five-year period.

DEPUTY PRIME MINISTER: John Briceno. He is appointed by the Prime Minister and is a member of the cabinet and the ruling party.

POPULATION: 279,457 people. Forty-two percent of the population is under 14 years of age. Depending on which source you look at, the ethnic groups are as follows: 29-40% Creole, 33- 43.7% Mestizo, 10% Mayan, 8% Garifuna, 8% white and 1% other (mainly East Indian and Chinese).

AREA: 8,868 square miles. Of that, 62 square miles is water. Belize is smaller than Massachusetts.

BORDERS: Guatemala 165 miles/264 km, Mexico 155 miles/248 km.

COAST: 240 miles/384 km.

CURRENCY: Belizean dollar; US $1 = BZ $2 (2006). This is a fixed rate.

HOSPITALS: There are eight government-run hospitals, one in Belize City, one in Belmopan and one in each of the six districts.

RELIGION: 92% Christian, with 62% of that being Catholic.

EDUCATION: Compulsory for everyone between six and 14 years of age. The literacy rate is 70.3% and is equal for men and women.

LIFE EXPECTANCY: 69 for men and 73.5 for women. On average, four children are born to each woman.

NATURAL PRODUCTS: Bananas, cocoa, citrus, sugarcane, lumber, fish and cultured shrimp. Industrial production includes garment factories, food processing, tourism and construction. Belize produces its own electricity from fossil fuels (43%) and water (57%).

GDP: $6,800 per person, per year in 2005, but the unemployment rate is 11.8% of the adult population.

WHEN TO GO

■ SEASONAL CONSIDERATIONS

 The climate in Belize is pleasant at any time of year. The off-season, from mid-May to mid-September, brings the best prices for hotels and tours, as well as fewer divers at the reefs or amateur archeologists at the ruins. Mid-May is also the start of the rainy season. However, it does not rain all day every day during that time. Usually, there are a few torrential downpours during the night or for an hour during midday. This is the most hot and humid time of year. One local told me that during the rainy period (she called it summer) Belize gets heavy but brief squalls, while in the dry season it can suffer from a miserable drizzle all day long. September and October are the worst months for hurricanes.

Temperatures peak at 90°F (32°C) and can go as low as 66°F (19°C). If a north wind blows, even the cayes can have temperatures as low as 70°F (21°C). **Humidity** is always high, averaging between 87% and 90%, and **rainfall** can be anywhere from 1.5 inches (38 mm) to 12 inches (305 mm) per month.

Christmas and **Easter** are the times when Belizeans like to vacation so getting hotel rooms not previously booked will be difficult. This is also high season.

If bike racing is your thing, come in April for the famous **Classic Bike Race** in Belize City. If you want **lobster** for every meal, then plan your visit to avoid the closed season, February 14th through June 15th.

■ NATIONAL HOLIDAYS

 National holidays are a big thing in Belize. Shops are closed, restaurants are full and everyone is out enjoying the festivities. Special foods are brought out and sold on the streets. People are friendlier than usual. Baron Bliss Day is especially good as the entire nation participates in events like bike, horse or sailboat racing.

For information about particular events during national holidays, contact the **tourist office** in Belize City, New Central Bank Building, Gabourel Lane, ☎ 223-1913. For information in Corozal, ☎ 422-3176; New River Orange Walk, ☎ 322-

Maya girls gather for a celebration.

0381; Punta Gorda, ☎ 722-2531; and San Ignacio, ☎ 824-4236. Or you can e-mail them at info@travelbelize.org.

■ FEBRUARY

One week before Lent the **Fiesta de Carnival** is held. The carnival has evolved into a costume party where people use paint and face makeup to hide their identity. There is usually lots of noise attached to this event.

■ MARCH

March 9 is **Baron Bliss Day**. Henry Edward Ernest Victor Bliss IV was a wealthy Englishman who received his title from the Portuguese. Bliss originally came to Belize in 1926 to sail and fish, but he fell in love with the country so he brought his wife over and they made it their home. When Bliss learned of his impending death due to food poisoning he willed all his money, rumored to be about one million pounds sterling, to Belize. The country received it after Bliss's wife died. Each year a ceremony is held at his tomb below the lighthouse in Belize Harbor, Belize City. This is followed by sailing regattas.

■ MARCH/APRIL

There is a four-day holiday for **Easter** sometime during March or April; the exact date depends upon when Easter falls. The vacation includes Friday, Saturday, Sunday and Monday, and everything is closed, including shops and tour companies.

■ MAY

May 1st is **Labor Day**, celebrated (after a speech from the Minister of Labor) with kite-flying contests, a sailing regatta, horse races and a bicycle race.

May 24th is **Commonwealth Day**. This was once Victoria Day and celebrated Queen Victoria's birthday. Now the holiday is a general celebration of Belize's place in the British Commonwealth. The most popular events are the horse races in Belize City and Orange Walk.

■ JUNE

June in San Pedro offers a three-day festival in honor of St. Peter, the town's patron saint. All the people who fish for a living are blessed at a special mass, followed by music, dancing and food.

■ AUGUST

San Antonio in the Toledo District celebrates the **Maya Deer-Dance Festival**. The celebration, which lasts for one week, offers historical plays, music and dancing.

The **Costa Maya** Festival (formerly the International Sea & Air Festival) is held in San Pedro in mid-August to celebrate the friendship of all neighboring countries. There is music, dance and food. San Pedro likes a party.

■ SEPTEMBER

September 10th is **St. George's Caye Day**. This national holiday commemorates the battle of St. George in 1798 (see *History*, page 11). There are carnivals, sporting events, parades and music concerts. This is a very big celebration.

September 21st is **Independence Day**. Independence from Britain was granted on that day in 1981 and is when the Constitution of Belize came into effect.

■ OCTOBER

October 12th, **Columbus Day**, brings a two-day, international cross-country hike and bike race to bring attention to the national rainforests.

■ NOVEMBER

November 19th is **Garifuna Settlement Day**. It was on this day in 1823 that Garifuna first arrived in Dangriga. To commemorate this event, they paddle in canoes laden with traditional foods, drums and household utensils. Once at the village they dance, sing and eat until late into the night.

■ **DECEMBER**

December 25th and 26th has the festival of **Christmas** followed by the English holiday called **Boxing Day**. Originally an English tradition, Boxing Day or St. Stephen's Day was when those of lower classes received boxed gifts of goods or money from their bosses/lords/employers. Giving a gift to an employer or boss was never done because that would suggest equality.

WHAT TO TAKE

■ REQUIRED DOCUMENTS

 You must have a valid **passport** that will be good for six months after your entry into the country. No visas are required for citizens coming from Canada, the United States, England, Belgium, Denmark, Finland, Greece, Iceland, Italy, Liechtenstein, Luxembourg, Mexico, Spain, Switzerland, Tunisia, Turkey and Uruguay for stays of up to 30 days. If your visit exceeds one month, a stay permit must be obtained from the Immigration Authorities at the airport.

Everyone entering Belize must apply for a travel permit, given free of charge at the border or port of entry. If you arrive by plane, the application form is distributed prior to landing. You will be returned a portion of the form to carry with you. This tiny piece of paper must be submitted to the border guard on your departure. Loss of the paper could cost you in time and headaches.

The border guards will usually give a visitor a 30-day visa with no problems, but not always. On my last visit, I was given 10 days and when I explained that I needed 30, they said I would have to pay the US$25 to extend my visit. I spoke with Gareth Murillo, the Assistant Director of Immigration in Belmopan, and he smiled and said, "The guards can make this decision and if you want to stay you will have to pay the extra money for a visa extension." I later learned that overstaying your visa could cost US $1,000.

Technically, you must also have an onward ticket when entering Belize, although this is seldom checked.

If bringing an animal with you, it must have all shots and vaccinations required for international travel. Rabies shots must be no older than six months.

An AIDS test is required for those staying more than three months in Belize; a US test is accepted if it was done within three months of your planned visit.

A six-month extension is possible for a mere US $25, but you can get this extension only once. Then you must either leave the country and start all over again or apply for permanent residence at a cost of US $500 for those from the US and Commonwealth countries. After you have been accepted for residency, you must pay an additional $62.50 for a card. Those from mainland China must pay US $1,500 to apply for permanent residency, while anyone from Mexico or Guatemala pays only US $125.

For other information, contact the **Embassy of Belize**, 2535 Massachusetts Avenue, NW, Washington, DC 20008, ☎ 202/332-9636, or the **Belize Mission** in New York at ☎ 212/599-0233.

For further information about regulations, call one of the **Immigration and Nationality Departments**: ☎ 822-2423 in Belmopan; ☎ 222-4620 in Belize City. Or see the websites www.travel.state.gov or www.ambergriscaye.com/economics/entryreq. This second site also has a list of Belize Foreign Offices around the world.

■ PACKING LIST

 Binoculars are a must, even if you are not a bird watcher. I have never seen such an abundance of interesting feathered creatures in my life. Pooh pooh this all you wish (as I once did), but if you go without binoculars you will be sorry. Binoculars are also fun to use on the beach to watch boats (and those on the boats) as they pass by.

Everyone in Belize wears shorts, so pack **shorts** and **t-shirts**. However, the most revealing outfits are not acceptable; your shorts should fall to mid-thigh at the shortest. Keep your clothing loose and comfortable.

If you're visiting during rainy season, bring some type of rain protection. I recommend an umbrella because it is cooler than a rain jacket and can also be used as shade from the sun.

Sandals are good at the beach and on the cayes, but **running shoes** or light **hiking boots** are needed for jungle walks.

On public beaches you will need a **bathing suit**. Most beach-goers bring a beach towel or grass matt to lie on.

Cameras are a great way to record a memory. Humidity is high in Belize, so keeping the camera dry is a concern; I use a foam-padded carrying bag and a desiccant. Putting cameras in plastic bags where the moisture seems to condense is not advisable. Bring your own **film**, as any film in Belize is expensive and you probably won't be able to find specialized film such as transparency or high quality print film. Because there is so much intense sunlight, a slow-speed film is recommended.

> **AUTHOR TIP:** *A flash should be used when photographing people during the day so that the harsh shadows are eliminated.*

The underwater photography is splendid in Belize. However, I suggest you take an introductory course before leaving home. One lady I spoke with threw out the first 100 images she took because they were so bad. The second hundred were great photos of sand and water and blurred sand and blurred water. That's a lot of money wasted.

A **money belt** should always be made of a natural-fiber so that it's comfortable worn around the midriff under your clothes. Ladies, you can wear a sports bra of the kind with back pockets meant for carrying water bottles. Place a piece of Velcro across the opening of the pocket and put your money/traveler's checks inside. The bills folded in half fit perfectly. You must place your money/traveler's checks/credit cards into a plastic bag first, otherwise they will get wet from perspiration.

KEEP IT SAFE

Keep important documents (such as your passport) in plastic bags inside the money belt, protected from sweat. Always place money and/or travelers' checks in different places, so if you are robbed you will have mad money to live on. There are belts sold today that have zippered pockets sewn on the underside. These comfortable and inconspicuous belts are worn as ordinary belts through the loops of your pants or skirt. Money must be folded lengthwise to fit into the pockets. Tiny pockets can also be sewn into your clothing, in the hem of your skirt, or the cuff of your shirt. A few bills can also be placed in a plastic bag, under the inner sole of your shoe. My husband did this one time but neglected to put the bill into a plastic bag. The impression on the bill was erased and the money became good only for fire starter.

Daypacks are far more convenient to carry than handbags. They are also harder to pickpocket or snatch. In cities, on buses or crowded places like markets, wear your daypack at the front, with the waist strap done up. That way, your hands can rest on the bag while you walk. In this position, it is almost impossible for pickpockets to access the pack. Keep only the amount of money you need for the day in your daypack and the bulk of your money elsewhere. If you keep your camera in the pack, the camera is easily accessible and then slipped out of sight again. Never wear your camera around your neck when touring in cities.

It seems to me that a map is really hard to follow if you don't have a **compass**. They are not heavy and you need not buy one that can do triangulation measurements. A simple one will do.

Should you find yourself stuck in a hotel room facing the front street, over a bar, or next to the parrot cage, **earplugs** are essential. Dogs seem to start barking when you turn your bedroom light off and they don't stop until morning.

Diving gear, like wetsuits and face masks, can be brought from home or rented from the dive shops at around US $25 for a complete diving outfit ($8 for a wet suit). Remote shops like the one on Glover's Reef can outfit up to 30 people at any one time, so bringing your own would be only to save money. You will need your **PADI diving certification** ticket. The tour operators check this certificate every time you go out.

An **umbrella** is good if you plan to walk, regardless of the time of year. It keeps off both sun and rain. It is also a nice little defense tool.

A **walking stick** is useful if you plan to visit caves, or go hiking or walking along rivers, where rocks are usually slippery.

Your **first aid kit** should include things like mole skin (for skin sores), Advil (hikers' candies), bandage, antihistamines, topical antibiotic cream, Band Aids. All prescription medications should be carried with you in their original bottles.

Make **photocopies** of your passport and other documents and store them somewhere other than with your passport. Memorize your passport number. Keep a record of the numbers on your traveler's checks and record where and when you cashed them. If they are stolen, you have a record to give the company that issued the checks. International ATMs were introduced to Belize in early 2006. You can now access your bank account anywhere in the world, so traveler's checks will soon become extinct. Keep important addresses and phone numbers in two places.

In our technological age you may also scan your passport and e-mail the scan to your traveling e-mail address (i.e., Yahoo or Hotmail). This way, you always have a copy.

Reading material is available in English at magazine stands and book stores and many hotels have book-trading services. But for the most part, Belize is in need of books. Take some and leave them there.

A **sleeping sheet** is advisable if staying in the cheaper places or camping out. Because the climate is hot and humid, anything warmer than a sheet is not necessary.

Sunglasses and **sun hat** should be brought and worn all the time you are in the sun because the intense ultraviolet light can damage your eyes. Paul Theroux, author of the famous *Patagonia Express*, has problems with his eyes due to the damage caused by ultraviolet rays. He often kayaked without sun glasses.

Sunscreen and **insect repellent** are necessities. Do not let yourself become cancer red or take the chance of getting dengue fever and malaria because you don't like chemicals.

HEALTH CONCERNS

Belize does not have the same quality of medical services as North America, so it is advisable to have **medical insurance**. The cost is anywhere from US $1 to $5 per day, and many policies include ticket cancellation insurance and coverage against theft. In the event of a serious illness or accident, you will want to get to your own country fast. Without insurance, the cost could be prohibitive.

Before purchasing travel insurance be certain your own insurance does not cover what you need. See which insurance companies give discount coupons for museums/parks. Also, check to see if evacuation is covered. There is one travel company that will cover you for adventure sports like climbing, but only if ropes are NOT used. I have used the RBC Travel Insurance ($1 a day for a period of six months) because their policy will pay for hospital/doctor bills without my doing any paperwork. The insured person must contact them (at a 24-hour toll-free number) as soon as an injury or sickness occurs and RBC Travel looks after the costs. To check out more options, a good starting place on the Internet is www.internationalplan.com.

Bring with you anything you may need in the way of prescriptions, glasses, orthopedics, dental care and batteries for hearing aids. Things like vitamins, bandages, antihistamines, or topical creams are readily available in Belize City.

■ COMMON AILMENTS

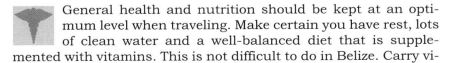

General health and nutrition should be kept at an optimum level when traveling. Make certain you have rest, lots of clean water and a well-balanced diet that is supplemented with vitamins. This is not difficult to do in Belize. Carry vitamins, eat meals with all the food groups and drink more liquids than you would at home. The tap water is safe to drink. It is collected rain water. If you feel squeamish about drinking tap water, bottled mineral water is available everywhere. The rule is to pee clear.

Salt intake is important in the tropics as it helps prevent **dehydration**. Carry some powdered electrolytes in case you do become dehydrated.

Should you get a mild case of **diarrhea**, take a day of rest, drink plenty of water and do not consume alcohol. This common condition, often caused by the change in diet, usually clears up quickly. The mineral water can be supplemented with yogurt tablets. In the event that you must travel, you may chance taking Imodium AD, but be aware that this too can cause problems. Use this drug only as a last resort. Eat at places where locals are eating. If they remain healthy, you should too. If the sanitation looks dubious, don't eat the salad; have some hot boiled soup instead.

FEVERS & WORSE

Malaria, according to the World Health Organization, is a possibility in Belize any time of the year and anywhere at elevations below 400 feet (120 meters). The danger of infection increases during rainy season. In other words, a prophylactic is crucial.

Belize has both chloroquine-responsive and chloroquine-resistant malaria. About 14% of the malaria is the falciparum strain (the chloroquine-resistant type), the most dangerous. You should see your doctor and read the IAMAT (International Association for Medical Assistance), www.IAMAT.org, reports before deciding on the type of protection you will need.

Mephlaquine is the recommended prophylactic against chloroquine- resistant malaria. One person in 15,000 may develop side effects, such as severe paranoia or panic attacks, from using mephlaquine. Most people have little or no reaction to the drug.

In the event that you develop a fever for no explicable reason, like a cold or flu, especially if you are in mosquito country or have been bitten by a mosquito, you should treat the condition as if it is malaria. Some forms of malaria are lethal, so immediate attention is imperative. The possibility of malaria should be considered for up to three months after leaving an infected area.

In the event of suspected infection, a person between 100 and 130 pounds (45-60 kg) should take five mephlaquine tablets within 24 hours. Larger people should take one tablet for every 25 pounds (10 kg) over the above recommendation. The tablets should be taken in three separate doses of two tablets, two tablets and finally one tablet, eight hours apart. If vomiting occurs within 30 minutes of ingestion, take another half-dose. Should you have ringing in the ears, reduce the dosage until there is no ringing. Get to a doctor or clinic as soon as possible.

CAUTIONARY TALE

While traveling in Honduras a few years ago, I met a lady who had refused to take a prophylactic for malaria thinking (I believe) that the medicine would be harder on her than the disease. She caught the disease. Her tremors were so severe that they ripped all the muscles in her legs and arms. I met her six weeks after the fevers subsided and she was hobbling along with a cane, still not healthy enough to head home.

Other protections against malaria-bearing mosquitos are to spray or soak your clothes and sleeping gear (including net or tent) with permethrin. Protection lasts for up to three washings. The recommended dose is a half-ounce (20 milliliters) of permethrin (13%) in two liters of water. For tents and mosquito nets, spray the item with a solution of 10 mils in a half-gallon (two liters) of water. Permethrin can be purchased in any garden shop that sells pesticides. If traveling for a long time, carry some concentrated permethrin and dilute it only when you need it.

Keep exposed skin covered early in the morning or at dusk when the mosquitoes are most active. Using repellents laced with DEET is also recommended. Although traces of DEET have been found in the livers of users, it is still better than the instant death of malaria. Using a sleeping net in infected areas is highly recommended.

Dengue fever and **dengue hemorrhagic fever** is caused by four related but distinctly different viruses that are spread by daytime-biting mosquitoes. Infection from one of the viruses does not produce immunity toward the other three. Dengue cannot be transmitted from person to person. Symptoms of dengue are high fever, headache, backache, joint pain, nausea, vomiting, eye pain and rash. There is no treatment except to take painkillers with acetaminophen rather than those with aspirin (acetylsalicylic acid decreases your blood's clotting abilities thus increasing the possibility of hemorrhage). Drink plenty of fluids and rest. If dengue hemorrhagic fever is contracted, fluid replacement therapy may be necessary. The illness lasts about 10 days and total recovery takes two to four weeks.

Yellow fever is present in all the jungles of Central America. Though inoculation is not required for entrance to Belize, it may be required for re-entry to your own country (check with your immigration office). Inoculation, good for 10 years, is recommended if you want to avoid a lengthy stay in quarantine. Children must also have a certificate of inoculation, but it is not recommended to inoculate those who are less than one year of age.

Routine inoculations common in your home country should be up to date. Besides these, immune globulin is recommended against **viral hepatitis**; the shots are good for about six months. If you have had viral hepatitis, you are already immune. Inoculation against **typhoid fever** is highly recommended. This inoculation is good for 10 years.

BUGS

Worms and **parasites** can be a problem anywhere in the tropics. To name and describe them all would be impossible. Keep your feet free of cuts or open sores so that worm larva or parasites cannot enter. Use sandals in the showers, especially if cleanliness is in question. Wear closed shoes (running shoes or hiking boots) when outdoors, especially in the jungle.

If staying in lower-end hotels, where **bed bugs** or **fleas** can be a problem, keep your sleeping gear in mothballs during the day. You will find that bed bugs do not cross that smelly barrier no matter how succulent the impending meal is. The mothball smell dissipates within a short period of time.

The **tumbu fly** transports its eggs into its host by way of the mosquito. Once in its host, the egg hatches and the fly lives under the skin. However, the fly must have air. If you have a red swelling that is larger than something from a mosquito bite, look closely. If you see a small hole in the swollen area cover it with petroleum jelly to prevent the fly from breathing. Without air, it dies.

Chagas, also known as the kissing bug, exists in Central America and infection can become either chronic or acute. The parasite enters the bloodstream when the infected oval-shaped insect inserts its proboscis into your skin. As it sucks your blood, its excretion is forced out and into the opening it has formed in your body. It is the excretion that carries the larva of the parasite. Once in your bloodstream, the larva migrates to the heart, brain, liver and spleen, where it nests and forms cysts. If you wake up one morning after sleeping under a thatched roof and you have a purplish lump somewhere on exposed skin, you may have been bitten. Symptoms include fever, shortness of breath, and vomiting or convulsions. See a doctor immediately.

■ TREATMENT OPTIONS

If you become sick, contact your own consulate for the names of doctors or medical clinics. The consulates can usually recommend doctors who have been trained in your place of origin. For minor ailments that need attending, you may want to try one of the local clinics or hospitals in Belize. See *Emergency Contacts*, page 541, for a complete list of embassies and consulates.

HOSPITAL CONTACT INFORMATION	
To reach these hospitals by phone, you need dial only the number given here if you are in Belize. There are no area codes to incorporate.	
Karl Heusner Memorial Hospital, Belize City	☎ 223-1548
Cleopatra White Outpatient Clinic, Belize City	☎ 224-4012
Matron Roberts Health Center, Belize City	☎ 227-7170
Port Loyola Health Center, Belize City	☎ 227-5354
Rockview Hospital, Rockville	☎ 220-6074
Orange Walk Hospital, Orange Walk	☎ 322-2072
Corozal Hospital, Corozal	☎ 422-2076
Dangriga Hospital, Dangriga	☎ 522-2078
Dr. Price Memorial Clinic, Independence	☎ 523-2167
Punta Gorda Memorial Hospital, Punta Gorda	☎ 722-2026
Belmopan Hospital, Belmopan	☎ 822-2264
Caye Caulker Health Center, Caye Caulker	☎ 226-2166
San Pedro Health Center, San Pedro	☎ 226-3668
San Ignacio Hospital, San Ignacio	☎ 824-2066

You may also contact the **IAMAT** (International Association for Medical Assistance to Travelers) clinic at 99 Freetown Road in Belize City, ☎ 224 5261. The coordinator is Manuel Cabrera, MD. IAMAT's mission is to provide competent medical care to travelers anywhere in the world by doctors who have been trained in Europe or North America.

The information reported in this section is taken from either IAMAT or World Health Organization publications. If you are a frequent traveler and feel inclined, please become a member of IAMAT by sending them a donation. Some of the money they raise goes toward a scholarship to assist doctors in developing countries go to medical training sessions in more advanced parts of the world.

Travel Information

Herbal medicines are popular among the Maya and Garifuna. If you are away from the kind of medical care you are accustomed to, you may want to try a local "curandero," or healer. You will need to ask a local where one can be found.

> **HERBAL LAXATIVE:** *Tamarind is a fruit found in a long brown pod that is often seen in the market. From this fruit a tart drink is made. If the fruit is soaked in water for a while, the water can be used as a laxative.*

As North Americans get more and more into the natural health methods, this type of treatment for minor ailments may be a priority. I had a severe case of prickly heat on my arms while I was in Laguna. A Maya lady looked at my arm, reached down, picked seeds from a grass and rubbed them on my arms. Within minutes, I had no bumps (and they never came back). However, I don't think I would go to her with a ruptured appendix or suspected malaria, no matter how good my experience.

For official government updates on outbreaks, advisories and more, visit the Centers for Disease Control & Prevention run by the US Health Department at http://www.cdc.gov.

■ WATER

Tap water is considered safe to drink in Belize. It is usually rain water collected from roofs and stored in wooden or cement vats. If you feel uncomfortable with this, purified water is available throughout Belize. The cost is about BZ $1 per liter.

> **STAYING HEALTHY:** *Signs decorate many buildings in Belize warning people to pay attention to thirst, and not to dehydrate themselves.*

If traveling where creek/lake water must be used, add a chemical such as iodine for purification. There is also a tablet available with a more palatable silver (as opposed to an iodine) base. Chlorine bleach can also be used as a purifier. It is the least effective of chemicals for water purification, but it is also the most available in Belize.

Mechanical filters take a long time to process the water and they do not filter out all organisms that could cause problems. They are also much heavier to carry than chemicals.

MONEY MATTERS

Belize is not a cheap place to visit. It is the most expensive Central American country and costs about double that of Gutaemala. The (almost) all-inclusive resorts are expensive, ranging from about US $100 to $200 per day. Plus, the non-inclusive part of these packages are drinks, tours and diving. Budget travelers will have a hard time living in Belize for less than US $25 a day, which puts it almost on par with Canada.

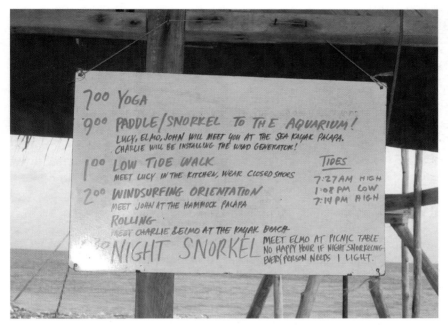

A rustic board displays the offerings of a local watersports vendor.

Always be aware of which currency is being quoted. Occasionally, a taxi driver will tell you that your fare is $5, and he silently hopes you pay in US dollars even though he meant the fare to be in Belize dollars. On the other hand, as soon as a hotel owner sees that you are a foreigner, he will almost always quote you a price in US dollars. Since Belize has an informal policy of double-pricing for tourists, deliberately confusing US and Belize dollars is common.

■ PRICE SCALES

In the hotel/restaurant/tours sections of this book, I give a price range, rather than a fixed rate. The price for a single and double room is the same, unless otherwise stated, and all prices are in US dollars. Use these rates as a guideline only; always call and verify current prices.

For each restaurant/hotel, I give my personal impression, followed by a brief review. My impressions may have been influenced by who I saw and how they treated me. Once you have used the book for a while, you will have an idea as to what events and experiences interest me and what level of service impresses me.

HOTEL PRICES	
$	$20 to $50
$$	$51 to $75
$$$	$76 to $100
$$$$	$101 to $150
$$$$$	over $150

RESTAURANT PRICES	
$	$5 to $10
$$	$11 to $25
$$$	$26 to $50
$$$$	$51 to $75
$$$$$	over $75

■ BANKING/EXCHANGE

One domestic (**Belize Bank**) and three foreign-owned banks (**Barclays**, **Nova Scotia** and **Atlantic**) operate in Belize. Banking hours are from Monday to Thursday, 8 am to 2:30 pm and Friday from 8 am to 4:30 pm. You can exchange foreign currency in either cash or traveler's checks and draw money from your Visa/MasterCard account.

ATMs have finally arrived, although not all banks have got the technology. The Belize Bank has 12 locations with a total of 15 machines throughout the country. Their machines accept Visa, Master Card, Cirrus, Plus and Visa Electron. Other banks accept fewer cards but machines are starting to appear in grocery stores and service stations. Be aware that, at time of writing, machines at Scotia Bank accepted only local cards.

The Belize dollar is tied to the American dollar and is half the value. In other words, BZ $2 = US $1. Both currencies are readily accepted anywhere in the country. If you want to use Belize dollars you can change foreign currency at the airport, at your hotel or at any bank in the country. It is best to carry US dollars. Money changers at the borders now accept traveler's checks and charge no commission.

Belize dollars can be exchanged back into US dollars at the airport in Belize City or with money changers at all land borders (although anything less than BZ $5 will not be accepted at the airport). Belize dollars can also be exchanged at some US airport money exchange offices for a charge.

Traveler's checks in American currency can be cashed almost anywhere, including with money changers at the borders. If you carry American Express Travelers' Checks and you are charged a fee for cashing them, insist on obtaining a receipt. Send the receipts into American Express, Salt Lake City, UT 84184-0401 and they will refund these charges.

If you are charged an extra fee (some merchants charge up to 8%) for using Visa/MasterCard, report this to the Visa/MasterCard office in your home city or call the international office at ☎ 800-336-3386. This extra charge violates the contract agreement between the credit card companies and the merchant and there could be repercussions for the merchant.

Should you run out of all financial resources and need money sent from your home country, try **American Express Travel Service**, 41 Albert Street, Belize City, ☎ 227-7363, or **Western Union**, 63 Regent Street, Belize City, ☎ 227-0014. There are four Western Union substations in the city at: Bi-way Gift Shop, Douglas Jones Street and Freetown Road, ☎ 223-1341; Marine Terminal on North Front Street, ☎ 203-1969; Dooneys, 15 Albert Street, ☎ 227-3039; and Eighty-Eight Trading Center, 66 Neal Pen Road, ☎ 227-8688. There are also Western Union substations throughout the country and they offer the quickest service.

Working through banks could take up to two weeks, while the money transfer companies offer same-day service. However, this service costs up to $100 for each transaction and is dependent on someone at home sending the cash.

■ TAXES & TIPPING

% Sales tax is 15% on all goods and services (called the VAT, or value added tax) except on food (no tax) and accommodations (8%). Some hotels and restaurants charge a 10% service charge over the quoted price and tax of the room or meal. Be sure to check your bill before adding a tip.

Once you have paid the foreigner's fee, the tax and the service charge, tipping is not necessary. Taxi drivers do not expect a tip. However, if you receive good service in a local restaurant, a tip is a nice gesture of appreciation. Ten-15% of your bill is a reasonable amount to tip.

Travel Information

DUAL PRICING

Dual pricing is in effect and, in fact, is encouraged by the government. This means that Belize citizens are charged a much lower price for some hotels and all park entrance fees. For example, the entry fee to Cockscomb Basin Wildlife Reserve is BZ $4 for nationals and US $8 for foreigners. This makes the price four times as high for you and me than it is for locals. Some hotels also use the dual pricing scheme, again with encouragement from the government. When hotels fill out their application forms for licensing, one of the questions asked is what will the proprietor charge locals and what will he charge foreigners for the same room. For me, this says that tourists are nothing more than cash-cows to be exploited. If you think this dual pricing will bother you, then Belize is not the country to visit and I would advise you to choose another destination.

The official justification for dual pricing is that Belizeans would not be able to afford to go to the tourist attractions if the prices were not lower. Ironically, what is happening is that Belizeans are buying the entry tickets to attractions at their lower price and selling them to the tourists for a significant mark-up, though still lower than the suggested tourist price.

■ PLANNING YOUR EXPENSES

If you make all your own arrangements, your cheapest day could run about US $50. This would include a basic room with a slow-moving fan, two good meals in a traditional restaurant and a visit to one tourist attraction that you reached by walking or riding your own bicycle. If you had to rent a bike your costs would increase considerably. Taking a taxi, a water taxi or a bus will add another $10 to your amount. Should you want to do some of the fun things like snorkeling or diving, you will have to budget US $50 to $75 a day.

To go first class in Belize – enjoy a rum punch at sunset and spend a few hours scuba diving with rented gear – budget US $200-$400+ per day.

MEASUREMENTS

Officially, Belize recognizes the metric system. However, car odometers show miles, and everyone talks in miles, so we use miles as forms of measurement in this book. Other measurements are not so cut and dry, so we give both. If ever you are in doubt, use this chart to convert the figure into a measurement you can work with.

GOING METRIC

General Measurements

1 kilometer	=	.6124 miles
1 mile	=	1.6093 kilometers
1 foot	=	.304 meters
1 inch	=	2.54 centimeters
1 square mile	=	2.59 square kilometers
1 pound	=	.4536 kilograms
1 ounce	=	28.35 grams
1 imperial gallon	=	4.5459 liters
1 US gallon	=	3.7854 liters
1 quart	=	.94635 liters

Temperatures

For Fahrenheit: Multiply Centigrade figure by 1.8 and add 32.

For Centigrade: Subtract 32 from Fahrenheit figure and divide by 1.8.

Centigrade		*Fahrenheit*
40°	=	104°
35°	=	95°
30°	=	86°
25°	=	77°
20°	=	64°
15°	=	59°
10°	=	50°

Travel Information

DANGERS & ANNOYANCES

Every country in the world has its robbers and petty thieves, whether you are in the polite society of Japan or the northern wilds of Canada. If you hang out in the very poor sections of a city where you are unknown, if you are staggering drunk in a back alley, if you trust a stranger to hold your cash while you run to the washroom, you are going to have a sad tale to tell.

■ COMMON-SENSE PRECAUTIONS

 When out, **be aware** of what is around you. If you are being followed, go into a store or knock on someone's door. Most predators are looking for single travelers.

Make certain that expensive items like your camera or Rolex watch are **out of sight**. Carry only a bit of cash in your pocket and the rest in your money belt.

Be inside at night and take a **taxi** back to your room if you have been out late. **Don't be drunk** in public. A drunk is a great target. Don't get mixed up in the **dope** trade. Save booze and dope for home. If you do get into trouble at home, you know the rules, you have friends to help and the prisons are far more comfortable than they are in places like Belize.

Women should walk with confidence. If you appear frightened or lost, you are a target. Don't walk alone in non-populated places like the jungle or along a secluded beach. In the event that you are grabbed or accosted in any way, create a scene. Holler, scream, kick and fight with all your might. However, if you are approached by someone with a weapon, let them have it all. Being dead or seriously maimed isn't worth any possession you may have, including your virginity.

■ IN THE CITY

Belize City has the reputation of being dangerous. With an unemployment rate of almost 13% and with the average employed person earning about US $3,200 a year, money is in short supply for many people. The young seem to be especially vulnerable to the temptation of robbery. They want all the glitz that comes with a richer life; they want the things you are flashing around. Your cash and camera are ways of getting that wealth.

I personally have never had a problem in Belize City or anywhere else in Belize. However, caution is advised. Be alert, confident and careful.

■ EMERGENCY ASSISTANCE

In the event of a **robbery**, call the police in the town you happen to be in. Phone numbers are given at the beginning of every telephone book. The police, for the most part, are not corrupt. If you are unable to call the police, ask a local for help. Belize is full of kind people. Once you have reported the incident, call your embassy or consulate. All incidents should be reported to your own country's officials. See the *Appendix*, page 541, for a list of embassies and consulates in Belize.

COMMUNICATIONS

■ TELEPHONE

Belize has a new phone system. To call anywhere in Belize, you dial only the seven-digit number. If calling from out of the country, you need to dial your country's international access code (in the US, this is 011), the country code, which is **501**, and then the seven-digit number.

Of the seven numbers, the first three are the national destination code, or area code, as it is commonly called in the US and Canada.

Using the telephone in Belize is not difficult. First you must purchase a **telephone card**, available in BZ $5, BZ $10 and BZ $20 denominations. Go to a telephone that is programmed to accept telephone cards, pick up the receiver and wait for the operator to tell you to punch in the PIN shown on the back of the card (you must scratch off the silver when you first purchase the card in order to see the PIN). Assuming the number is accepted (often it is not, so you have to punch it in again), you will be instructed to enter the number you are calling. If you wish to make more than one call, you need to hit the pound sign after you finish your call and then punch in the next number. If you run out of funds during a call (the operator will tell you how much money is left on the card at the beginning of your session), the operator will come on the line, tell you that you are out of money, and then cut you off. There is very little time to punch in another PIN; you will need to redial the call.

■ INTERNET

 It is usually much cheaper to go to the Belize Telephone Limited (called BTL) office in any town and use their Internet services than it is to use an Internet café.

The price for Internet access at BTL offices is US $3 an hour. The machines are generally fast, but the downside is that you can use them only during business hours, Monday through Friday, 8 am to 5 pm.

The cost of service at commercial Internet cafés range from US $6 for five minutes (on Ambergris Caye) to US $3 per hour (San Ignacio).

■ POSTAL SERVICE

 Postal service is good. It takes about a week for a letter to reach North America and costs about 30¢ for a card or one-page letter. Parcels do not have to be inspected before being mailed and insurance is available. You may have mail sent to General Delivery at any post office in Belize and it will be held for you.

CULTURE SHOCK

■ PUBLIC AFFECTION

 Belize is a conservative country, so physical affection in public is not encouraged. Remember, this is a country with a strong religious tradition and a place where even abortion is not yet legal.

■ GAY & LESBIAN TRAVEL

 It is illegal to be gay in Belize. My feeling is that until we stop making distinctions, there will be discrimination. However, I understand the need for discretion so I mention whether a hotel is gay-friendly in my review (there are just a few) by referring to their liberalism.

■ HUMAN RIGHTS

Although women are not considered equal to men in any setting, for the most part human rights are respected. The government never stops international groups from checking on the rights of Belizeans and women's groups are free to educate and promote equality.

There have been few reports of **police brutality**. Arbitrary arrest, limited to 72 hours, is seldom abused. All accused are innocent until proven guilty and family court issues are usually settled behind closed doors. There have been no political assassinations nor are there any political prisoners in Belize.

The only **prison** is in Hattieville and the conditions are poor. The building was designed for 500 people, but actually holds 1,100. Each cell holds six men in a 10- x 12-foot space. There are no showers or toilets in the cells; men are given a five-gallon bucket to use. Although there is a separate area for women, it is accessible by male guards and some male prisoners. There are no special areas for mentally ill prisoners.

FOOD

Traditional foods in Belize are often good and some are exceptional. Chicken, beef, pork and seafood can be purchased almost anywhere, and its the way they are prepared that makes for a culinary adventure. Always go to an eatery that is patronized by locals.

If you are on the islands, seafood will be your main staple and Creole food may be more common than anything else. These dishes are usually spicy and hot.

Chinese restaurants are abundant and there are even some ethnic places, including a Lebanese restaurant on Ambergris Caye and an Indian restaurant in Belize City.

■ TRADITIONAL DISHES

I wouldn't hesitate to eat food cooked over a fire by street vendors, nor would I ever go hungry if a market stall serving food was nearby. Belizeans are clean and their food is no exception.

Cassava (or yucca) is a root that is boiled and then strained for the pulp. It is dried and pounded into a white flour which, in turn, is made into a bread. Cassava is a traditional food of the Garifuna.

Fry jacks are a cornmeal bread substitute that's fried to a crisp. They are half moon-shaped and hollow inside. For breakfast, fry jacks are often served in restaurants instead of toast.

Rice and **refried beans** are the national staple. Since they have no taste they need no explaining.

Tamales are made from a gob of corn paste with a spicy piece of meat in the center rolled into a banana leaf and boiled. These are very good. Tamales are usually served by ladies during festivals. Look for a lady with a basket over her arm. If she has something wrapped in green leaves, it is probably a tamale.

Escabeche is an onion soup flavored with copious amounts of spices. It is not only spicy hot, but the flavor is such a complicated mix of spices, it is difficult to put a finger on any particular one.

Relleno soup is made with stuffed chicken, ground pork and eggs. This is one of my favorites.

Gacho is a flower tortilla stuffed with vegetables, cheeses or meats and baked in the oven.

Sere is a soup made with fish and coconut milk.

Conch and **lobster** are offered almost everywhere. **Stewed chicken**, like rice and beans, is on every menu.

Ice cream is often homemade and very good. But even the commercially made ice cream is good in Belize. The heat makes it taste even better.

BOOKING A ROOM

Many people book their accommodations over the Internet. This is okay, but beware that not everything on the Internet is true. Photos probably show only the best side of an establishment, and lighting plays a big part in making something look far more attractive than it is. You may not see the cockroaches in the corners or the bus terminal next door. Rates quoted may be off-season, with no indication of what on-season rates are, and taxes may not be mentioned.

Ask some questions.

- Is there air conditioning or a fan? In a thatched-roof hut, air conditioning is useless because the cold air goes out through the roof.
- Is there hot water? How is it heated? Water heated on the roof by the sun is far cooler than water heated in an electric tank.
- Where is the water obtained and is there a cost for it? Water stored in a vat is different from water in a well.

Water on an island may be filtered by the sand and dis-colored by the roots of the palm trees.

■ Is there electricity, or will you listen to a generator all night? Some islands do not have any electricity, while others use solar paneling to generate it.

■ What exactly does "meals included" mean? Is it three orders of rice and beans or will there be other things available? Is there a bar and, if so, can you bring your own alcohol (which is much less expensive than buying alcohol from a bar)?

■ How far is this establishment from other life? Isolation is great for a few days, but if you would like to eat out one evening, you need a restaurant.

■ Do the prices include taxes and service charges? If not, those costs can add up to 20% of the total bill.

■ Does the hotel accept credit cards and do they add a fee for this? Charging for this service is against their con-tract with the credit card companies, but some places do it anyway.

■ What kind of fun activities are nearby? Can you ride a horse, windsurf or fish? Are guides licensed? Note that it is illegal for a person to act as a guide without being licensed. All guides have picture IDs stating that they are qualified to offer guiding services.

If you do book ahead, print out all correspondence and keep the documentation with you. Some proprietors have been known to of-fer one rate, but charge another after the customer has arrived.

GETTING HERE

There are many options. For a luxurious stay near the beach, you can have a tour agent book your flight and hotels so all you need to do is pack, grab your cash and credit card, and get yourself to the airport. Or you may be on a long trip and arrive in Belize overland. You may want to do nothing but drive or cycle from one archeologi-cal site to the next before heading to Guatemala or Mexico. If you have specialized activities you'd like to pursue, like kayaking around Glover's Reef or diving the Blue Hole, consider using a tour group, such as Slickrock Adventures or Island Expeditions. They do all the work while you have all the fun.

Travel Information

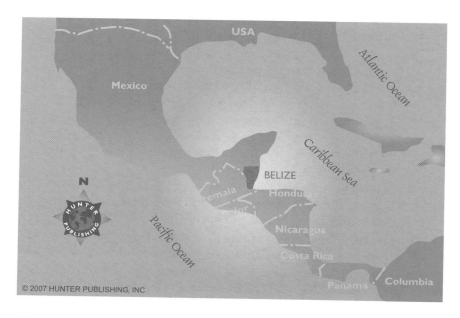

© 2007 HUNTER PUBLISHING, INC

■ OUTFITTERS WHO DO ALL THE WORK

 Some tour companies will be mentioned more than once in this book because they specialize in many types of tours. All offer photography, wildlife viewing and natural history information.

Slickrock Adventures, PO Box 1400, Moab, UT 84532, ☎ 800-390-5715, www. slickrock.com, US $200+ per day. Slickrock has been around for more than 25 years. For 20 of those years, it has been offering tours into Belize. What impressed me the most about this company is the professional instruction they offer in sea kayaking and windsurfing. The company is also safety conscious, permitting, for ex-

Slickrock's windsurfing courses are recommended.

ample, only those able to run the whitewater of the Macal to do it. They are the only company that takes canoes and kayaks down a Class IV river. The food is splendid, with everything from fry jacks to key lime pie. This company is highly respected in Belize and is recommended.

Eco Summer Expeditions, PO Box 1765, Clearwater, BC, V0E 1N0, Canada, ☎ 800-465-8884, www.ecosummer.com, US $100-200 per day. This company offers a number of expeditions. Some are in Canada, some in Tonga and Chili, and some in Belize. Included activities are visiting ruins, jungle hiking, canopy viewing, drumming, sailing and tubing. Their reputation for safety in Canada is excellent. Their meals are popular too.

A traveler explores a new world with Island Expeditions.

Island Expeditions Co., 1574 Gulf Road, #156 Point Roberts, WA 98281, ☎ 800-667-1630, www.islandexpeditions.com, US $100-200 per day. Island Expeditions has been running specialized kayak tours into Belize for about 20 years, so they must be doing something right. Each year they offer trips ranging from seven to 12 days, and these can include hiking, sea kayaking, river rafting or exploring Maya sites. Trips are all-inclusive (except for airfare, departure taxes and diving costs) and accommodations are in either tents or lodges.

Their most spectacular tour is an eight-night adventure that includes a trip to the Actun Tunichil Muknal or the Cave of the Stone Sepulcher (burial vault). Once inside the ceremonial chamber, in addition to the incredible geological features of the cave, you get to see artifacts from the Maya world. From the cave you hike in the jungle and then take a wild river trip down the Swasey River. All the guides are local Belizeans.

GAP Adventures, 19 Duncan Street, Toronto, ON M5H 3H1, Canada, ☎ 800-465-5600, www.gap.ca, US $75-100 per day. If you are looking for a more relaxed adventure, GAP kayaks around the southern cayes for about four hours a day, leaving you lots of time to read a book or enjoy a rum punch. Sleeping accommodations are in a tent or hammock and meals include a lot of fresh fish, fruit and veggies. Over the years GAP's reputation has improved to such a high degree that many people I know now book with no one else. They take small groups and have experienced and knowledgeable guides and gourmet cooks. Their staff has a great sense of humor and those involved with the company are sensitive to the environment. This is a good choice.

GAP offers a more relaxed adventure experience.

Peter Hughes Diving Inc., 5723 NW 158 Street, Miami Lakes, FL 33014, ☎ 305-669-9391, www.peterhughes.com, US $300+ per day, offers live-aboard charters on a Dancer yacht. This tour includes almost everything – meals, a stateroom with private bath, all drinks, bathrobes, access to photo labs, and five half-days of diving with up to five dives a day. The boat has its own SSB equipment for the manufacture of fresh water. Not included are airfare to Belize, equipment rentals, instruction, tips, departure tax, use of the hyperbaric chamber and onshore drinks. This is a first-class service that specializes in diving around the cayes.

Sunny Skies Adventures, TMM Bareboat Vacations, Coconut Drive, Ambergris Caye, Belize, ☎ 226-3026, www.sunny skyadventures.com, US $200 per person, per day. This company offers a bareboat (that means no crew and you do everything) catamaran that holds eight people comfortably or 10 people if using the crew's quarters. To hire a captain or cook will cost another $100 per day. You supply all food and drinks plus personal equipment. All boats have GPS, dinghy, outboard, snorkel gear and some linen.

Journeys International uses knowledgeable guides on its ruins tours.

Journeys International, Inc., 107 Aprill Drive, Suite 3, Ann Arbor, MI 48103-1903, ☎ 800-255-8735 or 734-665-4407, www.journeys-intl.com, US $300 per day. In addition to trips visiting the cayes and atolls, Journeys offers a cultural tour to the ruins of Tikal and Caracol (with knowledgeable guides), a visit to a cave that reveals Maya artifacts, and a walk in the rainforest along a Maya medicine trail.

Global Travel, 1 Kiln Shaw, Langdon Hills, Essex, SS16 6LE, England, ☎ 01268-541732 or Southern Foreshore, Dangriga, Stann Creek District, Belize, ☎ 522-3262, www.global-travel.co.uk, US $100-200 per day. Global has a family-run office in Dangriga that helps to make efficiency the norm. If there is a request/complaint by a client, it can be handled immediately. Global also uses local hotels, transport services and guides without going through an outside agency, which means that more Belizeans are hired. Economically aware, Global makes certain all monies earned from their company are put into Belize bank accounts. This way full taxes are paid (18% of Belize's income is from tourism).

Looking for a romantic tropical wedding? Global specializes in marriage arrangements in Belize. They can take care of almost any budget when doing these preparations.

Sea and Explore Belize, 1809 Carol Sue Avenue, Suite E, Gretna, LA 70056, ☎ 800-345-9786, US $200 per day, depending on what you do and what you opt to include. Sea and Explore specializes in customized tours for both individuals and groups. One of the owners is a native Belizean, so she knows where to go and what to do on a trip around the country.

■ ARRIVING BY AIR

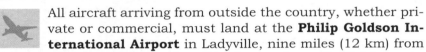

All aircraft arriving from outside the country, whether private or commercial, must land at the **Philip Goldson International Airport** in Ladyville, nine miles (12 km) from Belize City. Those transferring directly to a domestic flight for another destination within Belize must pay a US $7.50 security charge. When leaving Belize by air, the departure tax is US $35.

REFUND ALERT

Be aware that if you must cancel a ticket with an airline, getting a refund may take awhile. I had a ticket canceled by American Airlines because the country I was going to had a violent coup and they didn't want to take me in. I waited over five months to get my money back. This ended up being the fault of the agency with whom I booked.

Many major centers in North America and most capital cities in Central America have direct flights to Belize. **American** (☎ 800-433-7300, www.aa.com), **Continental** (☎ 800-525-0280, www.continental.com) and **TACA Airlines** (☎ 800-535-8780, www.grupotaca.com) all fly out of at least one major North American city. **Mexicana** (☎ 800-531-7921, www.mexicana.com) and **Aeromexico** (☎ 800-237-6639) also have flights from many of the major North American cities, although they don't offer direct flights to Belize (they stop in Mexico). As of 2002, **Cayman Airways** (☎ 800-422-9626, www.caymanairways.com) started flying a charter plane to Belize. Starting November 2002, **Air Jamaica** will be flying into Belize four times a week. They will make connections from any major American city and their prices are good. www. airjamaica.com, ☎ 800-523-5585.

Instead of flying directly into Belize, a more economical option is to take a flight to Cancún, Mexico, and bus/drive/cycle/hitch down to Belize. Since Cancún receives two million vacationers a year, hundreds of planes go in and out of there daily from places around the world, and deals are relatively easy to find.

There are air-conditioned, first-class buses leaving for Chetumal from the main terminal in Cancún five times a day. You must check the schedule in Cancún as it changes almost daily. The cost to ride from Cancún to Chetumal is US $20. Once in Chetumal you can catch a bus to Belize City or any destination along the Northern Highway. Buses run almost every hour from 10 am until 6 pm. However, only two are express buses. Be aware that all overland border crossings now cost US $20 when leaving Belize and the border guards have the right to give you only a few days in the country. If you wish to extend your visa, you will have to pay an extra US $25.

There are no flights arriving or departing Belize City after dark. This is why it's so difficult to get a flight into the country without spending a night en route. Of course, if you live in a major US city (Houston, Dallas, Miami), direct flights are available.

The best way to find a flight suitable for your needs is to search the Internet. The more flexible you are with times and flight schedules, the easier it will be to get a suitable price. If you don't surf (the net), try a reputable travel agent in your city.

AN AGENT ON YOUR SIDE

I have used a travel agent for years. However, with the new Internet, self-find/pay, many people are bypassing the agents. I ran into a complication recently that resulted in the airline having to refund my payment for a ticket. The agency (from Vancouver) my home-town agent worked with wasn't able to refund my money for a number of vague reasons. When, after waiting for six months, I threatened to call a lawyer, the Vancouver agency called and convinced me that hiring a lawyer was a waste of money. The agency told me that I would eventually get a voucher from the airline in place of the canceled ticket, probably within a year, and I'd then have to use the voucher within the next year – even if I didn't want to travel. The Vancouver agency also assured me that the voucher would be nontransferable. I was unhappy with this resolution and called Transport Canada. They got involved and I received a check for the entire amount within a week. However, without the documentation and force of the agent I work with, I may not have been so successful. I recommend using an agent.

INTERNET SEARCH SITES

The cost of flights changes all the time. Although this can be frustrating, it can also work to your advantage, especially if you're willing to book on-line. Use the travel-oriented sites listed below or go to each individual airline (see websites listed above). Alternately, go to a general search engine, such as www.google.com, type in "discounted airline tickets" and let your search engine start the process.

www.cheapflights.com sells to those in Canada and the US.

At **www.priceline.com**, you place a bid on an airline ticket. The bid, if accepted, is a binding contract.

www.latintickets.com sells to those in the United States only.

www.vacationweb.com, which sells to those in the US or Canada, offers the best prices of all.

■ OVERLAND

 You can reach Belize by bus from either Mexico or Guatemala. Mexican lines go as far as Chetumal, and Guatemalan buses go as far as Melchor de Mencos on the Guatemala/Belize border. Buses in Chetumal are caught at the Mercado Nuevo, about six blocks from the ADO Terminal.

Once in Belize and after you have cleared immigration, the rest is easy. There are flocks of money changers who will exchange your foreign currency and bus drivers who will take you to the next town. The last express bus leaves Corozal at 3 pm for Belize City and the last bus going to San Ignacio leaves Benque Viejo at 5:30 pm. There are taxis at both borders that will take you to the closest town shortly after the land borders close at 6 pm.

If driving your own car, there are a few more things that must be done before you are on your way. You must fill out a form at immigration indicating the type and condition of your vehicle. You must post a bond on your credit card as insurance that you have the same vehicle when you leave the country. You must also purchase Belizean car insurance. The Insurance Corporation of Belize has agents at the border just waiting to take your cash. The largest company in the country is **F&G Insurance**, ☎ 227-7493, www. fandginsurance.com. Contact them for an insurance estimate on your vehicle.

Immigration officials are getting more accustomed to seeing cyclists crossing their borders. I have not heard about any hassles.

■ ARRIVING BY SEA

You can cross by ferry from Puerto Barrios, Guatemala to the Belizean ports of Punta Gorda or Placencia.

If you have your own boat, the options increase. You can also land at Belize City, Dangriga, Big Creek and San Pedro (Ambergris Caye). If you opt for the latter, you must pay the fare (US $110 to cover airfare and taxi) for a Customs officer to come out from the mainland and stamp you in.

GETTING AROUND

■ AIR TRAVEL

There is just one international airport in the country, in Ladyville, nine miles (12 km) out of Belize City. Both international and local flights use the international airport. Municipal airports vary in their regulations. Only local flights can use the municipal airport in Belize City.

> **AUTHOR NOTE:** *If transferring directly from an international flight to a domestic flight at the International Airport, there is a US $7.50 security charge.*

From the Ladyville airport, you can fly to many destinations within Belize with Tropic Air and Maya Air.

Tropic Air (☎ 800-422-3435, 226-2012 in Belize, www.tropicair. com) has numerous flights every day from either the international or municipal airports. They also offer air tours that fly over the cayes. There are no flights before 7:30 am or after 5:30 pm.

TROPIC AIR FLIGHTS

FROM THE INTERNATIONAL AIRPORT TO:

Dangriga - Nine flights daily, US $5.50 each way. From the Municipal Airport there are five flights daily, US $54 each way.

Flores, Guatemala - Two flights daily; no flights from the Municipal Airport. The cost is US $213 round-trip. There are no one-way prices.

Plancencia - Eleven flights a day, US $75 each way. From the Municipal Airport there are five flights a day, US $64 each way.

Punta Gorda - Four flights a day, US $93.50 each way. From the Municipal Airport there are five flights a day, US $81 each way.

San Pedro - Eleven flights daily. You may stop off at Caye Caulker on any of these flights. The cost to San Pedro or Caye Caulker is US $51 each way.

FROM OTHER POINTS:

Corozal to San Pedro - Five flights daily, US $40 each way.

Dangriga to Placencia - Five flights daily, US $39 each way.

Dangriga to Punta Gorda - Five flights daily, US $61 each way.

Placencia to Punta Gorda - Five flights daily, US $39.50 each way.

Maya Air (☎ 422-2333, www.mayaair.com) offers many flights to various points in Belize. Because the prices become repetitious, I have omitted them from all but the Belize City flights.

MAYA AIR FLIGHTS

FROM THE INTERNATIONAL AIRPORT TO:

San Pedro - Eleven flights a day, US $51.50 each way. From the Municipal Airport there are six flights a day, US $35.50 each way.

Caye Caulker - Three flights a day, US $51.50 each way. From the Municipal Airport there are five flights a day, US $31 each way.

Caye Chapel - Three flights a day, US $51.50 each way. From the Municipal Airport there are five flights a day, US $31 each way.

Dangriga - Five flights a day, US $49.50 each way. From the Municipal Airport there are five flights a day, US $35.50 each way.

Placencia - Five flights a day, US $75 each way. From the Municipal Airport there are five flights a day, US $61 each way.

Punta Gorda - Five flights a day, US $93.50 each way. From the Municipal Airport there are five flights a day, US $81 each way.

Corozal - Two flights a day, US $75 each way. From the Municipal Airport there is one flight a day, US $64 each way.

Big Creek - Three flights daily, US $80 each way. From the Municipal Airport there are three flights a day, US $69 each way.

Florez, Guatemala - Two flights a day, US $93 each way.

FROM OTHER POINTS:

San Pedro to: the International Airport, eight flights a day; to the Municipal Airport, 10 flights a day; to Caye Caulker, Dangriga, Placencia and Punta Gorda, five flights a day; to Corozal and Big Creek, three flights a day; to Florez, Guatemala, two flights a day.

Punta Gorda to: the International Airport, four flights a day; to the Municipal Airport, San Pedro and Placencia, five flights a day; to Caye Caulker, Caye Chapel and Dangriga, four flights a day; to Big Creek, three flights; to Corozal and Florez, Guatemala, two flights a day.

Big Creek to: the International Airport, San Pedro, Caye Caulker, Caye Chapel and Florez, Guatemala, two flights a day; to the Municipal Airport, Punta Gorder and Dangriga, three flights a day.

Caye Caulker to: the International Airport, Dangriga, Placencia, Punta Gorda and San Pedro, five flights a day; to Big Creek, three flights a day; to Florez and Corozal, two flights a day.

Placencia to: the International Airport, San Pedro, Dangriga, Municipal Airport and Punta Gorda, five flights a day; to Caye Caulker and Caye Chapel, four flights a day; to Corozal and Florez, Guatemala, two flights a day.

Dangriga to: the International Airport, Municipal Airport, San Pedro, Placencia and Punta Gorda, five flights a day; to Caye Caulker, Caye Chapel and Corozal, four flights a day; to Florez, Guatemala, two flights; to Big Creek, one flight a day.

Caye Chapel to: the International Airport, Municipal Airport, Dangriga, Placencia and Punta Gorda, five flights a day; to Caye Caulker, four flights; to Big Creek, three flights; to Corozal and Florez, Guatemala, two flights a day.

Corozal to: the International Airport, Municipal Airport, San Pedro, Caye Caulker, Caye Chapel, Dangriga, Placencia and Punta Gorda, two flights a day; to Florez, Guatemala and Big Creek, one flight a day.

Florez, Guatemala to: the International Airport and San Pedro, two flights a day; to Caye Caulker, Caye Chapel, Dangriga, Placencia, Punta Gorda, Corozal and Big Creek, one flight a day.

When leaving Belize by air, the departure tax is US $35, which includes a US $3.75 Protected Areas Conservation Trust fee. If crossing the border overland, you must pay about US $20 each time you cross and occasionally they will not give you a complete 30 days when you visit.

FROM THE AIRPORT TO YOUR HOTEL

Taxis run from the airport to the city for a set rate of US $17.50. You can share a taxi with up to three other people, but make arrangements before leaving the terminal building; the taxi drivers become quite hostile if they catch you trying to get a group together once outside.

A **shuttle van** goes from the airport to San Ignacio and costs US $5. The vans meet all TACA, American Airlines and Continental Airlines flights.

You can get from Ladyville (where the airport is located) by **public bus**, but you must walk from the airport to the main road and then wait for a local bus. This is for serious budget travelers only.

Water taxis are available at the Marine Building in Belize City if you want to go to the cayes. The last one leaves at 5 pm.

Caye Caulker Water Taxi, ☎ 203-1969 or 209-4992, www.gocaye-caulker.com, offers a good schedule:

> Belize City to Caye Caulker - 9, 10:30 am, 12, 1:30, 3, 5 pm
>
> Belize City to San Pedro - 9 am, 12 and 3 pm
>
> Caye Caulker to San Pedro - 7, 8:30, 10 am, 1, 4 pm
>
> San Pedro to Caye Caulker - 8, 9:30, 11:30 am, 2:30, 4:30 pm
>
> San Pedro to Belize City - 8, 9:30, 11:30 am, 2:30, 4:30 pm
>
> Caye Caulker to Belize City - all water taxis leave Caye Caulker half an hour after they leave San Pedro. It takes 45 minutes to reach Caye Caulker from BC and an additional 30 to go from Caulker to San Pedro. The cost is US $10 one way.

Caye Caulker Water Taxi also has boats for day-trips from Belize City to Burrell Boom to see birds, crocodiles, iguanas and howler monkeys (US $300) and Gales Point to see manatees (US $350). Half-day fishing trips for up to four people are US $125.

Thunderbolt Water Taxi (Captain Cesario Rivero) is based on Ambergris Caye, ☎ 226-2217. Thunderbolt goes from San Pedro to Belize City and back or from Corozal to San Pedro and back. They have their station on the lagoon side of the island in San Pedro and at the Tourist Village in Belize City.

> Belize City to San Pedro - 8 am, 1 and 5 pm (US $10)
>
> San Pedro to Belize City - 7, 11 am and 4 pm (US $10)
>
> San Pedro to Corozal - 7 am (US $15)
>
> Corozal to San Pedro - 3 pm (US $15)

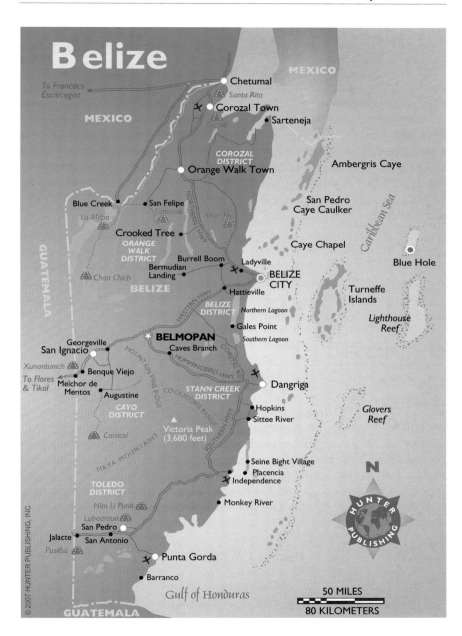

© 2007 HUNTER PUBLISHING, INC

■ BY BUS

Three major bus companies travel to different parts of the country. **Venus Bus**, ☎ 207-3354, travels north to Corozal and the Mexican border; **Novelos**, ☎ 207-2025/3929, travels west to the Guatemala border; and **James**, ☎ 702-2049, travels south to Punta Gorda. Smaller companies will take you to outlying villages, usually a minimum of three times per week; ask the locals.

Novelo buses leave from the Guatemalan border every 30 minutes starting at 3 am and arrive in San Ignacio one hour later. The last bus leaves the Guatemalan border at 5:30 pm. The cost is US 25¢ for the regular and US 50¢ for the express bus.

They also run from San Ignacio to Belize City every 30 minutes and the last bus leaves San Ignacio at 5 pm. Nonstop express buses take 2.5 hours to reach Belize City (45 minutes quicker than the regular bus). The cost is US $2.50 for the regular and US $3 for the express.

At time of writing, Novelos Bus Company was on strike and the general belief was that the government would take it over. During the strike bus travel was interrupted although not discontinued.

Buses leave the Mexican border starting at 4 am, and run every half-hour until 7:30 pm. The cost to Belize City is US $5 for the regular and US $6 for the express.

■ CAR RENTALS

 Four big American franchises offer service in Belize – **Budget** (☎ 800-404-8033, www.budget.com), **Hertz** (☎ 800-654-3131, www.hertz.com), **Thrifty** (☎ 800-847-4389, www.thrifty.com) and **Avis** (☎ 800-230-4898, www.avis.com). Additionally, you can rent a vehicle from one of a handful of smaller companies in Belize City or San Ignacio. Prices are always quoted in US dollars and you must have a major credit card. At some places, a charge of up to $1,500 may be written on the credit card imprint as a form of security; this will be destroyed upon the car's safe return.

Some companies allow you to take your rental vehicle off the major highways and onto secondary roads. Some don't. Only one company (Crystal) will allow you take the car into Guatemala or Mexico, but you must inform the company of your plans before you sign the agreement. (Agreement and vehicle type differ if going out of the country.)

Insurance is mandatory; a deductible of US $750 is payable by both parties involved at the time of an accident. A refund is forthcoming if you are proven the innocent party.

The only other document you will need is an International Driving Permit or a legal **driver's license** from your own country.

Gasoline is expensive, about US $4.25-$4.50 per gallon. This works out to about a dollar per liter.

Crystal Auto Rental, International Airport, ☎ 223-1600 or 800-777-7777, www.crystal-belize.com. Crystal charges US $88.45 per day and offers a 10% discount for rentals of over three days. This includes your insurance and unlimited mileage. If you pay in cash, there is an additional 5% discount. I rented from Crystal and the vehicle was a new four-cylinder Chevy Tracker with high clearance so I could go on the back roads. It had air conditioning, was economical and suited me fine.

JMA Motors Ltd., 771 Bella Vista, Belize City, ☎ 223-0226, jmagroup@btl.net. If reserving a vehicle through this company, you may work through Budget (see above). A small car costs US $90 per day for the first three days and the fourth day is free (except for the cost of insurance, about $14/day). This price includes unlimited mileage. JMA has vehicles ranging from 4WDs and pickup trucks to 12-passenger vans. The staff was helpful and supplied a car within an hour.

Safari Car Rentals, 11A Cork Street, Belize City, ☎ 223-0886 www.gocaribbean.about.com/cs/belizecars. The cost of a car is $80 a day, plus $14 per day for insurance. There is also an added 8% tax (which, incidentally, is not charged by other companies).

Thrifty Car Rental, Cental American Boulevard/Fabers Road, Ladyville, ☎ 207-1271, 800-847-4389, www.thrifty.com. I called this company looking for a car. Their prices were competitive, but I am still waiting for them to let me know if they have a car available.

For more companies, see the section on San Ignacio (page 277).

WATCH YOUR CAR, MISTER?

If asked by a local if your vehicle needs to be watched (for a fee) I would suggest paying and, after you leave with your vehicle intact, report the incident and give a description of the "protector" to the police. If you elect not to pay the protection fee, you may find your tires poked full of holes from an ice pick.

DRIVING

In Belize City the traffic is heavy during rush hours. Most streets are narrow and all are one-way. The roads often have potholes and everyone travels slowly.

Of the 1,678 miles (2,685 km) of highway in the country, only 311 miles (498 km) is paved. The traffic is sparse and people travel quite slowly (except for the odd hot-rodder). Once out of the city, the highways are narrow, with little shoulder room. Off the highway, the roads are deplorable – all gravel with huge potholes. While bumping along, my teeth banging in my head, I devised a new rating system. The roads fall between a 5 mph road and a 30 mph road. Most fall in the 5 to 15 mph category. Take this into consideration when planning your day.

Driving is on the **right side** of the road and road signs are international. However, if making a left turn on the highway, you first pull onto the right-hand shoulder. Check both ways and wait until there is no traffic. Then pull across both lanes and onto the road you want. This seems like a recipe for disaster, but it is actually an indication of how few cars there are on the roads.

Seat belts are mandatory for everyone in the front seat and failing to use them can result in a fine of US $25.

■ HITCHHIKING

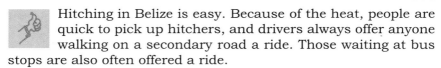 Hitching in Belize is easy. Because of the heat, people are quick to pick up hitchers, and drivers always offer anyone walking on a secondary road a ride. Those waiting at bus stops are also often offered a ride.

However, any opportunist will recognize you as a foreigner, and would know you have at least some money. The person may be quick to exploit you once they have picked you up. There are stories about rapes of female hitchers along the road to Sarteneja, Bullet Tree and other isolated places. Hitching is probably safe if you are a group of two or three people. I would avoid hitching when alone. On the other hand, I walked along the back roads in Toledo district and was often offered rides that I took. It never occurred to me that I could have been in danger; the lack of tourists in that part of the country means that crooks are less likely to be prepared to rob.

> **AUTHOR NOTE:** *A new website, launched in 2005 and run by the Belize Tourism Association, called the **Toucan Trail**, www.toucantrail.com, has affordable accommodations listed along with information on what to see and do while in Belize. The site is directed to the independent traveler. Those needing more information than is provided here should visit the site.*

DIRECTORY

GENERAL DIRECTORY

■ OUTFITTERS & TOUR OPERATORS

Eco Summer Expeditions . . . . ☎ 800-465-8884 . . . . www.ecosummer.com

Gap Adventures . . . . ☎ 800-465-5600 . . . . www.gap.ca

Global Travel . . . . ☎ 01268-541732 (UK) . . . . www.global-travel.co.uk
. . . . ☎ 522-3262 (Dangriga)

Island Expeditions . . . . ☎ 800-667-1630 . . . . www.islandexpeditions.com

Journeys International . . . . ☎ 800-255-8735 . . . . www.journeys-intl.com
. . . . ☎ 734-665-4407

Peter Hughes Diving . . . . ☎ 305-669-9391 . . . . www.peterhughes.com

Sea and Explore Belize . . . . ☎ 800-345-9786 . . . .

Slickrock Adventures . . . . ☎ 800-390-5715 . . . . www.slickrock.com

Sunny Skies Adventures . . . . ☎ 226-3026 . . . . www.sunnyskyadventures.com

■ WATER TAXI SERVICE

Caye Caulker . . . . ☎ 203-1969, 209-4992 . . . . www.gocayecaulker.com

Thunderbolt . . . . ☎ 226-2217 . . . .

■ CAR RENTAL COMPANIES

Avis . . . . ☎ 800-230-4898 . . . . www.avis.com

Budget . . . . ☎ 800-404-8033 . . . . www.drivebudget.com

Crystal Auto Rental . . . . ☎ 223-1600, 800-777-7777 . . . . www.crystal-belize.com

Hertz . . . . ☎ 800-654-3131 . . . . www.hertz.com

JMA Motors . . . . ☎ 223-0226 . . . . jmagroup@btl.net

Safari Car Rentals . . . . ☎ 223-0886

Thrifty Car Rental . . . . ☎ 207-1271, 800-847-4389 . . . . www.thrifty.com

■ AIRLINES

Air Jamaica . . . . ☎ 800-523-5585 . . . . www.airjamaica.com

Aeromexico . . . . ☎ 800-237-6639 . . . . www.aeromexico.com

American Airlines . . . . ☎ 800-433-7300 . . . . www.aa.com

Cayman Airways . . . . ☎ 800-422-9626 . . . . www.caymanairways.com

Continental . . . . ☎ 800-525-0280 . . . . www.continental.com

Maya Air . . . . ☎ 422-2333 . . . . www.mayaair.com

Mexicana . . . . ☎ 800-531-7921 . . . . www.mexicana.com

TACA Airlines . . . . ☎ 800-535-8780 . . . . www.grupotaca.com

Tropic Air . . . . ☎ 800-422-3435, 226-2012 . . . . www.tropicair.com

■ BUS COMPANIES

James Bus . . . . ☎ 702-2049

Novelo Bus . . . . ☎ 207-2025

Venus Bus . . . . ☎ 207-3354

Travel Information

GENERAL DIRECTORY

■ EMBASSIES

Belize Embassy . . . . ☎ 202-332-9636 . . . . www.embassyworld.com/
. . . . or 212-599-0233 . . . . embassy/belize

For foreign embassies within Belize, see *Emergency Contacts*, page 541, in the *Appendix*.

■ EMERGENCIES

American Express . . . . ☎ 227-7363 . . . . www.americanexpress.com

US Center for Disease Control & Prevention . . . . www.cdc.gov

Visa/Mastercard . . . . ☎ 800-336-3386. . . . . www.visa.com
. . . . www.mastercard.com

Western Union . . . . ☎ 227-0014 . . . . www.westernunion.com

■ INSURANCE COMPANIES

F & G Insurance. . . . . ☎ 227-7493 . . . . www.fandginsurance.com

International Plan . . . . ☎ 888-825-9777 . . . . www.internationalplan.com

RBC Insurance . . . . ☎ 800-565-3129 . . . . www.rbcinsurance.com

■ USEFUL WEBSITES

Belize Discover. . . . . www.belizediscover.com

Belize Now . . . . www.belizenow.com

Belize Online Tourism & Investment Guide . . . . www.belize.com

General Travel Information. . . . . www.belizereport.com

Travel Belize . . . . www.travel-belize.com

Belize City

INTRODUCTION

Although not the capital of the country, Belize City is the largest city in the nation. It is also the center of commerce, culture and transportation. The census showed a population of 68,197 in 2004, although unofficial estimates go as high as 84,200 residents, a third of the country's total population.

BC, as the city is commonly called, is a collection of majestic colonial houses interspersed with clapboard shacks rigged with huge wooden vats that collect rain water from the tin roofs. Decorating the vats and roofs of these buildings are palm trees and flowering bougainvillea. Mosquitoes breed in the open sewers bordering the black-topped streets and in the swamps beyond the sea walls.

The city's populace is as colorful as its buildings. It is a mixture of black and white, brown and yellow. For a developing nation, Belize has citizens that look healthy and dress in very clean clothes. All have smiles (even if they rob you) and the time to talk.

■ CITY LIFE

In the past, Belize City was considered a dangerous and crime-riddled place. Built on a history of rum running and buccaneering pirates, at one time it may have been more intimidating. Today, there are fewer pan-handlers in the crowded and busy streets than there are in Seattle or Vancouver. On my most recent visit, I was not bothered even once by hustlers trying to sell me something.

Like any major center in the world, Belize City does have robberies and murders. There are organized gangs and drug runners, thugs and petty criminals. As an obvious foreigner, you should be as cautious in Belize City as you would in Los Angeles, London or Nairobi.

Because tourism is an important part of the economy, Belize established a **Tourist Police Force** in 1995. These officers can be seen walking or riding bicycles on the streets in the core of the city, alert to the presence of trouble. Since their formation, petty crime against foreigners has decreased. They will come and speak with you or shadow you if they feel you are in a dangerous situation.

But don't let potential crime deter you. I hope you take the time to enjoy the city by exploring historical spots, eating in great restaurants, and talking with those who call BC home. It is an interesting and friendly place to be.

■ ORIENTATION

The heart of Belize City is split by **Haulover Creek**, at the mouth of the Belize River. The most common landmark and reference point is the **Swing Bridge** that goes over the river as it flows into the Caribbean Sea. The only one of its kind in the Americas, the bridge separates the residential north part of the city from the commercial south. Once a day, at around 5:30 pm, this hand-operated bridge swings open to allow ships up or down the river.

In contrast to the rest of the country, which is laid back and easy going, the southeastern side of the Swing Bridge, in the commercial area of Regent and Albert Streets, is a cauldron of human activity. It's an interesting part of town during the day, but a place that foreigners should avoid at night as this is where a lot of the crimes occur. Taxis are plentiful and cost US $2.50/BZ $5 to anywhere in the city. Use them as an inexpensive safety precaution.

Another area that seems busy and intimidating is where the out-of-town buses arrive and depart near the Belchina bridge, also in the southeastern part of town. Again, take a taxi to and from this area, especially if you have baggage that makes you look like a tourist.

AVERAGE TEMPERATURES & RAINFALL			
	Daily temp.	Humidity	Monthly rainfall
JAN	74.6°F/23.7°C	74%	54.9 inches/139.6 cm
FEB	77.2°F/25.1°C	69%	26.6 inches/67.8 cm
MAR	80°F/26.6°C	68%	21.8 inches/55.4 cm
APR	82.1°F/27.8°C	71%	24.1 inches/61.5 cm
MAY	84.0°F/28.9°C	69%	42.7 inches/108.6 cm
JUN	84.4°F/29.1°C	75%	25.5 inches/65 cm
JULY	83.7°F/28.7°C	73%	92.4 inches/235.2 cm
AUG	83.8°F/28.8°C	74%	72.5 inches/184.4 cm
SEPT	83.3°F/28.5°C	76%	72.5 inches/184 cm
OCT	81.5°F/27.5°C	74%	98.3 inches/250.1 cm
NOV	79.2°F/26.2°C	77%	77.9 inches/198.3 cm
DEC	77.2°F/25.1°C	76%	69.1 inches/175.8 cm

Information provided by Historical and current records at the National Meteorological Service at Philip SW Goodson International Airport in Ladyville.

HISTORY

Some locals claim that Belize City is one of the swampiest, hottest and most humid places in the country, but is in no danger of sinking into the bog because it is built on a solid foundation of mahogany chips, sand ballast and empty rum bottles.

■ TRADE

During the 1600s the wealth of the **mahogany logwood trade** was established. Logs were floated down to Belize City, so warehouses and wharves were built. Logging was hard; by 1690, the British realized that slaves would be needed to make this industry lucrative. Slaves were brought from Africa for the industry. The population quickly increased to an estimated 400 people and the capital city was moved from St. George's caye just offshore, to the present site of Belize City.

By 1786 enough sand and brick ballast (it was replaced with mahogany for the return voyage) was dumped into the swamp at the mouth of the creek to create solid ground. The city soon had an influx of people interested in the logging industry either directly or indirectly. As a consequence, the population increased to over 2,000. In 1787 a hurricane obliterated the entire town except for one building. In an attempt to protect the people from future hurricanes, a second city was established 15 miles upriver. However, because of its location on the Caribbean Sea, Belize City continued to flourish.

"BELIZE"

The name Belize has at least three possible origins. The first is from the Maya words "beliz," which means muddy water, or "belekin," which means towards the east. The second origin could be from the French word "balise," which means beacon. Because of its importance to the trade routes in the Caribbean, there was always a beacon on or near the mouth of the Belize River. The third possible origin (and the least likely) is that the word was a corruption of the name Wallace. Wallace was either a notorious pirate who landed on the city's shores in 1638, or Peter Wallace, the founding father of the city.

■ DEVELOPMENT

By 1790 there were 2,656 residents and Yarborough Cemetery, the city's first, was opened. The 1800s saw the formation of **Fort George Island**, an area north of the Belize River that is now part of Belize City. There was also the building of **St. John's Church**. A wooden bridge was built across the river and development of the south side of the city began. A new **court house** was constructed on Regent Street in 1819 and by 1857 a **prison** was built out of the bricks that had been brought from England as ballast in the bowels of the ships. By 1859 the population was at an explosive 6,000 people and before the turn of the century three **newspapers** had been established.

■ PEAKS & VALLEYS

Through all this development, Belize City suffered from hurricanes and devastating fires but, like the phoenix, she rose again and again. The first hurricane, in 1787, destroyed everything except one building. A fire in 1806 got rid of many buildings and then another in 1856 destroyed almost everything on the north side of the city.

In 1862, the city was made the capital of **British Honduras**, an official British colony. Arson in 1863 caused the destruction of the south side of the city and then again in 1918 most of the public buildings were burned when soldiers rioted against the racism they were experiencing.

But by 1918 Belize City was built into a modern metropolis with banks and poorhouses, newspapers and motor cars. There were street lights, a telephone exchange, radio station and telegraph system. By 1931, important people like **Marcus Garvey** and **Charles Lindbergh** had come to visit and the population had risen to 16,687.

MARCUS GARVEY

Marcus Garvey was born in St. Ann's Bay, Jamaica in 1887 to a poor black family. He finished grade six and went to Kingston as a printer's apprentice. It was the influence of the printed word that inspired him to start writing and publishing. He wrote about what he knew – the need of black people to rise above their oppressors.

In his early years, Garvey traveled around Central America publishing articles and speaking to others who believed the blacks needed better living conditions. Finally, in 1914 he and his future wife Amy Ashwood co-founded the **Universal Negro Improvement Association** (UNIA). This earned him a small but loyal following.

Garvey knew that a better life for blacks in the Caribbean would never occur unless he could first convince American blacks that they should follow his philosophy. He went to New York penniless and lived with a family in Harlem. After working in a print shop all day, Garvey would stand on a street corner and preach his beliefs.

Eventually, his following grew to about four million people. The UNIA needed money, so he started publishing the *Negro World Newspaper*. After six months the newspaper had a subscription list of about 75,000. The money earned from this helped Garvey promote his beliefs. He purchased ships so that he could transport and trade with other countries that had large black populations.

Corruption within the organization and opponents like J. Edgar Hoover of the FBI soon caused the fall of Garvey. He was imprisoned, his publications were banned and he was deported from the US.

In 1940, as he was sitting at home after suffering a stroke, he died while reading about his death. The newspaper had gotten the facts wrong about his stroke.

Belize City

> Garvey always maintained an active chapter of the UNIA in Belize. It was in support of this chapter that Garvey was inspired to visit the little country in 1922 and again in 1928.

The year 1931 was disastrous for the city. On September 10th, the residents were celebrating the Battle of St. George's Caye when a hurricane hit, ripping away houses and smashing down trees. More than 2,000 people were left dead or missing and the cost of rebuilding almost broke the city financially. But strong will prevailed. The city prospered and continued to grow until 1961 when Hurricane Hattie's tidal wave and 96 mph/155kmh winds destroyed so much that the government moved its headquarters to the new capital of Belmopan, a few miles inland. Again the city was rebuilt and the residents, through these hardships, became possessive and proud of their town.

The country won **independence** from Britain and the first Belizean flag was hoisted over Government House on September 21, 1981.

EMORY KING

Emory King, a colorful local character, was shipwrecked on the cayes of Belize in 1953. This compelled him to make Belize his home and, as it turned out, the country became his passion. He has authored many history and travel books about Belize, is a newspaper columnist, a broadcaster and realtor. King is quoted by Fodor as saying, "In the north we raise sugar cane. In the south we raise citrus and bananas and rice. In the west we raise cattle and pigs and corn. In Belize City we raise hell."

GETTING AROUND

Walking is the best way to get around in the center of the city. Most places of interest are within a short distance of each other.

> **AUTHOR NOTE:** *Cycling in the city is not advisable because the streets are narrow and the traffic heavy. Also, motorists are not accustomed to cyclists, so courtesy toward them is not common.*

Public **buses** go anywhere in the city for BZ $1. You may have to take more than one bus to get where you want to go, but those living in the city can give you directions on which bus to take and where to catch it. As a general rule, once out of the heavy traffic common in the core of the city, the bus will stop to pick you up almost anywhere; just put your arm out to indicate that you want the bus to stop. Otherwise, you must go to a marked bus stop – there will be a sign on a post indicating the spot.

Taxis have green license plates (as opposed to white ones on private vehicles) and will go anywhere in the city for BZ $5. Because the price of gas is high (BZ $9-$10/gallon), taxis often take more than one passenger along a route. If you are coming from the bus station, a popular point of origin, you can be almost certain there will be more than one person riding with you. Each person will pay BZ $5. Taxis from the airport to anywhere in town cost BZ $40 and the drivers get very angry if you try to share a taxi with someone not in your party. I suggest teaming up with others *before* you leave the terminal building. These drivers have a monopoly on the trade and are protective of their fares.

Driving your own vehicle in the core of Belize City requires a lot of nerve. The streets are all one way, narrow and busy and there are also a few traffic circles to tackle. However, once in the suburbs and not during rush hours, driving is no problem.

The city harbor.

Belize City

1. Marine Terminal & Marine Museum/ Coastal Zone Museum
2. Image Factory
3. Tourist Village
4. Audubon Society
5. Fort George Lighthouse & Barron Bliss Tomb
6. Radisson Fort George
7. National Handicrafts Center & Memorial Park
8. National Museum/Tourist Office
9. Charles Lindbergh Park
10. Police Station
11. Covered market
12. Supreme Court
13. Belize Telephone Limited (BTL)
14. Bliss Institute/National Library
15. St. John's Cathedral
16. House of Culture
17. Santino's Bike Shop
18. Bus Station
19. Flag Circle

NATIONAL STADIUM

NEWTOWN BARRACKS ROAD

NEWTOWN BARRACKS

HUNTER

ER ST

FULLERS

WILSON ST

CALLE AL MAR

FREETOWN RD

MATRON ROBERTS

KELLY ST

NURSE SEAY ST

SIMON LAMB ST

CRAN

SLAUGHTER HOUSE ROAD

HAULOVER CREEK

BELCAN BRIDGE

N ST

NORTHERN HWY

To International Airport, Belmopan & Corozal

PRINCESS MARGARET DRIVE

MOGUEL

VASQUEZ

GENTLE AVE

LIZARRAGA AVE

MEIGHAN AVE

SMITH ST

LOTTIE WAIGHT

LESLIE ST

ST. THOMAS ST

ST. MATTHEW

ST. CHARLES

ST. MARK

ST. LUKE

ST. JOHN

ST. EDWARD

PRINCESS MARGARET DRIVE

K ST

19TH ST

1ST H

H ST

12TH ST

8TH ST

6TH ST

4TH ST

3RD ST

1ST ST

DUNN ST

ST. PETER'S ST

GUADALUPE ST

ST. JOSEPH ST

HELSNER

G ST

F ST

E ST

D ST

A ST

18TH ST

17TH ST

16TH ST

15TH ST

14TH ST

13TH ST

11TH ST

9TH ST

7TH ST

5TH ST

2ND ST

C ST

HOPKINS ST

LANDIVAR ST

ST. JAMES

BAYMEN AVE

Caribbean Sea

600 YARDS
550 METERS

MARINE PARADE
HONDURAS
SOUTH PARK
NORTH PARK
CORK ST
DREDGE ST
FORT ST
EYRE ST
HUTSON
GABOUREL
HANDYSIDE
NORTH FRONT ST
ANGEL
EVE ST
MORTUARY
GAOL LN
CRAIG
DALY ST
ALBERT ST
BARRACKS RD
QUEEN ST
NORTH SIDE CANAL
SWING BRIDGE
HYDES LN
PETTICOAT ALLEY
PICKSTOCK ST
RHABURNS
CRADLE ALLEY
USHER
PRICE
NEW RD
NORTH FRONT ST
BELCHINA BRIDGE
ADAMS
REGENT ST
RECTORY
PALM
ALBERT ST WEST
COCKBURN
BERKLEY
WAGNER
SOUTH
DEAN
PRINCE
KING
BISHOP
CHURCH
DICK LN
REGENT ST WEST
WATER
RICHARD
ALEXANDRA
LINDOS
VERNON ST
EBONY ST
WOODS
BAGDAD
ORANGE ST
GLYN ST
CAIRO
MOSUL
FAR WEST ST
WEST ST
GEORGE ST
PLUES ST
WEST CANAL ST
EAST CANAL ST
BASRA
SOUTH SIDE CANAL
EAST CANAL CANAL
ROCKY
DICKENSON
QUEEN CHARLOTTE ST
CEMETERY LANE
RACECOURSE ST
SOUTHERN FORESHORE
BIRDS ISLE
ALBERT ST EAST
TIGRIS ST
EUPHRATES ST
AMARA AVE
ALLENBY ST
EAST COLLET CANAL ST
WEST COLLET CANAL ST
JOHNSON ST
MAGAZINE RD
HICCATEE
WELCH
DOLPHIN ST
ARMADILLO
BOCCOTORA ST
CURRASOW ST
SEAGULL ST
RACOON
PELICAN
IGUANA
ANTELOPE
GIBNUT ST
CEMETERY RD
BANAK RD
LOGWOOD ST
LAKE VIEW ST
VERNON ST
SITTEE ST
PINE
MAYFLOWER ST
EBONY ST
MARGUSTA ST
CENTRAL AMERICAN BL
CENTRAL AMERICAN BLVD
NORTH CREEK RD
SOUTH CREEK RD
RAMSEY
BEN BOW ST
NEAL'S PEN RD
MONROE
FABER'S ROAD
WAIGHT ST
RIVERO
BARNETT
HAYNES
KRAAL
FAIRWEATHER
MEX AVE
YOUNG
KUT AVE
CAESAR RIDGE RD

1 2 3 4 5 6 7 8 10 11 12 13 14 15 16 17 18

ADVENTURES & SIGHTSEEING

■ ADVENTURES ON FOOT

WALKING TOUR ~ DAY 1

 Start at the swing bridge and walk on the northwestern side of the city. This will introduce you to the sometimes intimidating pace and activities of the city.

The first **wooden bridge** over Haulover Creek was built in 1818 so that those transporting cattle would no longer have to drag them across the water with ropes. Because of the humidity and constant use, the first bridge soon rotted and a second wooden structure was built in 1859. When this had to be replaced, residents built a swing bridge to accommodate boats that now traveled up and down the Belize River. Finally, a metal bridge, made in Liverpool, England, was brought over and put across the water. This too could be moved so boats could pass. It is one of only a few hand-operated bridges in the Americas and Belizeans are reluctant to have it removed or replaced for any reason.

Water taxi stand, Ambergris Caye.

On the corner of North Front Street beside the swing bridge is the **Marine Terminal**, where the water taxis depart for the offshore cayes. **Thunderbolt**, **Andrea** and **Triple J Ferries** offer several fast boats between BC and San Pedro on Ambergris Caye. The most accessible boats are those in the Water Taxi Association. All ferries leave from the Swing Bridge area.

The terminal has always been a bustling and colorful place. Logs were floated down the river and sold to waiting merchants here who, in turn, shipped the logs around the world. The terminal is also where slaves were displayed before they were sold to landowners. Fishermen have always congregated at this junction of fresh and salt water, offloading and selling their daily catch. Built in 1923, the building was originally the city's fire station.

The terminal also houses the **Maritime Museum** and the **Coastal Zone Museum**. Both are open daily from 8 am to 4:30 pm; tickets are sold just outside the door, at the same booth where water taxi tickets are sold, and are good for both museums. The cost is BZ $4 per person, but US $4 for foreigners. The museum's main floor has model boats and documents on display in dusty glass cases with little lighting. It offers a historical account of the maritime history of Belize. Upstairs is a collection of shells and corals illustrating the oceanography of the area. The entire museum is in dire need of repair and care. ☎ 223-1969.

Across North Front Street from the terminal building where there is now an empty lot, was the old Paslow Building. On September 29, 2002, a court clerk who had been falsifying records for his own financial benefit set fire to the building in order to destroy any traces of his fraud. To date, there are no plans to rebuild.

THOMAS PASLOW

Thomas Paslow was a slave owner known for mistreating his slaves.

Continuing along North Front Street to the northeast is the Sea Sports Belize office (an easy-to-spot landmark) and just beyond, at 91 North Front Street, is the **Image Factory**, ☎ 223-4151. This fairly new gallery was actively promoted by the Prime Minister's son, Yasser Musa and his co-supporter Gilvano Swasey. Since its inception in 1995 it has had over 30 exhibitions, some from as far away as New York, England and Australia. Locally, the gallery promotes artists such as Pamela Braun, a natural-life painter who has worked hard to raise public awareness of women artists in Belize. Numerous Belizian artists display their work here, including Richard Holder, a street-life photographer, Hugh Broaster, a sculptor, and Betty Cooper, a painter from Dangriga.

Continue along until North Front Street hits Handyside. Cross over and follow Fort Street past the **Wet Lizard** (where you might like to stop for lunch), and you will come to the entrance of the new **Tourism Village**, www.belizetouristvillage.com, built in part by the rich Belizean entrepreneur Barry Bowen as a duty-free shopping center. His plan was to attract the cruise ship tourist business. To date, he has been only moderately successful and many of the rental spaces in the tourist village are empty. Locals throughout the country are complaining about the cruise ship business, whose passengers, known as "flushers," come to Belize, benefit only a few people in the tourist trade, and leave nothing but their ship's bilge content for the rest of the people in the country.

But the village is worth a visit. There are restaurants with live entertainment, an Internet café and shops selling everything from alcohol to imported tobacco or souvenir trinkets. The mall is open until 6 pm daily. As this shopping center catches on, more people will patronize it. At the moment it is kind of spooky unless there is a cruise ship in harbor.

She Sells Sea Shells, ☎ 223-7426, open same times as the Tourist Village, is in booth 21A. It's an exquisite shop that sells and trades in rare shells. The owner displays shells like the **paper nautilus** that weighs less than a feather. The **helmet** comes from a female squid, who uses the "helmet" as a floatation device. One rare shell, called **Glory of the Sea**, sold for US $1,800 to an American collector. My favorite was the **Venus comb**, a conch shell with spines. Be certain to stop here and perhaps buy something.

Continuing along Fort Street you will come to the **Audubon Society**, ☎ 223-4987. Stop in and get the latest information about the parks and reserves for which the society is responsible. Maybe make a small donation or purchase an item for sale in the little shop.

The next landmark is the **Bliss Lighthouse** and **Tomb of Baron Bliss**, Belize's greatest benefactor. Each year on March 9th a ceremony is held at his tomb below the lighthouse in Belize Harbor. This is followed by sailing regattas. You cannot go inside the lighthouse. Read the full story of Baron Bliss on page 65, *National Holidays*.

Across from the lighthouse is the **Radisson Fort George** as well as numerous colonial mansions. Take a look at the Fort Street Guest House and Restaurant, which is now closed. It looks to be in a state of disrepair. Next, continue up Cork Street to **Memorial Park**, where World War I heroes are commemorated. The park is a pleasant place to sit and rest before continuing your tour of the city.

The **National Handi-crafts Center**, 2 South Park Street, ☎ 223-3636, bcci@btl.net, was established in 1992 to help local artists. It is a cooperative that has a wide range of goods such as zericote and mahogany carvings, slate sculptures, oil paintings and jippi jappa baskets. Jippi jappa is the green palm leaf you'll often see used in woven articles. There are a total of 550 artists in the cooperative and they all live in Belize. The co-op takes goods on consignment and is presently working hard to export some of the works. I encourage you to purchase pieces from a cooperative

Baron Bliss Lighthouse & Monument.

like this because more of the profits go directly to the artist. Also, it allows you to see first-hand the high quality of work available, as compared to cheaper imitations.

The **Chamber of Commerce** is in the same shop/building/office and shares the same staff. Both places are open from Monday to Friday, 8 am to 5 pm and Saturday from 8 am to 1 pm.

Walk south past the American Consulate on Gabourel Street until you see the Central Bank building, where the **tourist board** (☎ 223-1913 or 223-1910, www.travelbelize.org) is located. This office, open from 8 am to 5 pm, Monday to Friday, has information about upcoming cultural events in town, but few advertising pamphlets. The Central Bank building in front of it is the old prison that has been converted into the new **Museum of Belize**, ☎ 223-4524, www.museumofbelize.org. It opened in February of 2002 and is Belize's first national museum. The building was constructed in 1857 from ballast bricks and was used as a prison until 1993. Extensive renovations had to be completed before the building was safe to open as a museum. There was no wiring and many of the bricks and support beams needed securing. The work took eight months to complete.

To provide us with a glimpse of what the building once was, one cell has been restored. A cell was originally built to hold one man; at the time of the prison's closing each cell held six to eight men. Among other things, the museum's exhibition shows how, in the 1870s, hard prison labor included chopping mangroves at Prisoners' Creek. Another display shows how the prisoners soaked cocoa husks overnight and then beat them dry the following day. From these they made pillows and mattresses. If each man didn't reach his production quota, the missing amount was added to the next day's work, making it hard for the prisoner to ever catch up.

The country's 21st anniversary of independence was celebrated in 2002, and the museum had an exhibition around this theme. The curator, Gil Vano, is trying to change the exhibitions every six months or so.

The second floor of the museum is dedicated to Maya culture and holds such treasures as the buenavista vase found in Cayo. The polychrome vase depicts two male dancers dressed as corn gods. They have tricked the lords of death and are on their way out of hell. The exhibition also displays the famous carved jade head found by Prentergats's wife at Altun Ha and the jade mosaic mask found at Santa Rita.

 If Maya history intrigues you, pick up a copy of the excellent full-color book called **Maya Masterpieces** for sale at the museum. It describes some of the treasures found in the Maya display.

The entrance fee to the museum is US $5 (for foreigners) and it is open Tuesday to Friday, 10 am until 6 pm, and Saturdays, 10 am until 4 pm. All the staff, from the curator to the janitor, is fully trained to answer any questions you may have about the museum or its contents.

Going north from the museum to the sea wall and beyond, you will come to the **Charles Lindbergh Park**. The park was dedicated to Lindbergh because he landed his famous plane, *Spirit of St. Louis*, in Belize in 1927. This event, apparently, sparked the idea of an aviation industry in Belize, though it seems the spark wasn't that bright.

This completes the first day of your walking tour. Meet again at the swing bridge in the morning and we'll head over to the other side of the city.

WALKING TOUR ~ DAY 2

Cross the swing bridge and walk along Albert Street, going first past the **covered market**, built in 1993 to replace the original one that was established in 1820. There is mostly produce for sale here, but just outside the door and beside the swing bridge local artisans sell handmade jewelry, hats, carvings and beaded works. These are good to pick up for souvenirs. Next to the market is the banking district, set in the pie-shaped corner where Albert and Regent Streets meet. This was the location of the original courthouse, but the fire in 1918 destroyed the building.

Cutting across to Regent Street, you will come to a white colonial building with ornate iron works along the stairs and balcony. This is the **Supreme Court Building**, featuring a four-sided clock as its crown. The original building was constructed in 1818, but the court was not used until 1820. In 1918 the building was destroyed by fire. During the fire, the governor at the time, Hart Bennet, was struck by the burning flag pole and was killed. The building is across from Central Park, now called **Battlefield Park**, where a bust of labor leader **Antonio Soberanis** sits.

Before labor laws changed in the 1940s, a man could be forced into hard labor for three months if he left his job or broke his contract. Pay was low and days were long. Conditions didn't improve and the end of World War I left many men unemployed. Then came the Depression and more starvation for workers. In 1934 Soberanis organized and united workers to hold demonstrations against the government and wealthy merchants. Only after many workers were imprisoned and killed, did these demonstrations and riots lead to better working conditions for laborers.

Just beyond the Supreme Court and down along the ocean on Southern Foreshore Street is the **Bliss Institute**, named after the famous benefactor Barron Bliss. Today, it is the cultural center of Belize City and it hosts plays, concerts, and exhibitions. There is a permanent exhibition of Maya artifacts from Caracol. The display is open Monday to Thursday from 8 am to 5 pm and Friday until 1 pm. ☎ 227-2458. The Institute also houses the Belize Arts Council (same phone number).

Leave the ocean and go inland on any appealing street to Albert Street, where you will find **St. John's Cathedral**, the oldest Anglican church in Central America. It had its foundation stone laid in 1812. Like the prison, the church was constructed with ballast bricks. It was in this church between 1815 and 1845 that the kings of the Mosquito Coast were crowned. This is the only cathedral outside of England where the crowning of kings has occurred.

Belize City

West of the cathedral is **Yarborough Cemetery**, which has grave-stones dating back to 1781. Unlike other cemeteries, where bodies have been buried on top of one another when space got tight, Yarborough was declared full in 1870 and a new cemetery, located on Cemetery Road by the bus stations, was established.

Turn back toward the water to Regent Street and Government House, now renamed the **House of Culture**, ☎ 227-3050. Built in 1814, it is one of the oldest buildings in the city and was the seat of government for over 150 years. Since Hurricane Hattie, however, officials now hold office in Belmopan. In its day, the house saw visitors such as Queen Elizabeth and Prince Phillip, who stayed here during their 1994 visit. In 1839 Frederick Catherwood and John L Stephens stayed here en route to Central America and Mexico, where they uncovered and recorded the findings of numerous Maya sites.

Today you can go inside this historical museum (for a small fee) and see unique colonial antiques that include wine glasses used by Queen Victoria and paintings of past government officials. But the elegant building alone, with its mahogany staircases and hardwood furniture, is worth strolling through. The house is open Monday to Friday, 8:30 am to 4:30 pm. The gardens are open to birdwatchers for a mere US $2.50, so they can get a glimpse of some less common feathered creatures that may be hiding in the thick vegetation.

At the very end of land is a causeway joining Bird's Isle with the mainland. The island is a favorite spot for impromptu outdoor concerts.

As you stroll back along Albert Street toward the swing bridge, take note of the colonial houses that have what appear to be brick basements. In fact, it was here that slaves were chained at the end of their working days. Stop for lunch/dinner at **Macy's Café**, 18 Bishop Street, a popular restaurant for travelers and locals alike.

■ ADVENTURES ON WHEELS

CYCLING

 Although I don't recommend cycling in the city itself, I do encourage cyclists to connect with Belizean cycling groups and get to places out of town. If you must cycle in Belize City, you should bring your own bicycle; rentals are not available.

Santino's Bike Shop, 18 New Road, ☎ 223-2500, santinos@btl. net, is a great repair shop. Stop here to catch up on the latest cycle news or to make a connection so you can enter one of their monthly races.

For the latest schedule of events, including bike races throughout the year, visit www.belizeweb.com/calendar-of-events.htm.

Organized cycling events have a huge number of contestants and some of the races offer large prizes. Other races have prizes that you couldn't take home with you, such as goats and chickens; however, the fun of participation is worth forfeiting your winnings. Scheduled races throughout the year are detailed below. If you'd like to participate, visit Santino's Bike Shop.

 A great little book, reproduced by Emory King, is *Blazing Trails, on Bicycles and Motor Cars in British Honduras*. This book was first published in 1928 and describes, among other things, the Cross Country Classic Bike Race held that year. The book can be purchased for US $5 and has some great photos, poems, lists of competitors' names and tales of the event.

SHOPPING

Most tourists buy sculptures made from mahogany or zericote hardwood. There are men throughout the country who can sculpt your profile onto something like the handle of a cane or into a bust. **George Gabb** is the most famous carver in Belize, but if you want to commission him you will have to pay upwards of US $1,000 for a bust.

Another common art is **slate carving**, drawn from the Maya tradition. The reproductions are all copies of those found at one of the ruins in Belize. A carved slate sitting on a plate holder looks elegant in any living room.

Calabash painting is another popular craft. Calabash is a piece of dried gourd that Belizean artists use as a medium. These can be purchased at souvenir shops.

The **National Handicraft Center**, 2 South Park Street, ☎ 223-3636, has many unique designs on display and they vary from finely crafted toy sailboats to smooth wooden tapirs.

In Belize City you can buy **handmade jewlelry** and a few crafts from the artists located outside the market beside the swing bridge. For these items you must barter.

Belize City

BIG ON BARTERING

- Look the artist in the eye and suggest that you have seen better art just down the street.
- Try to get the piece on commission, a price to be paid only when you find out that the artist is as famous as she/he claims.
- Ask if you can pay in full only after you sell the art in the New York art gallery (which you own).
- Talk about the weather, the cost of peanuts and the political situation in Belize.
- Point out flaws, like the fact that the color of the wood does not match the color of your shoes.

I was amazed at the variety and quality of products at the **Wet Lizard Gift Shop**, 1 Fort Street, ☎ 223-5973. Many of the pieces cannot be found anywhere else in Belize. There are handmade paper books with painted wooden covers and locally crafted letter openers with exquisite designs on the blades. The goods are tastefully displayed and the staff is friendly.

The Tourism Village next door to the Wet Lizard has many craft shops that carry things like clothes made from local cotton, painted gourds (calabash), sea-shell chimes, black coral jewelry and paintings by local artists. The top painters in Belize are Jason Bennett, Carole Bowman, Carolyn Carr, Edwardo Alamilla, Marcos Larios and Walter Castillo. I have seen samples from most of the artists mentioned here, and they're good. Prices start in the hundreds and run into thousands of dollars. Many of these paintings can be found at **Fine Arts**, ☎ 227-5620.

My favorite shop is **She Sells Sea Shells**, ☎ 223-7426, described in the walking tour of Belize City, page 116.

Gallon Jug Agro-industry Ltd., #1 King Street, ☎ 227-7031, has many items for sale that are grown and produced on the Chan Chich estate. The most popular is their Mango Tango Gourmet Coffee, grown without the spraying of pesticides or herbicides. Also for sale are Lissette's Sweet Mango Jam and Secret Sauce of Spicy Mango that would taste good on any dish at home. Try the jam on your morning toast to remind you of your stay in Belize.

Belizean Style, 6238 Park Avenue, Buttonwood Bay, Belize City, ☎ 223-4660, www.gotees.net, is a high-end shop that screen print t-shirts, tanks, ladies tops, caps, visors and any other item you may want with a specific design. They also sell casual apparel to go with their well-designed shirts and silver jewelry to complement an entire outfit. The shop was formerly called Go Tees, when it was located downtown. Now it is 2.5 miles along the Northern Highway. To get there, turn right at the first corner past the traffic circle with all the flags. There is a sign at the turnoff. The store is three blocks down at Park Avenue.

PLACES TO STAY & EAT

■ ACCOMMODATIONS

 Accommodations are scattered throughout the city and run from basic to luxurious. Price ranges are per room, per night. Usually the price for a single and a double is the same.

HOTEL PRICES	
$	$20 to $50
$$	$51 to $75
$$$	$76 to $100
$$$$	$101 to $150
$$$$$	over $150

Mama Chen's, 7 Eve Street, ☎ 223-2057, $, was originally the Downtown Guest House. That property burned down and Miss Kinny sold the land to the present owners who re-built the house with the same cell-like rooms containing just a bed and fan and without private bath. However, it is new and clean. There is a very tiny TV area where you can watch the tube. Across the hall is a small restaurant where you can order a snack or breakfast or just enjoy a beer.

Sea Guest House, 18 Gabourel Lane, ☎ 223-9075, $, is across from the American Embassy. It's an odd place, but safe. Most rooms in this old colonial house have a shared bath. Off-street parking is available.

Barrack Guest House, 8 Barrack Road, ☎ 223-6671, $, has five dingy rooms, three with baths. All have fans. Rooms are located at the back of the building and you will have to be shown how to get inside the first time you arrive.

North Front Street Guest House, 124 North Front Street, ☎ 227-7595, thoth@btl.net, $, is a rambling old building run by Miss Matilde Speer who has lived in the house all her life. The eight rooms have shared bath and there's a large porch where you can sit at night and enjoy the street action.

Belize City

BURIED TREASURE

Henry Robateau was a pirate who ran rum between Jamaica and Belize in the fastest schooner on the high seas. During his last visit to Jamaica he got into too much rum and wild women, which resulted in his losing every penny he had. He decided that to get his money back he would have to put up a wager and race his boat against anyone willing. The challenge was met, the wager set and the men took off. Robateau won the race and with his winnings bought the house on 124 North Front Street. He buried the keel of his boat under the house and never left home to carouse again. As far as everyone knows, the keel is still under the house.

Seaside Guest House, 3 Prince Street, ☎ 227-8339, seaside belize@btl.net, $$, was once run by Quakers who enforced a strict curfew. But the place has since changed hands and the curfew is no longer in effect. The house is well decorated in bold colors and is safe, even though it is not in the best area of town. The six tiny rooms are all basic and there are dorm beds available for less money. You may order breakfast or purchase refreshments on site.

Freddie's Guest House, 86 Eve Street, ☎ 223-3851, $$, has been run by Mrs. Griffith for over 33 years. She must be doing something right. There are three rooms, two that share a bath and a

third with private bath. This clean and spacious house is only one block from the sea, and even offers its guests a garden in which to sit. Call ahead to book, as this is a popular place. However, do not pay with a wrinkled or torn bill as Mrs. Griffith will not accept it.

Three Sisters Guest House, 55 Eve Street, ☎ 223-5729, $$, is set in a large wooden house across the street from Freddie's. Its guest rooms are set around a main common area, where cable TV is available. The four rooms are large and two have private baths. Although not as bright as those at Freddie's, each room has a good fan.

Mopan Hotel, 55 Regent Street, ☎ 227-7351, hotelmopan@btl.net, $$, is across the street from the Coningsby. This 200-year old colonial house is newly painted in bold colors. Be aware that the warped floors may give you vertigo! There is a bar and restaurant on site, along with a tour agency that can arrange trips to a variety of interesting places.

D'Nest Inn, 475 Cedar St., ☎ 203-5416, $$, has three large, sunny rooms tastefully decorated with antique furnishings. Each room

has a private bath and air conditioning and some rooms overlook the river. Breakfast, cooked and served by owners, Gaby and Oty, is a culinary delight. The well-tended gardens are shared with wildlife such as iguanas and colorful birds. The only downfall is that the house is a bit distant from the center.

Bellevue Hotel, 5 Southern Foreshore, ☎ 227-7051, bellevue@btl. net, $$$, under new management, is now glistening with charm. Located on the south side of town on the water, the newly renovated hotel offers large, clean rooms with private bathrooms. There is a pool, bar, restaurant and Internet café. A few suites are also available.

Coningsby Inn, 76 Regent Street, ☎ 227-1566, coningsby_inn2001@yahoo.com, $$$, is a well-kept colonial home with comfortable rooms, air conditioning, private baths and a view that overlooks a littered backyard. The restaurant is famed for its good food, although one reader recently told

me that he was served leftovers for dinner and the same breakfast every day. The hotel was named by the owner's father (it was his middle name).

Bakadeer Inn, 74 Cleghorn Street, ☎ 223-0659, $$$, has 12 rooms, all with private bath, air conditioning, king-size beds and cable TV. There is secure parking and a common room and garden for guests to enjoy. This tutor-style house sits alongside the river and its name is tied into the lumber business. Bakadeer is Creole for "landing area." The McFields are an active family in Belize. Kent has an art/frame shop across the street from the hotel where local artwork can be purchased. Ian is involved in the real estate business. If you want to be in Belize on a more permanent basis, he will help you out. Melony is a marine biologist who has been the director of the Shipstern Reserve in Corozal District.

Grant Residence Bed & Breakfast, 126 Newtown Barrack Road, ☎ 223-0926, www.grantbedandbreakfast.com, $$$, is a family run establishment that makes personalized service their greatest feature. This spacious colonial home, luxuriously decorated, offers an open living/dining room for guests to use. Each bedroom faces the sea, has private bath, ceiling fan and cable TV. There is private parking and Internet service, and the house is just one block from the casino at the Princess.

Breakfast is a culinary adventure at this B&B. The owners, Ward and PJ, offer exciting dishes like a papaya boat – half a papaya topped with banana slices and drizzled with lime and coconut yogurt. Fry jack fans will be pleased to hear that their favorite Belizean breakfast item is also available here. In the evenings, Ward and PJ offer guests a complimentary drink. This gesture seems to reinforce the hosts' desire to make everyone feel welcome. Longer stay guests get every eighth day free.

At time of writing, this place was for sale. I hope the new owners can keep up the reputation of the present owners.

Villa Boscardi, 6043 Manatee Drive, Buttonwood Bay, ☎ 223-1691, www.villaboscardi.com, $$$, has five rooms. The spacious rooms, decorated in the finest European style (with cleanliness to match) all have private bath, cable TV, hardwood floors and air conditioning. There is also Internet service. Complimentary transportation to and from the airport is available every day except Sunday and on holidays, and a shuttle service runs into the center of the city for a small fee. They can also arrange a rental vehicle or special tours for their guests. This is one of the better places to stay in BC.

Chateau Caribbean, 6 Marine Parade (next to Memorial Park), ☎ 223-3888, www.chateaucaribbean.com, $$$$, is a colonial house that was once a hospital. It overlooks the ocean and has recently been renovated. Each room has air conditioning, a tiled bathroom, cable TV and a good view. The wrap-around porch dotted with wicker furniture is a draw. The restaurant has a notably good reputation. I did not find the staff particularly friendly.

Belize Biltmore Plaza (Best Western), Mile 3, Northern Highway, ☎ 223-2302, www.belizebiltmore.com, $$$$, is elegant. It has 80 spacious, air-conditioned rooms with cable TV and private baths. There is a safe deposit box, parking lot, business center, pool and gardens, gift shop, bar and restaurant. The staff is friendly and helpful and the tour office can arrange all trips from horseback riding to jungle river expeditions and fishing.

Radisson Fort George Hotel & Marina, 2 Marine Parade, ☎ 223-3333, 800-333-3333 (US), www.radisson.com, $$$$$, has 102 rooms in two buildings. Each room has air conditioning, private bath, coffee maker, hair dryer, mini bar, radio, data port, direct-dial telephone and cable TV. The rooms overlook either the Caribbean Sea or a well-tended garden. There is a restaurant, tavern, pool, dive shop, tour agency and gift shop. Even if you don't stay here, you should visit for a cocktail one evening.

Princess Hotel & Casino, Newtown Barracks in Kings Park area, ☎ 223-2670, www.princessbelize.com, $$$$$, has a total of 181 first-rate rooms with all the amenities of a first-rate hotel. It also has a plethora of entertainment facilities. There is the usual dining room and bar, along with a conference room and business center (for Internet and e-mail), swimming pool and air conditioning throughout. It also has a casino with dance hall girls, two of the largest movie theaters in Belize, a fitness center with massage parlor, a bowling alley and an arcade room. The staff can be quite aloof.

The Great House, 13 Cork Street, ☎ 223-3400, www. greathousebelize.com, $$$$$, is a colonial masterpiece that was built in 1927 as a family home. It still holds its original charm. There are 12 rooms with glistening hardwood floors, balconies, private baths, air conditioning, cable TV, mini-bars and fridges, coffee makers and hair dryers. The colonial-style décor is pleasing. Shops on the main floor offer souvenirs and newspapers, and you can also book a tour here. The hotel's Smoky Mermaid restaurant is a popular place to hang out (see below).

BELIZE CITY ACCOMMODATIONS	
ACCOMMODATION	PHONE
Bakadeer Inn ($$$)	☎ 223-0659
Barrack Guest House ($)	☎ 223-6671
Belize Biltmore Plaza ($$$$)	☎ 223-2302
Bellevue Hotel ($$$)	☎ 227-7051
Chateau Caribbean ($$$$)	☎ 223-3888
Coningsby Inn ($$$)	☎ 227-1566
D'Nest Inn ($$)	☎ 203-5416
Freddie's ($$)	☎ 223-3851
Grant Residence B&B ($$$)	☎ 223-0926
Great House ($$$$$)	☎ 223-3400
Mama Chen's ($)	☎ 223-2057
Mopan Hotel ($$)	☎ 227-7351
North Front St Guest House ($)	☎ 227-7595
Princess Hotel & Casino ($$$$$)	☎ 223-2670
Radisson Fort George ($$$$$)	☎ 223-3333
Sea Guest House ($)	☎ 223-9075
Seaside Guest House ($$)	☎ 227-8339
Three Sisters ($$)	☎ 223-6729
Villa Boscardi ($$$)	☎ 223-1691

Belize City

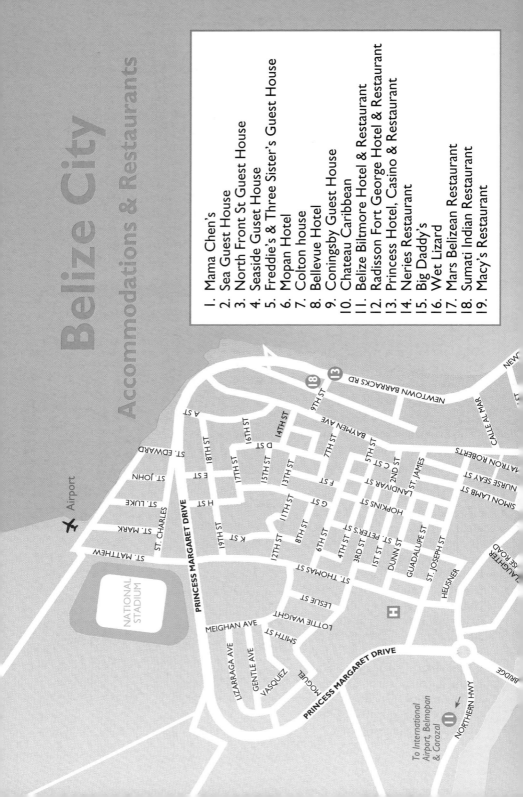

Belize City

Accommodations & Restaurants

1. Mama Chen's
2. Sea Guest House
3. North Front St Guest House
4. Seaside Guset House
5. Freddie's & Three Sister's Guest House
6. Mopan Hotel
7. Colton house
8. Bellevue Hotel
9. Coningsby Guest House
10. Chateau Caribbean
11. Belize Biltmore Hotel & Restaurant
12. Radisson Fort George Hotel & Restaurant
13. Princess Hotel, Casino & Restaurant
14. Neries Restaurant
15. Big Daddy's
16. Wet Lizard
17. Mars Belizean Restaurant
18. Sumati Indian Restaurant
19. Macy's Restaurant

Caribbean Sea

600 YARDS

550 METERS

© 2007 HUNTER PUBLISHING, INC

HUNTER PUBLISHING

MARINE PARADE
HONDURAS
HUTSON
EYRE ST
NORTH PARK
SOUTH PARK
CORK ST
7
DREDGE ST
10
FORT ST
16
12

MORTUARY
EVE ST
1
GAOL LN
2
GABOUREL
17
HANDYSIDE
5
DALY ST
14
ALBERT ST
QUEEN ST
NORTH SIDE CANAL
BARRACKS RD
CRAIG
HYDE'S LN
SWING BRIDGE
NORTH FRONT ST
ANGEL

ADAMS
8
REGENT ST
4
PALM
RECTORY
9
ALBERT ST WEST
DICK LN
15
CHURCH
BISHOP
KING
PRINCE
DEAN
SOUTH
WAGNER
BERKLEY
COCKBURN
ALBERT ST EAST
6
SOUTHERN FORESHORE

LOVELY
VICTORIA ST
NEW RD
CRADLE ST
RHABURNE
USHER
PRICE
PICKSTOCK ST
PETTICOAT ALLEY
REGENT ST WEST
WATER
RICHARD
ALEXANDRIA
BAGDAD
MOSUL
ORANGE ST
GLYN ST
CAIRO
FAR WEST ST
WEST ST
GEORGE ST
PLUES ST
BASRA
EAST CANAL ST
WEST CANAL ST
SOUTH SIDE
ROCKY
RACECOURSE ST
QUEEN CHARLOTTE ST
DICKENSON
CEMETERY LANE

LANC
CASTLE ST
PITTS ALLEY
DOUGLAS JONES
EGHORN
NORTH FRONT ST
BELCHINA BRIDGE
3
LINDOS
EBONY ST
VERNON ST
WEST COLLET CANAL ST
EAST COLLET CANAL ST
TIGRIS ST
EUPHRATES ST
AMARA AVE
ALLENBY ST

MAPPS
WOODS
JOHNSON ST
MAGAZINE RD
HICCATEE
BOCCOTORA ST
DOLPHIN ST
ARMADILLO
WELCH
CURRASOW ST
KUT AVE
YOUNG
FAIRWEATHER
MEX AVE
HAYNES
KRAAL

SARSTOON RD
SITTEE ST
VERNON ST
LOGWOOD ST
LAKE VIEW ST
SEAGULL ST
SOUTH CREEK RD
NORTH CREEK RD
RAMSEY
BEN BOW ST
NEAL'S PEN RD
MONROE

MOP
ST JUDE ST
MAHOGANY ST
MARGUSTA ST
EBONY ST
MAYFLOWER ST
PINE
BANAK RD
CEMETERY RD
GIBNUT ST
ANTELOPE
IGUANA
PELICAN
RACOON
19

CENTRAL AMERICAN BLVD
CENTRAL AMERICAN BLVD

■ RESTAURANTS

While there is good food in Belize, no one comes here to eat. Rice and beans often alternates with beans and rice. This, of course, can be spiced up with hot sauce. The plus is that there is real coffee, as opposed to instant Nescafé, country-wide, and this is a real attraction for me. But unless you dine at resorts, you will have to work hard to find culinary excitement. If you are unsure of where to go and nothing in this book appeals to you, follow the locals. Their restaurants often look shabby, but the rice and beans at least will be good.

RESTAURANT PRICES	
$	$5 to $10
$$	$11 to $25
$$$	$26 to $50
$$$$	$51 to $75
$$$$$	over $75

Another option is to purchase your food in the market and prepare it at your hotel. Cooking can be a problem, but I found that salads were seldom on café menus and, since I craved them, I had to purchase veggies in the market and eat them at home.

WHAT'S THE SEASON?

Lobster is unavailable from Valentine's Day on the 14th of February to the middle of June. However, if **cashew** is your culinary dream, this pepper-shaped fruit with a large seed hanging from the bottom is ripe in May. The Guatemalans claim that they gave the English the seed and kept the succulent fruit for themselves.

Most eateries do not require reservations. However, I suggest you avoid the main rush hours as the more popular places fill up quickly for lunch and dinner. Places like Capricorn on Ambergris Caye need as much as two day's notice before you can get a table. During high season, all up-scale restaurants require reservations except those with a buffet.

Neries 2 Restaurant on the corner of Queen and Daly Streets, ☎ 223-4028, $, is by far the most popular and famous place in BC. Offering traditional foods, it opens at 7:30 am. They make fry jacks for breakfast and cow foot soup for lunch. Sere, made with fish and coconut milk, is a favorite soup. According to the menu, relleno soup, made with stuffed chicken, ground pork and eggs, is available only on government paydays. There is a second Neries at 124 Freetown Road near the Cinderella Plaza.

Big Daddy's Diner, ☎ 227-0932, $, is on the second floor of the Commercial Center. Take the stairs at the back of the Albert Street market on the south side of the swing bridge. If going for lunch, arrive by 11:30 am because workers from the downtown area flock to this popular place and it holds only 66 people. Big Daddy's is famous for its fresh salads.

The Wet Lizard, #1 Fort Street, ☎ 223-5973, $, is next door to the Tourist Village. The restaurant overlooks the Village and the water. This is a good place to stop for lunch and a rest on your walking tour of the city.

Mars Belizean Restaurant, 11 Handyside, ☎ 203-7850, $, has good traditional foods. It also has one computer that is available for a reasonable US $5 per hour.

Macy's Café, 18 Bishop Street, ☎ 207-3419, $$, specializes in wild game such as venison. Iguana (banana chicken) and seafood are also on the menu. Once you are seated, look for the photo of Harrison Ford taken while he was starring in the film *Mosquito Coast*. His table was the one by the door. This is a busy restaurant during lunch hour, when it gets packed with locals.

Sumathi Indian Restaurant, 190 Newtown Barracks, ☎ 223-1172, sumathi@btl.net, $$, has moved here from its old location in the center of town. It also changed its name; it was previously called Memories of India. The restaurant opens from 10:30 am to 11 pm and features north Indian foods, even though the owners are Tamil, from southern India. Sumathi means "bright light" in Tamil. The prices are reasonable and, much more important, the meals are a welcome change from beans and rice.

Radisson's St. George's Dining Room, 2 Marine Parade, ☎ 223-3333 ext 654, $$$. The Sunday brunch, open from 11:30 am to 2 pm every week, always has a huge variety of foods. The restaurant also has theme nights like the Seafood Dinner Buffet, the Mexican Dinner Buffet or the Oriental Lunch Buffet. You can call for information or stop in the lobby and ask for a calendar that shows the features for the month.

Princess Hotel Restaurant, Newtown Barracks in Kings Park, ☎ 223-2670 or 800-451-3734, www.princessbelize.com, $$$, has an all-you-can-eat buffet for less than US $10. In competition with the Radisson, the Princess also tries to do theme nights. However, the Radisson has a better reputation. For the most part, the food here is North American in style and content – chicken, steak and roast beef.

Biltmore Plaza Hotel, Mile 3, Northern Highway, ☎ 223-2302, $$$, has both good food and good service in an elegant setting. It opens at 6 in the morning and serves a bottomless cup of coffee. The North American-style food is well prepared and tasty.

The Smoky Mermaid, 13 Cork Street, ☎ 223-4759, $$$$, is open from 6 am to 10 pm every day and offers special dishes like coconut shrimp, Jamaican chicken and ribs, and Smoky's banana chimichanga, their specialty. I am not going to tell you what this is. You must give it a try.

Pop-n-Taco, King and Regent Streets, ☎ 227-3826, $, is a tiny hole-in-the-wall Chinese restaurant that offers the best food with the largest portions for the lowest prices in all of Belize City. However, there are only four bar stools and one table in the restaurant. Go during, before or after meal times and you'll get good service and great food.

Chon Saan Palace, 1 Kelly Street, ☎ 223-3008, $$, is open from Monday to Saturday, 11 am to 2:30 pm and again from 5 to 11:30 pm. Sundays they are open from 5 to 11:30 pm. This restaurant has been open since 1974 and is one of the oldest ethnic restaurants in the country. It has fish holding tanks in the dining room so that all seafood is fresh when cooked. There are about 200 dishes from which to choose and the cooking is authentic Chinese, similar to what you would find in Hong Kong.

Harbor View Restaurant, Fort Street next door to the Tourism Village, ☎ 223-6420, $$$$. It faces the water at the mouth of the Belize River. This is a restaurant for those in search of a romantic atmosphere. Tables interspersed around the verandah allow you privacy to enjoy a gourmet meal of steak or lobster. Between the soft light, the breeze off the ocean and the food, you will have a meal to remember.

Bob's Bar & Grill, 164 Newtown Barracks Road, ☎ 223-6908, www.angel fire.com/biz7/chefbobs, $, has a verandah where you can sit and watch the action on the street. This

BELIZE CITY RESTAURANT DIRECTORY	
EATERY	PHONE
Big Daddy's Diner ($)	☎ 227-0932
Biltmore Plaza Hotel ($$$)	☎ 223-2302
Bob's Bar & Grill ($)	☎ 223-6908
Chon Saan Palace ($$)	☎ 223-2308
Harbor View Restaurant ($$$$)	☎ 223-6420
Macy's Café ($$)	☎ 207-3419
Neries 2 Restaurant ($)	☎ 223-4028
Mars Belizean Restaurant ($)	☎ 203-7850
Planet Hollywood ($$)	☎ 223-2429
Pop-n-Taco ($)	☎ 227-3826
Princess Hote l Restaurant ($$$)	☎ 223-2670
Radisson St. George's ($$$)	☎ 223-3333
Sumathi Indian Restaurant ($$)	☎ 223-1172
Smoky Mermaid ($$$$)	☎ 223-4759
Wet Lizard ($)	☎ 223-5973

is a comfortable and popular place to hang out. Reservations are recommended. Bob was at the top of his graduating class from the Culinary School of Washington.

WINES

Premium Wines & Spirits, 166 Newtown Barracks, ☎ 223-4984, price@btl.net, is the place to go if you want to buy some wine. In addition to Belizean selections, there's a large choice of imported wines. Although I found wine in the heat of Belize far too dehydrating to be appreciated, you may want some in your air-conditioned hotel room.

> **NOTE:** *You must be 18 years of age to consume alcohol legally in Belize.*

NIGHTLIFE

The nightlife in Belize City is fun and a lot of it revolves around the strip of **Newtown Barracks Road**. If you plan to bar-hop or be out late, take a cab.

■ PERFORMING ARTS

If you are a concert/symphony/theater fan, call the **House of Culture**, ☎ 227-3050, or the **Belize Arts Council**, ☎ 227-2458, to learn what's happening in the city.

■ LADY LUCK

Princess Hotel Casino on the strip (Newtown Barracks in Kings Park), ☎ 223-2670, is open daily from noon to 4 am. Near the door are almost 500 slot machines and video poker games. The serious gamblers are farther back. You can play blackjack, roulette or get into a game of poker. All players get free drinks and snacks. Twice a night Russian dance hall girls do a Los Vegas-style performance. Why Russian? I have no idea. Belize is known for its No shoes, No shirt, No problem policy, but that doesn't apply here, where there is a conservative dress code and no sandals are allowed.

■ FLICKS

You'll find **movie theaters** at the Princess Hotel, Newtown Barracks in Kings Park, ☎ 223-2670. The two theaters, which hold 200 people each, show first-rate movies that change every week. Belizeans have great pride in these theaters.

■ SPORTS

 Soccer (called football, and pronounced fooot-BAL) is popular throughout Central and South America. Belize is no exception. To see a game, go to the MCC grounds on Newtown Barracks Road (past the Princess). Call ahead to see who is playing and when, ☎ 223-4415.

Bowling is offered at the Princess Hotel, Newtown Barracks in Kings Park, ☎ 223-2670. There are two lanes with all the latest equipment.

Ping Pong at Pop-n-Taco, King and Regent Streets, ☎ 227-3826. You can play the champ every Saturday night at this restaurant and, while playing, enjoy a Belikin. This is a popular place that may soon expand.

■ MUSIC, BARS & CLUBS

 The Tourist Office, Central Bank Building, Gabourel Lane, ☎ 223-1913 or 223-1910, www.travelbelize.org, keeps track of **local bands**. Contact them to find out where the best Belizean pop music bands are playing. The office is open from 8 am to 5 pm, Monday to Friday.

Bars are everywhere in Belize and they range from sleazy, smoky dumps to sophisticated verandah lounges. There is live music poolside at the Radisson and Biltmore every weekend. The Radisson often has local musicians like the popular **Sandino's Band**. The band almost always plays at the San Pedro Costa Maya Festival (see page 449), and also performs around the country. If at all possible, make time to see them.

Belize Biltmore Plaza offers the prize-winning Blue Hole Drink, which consists of dark rum, blue cacao, grapefruit juice, lime concentrate and coconut cream. The drink was first created by manager Jason de Ocampo, who entered in the contest during the Belize Tourism Week festivities and won the Belize Signature Drink Award.

Planet Hollywood, 35 Queen and Handyside Streets, ☎ 223-2429, and the **Ambassador Lounge**, 69 Hydes Lane, ☎ 223-1723, are places to try for a drink if you want familiar surroundings.

Along the strip (Newtown Barracks Road), try the **Eden Night Club**, 190 Newtown Barracks, ☎ 223-4559. If that isn't any good, head to **Caesar's Palace** in the same block, ☎ 223-7624.

If you want to hang out with the university crowd, take the little ferry from the landing just two blocks from the university (walk down University Drive until you hit the water). The ferry takes five minutes and costs US $2.50 for a round-trip ticket to **Moho Caye** (don't confuse this with a different Moho Caye just out of Placencia). The ferry goes once every hour.

You can sit on the deck of the restaurant, ☎ 223-5350 (the name and owners keep changing but the phone number stays the same) overlooking the ocean with the trade winds fluffing your hair while you schmooze (and drink) with the up-and-coming intellectuals of Belizean society.

DAY TRIPS

Except for visiting the more distant cayes, these trips can be done using public transportation, your own bicycle, a car or with a tour.

SUGGESTED DAY TRIPS

- Hike to and around the education center at the **Belize Zoo**; see page 224 in the chapter, *The West.*
- Go horseback riding at **Banana Bank Lodge**; see page 229 in *The West* chapter.
- Cycle or drive to **Altun Ha ruins**; see *The North* chapter, page 142.
- Paddle through the **Barton Creek Caves**; see page 246.
- Windsurf off **Caye Caulker**; see page 485, *The Cayes* chapter.
- Take an historical exploration of **St. George's Caye**; see page 503 in *The Cayes* chapter.
- Play golf at **Chapel Caye**; see page 502 of *The Cayes.*
- Bird watch in a protected area of **Swallow Caye**; see page 505.

Belize City

■ TOUR OPERATORS

 Sea Sports Belize, 83 North Front Street, ☎ 223-5505, www.seasportsbelize.com, are experts in water sports and should be the first you speak with when trying to arrange a trip. The company was nominated for Best Tour Operator in 2000 and 2001. Not only are they experienced in taking you out on the water, but Linda Searle is a font of knowledge about things to see and places to visit. Be sure to stop in.

Slickrock Adventures are highly experienced. They suggest that, before choosing a tour, you make certain you will see what you want.

- If you want **ruins**, the best are Actun Tunichil Muknal, Xunantunich, Caracol, Lamanai and Altun Ha.
- For **wildlife** go to the Belize Zoo, Crooked Tree Baboon Sanctuary, Manatee Lodge or Lamanai Outpost.
- For **jungle hiking** go to Chaa Creek, Jaguar Preserve and Chan Chich.
- And I must add that for the best **diving/snorkeling**, go to Glover's Reef.

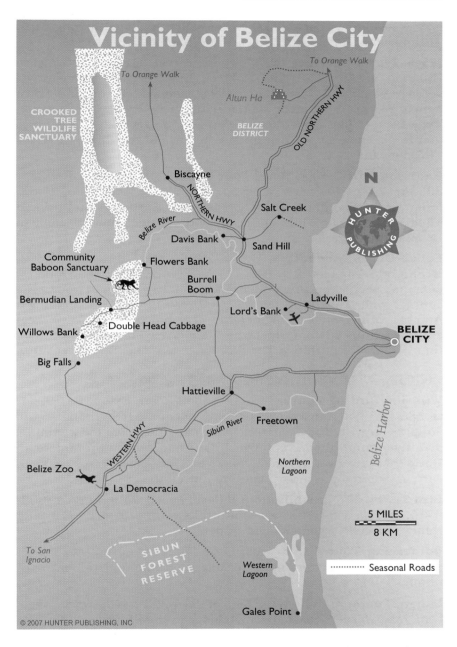

Vicinity of Belize City

Action Belize Travel Service, Mile 2 New Northern Highway, ☎ 223-3987, www.actionbelize.com, at the Biltmore Hotel, offers half-day tours around the city and to the zoo, the baboon sanctuary or the Altun Ha ruins. Their prices are reasonable and their guides are knowledgeable. Their specialty is guided fishing trips. The office also offers Internet, fax and photocopying service.

Maya Travel Services, 42 Cleghorn Street, Caribbean Tobacco Building, ☎ 223-1623, 223-1241 or 223-2886, www.mayatravel services.com, have "hiked, paddled, galloped, driven and flown across Belize." They offer all the usual trips around Belize City. They seem to like river travel; if you want to visit one of the ruins and to get there by river (a must while in Belize), then give Maya Travel a call.

Radisson Fort George Hotel Tour Office, Fort Street, ☎ 800-333-3333 or 223-3333, www.radisson.com/belizecitybz, offers 27 different tours around the country. They will go as far as Caracol and Tikal or as close as a tour of the city with a guide knowledgeable in Belizean history.

Belize Close Encounters, Box 1320, Detroit Lakes, MN 56502, ☎ 888-875-1822 or 218-847-4441, www.belizecloseencounters. com, has been operating in Belize for over 15 years and knows the country well. They represent over 60 resorts and can combine a number of activities with suitable accommodations. Their best skill is creating custom trips, whether it be caving or diving, museums or horseback riding. The San Ignacio area is their specialty.

BIRDING TOUR AGENCIES

Wildside Birding Tours, 14 Marchwood Road, Exton, PA 19341, ☎ 888-875-9431, www.wildsidebirding.com. This company will supply you with any accessories you may not have for watching, identifying and photographing birds. Endorsed by the American Birding Association, Wildside offers educational courses that can earn you a credit at a participating university.

Bird Treks, 115 Peach Bottom Village, Peach Bottom, PA 17563-9716, ☎ 717-548-3303, www.birdtreks.com, is run by Bob and Nancy Schutsky, who are avid birders.

Borderland Tours, 2550 West Calle Podilla, Tucson, AZ 85745, ☎ 800-525-7753, offers one specialized birding tour to Belize annually.

Caligo Tours, ☎ 800-426-7781 or 914-273-6333, www.caligo. com, takes birders to Chan Chich lodge in the Rio Bravo area. The price of this easy-going tour is about the same as if you went to Chan Chich on your own.

BIRDING GUIDES IN BELIZE CITY

If you want a private tour, hire one of the bird specialists living in Belize City. The cost of a birder is usually US $100 - $200 per day.

- Edward Allen, 6413 Fer Lane, ☎ 223-4660
- Ed Herrera, 98 George Street, ☎ 227-7413
- Hector Bol, a Belize native who studied in Mexico, charges $150-$250 per person, depending on where you wish to go. He can be reached at birdjaguar2003@ yahoo.com.
- Peter Faria, 11 Belama Site, ☎ 223-1745
- L. Hunter, a birding pal, can be reached at belize hunter@yahoo.com.
- Nathan Forbes, 7061 Racoon Street, ☎ 227-0049

DIRECTORY

BELIZE CITY – GENERAL DIRECTORY

■ INFORMATION SOURCES, WEBSITES

Audubon Society	☎ 223-4987	www.belizeaudubon.org
Belize Arts Council	☎ 227-2458	
Chat About Belize		www.chatboutbelize.com
Nationality Dept	☎ 822-2423	www.travel.state.gov
Tourist Office	☎ 223-1913	www.travelbelize.org

■ TOUR OPERATORS & OUTFITTERS

Action Belize Travel Service	☎ 223-2987	www.actionbelize.com
Belize Cycle Association		wallen@btl.net
Bird Treks	☎ 717-548-3303	www.birdtreks.com
Borderland Tours	☎ 800-525-7753	
Caligo Tours	☎ 800-426-7781, 914-273-6333	www.caligo.com
Close Encounters	☎ 888-875-1822	www.belizecloseencounters.com
Maya Travel Services	☎ 223-1623, 223-1241	www.mayatravelservices.com
Radisson Fort George Tours	☎ 223-3333	www.radisson.com/belizecitybz
Sea Sports Belize	☎ 223-5505	www.seasportsbelize.com
Slickrock Adventures	☎ 800-390-5715	www.slickrock.com
Wildside Birding Tours	☎ 888-875-9431	www.wildsidebirding.com

Belize City

BELIZE CITY – GENERAL DIRECTORY

■ SHOPS & ART GALLERIES

Belizean Style . . . . ☎ 223-4660 . . . . www.gographicsbz.com

Fine Arts Shop . . . . ☎ 227-5620

Gallon Jug Agro-industry Ltd. . . . . ☎ 227-7031

Image Factory Art Gallery . . . . ☎ 223-4161

National Handicrafts Ctr . . . . ☎ 223-3636 . . . . bcci@btl.net

Premium Wines & Spirits . . . . ☎ 223-4984 . . . . price@btl.net

She Sells Sea Shells . . . . ☎ 223-7426

■ NIGHTLIFE

Ambassador Lounge . . . . ☎ 223-1723 . . . .

Caesar's Palace . . . . ☎ 223-7624

Eden Night Club . . . . ☎ 223-4559

Princess Casino . . . . ☎ 223-2670 . . . . resprincess@btl.net

■ ATTRACTIONS

House of Culture . . . . ☎ 227-3050

Marine/Coastal Museum . . . . ☎ 223-1961

MCC Soccer Grounds . . . . ☎ 223-4415

Moho Caye Bar . . . . ☎ 223-5350 . . . .

National Museum . . . . ☎ 422-4524 . . . . www.museumofbelize.org

The North

The Northern Highway and its side roads take you from Belize City to the northern region of Belize. Whether you go by bicycle, bus, canoe or car, the lands surrounding the Northern Highway will give you a different view of Belize than you get from the Cayes or Pine Mountain Ridge areas. The easy-going Colonial town of **Corozal**, for example, has never been promoted enough. The quiet fishing villages near **Orange Walk** are beautiful, but seldom visited by foreigners.

In the north, there are **Maya ruins**, some of which are not yet excavated. It is a popular sport to cycle to Altun Ha and tent at Pueblo Escondido. Opportunities to spot rare wetland birds are found at places like **Crooked Tree**. Virgin jungle foliage can still be found around places like **Gallon Jug**. **Cycling** is safe and a pleasant method of travel, and **canoeing** at least once on a jungle river in Belize is a must. In the north, the New River runs to Lamanai and the Belize River goes from Bermudian Landing to the sea. Both are gentle runs.

Although there are some upscale accommodations available in unique settings, they

The North

are the exception in this area. Often, food is local rather than international. The people seem friendlier because they haven't been tainted by too many travelers asking, "Is there a MacDonald's nearby?"

I recommend spending time in the north and getting to know some of country's unique attractions.

ALONG THE HIGHWAY

Below, I describe the road going north from Belize City. As we come to secondary roads leading to other places of interest, we detour to visit them before returning to the New Northern Highway.

MILEAGE FROM BELIZE CITY TO MEXICAN BORDER	
Mile 10	**Airport/Ladyville**
Mile 15.5	Turn west onto a secondary road for **Burrel Boom/Bermudian Landing/Baboon Sanctuary**
Mile 18	**Sandhill**
Mile 19	Turn east onto the Old Northern Highway/**Altun Ha**
Mile 30	Turn west onto a secondary road for **Crooked Tree**
Mile 49	Old Northern Highway joins New Northern Highway
Mile 52	Turn west onto a secondary road for **Guinea Grass/Lamanai** and **Blue Creek**
Mile 57	**Orange Walk Town**. Turn east (over the New River) onto a secondary road for **Copper Bank/Progresso/Sarteneja**
Mile 67	Turn east onto a secondary road for the **Libertad Sugar Factory**
Mile 83	**Corozal Town**
Mile 92	**Mexican border**

Although there are few mileage signs on the Northern Highways, people refer to locations by the number of miles along the road. To make things easy, I give all directions this way. If you lose track, ask a local resident.

LEAVING BELIZE CITY

■ HOW TO TRAVEL

If traveling by **bus**, take a taxi to the **Venus bus station** at the main terminal and buy a ticket for the town you wish to

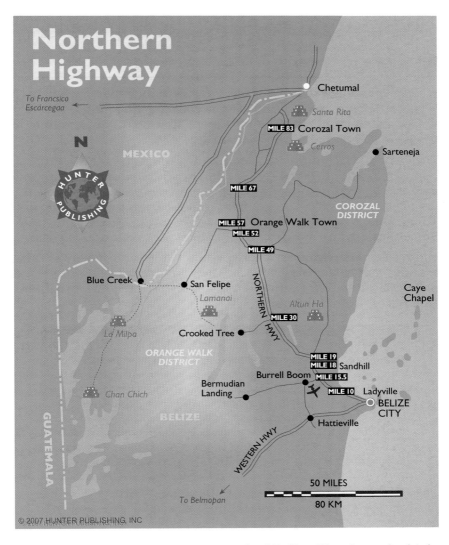

Northern Highway

To Francsico Escárcegaa ←

Chetumal

Santa Rita

MILE 83 Corozal Town

Cerros

Sarteneja

MEXICO

N

HUNTER PUBLISHING

MILE 67

COROZAL DISTRICT

MILE 57 Orange Walk Town
MILE 52

MILE 49

Blue Creek

San Felipe

Lamanai

Altun Ha

Caye Chapel

NORTHERN HWY

MILE 30

La Milpa

Crooked Tree

ORANGE WALK DISTRICT

MILE 19
MILE 18 Sandhill

Burrell Boom MILE 15.5

Chan Chich

Bermudian Landing

MILE 10 Ladyville

BELIZE CITY

BELIZE

Hattieville

GUATEMALA

WESTERN HWY

50 MILES
80 KM

To Belmopan ←

© 2007 HUNTER PUBLISHING, INC

The North

visit. Corozal, the farthest town north of Belize City along the highway, is only three hours by express bus. All buses will stop anywhere along the road, except for express buses, which stop only in the major centers.

Driving, **cycling** or **hitching** requires a bit more work. From the Swing Bridge in Belize City, follow Queen and then Albert Street to Eve Street. Turn north and continue along the road that skirts the water. Eve Street becomes Barracks Road and, after it curves, turns into Princess Margaret Drive. When you arrive at a large traffic circle that has many flags in its center, take the first road to the right off the circle. This is the New Northern Highway.

BELIZE CITY TO BERMUDIAN LANDING

■ ATTRACTIONS

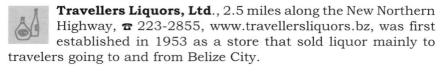 **Travellers Liquors, Ltd**., 2.5 miles along the New Northern Highway, ☎ 223-2855, www.travellersliquors.bz, was first established in 1953 as a store that sold liquor mainly to travelers going to and from Belize City.

The owner, Mr. Omario, blended his own rums and they became so popular that he decided to experiment with vodka. This product was also successful and, as its reputation increased, it became the first Belizean liquor to be exported into the United States. The first 1,600 gallons of Cane Juice Vodka were sent to 39 states in 1995. Since that day the status of the distillery has continuously risen.

Today, Travellers makes colored rums, white and flavored rums, brandy, vodka, wine and liquors. Their liquors are all naturally fermented and double distilled. I personally love the award-winning One Barrel Rum, taken neat.

LIKE YER LIQUOR?

Each year there is an international competition in the Caribbean to determine the best liquors made during the year. In 2001, 175 rums from around the world were entered in the contest. At the same time, Bacardi's unveiled 3,000 bottles of its Millennium Rum. Each crystal bottle sold for $800. However, it was Great Spirits Company of New York that won the top price of $6,000 for a demijohn (4.54 liters) bottle of flagship British Royal Navy Imperial Rum. Until 1970, this was the rum given as a daily drink to sailors in the Royal Navy. Since the practice ended, the remaining rum has been stored in an underground warehouse. At $6,000 a bottle, I think I'd leave it there.

Travellers' One Barrel Refined Rum won a Gold in the Dark Rum category in 2001. In 2000, their 151 Two for One won a Gold in the Overproof category, Caraboo Cream won a Gold and Tropicanah Coconut won a Bronze in the Spiced and Flavored category, One Barrel Refined won a Gold in the Regular category, Durrly's Parrot Cristal won third place in the White Rum category, and Nanche Liqueur won third place in the Spice and Flavored category.

Ladyville, 10 miles from Belize City along the New Northern Highway, is a small suburb with about 1,500 residents. Because Belize is growing fairly rapidly, Ladyville is now almost a suburb of Belize City.

The most notable landmark in Ladyville is the **Philip S.W. Goldson Airport**. Goldson was the Minister of Human Resources, Youth Development and Women's Affairs. His work in fighting poverty was so notable that he became a national hero and the international airport was named after him. An extension of the airport runway in 1998 added 3,060 feet (930 meters) to its length. The construction took 14 months to complete and cost US $4.5 million. It was done by M.A. al-Kharafi, a Kuwaiti contractor.

A trip to the **Belikin Brewery and Coca-Cola plant** (in the same building) just a mile or so past the airport on the old airport road (turn left off the New Northern Highway) may also be of interest. ☎ 225-3195. You may have to book a tour with an agency. Tours usually run about four hours and require some walking on uneven surfaces and climbing of stairs.

Owned by the Bowen family, Belikin Beer has a monopoly in Belize. However, the monopoly is justified by the affordable price and quality of beer. Made with hops from Washington state, barley from Canada, and water from Belize that has not been treated with chemicals, the beer ferments under the watchful eye of a brewmaster who has worked in Germany, Bolivia and Canada.

The company was founded in 1971 and now produces 52,000 barrels of beer a year. These barrels include a 4% lager, a 5% premium, a 6% stout and an 8% stout, all served in 12-ounce recycled bottles. The average life span of a bottle is 10 fillings.

Besides the beer production, the brewery houses the Coca Cola and Crystal Water bottling plants.

■ PLACES TO STAY

 There are a few places to stay as you head out of town. **Belize River Lodge**, Mile 8.5 Belize River Road, ☎ 225-2002, bzelodge@btl.net, $$$$, is a first-class fly-fishing lodge that has been operating since 1960. Situated on the Belize River, the lodge is just four miles from the Caribbean.

Each mahogany cabin has air conditioning, private bath and a porch overlooking the river from which fishers can cast their lines. Should you want to hit the Grand Slam (by catching a permit, bonefish and tarpon all in one day) expert guides are available to help. Of course, there are no guarantees.

The North

Besides a **restaurant** and bar, the hotel offers tours to other must-see spots in the country. All-inclusive prices are available.

Embassy Hotel, Airport Ring Road, ☎ 225-3333, www.embassy-hotelbelize.com, $$, is the only hotel close to the airport. Since there is no flying after dark in Belize, there is no possibility of the planes keeping you awake. There are 20 rooms available and more are being constructed. Each has air conditioning, fan, TV and private bath with hot water. Private parking is offered and there's a restaurant that opens early for breakfast, a roof-top courtyard and hammocks around the verandah. The hotel is clean and the hosts are hospitable. This is one of the best deals for an airport hotel that I have ever discovered. It also offers luggage storage for US $1 per day; parking for non-guests at US $2.50 per day. You may rent a sports utility vehicle for US $80 a day or $70 a day on a weekly rental. A small car goes for US $60 a day or US $50 a day (weekly). These prices include taxes and insurance. For the economy-minded you can have a car, room and breakfast for US $99 a day. I don't think a better deal is available anywhere in the country.

▶▶ *To reach **Burrel Boom** and **Bermudian Landing**, turn west off the New Northern Highway at Mile 15.5 onto the secondary road. The communities along this stretch of road each have a population of between 500 and 1,500 residents.*

BERMUDIAN LANDING AREA

■ GETTING HERE

BY CAR OR BICYCLE

From the New Northern Highway, turn west at Mile 13 onto an unnamed secondary road. Drive for three miles and cross the Belize River. Less than two miles farther, you will pass a road going south (it leads past a Methodist school and the El Chiclero Hotel). Continue straight ahead on the secondary road and you will arrive at Bermudian Landing and the farming villages beyond.

> **AUTHOR NOTE:** *A "sleeping policeman" is the local name for those irritating speed bumps found at the entrance and exit of every town.*

BY BUS

There are two bus companies that travel to this area; **Pooks** leaves from the main bus station area in Belize City and **Russells** leaves from Cairo Street, two blocks east of the main station and one block north. Pooks buses leave at 5:10 pm, Monday to Friday, and at 2 pm on Saturdays. Russells buses leave at 12:15 and 4:30 pm, Monday to Friday, and 12:15 and 1 pm on Saturday.

TAXI OR TOUR

Almost every tour agency or taxi driver will take you to the Baboon Sanctuary. A half-day tour would include only the sanctuary. A taxi would charge about the same as a tour. If taking a taxi one way (you'd probably be charged for the return even if you didn't use it), you could walk to some of the communities and then enjoy a home stay for a night. But this would be my last choice. It is hot in Belize, there's not much shade, and walking along country roads is difficult. Hitching is possible, but there is little traffic to the villages.

■ INTRODUCTION

The greatest draw to this area is the **Community Baboon Sanctuary**. The sound of these animals howling through the jungle is a thrill that should not be missed. If you happen to be alone when they start their lament, it will raise the hair on your neck.

Having your own transportation here makes it easier for you to visit villages. Tenting is permitted near the sanctuary. If you decide to camp, you'll get the thrill of staying in the jungle at night while the howlers sing.

There are also two **canoe** routes that can be enjoyed along this stretch of the **Belize River**. One is the 60-mile run from Bermudian Landing to the Haulover Bridge in Belize City and the other is the 60-mile run from Guanacaste Park to Bermudian Landing. If you are really ambitious, have the time, and enjoy jungle rivers, do both of these trips.

■ HISTORY

This area was a logging center from the 1700s until the end of Belize's mass-logging period. Now the area is farmland. Burrel Boom got its name from a time when logs that were floating loose down the river were "boomed." Booming is the process of grouping a large amount of logs and holding them together by a chain or rope. The "boom" is then floated downriver in a controlled fashion. Loose timbers were stopped from floating past Burrel Boom by a huge chain strung across the river. Parts of the

The North

chain and chain anchors can still be seen along the river near the village.

Bermudian Landing is said to have gotten its name from the Bermuda grass that was planted for cattle by the Scottish settlers who came in the mid-1800s. The village across the river is called Scotland Halfmoon – it seems that a settler who arrived during the half moon was feeling homesick for Scotland.

Flowers Bank, just upstream from Bermudian Landing, is believed to be named after Adam Flowers who, in 1797, cast the deciding vote in Belize City to defend the area against the threat of an invasion by Spain. The following year resident Belizeans fought at the famous Battle of St. George's Caye.

During Hurricane Keith in 2000 the Belize River rose 25 feet (7.5 meters) at Flowers Bank and 30 feet (nine meters) at Isabella Bank. Burrel Boom had water running down its main street and Mussel Creek overflowed its bridge, thus cutting off all the villages upstream. The devastation resulted in better ecological practices being implemented in the hope of preventing further damage if another flood should hit.

At the end of the road beyond Bermudian Landing are the villages of Big Falls and St. Paul's Bank, known for the rock outcroppings in the Belize River that cause churning rapids during high water. In dry season, many people sit on the rocks to sunbathe.

■ THINGS TO DO

COMMUNITY BABOON SANCTUARY

A **Natural Wildlife Museum and Visitor Center**, at the far end of Bermudian Landing (there's only one street), is the official headquarters for the sanctuary. Their mailing address is PO Box 1428, Belize City, ☎ 220-2181 or 220-2158. The center is open daily from 8 am to 5 pm. With your entrance ticket, you may walk on the trails until it is almost dark. The entry fee is US $5 and the ticket is good all day. You can leave and return to the sanctuary at no extra charge. Online, visit www.howlermonkeys.org.

You must hire a local guide, available at the center, to take you through the jungle. I was escorted by Camile Young and he not only showed me monkeys, but also shared his lifetime knowledge of them with me. Fallet Young is the head guide and he specializes in local medicinal plants. If that is your interest, ask if he is available. The best time to see the monkeys is in the early morning or at dusk. The shorter trails take as little as 10 minutes, while longer ones can take two to three hours.

The modest natural wildlife museum, opened in 1989, takes only a few minutes to visit, but the information will fill in details not always available elsewhere. The museum is open during the same hours as the park.

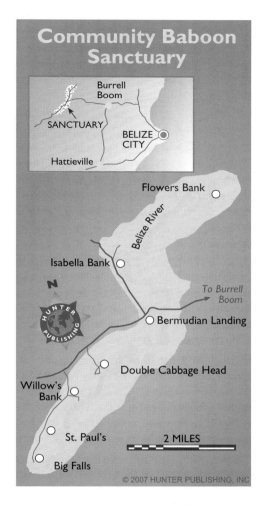

MONKEY BUSINESS

Beware! The sanctuary offers a Sponsor a Monkey program for those interested in helping these animals. This is a noble cause, but the workers at the sanctuary do not keep up their part of the deal. They will take your money – $25 for adults and $15 for children – but they will not send photos and updates of the animal you have sponsored. This may be because the entire sanctuary is run by volunteer staff.

The North

The center also sells the book, ***Belizean Rain Forests; Community Baboon Sanctuary, 3rd edition***, by Robert Horwich and Johnathon Lyon. Previously used copies are available at www.amazon.com.

The sanctuary is operated by the citizens of the surrounding communities who have cooperated with each other to create an environmental haven for the black howler monkey. The management of the sanctuary is completely voluntary, as is the agreement to practice farming techniques that will not harm the natural habitat of the monkeys. Before the formation of the sanctuary, these creatures were endangered due to loss of habitat.

In 1981, Dr. Robert Horwich of the University of Wisconsin came to the area to study these endangered animals. He became so enamored with them that he worked tirelessly to create an environment in which they could thrive. Horwich educated local farmers on non-erosive soil techniques and irrigation methods to enhance sustainable crops. This, in turn, stopped the slash-and-burn practices so common at that time. He also applied for monies and got environmental groups interested in helping with the project.

Finally, in 1985, the sanctuary was official. It covered 11,520 acres. Sixty landowners were part of the original group who worked at maintaining the sanctuary. Thirty more were willing to follow conservation practices on their farms. The sanctuary soon grew to 12,980 acres in size with 70 landowners actively participating in its management. The land is all privately owned by the farmers.

Those contributing to the project come from Bermudian Landing, Big Falls, Double Head Cabbage, Flowers Bank, Isabella Bank, St. Pauls, Scotland Halfmoon and Willows Bank. The original sponsors for the idea were the Belize Audubon Society, the World Wildlife Fund and the Zoological Society of Milwaukee County. Current sponsors include Conservation International, Margo Marsh Biodiversity Foundation, Columbus Zoo and Give to the Earth Foundation.

The sanctuary has also been generously supported by the United Nations Development Program. The UN's latest project is to set up an education center at the museum so that both locals and visitors can learn more about the area in general and the monkeys in particular.

The sanctuary is bordered by the banks of the Belize River, with its riparian and broad-leafed forests that are abundant in vines so popular with baboons. Inland from the river are marsh, pasture and farmland. The eastern end of the sanctuary has cohune palm, while the west is bordered by pine trees and savanna.

The monkey species found in the sanctuary is one of six similar types living in Central and South America. This particular species dwells only in southern Mexico, northern Guatemala and Belize. After the sanctuary had been in operation for three years, the monkey population had grown to about 1,000. But there were still many unnecessary deaths. Monkeys were caught in barbed wire fences or run over by cars at night. Bridges, ropes and wooden ladders were placed in strategic places so the animals could travel over and around these hazards safely. This has contributed to the increase of the population that is now believed to be over 4,000. One such bridge can be seen strung high above the road as you enter Bermudian Landing.

Besides the howler monkey, the sanctuary has Baird's tapirs, Morelet's crocodiles, iguanas and Central American river turtles. There are over 250 birds hanging around the 100 or so species of trees that border many of the unexcavated Maya house mounds in the sanctuary.

ADVENTURES

Crocodile Hunting, ☎ 220-2158, www.howlermonkeylodge.com, is a one-hour boat trip through dense jungle where howler monkeys' serenade competes with tropical bird calls for air space. Iguanas stare at the odd creatures sitting on this 26-foot pontoon boat that hardly makes a ripple on the water. The elusive crocodiles move only their eyes as you pass and the blooming flowers offer a pungent scent. The sounds of the cicada help make this trip more a Hemingway adventure than a simple excursion. This is a great trip that costs $7.50 for children and $15 for adults. The boat operates every day from 8 am to 5 pm. Reservations are recommended.

© Howler Monkey Lodge.

Canoeing from Big Falls to the sanctuary takes one day and is highly recommended. If you want a longer paddle, I suggest starting from Guanacaste National Park (near Belmopan). Another option is to start at Bermudian Landing. All trips end at Haulover Bridge in Belize City. The distance from Guanacaste is about 120 miles. Canoe rentals and shuttles can be arranged from either lodge in Bermudian Landing or from the sanctuary. The cost is dependent upon the length of your trip.

The canoe ride from Bermudian Landing to Belize City is in deep water that is slow and flat. There is lush jungle on both banks. There are a few spots where the water speeds up a bit (between Black Creek and Flowers Bank is one such place), but nothing that takes great skill to pass. After Flowers Bank the river really gets boring (there isn't even a riffle) as you push your way through mangrove swamp. If you are a birder, this section will be anything but boring. The greatest draw during dry season is the possibility of seeing sharks that come up the main channel from the coast. However, keep your eye on the river as you watch. Don't end up in the water with the sharks.

The best place to pull out is at Haulover Bridge. If you would like to avoid the last 15 miles of swamp, you can also pull out (after 45 miles) at Burrell Boom. The river makes a huge curve between Bermudian Landing and Burrell Boom, so the shuttle for this loop is only 15 miles and will cost less than if you went all the way to Belize City.

I highly recommend at least one river trip while in Belize and if your skills and confidence are low, this may be a good one. The worst that could happen is that you could tip, get wet and then be attacked by a shark.

Horseback riding through the sanctuary is available, but should be booked ahead of arrival. Call the sanctuary, ☎ 220-2181 or 220-2158, for information. Rates are US $10 per hour.

Double Head Cabbage, on the road beyond Bermudian Landing, is worth a visit just so you can go to **Uncle Charlie's Winery** for some locally brewed wines. At **Isabella Bank**, just a bit farther, you can visit **Country Can Producers**. They sell jams, jellies and juices that are canned without preservatives. Both places are friendly and the proprietors will take time to answer questions, give samples or show you some of the processing methods.

■ PLACES TO STAY

 The Nature Resort, next to the sanctuary's visitor center, ☎ 610-1378, www.toucantrail.com/nature-resort.html, $$, has spacious and clean cabins beside the river. Each thatched-roof building has a fan, writing desk and fridge. The shared bath is about 20 feet from the front door.

Howler Monkey Lodge, ☎ 220-2158, www.howlermonkeylodge. com, $$, is just before the visitor center and a short distance off the main road. Each little cabin, nestled in the jungle on the banks of the river, has two double beds, a fan and a private bath with hot water. The lodge has a reference library and a one-for-one book exchange. There is a short jungle trail on the property that can be walked alone. Howlers are often seen right from the porches of the cabins.

© Howler Monkey Lodge.

Tenting, $, along the river at the Howler Monkey Lodge is permitted. Camping in the sanctuary is not permitted. But set your tent up at the lodge and you'll fall asleep to the roar of howlers during the night.

The **Home Stay Program**, $, is run through the visitor center, ☎ 220-2181. The program is designed to encourage travelers to mix with and get to know local residents. The center arranges for you to stay with a Creole family in any of the seven villages that surround the

HOTEL PRICES	
$	$20 to $50
$$	$51 to $75
$$$	$76 to $100
$$$$	$101 to $150
$$$$$	over $150

sanctuary. You will be able to taste authentic food (better than rice and beans), watch the farming methods and listen to stories the host family may wish to share. It is a good way to exchange cultural information for both the host and the guest.

> **AUTHOR NOTE:** *If in a large group, you may have to separate as each village can accommodate no more than five people at one time. All home stays include meals. This is a real deal.*

Working with the organizers of this program, I was impressed by the cheerful enthusiasm and diligent work each member contributed in order to make the visitor's stay a success. If you have no other opportunity for a home stay while in Belize, try this one.

If you wander into **St. Paul's Bank** or **Flowers Bank**, both have basic cabañas for rent ($). If you're canoeing and a home stay doesn't appeal to you, a stop in either of these villages would allow you to observe the local way of life while still enjoying your own space.

The North

El Chiclero, Burrell Boom, ☎ 225-9005, elchiclerol@yahoo.com, $$, is a stucco building, clean and neat, with air conditioning. Each room has two double beds, private bathrooms with tile floors and hot water. There is a swimming pool on the grounds and the sundeck overlooks the town. Special weekly or monthly rates are available. There is 24-hour Internet service. This is a comfortable base from which to explore. The restaurant serves excellent home-cooked food, although it is not cheap.

■ PLACES TO EAT

The **Baboon Sanctuary Restaurant**, $$, beside the visitor center, is open from 8 am to 5 pm seven days a week. The food is cooked and served by local women, who use their own secret recipes to deliver unforgettable flavors.

RESTAURANT PRICES	
$	$5 to $10
$$	$11 to $25
$$$	$26 to $50
$$$$	$51 to $75
$$$$$	over $75

Howler Monkey Lodge, $$, run by the Womens' Conservation Group, offers Creole and international cuisine, all home-cooked. Vegetarian and special dietary requirements can be met as long as the cook knows in advance. The meals are family style; you get what everyone else gets.

There's a **supermarket** just half a mile past the visitor center on the road going to Double Head Cabbage. It's not a long walk and is a good spot to buy groceries and snacks for your cabin.

El Chiclero, Burrell Boom, ☎ 225-9005, $$. Carl and Mary Lynn Faulkner, American ex pats, have lived in Belize for 25 years and in 1992 built this hotel. They take pride in serving some of the best meals available in the north. They also like to have their guests sit with them around the dinner table so they can exchange stories. This event is always a highlight with travelers. El Chiclero is famous for its cashew pie and cake, so much so that people drive from BC just for a piece. They also have home-made jams to slather over your bread.

▶▶ *Return to the New Northern Highway at Mile 15.5 and continue north to **Sandhill** at Mile 18.*

Sandhill is a little village just before the junction of the Old and New Northern Highways.

OLD NORTHERN HIGHWAY

Turn east off the New Northern Highway at Mile 19, just past Sandhill. The Old Northern Highway is single lane and paved for most of the way, but also dotted with numerous potholes. Occasional extensions in the width of the road allow vehicles to pass each other. There is one bridge with no side guards. This style of roadway encourages careful driving. However, the road is excellent for cycling.

A bus goes from Belize City, past the turn for Altun Ha, to the village of **Maskall** three times a day; at 1, 3:30 and 5:30 pm. The **Maskall Bus Company** vehicles leave from Mosuel Street, just off Princess Margaret Drive (near the Flag circle) in the city and **Russell's** buses leave from Cairo Street, just two blocks from the main bus terminal. The bus drivers will let you off at the road to Altun Ha and you can walk the rest of the way.

▶▶ *If driving or cycling, turn off the Old Northern Highway at Mile 10.5 to reach Altun Ha.*

ALTUN HA

Altun Ha Maya ruins are three miles along an unnamed secondary road. The ruins are open daily from 8 am to 4 pm and the entrance fee is US $5 per day for foreigners. Trained tour guides are available and they can give you tons of information about the area. There is also a confectionary, a gift shop and toilet facilities at the entrance.

© Howler Monkey Lodge.

The North

HISTORY

In 1963 A.H. Anderson, an archeologist, was in the market in Belize City when he noticed a peasant selling a jade pennant that looked interesting. He purchased the piece and gave it to Dr. David Prendergast, another archeologist, who was working in western Belize at the time. The two men went to the Altun Ha site, where the peasant claimed he found the pendant, and did some testing. After reporting their find to the Royal Ontario Museum in Canada, the ROM decided to revive its Belize research program that it had previously canceled. By 1964, the excavations were back in full operation with funding from the ROM, the Wenner-Gren Foundation, the Globe and Mail Newspaper and the Canada Council. Dr. Prendergast worked until 1970 and under his leadership the project became the biggest archeological endeavor in Belize.

In 1968, while excavating the Temple of Masonry Altars, they found seven tombs, six of which had been vandalized. The seventh, which was tucked under some stairs, had a stone table with cable markings beside it. It is believed cables were used to lower the table and body into the tomb. These tombs were different than those of other sites in that they were lined with rough quarried limestone and only a few facing stones. The ceilings were made of flint and limestone and the floor was limestone soil. The seventh tomb was the only one with a body inside. It was that of an elderly priest who was covered in animal skins and dressed in robes that had been decorated with red dyes. There were numerous wooden and jade objects beside him and a cloth book that had totally disintegrated. Archeologists believe the priest had been buried around AD 600.

But the most valuable treasure buried with the priest was a 9.75-pound (4.4-kilogram) jade head carving of Kinich Akau, the Maya Sun God known for his dedication to poetry and music. The carving turned out to be the largest of its kind ever found in the Maya world.

Belize has no natural jade. The discovery of the head indicated that people living at Altun Ha had traded with those living in Guatemala and others as far away as Mexico. Also, John Stephens and Frederick Catherwood, during their explorations of Central America in 1839, had found and recorded the same face carved on the walls of Uxmal in the Yucatán Peninsula of Mexico. The people at Altun Ha also traded with people as far away as Panama. A metal disc was found at Altun Ha that was from the Cocle region of Panama.

Although the earliest settlements are thought to have been around 200 BC, most of the large structures were built about AD 100. At its peak Altun Ha had over 3,000 people living in the center and an additional 5-7,000 people living in the vicinity.

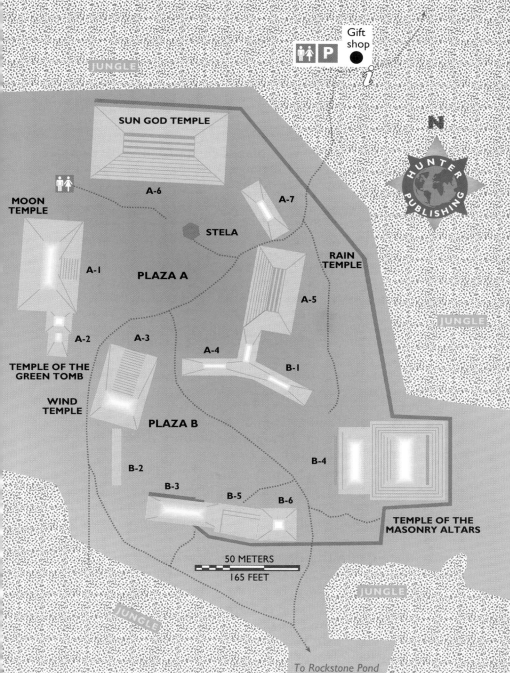

Altun Ha

To Old Northern Hwy (1.5 miles)

Gift shop

JUNGLE

N

HUNTER PUBLISHING

SUN GOD TEMPLE

A-6

A-7

MOON TEMPLE

STELA

RAIN TEMPLE

A-1

PLAZA A

A-5

JUNGLE

A-2

A-3

A-4

B-1

TEMPLE OF THE GREEN TOMB

WIND TEMPLE

PLAZA B

B-4

B-2

B-3

B-5

B-6

TEMPLE OF THE MASONRY ALTARS

50 METERS
165 FEET

JUNGLE

JUNGLE

To Rockstone Pond

MYSTERIOUS MAYA: *Kinich Akau was the patron God of Uxmal and father of Itzamna, lord of night and day. It is believed that Kinich Akau descended into the city of Uxmal every day at noon in the form of a macaw and ate the offerings left on the altar. Kinich Akau often appears with filed teeth similar to those of a jaguar and wearing Kin, the symbol of the Maya day.*

EXPLORING THE RUINS

The ruins consist of two main **plazas** surrounded by 13 **temples**. The ceremonial center sits inside a 1.5-square-mile area and is surrounded by about 500 **residential mounds**.

"ALTUN HA"
Altun Ha means "stone water" and was named after the rockstone pond beside which a small reservoir was built. However, the main 71,000-square-foot reservoir is southwest of the ceremonial complex along a trail leading from Plaza B. It has a stone and clay dam at its south end. Beside it was the first temple built here. Because of the abundant water supply, the housing density near the reservoir is higher than elsewhere in the site.

Altun Ha's temples are unique in structure. Most were built in four phases and each phase had an altar on top. At the altar, carved jade objects were thrown into a fire and burned, along with incense. The next phase was then built over the altar and sacrificial objects. In Plaza B at the **Temple of Masonry Altars**, there were eight phases of construction.

In Plaza A, at the **Temple of the Green Tomb**, which was built around AD 550, over 300 items were found. Some items were of carved jade, others were pieces of stone jewelry. Numerous stingray spikes were also found. These were used by the Maya for bloodletting.

It is believed that Altun Ha fell due to peasant revolts in the Late Classic Period. Following that, the trade center for the region moved to Lamanai.

Today, under the leadership of German archeologist Andrea Ruf, many of the temples and masks are being restored. She informed me that there are also plans to build a new information center. While talking to Andrea, my eyes were drawn to a tin of smoldering cahoon nuts. The smoke was supposed to stave off mosquitoes, but it was far more effective as a perfume.

■ BELIZE JUNGLE GARDENS & AQUARIUM

 The Jungle Gardens, Rockstone Pond, ☎ 609-5523, are open Sunday to Friday, 9 am to 5 pm and are located a half-mile from the ruins on the way back toward the Old Northern Highway. This tastefully designed garden has a river-to-reef aquarium, and cages that contain reptiles and amphibians. Another building displays insects and plants, and a saltwater touch tank is filled with touchable marine animals and plants. There's also a butterfly garden, nature trails, reptile cage, gift shop and a healing herb garden.

Belize Jungle Gardens offers educational workshops and river snorkeling tours or survivor-island (as in the TV program on Discovery Channel) camping. Ask at the desk or phone for details.

■ PLACES TO STAY & EAT

 El Pescador Restaurant, ☎ 609-5523, $$, on the Belize Jungle Garden's grounds, can seat 70 people in its covered gardens. It serves gourmet food and specializes in seafood. I recommend you stop here for a beer, a pop, a snack or a full six-course dinner.

Maya Wells Restaurant, ☎ 209-2039, $$, opens Tuesday to Saturday from 9 am to 5 pm. They were closed when I visited, but are reputed to serve good local cuisine. The restaurant itself is in a covered garden similar to El Pescador.

▶▶ *Return to the Old Northern Highway and continue north. The road is riddled with potholes.*

You'll pass Corzalito Village Community Center, which was built mostly by locals and funded by Raleigh Group Events from the United Kingdom. At Mile 19 is the village of **Maskall** and north of Maskall, at Mile 27, is the **Rancho Creek Farm** and the **Colha Maya ruins**. If you are truly a Maya ruins enthusiast you may want to ask the owners if you can poke around. Colha means water cabbage.

This laborers' site, built in the Late Classic Period, sits on a chert outcrop so workers were close to the valuable stone that was used to make knives and axes. Some tools found at the site are 4,500 years old. It is believed that in about AD 1300 work ceased because

The North

the bow and arrow became the popular hunting weapon and chert was no longer needed to make tools.

At the site, there is a single ceremonial pyramid and ball court with living quarters nearby. All the houses are built around courtyards, not a common design in those days.

Three miles farther north along the Old Northern Highway at Mile 30 is the popular cycling destination of **Pueblo Escondido**, ☎ 614-1458, www.pueblo-escondido.net, $, a "farm and observation garden," where **tenting** is permitted. Some sites are under covered huts for protection against rain. There are hiking trails, fishing ponds and wetland birding sites on the property. There is also a good cycling road at the back of the property that leads to the Altun Ha ruins. Pueblo Escondido is a great destination from which to explore the entire Old Northern Highway and its side roads.

Continuing north along the Old Northern Highway at Mile 39 is the **Pretty See Jungle Ranch**, ☎ 209-2005, $$$$, which was once a macadamia nut plantation. It is located on 1,300 acres of pasture land and jungle. The opportunity for seeing wildlife along its many trails is good. The hardwood, octagonal-shaped cabins sleep four. There is a bar and restaurant on the premises.

COOL ABODE

It is believed that houses built in an octagonal shape are easier to keep cool. Thatch huts should never have air conditioning as the cold air goes up through the roof. It is much better to have a fan.

Maruba Jungle Resort and Spa, Mile 40.5 on the Old Northern Highway, ☎ 322-2199, www.maruba-spa.com, $$$$$, is *the* luxury accommodation on this stretch of road. There are standard rooms, suites and villa suites ($450/day) tucked into the jungle on the property. For entertainment, you can go to a Maya psychic reader, rent a car with a chauffeur, ride horses or soak in the Japanese hot tub. There is a mineral bath and a viewing tower. For those who want to relax by the pool but have gone through all their reading material, there is a one-for-one book exchange. Other amenities include a restaurant and bar, laundry service and airport pick-up service. The resort offers honeymoon and wedding packages, as well as "mood mud therapy." Best of all, a waiter can deliver tropical drinks made from local fruit to anywhere on the property. The owners speak Spanish, English and German, and any tour you may want can be arranged from the reception desk.

The Old Northern Highway joins the New Northern Highway at **Carmelita**. This little village, with its great community spirit, uses some of the profits from its sand pits to fund the primary school.

▶▶ *You'll return to the New Northern Highway at Mile 19 and continue to Mile 31. Turn west onto a secondary road that leads to Crooked Tree Village and Sanctuary. The secondary road goes for three miles until it reaches a causeway that takes you across the Northern Lagoon to the village. Prior to the building of the causeway in 1984, the village was accessible only by boat.*

CROOKED TREE VILLAGE & SANCTUARY

Crooked Tree Village and Wildlife Sanctuary is located on an island that covers about 20 square miles and has a population of about 900.

INTRODUCTION

Serious **birders** can't afford to miss this spot. The wetland bird population is second to none, plus there are two families of the rare jabiru storks that make the sanctuary their yearly nesting place.

A second important draw to this little island is the **Cashew Festival** that takes place over the first weekend in May every year. Attending will give you a pleasant memory of Creole culture (see below).

Eight miles or so south of the village is another Maya site, **Chau Hiix.** This ruin is still only half-excavated and, if you visit, you will get the feeling of being deep in the jungle, isolated, away from the rest of Belize. Animals abound, as do birds, and the vegetation is lush. Snails eggs are abundant on the trees near the lagoon and leaf cutter ants stomp through the jungle over any obstruction.

Crooked Tree is set up for outdoor exploration. Tenting, canoeing and hiking are popular pursuits. If isolated outdoor freedom is what you want, this is a good place to get it.

HISTORY

The village of Crooked Tree has been around for over 300 years and is thought to be the country's oldest modern-day settlement. There are three popular stories about the naming of the community.

The North

■ The first is that three **buccaneers** came to the area and called themselves the "crooked three." It is reported that the three hid a bucket of gold in the swamps north of the village.

■ The second story is that it was the **logging** industry that first settled in the area and named the place after the crooked branches of the logwood trees.

■ The third story concerns the **cashew tree**, which grows abundantly in the area. During storms, it has been known to topple over but continue to grow, crookedly.

Because the area is rich in logwood, the settlers came to harvest the wood and ship it to Europe, where it was used to make expensive dyes. Logwood is a shrub with crooked branches. The trunk is corrugated and dark rust in color, with white patches. The wood was logged, chipped and fermented. It was then made into red, blue, violet, gray or black dyes. The actual dye found in the heart of the wood is called hematoxylin and has been used on wool, cotton, silk, furs and leathers. It is also used as an ink and as a dye to stain cells on microbiological slides so the organism can be seen under a microscope.

Local people make a tea from the wood and use it to cure chronic diarrhea, dysentery and hemorrhages of the uterus, lung or bowel. The drink makes the urine and stool blood red. This was enough to prevent me from trying it.

LUCRATIVE LOADS

During the 1500s logwood sold in England for £100 per ton. One ship could carry about 50 tons of logwood, which could be sold for a total of £5,000, more than a year's profit from any other merchandise shipped during that time. In the mid-1700s a total of 13,000 tons of logwood left Belize in one year. That comes to a total £65 million paid for the one export product. It was only after the aniline dyes made from coal tar were discovered that the use of logwood decreased.

■ GETTING HERE

BY BUS

There are four direct **Jex Busses** going from Belize City to Crooked Tree. They leave daily at 10:30 am, 4:30 and 5:30 pm from Pound Yard Bridge in Belize City. The fourth bus departs at 4 pm from the main terminal.

If these times are not convenient, take any non-express bus going north and ask to be let off at the junction going to the sanctuary. The walk to the village takes about an hour, and you stand an excellent chance of seeing a lot of birds along the way. Returning buses leave Crooked Tree at 6 am, 6:30 and 7 am daily.

■ THINGS TO DO

CROOKED TREE WILDLIFE SANCTUARY

Crooked Tree Wildlife Sanctuary is under the care of the Belize Audubon Society, 12 Fort Street, Belize City, ☎ 223-5004 or 223-4987, www.belizeaudubon.org. The visitor center, located beside the causeway at the entrance to the village, is open daily from 8 am to 4:30 pm. The cost to enter the sanctuary is US $5 per day for foreigners. The first visitor center was built in 1984 and it was replaced in 1995 with the help of the Audubon Society. It features a small display of local birds and has a registration book that should be signed.

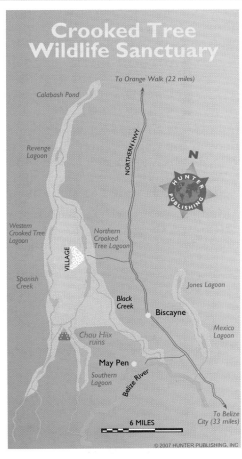

There are three ways to visit the sanctuary: on foot, by boat or on horseback. Boats and horses are available in the village and at the resort within the sanctuary.

The North

The 16,400 acres of waterways and swamps make up two groups of lagoons that, in turn, make up the sanctuary. The largest group includes the Calabash Pond, Southern Lagoon, Western Crooked Tree, Revenge and Spanish Creek. They are linked to the Belize River by Black Creek. The second group, located south and west of the first group, includes Jones and Mexico Lagoons. They run into the Belize River via Mexico Creek. Until 1984 when the causeway was built, these linking waterways were the only highways into the area.

The lagoons are as much as one mile wide and 20 miles long (1.6 km by 32 km). During high water the Northern Crooked Tree Lagoon reaches a depth of eight feet (2.4 meters), while in May, at the end of dry season, it can become completely dry.

The lagoons and creeks of the sanctuary are inundated with logwood thickets, marsh and broadleaf forests and pine/oak savannas. This makes them a haven for both migratory and indigenous birds. The lagoons also house manatee, crocodiles, iguanas and every species of freshwater turtle found in Belize.

> **AUTHOR NOTE:** *In 1998 the sanctuary became the 108th member of the Ramsar Convention, at which time it was declared the first wetland of international importance.*

Interpretive hiking trails lead through the sanctuary. Ask for directions at the visitor center or follow any of the sandy trails from the village – they go for miles. The sanctuary has the longest elevated boardwalk in Belize and it stretches .5 miles across a section of the wetlands. This walk has signs along the way.

Although waterfowl are the most prominent birds found at the sanctuary, the greatest draw for birders is the possibility of spotting a jabiru stork with its three- to four-meter (10- to 12-foot)

© Howler Monkey Lodge.

wingspan. Belize has the largest nesting population of jabirus in all of Central America and the sanctuary has two pairs that nest there every year. They arrive in November and build stick nesting platforms in the lowland pine savannas. The birds remain until April or May, when they join other jabirus and head out, leaving just as the rains arrive.

April and May is also when migratory birds are passing through. The bird population at this time is immense; to date, a total of 276 species have been seen.

CHAU HIIX RUINS

Chau Hiix ruins are about eight miles south of the village and can be reached by canoe in three or four hours or by motorboat in about half an hour. There are no extra entry fees to visit the ruins. Boats can be rented from Tillett's Hotel or Bird's Eye View Lodge (see below).

While doing some cultural anthropology at Crooked Tree in 1989, Dr. Welks of the United States was encouraged by villagers to see a mound south of the village. He was uninterested, but finally gave in to their coaxing and was pleasantly surprised. He informed his wife, Dr. Anne Pyburn, an archeologist with Indiana University, of the mound and when she saw it she became quite excited. She thought that it might be the last unlooted Maya village in Belize. Excavations began shortly after.

After excavations began, Dr. Pyburn realized that the ruins needed a name. She called them Chau Hiix, the Maya word for jaguarundi, the animal of which she saw the most when she first arrived.

 MYSTERIOUS MAYA: *The Maya believed that their era began on August 11th, 3114 BC and will end on December 21st, 2012.*

Chau Hiix was a small city covering three to four square miles. From the findings, Dr. Pyburn felt that the people had a high standard of living. Among other things, it was discovered that these Maya practiced dentistry and actually filled cavities.

The central pyramid is 75 feet high (20 meters), surrounded by six buildings from the post-classic period, and there are 25 large structures in all. Two tombs have been uncovered so far. Inside were two carved plaques made of jade and some hematite earrings. Obsidian blades were also uncovered indicating that the city traded with other communities living some distance away (there is no obsidian in this area).

Although this is not a major ruin, a boat ride or canoe paddle to the ruins is recommended for birders as there are many birds along the way. Groups interested in archeology go to the ruins to help with excavations and to study. If you are interested, visit www.indiana.edu/~overseas/flyers/chauhiix.html.

ADVENTURES

 Canoe rentals and **horseback riding** can be arranged either at **Sam Tillett's Hotel**, ☎ 220-7026, or at the **Bird's Eye View Lodge**, ☎ 225-7027. The cost of a canoe is US $15 per day. Taking a motorboat tour with four people will cost the same (per person) and you have the advantage of a guide. However, the canoe is far more ecologically sensitive to the lagoons and less intrusive to the birds. Horses can be rented from both places and cost US $10 an hour from Bird's Eye without a guide and US $15 from Tillett's with a guide.

The **Cashew Festival**, on the first weekend of May, is actually a three-in-one event. There is the harvest of the cashews, an agricultural show and a display of Creole village life at its best. During the festival, cashew wine (which is sweet) flows into the mouths of all except the very young or very weak and counters the spices of the Creole foods that are served. The wine, in turn, makes the Punta Rock music (see callout, page 354) less abrasive and the greased pole climb more appealing. There is also a story-telling event, a beauty pageant and Creole games of every kind.

One of the highlights for visitors is the opportunity to watch the harvest of the cashew. The nut is picked off the bottom end of the fruit and thrown into a fire to neutralize the acidic juice found between the shell and the meat inside. The nut is then shelled and the meat roasted to perfection. It will give you an appreciation for the high cost of cashews the next time you purchase a bag at home.

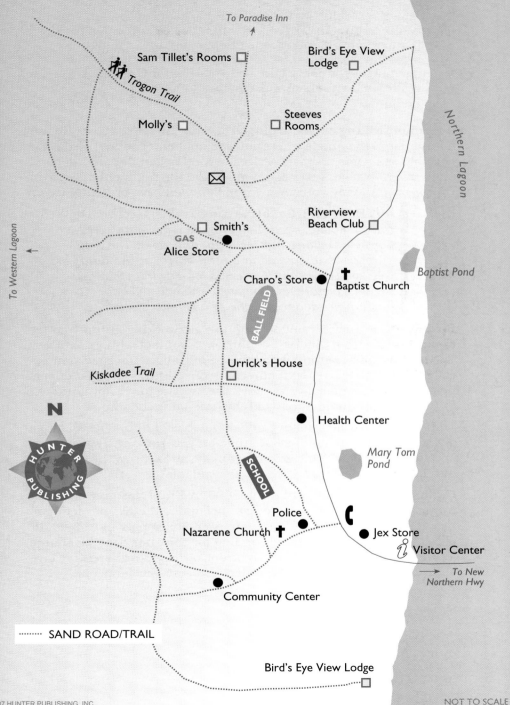

Crooked Tree Village

To Paradise Inn

Sam Tillet's Rooms ☐

Bird's Eye View Lodge ☐

Trogon Trail

Steeves Rooms ☐

Molly's ☐

Northern Lagoon

☒

Riverview Beach Club ☐

☐ Smith's

GAS
Alice Store ●

Baptist Pond

Charo's Store ● ✝ Baptist Church

BALL FIELD

To Western Lagoon

Kiskadee Trail

☐ Urrick's House

● Health Center

Mary Tom Pond

SCHOOL

N

HUNTER PUBLISHING

Police ●

✆

Nazarene Church ✝

● Jex Store
𝑖 Visitor Center

To New Northern Hwy

● Community Center

········· SAND ROAD/TRAIL

Bird's Eye View Lodge
☐

NOT TO SCALE

IN THE EYE OF THE BEHOLDER

During the beauty contest, "E too maaga," meaning "she's too thin" in Creole, can be heard often as the beauties line up for the pageant. "Manfi" is the desired requirement. Manfi means shapely bust and hips. Besides not being too thin, the beauty pageant contest winner must be a local girl with good moral conduct, top grades at high school and a polite manner.

Overnight hiking can be arranged at **Sam Tillett's**, above. He will take you into the jungle where you can spot many inland birds and possibly see some animals. Prices can be negotiated and depend upon where you go, services required and the number of people in your group. Having your own equipment will save on rental fees.

> **AUTHOR TIP:** *Gasoline can be purchased from a private house, even though there is no service station in the village. Ask locals for directions. The lady purchases the gasoline by the barrel in the duty-free zone and sells it to locals for less than the cost at service stations. However, she will sell only the amount needed to get you to a service station.*

Birding Pals, www.birdingpal.org, is a networking group who try to put birders from different countries in contact with each other. The purpose of the group is to have people share the special interest in birds and learn about one another's cultures. The list of participants is growing daily, so check the website just before heading to Belize if you would like to develop such a friendship.

The group lists professional guides available for hire. These listings give the qualifications of each guide so you can satisfy your own special needs. This list is growing rapidly, so log on to their website just before you leave and see who's available.

Birding Pals was started in April, 2000 by Knud Rasmussen of Toronto, Canada. Since the group's inception, the list of members has become substantial. There are over 1,500 pals in 166 countries. Mr Rasmussen gets no funding for this, nor does he charge for the immense amount of work he does. His motivation is his love of birds and he believes that birders are very special people.

■ PLACES TO STAY

 Bird's Eye View Lodge, at the south end of village along the lagoon, ☎ 225-7027 or 570-588-1184, www.belizenet.com/birds-eye, daacker@ptd.net, $-$$$. This is a bustling place where excited birders gather in the guest lounge to talk about

HOTEL PRICES	
$ . . . . $20 to $50
$$ . . . . $51 to $75
$$$ . . . . $76 to $100
$$$$ . . . . . $101 to $150
$$$$$ . . . . . . over $150

the day's sightings. There is a mixed selection of accommodations, from inexpensive dormitory beds or tenting space to rooms that offer private baths.

Sam Tillett's Hotel is in the center of the village, set back from the lagoon. ☎ 220-7026, samhotel@btl.net, $-$$$. Tillet's is another busy spot. It offers comfortable suites and single rooms with fans and private bathrooms. There is also tenting in the yard with access to a shower. If Sam is full and you have no place to stay, he may rent you a hammock on the porch. There is a restaurant at the hotel. Sam is known as the best bird guide in the village and his zest for life is infectious.

Across the street from Tillett's Hotel is a nameless, locally owned shop selling natural skin-care products.

Rhaburn's Rooms, $, in the center of town (ask a local for directions), is a basic accommodation with high-quality hospitality.

Paradise Inn is right on the lagoon at the north end of the village. ☎ 225-7044, www.adventurecamera.com/paradise, $$$$. There are a group of palmetto palm and thatch cabins with private baths and balconies overlooking the lagoon. Owner Rudy Crawford and his family run this establishment by welcoming everyone as if they were personal friends. The food served in the dining room is excellent. The hotel has been recommended by many travelers.

Tenting is available at Tillett's and at Bird's Eye View Lodge. A home stay can be arranged at the visitor center if you would like to be with a family. The center closes at 4:30 pm, so plan to be there at least an hour before closing to give the worker time to arrange a place for you. However, if you arrive late, ask for help from a friendly local.

■ PLACES TO EAT

 The hotels listed above all offer meals that can be ordered and/or included with your room package.

Tree's & Vee's, $, in town, serves traditional Creole food with fresh seasonal wines (cashew and berry).

Ms. Suzette's, $, offers the best fried chicken and fries, or fresh fish and fries, in the village. Both dishes come with a coleslaw that has a unique dressing and an admirable reputation.

RESTAURANT PRICES	
$	$5 to $10
$$	$11 to $25
$$$	$26 to $50
$$$$	$51 to $75
$$$$$	over $75

Ms. Judith's, $, offers the traditional beef, pork or chicken with rice and beans. Although the choice of dishes is limited, the quality of food is high.

If you're looking for something to do after dinner, head to the disco near the lagoon on the north side of the island.

▶▶ *Return to the New Northern Highway at Mile 31, the Crooked Tree Village turnoff, and head north. The next 24 miles of highway goes through farmland.*

CROOKED TREE VILLAGE TO ORANGE WALK

The toll booth at **Tower Hill Bridge**, Mile 51, will cost about US 75¢ if you are driving. Tower Hill is the only toll bridge in the country.

The sugar cane area around Orange Walk is also known as **Little Columbia** because of the ganja and coca that is illegally grown and shipped from here. The side roads in this area should not be traveled at night either by foot, bike or car. Drug enforcement officers are often in the area, but they may not be around when you need protection.

▶▶ *Just after the toll booth on the New Northern Highway is the secondary road going west to **Guinea Grass** and the Mennonite community of **Shipyard**. It's nine miles to Guinea Grass and 18 miles to Shipyard.*

About four miles west of Guinea Grass is a minor ruin, **El Posito**. If you need to walk, it is a destination. (Driving would be slow and in rainy season it would be impossible.) Otherwise, it is little more than a mound.

If you are interested in Mennonite culture, be sure to stop in Shipyard. This is where the conservative Mennonites live. They reside in simple houses without electricity or telephones. They consume no alcohol, nor do they listen to the radio. They are forbidden to ride bikes or cars and their tractors must not have rubber wheels.

They speak Platt Deutsch (low German) as their first language and Spanish as their second. Should you decide to visit, you will be made welcome. Their farms are successful and the people are friendly. If you need something made or fixed and can't get it done in Belize City, come to these fix-it wizards. The greatest fame this group has earned is for the building and carving of mahogany furniture. The down side of this is that most of the timber that is over eight inches in diameter is gone.

Boats can be hired to go up the New River to the Maya ruin of **Lamanai**. However, I suggest hiring a boat at Orange Walk or catching one at the New River beside the Tower Hill toll booth, where there are more boats available.

▶▶ *From the toll booth on the New Northern Highway at Mile 51, it is another four miles to Orange Walk Town.*

ORANGE WALK TOWN

Orange Walk town has a population of about 12,300 people and is locally called **Sugar City**.

AVERAGE TEMPERATURES & RAINFALL		
	Daily temp.	**Monthly rainfall**
JAN	74.6°F/23.7°C	30.2 inches/76.8 cm
FEB	77.0°F/25.0°C	13.3 inches/33.7 cm
MAR	78.8°F/26.0°C	11.3 inches/28.8 cm
APR	82.6°F/28.1°C	18.1 inches/45.9 cm
MAY	84.2°F/29.0°C	39.0 inches/99.1 cm
JUN	84.9°F/29.4°C	79.7 inches/202.5 cm
JULY	84.0°F/28.9°C	75.5 inches/191.7 cm
AUG	84.2°F/29.0°C	80.9 inches/205.6 cm
SEPT	84.2°F/29.0°C	67.3 inches/171.0 cm
OCT	82.2°F/27.9°C	74.3 inches/188.7 cm
NOV	79.5°F/26.4°C	40.0 inches/101.6 cm
DEC	76.8°F/24.9°C	30.5 inches/77.4 cm

Source: Belize Sugar Industries located at Towerhill, two miles from Orange Walk Town.

The North

■ GETTING HERE

If **driving** or **cycling**, stay on the New Northern Highway. The road is good and decorated on each side by sugar cane fields.

> **TAKE NOTE:** *Do not drive at night, especially on the secondary roads. This is a drug-running area and night travel is not for visitors.*

Buses going north and south pass along the New Northern Highway through Orange Walk every half-hour. Take a bus from the main terminal in Belize City. An express bus will take half as long as a regular bus, but it isn't nearly as interesting. Regular buses can be caught anywhere along the highway. Flag one down and the driver will stop.

■ INTRODUCTION

The town, sitting on the banks of the New River, is a bustling hodge-podge of animals, cars, buses, sugar cane trucks, garden goods and friendly people. It's also the transfer place if you want to reach some of the fishing villages on the Caribbean coast.

Orange Walk is believed to have gotten its name from the orange trees that at one time decorated the banks of the New River. If this is true, the town council should plant more because the quiet walk near the river is a delightful contrast to the bustle of the center and orange trees would add to the beauty.

There are two fairly important Maya sites near Orange Walk. **Lamanai** is best reached by taking a boat up the New River and **Cuello** is close enough to town that it can be reached by bicycle. Other attractions are the **Rio Bravo Conservation Area** and the **Chan Chich Lodge**. Both are exquisite for wildlife viewing.

Orange Walk itself has decent hotels, good restaurants, Internet cafés and sleazy bars. The surrounding area is dedicated mostly to sugar cane farming or Mennonite settlements. The drug running mentioned earlier seems to be just an extension of the rum running that was done during the 1800s.

■ HISTORY

Prior to Europeans arriving in Belize, this area was densely populated with **Maya**. For some unknown reason they abandoned most of the area before Columbus arrived. The latest theory is that severe drought caused starvation.

The re-entry of the Maya occurred in 1849 when they were fleeing from the wars in Mexico caused by the Spanish elite enforcing servitude and confiscating land. These acts of oppression left the Maya in poverty.

The **British** welcomed the Maya, hoping that they would set up farms and grow much needed produce for the loggers who were denuding the forests at that time. As the wood disappeared and the prices for logs dropped, the landowners rented their land to the Maya. But not all was amiable and peaceful. Fort Cairn and Fort Mundy were built to protect the settlers from the warring Mexicans, who felt that a lot of Belize belonged to them. The final battle occurred in 1872 and a sort of peaceful co-existence began until 1892 when an actual treaty was signed between the British and the Mexicans.

As logging disappeared, the **chicle** business flourished. It was later replaced with **maize**. In the early 1900s an old sugar mill was imported from Leeds Foundary in New Orleans and installed north of town. The **sugar** business was started and is still the main source of income today.

Sugar cane trucks.

Orange Walk and Corozal Districts were one large district until 1955, when Orange Walk split from Corozal and became a separate district with its own government. This seems to have been good for the area. In the last 50 years, Orange Walk District has quadrupled its population to about 40,000 people, one quarter of the population of Belize.

■ THINGS TO DO

 Godoy's Orchid Garden, 4 Trial Farm, ☎ 322-2969, has a huge display of orchids and bromeliads. There is no charge to visit and Godoy's is open during regular business hours. In its fall blooming season, the national flower, the black orchid, can be viewed.

La Immaculada Church is in the center of Orange Walk. It's a catholic church with a children's school attached and is most impressive. Although not open all the time, it is a good landmark.

> **AUTHOR NOTE:** *Belize has nine major religious groups practicing in the country. Churches are exempt from paying property taxes and this may be one reason there are so many.*

CUELLO RUINS

Cuello ruins, ☎ 322-2141, are just 1.8 miles along Yo Creek Road, west of Orange Walk Town and easily walked to in less than an hour. Cycling would take even less time. The ruins are on the Cuello family land, where rum is made at the distillery. You must ask permission to enter the ruins. Call ahead.

To visit the ruins, go west on Baker Street, cross the highway and continue along San Antonio Road (Yo Creek Road) until you arrive at the Cuello Farm, about two miles along the road. If you haven't phoned ahead and asked permission to wander the ruins, stop at the first building you pass on the property.

The ruins are not very interesting, but quite old. If you have time to spend and would like a destination for a walk, then go to Cuello and have a picnic lunch. The trip takes a few hours.

Cuello was first discovered in 1973 by archeologist, **Dr. Norman Hammond**, an acclaimed researcher who has been affiliated with numerous universities, including Cambridge and Rutgers.

The oldest pyramid on the site, built in nine layers, is believed to have been constructed about 2600 BC. This date is controversial; other experts think the pyramid was built about 1000 BC. Regardless, the ruins are an early example of how the Maya plastered over their structural stones to give the pyramid a smooth finish. This style of finishing is similar to the Cahal Pech ruins in San Ignacio, Cayo District and to the Zaculeu ruins, located just out of Huehuetenango in Guatemala. The Zaculeu ruins are believed to date from the Mam Dynasty, built during the late post classic period (AD 1400).

The style of pottery that was produced here is the oldest example of this kind ever located in the Maya lowlands. The style is called the **Consejo red Swasey** and there is evidence that similar monochrome pieces were used at Cahal Pech at San Ignacio, Cayo District. This could mean that the two communities traded with each other; not an unreasonable assumption. They also found a bowl, now at the National Museum, that was manufactured using a coil technique and then polished to a luster.

The most interesting discovery was the bodies with ceramic head coverings found at some of the 180 unearthed graves. There were also bodies showing evidence of torture found in a mass grave.

Damage to Cuello happened due to road construction in recent times. Building stones were removed for this work and graves were looted. The remaining objects found here are now part of the national exhibition.

 MYSTERIOUS MAYA: *The Maya are believed to have domesticated several breeds of dogs, one of them being barkless. Too bad they aren't still around. The Maya used to fatten the dogs and sacrifice them. I'd love to sacrifice some of the barking dogs found in Belize City, especially around 3 am.*

NOHMUL RUINS

The Nohmul ruins are just north of Orange Walk Town. To get there, take any vehicle heading north and get off at San José, just seven miles from town along the New Northern Highway. At the crossroads, walk west for one mile. This stroll will take less than 20 minutes each way.

Nohmul, meaning Great Mound, was at one time a major ceremonial center. However, its greatest fame comes from the ability of the Maya living there to conquer the Pulltrouser Swamp area and transform the land into productive farms.

Occupied from about 350 BC to AD 250 and then again from about AD 600 to 900, the town was the government seat for the settlements around San Estevan and San Luis.

The two ceremonial sites contain 10 plazas connected by a raised causeway. In total there are about 81 buildings in the city. The site covers 12 square miles and overlooks the Hondo River. Some of the architecture found at Nohmul is similar to that of the Yucatán in Mexico. This supports the idea that the Maya did migrate to the area from the north.

This site was first explored by **Thomas Gann** in 1897. He came back often and finally, in 1935, he excavated the main settlements and found tombs that contained jewelry, sea shells and painted containers.

LESSONS

Before Nohmul was established, trading was already popular between those living in Mexico and those near Corozal. Mik Chan (850 BC) was one such Maya trader, but during a drunken spree someone went off with all his goods, leaving him with nothing. Times have not changed. Get drunk in public and you could lose all your money.

Lamanai Ruins can be visited from here as a day-trip by either walking or taking a river tour. See Lamanai Ruins description on page 180.

■ ADVENTURES

A **canoe race**, called the **Lamanai Adventure Challenge**, is held every September. It goes from Lamanai to Orange Walk, 32 miles of grueling work to get to the finish line on the same day, never mind in the winner's circle. Contact the Lamanai Outpost Lodge, ☎ 223-3578 or 888-733-7864, for more information.

Light up the Holiday House decorating contest is held in December and is sponsored by (who else?) the Belize Electrical Company. If you're here around Christmas, walk through the residential part of town and look at the decorations.

■ PLACES TO STAY

D' Victoria Hotel, 40 Belize/Corozal Road, ☎ 322-2518, www.d-victoriahotel.com, $$, is at the south end of town. There is air conditioning, cable TV, parking, private bath with hot water and also a swimming pool in the courtyard. Al-

Orange Walk

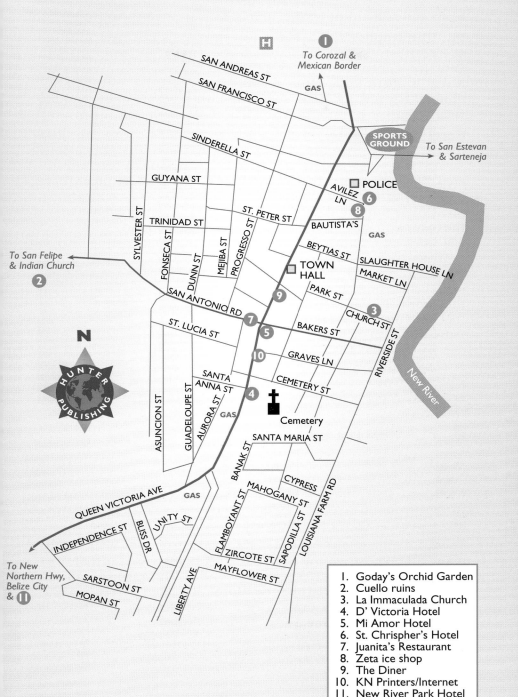

1. Goday's Orchid Garden
2. Cuello ruins
3. La Immaculada Church
4. D' Victoria Hotel
5. Mi Amor Hotel
6. St. Chrispher's Hotel
7. Juanita's Restaurant
8. Zeta ice shop
9. The Diner
10. KN Printers/Internet
11. New River Park Hotel

NOT TO SCALE

© 2007 HUNTER PUBLISHING, INC

though a bit run down, the hotel is not noisy and it has pleasant staff. There is a bar and restaurant on the premises.

HOTEL PRICES	
$	$20 to $50
$$	$51 to $75
$$$	$76 to $100
$$$$	$101 to $150
$$$$$	over $150

St. Christopher's, 10 Main Street, ☎ 302-1064, $$$, is across from the Zeta Ice Factory and faces the New River. It offers fairly clean rooms (although they are in need of some care), with private baths and hot water. There is a restaurant and bar on the premises.

Hotel de la Fuente, 14 Main St., ☎ 322-2290, www.hoteldela fuente.com, $$, is a brand new place that won the "Small Hotel Award" last year – and justifiably so. Every detail has been considered. The bathrooms are tiled and have coordinated fixtures. There is hot water all the time and remote controlled air conditioning. The TV has numerous English channels and there is a data port in the room with instructions on how to configure your computer so it will work on this system. The floors are tile and every corner is

spotless. Included in the room is a fridge, microwave, coffee maker (with coffee) and shaving plug-ins that work. The mirrors are set at the right height. Workers at the hotel will arrange your New River trip to Lamanai for a reasonable price. Staying here will give you a whole new view of Orange Walk. It is highly recommended!

■ PLACES TO EAT

The Diner, 44 Queen Victoria Avenue, ☎ 302-3753, $$, is by far the best place to eat in Orange Walk. Presented buffet-style, the food is better and the variety larger than the usual fare found in other restaurants. Dishes such as pepper steak and fish in a rich white sauce, are on the menu too.

There are numerous **Chinese restaurants** in Orange Walk. Of the many around, I tried the **Belize Road Chinese Restaurant**, 151 Belize Road, ☎ 322-3159, $, and wasn't enthralled or disappointed. The **St. Christopher's Hotel**, 10 Main Street, ☎ 302-1064, $$, also serves fairly decent food. Excellent ice cream is available at the **Zeta Ice Shop**, 31 Main Street.

Caye Caulker Restaurant, Main St., no phone, $$, open every day except Sunday, 7 am to 9 pm. The salads are excellent and the portions large. However, if you order the steak, they will overcook it to shoe-leather quality.

White Gold Café, Main St. across from the Caulker, $$, appears a bit grotty but the food and service are very good. The beef chow mien is recommended. Portions are large – don't order too much.

■ NIGHTLIFE

 Mi Amor Hotel has a disco where Punta Rock isn't quite so popular as Latin music. If you don't like marimba, maybe do the nightlife in some other town. (See page 354 for some information about the history of Punta Rock.)

■ SERVICES

 Sugar N Cream Internet Café, 22 Main St., ☎ 322-0020, Monday to Friday, 8 am to 8:30 pm, and Saturday, 8 am to 6:30 pm. The machines are fast and the owners friendly.

▶▶ *From Orange Walk to Lamanai, the road is very rough during dry season and impassible during rainy season. To get here, turn west onto the road just north of the New River Bridge. The road is paved to the first tiny village then it becomes bad gravel or mud. At Shipstern, where the road ends, turn left and follow that road for about 12 km – it will get quite bad in places – until you come to a sign indicating a turn to Lamanai. The ruins and lodge are a few kilometers down that road. If you continue ahead, you will go to La Milpa and Gallon Jug.*

ORANGE WALK TO INDIAN CHURCH

■ GETTING HERE

 A **bus** goes to Lamanai three times a week, on Monday, Wednesday and Friday. It leaves Orange Walk Town around 4 pm from the fire station. Traveling by bus usually means that you will stay at the lodge near Lamanai for three nights (one when you arrive and the next day while you tour the ruins), then catch the 6 am bus back on the morning of your return.

Jungle River Tours, 20 Lovers Lane (southeast corner of the park in Orange Walk), ☎ 302-2293, runs a boat service for the 26-mile run upriver. The cost is US $50 per person, with a minimum of four persons sharing the boat. The trip takes about 1.5 hours and includes lunch and pop. The owners, Herminio and Antonio are knowledgeable and will give you a complete guided tour along the river and through the Lamanai ruins site. They are enthusiastic and interested in their work, which makes the trip even more enjoyable for you.

Lamanai Lady Boat will pick up passengers at the Tower Hill toll bridge where it crosses the New River along the highway. The boat leaves at 9 am and a round-trip costs US $80 per person. Again, the trip upriver takes 1.5 hours. I have heard reports that if there are not enough passengers to fill the boat, it will not go.

Road to Lamanai in rainy season.

■ INDIAN CHURCH

 Indian Church is the village where Lamanai ruins are located. Of the few buildings in town, some contain attractions. You might like to stop at the **Xochil Ku Butterfly Farm** (no phone). Built especially to promote ecological ideas among the local children, the farm is open during daylight hours at no cost to locals. You, on the other hand, are asked for a small donation.

Another in-town attraction is the **Chujue Xux Honey Project** (no phone). Here, African bees make honey, which is available for sale and makes a great gift. African bees are used because of their high quantity of production.

DOING GOOD

The **Tropical Rainforest Coalition**, 21730 Stevens Creek Boulevard, Cupertino, CA 95014, www.rainforest.org, has been very active and successful in this area. Not only have they preserved land here at Indian Church, but they also have land in Trinidad, the village missed by a blink back along the road. For US $50 you can preserve an acre of rainforest. The donation is tax deductible. Should you donate more than US $200, your name goes on their website.

■ LAMANAI RUINS

 Lamanai ruins are open daily from 8 am to 5 pm and the entry fee is US $5. The ruins are impressive, especially if arriving by boat. I recommend doing at least one river trip while in Belize and if Lamanai is a desired destination then I urge you to consider taking a boat, rather than a bus or car.

This is not only one of the oldest Maya sites in Belize, it is the one that had the longest continual occupation. This occupational span started about 1500 BC and continued until the 1800s.

Lamanai is the original Maya name for this city and it means "submerged crocodile." The name was recorded in church records when two priests visited the city and then described their findings.

Lamanai Ruins.
(Photo courtesy Lamanai Outpost Lodge)

The 950 acres that the city occupies have 720 structures mapped, but only 70 excavated. Eight plazas have been located. First worked by Dr. **David Prendergast** in 1974, the project was continued by Dr. Elizabeth Graham, also from Canada. Prior to that there was a British archeology buff, Thomas Gann, who in 1917 came to the site and found a stele that had been plastered over with clay by the Catholic church. A few others came but nothing serious was done on the site until Dr. Prendergast arrived.

 MYSTERIOUS MAYA: *The Maya used the concept of "zero" one thousand years before Western civilization started using it.*

Lamanai sits on the New River Lagoon and some ceremonial sites are close to the water. This is unusual; Maya usually have the ceremonial temples and plazas in the center of town with the residences circling beyond. However, at Lamani, the houses splay out from the water to the south, north and west.

The most dominant structure and the one most thoroughly excavated is called N9-56 or the **Mask Temple**. It is so named because of the large mask on one corner of the building. A second mask that has no face (only the back panel remains) is on the upper side. These masks were cut from blocks of limestone, rather than the more common method of sculpting from a stone covered in plaster. The mask here is believed to depict someone from the Olmec society in Mexico. It is also believed by some to depict Kinich Ahau, the Mexican Sun God. The mask is adorned with a crocodile crown or headdress. This building, from the early classic period, stands at 56 feet (17 meters).

A tomb uncovered in this building had jade earrings and wooden figurines inside. One necklace found at the site has 90 jade beads, some carved, and is occasionally on display at the National Museum. The coffin, in which one body was found, was covered in chert chips, possibly from Colha ruins near Altun Ha.

Detail on Lamanai's Mask Temple.

MYSTERIOUS MAYA: *Because no croc-odile remains have ever been found in any Maya tombs, it is believed that the creatures were actually protected.*

P 9-25 is the largest set of buildings. They sit around a plaza that is over 300 feet long (90 meters). The tallest building around this plaza is 30 feet high (10 meters).

High Temple is the tallest building at Lamanai. Standing a majestic 108 feet (33 meters), it is understandably often called "the castle." Built around the 2nd century BC, it was the Empire State building of the Maya. This pre-classic building was as tall then as it is now. In other words, no layers have been added. The transition from the lower buildings like those located around other groups to the huge one here suggests an economic upswing.

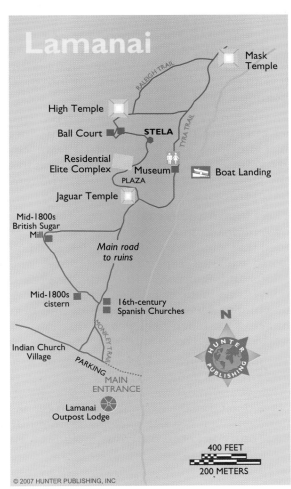

A climb to the top of this temple is recommended, but challenging. The views of the lush jungle surrounding Lamanai and of the lagoon cutting through the green makes this site reminiscent of Tikal in Guatemala.

Just to the north is a small **ball court**. Under the court's marker disc was a vessel sitting on a container of mercury, a substance believed to be known only to the highland Maya. The vessel had smaller vessels inside, along with shells and jade.

The North

POK A TOK

The ball game, called Pok A Tok in the Maya language, was played by young warriors who wanted their blood sacrificed to the Sun God. It was believed that the sacrificed blood could renew the god's life. The winners/losers(I've never been sure which is which) were the ones who died on the high altar.

Farther south of the ball court are about 50 burial sites believed to be from the post classic period. The identifying trait for these tombs was the breaking of a clay vessel over the burying container before final covering. Another tomb found in the vicinity had a mirror, a copper bell and wooden objects inside.

To the south is a stelae that was found face-down over the stairs of a small temple. The figure on the now upright stelae is known as **Lord Smoking Shell** and incorporates a date, "tun 7 ahau 3 pop," which translates into a festivity that ended on March 7th AD 625. It is an elaborate carving, with the lord dressed in rich adornments holding a shell.

The final ruin, to the south, is from the Spanish period. Missionaries built two **churches**, the remains of which can be seen. The colonial graveyard, used for about 70 years, covers a Maya ceremonial structure. The original church was built in 1560 but was burned to the ground by the Maya in 1641. The remains here are from the later structure.

There is also a **sugar mill**, the first ever built in Belize, constructed by American refugees after the Civil War. It is located along a side road that winds through the jungle and back to the main trail. It is worth walking, especially for birders. The mill was built in the 1850s and abandoned in the 1880s because of its poor construction. It was made of bricks that rattled and moved when the heavy machinery was running, causing the bricks to shatter. Maintenance of the machinery was an unknown skill in these parts of the world, so it too soon fell apart, at which time it was abandoned.

The museum, near the wharf, was built in 2005 to replace the original that was vandalized a few years before. All artifacts here are original and most were found at the site. There are historical displays depicting life from about 7000 BC to the present. One fascinating artifact is a necklace made from hundreds of human teeth. Your entry ticket to the ruins includes a visit to the museum.

■ PLACES TO STAY & EAT

Lamanai Outpost Lodge, ☎ 223-3578 or 888-733-7864, www.lamanai.com, $$$. The lodge, just 15 minutes from the ruins, is an upscale luxury place sitting on a knoll above the lagoon. The screened mahogany huts have thatched roofs and come with good ceiling fans, 24-hour electricity, laundry service and private baths with hot water. E-mail access is offered. There is a gift shop, swimming dock, bar and **dining room** ($$$) called **Bushey's Palace** that serves excellent food. The owners, Mark and Monique Howells, rescued two orphaned black howler monkeys and, with the help of those at the Lamanai Research Field Station, got them ready for reintegration into the jungle. The lodge won the 1999-2000 Hotel of the Year award. Their Spotlight River Tour allows guests to see a bulldog bat, the world's largest fishing bat, a flowering cactus whose flower opens only at night, or the Morelet's crocodile. It is believed that the world's largest population of Morelet's crocs lives around Lamanai.

© Lamanai Outpost Lodge

This is the only place in Lamanai at which I could recommend eating. It is excellent. If you plan to stay at the lodge, book in advance as it is often full of people on birding tours.

MYSTERIOUS MAYA: *According to Maya legend, the Creation Tree (bearer of all life) came from the head of a crocodile.*

Lamanai Research Field Station runs study courses with credits from York University in Canada. Each year the station offers a chance to partake in archeological excavations, bird research studies, howler monkey research and other studies pertinent to jungle conservation. The station is based near the lodge.

■ RIO BRAVO MANAGEMENT AREA

Programme for Belize, 1 Eyre Street, Belize City, ☎ 227-5616 or 227-1248, www.pfbelize.org, was established in 1988 to protect the forest that is now the Rio Bravo Management Area. The forest was under threat of being cleared by an international company. Environmentalists stepped in and convinced the company to use other land for their purposes.

The North

Programme for Belize then had to convince local farmers that it was better to use the forest as a tourist destination, for scientific study and for other sustainable purposes, than to slash and burn for agriculture.

To date there are 260,000 acres holding two research stations. Hill Bank is at the far end of the New River Lagoon and La Milpa Field Station is on the road to Gallon Jug. According to reports procured by these stations, this land holds around 400 species of birds, 200 varieties of trees and about 70 different kinds of animals. That makes it quite a natural zoo.

Programme for Belize has grown and now they try to educate anyone interested in learning about using natural resources wisely. For an example, they are trying to develop a laboratory procedure to propagate orchids for export. If you stay at the field station, the profits go into helping the program promote environmental awareness.

Hill Bank Field Station, ☎ 221-2060, at the south end of New River Lagoon, is best reached by boat. Some boats that go from Orange Walk will also go to the station if they know ahead of time. Otherwise, you may be able to hire a boat at Lamanai Outpost Lodge. Profits from overnight guests go to the preservation of the rainforest. The purpose of the station is to give the visitor an introduction to and education about the delicate balance of the rain forest and to promote environmental awareness.

At the station there are dorms that sleep 30 people. The dorms cost US $80 per person, and the fee includes three meals. There are compost toilets and showers heated by solar panels.

SAN FILIPE TO BLUE CREEK

▶▶ *If you wish to drive or cycle to the Mennonite settlement of Blue Creek and then continue on to Gallon Jug, you must backtrack from Indian Church 12 miles to San Filipe.*
At San Filipe, turn left (west) onto that road. Continue along the road (rather than going back to Orange Walk) for about five miles and cross the Rio Bravo River Bridge. After 2.5 miles, turn left and you will be in the center of Blue Creek, by the Linda Vista Shopping Center.

■ BLUE CREEK

 Blue Creek has gasoline available. The town is on the Rio Bravo Escarpment and on the confluence of the three waterways – the Rio Bravo, the Rio Hondo and Blue Creek.

There is a border crossing into Mexico on the Honda river, but it is open only to local Belizeans. The river is the border. The area of Blue Creek includes about three square miles of surrounding settlements.

There is an interesting artifact found close to town. In 1976 a **Lockheed Super Constellation plane**, originally built in 1958, was flying from Mexico to Guatemala City when it ran into trouble. Propeller #1 fell off and struck engine #2. This caused the engine to run out of control so the pilot, one of three on board, decided to land in Belize City. However, the wheels wouldn't come all the way down, so the plane skidded on its belly past the edge of the runway. It was not a good day. All three pilots were killed. There were no passengers on board.

The men from Blue Creek decided that they could use the remaining parts of the plane to repair and make things for their farms around Blue Creek. They went to Belize City and hauled the wreckage to the farm of Abe Dick near the village.

Although the wreckage has never been restored, it is still of interest to pilots or airplane buffs. If you want to see it, contact Abe Dick, ☎ 323-0337, to make an appointment.

■ PLACES TO STAY & EAT

 Hillside Bed and Breakfast, ☎ 323-0155, $$, is the first Mennonite B & B established in Belize. Ask in town for directions to the house. If you are interested in the Mennonite way of life, you can get first hand experience by partaking in the ranching life of the Klassens. The food at Hillside is exceptional and the hospitality is the same.

HOTEL PRICES	
$	$20 to $50
$$	$51 to $75
$$$	$76 to $100
$$$$	$101 to $150
$$$$$	over $150

La Rosita Store, about two miles west of Linda Vista Shopping Center, ☎ 323-0445, $$, has rooms for rent above the store. The rooms are basic and very clean. They are run by Jacob Neufeld and his wife, who will make you feel welcome. I suggest you try them out if the Hillside is full.

Cornerstone Café, ☎ 323-0905, $, near the Linda Vista Shopping Center, has meals and refreshments. Prices are low and portions are big.

BLUE CREEK TO GALLON JUG

▶▶ *The all-weather road continues west out of Blue Creek through small settlements to Newstadt. A three-season road heads south. The one going to Gallon Jug and Chan Chich starts just before the village of Tres Leguas. This is a well-maintained road. To go to La Milpa, phone ahead to find out about the road conditions.*

■ LA MILPA RESEARCH STATION & RUINS

La Milpa Research Station, ☎ 323-0011, www.pfbelize.org, is one of two stations in the Rio Bravo Management Area. La Milpa charges US $20 for foreigners to visit (it's free for nationals). This is where I think the "scalp the tourist" game has gone too far. However, the money goes for a good cause and Programme for Belize needs the local support. If you want to visit, let them know in advance by either phoning or sending an e-mail. The entry fee includes a guided walk along one of their trails, plus a guide at the ruins. Lunch will cost another US $8. There are thatch hut cabañas for overnight stays (US $100 per person) or dorm beds (US $80). These prices include three meals.

This field station has some sponsorship from National Geographic Society and from Boston University and works in cooperation with Programme for Belize (see above) and all the profits from tourists' visits are going into more conservation for Belize. This site is deemed so important that when Princess Anne of England visited in 2001, she was given a tour. I wonder if she had to pay the twenty bucks.

From the visitor center at the station it is a one-hour walk through the jungle to La Milpa ruins. The name means corn field in Mayan. The land that holds the ruins was destined to be made into a corn field by local farmers before the area was saved by the Programme for Belize.

Under the leadership of Drs. Norman Hammond, Francisco Estrada-Belli and Gair Tourtellot, excavations at the site uncovered the **Great Plaza**, believed to be the largest Maya plaza ever discovered in Belize. It covers six square miles. The plaza is surrounded by four temples, three of which stand about 80 feet (24 meters) high. The plaza also contains two ball courts.

During its peak, it is believed that about 46,000 people lived in the 20,000 houses surrounding the center. There was also terracing done in the nearby fields.

So far, 19 stelae and 20 courtyards have been found. One building that was never completed had a stone throne in it. But the most important find was a **royal tomb** with a man inside. Archeologists think his name was **Bird Jaguar**. Across his chest was a huge jade necklace. They think he lived around AD 450, just before La Milpa started its first decline. There was a revival in about AD 600 and then habitation continued until 1600. La Milpa peaked around AD 900.

▶▶ *To reach Gallon Jug, continue along the well-graded gravel road above the Rio Bravo for 35 miles to Barry Bowen's exquisite resort, Chan Chich.*

GALLON JUG/CHAN CHICH

Chan Chich, ☎ 800-328-8368, www.chanchich.com, $$$$$, is reputed to be one of the world's best lodges. Owned by Barry Bowen, the richest man in Belize and owner of Belikin Beer, the 250,000 acres of land backs onto the Rio Bravo Management Area. Because the lodge is ecologically sympathetic, it makes the two parcels of land one huge environmental reserve. Ten thousand acres of Bowen's land is being managed by the Programme for Belize.

The history of Bowen's 250,000 acres is interesting. Up until the 1960s Belize Estates, an international logging company, owned about one-fifth of the land in Belize, some of it around Gallon Jug. The main headquarters for the area was at Hill Bank on the New River Lagoon, not far from Lamanai. Logs were cut and hauled to the lagoon and then shipped downriver to the ocean.

However, in 1943 it was decided to move the headquarters from New River Lagoon to the Gallon Jug area. The foreman from New River Lagoon, Austin Felix, wanted to move to the new location. He chose a spot in the high bush near the present site of Gallon Jug. After the logging crews moved into the area, they called their home town many names, but nothing fit. Then Felix found three old jugs beside his house. It is believed the jugs were left many years before when the area was a Spanish camp. Felix named the area **Campamente Galon de Jarro**, but that name was too long. Gallon Jug was the name that stuck.

In 1988, Bowen completed the lodge facilities on one of the plazas in the Chan Chich Maya ruins. The thatched-roof cabins are surrounded by jungle and grass-covered temples. Made of local hardwoods, each cabin has two beds, screened windows, a ceiling fan and a large bathroom with hot water.

The North

BELIZE ESTATE & PRODUCE CO.

The British Honduras Company bought land in the Corozal District in 1859 from the early settlers, James Hyde and James Bartlett. Fourteen years later the company changed its name to the Belize Estate and Produce Co. (BEC). They also purchased all available land that had hardwood growing on it. Their estate soon covered over one million acres.

The BEC was not a good landowner. They destroyed many Maya villages and left hundreds of people homeless so that the company would have access to the hardwoods. They also fought strongly against workers' rights and kept the wages of the workers at starvation levels. It wasn't until the 1960s and 1970s that the land passed into other hands. It was purchased by the Bowen family during BEC's sell-off in the 1960s.

The jungle outside the cabins is home to about 350 species of birds and 150 different types of butterflies. A large number of cats also live here. If you want to walk in the jungle, guides are available all day long.

This resort offers numerous packages, all of which include birding. Some packages also have diving, some have ruin tours, some focus more on animal sightings. There are horses available for riding and the coffee served at the lodge is grown on the property. You may also rent a cabin without any other services.

> AUTHOR NOTE: *Humans use only 7,000 of the 75,000 known edible plants found in the rainforests around the world.*

There are nine miles of trails through Bowen's jungle that can be hiked or ridden. There are canoes for use at the spring-fed Laguna Verde and the larger Laguna Seca. There are unexcavated ruins to explore and birds to spot. Don't forget to look for jaguars and the fer-de-lance snake.

▶▶ *Return to Orange Walk at Mile 56 on the New Northern Highway. To get to **Sarteneja**, follow Main Street north through Orange Walk and over the old New River Bridge. This secondary road leading to Sarteneja starts to get bad at the bridge and gets progressively worse all the way to the village. Once across the bridge, take the left fork after one mile. Drive 5.5 miles to the town of San Estevan. Stay on the pavement. Six miles past San Estevan, take the road to the right. The road straight ahead goes to Progresso and Copper Bank (directions to these villages are below). Going to Sarteneja, take the left-hand turn at the next crossroad and drive past the Progresso Lagoon, Chunox Village and finally the Shipstern Reserve. Sarteneja is next.*

SARTENEJA

■ GETTING HERE

Buses for Sarteneja leave the Zeta Ice Factory in Orange Walk Town, 31 Main Street, at 2 pm, 3 pm and 3:30 pm. It takes almost two hours to reach Sarteneja. This road is the worst in Belize.

Returning to Orange Walk Town, the buses leave Sarteneja at 4:30, 5:30 and 6:30 am. They drive around town quite a few times, making sure no one has been missed before they start down the highway.

The North

Boats can be hired at Ambergris Caye, Caye Caulker and Corozal Town for the short trip to Sarteneja. It takes about 30 minutes from Corozal and about an hour from Ambergris. The boat should be arranged with a tour agency of your choice. The cost by boat from Corozal to Ambergris Caye is US $20, so expect to pay around that price from the cayes to Sartenejo and less from Corozal.

■ INTRODUCTION

 A sleepy fishing village with about 700 residents on Corozal Bay, Sarteneja is just waiting for the tourists to start flocking in and, when they do, the village will loose a lot of its charm. However, I can't be selfish. My job is to tell you about such places. There are three hotels and one restaurant in town. Fishermen sit on the sandy beach mending nets and boats bob in the bay, waiting to be photographed. A constant breeze comes in off the bay and the dogs don't bark all night. The people are friendly and helpful; they want to please. If you need to chill out, this is one of the villages where you can. Spanish is spoken more than English.

■ HISTORY

 "Tzateb-ey-ha" means water between the rocks or pool in the Mayan language. Two Mayans, Mr. and Mrs. Aragon, came to Sarteneja from Valladolid to escape the hardships in Mexico. As they walked through the jungle, they came upon a spring that had formed a pool of fresh water. The Aragons decided to settle near the pool. They were joined by others from Tulum, who were also escaping harsh treatment from the Mexicans.

The new settlers started farming and built thatch huts in which to live. A hurricane came and, like the big bad wolf, blew the houses down. So the settlers rebuilt, this time with stone and mortar. Unknowingly, they built over other Maya homes that had disappeared into the ground.

The next hardship that hit the area was severe drought, so the adaptable Aragons started selling firewood for a living. As time passed, they switched to the more lucrative fishing industry. This proved to be a good move. Soon others came and the village grew to its present size.

THINGS TO DO

The two **graves** of the Aragons can be visited. The white plaster graves sit above ground near the ocean, within view of Krisami's Hotel. The fresh water **well** that the Aragons found is still being used, although it is now encircled with cement. It is on Cola Aragon's property at 114 Conlos Street. Ask for directions. Drinking the water from the well will ensure that you return to Sarteneja before you die.

At Camdalie's Sunset Cabañas, there is a mural depicting the history of the town.

Bicycles can be rented from Krisami's Rooms. These bikes are available for guests first so you may have to wait. Cycling to Shipstern Nature Reserve is highly recommended. You see so much more along the way when on a bike or walking.

SHIPSTERN NATURE RESERVE

Shipstern Nature Reserve is three miles from Sarteneja. The bus will let you off at the reserve if you want to stop on your way to the village. Entrance fees are US $5 per person, payable at the park. The visitor center is open 24 hours a day.

The reserve covers 22,000 acres of unique land. It has north-wood forests, salt-water lagoons and mangrove shorelines. The forests are interspersed with limestone hillocks.

First purchased in 1989, the reserve was managed solely by the International Tropical Conservation Foundation, Box 31, Ch 2074 Marin, Neuchatel, Switzerland. In 1996, the Belize Audubon Society joined in management of the reserve.

The **butterfly breeding center**, next to the visitor center, was started by two English people who eventually sold the entire reserve to the ITCF. It was established to help local people with sustainable development. By breeding the butterflies and selling the pupae to European butterfly houses, the locals attempted to make a little money. However, it was not cost-efficient and the export of the pupae was stopped.

About 200 species of butterflies are found on the reserve and, because they are enclosed at the station, the different stages of development can easily be seen and photographed. The best time to visit is on a sunny day. Rain and clouds cause the butterflies to hide in foliage.

The visitor center has an interesting quiz for tourists. There are six different samples of scat to be matched up with the creature that

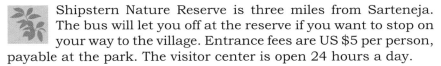

donated it. Would you like to know what a boa's poop looks like? Try the test.

There is also a short trail called the **Chiclero Botanical Trail** that leads from the parking lot into the forest. Because of the hurricane in 1955, much of the area's forest was destroyed and reforestation practices can now be observed. Along the trail you will encounter three different types of hardwood forests with about 100 varieties of trees. Many are labeled with their Latin names, their family names and their local names. A booklet available at the visitor center has a detailed description of the trail.

Just past the forested area is a wide savanna with mudflats and hillocks of limestone, vegetated with palms and hardwoods. The savanna is visited by white-tail deer and brocket deer. Tapirs, ocelots and jaguars are also reported to cross this area, although tracks are seen more often than the animals themselves.

Beyond the savanna is **Shipstern Lagoon**, where large numbers of North American birds take refuge before continuing their migration either north or south, depending on the time of year. One of the most fascinating birds that can be seen here is the black catbird, so named for its mew that often fools people into thinking that a cat, rather than a bird, is in the vicinity.

There are also about 60 species of reptiles and amphibians lurking about the lagoon. The Morelet's crocodile, an endangered species, has been spotted here.

At the very south end of the park is an abandoned village called Shipstern, from which the park derived its name.

■ TOUR OPERATOR

Wildtrack, ☎ 423-0232, at the Environment Center in Sarteneja, is run by Paul and Zoe Walker. It's associated with Raleigh International, 27 Parsons Green Lane, London SW6 4HZ, www.raleighinter-national.org. The Walkers will take you on an overnight trip to Fireburn Village, where the mostly unexcavated Shipstern Maya ruins are located. In this area, Raleigh is known for its work on the ruins, measuring and recording elementary details before intense excavations can take place.Raleigh International is also credited with radio tagging a fer-de-lance snake for the first time, a female 5.5 feet long. They hope to tag more so studies can be done on these highly poisonous creatures. At Fireburn Village, Raleigh found a shell figurine with the head of a bird at one end. No one knows what the object was used for, but it is different than most relics found in Maya sites in Belize. To work as a volunteer or a sponsor in a similar project, contact Raleigh International. The cost of working with Raleigh is about US $500 a week.

For US $50 per trip, the Walkers may also take you to Xo-Pol Pond for wildlife viewing. Overnight excursions are more.

Fernando/Verde Tours, Sarteneja, ☎ 423-2085 or 423-2283, will take you on a snorkeling trip to the reef or out fishing for snapper, grouper and tarpon. Since the men operating the tour agency have lived near these waters almost all their lives, they know where the fish are. The cost for fishing is US $150 a day, while a snorkeling trip with other people cost US $40 for each person for half a day.

■ PLACES TO STAY

Fernandos Rooms, on the main street facing the water, ☎ 423-2085, $$, has four rooms, all with double beds, private bath, hot water and fans. The establishment is very clean and the owners are friendly. There is a common room and a balcony on the second floor where you can sit. Guests may order meals from Ciela, Fernando's wife, for reasonable prices. A large portion of fresh fish with vegetables and rice is about US $7.

HOTEL PRICES	
$	$20 to $50
$$	$51 to $75
$$$	$76 to $100
$$$$	$101 to $150
$$$$$	over $150

Krisami's Motel, on the main street beside the water, ☎ 423-2283, www.krisamis.com, $$, has only two rooms available. Each is immaculately clean and exquisitely decorated, with private bath, hot water and cable TV. This is a family-run establishment and Maria Verde, the owner, goes out of her way to make guests welcome.  She also has family-style meals (often fresh fish) available for her guests. In fact, if you spend a day fishing and catch something good, Maria will cook it up for you. Her costs are reasonable.

Camdalie's Sunset Cabañas are next to Kisami's, no telephone, $$. There are two thatched-roof cabins with two double beds, a private bath and hot water in each. One has air conditioning, while the other has a fan. The main room next to the cabins contains the mural mentioned above.

Shipstern Nature Reserve has dormitory beds for US $10 per person and all profits go into the maintenance of the reserve. The beds are rented on a first-come, first-gets basis. Contact the Audubon Society for availability.

■ PLACES TO EAT

Lily's Restaurant is just off the beach. Follow the water to the east until you see a blue building with one or two tables outside. There is a sun porch and inside there are two booths. Lily's is a tiny establishment. Order your meals ahead of time

RESTAURANT PRICES	
$	$5 to $10
$$	$11 to $25
$$$	$26 to $50
$$$$	$51 to $75
$$$$$	over $75

and give her about two hours to prepare. She makes traditional rice and beans, eggs and tortillas, but she also offers a fish dish cooked in foil with vegetables and rice or French fries. Her meals are not scanty and her costs (US $3.50) are not high. Because restaurants are not abundant in Sarteneja, you can also order from your hotel. Again, about two hours notice is required.

■ NIGHTLIFE

Nightlife in Sarteneja consists of a book which you brought yourself, a hammock swinging in the ocean breeze and a rum punch that you made yourself.

▶▶ *Return to Orange Walk at Mile 56 on the New Northern Highway. To reach Progresso and Copper Bank, follow Main Street north through Orange Walk and over the old New River Bridge. After crossing the bridge there is a fork within the first mile. At this fork go to the left and then drive 5.5 miles to the town of San Estevan. Stay on the pavement. Six miles past San Estevan there is a road to the right. Do not take this one. Take the road straight ahead. Belize First magazine rates this stretch of road as the third most beautiful in the country.*

PROGRESSO & COPPER BANK

Progresso and Copper Bank are two tiny villages situated on Progresso Lagoon, one of the prettiest stretches of water in the country. The villages can be reached from either Orange Walk Town or the shorter route from Corozal.

■ GETTING HERE

BY FERRY

 From Corozal, the trip is eight miles and includes a ride on the largest ferry in Belize. Leave Corozal going south and turn left at the sign indicating "Tony's." Turn right at the end of the road. After driving/cycling about 4.5 miles, make a left. Follow this road along the river for three miles.

The ferry is an old sugar barge donated to Belize from the Belize Sugar Industry. The government supplied workers for the restoration of the barge. This ferry has cut the distance to Copper Bank from 42 miles to eight miles.

BY BUS

A bus leaves daily from Zeta Ice Factory in Orange Walk Town at 11:30 am and 5:30 pm or from the bus terminal in Corozal at 11 am and 4:30 pm.

■ HISTORY

 The lagoon has been occupied by **Maya** for centuries. During the early time of the **Spanish**, a group of soldiers commissioned to rule over northern Belize and the Lake Bacalar region near the border took control of the town of **Tiper**. The soldiers were hoping to use the town as a base to subdue the Maya in Petén. But the Maya living on the lagoon rebelled and killed the Spanish invaders and started a huge rebellion in Belize against the Spanish.

The small islands of Caye Coco, Caye Muerto and Caye On in the lagoon have Maya **ruins**. The ancient Maya city of **Chanlacom** is believed to be on the western shore of the lagoon. The Maya lived in small settlements around this lagoon and worked as farmers who traded with fishers along the Caribbean. These settlements were occupied until the 1600s.

■ ADVENTURES

 Rent a canoe from **Last Resort** in Copper Bank (see page 198) and visit one of the cayes. The ruins are still being excavated and burial sites have been found containing ceramics and spindle beads, bowls and, of course, skeletons of early people who lived here. The wildlife on this lagoon is exceptional and the area is not densely populated with locals or foreigners.

The North

Canoeing from Copper Bank to Progresso during orchid season is one of the best trips in Belize. The plants hang from the banks and trees over the river, making them visible right from the canoe. Manatees and crocodiles are also living along this stretch of water. Because the lagoon hasn't yet been developed and inundated with visitors,

Orchids.

the area is quiet. Rent a canoe at the Last Resort in Copper Bank, ☎ 606-1585. The cost is US $50 a day.

If you are not an experienced canoeist, join a guided tour organized by Last Resort. The guides will point out things that you would probably otherwise miss.

Ernesto Villas' House, in the village of Progresso, is a kind of historical site. Villas was known for helping the Maya and the black slaves escape from oppression. The house is a small wood shack, but there is part of a wall behind the house that is supposed to be from the Caste Wars.

Hikers may want to undertake the three-mile trail from Copper Bank to Cerros ruins. The trail meanders through the jungle. Donna, at the Last Resort, will give you directions to the trailhead. Take a bird book to help you identify some of the birds.

Fishing for tarpon on the New River is highly recommended by those experienced in fishing. I understand their luck has been better here than in most places in Belize.

Although there is not a tremendous amount to see, the area is a good place for a restful Caribbean experience.

▪ PLACES TO STAY & EAT

Last Resort, PO Box 260, Copper Bank, Corozal, ☎ 606-1585, www.belizenorth.com/last_resort.htm, $. The people who run the resort, located just past the village, describe their establishment as offering "primitive luxury." It has 10 thatched-roofed cabins that have fans or air conditioning, shared baths and hot water. **Tenting** is also available for a reasonable price. The rooms are bright and clean and overlook the lagoon. The place is homey and was recommended by some foreigners working in Belize. There's a reference library and a **restaurant** that serves a great variety of dishes, from lasagna to beef to lobster and homemade ice cream.

Regular live entertainment is available by the almost-famous Paradise Wranglers. This fun group started their musical career at Last Resort and have now been invited to play at other resorts in Belize. The hospitality here is exceptional.

Last Resort's restaurant.

Fantasy Point, #1 Freedom St., ☎ 420-6033, www.fantasypoint progresso.com, $$$, has six rooms/casitas available and meals can be included in a package. Note that air conditioning costs an extra US $25 per night. The resort is within walking distance of the village of Progreso and located on the lagoon where peace and quiet are constant. The delicious meals are served in a large dining hall that is separate from the sleeping areas. This family is related to Mama Noot, located south of Dangriga, and to the owner of Mark Anthony Hotel in Corozal. In previous generations, they were known as rumrunners, but have given that up and become a family of hoteliers. They do the second occupation much better than the first.

▶▶ *Return to Orange Walk at Mile 56 on the New Northern Highway. Continue north to Corozal, Consejo and the Mexican Border. About 20 miles on the New Northern Highway takes you from Orange Walk Town to Corozal Town. You'll see sugar cane fields that support the Libertad Sugar Refinery just beyond San Pablo. The area is dotted with houses on stilts that seem well cared for. The roads are often cycled by both locals and foreigners. Once past Concepcion, just east of Louisville, the New Northern Highway ends. Turn left for Corozal.*

COROZAL

■ GETTING HERE

Driving/cycling is described here from south to north. If you are fresh from Mexico, you will find driving/cycling in Belize a cake walk.

BY AIR

Maya Air (☎ 422-2333) and **Tropic Air** (☎ 800-422-3435, 226-2012) fly between Corozal and Belize City, Ambergris Caye and Caye Chalker. See *Getting Around*, pages 96-97, for schedules.

BY BUS

Buses from Chetumal go to Corozal daily. They leave from Mercado Nuevo in Chetumal, about six blocks from the ADO station. Take a taxi or ask locals for directions. Buses leave about once every hour and it takes 20 minutes to get to the border. The bus will wait as you process your documents and then take you to Corozal. Buses also go to Belize City, three hours away, every hour, beginning at 5:30 am and quitting at 5 pm.

BY WATER TAXI

A water taxi/boat from Ambergris Caye and Caye Caulker arrives at the town wharf just beside the museum. It leaves daily at 7 am and costs US $20 per person. It takes 1.5 hours to reach San Pedro. Returning, the taxi leaves San Pedro at 3 pm.

■ INTRODUCTION

 Corozal is a clean colonial town on the Caribbean Sea in **Chetumal Bay**. It has the lowest crime rate in all of the country and residents are rightly proud of this fact.

This little city has been ignored by tourists for far too long. Although there isn't enough to keep one busy for weeks, it is a place for those who want a break after or before the hassles of Mexico.

Corozal has a population of around 10,000 people; most are fishers, farmers or sugar production workers.

This metal bowl, called a *pila*, was donated to the Corozal museum by photo-journalist, Manolo Romero's family. It was originally used to store extracted cane juice. The belt of the cane crusher was powered by a kerosene-operated tractor. The juice was transferred from the bowl to wooden vats and fermented. It then went to the Scottish-made, wood-fired still where it was made into liquor. This production made Romero's grandfather boatloads of money. In its retirement, the bowl was used to store water for cattle and then to store water for the family's modern column distillery.

■ HISTORY

Originally, Corozal was the Maya city of **Santa Rita**. The old city was sporadically occupied and deserted for about 2,000 years. Then, in the mid-1800s when the Caste Wars of Mexico were at their height, about 10,000 refugees crossed the Rio Hondo into Belize and made their home at the present site of Corozal. Some of these refugees were helped by the gun runner James Blake.

THE LIFE OF JAMES BLAKE

James Humes Blake became the Magistrate in Corozal during the Caste Wars. He married and had two children and lived his life accumulating wealth.

Meanwhile, on the other side of the border, a Spanish soldier by the name of José Andrade fought for the Spanish against the Maya. One day, the Maya invaded the village where José and his family lived and José was killed. His wife Juanita and their two daughters managed to escape over the Rio Hondo into Belize. Juanita and her daughters settled in Corozal.

After Blake's first wife died of influenza, he met and married Juanita. Their family grew and Blake became quite prominent. He eventually bought Ambergris Caye for US $625.

As the years passed, the Blake family became a dynasty. Many Belizeans didn't like the way the Blakes ruled Ambergris Caye, so the people pressured the government to expropriate the Caye. The government did this and, in turn, sold the confiscated land for a reasonable price to anyone who could buy.

Mexico wanted the territory that was now in the hands of the British, so skirmishes occurred often, forcing locals living near Corozal to build **Fort Barlee** for protection. That was 1870 and part of the fort still sits where the present day central park is located. The bricks used for construction of the fort and its adjoining buildings were originally used as ballast for ships that were coming from Europe to pick up wood.

The Caste Wars ended, but the fort continued to be the mainstay of the village. A courthouse was built across from the fort in 1879 and a post office and bank were placed nearby in 1881. By 1883 a hospital was built inside the walls of the fort and finally, in 1886, the Customs warehouse and market were erected by the water. Today, the old hospital building is part of the post office, treasury and courthouse.

As the village grew, residences were built over Maya houses. Stones from Maya buildings were used as road fill. Today, the Maya city has but one pyramid left, about a mile northwest of town.

> ### "COROZAL"
>
> Corozal derives its name from the Maya word for the Cohune Palm, once abundant in the area. The Maya considered the palm a sign of fertility.

In 1955 Hurricane Janet struck and destroyed almost everything. Five buildings from a town of 2,500 people survived. The storm also took 16 lives. When the hurricane hit, there was a rum distillery on the Santa Rita hill. One woman was hiding in the factory when the roof blew off. The owner decided to turn the water reservoir upside down and have the people go inside for protection. This worked. None of those hiding in the vat (reservoir) were killed.

The upside of Hurricane Janet is that the town had to be rebuilt. The town council hired professional planners to design the new city. The rebuilding cost US $3.5 million and Corozal was the first town in Belize to have electricity, water and sewer throughout. It also has a logical grid street pattern.

AVERAGE RAINFALL	
JANUARY	37.1 inches/94.2 cm
FEBRUARY	13.2 inches/33.6 cm
MARCH	8.97 inches/22.8 cm
APRIL	17.4 inches/44.3 cm
MAY	31.7 inches/80.6 cm
JUNE	75.2 inches/190.9 cm
JULY	75.5 inches/191.7 cm
AUGUST	63.8 inches/162.3 cm
SEPTEMBER	87.3 inches/221.7 cm
OCTOBER	68.7 inches/174.5 cm
NOVEMBER	41.2 inches/104.7 cm
DECEMBER	36.9 inches/93.8 cm

Consejo, Corozal District, period 1978-2000.

> **AUTHOR NOTE:** *Corozal District was the first area in Belize to have a sugar cane industry and it is still the largest area for production of sugar.*

■ THINGS TO DO

SANTA RITA RUINS

Walk to Santa Rita ruins just north of town (about one mile). The ruins are open from 8 am to 5 pm and entry fee is US $5. From the central park on 1st Street, walk north past the Venus Bus Station, veering half a block east at the station. Continue northwest along the Santa Rita road. You'll pass the hospital and town reservoir before you reach the ruins and, just beyond them, is the New Northern Highway.

At the beginning of the 20th century, Thomas Gann, a serious archeology buff, drew pictures of the frescoes he found at Santa Rita. The paintings showed figures roped together at the wrist. They were decked in tassels, garlands and jewelry – a distinctive characteristic of the Santa Rita frescoes. The paintings here resemble the paintings found on copper disks at Chichen Itza.

Before the value of the paintings, frescoes and stone carvings was really appreciated, they were destroyed; mostly they were used as road fill. This is why Gann's pictures are so important. Later (1979-85) Dr. Chase from the University of Southern Florida excavated the remaining post classic buildings.

Early-style pottery found in graves indicates that the site has been occupied since about 2000 BC. As time passed, trade replaced some of the agricultural activity and the city grew. It is guessed that the city was continuously occupied right up until the Spaniards came in the mid-1500s. At the peak of their trading years, the Maya of Santa Rita included the Rio Hondo and the New River in their territory. They called their city **Chetremal**.

There were two significant **burial chambers** found at the site. One contained an elderly woman decorated with turquoise jewelry. In the other was a warrior who died around AD 500. He had a flint bar and stingray spine in the tomb with him.

The main attraction, however, is a smaller pyramid that had a **ceremonial room** from the late classic period. In this room, offerings were made to the gods. This pyramid and ceremonial room are a good example of the architecture from that time and the offerings were an indication that the people were fairly prosperous.

But even more impressive (for me) is the **jade mosaic mask** that was found in one tomb. The mask, now in the National Museum, is 11 cm (four inches) by 16 cm (six inches) and has pieces of jade pasted onto a base. The eyes and mouth are made from shell and iron pyrites. A vase from the early classic period (about AD 500-600) has exquisite decorations painted in dark brown paint on a cream background. The painting is of glyphs inside rectangles. The vase may now be found in the National Museum.

My favorite piece, also in the National Museum, is a set of gold earrings with gold bells attached to the bottom and turquoise chips glued into the main body.

It is believed that in the late classic period the Maya from this site traded with people as far away as the Aztec cities in Mexico and the Aymara cities in the Andes. Pottery found on-site supports this theory.

Although some of the buildings had excellent frescoes and wall murals, those buildings have been destroyed. The only records we have of them even existing are the drawings of Thomas Gann. The remaining structures at Santa Rita are barely worth the walk to see, but the view of the city is good from the top of the temple.

CERROS RUINS

Cerros ruins are located across Chetumal Bay from Corozal. To reach them during rainy season you must hire a boat; during dry season you can take a car along the road to Progresso and Copper Bank. To hire a car will cost $250 for up to four people. There is a US $10 entry fee to the ruins. Exploring the ruins (unless you are a professional) will take about two or three hours. The boat will have to wait for you. Tour agencies from other cities offer trips to the ruins. You can contact **Menzies Travel Agency**, ☎ 422-2725, in town near the south end. Also, a boat can be rented at the dock behind Corozal Bay Inn on the road to Progresso. The cost is under $100 for the trip there and back for three people.

Cerros (which means hill in Spanish) sits on 53 acres by a cliff overlooking the Caribbean Ocean, a setting much like Tulum in Mexico. The community was at its height between 400 BC and AD 100. At that time the people there specialized first in fishing and then in the marine trade along the coast. Some archeologists believe that salt was an important trade item. As other cities became more prominent, Cerros lost power. Today, the ruins are showing serious erosion due to their proximity to the ocean.

The largest building at the site stands 69 feet (21 meters) above the plaza floor; it still has some walls intact. It's one of the best examples of pre-classic architecture, with **sculptures** on the walls beside the stairs. The four friezes are named Evening Star Setting, Morning Star Rising, Sun Setting, and Sun Rising.

Around its outer perimeter Cerros had a **canal** almost 20 feet wide (six meters). The main purpose of the canal was to drain the surrounding land so it could be used for agricultural purposes. Encompassed by the canal were two **ball courts**, three **pyramids** and over 100 public and private buildings. Today, maintained trails go from the center of the ancient city out to the canal.

Found at the site were jade and obsidian objects, tombs and a pendant made of exquisitely carved jade. The carving represents a human face. Because of the slanted eyes and the high cheek bones it is believed to have come from the Olmec civilization farther north.

Some carvings could not be removed from the site and placed in the museum, so another method of preservation is being tried. Two huge masks carved from stone and placed in the walls of the structures near the main plaza are now covered in plaster so you can't see the carving.

Again, the work of Thomas Gann brought attention to this site. A little more interest was generated in the late 1960s and an American developer started excavations and planned on making Cerros a big tourist attraction, complete with expensive hotel and museum. However, that plan eroded much more rapidly than the stones on the buildings. Cerros now sits overlooking the ocean and much of its historical information is hidden under the jungle's growth.

COROZAL TOWN

Across from the park on 5th Avenue is the Fort Barlee **police station** and the **post office** – once the hospital of Fort Barlee.

On 1st Street South is the **library** and **town hall**. Inside the hall is a mural painted by Manuel Villamor Reyes. He originally painted it in the 1950s, then decided to re-do a lot of the scenes within the mural when it was restored in 1986. Reminiscent of a Diego Rivera painting, the mural has a lot of historical detail, starting with the life of the Maya and covering major events up to the present sugar cane production.

EASY MONEY

Prior to 1884 Belize used any currency traded in the world. Most of it was made from Potosi silver minted near the mines of the same name in Bolivia. Finally, Belizeans decided to form a currency of their own and the British Honduras dollar was minted.

Corozal's **Central Park** has a fountain in its center, from which six walkways splay out to the surrounding streets. A wander through these streets reveals many different trees. The triangle that has its base on 1st Street South has kinip trees, strangler figs, royal flame trees and Christmas palms, while the triangle facing 1st Street North features, in addition to the above, ficus and almond trees. The two triangles facing 4th Avenue also have hibiscus and fan palms. On the triangles facing 5th Avenue there's also an erythrina tree, the plant that is used to shade cocoa trees. Pick up a map at the town library (US $1); it covers the Tree Tour, below, and indicates which tree is which.

The Walking Tree Tour of Corozal waterfront starts at the east end of town and mostly follows the shoreline all the way to Tony's Inn at the west end of town. 1st Avenue turns into South Street after going west past 8th Avenue. It then turns into 7th Avenue. The walk can be done in whole or in part. See how many of the 30 trees you can find and identify. There are some descriptions at the front of the map, but by no means does that section cover all the trees along this walk. You may need to purchase a book that describes tropical trees.

 The best book I can suggest is **Cockscomb Basin Wildlife Sanctuary, Historical and Botanical Guide to the Area** by Katherine Emmons, Orangutan Press, Gay Mills, Wisc. 1996. Although it covers mostly the rainforest around the Cockscomb Basin, some trees are found on this walk.

At the corner of 1st Avenue and 2nd Avenue is a mayflower tree. Continuing along 1st Avenue past the curve between 3rd and 2nd Street North is a royal palm which, by the time you get there, may be dead due to an infection. The dying royal palm is being replaced by a dwarf royal palm, which has a strong resistance to the bacteria. A sago palm and lime tree are next. On 2nd Street North, half a block up from the water, is a ziricote and a mamey tree. Between 1st Street North and South is an orchid tree, a mahogany tree and a Norfolk Island pine. Just after the water taxi stand is a breadfruit tree.

The **Museum of Corozal**, also called the Cultural Center, is along the water between 4th Avenue and 1st Avenue. The museum is open from 9 to 12 and 1:30 to 4:30 pm, Tuesday to Saturday. The entry fee is US $5. The museum was renovated in 1996 and opened in February of 1997. The staff here will answer just about any question you may have about the region.

First built in 1886 as the Customs House, the building is the only colonial structure of this design in Belize. Everything in the building is made of iron that has been bolted and riveted together. When first built, it was the only legal entry place into Belize.

Inside the building, an ornate stairway leads to the town's four-faced clock. Originally, a keeper of the clock would climb the stairs and wind it every day. However, the four clocks were always running out of synchronization so the town recently had it computerized. It now gives accurate time regardless of which face you look at. The building's clock tower was also used as a light-house. The keeper of the clock rang a bell to let fishers know that they were near land.

The displays in the museum are well done. Many of the bottles on exhibit were found in the bay just offshore, left by the pirates of earlier days. There are ink, perfume, rum and medicine bottles of colored glass made in every shape. The most recent bottles date back to the mid-1800s.

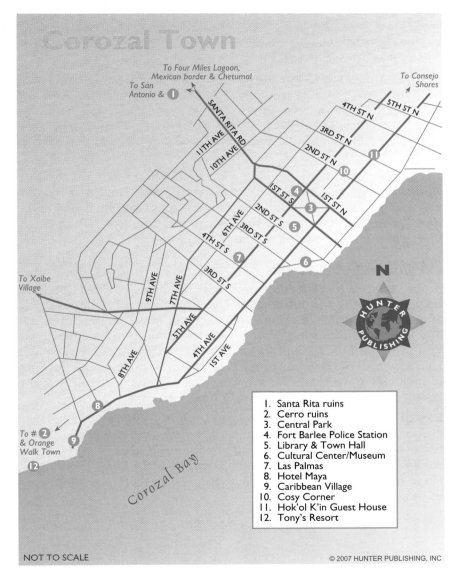

Corozal Town

To San Antonio & ①
To Four Miles Lagoon, Mexican border & Chetumal
To Consejo Shores

SANTA RITA RD
11TH AVE
10TH AVE
4TH ST N
5TH ST N
3RD ST N
2ND ST N
1ST ST S
1ST ST N
2ND ST S
3RD ST S
6TH AVE
4TH ST S
3RD ST S
9TH AVE
7TH AVE
5TH AVE
4TH AVE
1ST AVE
8TH AVE

To Xaibe Village

To # ② & Orange Walk Town ⑫

Corozal Bay

N

HUNTER PUBLISHING

1. Santa Rita ruins
2. Cerro ruins
3. Central Park
4. Fort Barlee Police Station
5. Library & Town Hall
6. Cultural Center/Museum
7. Las Palmas
8. Hotel Maya
9. Caribbean Village
10. Cosy Corner
11. Hok'ol K'in Guest House
12. Tony's Resort

NOT TO SCALE
© 2007 HUNTER PUBLISHING, INC

The North

The house next to the museum is a colonial structure built in the early 1900s.

FOUR MILE LAGOON

The lagoon is just four miles south of the Rio Hondo. Jump on your bike, take the Santa Rita road north and then branch off to the right onto a secondary road. There is a sign indicating the turn-off to the lagoon. Bike rentals are available from **Hok'ol K'in Guest House**, 89 4th Avenue/4th Street South, ☎ 422-3329, at US $5 per day. This is a deal. However, guests of the hotel get first dibs on the bikes.

People come to swim, windsurf and fish. Since the lagoon has fresh water, it is a treat to swim in after the ocean's salt water.

Bill Dixon owns the **Four Mile Lagoon RV** and **tenting** site that is fully serviced. To get there, follow the road going to Santa Rita and turn north (right) onto a gravel secondary road. The site is alongside the lagoon. Tenting is US $5 per person. On Sundays you can go to Riverol's Cool Spot along the beach for a beer, pop and/or snack.

Cycling on a more challenging road from Chan Chen on the New Northern Highway to Santa Rosa on the Rio Hondo is recommended for a short nine-mile run. Follow the Santa Rita road to the New Northern Highway and turn south for .6 miles to Chan Chen. Turn right and follow the dirt road to the river.

XAIBE

Xaibe boasts a resident naturopath by the name of Peter Singfield, commonly called the "snakeman," who specializes in natural medicines derived from the jungle. He uses old Maya healing methods and incorporates specially prepared snake bones in his medicines. You can read about his practices at www.tzabcan.com. Singfield is also into a lot of recycling projects. It is worth the five-mile journey to his place northwest of town. Take the road past the airport and keep going north. Peter also has a boat for rent.

Day of the Dead is an interesting event in the village of Xaibe. Traditional Maya food is made and served after a service is held at the cemetery. If you are around on November 2nd, this is a good place from which to observe this event. The Day of the Dead is when the Maya make contact with ancestors and wish them a good journey in the next world.

CONSEJO SHORES

Consejo Shores is six miles north of Corozal along a secondary road. It is also just 10 minutes by boat from Chetumal, Mexico. Consejo is a sleepy little fishing village similar to Sarteneja, but it wasn't always so placid. Once it was a major seaport for the logwood industry. It was also the first village that the Spanish attacked before continuing south to fight the Baymen at St. George's Caye.

You can walk, cycle or drive to the village, then pitch a **tent** or take a rest at the Casa Blanca resort. The village is an expatriots' suburb. Like Four Mile Lagoon, it is a nice place to swim and windsurf.

■ PLACES TO STAY

 Las Palmas, 123-5th Ave, ☎ 422-0196, www.laspalmas hotelbelize.com, $$, is the hotel that resembles a cruise ship surrounded by a secure wall and locked gate. It is in the same spot where Nestor's used to be, but is far classier and comfortable. Owned by an American married to a Columbian lady, the hotel has been built to North American standards and comfort. Not only is it affordable, but the owners will go out of their way to give you special service (they popped some microwave popcorn for me).

HOTEL PRICES	
$	$20 to $50
$$	$51 to $75
$$$	$76 to $100
$$$$	$101 to $150
$$$$$	over $150

The rooms have tiled floors, fridges, hot water all day, remote conrolled air conditioning, cable TV (with a movie channel in English!) and a sitting area with table and chairs. Good place to stay.

Hotel Maya, between 9th and 10th Streets South on South Street, ☎ 422-2082, $$, is clean and friendly. The hotel first opened in 1980 with just two rooms. It did so well that there are now 20 rooms. There is air conditioning, cable TV and private bath with hot water in every room. The hotel is half a block from the beach.

An on-site **restaurant** is open from 7 am to 9 pm daily. The downside of this place is that occasionally you may find the hotel closed.

The North

Caribbean Village, 7th Avenue, ☎ 422-2725, $, is two blocks southwest of Hotel Maya. This is an RV park with tenting spots available. Located in an open grassy field across from the water by about half a block, the park has electricity and a shower/bath facility. Directly across is the **Celest Restaurant**, an open-air place serving good food. Just up the road is a tiny spot called **Jam Rock**, which is good for refreshments. There are also two thatched-roof cabins for rent; they are basic but have fans.

Corozal Guest House, 22 6th Avenue, ☎ 422-0634, $$, www. corozal.bz/guesthouse, is just around the corner from the bus station and within easy walking distance to everything in town. Under new ownership, the guesthouse is working hard to keep guests happy. The spotless rooms have private bathrooms and standing fans, as well as night tables and comfortable beds. The owner can help arrange a guide for trips.

Corozal Bay Inn, Almond Drive, ☎ 422-2691, www.corozalbayinn. com, $$$, has four thatch-roofed cabins sitting beside a fine sandy beach. There are also rooms in the hotel area of the resort. The cabins have air-conditioned bedrooms and the beds have mosquito nets. The sitting rooms include wireless Internet connections, and both the bathrooms and kitchens are tiled. The restaurant and bar on site is excellent in service, quality and quantity. This is a very good place to stay.

Hok'ol K'in Guest House, 89 4th Avenue/4th Street South, ☎ 422-3329, maya@btl.net, $$, is near the water. It is clean, comfortable and highly recommended by those who like comfort without paying big bucks. The hotel has a nice porch where you can sit and watch the sunset (or sunrise) over the Caribbean while sipping on some rum punch. There is a **restaurant** on site, and they also have bikes for rent. Hok'ol K'in is wheelchair accessible.

Pirates Cave, ☎ 501-422-6679, dixiemoss@aol.com, $$$$, is a 30-minute boat ride up the Rio Hondo, close to where pirates long ago went to hide. Just opened in December, 2002, this tiny resort has two cabañas. Each cabaña has two bedrooms so it can accommodate two couples in each. The cabañas are luxurious and tastefully decorated with Maya weavings. The price includes transportation to the lodge, meals, room service and tours on the Rio Hondo and along the Caribbean coast into Corozal.

Stephen Ambrose and Ustace Danials are the owners and both are artists. Stephen is a wood carver and Ustace is a painter. They encourage artists to come and enjoy the serenity and beauty of the jungle river. Meals are cooked by a professional chef and served on a two-story palapa, where the breeze will ensure there are no mosquitos. The owners like to take their guests fishing and the chef loves to cook the catch. There are hundreds of birds around this isolated resort. Jaguar prints have been seen along the river and crocs are common.

Tony's Inn and Beach Resort, South End (on Corozal Bay Road), ☎ 422-2055, $$$, www.tonysinn.com, is the town's common landmark. It is about a half-mile down the bay from the center of town. The rooms are big, the service excellent, and the owners friendly. There is safe parking for your vehicle, as well as a bar and **restaurant** on the premises. Tony's, where the customer comes first, is a classy place to stay. Boats can be hired behind Tony's for a trip to Cerros.

Mark Anthony Hotel, Corner of 4th St. North and 2nd Ave, ☎ 422-3141, www.markanthony belize.com, $$, just opened. It has 10 rooms with air conditioning, overlooking the water. The big draw is the in-house restaurant. Butchie, the owner, had a successful restaurant before opening the hotel and serves the same delicious food he did before. This is another great place to stay while in Corozal.

© Farworld Tech

Casa Blanca Hotel, PO Box 212, Consejo Village, Corozal, ☎ 423-1018, www.casablanca-bythesea.com, $$$. Chosen by Lan Sluder's *Belize Guide Book* as one of the 10 most romantic places to stay in Belize, Casa Blanca certainly deserves this status. The hotel is exceptionally comfortable and the rooms offer air conditioning, fans, private baths with hot water, satellite TV, queen-sized beds and exceptional views. There's a **restaurant**, postal service, e-mail facilities and tour office. The resort will also cater to weddings that can be held on its private beach. All-inclusive package deals are available.

© Casa Blanca By The Sea

The North

Kayaking, waterskiing and windsurfing equipment is available for rent. The bay on which the resort sits is one of the best in the country for windsurfing, but it hasn't yet been discovered by the crowds who seem to chase the wind around the Caribbean.

■ PLACES TO EAT

Al's Café, 5th Avenue between 2nd and 3rd Streets, $, is where the locals eat. The restaurant serves Belizean food: rice and beans with either pork, beef or chicken, but it is good rice and beans. However, the waitress can be a little impatient with tourists. Refrain from leaving a tip if she is this way when you are here.

Hok'ol K'in Guest House, 89 4th Avenue/4th Street South, ☎ 422-3329. The restaurant is great if trying to escape the heat. It is clean to a sparkle and the salads are made with crisp fresh vegetables. One gentleman I spoke with enjoyed the rum punch far too much. He ended up staying in one of their rooms too. Hok'ol K'in offers bikes for rent at US $5 per day. Guests of the hotel get first dibs on the bikes.

COROZAL TO SANTA ELENA & THE MEXICAN BORDER

▸▸ *If leaving Corozal at Mile 79 on the New Northern Highway, go past the service station and bus terminal. Stay on the road, but do not go to the Santa Rita ruins (up the hill). Instead, veer to the right and continue to the junction five miles beyond Corozal. Turn right. It is four miles to Santa Elena and the Mexican border. From Corozal to the border takes about half an hour and the crossing is usually non-eventful. There is a US $20 fee to leave Belize. There is no fee to enter Mexico.*

Belize **buses** cross the Mexican border and go as far as Chetumal. The money changers at the border are good. Get rid of your Belize dollars before crossing.

If you need a taxi service anywhere in Corozal or to Chetumal, call **Leslie's Taxi Service**, ☎ 422-2377, and ask for Alvin. If calling from Mexico, ☎ 501-422-2377 or 501-602-2583 (cell). I used Alvin. He drives carefully and does not overcharge.

AUTHOR TIP: *Do not take Belize dollars too far into Mexico unless you collect foreign currency.*

If coming into Belize from Mexico, there is no charge to enter. You will be given a tourist card that must not be lost. (Should you lose your card, you will need to go to the police station wherever you discover the loss and try to get another.) You will have to pay an exit fee of $20 every time you leave Belize. Often, border guards will not give the full 30 days that you should be entitled to. You then have to pay another $25 to extend your visa.

For information on **Chetumal** and the Yucatán Peninsula, see the award-winning book by Bruce and June Conord, *Adventure Guide to the Yucatán, Cancun & Cozumel* (2nd edition), by Hunter Publishing.

DIRECTORIES

■ GENERAL DIRECTORY

THE NORTH – GENERAL DIRECTORY		
■ OUTFITTERS & TOUR OPERATORS		
Birding Pals		www.birdingpal.org
Fernando/Verde Tours	☎ 423-2085 or 423-2283	
Jungle River Tours	☎ 302-2293	
Paradise Inn (birding)	☎ 220-7044	www.adventurecamera.com /paradise
■ ATTRACTIONS		
Belikin Brewery & Coca Cola	☎ 225-3195	
Belize Jungle Gardens/Aquarium	☎ 609-5523	
Burmudian Land. Baboon Sanct.	☎ 220-2181	www.howlermonkey.bz
Cuello Ruins	☎ 322-2141	
Crooked Tree Wildlife Sanct.	☎ 223-5004	www.belizeaudubon.org
Godoy's Orchid Garden	☎ 322-2969	
Pueblo Escondido	☎ 614-1458	www.pueblo-escondido.net
Travellers Liquors	☎ 223-2855	ww.travellersliquors.bz
■ TRANSPORTATION		
Venus Bus	☎ 402-2132	
■ GROUP RESOURCES		
Programme for Belize	☎ 227-5616	www.pfbelize.org
Tropical Rainforest Coalition		www.rainforest.org
Wildtrack	☎ 423-0232	www.raleightinternational.org
■ USEFUL WEBSITES		
Corozal District Information		www.corozal.com
Corozal Business & Tourist Information		www.corozal.bz
Belize Tourism		www.belizetourism.org

The North

■ ACCOMMODATIONS DIRECTORY

THE NORTH – PLACES TO STAY	
Belize River Lodge ($$$$)	☎ 225-2002; bzelodge@btl.net
Bird's Eye View Lodge ($-$$$$)	☎ 225-7027; www.belizenet.com/birdseye
Caribbean Village ($)	☎ 422-2725
Casa Blanca Hotel ($$$)	☎ 423-1018; www.casablanca-bythesea.com
Chan Chich Lodge ($$$$$)	☎ 800-328-8368; www.chanchich.com
Corozal Bay Inn ($$)	☎ 422-2691; www.corozalbayinn.com
Corozal Guesthouse ($$)	☎ 422-0634; www.corozal.bz/guesthouse
D' Victoria Hotel ($$)	☎ 322-2518; www.d-victoriahotel.com
Embassy Hotel ($$)	☎ 225-3333; www.embassyhotelbelize.com
Estelle's Airport Hotel ($$$)	☎ 205-2282
El Chiclero ($$)	☎ 225-9005; elchiclerol@yahoo.com
Fantasy Point ($$$)	☎ 420-6033; www.fantasypointprogresso.com
Fernandos Rooms ($$)	☎ 423-0285
Hill Bank Field Station ($$)	☎ 221-2060
Hillside B & B ($$)	☎ 323-0155
Hok'ol K'in Guest House ($$)	☎ 422-3329
Home Stay Program ($)	☎ 220-2181
Hotel de la Fuente ($$)	☎ 322-2290; www.hoteldelafuente.com
Hotel Maya ($$)	☎ 422-2082
Howler Monkey Lodge ($$)	☎ 220-2158; www.howlermonkeylodge.com
Krisami's Motel ($$)	☎ 423-2283; www.krisami.com
Lamanai Outpost Lodge ($$$)	☎ 223-3578; www.lamanai.com
La Milpa Research Station ($$$$)	☎ 323-0011; www.pfbelize.org
La Rosita Store/Rooms ($$)	☎ 323-0445
Las Palmas ($$)	☎ 422-0196; www.laspalmashotelbelize.com
Last Resort ($)	☎ 606-1585; www.belizenorth.com/last_resort.htm
Mark Anthony Hotel ($$)	☎ 422-3414; www.markanthonybelize.com
Maruba Jungle Resort ($$$$$)	☎ 322-2199; www.maruba-spa.com
Nature Resort ($$)	☎ 610-1378; www.toucantrail.com/nature-resort.html
Paradise Inn ($$$$)	☎ 225-7044; www.adventurecamera.com/paradise
Pirates Cave ($$$$$)	☎ 501-422-6679; dixiemoss@aol.com
Pretty See Jungle Ranch ($$$$)	☎ 209-2005
St. Christopher Hotel ($$$)	☎ 322-3987
Sam Tillett's Hotel ($-$$$$)	☎ 220-7026; samhotel@btl.net
Shipstern Nature Reserve ($)	no phone
Tony's Inn ($$$)	☎ 422-2055; www.tonysinn.com

■ RESTAURANT DIRECTORY

THE NORTH – PLACES TO EAT	
Al's Café ($)	no phone
Baboon Sanctuary Restaurant ($$)	☎ 220-2181
Belize Road Chinese Restaurant ($)	☎ 322-3159
Bushey's Place Restaurant ($$$)	☎ 223-3578
Caye Caulker's Restaurant ($$)	no phone
Cornerstone Café ($)	☎ 323-0905
Diner, The ($$)	☎ 302-3753
El Chiclero restaurant ($$)	☎ 225-9005
El Pescador at Jungle Gardens ($$)	☎ 609-5523
Howler Monkey Lodge Rest. ($$)	☎ 220-2158
Juanita's Restaurant ($)	☎ 322-2677
Lily's Restaurant ($)	no phone
Maya Wells Restaurant ($$)	☎ 209-2039
Ms. Judith's ($)	no phone
Ms. Suzette's ($)	no phone
St. Christopher Hotel Rest. ($$$)	☎ 302-1064
Tree & Vee's Restaurant ($)	no phone
White Gold Café ($$)	no phone

The North

The West

The Western Highway goes from Belize City to San Ignacio and on to Guatemala. It is 76 miles from Mile Zero at the traffic circle on Cemetery Road and Central American Boulevard in the city.

Outdoor adventure is the most attractive feature of the Western Highway area. **Pine Mountain Ridge** is easily accessible and a real draw for the mountain bike enthusiast. Many

of the **cave systems** are not far off the Western Highway and a run down the Macal River will give every **whitewater** kayaker/canoer a thrill. Places like **Xunantunich and Caracol ruins** (below) are must-sees, as is **Belize Zoo. Horseback riding** at the historical Banana Bank Lodge is the best in Belize, and photography around Roaring River provides unique opportunities for shutterbugs.

The landscape is diverse, ranging from swamp to savanna to mountains. And each landscape has different birds and animals.

The west is prepared for tourists and the area offers something for every budget. However, if you are going west during high season, October to February, you may want to book ahead for places to stay.

ALONG THE HIGHWAY

The road going west from Belize City is described below. When we come to secondary roads that lead to other places of interest, we detour and explore them before returning to the highway.

Although there are few mileage signs on the Western Highway, people refer to locations by the number of miles along the road. To make things easy, I give all directions this way. If you lose track of where you are, just ask a local resident.

MILEAGE FROM BELIZE CITY TO TIKAL, GUATEMALA	
Mile Zero	Traffic circle at Cemetery Road & Central American Blvd.
Mile 5	**Beach** access
Mile 6	**Sir John Burdon Canal**
Mile 10	**Almond Hill Lagoon**
Mile 15.5	Turnoff to **Community Baboon Sanctuary** (see *The North*, page 148)
Mile 16	**Hattieville Village**
Mile 26	**Big Falls** turnoff
Mile 29	**Belize Zoo**
Mile 31.5	**La Democracia** and **Monkey Bay Sanctuary & Park**
Mile 37	**Jungle Paw Resort** turnoff
Mile 47	**Banana Bank Lodge and Equestrian Center**
Mile 48	**Guanacaste Park** and **Belmopan**
Mile 50	**Carmelote Village**
Mile 52	**Teakettle Village**
Mile 52.5	**Roaring Creek** and **Xibalba**
Mile 54.5	**Warrie Head Resort**
Mile 57	**Spanish Lookout** turnoff
Mile 59	**Unitedville**
Mile 60	**Caesar's Palace**
Mile 66	**Georgeville**

MILEAGE FROM BELIZE CITY TO TIKAL, GUATEMALA	
Mile 69.6	Cristo Rey Road
Mile 70	**Santa Elena/San Ignacio/Bullet Tree** turnoff
Mile 71.2	**Clarissa Falls** turnoff
Mile 72	Hydro Dam Road
Mile 72.8	**Tropical Wings Nature Center**
Mile 73.1	**San Jose Succotz**
Mile 74.5	**Benque Viejo del Carmen**
Mile 76	**Guatemalan border**

LEAVING BELIZE CITY

■ HOW TO TRAVEL

 To get anywhere along the highway by **bus**, take a taxi to the **Novelo bus** station at the main terminal in Belize City and buy a ticket for the town you wish to visit. Buses stop anywhere along the road, except the express bus, which stops only in the major centers.

For those **driving, cycling or hitching**, I describe the simplest way to get out of Belize City, not the shortest. This is because of the many one-way streets requiring a lot of turns along the way.

From the swing bridge in Belize City, follow Albert Street to Eve Street. Turn north and continue along the road that skirts the water. Eve Street becomes Newtown Barracks Road. It curves and turns into Princess Margaret Drive. At the large traffic circle with many flags in its center, go straight ahead onto Central American Boulevard.

Cross the Belcan Bridge (built by Canadians and Belizeans in the 1970s) and continue to the next traffic circle. Take the first exit off the circle. This is Cemetery Road and Mile Zero of the Western Highway.

■ AS YOU LEAVE TOWN

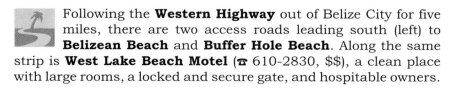 Following the **Western Highway** out of Belize City for five miles, there are two access roads leading south (left) to **Belizean Beach** and **Buffer Hole Beach**. Along the same strip is **West Lake Beach Motel** (☎ 610-2830, $$), a clean place with large rooms, a locked and secure gate, and hospitable owners.

This motel is a 10-minute walk from the water. If you have a vehicle, it will be safe here.

Old Belize Historical Center/ Cucumber Beach, Mile 5, Western Highway, ☎ 222-4286, www.oldbelize.com, is a museum, marina, and beach. There is also a gift shop and restaurant. This is one of the cruise ship destinations, so if you can, avoid going on a day when there's a ship in port. The 45-minute tour of the museum will take you through a simulated rainforest with waterfall and cave, through traditional scenes during the time of the Maya, into a traditional Garafuna home and along a 20th-century street scene. One of the exhibitions is of a tomb like that found at Lamanai. You will see how chicle was collected, how mahogany was logged, how logwood dye was produced and how sugar is extracted. The cost to enter is US $10 per person, which includes the museum and the beach. To visit just the beach or just the museum, it's $5. Children under six enter the museum for free and children under 12 can enter the beach at no cost.

© Old Belize Cultural & Historical Center

The marina, ☎ 222-4129, has a dry dock, a gas station, electricity, water, telephone, wireless Internet, cable TV, laundromat and showers. Boat fees are US $1.50 per foot, per day, with discounts for longer stays.

Sibun Bite Bar and Grill opens at 7 am and closes at 9 pm weekdays and 10 pm on weekends. They offer all traditional foods plus burgers, fried chicken and fish. On weekends you may find entertainment there.

The sandy **Cucumber Beach** has palapa huts, canoe rentals and beach lounges. You can snorkel, dive, sail or take the glass-bottom boat for a tour of the bay. Prices for activities are comparable to those offered on the islands. If you want to exclude the museum and just take in the beach, the cost is still US $5 per person.

© Old Belize Cultural & Historical Center

Vicinity of Belmopan

N

© 2007 HUNTER PUBLISHING, INC

To Belize City

Freetown
Sibún

Hattieville

Butchers
Burns

Cedar Bank

Big Falls Farm

Belize
Zoo

La Democracia

New Road

Northern
Lagoon

Monkey Bay
Wildlife
Sanctuary

Churchyard

SIBUN
FOREST
RESERVE

Southern
Lagoon

Gales Point

Shores Lodge

To Dangriga

HUNTER PUBLISHING

5 MILES

8 KM

FIVE BLUE LAKES
NATIONAL PARK

BLUE HOLE
NATIONAL PARK

Cotton
Tree

WESTERN HWY

BELMOPAN

HUMMINGBIRD HWY

Caves
Branch

St. Herman's Cave

To Dangriga

Banana
Bank

GUANACASTE
NATIONAL PARK

Roaring
Creek

Teakettle
Village

Xibalba
Cave Group

Spanish
Lookout

To San
Ignacio

Tapir Mtn Nature
Reserve & Pooks Hill
Archeological Site

Cara Blanca
Camp

- - - - - Seasonal roads

BELIZE CITY TO THE ZOO

■ SIR JOHN BURDON CANAL

At Mile 6 is the Sir John Burdon Canal. The canal, named after the man who was Governor of British Honduras between 1925 and 1932, is part of a tiny reserve protecting the red mangroves. The mangroves are so lush along this area that they form a tunnel over Haulover Creek (the Belize River) at the creek's entrance.

The canal was originally built in the 1920s so farmers could get their crops to market. Today it is used by visitors who have little time to go to other places in Belize, but would like to do some wildlife watching. These visitors are often rewarded with seeing reptiles such as crocodiles and iguanas, mangrove skipper butterflies with their dark brown wings decorated with one huge orange dot, and up to 50 species of birds. You are also certain to see some blue land crabs digging in the banks for food.

The canal starts at the Belize River and passes through Fabers Lagoon Bird Sanctuary with 108,000 acres of protected land. The canal then flows into the Sibun River and eventually to Manatee Lagoon, where Gales Point is situated.

Boats for the canal and lagoons can be hired either in Belize City or in Gales Point. No companies offer this as part of their scheduled service, but anything is possible. The cost of a full day depends on how many people share the boat. It should not be more than US $250 for up to six people. If starting at Gales Point, you will probably have to hire a private boat from a local fisher.

A PLACE TO STAY

Another four miles along the Western Highway at Mile 9 is the **Almond Hill Motel**, ☎ 225-1088, obsession@btl.net, $$, and the Almond Hill Lagoon. According to Emory King, this lagoon is believed to have been hand-dug by the Maya. Almond Hill has a population of 500, so few amenities are available. However, the motel has four clean rooms for rent.

▶▶ *The Western Highway continues to Hattieville at Mile 15.5. The Bermudian Landing Baboon Sanctuary turnoff is on the right (see The North, page 148).*

> AUTHOR NOTE: *On your left along this stretch, the high limestone outcropping is where a scene from The Mosquito Coast was filmed.*

■ HATTIEVILLE

 Hattieville was originally a temporary settlement for the refugees left homeless after hurricane Hattie hit Belize. Some of the refugees stayed and made this their permanent home. Today the population is around 500 people.

HOMES FOR THE HOMELESS

Many of the houses between Belize City and Hattieville have been built by Habitat for Humanity, an organization that believes everyone should have an acceptable place to live. If a family has insufficient funds to live decently and they qualify under the organization's mandate, Habitat will build them a home. They are simple, constructed from cinder blocks, with two or three bedrooms, and a small porch. Should you wish to support this worthwhile cause, contact **Habitat for Humanity**, #146 E. Collet Canal, Belize City, ☎ 227-6818, habelize@btl.net, www.habitat.org. Habitat loves visitors.

Hattieville is best known for the high-security prison, commonly called the Hattieville Ramada, that sits just out of town on a secondary road that runs north to Bermudian Landing. According to Amnesty International, this prison is far too crowded and the conditions are below international standards. The latest reports in newspapers are that the government is improving things.

The road to **Freetown Sibun** goes to the south (left) and ends at the Sibun River. June and Hubert Neal and the Community Conservation Society managed to lobby the government during the 1990s to have laws changed with regard to the endangered Hiccattee River turtle. Before the laws were changed this turtle was hunted for its delicious meat. However, in 2000 the work of these people resulted in the turtle being protected. The society that was formed also got a substantial grant from the government to help educate others about the importance of protecting the turtle. If you have time, stop at the town, less than five miles off the Western Highway, and see if you can spot one of these little turtles.

▶▶ *The scenery continues to improve as the Western Highway rises into rolling, rocky, forested country. At Mile 26 there is a secondary road going north to the little village of **Big Falls**. If there is even a single cloud in the sky, I would suggest you not try this road as it can disintegrate quickly. Instead, take the road going through the Bermudian Landing Baboon Sanctuary.*

*At Mile 29 of the Western Highway you will reach the Belize Zoo and the Tropical Education Center. If you don't have your own transportation, **public buses** are the easiest way to reach the zoo and the Tropical Education Center. Take any bus going west from the main terminal and ask the driver to drop you off at the zoo. The walk from the road to the zoo is short, but the walk down to the Tropical Education Center is about 1.8 miles. Follow the signs on the opposite side of the road to the zoo.*

■ BELIZE ZOO & TROPICAL EDUCATION CENTER

This zoo, built in 1983, is considered the best in Central America. It was originally built to accommodate 17 animals that were used in the making of a film called *Path of the Rain Gods*. Tamed and no longer able to fend for themselves in their natural environment, the animals were housed in a temporary zoo after the film was made. When the official zoo was built, these 17 animals were the first conscripts. Now there are over 150 different animals and birds.

Today, the zoo will accept only those animals whose life is in danger. They will not accept animals captured from their natural habitat to be sold.

What makes this zoo more attractive than most is that many of the animals are kept in jungle-like surroundings with only a wire-mesh fence to keep them enclosed. They are not in cages behind concrete ditches.

An outspoken environmentalist, Sharon Matola, is the founder and present director of the zoo. She also contributes articles to a popular newsletter sent to members (sign up at www.belizezoo. org). The zoo offers a program that gives you the opportunity to adopt an animal. For example, for US $60 foreigners can adopt a howler monkey. The money goes toward your adopted animal's food and medicine and the upkeep of his home. You don't get to take the monkey home.

You can see more animals here than you could possibly see on a guided jungle tour. It's much cheaper, too, although not as pleasant as a walk through the rainforest. You may take a guided tour or

Belize Zoo

1. Deer
2. Spider monkey
3. Tapir
4. Keel-billed toucan
5. Hawk-eagle
6. Ocelot
7. Tayra
8. Paca
9. Agouti
10. White-lipped peccary
11. Puma
12. Collared peccary
13. Howler monkey
14. Jaribu stork
15. Aviary
16. Crocodile
17. Margay
18. Otter
19. Jaguar
20. Coatimundi & raccoon
21. Kinkajou
22. Red deer brocket
23. Tapir
24. Jaguarundi
25. Gray fox
26. Curassow
27. Hawk
28. Barn owls
29. Yellow-headed parrots
30. Red-lored parrots
31. Crested guan
32. Mottled owls
33. Scarlet macaw
34. Vulture

RESTROOMS

PLANT TRAIL

RIVER FOREST

Lagoon

DISPLAY

ENTRANCE

TICKETS & GIFTS

walk yourself with a map of the area. April, the famous tapir, is the most popular celebrity of the zoo. She celebrates her birthday every April and the birthday bash usually includes hundreds of school students. April's gourmet cake is made with horse pellets, grated carrots and cabbage, corn and hibiscus flowers. This mixture is topped with honey.

Besides April, there are jaguars (both the spotted and black variety), deer, macaws, pumas, ocelots and monkeys. The birds include a new resident barn owl called Screech who, during the visitors' night walks, loves to fly over and land on the hand of a staff member.

The 29-acre facility takes less than two leisurely hours to visit, ☎ 820-2004, www.belizezoo.org. It's open daily from 8 am to 5 pm, except during major holidays. The entry fee is US $7.50 for foreigners. Your tour can be stretched out to a full day if you walk to the Tropical Education Center and spend time there also.

The Tropical Education Center is across the road from the zoo and covers 84 acres of savanna. It has observation decks that can be used for bird watching, a labeled self-guided trail, and an iguana breeding center. Here, you can sign up for a half-day guided canoe trip down the Sibun River or join the zookeepers for a night tour of the zoo.

The center is geared toward environmental education and scientific research. For an added US $50 you can join in on the natural history lectures.

■ PLACES TO STAY & EAT

The Tropical Education Center, PO Box 1787, Belize City, ☎ 220-8003, $$, has dormitory accommodations that holds 30 people. There are showers and kitchen facilities.

There is a small **restaurant** at the zoo that can supply refreshments and a basic meal.

Cheers Restaurant, Mile 31, Western Highway, ☎ 614-9311, $, west of the zoo by about three miles, is the closest place to eat. I had heard high praise of this restaurant and knew it was haunted by expats so I assumed it was good. When I got there, I think they accidentally served me a tough old rooster instead of a younger chicken. The restaurant is open-air and it has a small gift shop.

Belizeous Cuisine is a book put out by the LABEN Scholarship Foundation. Profits from the books are used to help needy kids further their education. The book has 200 authentic Belizean recipes, including the best one for rice and beans. It also has recipes for dishes like panades and dukunu. Don't know what these are? Try them at the next Creole restaurant you visit. The book sells for US $17.95 and may be ordered from LABEN, PO Box 191701, Los Angeles, CA 90019, ☎ 323-732-0200.

▶▶ *Just beyond the zoo the* **Western Highway** *is joined by a secondary road called the Coastal Road or the Manatee Road. This goes to Gales Point and Dangriga farther south. It is a dry-weather, gravel road. See The South chapter, page 333, for these towns.*

LA DEMOCRACIA TO GUANACASTE NATIONAL PARK

▶▶ *The turnoff for Monkey Bay Wildlife Sanctuary & Park is at Mile 31.5 on the Western Highway.*

■ MONKEY BAY WILDLIFE SANCTUARY & PARK

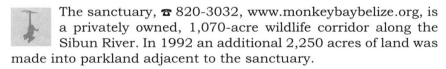

The sanctuary, ☎ 820-3032, www.monkeybaybelize.org, is a privately owned, 1,070-acre wildlife corridor along the Sibun River. In 1992 an additional 2,250 acres of land was made into parkland adjacent to the sanctuary.

The sanctuary's main focus is environmental education. The organizers work with students in Belizean high schools. However, all visitors are welcome to participate in the educational activities or to just stay and enjoy the area.

ADVENTURES

Once at the sanctuary you can hike along the interpretive nature trails or swim in the Sibun River. The new **Indian Creek Hiking Trail** is a 14-mile jungle trek that connects Monkey Bay with Five Blue Lakes National Park. There is an additional five miles walk out to the highway from Five Blue Lakes Park, where you can catch a bus. This is a three-day, two-night hike that will take you past limestone karst towers, with their nesting birds, and through

The West

three caves along Indian Creek. You must carry your own food. The adventure requires you to purchase a one-time trail access fee of US $25, plus US $5 per night camping fee. You must have a guide, available for hire at the sanctuary at a cost of US $35 a day for your group.

You can also canoe **Cox Lagoon Crocodile Sanctuary**. Six miles from Monkey Bay, the lagoon has excellent wildlife viewing opportunities. You can camp overnight at the lagoon. As with the Indian Creek Hiking Trail, the canoe trip to the lagoon costs US $35 for the one-time lagoon access fee, plus US $40 per canoe for rental and transportation. A local guide is US $35 per day.

Canoes are available at the sanctuary's office for those wanting to paddle on the river. The cost is US $20 for each canoe and US $20 if transportation is required.

Three **cave systems** were discovered recently in the karst hills surrounding the western end of the Sibun River. They are the Actun Ik, the Tiger Cave and the Glenwood Cave. Inside each, besides huge families of bats, are Maya wall paintings, shrines, altars and pottery shards. For the complete story about the finding of these caves, go to www.pobonline.com and read the article *Under the Canopy*, by Patricia A. McAnany. To enter the caves you must hire a guide at the sanctuary office.

BATTY FACTS

Bats mate for life and become distraught when separated from their partners for long periods of time. Bats can hibernate at will, especially during times of food shortages. They can soar at elevations of up to 10,000 feet (3,000 meters).

PLACES TO STAY & EAT

At **Monkey Bay Lodging** field research station, ☎ 820-3032, www.monkeybaybelize.org, there is **tenting** available on raised platforms under thatched roofs for US $5 per night. This is in your own tent. Using the station's tent and bedding costs US $10 per night per person. A **bunkhouse** has beds for US $ 10 per night and US $25 for a small basic cabin with toilet. The cabin will hold two people. Meals are prepared at the lodge and served in a common dining room. The food is excellent and costs $16 for dinner and $12 for breakfast or lunch. The owners of the sanctuary will take you on birding tours and on some adventure camping tours. They are totally focused on the natural environment of Belize. There are showers, a library and a natural history display. Meals are available at the station or you can walk to the restaurant that is less than a mile away.

JB's Watering Hole (aka Amigos), ☎ 820-2071, $, Mile 32 along the Western Highway, has very good food and is just a 10-minute stroll from the field research station. It has large meals, low prices and skunky coffee. Have coffee at the research station as the stuff served here is terrible.

To reach the **Jaguar Paw Jungle Resort**, ☎ 820-2023, $$$$$, turn at the sign at Mile 37 on the Western Highway and follow the gravel road for about seven miles, veering to the right whenever there is a junction. This will be either a long dusty ride or a muddy one, depending on the season.

The lodge is run by Donna and Cy Young. The 16 air-conditioned cabañas sit on 215 acres of jungle at the edge of the Caves Branch River. The lodge has all the amenities you could wish for, from large bedrooms with private baths to a bar where you can enjoy a rum punch. However, it is the exquisite African décor that adds to the romance of the jungle. The resort is also a privately owned nature reserve that offers **river tubing, hiking, mountain biking, birding** with a guide and instruction in **rock climbing**. Equipment is available at the lodge.

The **caves** on the property are thought to be 150,000-200,000 years old and show signs of use by the Maya. Trips to the caves located on the property are possible, but you may enter the cave only with a guide, available at the resort. Some caves are reached by tubing down the river.

> ▶▶ *Farther along the Western Highway over Beaver Dam Creek at Mile 39 and past Cotton Tree is a sign pointing right (north) to the Banana Bank Lodge.*

Banana Bank Lodge, Mile 47 Western Highway, ☎ 820-2020, www.bananabank.com, $$$$, sits on the Belize River. When you come to a fork, take either one. Left leads to a parking lot from which you must walk to the main part of the lodge. The right-hand fork will take you down to the river where a boatman will ferry you across. In the 1800s, the outpost was a *barquadier*, a place where mahogany logs were sorted and marked. Logs that were of the same quality were then tied together and floated downriver to Belize City. The main lodge is the original house.

The thatch-roof cabañas have two rooms with fans and a private bath with hot water. They can sleep four people comfortably and are great for families. Additional rooms are available in the new bright pink colonial building. Although built in the old style, it has

The West

all new amenities and is decorated in cultural themes taken from the Maya, Mestizo, Creole, Garifuna, Chiclero, Bayman or Bacadeer styles of life. The rate includes breakfast; a **restaurant** ($$$) serves lunch and dinner.

The lodge is the home of **Carolyn Carr**, one of the most famous artists in Belize. Her brightly colored paintings display the natural and political history of Belize and of Maya civilization. Even if you can't purchase a painting, you will find pleasure in looking. Because of Carolyn Carr, photography and painting are highly

respected activities at the lodge. Conversations on equipment and technique are easy to find. Birdwatching and trekking along the trails are encouraged, as is star gazing. Near the river is an observation tower with a 12-inch, computer-controlled, Schmidt Cassegrain telescope available for guest use. Here you can watch the stars unbothered by light pollution.

> **AUTHOR NOTE:** *In Belize, non-poisonous **snakes** outnumber the poisonous by six to one. To avoid an unpleasant encounter, never reach inside a hole without looking first and always check the unseen side of a log or rock before stepping there.*

On the property there are 4,000 acres of land, half of which is still virgin forest where birds nest and orchids bloom. But it is mostly the **equestrian** who is drawn to Banana Bank. The co-owner, Carolyn's husband John, has been involved with horses since he was seven. His enthusiasm is infectious. The Carrs have over 70 horses, many of them with long pedigrees. Warrior Chief, for example, has a line almost as long as the Banana Bank's guest list. John's experience with horses gives him the understanding needed to have well trained animals. This is reassuring for inexperienced and horse-shy riders like myself.

Horses with Western or English saddles can be rented by the day or by the hour. You may go on a guided trip through the jungle or take lessons to learn how to run an obstacle course. Trips can last two or three hours or all day and range in price from US $50-$90 per person. The jungle trails seem to be the most popular. You need not be a guest of the resort to rent a horse.

An added attraction to Banana Bank is the resident jaguar, Tika, who has been around for quite a while. She is friendly and beautiful to photograph.

Banana Bank will arrange stays that include caving, riding, ruins, jungle trails, accommodations, and meals. Go to their website, www.bananabank.com, for more information or contact them directly, ☎ 501-820-2020.

Belize Jungle Dome, Banana Bank, Mile 47 Western Highway, ☎ 822-2124, www.belizejungledome.com, $$$$, has five poolside rooms in its first class lodge. There is satellite TV and lovely tiled floors accenting the furniture that includes a king- or queen-sized bed, chair and table. The clean rooms have large closets, private baths, air conditioning, fans and places to hang things. There is also a wireless Internet hotspot and free Internet access for those staying at the lodge. The staff takes pleasure in small important things, like putting flowers in the rooms.

The swimming pool is just off the deck that is partially surrounded by jungle vegetation. Meals can be part of a package deal and are recommended as the food is exceptional. If your meals are included, you will have breakfast served on the deck just outside your room. Supper too, is served shortly after you return from your day-trip. They give you just enough time to freshen up before pouring your desired drink. The Dome is also very kid-friendly, with many things to keep youngsters busy. The dome will arrange every possible vacation adventure you could imagine, including caving, canoeing, birding, yoga, temple viewing, cave rappelling and biking. They can also take you whale-watching (in season), fishing or snorkeling. Just ask and they will try to fulfill your wishes.

I have nothing but praise for this establishment.

The Green Dragon Internet Café, ☎ 822-2124, from San Ignacio is presently being purchased by the owners of the Jungle Dome. This was the best café in Belize in for cappuccino, an ice cream, a latte or a plain old coffee while doing your e-mail or recuperating from an adventure. After the takeover it will return to its original high standards.

▶▶ *Return to the Western Highway. At Mile 48 is the junction of the Hummingbird Highway going south. Guanacaste National Park is at the junction and just two miles north of Belmopan.*

The West

■ GUANACASTE NATIONAL PARK

 Guanacaste National Park is a mere 50 acres of tropical forest bordered by the Belize River on the north, Roaring Creek on the west and the Western Highway to the east. The northern boundary features a walking trail called **Rustlers' Walk**.

TWISTED BEGINNINGS

The park derives its name from a giant guanacaste tree with a triple trunk. During its youth, the tree's trunk split and, as it grew, became twisted. Loggers decided that it wasn't worth cutting down. The famous tree is found growing at the western end of the park near the junction of three walking trails.

The guanacaste tree is fast-growing and will often reach a height of 130 feet (40 meters), with a 30-40-foot (10-12-meter) trunk. The seed pods are dark brown, about three inches across and coiled into a circle. Their shape may be one reason why the tree is sometimes called the "monkey's ear" tree. The tree is not susceptible to worm rot and is often used for making dories or dugout canoes.

ADVENTURES

Hiking

The maintained hiking trails in the park are short and interspersed with seating areas and wooden stairs that help prevent erosion from walking traffic. Many of the trees are identified with labels.

Near the parking lot a **visitor center** has a display of natural flora and fauna found in or near the park. There is also a picnic site, washrooms and a new birding deck.

The **Riverview Trail** takes you down to the Belize River where there is a large pool for swimming, a popular spot with Belizeans. The marked **Guanacaste Trail** will take you to the celebrity tree and beyond along the **Amate Trail** to the Roaring River. When you arrive at the Amate Trail you can go either right or left. The trail to the right will take you to the river much quicker than the one on the left. However, even if you decide to walk all the trails in the park, it should not take you more than an hour or two, depending on how long you spend watching the critters hidden in the foliage.

Watching Nature

The **leaf cutter ants** in the park are phenomenal. If you are at all interested in these little creatures, be sure to study them here. There are also **giant iguana, bats, rodents** and **opossums** roaming in the vegetation that includes trees such as the mammee apple, bookut and quamwood.

LIFE OF A LEAF CUTTER ANT

Leaf cutter ants started their quest to denude the jungle somewhere around five to 15 million years ago. Although they haven't succeeded, one colony can eat the foliage of a giant guanacaste tree (actually, they will eat any tree) in a single day. They chew the leaves (like snuff) and then spit the chewed leaf onto a leaf fragment. A fungus grows and the ants eat the fungus. The excretion from the ants helps to fertilize the rainforest.

The park is host to many types of birds, including the rare **blue-crowned motmot** and **black-faced antthrush**. I heard **woodpeckers** and **cuckoos** too when I was here.

There is no place to stay inside the park. You can either continue on the highway to Belmopan (see below), or head back to the lodgings mentioned above.

BELMOPAN

The capital city of Belmopan, with a population of 7,000, is growing and Belmopanians are hoping that the outskirts will reach the Western Highway in the near future. With their encouragement, I have included Belmopan along the Western Highway.

After hurricane Hattie wrecked Belize City, the government decided to move the capital inland where future destruction would be far less likely. Belmopan comes from the conjunction of Belize and Mopan. Mopan is the name of the Maya group living in the Cayo district.

Although the main government offices and the university have been moved to

AVERAGE DAILY TEMPERATURES	
JAN	73.0°F/22.8°C
FEB	75.6°F/24.2°C
MAR	78.1°F/25.6°C
APR	81.0°F/27.2°C
MAY	83.7°F/28.7°C
JUN	83.1°F/28.4°C
JULY	81.2°F/27.7°C
AUG	82.2°F/27.9°C
SEPT	82.2°F/27.9°C
OCT	80.6°F/27.0°C
NOV	77.9°F/25.5°C
DEC	75.6°F/24.2°C

The West

Belmopan, the people of Belize City weren't interested in following along. The city is considered the smallest capital in the world. However, it is one of the most attractive, largely because so many citizens got involved in gardening. Belizeans occasionally refer to the place as the Garden City.

Belmopan is built around a central plaza, much like a Maya city. **Independence Plaza** is surrounded by the Governor General's House, the Foreign Ministry, the National Assembly and Government offices. Grouped around the government buildings are the police station, the fire hall, the telephone office, the banks, the Belize Government Immigration Office, the market and the bus terminal. The entire city feels spacious.

To get anywhere in Belmopan does not take a long time, maybe 15 minutes to walk from one side to the other.

■ THINGS TO DO

 The only thing of interest to visitors is the **National Archives**, 26-28 Unity Boulevard, ☎ 802-2247, open from Monday to Friday, 8 am to 5 pm. The Archives welcome researchers interested in the history of Belize.

The **agricultural fair grounds** are at the junction of the Western and Hummingbird Highways. There is a national fair here every year toward the end of May. This is not a tourist attraction, but it is a place where you can see Belize at its best. There is livestock on display and crafts and food for sale. There is also a midway, where the wildest ride is the Ferris wheel. Live entertainment by local artists is a highlight and you can join the locals in a dance or two. If you want a taste of the real Belize, try to work this local event into your schedule. Call the tourist office in Belize City for exact dates, ☎ 223-1913.

> **AUTHOR NOTE:** In Belize, "patchwork children" are kids from blended families.

■ PLACES TO STAY

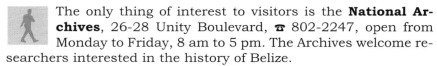

Bull Frog Inn, 23-25 Halfmoon Avenue, ☎ 822-2111, bullfrog@ btl.net, $$$, is clean and comfortable. Once the home and plant nursery of the prominent Belizean D'Silva family, the building was made into a restaurant in 1981. In 1984 the family decided to make it into a com-

HOTEL PRICES	
$	$20 to $50
$$	$51 to $75
$$$	$76 to $100
$$$$	$101 to $150
$$$$$	over $150

plete hotel, starting with two rooms. It has now expanded to hold over a dozen. The rooms have private bath, air conditioning, and cable TV. They have sheltered prominent people like the president of the Dominican Republic and Belize's Prime Minister Musa.

There is a drug store, travel agent and gift shop in the small strip mall next door.

Belmopan Hotel, Bliss Parade and Constitution Drive, ☎ 822-2130, $$$, has the only swimming pool in town. Each room has air conditioning and private bathroom. The staff seems a bit indifferent. The parking lot is fenced.

El Rey Inn, 23 Moho Street, ☎ 822-2841, $, has clean budget rooms with private baths, and hot water but no TV (bonus!) or air conditioning. The owners are pleasant and the place is clean. This is where I would stay if I had to spend time in Belmopan. It has an easy way about it.

Hibiscus Hotel, Market Square, ☎ 822-1418, hibiscus@btl.net, $$, has clean rooms with private bath and hot water. There is air conditioning and cable TV, tiled floors, a dresser and a patio door opening onto a large grassy courtyard. This and the El Rey are owned by the same people.

■ PLACES TO EAT

La Cabaña Restaurant on the highway coming into town has a lively bar and karaoke stage. This may not be a draw for many.

Alhoa Restaurant, Market Square, no phone, is a small restaurant in the strip mall next to Scotia Bank, across from the square. This is a very clean restaurant that serves the most popular meals in town. The coffee is filtered and tasty and the prices are affordable.

Caldium Restaurant on Market Square, ☎ 822-2754, $$, is open from Monday to Saturday, 7 am to 8 pm. This air-conditioned establishment is the best in town and offers things like fresh conch soup, sweet and sour chicken, or shrimp Creole with coconut rice. The del Valle family takes pride in serving guests and make them feel welcome.

Bull Frog Inn, 23-25 Halfmoon Avenue, ☎ 822-2111, $$, has a restaurant open daily from 7 am to 9:30 pm. It serves many dishes, including treats like tandoori chicken and curried beef, at reasonable prices (US $7-8). The bar is the most popular in town and offers live entertainment on Friday nights.

The West

International Café on Market Square, no phone, $, is where you can pick up the latest travel information and/or exchange a book. They are open daily from 7:30 am to 4:30 pm. Besides ordinary foods like soup and sandwiches, they also offer many vegetarian dishes.

■ OTHER SERVICES

i Market Square is where all **buses** servicing the west or the south stop to pick up and drop off passengers while the drivers have a meal. If in transit, you may have five minutes to poke around. If you can, spend one day in this tiny city. Be sure to shop in **Market Square**, which has small stalls offering local crafts and often something just a bit different than you find in many other places. The **Caldium Restaurant** also has a gift shop and boutique, just in case you need a new pair of shorts or a cooler skirt.

The Art Box, on the road into town, before the circle, ☎ 822-2233, www.artboxbz.com, is a cooperative that sells the highest quality (and quantity) of art made in the country. They also help promote local writers and singers by selling books and CDs. Be certain to stop here.

Techno Hub, ☎ 822-0061, on the square, has an Internet service. **BTL**, across the street and up about half a block, offers the same service but their two machines are often occupied.

BELMOPAN TO GEORGEVILLE

▸▸ *Back on the Western Highway heading west, you will cross Roaring Creek Bridge and then, three miles farther at Mile 50, the village of Camelote, where a secondary road goes left (south).*

Roaring River Golf Course, ☎ 614-6525 or 820-2031, martin@ btl.net, is reached by turning off the Western Highway at Mile 50, near Camalote Village. Follow the signs. The first public golf course in Belize, it is a nine-hole, 1909-yard, par-32 course adorned by indigenous trees and jungle growth. The water traps include crocs and iguanas. According to Lanz Shuderman, it is the "eccentric's delight." Owner, Paul Martin, is not the former Prime Minister of Canada but a South African who had a love for golf and some land in the bush. There is a clubhouse where you can enjoy a beer after the game (which costs US $40 per person).

■ CAVES AT ROARING CREEK, XIBALBA

AUTHOR NOTE: *Even though you could reach these caves on your own, you are not permitted to enter unless you have a guide. The reason for this is that Belize wants to preserve as much of this history as possible while still allowing visitors to get a sense of the Maya culture.*

My suggestion is to hire a tour company such as **Mayawalk** from San Ignacio, ☎ 824-3070, www.mayawalk.com, or come with a group such as **Slickrock**, ☎ 800-390-5715, www.slickrock.com, or **Island Expeditions**, ☎ 800-667-1630, www.islandexpeditions.com, from North America. They have climbing gear and strong lights so you can see. They know their way around the caves, so that you won't be wandering in the Maya underworld for eternity.

Knowledgeable guides take you to cave highlights.

To get to base camp, commonly known as Xibalba (shee-BAL-ba) Hilton, you must walk 1.8 miles along Roaring Creek. There is no road to the Hilton. The alternative to walking is to take a canoe down river. Xibalba means Place of Fright.

This group of three caves splays out from Cahal Uitz Na ruins, a small site that was in use around AD 250-900. There is a plaza and a ball court at the ruins and six very weathered stelae. The name means Place of the Mountain House.

The West

Before going into the caves be certain to have face masks (respirators) because of the bat guano (feces) that could contain spores that cause serious illness.

ACTUN TUNICHIL MUKNAL

This is by far the most impressive of the three caves in this group. Some say it is the most impressive in all of Belize. The cave sits on a tributary creek north of Cahal Uitz Na. The mouth has jagged limestone hanging from the ceiling and vegetation decorating the surrounding rocks.

From the inside, looking out of the cave entrance.

The entrance is often engulfed in mist and the Maya believed that the rain god, Choc, lived inside. The mist is suspected to be the reason the Maya called the cave the place of fright. This cave was especially popular during a period of drought that occurred just before the abandonment of many sites in Belize around AD 1000. Scientists believe that the Maya came to appease the rain god so he would end the dry spell. As the droughts got worse, the Maya went farther into the three-mile-long cave.

To enter the cave you must swim across a pool at the entrance and then trek along a rock shelf for half an hour in water that varies from ankle to waist deep. There are sharp edges and rocks in the water, so sandals must be worn. Although Belize is in the tropics, water flowing through caves is usually cooler than surface water in creeks or the ocean. You may get cold.

After you finish wading through the water, you must climb onto a shelf above the river. Off to one side of the main walkway is a burial chamber where the remains of a man were found. He had his teeth filed and his forehead flattened. There is another burial site where seven adults were found with seven young girls under the age of five. It was believed that young girls were pure and clean so they could be sacrificed to appease the gods.

A second chamber is found about a third of the way in. This chamber has a stone altar, a carved slate and many stingray spines, used to let blood. The Maya would bleed onto a piece of material and then burn the material as an offering to the gods.

All in all there have been over 1,400 artifacts located in this cave, including about 200 ceremonial vessels. Some of the bones and artifacts have been cemented into the cave due to the calcification that occurred. The chemical reaction is the same as when stalagmites and stalactites are formed.

The final section of this cave is reached by climbing fixed ladders on a rock wall. You will see where pottery pieces, broken to release the spirits, have been placed in crevasses. You will then enter a huge chamber where the crystal sepulcher is located.

Actun Tunichil Muknal means cave of the crystal sepulcher. It was named after the calcified skull of a young woman that is in the chamber. Archeologists believe the woman was about 20 years old when she was clubbed to death and left in the cave. They found a stone axe beside her body and an indentation in her skull.

A tour of this cave takes about three hours, longer for those who really want to poke around. Make certain your tour guide will stay as long as you do.

ACTUN NAK BEH

Acten Nak Beh is directly south of the Xibalba Hilton along Roaring Creek. It was found in 1997 by a worker who accidentally made a wrong turn and ended at a 25-meter (75-foot) wall that opens to passages leading to burial sites. Although much of this cave had been looted, the archeologists found one adult and two adults with a child in two separate graves. Because of the pottery found, the cave is believed to have been used by the upper classes who traded with others at Boiling Pot, Pook's Hill and Cahal Pech. There is also a causeway being uncovered and investigated.

ACTUN UAYAZBA KAB

Actun Uayazba Kab means "handprint" and the cave is named after the pictographs found inside. The entrance is .4 miles south of Xibalba Hilton along trails through the jungle. This cave opening is near the top of a cliff that rises about 200 feet (60 meters) above the jungle floor. It requires a steep uphill climb to the entrance. There is a large overhang at one of the two entrances and, from a distance, the two entrances make the wall look like a human skull. Inside, jugs were placed on ledges; you must use ropes to belay down in order to see them. Just inside the entrance is a carved turtle with its head missing.

 MYSTERIOUS MAYA: *It is believed that when boys were coming of age they climbed up one side of a turtle's back and once they got over to the other side they were transformed into men.*

Many of the passages along this cave system are so low you have to squirm through on your belly. Inside, some of the chambers have plaster floors. Petroglyphs depicting human faces and pictographs of handprints are etched into the walls of the cave. The remains of 11 people have been found in this cave system. A similar cave, found in 1999 near this area, is called Actun Holal. It has two entrances and carved faces inside.

Also near Xibalba Hilton is **Actun Yaxteel Ahau** cave, but it is difficult to enter because the collapsed entrance is full of water.

Place to Stay

At Mile 54 of the Western Highway is **Warrie Head Lodge**, ☎ 227-7185, www.warriehead.com, $$$$. Located on the Belize River, this was once a logging camp. After the price of wood fell, the 639 acres were made into a plantation with a sugar mill. In the middle of the 20th century, a man by the name of Dan Davis purchased the property and used it as a cattle ranch, but his premature death in 1950 resulted in the land being used as an American Missionary retreat center. Finally in 1988, John and Elvira Searle purchased the property and restored the old house. They cultivated the grounds and developed a botanical garden. The sugar mill's machinery was dug out of the ground and cleaned up and a Fowler engine, once used to move logs, was restored. Now visitors can **canoe** on the Belize River, **swim** in Warrie Creek or **hike** the mountain trail to a waterfall. Nothing offered here is strenuous and the artifacts scattered around give a real view of Belize history.

> **AUTHOR NOTE:** *During the 1700s Belize was called the Bay Settlement and people living here, mostly loggers, were called Baymen. The riverside logging camps were called "banks."*

▸▸ *Return the Western Highway. A short distance farther west is the village of* **Teakettle**, *Mile 52, where you have an access to the Tapir Mountain Nature Reserve, Pook's Hill Lodge and Pook's Hill archeological site.*

TAPIR MOUNTAIN NATURE RESERVE

 The Tapir Mountain Nature Reserve, previously called the Society Hall Nature Reserve (see ITMB map), is not open to the visitor. However you may drive/cycle past it by following the road that turns south at Teakettle or the road that turns south at Georgeville (Mile 66 on the Western Highway). This 6,741-acre parcel of reserve sits between Barton Creek and Roaring River.

The land was originally given to Belize by Svea and Tom Ward in 1975 to protect the Baird's tapir. It wasn't declared an official reserve until 1986 and, finally, in 1990 the land was leased to the Audubon Society for 99 years. Under the terms of the lease, the society must protect the land and use it only for scientific study or environmental monitoring. This includes educating both Belizeans and visitors about the area.

Besides a large number of tapir, the reserve has tropical and subtropical forests, numerous species of animals, reptiles and birds, ruins, caves and sinkholes. The Audubon Society is working with the 10 villages surrounding the reserve to promote the preservation of this naturally rich environment.

Dangers to the reserve are milpa farmers, who want to slash and burn as was traditionally practiced, poachers, marijuana growers using hidden patches to grow the illegal substance, and loggers.

The West

> ### TAPIRS 101
>
> The Baird's tapir, for which the reserve was named, is the largest land mammal in Central America, weighing in at up to 875 pounds (398 kg). The tapir loves water and bathes every day. It also runs to the water when threatened.

If you are on a bicycle along these secondary roads your ride will be smoother than in a car, and you will have a much better chance of seeing animals. To see a tapir, you should travel as late in the evening as possible.

Pook's Hill Lodge, ☎ 820-2017, $$$, www.pookshilllodge.com, is a 300-acre reserve that sits next to the Tapir Mountain Nature Reserve. To get here, follow the dirt road out of Teakettle for four miles. Turn right onto another road and follow it for .75 miles to the border of the reserve. The lodge is another .7 miles along this road. There are signs.

The lodge is composed of a number of cabañas surrounding a small Maya residential plaza. The white plaster cabañas are screened and have fans and private baths with hot water. The cabins are decorated with traditional Maya weavings. There is a library for guest use.

The bar and restaurant look like large cabañas and were designed in traditional Maya architecture. **Meals** ($$$) are European, with a splash of Caribbean influence.

The uniqueness of the lodge is its location, within walking distance (two hours) of the Actun Tunichil Muknal Caves and just steps from virgin forest.

For activities, there is **birding** and **swimming**. There are two **hiking** trails, one that takes less than an hour and follows the river. The other takes about two hours and goes through the jungle with flagging tape for directional markers. It is advised to take either a compass or a guide on this trek. The lodge has **horses** for hire for US $50 per person, per day. They also offer an overnight jungle **tenting** excursion (US $150) that includes gourmet camp meals and a tour of the Actun Tunichil Muknal Cave. Jungle camping is an excellent trip that was recommended to me by another traveler.

Svea, the original owner of the reserve, is also part of the **Green Iguana Project**. Started in 1996, the project was designed to help increase the number of iguanas in the jungle. Members collect iguana eggs and hatch them under controlled conditions. Once the iguanas are big enough to fend for themselves, they are released into the wild. Pook's Hill has released about 100 green iguanas every year since the project was started.

■ POOK'S HILL ARCHEOLOGICAL SITE

This archeological site was first investigated by the Western Belize Regional Cave Project. Their main objective was to find the relationship between the surface sites and the ritual cave sites near Pook's Hill along Roaring Creek.

Besides the four main temples around a little plazuela at Pook's Hill, archeologists found a **midden pile** tucked between temples 1 and 2A. A midden pile is important because it gives us a view of what the ordinary person (as opposed to the kings and elite) was eating, using and throwing away. This pile contained a lot of jute or freshwater snail shells. The snails are used to make a soup that is still cooked in Maya homes today.

Temple 2A was a banquet hall that was used for social gatherings. Here they found human teeth, grinding stones, ceramic figurines and musical instruments.

On the opposite side of the plazuela, they found burial sites in front of the building. This type of mass grave was common after the main burial sites were full. So far, nine skeletons have been found in this grave.

Pook's Hill is believed to have been abandoned shortly after the caves at Roaring Creek. The pottery found in the caves is of similar design to that found at Pook's Hill.

MYSTERIOUS MAYA: Popol na *means "Mat house" and the word seems to indicate a municipal building where public affairs were taken care of. Ah Hol Pop means "head of the mat."*

▶▶ *Back on the Western Highway near Mile 57, a road goes right (to the north), leading to Spanish Lookout and the Baking Pot Archeological site. The site is set on the south bank of the Belize River, close to the Western Highway.*

The West

■ BAKING POT ARCHEOLOGICAL SITE

 Baking Pot has two large temple complexes; one stands 45 feet high (17 meters) and is joined to a second temple complex by a causeway. The site, mostly mounds covered by vegetation, is under excavation by the Belize Valley Archeological Recognizance Project, under the direction of Mr. Jaime Awe who is a Belizean/Canadian archeologist and an authority on Maya sites in Belize.

 MYSTERIOUS MAYA: *Scribes were from the elite of Maya society and served to record a king's spiritual and earthly superiority. This writing blatantly extolled the king's powers. Scribes captured by an enemy were bound, semi-nude and had the pads of their fingers clawed away before they were finally put to death.*

■ VALLEY OF PEACE

 Just a bit farther up from Baking Pot is the Valley of Peace, a United Nations-funded refugee camp for Guatemalans, Salvadorians and Hondurans fleeing into Belize from oppressive governments. While traveling on a bus in the Petén of Guatemala a few years ago, I watched as a mother put two children on the bus. They were dressed in their best and were polite to everyone on the bus. The boy was about seven or eight and the girl about four. They had no money, so the driver let them ride for free. The little girl was sick with fever. I was told by the driver that the children would get off the bus just before the border and wait until dark to sneak across. They were headed for this camp.

■ SPANISH LOOKOUT VILLAGE

Spanish Lookout Village is six miles from the Western Highway up the same road as Baking Pot and Valley of Peace. It's a fairly large Mennonite community that includes both traditional and modern believers. The community is bustling. The only health food store in the country is in Spanish Lookout and you can get anything here from vitamins to wholewheat flour. The biggest draw to the village is the **Western Farms ice cream parlor**. The home-made ice cream flavored with fresh fruits is the best in the country. They also make a delicious yogurt that will cure any stomach problems – even those contracted by traveling. The cheese should be purchased just so you have something really good to snack on. Another side-line is automotive parts. People are known to come from as far away as Guatemala to purchase hard-to-find parts.

If you would like to stay in the village for a few hours (there is no place to stay overnight in the village itself) there are two restaurants, **Golden Choice Buffet**, ☎ 823-0421, and **Braun's Family Restaurant**, ☎ 823-0196. There is also a grocery store and an old-fashioned hardware store that seems more like a museum than a store.

> **AUTHOR NOTE:** *Mennonite women wearing white caps on their heads are from the more progressive groups and those wearing black caps are from the more traditional groups.*

Anyone on a **bicycle** is likely to be hungry, so for cyclists especially I recommend the short cycle into Spanish Lookout for food.

You will see mounds on the northern side of the road. These are part of a minor Maya ruin called **Floral Park**. It was probably a village, rather than a large center, during the peak of the Maya civilization. There is not much to see.

▶▶ *Continue west along the highway. The next hamlet is* **Unitedville** *at Mile 59 and then Caesar's Place at Mile 60.*

Caesar's Place, ☎ 824-2341, $$, has five rooms tucked well off the highway where it is quiet. The cabins are clean and spacious with fans and private bathrooms. There is a bar and **restaurant** on the property; these are so popular with both locals and visitors that if you come after seven you won't find a seat. Live jazz is featured on the first Saturday of every month. Internet service is also available.

The hotel is set on five acres of groomed land with fruit trees throughout and a small creek in the back. Julian Sherrard, the owner, is a natural outdoorsman who loves to show visitors where to find birds or animals hidden in the trees. He is also an avid whitewater/racing canoeist.

If cabins are not what you want, you can also **tent** at the back of the property. There are four **RV sites** with full hook-up services available.

For carved wood products **Caesar's Place Gift Shop**, ☎ 824-2341, www.belizegifts.com, has a woodworking shop on the property. The family does not cut down trees to be used for carving. Instead, Julian Sherrard scavenges the entire country for pieces of wood like logging stumps or branches that have been discarded by other

The West

wood users. The pieces are brought to the shop and worked into unique objects like bowls or masks. It was Julian's father who modified and sold the "Clam Chair" that has since been copied by hundreds of manufacturers in North America. The chair was originally a Mosquiti Indian invention. Some of the bowls found in the shop are not carved, but hand dug and then smoothed over to a marble polish. This design is a specialty from the Maya living in Crique Sarco in southern Belize. Maya slate carvings are also offered for sale. The gift shop will take special orders and mail them to your home.

▶▶ *Return to the Western Highway at Mile 60 and continue west to Mile 66 in Georgeville. The* **Chiquibul Road** *(south/left) heads out to the Barton Caves and the Mountain Pine Ridge gate is 10 miles ifrom the junction. However, except as a way of seeing the Barton Caves I do not recommend this road as it is in deplorable condition. The Chiquibul Road and Mountain Pine Ridge area can be reached from San Ignacio. Although the road from San Ignacio is also rather rough, it is better.*

THE CHIQUIBUL ROAD

If you decide to take the Chiquibul Road, it will lead you through green, lush citrus farmland, acres and acres of it. The entire Mountain Pine Ridge is excellent **mountain bike** territory. Any enthusiast can spend an entire month exploring the many logging roads and interconnecting military roads throughout the area.

> **AUTHOR NOTE:** *Belize has 30,000 acres of good citrus farmland. This produces a total of 3,600,000 crates of fruit, 2,400,000 of them oranges and the rest grapefruit. Most of this is made into juice concentrate and exported.*

■ BARTON CREEK CAVE

You must have a canoe to go into the cave, and you should visit only with the services of a guide or rent at the entrance to the cave from the owners of the land. They have canoes with lights and batteries. ☎ 824-3674, www.peacecorner.org/tours. The cave was first discovered by a man called Crocodile, who now owns **David's Adventures**, in San Ignacio, ☎ 803-3674, and the property at the entrance of the cave. The entrance fee and guide cost US $65. To get here, you must travel five miles along the Chiquibul Road. When you pass a large orange grove on your right, take the first left onto a one-track trail. You will have to drive through the creek and then past an Amish Mennonite community. Continue along to the end of the road and the opening to the cave. It is just beyond a pool of green water and is surrounded by jungle vegetation.

Inside the cave there are almost 1.2 miles of passages, partly inhabited by bats. Everything is eerily quiet, so you will find yourself whispering. The beauty of this cave is staggering. The river flows through a narrow canyon with walls about 150 feet high (45 meters) and in other places the river is 20 feet wide (six meters) wide.

There are many Maya artifacts and burial sites hidden inside the cave. Stalagmites and stalactites often come down so far from the ceiling that you will have to lie down in the canoe to pass by them. For protection of the environment, it is imperative that you do not touch the cave walls.

The length of the trip depends on the time of year. Rainy season will result in more water in the cave, making the float through easier and also producing a waterfall. However, there are times that there is so much water that entry to the cave will not be possible.

Visibility is possible if your guide brings a large light, powered by car batteries (a small head lamp is not sufficient, so plan accordingly). The trip inside the cave should take about two hours.

Green Hills Butterfly Ranch, Mile 8 on the Chiquibul Road, ☎ 820-4017, www.belizex.com/green_hills.htm, is getting a world reputation for its work with butterflies. It's open from 8 am to 3:30 pm and the entry fee is US $5 per person for a guided tour (minimum of two people). A picnic spot is open to visitors.

The 3,000-square-foot enclosed flight area contains numerous breeding butterfly species, some of which will be shipped to centers in the United States. There are two researchers often attached to the center, Jan Meerman and Tineke Boomsma, who have found new species of insects living at the ranch. One is a damselfly and the other is a tarantula.

 Meerman has a book available about the butterflies of this region. ***Tropical Lepidoptera, Butterflies and Moths of Belize*** is sold for US $18 and is available at the ranch.

■ MOUNTAIN EQUESTRIAN TRAILS

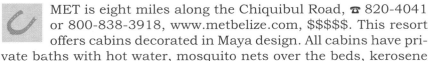 MET is eight miles along the Chiquibul Road, ☎ 820-4041 or 800-838-3918, www.metbelize.com, $$$$$. This resort offers cabins decorated in Maya design. All cabins have private baths with hot water, mosquito nets over the beds, kerosene lights, and decks with tables and chairs. There is a bar and a gift shop.

This is one of the few places in Belize where outdoor adventure in general and horseback riding in particular is part of the deal. The lodge has been rewarded for its efforts in these areas; last year, it received the Belize Eco Tour Award.

Marguerite Bevis, one of the owners, is a registered nurse (so less need to worry about snake bite) and an avid conservationist. Her husband Jim has lived in Belize since childhood and is at home in the jungle.

Marguerite is one of the founding members of the **Slate Creek Preserve**, a 3000-acre parcel managed by the surrounding communities. Started in 1992, the preserve is bordered by Barton Creek and the Tapir Mountain Preserve. It encloses waterfalls, unexplored caves and unexcavated Maya ruins. To date, there have been 244 species of

birds, 281 species of butterflies, 200 species of trees, 35 species of snakes and 18 species of amphibians spotted in the area. Traveling either on foot or by horse along the 60 miles of trails you will see many of these creatures.

Jim Bevis was the first man in modern times to cross the Mountain Pine Ridge divide on foot. He carried an inflatable kayak in his pack as he traveled for two days from MET to reach the Sibun River gorge, where he entered the water and paddled down the river to its end. On this trip he took a famous photographer, Tony Rath, and a scientist who was collecting fauna from freshwater creeks. Knowing the environment as well as he does, Jim is a good person to use as a guide to some wild jungle adventure.

Horseback riding trips can be either full-day or half-day events. The full-day trips run to **Big Rock Falls** and back; along the way, you will be shown different plants used by the Maya for medicinal purposes. At the falls, you can jump from the surrounding cliffs into the pool below, just to cool off. The **River Cave Ride** will take you through Maya farms to a river where you can swim into the cave. Inside are shards of pottery from ancient times. The **Mountain Pine Ridge Cave** trip takes you through the karst region to a cave with Maya pottery. Along the way you'll see many interesting limestone formations as well as medicinal plants used by the Maya. **The Vega Trail** is a half-day trip through a lush valley to a small waterfall along the Macal River.

▸▸ *This is as far as we go on the Chiquibul Road. Return to the Western Highway at Mile 66 and continue west. It is another one mile to the turnoff for the privately owned Matthew Spain Airport. It is just another 3.6 miles along the Western Highway to the Cristo Rey Road after the airport turnoff.*

THE CRISTO REY ROAD

The Cristo Rey Road forks at its beginning. The left fork goes to the Cahal Pech ruins, and ends there.

■ CAHAL PECH RUINS

 Cahal Pech is open from 8 am to 5 pm, and costs US $5 to enter. Information pamphlets (US $2) are available, but they were out of stock when I visited.

It takes no more than half an hour to walk to the ruins from San Igancio and touring should take no more than a couple of hours.

The site is believed to have been occupied by Maya from 1200 BC until the great collapse around AD 1000. Jade and obsidian from 100-600 BC have been found at the site. The acropolis on which the site stands is 900 feet (300 meters) above sea level. It probably gave those living there a spectacular view of the Belize Valley. But the view was important for more than just its beauty: it could show the approach of enemies.

It was not until the 1930s that exploratory records were written about Cahal Pech. These were largely ignored until the 1950s when Dr. Satterthwaite of the University of Pennsylvania studied the ruins and suggested that the Maya called it Place of the Ticks. Following Dr. Satterthwaite, there was little done at Cahal Pech except looting until 1969. It was then that Dr. Schmidt, Belize's second archeological commissioner, salvaged some artifacts from the main plaza.

In the 1970s, archeologist Dr. Jaime Awe, with the help of local police, caught some looters and had them convicted under the Antiquities Act of Belize. However, looting continued until the late 1980s. Finally, under the directorship of Dr. Awe, excavations are progressing well now.

If you walk from San Ignacio to the ruins, you will probably enter the site from the north onto Plaza B, where most of the **stelae** have been found. The earliest carved stele ever discovered in the Maya lowlands was found at this site. Besides the six stelae found here, 34 **ceremonial structures** have been uncovered, along with two **ball courts**. At its peak, the old city is believed to have covered about 10 square miles. Structure A1, just to the west of Plaza B, stands at a height of 77 feet (23 feet).

If you continue south from Plaza B you will see excavations taking place at structure F2. The diggers have unearthed some stairs facing Plaza F that lead to a platform with a door that opens to an interior room that measures three feet by nine feet (one meter by three meters). This room had traces of red paint on the walls. At first, the archeologists thought that the room would open onto Plaza G, but this has not happened.

A pre-Columbian plate with graffiti on it was found at Cahal Pech. Graffiti in Maya culture was very rare.

To the west of the main structures is a newly completed museum with some interesting diagrams. The grounds are kept in immaculate condition at this site and it is pleasant to walk around even if you are not an antiquities buff.

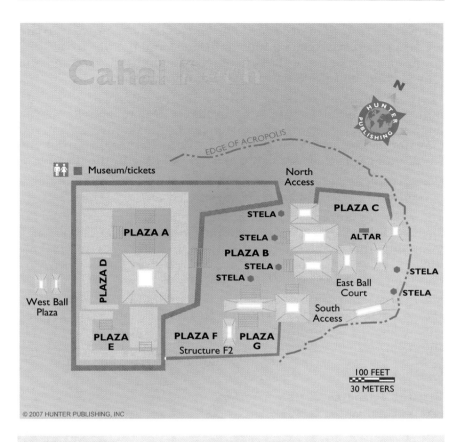

Cahal Pech

EDGE OF ACROPOLIS

Museum/tickets

North Access

PLAZA C

STELA

PLAZA A

STELA

ALTAR

PLAZA B

STELA

PLAZA D

STELA

STELA

East Ball Court

STELA

West Ball Plaza

South Access

STELA

PLAZA E

PLAZA F

Structure F2

PLAZA G

100 FEET
30 METERS

© 2007 HUNTER PUBLISHING, INC

▶▶ *Return to the fork at the beginning of the Cristo Rey Road. The right fork goes to Christo Rey and San Antonio before it hooks into the Chibiquil Road at Mountain Pine Ridge reserve. From there, it passes through recreational country with caves, relaxing resorts, splendid waterfalls, the greatest mountain biking in the country, canoeing, white-water rafting and outdoor camping sites that can be reached only by horse. If you have a car or bike, the way is easy. If not, you could hitch all the way to the Caracol ruins, but do it only during daylight hours. You should have a plan as to where you will stay if you are unable to get a ride all the way in and/or out.*

A bus goes to San Antonio from San Ignacio at 11 am, 1 and 6 pm daily. They leave San Antonio at 6 and 7 am and 4 pm daily. There are no buses going beyond San Antonio.

■ PLACES TO STAY

Maya Mountain Lodge, Box 174, San Ignacio, ☎ 824-2164, www.mayamountain.com, $$$, features white plaster and tiled cabañas that have fans and private baths with hot water. Tastefully decorated, these cabins offer privacy. There are less expensive rooms in the main lodge and there is a 40% discount for rooms during the off-season. Children are welcome and may stay for half-price up to age 12 and free up to age six.

There is a pleasant **walking trail** behind the lodge where you can find over 100 edible plants. A naturalist is available at all times to answer questions or to show examples of jungle plants that you may not be able to find on your own. The lodge has also printed a small trail guide that you can use when walking in the area.

Being family oriented, the lodge has a pool and library, and offers special activities for kids, such as shows and story times.

There is a **restaurant** and bar on the premises, or you can take the short trip into San Ignacio to eat. The food at the lodge is both high in quality and great in quantity. All tours for the Mountain Pine Ridge area can be arranged through Maya Mountain Lodge, who use some of the best guides available in the area.

Maya Mountain Lodge also offers a combination of custom-designed, all-inclusive packages that can take in things like visiting caves, waterfalls, the cayes and the ruins at Caracol. Some include canoeing and horseback riding. Their packages run from US $150 to $200 per person per day, depending on what you do and how long you stay. This is a good deal.

Crystal Paradise, Cristo Rey Village, Cayo, ☎ 824-2014 or 824-2772, www.crystalparadise.com, $$$, is just beyond Cristo Rey village, a Maya settlement at Mile 3. The family-run lodge has 20 units. There are thatched-roofed cabins, as well as traditional cabins and rooms in the main lodge. All have private baths, hot water, ceiling fans and verandahs. The décor of the cabins is in the Maya theme and the place is spotless. The Macal River flows behind the lodge.

Meals at Crystal Paradise are home-cooked and delicious. You may request traditional Maya dishes (in advance) and Mrs. Tut, the mother of the family, will try to accommodate you. Meals are served family-style in the central part of the lodge.

Several **birding** scopes are available to help you spot some of the 300 birds reported to live here. There are **horses** on the property, some of which can be ridden. To add to the beauty, the garden has over 150 plants, with about 50 species of orchids. If photographing flowers is your passion, this may be the best place around for you to do so.

Years ago, the Tut family were farmers. They wanted to get into tourism, so one of the sons started building traditional cabañas. Mr. Tut started digging a hole in the ground and water came up. The following morning, the murky water in the pool had turned clear. Thus the name "crystal." (The "paradise" is self explanatory.) This is a very traditional Maya family and staying here will give you a good insight into some of their ways.

■ SHOPPING

 Sac Tunich Gift Shop is another .3 miles down the road and is recognizable by the large carving of a Maya head on the upper stairs. The shop, located in a traditional Maya house, is run by local people and has many slate and wooden carvings that were made on the premises. The hosts are pleasant and reasonable to deal with. There is a small charge for photographing the carved head outside the shop.

SAN ANTONIO

San Antonio, at Mile 10, ☎ 824-3266 (public phone that may be used for contact), has a population of about 1,500. This Maya hamlet is nestled in a farming community and is worth a poke around. Not only does the village house the world famous Garcia Sisters (see below), but until 1996 it also was the home of Dr. Panti, the famous medicine man who lived for 103 years acting as the spiritual leader of the community and healer to all in need. While in the village you can visit with a Maya chiropractor, a snake doctor, a massage therapist or a midwife to learn about these areas of Maya medicine. The **Pacbitun ruins** and **Noj Kaax Panti National Park** are within cycling/walking distance. San Antonio also offers a home stay program, allowing you to stay with a family and learn traditional skills like patting tortillas or grinding corn.

■ HISTORY

 The five **Garcia Sisters** are Maya ladies who, years ago (1983), were working in the field when they uncovered a piece of slate. At the same time as the stone came to the surface, Pauahtun, the Maya God of art and writing, inspired them

The West

to carve on slate as their ancestors had done. Unable to control their new passion, they took the stone home and started carving.

However, their father, who had earned his food as a youngster by carving bowls out of limestone, didn't believe the girls should be carving. "People buy food," he said, "not stone." But the girls couldn't stop. They carved a whale and when that slate was finished they got more. Eventually they sold their carvings and became recognized for their artistry. Since then their work has been on display in England, Germany, Japan and many Latin American countries.

The Garcia sisters gather their slate from a secret location reached by a trek through the jungle, up and down streams, and through mud and thick vegetation. The sisters believe that gathering the stone replenishes their soul and rejuvenates their artistic spirit.

Only three of the sisters remain in San Antonio (one moved to live with her husband near the Jaguar Preserve and one passed away). However, there is an art gallery and shop at the Tanah Maya Art Museum in the village where you may purchase some of these carvings (see below).

■ THINGS TO DO

Take lessons in the practice of **Zaxtuns,** a form of healing that includes medicinal plants, prayers and secret stones. Practiced and taught by the Garcia Sisters' uncle Elejio Panti, this traditional way of healing is practiced not only among the Maya but also by foreigners as an alternative medicine. As an example of one of the practices, Dr. Panti uses the cohune palm root as a blood tonic.

Should you not have time for lessons, you can purchase herbs and tonics at the shop in the village. One controversial item is natural tobacco. The shop sells it in the form of cigars. It's not laced with addicting drugs, so this tobacco won't kill you quite as quickly as that found in North American cigarettes.

Besides learning about the gathering and use of medicinal plants, you can take a course in the art of slate carving using chisels, Exacto knives, hacksaws and machetes to etch out your creation.

Tanah Maya Art Museum and Community Collection, www.awrem.com/tanah/experience.html, is beside the Chichan Ka Lodge on the way into the village. The museum is often patronized by tour-bus companies. It has a collection of artifacts that have been donated by local villagers for the preservation and promotion of their culture. Be sure to see the ceremonial offering table and a carving from Xunantunich. The museum is not big. A donation of

US $5 is requested to support the museum and to establish a botanical garden in the village. Open 8 am to 4:30 pm daily.

The shop at the museum offers Garcia carvings that run anywhere from US $50 to $1,000. There are also necklaces, rings, plates, bowls and plaques, all with creative Maya designs.

Museum artifact.

All Saints Day is a fun celebration that starts on June 4th and goes for nine days. Also known as the Hog Head Dance, the celebration is given in honor of St. Anthony of Padua. The locals bake a pig head in the ground covered with banana leaves. Each villager decorates the head with flags and sweet breads. It's then placed on a large platter and given to a man dressed in traditional clothing. The man, holding the head, is paraded around town at the end of a rope. Others take a maraca and shake it in front of the man as if tempting him to follow. You'll have to ask locals the meaning of the dance. If you wish to partake in this festival, check with the sisters at the lodge for times.

Noj Kaax Panti National Park was inaugurated on February 23, 2001. The 13,000-acre park was named after the famous Dr. Panti from San Antonio who lived to 103 years of age and was the spiritual leader of the town until his death in 1996. The boundaries of this park are along the Macal River to the west, Barton Creek on the north, Mountain Pine Ridge on the east and Rio Frio Caves on the south.

Maria Garcia was instrumental in bringing this park into being, but only after three years of work and negotiations. The land, rich in trails, caves and wildlife, is cared for through the cooperation of three villages – El Progresso, Cristo Rey and San Antonio.

Before the area became a park, some farmers wanted to work the flat land that was going to be engulfed in the park. A dispute arose and finally the farmers were given a 500-acre parcel closer to the Mountain Pine Ridge. The redistributed land was previously a reserve where peanuts were grown.

In the park are the **Kaamcatun Ceremonial Caves**, reported to have large vessels inside. You will need a guide from the village to take you there or you can hire Mr Tzul (see below). There are also many old Maya and chicle trails that can be walked.

■ PACBITUN RUINS

 You can visit the Pacbitun ruins on your own, or with Mountain Rider tour operator (see below). If traveling independently, you will need to stop at Mountain Rider and pay the entrance fee of US $5.

Leave San Antonio and follow the Cristo Rey Road up the hill, veering to the left at the fork near the top. Continue to Mile 10.5 and turn left onto a secondary road to reach **Mountain Rider**, ☎ 820-4036, where horses and a guide can be rented. Jose Tzul, owner and licensed guide, can take you to the ruins, bathing pools and caves in the Mountain Pine Ridge area. Tzul's philosophy is that he uses horses to do interesting things, as opposed to riding for the sake of riding. His horses are as gentle as he is. You can arrange a half-day trip (US $35 per person) or full-day excursion (US $50 per person). Longer trips must be arranged in advance. Jose can accommodate children, but no younger than five years of age.

The family has owned the land on which the Pacbitun ruins are located since 1964. The farm sits on 500 acres of jungle, mountains and cultivated fields. The Tzuls have always used horses for work, so the animals are accustomed to the climate and the terrain. Now they are willing to take you on a ride to places not advertised by other outfitters.

MAYA GODS
■ Itzamna – God of Creation
■ Kinich Ahua – Sun God
■ Akab – Moon Goddess
■ Chac – Rain God
■ Ix Chell – Goddess of Medicine
■ Hacha – God of Fire
■ Pauahtun – God of Writing and Art
■ Ah Puch – God of Death
■ Yumkaax – God of Corn
■ Yum Kax-Ku – God of Mountains and Land
■ Xaman Ek – God of the North Star

Pacbitun ruins are beyond the Mountain Rider property by half a mile. There is a sign indicating the road to the ruins. At the sign, turn right and follow the road for about three miles.

Pay your entrance fee at the home of the Tzul family, where Mountain Rider is located. You may wander by yourself, although the family would much rather take you in by horse.

The name Pacbitun means "stones set in earth." The city is believed to have been occupied about 1000 BC and to be one of the oldest cities in the country.

Found on 75 acres of land on a limestone outcrop in the foothills of the Maya Mountains, the ceremonial center has 25 pyramids, the tallest standing about 56 feet (17 meters). This is a temple pyramid with a vaulted superstructure. There is also a ceremonial ball court, a causeway that is a half-mile long and an irrigation system. Because of the numerous musical instruments found here, it is believed that the city was occupied by an elite group of artists. The ocarinas, or wind instruments, made from pottery were the most common of the pieces, although drums were also found.

The site was originally excavated and mapped by Dr. Paul Healy of Trent University in 1986-87. He was studying the farming methods of the Maya and was interested in the terracing that is around the city for a distance of up to three miles. Instead, he found an acropolis with five plazas and 41 major structures. This distracted Dr. Healy from his original interests.

Another significant finding at the site was a small green arrow believed to have been traded with those living in Teotihuacan, Mexico.

Visiting Pacbitun from San Ignacio by bicycle is a great day trip.

■ PLACES TO STAY

Should you wish to stay in a **home** with a family, call ☎ 820-4023, and ask about the home stay program. It is run by the Itzamna Society, first headed by Maria Garcia (one of the sisters). The society was originally set up to form the Noj Kaax Elejio Panti National Park.

■ PLACES TO EAT

Regardless of where you stay, be certain to search out a glass of sugar-cane wine. This potent white wine is best sipped both slowly and sparsely.

THE CHIQUIBUL/CRISTO REY ROAD

■ PINE RIDGE MOUNTAIN RESERVE

▶▶ *Return to the Cristo Rey Road at Mile 10.5 and continue south for two miles. You will see the gate to the Pine Mountain Ridge Reserve where the Cristo Rey Road meets the Chiquibul Road that goes down to Georgeville on the Western Highway or continues south to Caracol. I advise you not to even consider trying the road to Georgeville. It was not passable at the end of the dry season when I was there. In rainy season you'd turn to mould before getting out.*

> **AUTHOR NOTE:** *The Cristo Rey Road and Chiquibul Road are the same route and locals use both names. To save repeating both names in the text, we use just Cristo Rey.*

The gate to the reserve is manually operated by a park warden who uses it to keep track of those coming and going. If you are wondering why there aren't more signs along the road indicating where you are, the warden at the reserve entrance told me that it was difficult to keep them from being stolen so they don't put any more up.

The reserve has 126,825 acres of controlled logging. However, in recent years a highly aggressive species of pine beetle has infested and killed 90% of the trees in the area and the hill tops in Mountain Pine Ridge look like they have tooth picks sticking in them.

UNDER ATTACK

The female pine beetle burrows into the bark of a tree so she can lay her eggs. On her head, she carries spores that produce a blue staining fungus. As she chews through the bark, she drops the spores. The fungus grows and blocks the vessels of the inner bark and the sapwood.

After the female successfully enters a tree and lays her 160 eggs, she spreads pheromones that attract males for fertilization of the eggs and other females so they too can drop their eggs into a safe place. It takes two months for the life cycle of the beetle to be completed and they can have three to four generations a year.

As the trees' sap stops flowing, the needles turn yellow and then a straw color. Finally, they turn a reddish-brown and the tree dies.

Woodpeckers like to eat developing larvae. Also, after a female sends off her pheromones, she attracts enemy beetles. But these are not enough to save the trees.

The "toothpick tree" problem is being addressed by replanting. As of August, 2002 officials have planted seedlings that are a bit more resistant to the beetle than the present trees. The reforestation program will continue for four years. Pine trees grow fairly quickly. At the end of four years, some of the trees should be almost as tall as you.

Dead pines.

Bol's Jungle Tours is on your right just before you come to the gate for the reserve. Bol's can take you for a hike into the jungle searching for wildlife or medicinal plants. They will take you by horseback to caves located on their property. The caves feature pottery and skeletons.

▸▸ *Inside the gate, at Mountain Pine Ridge Reserve, the road splits. You are at Mile 14 of the Cristo Rey Road. Veer to the left and follow the road signs for Hidden Valley Falls and the lodges along that road.*

■ LODGING, WATERFALLS INCLUDED

 Hidden Valley Inn, Box 170, Belmopan, ☎ 800-334-7942 or 822-3320, www.hiddenvalleyinn.com, $$$$. This is an exclusive lodge that has 12 cabins semi-circled around the main building, where the **restaurant** is located. Each cabin has a zinc roof, screened windows, fan, private bath with hot water, two twin-sized or one queen-sized bed, and tile floors. Rooms are tastefully decorated. The restaurant serves full-course meals at linen-covered tables decorated with fresh

HOTEL PRICES	
$	$20 to $50
$$	$51 to $75
$$$	$76 to $100
$$$$	$101 to $150
$$$$$	over $150

flowers, crystal glasses and candlelight. The price of the room includes meals.

The main draw, other than luxury, is access to the private waterfalls. Interspersed around 118,000 acres of private land are the **Tiger Creek** pools and falls, just a 30-minute walk from the resort, and the **King Vulture Falls**, a 45-minute walk away. The King Vulture Falls have a picturesque canyon on the opposite side of the river. **Bulls Point** allows a view all the way to Belmopan on a clear day. There is also a picnic shelter at Bulls Point. **Butterfly Falls** is a two- to three-hour round-trip hike. These falls drop 80 feet into a secluded swimming pool.

Lake Lolly Folly is a man-made lake 30 minutes from the lodge. If you catch fish here, the chef at the lodge will prepare it for your dinner.

Manakin Falls is 45 minutes along a two-mile trail. These falls were named after the bird frequently seen there. The luxury of these trips is that if you feel lazy, you can be driven close to each spot.

Hidden Valley Falls is just beyond the turnoff to Hidden Valley Inn, along the Cristo Rey Road and 4.5 miles from the gate. Follow the signs. The cost is US $2 per person. Tour buses frequent this site. The falls don't take long to photograph.

Hidden Valley Falls were previously called the 1,000-Foot Falls but, after the British Army measured them in 2000, they found that the drop was actually 1,600 feet (480 meters) in all.

There is a washroom, a covered sitting gallery and a gift shop with local artwork at the site. The cabins belong to the Hidden

Valley Institute for Environmental Studies. The caretaker is Pedro Mai and he loves to take interested visitors to the opposite side of the yard to look over at the surrounding hills. Four of the highest mounds that you see are unexcavated and unmapped Maya temples. Pedro will tell you stories if you give him the chance.

As you arrive at this government-controlled site you will see lush jungle, dying pine trees and the falls .6 miles away. If it is raining or if there is a mist, don't bother coming as you will see nothing. It is a steep descent to the bottom of the falls. Remember, you must climb back up in the heat.

The falls were known to the Maya and sat alongside a Maya Indian walking route. When the British Army pushed a road through in 1961, they spotted the falls and started showing them to others. However, it wasn't until 1975 that the falls became a tourist attraction. Most of the waterfalls up and down the Cristo Rey Road are on private property so if you do not go to the Rio On, a little farther up the road, these may be the only ones you see.

▶▶ *Return to the Cristo Rey Road at Mile 14 and go to the right.*

The first lodge along the way is **Pine Ridge Lodge**, ☎ 606-4557 or 800-316-0706, www.pineridgelodge.com, $$$$ (discounted in off-season). The lodge has seven fully screened cottages that have been refurbished to a sparkle and are decorated with Belizean pottery and Guatemalan textiles.

The cabins have private baths with hot water. Some are made with materials gathered in the jungle, some overlook the river and some are just plain nice. The grounds are well kept and dotted with orchids. The open-air **restaurant** serves gourmet meals, specializing in Italian and vegetarian dishes. However, I have heard that their soups are the big draw. Meals are served in a jungle-type dining room lit with kerosene lamps that add a romantic hue. The easy-going atmosphere is appealing.

Just beyond the property is the **Little Vaqueros Creek** and its 85-foot waterfall. It takes about

15 minutes to reach by walking. The lodge is also just 2.5 miles from Big Rock Falls, an excellent day-hike or a cycling excursion.

Pine Ridge Lodge has numerous people working for it. Some are very familiar with the Chiquibul area, including its caves, logging roads and rivers. If you are looking for a guide to that area, this is the place to find one. Or, contact the lodge in advance. Their knowledge of the back country and their willingness to help you enjoy it is admirable.

Big Rock Falls on the Privassion River has a 150-foot drop into a swimming hole. To get there, go about one mile along the Cristo Rey Road, following signs toward the Five Sisters Lodge. Turn right onto a secondary road after one mile and go another two miles until you see a cleared parking spot on the right. From there, follow the trail downhill for 10 minutes. You will come to a clearing where horses have been kept. Cross the clearing and follow the second trail until you come to the river. The falls are on the left. All in all the Privassion River has about 10 falls, most of them on private property. This trail description was given to me by Gary Seewalk of Pine Ridge Lodge. To go to the Vaqueros Creek waterfalls, you must stop in at the lodge and ask for directions. I suggest you also have "the last cold beer on the road to Caracol."

Blancaneaux Lodge, Box B Central Farm, Cayo, ☎ 820-3878, www.blancaneaux.com, $$$$$, is located .6 miles past Pine Ridge Lodge along the Cristo Rey Road (Mile 12.4 from San Ignacio) and is what film director and writer Francis Ford Coppola considers to be paradise. This is why he bought the place after he found it while hiking through the Mountain Pine Ridge area.

FRANCIS FORD COPPOLA

Known for winning the Oscar at the age of 31 for the movie *Patton*, Coppola also made such famous films as *The Godfather*. He won first place at the prestigious Cannes Festival for *Conversation* and *Apocalypse Now*. It was the resemblance to the Philippines, where he filmed *Apocalypse Now*, that attracted Coppola to Belize.

The lodge is first class. Each thatched-roof cabin, set on a ridge above the river, has antique colonial furniture, private Japanese bath, Maya weavings and hardwood floors. The entire lodge is surrounded by rock, jungle and water. With advance reservations, you can be picked up at Belize City International Airport in the lodge's private plane. Or, if you wish, you can drive.

The restaurant here will serve anything you want, but it specializes in the Coppola family's Italian recipes, like Neapolitan pizza or mother-in-law chicken. These are cooked on a wood fire in an oven imported from Italy. The chef won the Belize Tourism Board's Signature Dish award last year. I can't think of anything more romantic than eating these foods while sipping on some first class red wine!

There is also a Thai massage parlor and a grass thatched-roof building imported from Thailand, with authentic Thai therapists. Services include aromatherapy, wraps and facials. But if these activities don't use up enough energy, you can take a horse for a ride or hike along one of the jungle trails on the property.

Next along the Cristo Rey Road is **Five Sisters Lodge**, ☎ 800-447-2931 or 820-4005, www.fivesisterslodge.com, $$$/$$$$. The lodge sits above the Privassion River in a natural garden full of flowers that send an intoxicating perfume throughout the wilderness setting. The 14 screened cabañas have thatched roofs, hardwood floors, mosquito nets over the beds and private baths with hot water generated from a wood-burning boiler. There are also smaller rooms available in the main

© Five Sisters Lodge

lodge. A bar and **restaurant** serves excellent meals and a gift shop sells souvenirs. The resort also offers tour options or all-inclusive packages.

The five acres of property has trails down to numerous waterfalls, some of which drop more than 100 feet (30 meters). Bar service is available on the Garden of Eden Island, where natural swimming pools are located. The staff are all born and raised Belizeans who know how to provide the best service.

The Five Sisters Falls were named after the five braids the Privassion River takes as it cascades over the rocks into a pool that is used for swimming.

The Five Sisters Lodge has built a chapel at the river for romantic weddings in an exotic mountain setting back-dropped with a waterfall. The lush jungle surrounding and the tropical flowers used to decorate the chapel add to the ambiance. The bride enters the area by riding down the hydro-powered tram and then she walks across the bridge to meet her betrothed.

The West

Five Sisters will arrange everything including the application for a license, decorating of the chapel and the meals to be served to the guests.

MARRIAGE IN BELIZE

Foreigners must acquire a license costing US $100. You must be in the country for three days before applying for the license and those under age 18 need parental consent. Anyone previously married must have documents proving divorce or widowhood. More detailed information and valuable cautions can be found at www.travelbelize.org/honeym.html.

A **nature trail** that leads around the lodge has labeled medicinal plants. Bikes can be rented for a cycle to the Rio On and Rio Frio Cave. **Mountain biking** in the Mountain Pine Ridge is excellent and Rio On is about four miles past Blancaneaux Lodge along the Cristo Rey Road. The travel is slow but worth the joggling and abuse you must take to get there. Rio On's parking lot has a picnic shelter, so bring a snack. You must go down about 100 cement stairs to the river where it flows over granite rocks into a multi-faceted gorge. There are numerous swimming spots on the river although, during dry season, they have far less water in them. There is no charge for entering this site.

■ D'SILVA & RIO FRIO CAVE

 Augustine, now called D'Silva, is at Mile 25 on the Cristo Rey Road and has a population of less than 500. The town was named after Douglas Silva, the first ranger in the reserve. The name has been shortened by locals to D'Silva. I found nothing there but a few workers enjoying a bottle of spirits, and the abandoned reserve headquarters.

To reach **Rio Frio Cave**, turn right at the village (going left will take you to the research station) and right again at the first turnoff. Follow the signs and park at the end of the road.

The walk from the car park to the Rio Frio Cave is mystical (if by yourself) as jungle critters call like ghosts through the silence of the forest. There are numerous small caves at the side of the trail that you can explore. Take note of the scars on the sapodilla trees that were tapped for chicle many years before. It takes about 15 minutes to walk to the mouth of the cave, where you will find pools and sandy beaches along the river and the cave itself tucked into the side of a hill. The cave is huge and an easily followed path leads to the exit less than a quarter-mile in.

Continue along the river as it skirts the hill and you will find other caves. There is no charge to this site.

■ CARACOL

 From D' Silva it is another 10 miles to the Caracol ruins. Travel along the poor road averages five-15 miles an hour and you should keep alert to logging trucks. During wet season, the travel is even slower and sometimes the road is impassible.

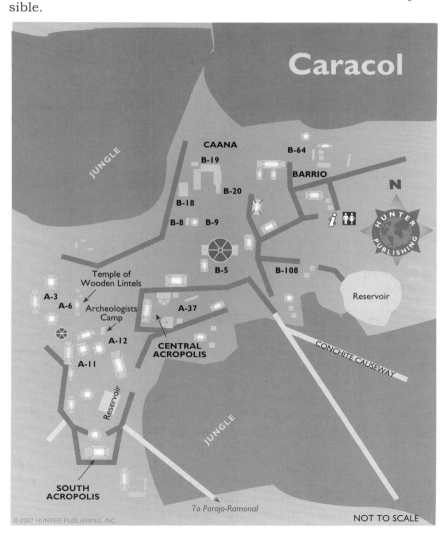

NOT TO SCALE

The West

Close to Caracol is the Guacamallo Bridge over the Macal River. Guacamallo is the Spanish word for macaw parrot and Macal is the English Creole word for the same bird. The bridge marks the border for the Chiquibul Forest Reserve, which houses the longest cave system found in Central America. At the Chiquibul Reserve's border with the Bladen Forest Reserve stands **Doyle's Delight**, the highest peak in Belize. Until recently it was believed that Victoria Peak was the king (queen?) of the mountains in Belize, but that has since been disproved.

Caracol's famous pyramid.

There are picnic tables at the entrance and a toilet. The visitor center, built with the help of Raleigh International, holds maps and artifacts found at the site. This mini museum is worth visiting. If you are there while the scientists are working, you will be taken on an informative tour.

HISTORY

The information about Caracol has been brought to light mainly through the work of two dedicated scientists, **Diane and Arlen Chase**, from the University of Central Florida. They started digging in Belize in 1979 (they were in Guatemala before that) concentrating on the Orange Walk district. It didn't take long for them to be drawn to the challenge of Caracol, the largest ancient Maya settlement in Belize. The site also contains the highest manmade structure in Belize.

Caracol was first noticed by *chicleros* working in the area. That was 1937. A year later, **Dr. Anderson** came to map the ruins and then **Dr. Satterthwaite** from the University of Pennsylvania came in the 1950s to excavate. He also named the city. Caracol means "snail" and was called this because of all the snails found on the site. However, it is suspected from glyphs uncovered more recently that the Maya name could have been "Place of Three Hills."

The Chases have written numerous accounts of their explorations at the site and they have also been filmed in a National Geographic documentary called *Hidden City of the Maya*. It is to them that we give credit for the information that allows us to walk through this city and accurately imagine the lives of those who lived there.

CARACOL'S TIMELINE

1200-250 BC. Caracol was a collection of small hamlets and farming sites.

900-600 BC. The first signs of a city appeared.

AD 70. Temples and burial sites were being used. A ritual complex was also present.

AD 150. Elaborate burial sites were developed.

AD 250-900. The city was at its peak with a population of around 150,000 people. By 800 the decline had started.

AD 331. Evidence was found of a Royal dynasty existing.

AD 480. An unknown ruler was buried in the city.

AD 553. Lord Water becomes the ruler. He is also mentioned at Tikal.

AD 562. Caracol's most prominent rival, Tikal, is defeated, either in a game or in battle.

AD 575-618. Smoke Ahau is born and comes to power.

AD 618. King Kan becomes the ruler.

AD 626-936. The Naranjo Wars (rival groups from Guatemala) start.

AD 658. Kan dies and Smoke Skull comes to power.

AD 680. The Naranjo's War of Independence.

AD 702. Ixkun is captured.

AD 859. The most recent date inscribed on a stele at Caracol.

AD 1050. Caracol is abandoned.

The city originally started as a small farming community. As it grew, there was a need for a central market place. The civilization became more sophisticated, temples were added near the market, burial sites were created and the need for a place of worship (rituals) was satisfied.

The West

As the population grew, a leader or king was chosen and a class system developed. The need for more plazas increased, sort of like shopping malls in today's civilization, until Caracol had five major plazas in the core of the city and numerous others around the outskirts. Through the investigations of the Chases, we know that the people who lived in the palaces in the center of the city ate the healthiest foods, while those living on the outside ring of the urban sprawl ate the worst. Those living in between were the largest class, the middle class, who ate neither badly nor well. We also know that the peasants who lived in the country ate well.

The city eventually became immense, covering over 88 square miles and holding over 30,000 structures. In the center plaza a pyramid was built that was higher than any other structure in the town. Its top still bursts out of the jungle canopy at a height of 128 feet (42 meters). From the top, you can see all the way to Guatemala. The city had no permanent water supply, so reservoirs were built and an observatory was erected. The ball courts took on a circular shape and stelae revealing the history of the city were inscribed.

As the wealth of the city grew, rival areas like Tikal fought with Caracol for power. At first, fights were common only among the elite classes. However, as the wars became more frequent and fierce, the lower classes were required to fight. The Naranjo wars continued for a long time until what is now Guatemala won its independence from Caracol.

In 895, for some reason, whether it was disease, famine or invasion, the city collapsed and the elite left. Some buildings were left unfinished and the body of a child was found in one room. The assumption is the parents didn't have the time to perform a burial ceremony. However, many of the peasants on the outskirts of the city remained.

ON MAYA TIME
Kin . . . . one day.
Uina . . . . one month, made up of 20 kins.
Tun . . . . . . one year, made up of 18 uinas or 360 days.
Katun . . . . 20 years or 7,200 kins.

EXPLORING THE RUINS

As you enter the city from the visitor center, the imposing **Caana Temple** (meaning sky place) is on the far right, to the north. At 128 feet (42 meters), the view from the top is breathtaking. The structure has 71 rooms and 45 of those rooms had stone benches inside. Some of the rooms had ceramic tiles on the floors and it was in this structure that the unburied body of the child was found. Two intricately carved stucco heads of people were found here and it is believed that they came from the upper facing of the building. This building contained only storage vessels and no drinking, eating or working vessels.

There have been more than 200 burial sites found under Caana, some with family plots. One such plot contained two adults, a 15 year old, a six year old and a one year old. These ages are approximate. All of them had either filed teeth or inlays of jadite put into the teeth. In some of these tombs, fragments of the original paint can still be found.

Around Caana are structures **B18** and **B20**, palaces where the elite lived. **B25** dominates the eastern side of the plaza and it has a room inside that is 35 meters long and seven meters wide. The door to the room is three meters wide and has eight steps leading to it. Inside, benches are set around three sides of the room and numerous vessels are strewn about.

It was believed by the Chases tht this room would open onto the west side of the plaza on the Barrio complex. However, excavation showed exactly the opposite. There was a solid wall between the

The West

two. Although there is a similar dividing of property found at Tikal, the feature is not usually found in Maya architecture.

To the south of Caana is a **ball court**, where a marker was found that describes the battle with Tikal. **Altar 23**, the largest found at the site, is southeast of the ball court. The altar was inscribed in 810 and shows captured prisoners. The glyphs tell of the war with Tikal.

To the east or the back of Caana is the **Barrio complex**; B26 is the tallest building in this complex. A new building was being erected on top of an older building, but it was never completed. Excavations showed that, if it had been finished, it would have stood nine feet (three meters) above the previous building.

Between **B26** and **B25** is a narrow alley. Inside this alley were shells and bones, indicating that it was a working area. There were also palaces under the main structures of B25 and B26. The altar found here had a carving of a person sitting inside the sign of the moon.

Continuing south of Caana, the main **acropolis** dominates the center of the city. It is surrounded by three plazas and two ball courts. **A39** had a bench inside similar to the one at Caana. This bench was painted red and inside the room were tripod plates, vases and a ceramic bird whistle.

Behind the central acropolis is the **temple of the wooden lintel**. The carved lintel was of sapodilla wood. Just to the west of this temple was the observatory where the elite studied the stars. To the north of this set of buildings is a **ceiba tree**, believed to be at least 600 years old. Its huge buttresses fan out far enough that they could be the walls of another temple. The Ceiba was sacred to the Maya, who believed it was the symbol of all creation.

Tombs and rooms throughout the city have been found with interesting treasures inside. One of the most interesting was a free-standing stucco statue of a person seated on a throne. Inside the statue's chest was a ceramic box. Both the box and the statue are rare objects for a Maya site.

One burial site found had a beehive chamber inside. The chamber at Saraguate, 1.2 miles from the center of Caracol, was looted, but the bones of a 25-year-old woman were not touched.

Of the interesting **stelae** found, one had a feathered serpent, and one describes a fire in 895. One of the altars suggests there was a female ruler for awhile. So far, 40 inscribed monuments covering 500 years of Caracol's history have been found. One held in the highest esteem is from 562, when people were rejoicing in the defeat of Tikal by Lord Water.

HIKING

Caracol is on the Vaca Plateau and stands at 1,500 feet (450 meters) above sea level. The causeways around it offer excellent walking and should not be overlooked. One of the causeways, an engineering masterpiece, still supplies water to the site.

The walks around the causeways can last an hour or two or up to half a day. The sounds of the jungle coming from the thick vegetation, the odd stone that is kicked could be another piece of the historical puzzle, the animals that cross the path in front of you are all worth experiencing. At present the ruins are being preserved rather than restored. However, you will find that Caracol rivals Tikal as a worthwhile Maya site.

INFORMATION

Caracol ruins, www.caracol.org, is open from 8 am to 4 pm and costs US $5 to enter (for foreigners). Belizeans do not pay on Sundays or any public holiday. The site was made into a national park in 1995 and shortly after it became a natural monument reserve.

There are **no facilities** or amenities at Caracol. Bring food and drink, plus enough gas to get home. If cycling (the best thing to do) you will need to camp between Caracol and town. You should have those arrangements made with one of the lodges (above) before you arrive at the ruins.

■ CHIQUIBUL CAVES

 The Chiquibul (CHICK-ee-bull) Cave system starts eight miles past Caracol and weaves in and out of about 265,000 acres of jungle on the Vaca Plateau, across the Guatemalan border and back. So far, 40 miles of connected passages have been mapped and there's a suspected 20 miles still to be done.

Hardly accessible because of the lack of maintained roads, the caves can be reached on horseback (see below) following old logging tracks and stream beds. Water is often inaccessible along the route, so carry some with you until the Chiquibul River is reached. You must have a guide and a permit from the Department of Archeology in Belmopan, ☎ 822-2106 or 822-2227. Failing to obtain a permit is punishable by a jail term. The jails are crowded in Belize and there is no TV.

This is the longest connecting cave system in Central America and includes the largest cave chamber in the western world. The chambers, which can be as wide as 260 feet (78 meters), are connected by narrow passages. Some passages stretch for almost two miles. The Chiquibul River runs through these connecting passages and, during rainy season, the water level can rise as much as 70 feet (20 meters), making passage quite dangerous.

By measuring a uranium isotope, scientists reckon that the caves were formed 800,000 years ago. The bones of a now extinct bear species, believed to have lived 10,000 years ago, were found in one of the caves. Bones from vampire bats dating to the same period were also found.

To date, four main caves have been explored in this system – **Kabal**, **Cebada**, **Tunkul** and **Xibalba**. Inside were pots and incense burners, whistles and grinding stones all belonging to the Maya.

The military explored the region around the caves in 2000 and found an M16 clip and a string from a military hammock tied to a tree. The British military was in the area prior to Independence and could have left the objects behind. But the clip could also belong to Guatemalan guerillas or marijuana farmers. One point is agreed upon: it is unadvisable to explore this region on your own. If you want a knowledgeable **guide**, inquire at the **Pine Mountain Lodge** (above), or contact **Peter Herrera**, a naturalist guide who has a world of experience. He has worked for Birds without Borders and assisted journalists on magazine assignments. His number in Belize City is ☎ 222-4802.

■ PUENTE NATURAL ARCH

To the south of Caracol, this natural phenomenon is difficult to reach without a four-wheel-drive or a bike. You follow an old one-lane road from Caracol to a gold mine near the arch. For explicit directions, see the owners of Pine Mountain Lodge.

▶▶ *This is the end of the Cristo Rey Road. Return to the Western Highway at Mile 69.6.*

SANTA ELENA

The little village of Santa Elena, Mile 70, is on the east side of the Macal River. It is quiet and non-imposing as compared to San Ignacio on the other side of the Hawksworth Bridge, the only suspension bridge in Belize.

AUTHOR NOTE: *From the Western Highway going west, turn right at the sign that says "Santa Elena," even if you are going directly to San Ignacio. If you go straight ahead, you will come to the Hawksworth Bridge and you will be going the wrong way. I did this and had to make an embarrassing U-turn in the middle of the road to the honking of numerous vehicles coming toward me.*

Once on the road to Santa Elena, go straight to the stop sign and turn left. Santa Elena is straight ahead. If going to San Ignacio, veer to the right after the stop sign and go down the hill to the wooden bridge.

Santa Elena has both hotels and restaurants.

■ PLACES TO STAY

The Aguada Hotel, ☎ 804-3609, www.aguadahotel.com, $$, is a first-class hotel in the center of town with very reasonable rates. The name means "watering place" in Mayan. This is a family run business that offers numerous styles of accommodations from the economical

HOTEL PRICES	
$	$20 to $50
$$	$51 to $75
$$$	$76 to $100
$$$$	$101 to $150
$$$$$	over $150

room to a family unit that has three double beds and a sitting area. One room even has queen-sized bunks. There is a swimming pool and a patio to sit on while enjoying a cool drink. The Aguada also offers Internet service and an excellent restaurant that pays attention to details. For an example, if you ask for extra garlic, you will get it. The cook and waiter have gregarious personalities yet they are never intrusive. The entire hotel is surrounded by jungle vegetation that also encompasses a nearby pond hosting birds, turtles and fish. The most interesting sound in the area comes from tree

The West

frogs who thump away with better rhythm than any Garafuna drummer. For kids, there is a play house and small park. The hotel is run by Bill and Cathie Butcher, who are training their daughter, Shalue, in the business. This is an excellent place to stay. To get here, turn off the main highway at the Plasmet Hardware store. The hotel is on "the boulevard," with a huge sign at the entrance.

The Touch of Class Comfort Inn, Perez Street, ☎ 824-4006, www.touchofclasscomfortinn.com, $$, is a two-storey motel-style building that has 10 rooms with access to the balcony, air conditioning or fans, cable TV, and private baths with hot water. There is a bar and **restaurant** on the premises. The rooms are clean, the hotel quiet, the walk to town not far. To get there, turn left at the first street past the La Loma Luz Hospital. Follow the signs. The hotel is about four blocks down Perez Street. They will arrange tours for you.

The Log Cabins, on the Western Highway past the Cristo Rey Road turnoff, ☎ 824-3367, www.logcabinns-belize.com, $$$, have rustic but clean cabins set in an orange grove on 45 acres. The nine cabins have private baths and hot water, fans and a deck. There is a swimming pool, bar, **restaurant** and gift shop on site. Internet service is also available. The owners offer packages that include meals.

SAN IGNACIO

San Ignacio, often called Cayo, is on the western side of the Macal River. It has a population of about 15,000 people, making it the second-largest town in Belize.

The Western Highway goes through San Ignacio, but because the Bridge is one way going east instead of west, you must turn right before the bridge and go toward Santa Elena. Instead of going into that village, take a left at the stop sign and then an immediate right onto the road going downhill. You will cross a wooden bridge and then come to the Savanna Sports Grounds in San Ignacio. Take any road to the left to get to the center of town. It becomes obvious once past the sports grounds.

■ INTRODUCTION

San Ignacio has a fair amount to offer. Nearby are the **Xunantunich ruins** with the towering palace of El Castillo. There are Maya medicine trails to walk and butterfly reserves to visit. **Cahal Pech**, an extensively excavated and well cared for ruin, is a short walk from the center of town. San Ignacio is also a place where guides can be hired to take you on specialty **adventures**, such as those to Barton Creek Cave or whitewater rafting down the Macal River.

Going to the different resorts and visiting their attractions like the medicine trail, the Belize Botanical Garden and the Museum at Chaa Creek, is easy to do. Taxis, buses or bikes are all possible means of transportation. Xunantunich and El Pilar ruins can be reached by bus or bike and caves can be visited by joining a tour. Canoeing down the Macal River is a great sport; canoes can be rented in town.

Nightlife is also exciting. There is a new **casino** and numerous hang-out bars where you can listen to local musicians. Coffee shops are located in garden settings and funky gift shops sell souvenirs. San Ignacio is also just nine miles from the Guatemalan border.

AVERAGE TEMPERATURES & RAINFALL		
	Daily temp.	**Monthly rainfall**
JAN	73.6°F/23.1°C	47.3 inches/120.2 cm
FEB	76.3°F/24.6°C	32.0 inches/81.3 cm
MAR	80.4°F/26.9°C	23.9 inches/60.7 cm
APR	81.3°F/27.4°C	16.9 inches/43.0 cm
MAY	84.2°F/29.0°C	27.9 inches/71.0 cm
JUN	83.7°F/28.7°C	84.8 inches/215.5 cm
JULY	82.2°F/27.9°C	88.6 inches/225.1 cm
AUG	82.6°F/28.1°C	62.9 inches/160.0 cm
SEPT	82.6°F/28.1°C	70.7 inches/179.8 cm
OCT	80.9°F/27.2°C	72.5 inches/184.6 cm
NOV	80.2°F/26.8°C	81.9 inches/208.2 cm
DEC	76.3°F/24.6°C	55.9 inches/141.9 cm

■ HISTORY

 Originally a **logging** community, San Ignacio during the mid-1800s became a sanctuary for the Maya fleeing from the Caste Wars in the Yucatán. They settled in the mountains and made money by selling their produce in San Ignacio.

After the logging market dropped off, **chicle** became the important commodity of the area. However, that too lost its attraction and now **citrus** or **cattle ranching** are the ways to earn a living.

It took San Ignacio a long time to be recognized as an important center. The first road wasn't pushed through until the 1930s and it wasn't paved until the 1980s.

Built on seven hills (like Rome), the town has an attractive setting and was once a tranquil place. However, after the recreational value of the area was discovered, every possible amenity was built to accommodate sports enthusiasts. Today, hiking boots, canoe paddles or climbing gear are often seen on the porches of the cafés and restaurants as the hikers and canoeists grab a quick bite to eat and share a tale before heading off for another adventure.

MACAL RIVER DAM PROJECT – HULA-HOOP DANCE

Fortis, a Canadian firm (from Newfoundland) that owns Belize Electric Limited, has a contract with the Belize Government to build a dam seven miles down the Macal River from its confluence with the Raspaculo River in Chiquibul National Park. The Chalillo Project involves Fortis flooding a 5.5-square-mile parcel of land that could hold back 120 million cubic meters of water. The cost of the project would be an estimated US $60 million. This land is also part of the Vaca Plateau, an exceptional area that is home to numerous birds and is the nesting spot for the endangered scarlet macaw. The park also has the largest number of jaguars in all of Central America. Unexcavated Maya sites in the park are innumerable. For all these reasons, recreationists are drawn to the area.

An environmental impact study was done by AMEC, a contractor from England. It was learned that AMEC was not disinterested; it hoped to net about US $12 million in construction jobs after the project got started.

Environmental groups who oppose the project have taken the Belize Government to court over the issue. This is a first-time challenge for the people of Belize. Sharon Matola, founder of the Belize Zoo, has received support from groups such as the US Natural Resources Defense-Based Council, Biogems Program and Probe International. Over 30,000 private citizens from as far away as Northern Canada have sent letters of opposition to the Belize Government and Fortis over the project.

In court, it has been discovered that many laws were broken in the agreement with Fortis. First of all, it is illegal to build a dam in a national park in Belize. The lawyers also found that the committee assigned to lead the required public meetings had nine government and two non-government members. All the government members voted for the project. But the public meetings were not held until after the project was approved by the government.

The environmental assessment document stated that the dam would be built on granite. In fact, it would be built on limestone, a much weaker rock. Despite this, part of the contract allowed Fortis to sell the dam for $1 and walk away from any liability charges if problems arose.

The contract also guaranteed Fortis 15-20% profit from its investment every year, regardless of whether electricity was supplied or not, and it gave Fortis a monopoly in Belize on the sale of electricity.

Fortis controls a lot of the electricity in Canada. In 2001 Fortis sold 100 gigawatts of electricity for CN $425,000; in Belize the cost of 100 giga-watts of electricity was CN $5.6 million. Robert Leslie, Secretary to the Cabinet is quoted as saying, "Some people want the entire country to become a zoo. We are simply trying to get electricity to people."

As of January 29, 2004, three out of five judges on the Privy Council decided to let the project go ahead. The dam was built and the huge area behind the dam was burned by Fortis, in anticipation of flooding that may never occur. But to add to this outrage, the cost of electricity to Belizeans is now US 20¢ per kilowatt-hour, an increase of 12% overall and 50% to the poorest families. In neighboring Guatemala and Mexico, electricity costs about 6¢ per kilowatt-hour and in Canada it is about 4¢. But the story is not over. Fortis wants to build a third dam on the river at Vaca Falls.

Visit www.stopfortis.org for photos and an in-depth description of the ramification of this dam. The one complaint I heard over and over in Belize this year was that the government has become totally corrupt. This story is said to be just one example.

■ GETTING HERE

 Buses go to San Ignacio or Santa Elena from Belize City every day starting at 4 am. They run every half-hour until 9 pm and every 45 minutes during slack times. The cost is US $2.50. From San Ignacio, buses leave for Belize City every half-hour starting at 4 am. The last one leaves at 5 pm.

Buses to and from Benque Viejo go every half-hour starting at 3:30 am and run until 11:30 pm at a cost of US 25¢.

CAR RENTALS

Safe Tours Belize Ltd., 287 Western Highway, ☎ 824-3731 or 824-4262, cell 614-4476, dcpil@yahoo.com, has vans or Izuzu Troopers, most of which are four-wheel-drive and have air conditioning. The vans, some of which can hold up to 15 passengers, rent for US $100 per day or $87.50 per day if taken for more than four days. The Troopers go for US $75 a day or $62.50 per day if taken for more than four days. There is an 8% tax on all car rentals. The vehicles are new and in good repair. These prices include insurance for driver and passengers (most companies do not include passenger insurance). The company will pick up and deliver anywhere in the Cayo district free of charge. If delivering to the international airport near Belize City, there is an additional US $25 charge. You can save money by taking the airport shuttle van (it meets all planes) from the airport to San Ignacio to pick up your vehicle.

You should book these vehicles about two weeks in advance, especially during peak season. Cancellation must be completed at least one week before pick up is due. Should you have problems with your vehicle, owner Emil Moreno will come out to where you are with a new one. This is a 24-hour service. The vehicles can take you almost anywhere you would want to go in Belize.

Western Auto Rental, 29 Burns Ave, ☎ 628-8987 or 620-6640, below the Venus Hotel, has a number of cars starting at US $50 per day, including insurance. Larger jeeps are available for $62.50 a day, including insurance. This is a real deal and I went for it. Although the vehicle, a Toyota Tracker, was not brand new, it was in good shape. The brakes worked very well, the steering was not loose and the engine purred like it should. It took me over some rough roads and kept me dry during torrential rains. The company does not have a huge fleet of vehicles but it was able to supply me with a vehicle on the same day I asked for it. The upside of the little vehicle I got was that it was economical on gas.

In addition to renting cars, this company runs tours to Caracol and the Hidden Valley of the Maya. You can also go canoeing or horseback riding with them. They are hospitable and eager to help.

■ SIGHTS

Hawksworth Bridge, built in 1949, sits over the Macal River and joins San Ignacio with its sister city of Santa Elena. Often called the roller coaster because of the noise this metal one-way suspension bridge creates when vehicles cross, it is the only one of its kind in the country. Vehicles coming from San Ignacio and going east must use it. Historically, the bridge was used as a two-way bridge with only one lane of traffic. But when conflicts arose as to who had the right of way, the city decided to put in a traffic light. But the light was often out of commission so the conflicts continued. Finally, the city decided to detour drivers

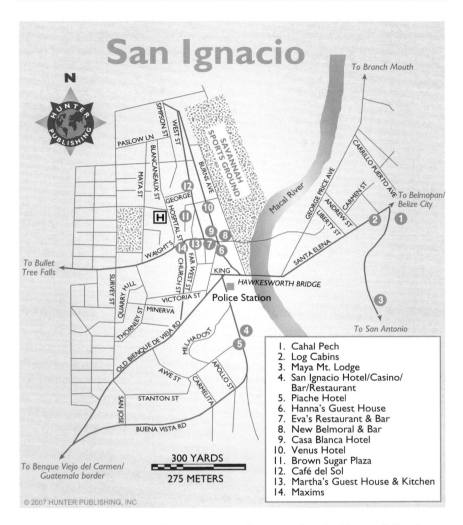

San Ignacio

N

To Branch Mouth

To Belmopan/
Belize City

To Bullet
Tree Falls

To San Antonio

Police Station

HAWKESWORTH BRIDGE

To Benque Viejo del Carmen/
Guatemala border

300 YARDS

275 METERS

© 2007 HUNTER PUBLISHING, INC

1. Cahal Pech
2. Log Cabins
3. Maya Mt. Lodge
4. San Ignacio Hotel/Casino/
   Bar/Restaurant
5. Piache Hotel
6. Hanna's Guest House
7. Eva's Restaurant & Bar
8. New Belmoral & Bar
9. Casa Blanca Hotel
10. Venus Hotel
11. Brown Sugar Plaza
12. Café del Sol
13. Martha's Guest House & Kitchen
14. Maxims

coming into San Ignacio over a smaller wooden bridge, while those leaving can have the Hawksworth at all times.

Foot and bicycle traffic can use the bridge both ways at any time. Sitting close to the bridge and watching the action is often better than watching television.

■ ADVENTURES

BIRDING

Birding Pals, www.birdingpal.org, is a networking group that tries to put birders from different countries in contact with each other. The purpose of the group is to have people share their special interest in birds and learn about one another's cultures. Since the list is growing daily, please check their website just before heading to Belize if you would like to develop such a friendship. There is a pal from San Ignacio who is registered. His name is **Jeronie Tut**, birdinginbelize.com. Contact him by e-mail before arriving and he will be glad to accompany you on a birding excursion. There is a charge for this service.

The birding pal website also lists professional guides who can be hired for a fee. These listings give the qualifications of each guide so you can find one to meet your needs. This list is also growing rapidly.

Birding Pals was started in April, 2000 by Knud Rasmussen of Toronto, Canada. Since the group's inception, the list of members has become substantial, with over 1,500 pals in 166 countries. Mr. Rasmussen gets no funding for this nor does he charge for the immense amount of work he does. His motivation is due to his love of birds and he believes that birders are very special people.

CANOEING

The Belize Canoe Association was formed in January, 2001 with Elvin Penner, Julian Sherrard and Luis Garcia as the founding members. Membership has increased quickly and their mandate is to promote canoeing while preserving the environment. For more information, go to www.blackrocklodge.com/bcanoe.htm.

Because of their good reputation, the canoe association, as well as each individual race that the association puts on, has a large number of sponsors.

Races

Ruta Maya Baron Bliss Canoe Race, the most famous international race in Belize, starts on the Thursday closest to March 9th, Baron Bliss Day, and finishes on the following Monday. Sixty to 80 teams enter the race with three people to each team. The cost is US $125 per team and the first prize for the men's professional category is US $5,000. The race route goes from San Ignacio to Belize City along the Macal and Belize rivers and the race is grueling.

There are both amateur and professional categories, as well as male, female or mixed classes. There are also categories for youth, 14-17 years of age, masters (40+) and a dory class. In other words, this race excludes no one.

The Ruta Maya is the longest race in Central America and the second-longest in the world, covering 170 miles of jungle waters. The section between Banana Bank and Bermudian Landing has some fairly rough whitewater. The race starts with a run overland, of about 100 meters, where the teams carry their canoes.

The racers use anything from a 200-pound wooden dory to a 110-pound, 16-foot fiberglass to a light-weight 52-pound, 20-foot Kevlar canoe. There are always over 20,000 specta-tors lining the shore, (almost 10% of the coun-try's population) to cheer these racers along. If you are in Belize during this  time, be certain to either enter the race or participate in the cheering. Profits go toward the preservation of the Belize River Valley.

For more information on this race, see www.larutamayabelize. com. The Big H juice company supplies drinks for competitors dur-ing the race.

The Belize Extreme Canoe Adventure takes place during the weekend closest to the full moon every September. Forty-five pro-fessional paddlers spend 18 continuous hours paddling from San Ignacio to Belize City. The prize (US $7,500) is worth the work. This is a new race in Belize and only for the strong competitor. For infor-mation on this and other Belize races, including those below, con-tact Julian at www.blackrocklodge.com.

Boom to City Race takes place on the Sunday before Valentine's Day in February and covers the 25 miles from Burrell Boom to Belize City along the Belize River.

The Agricultural and Trade Canoe Challenge takes place on the Saturday of the trade show at the end of May in Belmopan. The race is from San Ignacio along the Belize River to the mouth of Roaring Creek and then up the creek to the show grounds. At the grounds, canoers jump out of their canoes, and haul them up to the grandstand.

Around da Caye is the race to enter in July. It is run in conjunc-tion with the Lobster Festival. This race takes paddlers around the entire island of Caye Caulker.

The West

Cayo Canoe Safari and Canoe Festival takes place every October 12 in celebration of Columbus Day/Pan American Day. During this multi-sport event, teams of three cycle, run and paddle. The first person cycles from Spanish Lookout to Calla Creek via a dirt road through Billy White Village, Duck Run 1 Village, Santa Familia and Bullet Tree. The second person runs from Calla Creek to San Jose Succotz via Clarissa Falls. The third person runs from Succutz to the border via Benque Viejo. At the border, all three jump into a canoe and paddle down the Mopan through white water to Branch Mouth and then up the Macal to San Ignacio. Everyone is welcome!

Another real canoeing enthusiast is Julian Sherrard from **Black Rock Lodge**, ☎ 824-2341, www.blackrocklodge.com/bcanoe.htm. He will help visitors with legalities for entering the races. He also has a fleet of canoes for rent for about US $30 a day. When renting from Julian, there isn't the problem of getting the canoe to the mainland. Like Allie at Toucan Canoe, Julian advises that you bring your own paddle.

CANOE RACE HISTORY

During the logging days and before locomotives, people moved around in Belize by river. In those days it took one week to go by boat from San Ignacio to Belize City, longer if paddling a dory.

For entertainment, the dory paddlers would race. Eventually, one-man dories were replaced with eight-man dories and, finally, 15-20 men paddled in a grueling race from San Ignacio to Gales Point, north of Dangriga.

There was often a serious competition with the winning cup sometimes going to Gales Point and other times going to San Ignacio. In 1975, the races came to an end and canoeing of any sort in Belize became unpopular.

In 1997 Luis Garcia wanted to revive the racing spirit so he started a small race called the Up and Down. The race went down the Mopan River to Branch Mouth and then up the Macal to San Ignacio, finishing at the Hawkesworth Bridge. It became so popular that it was eventually made into the now world famous Ruta Maya from San Ignacio down to Belize City.

Canoeing Locales

The Mopan and Macal rivers are interesting and both have a little whitewater on them just to keep you on your toes. The Macal run starts at a gorge near Black Rock Resort and flows into San Ignacio down to the Branch Mouth, where it joins the Belize River for a run to the ocean.

The Mopan River run goes from the bridge at the Guatemalan border for 15 miles, through some bubbles but nothing too serious, until it joins the Macal near San Ignacio. This is a full day's run. If you wish to stop en route at El Pilar ruins near Bullet Tree, you must start very early.

Guacamallo Bridge to Negroman is a 21-mile run starting in the Vaca Plateau in the Mountain Pine Ridge. This rugged canyon run is for rafting or very skilled kayaking as there are numerous Class III and IV rapids, plus several Class V stretches. Portages take you around the two Class VI waterfalls. The run starts at the high end of the Hydro Dam Road and goes through the canyon, past Black Rock and on to Negroman, where the river flattens out.

Negroman to the Branch Mouth is an easy 11-mile float past white cliffs and good swimming holes. It ends at the car wash in San Ignacio.

You can rent equipment locally. See below.

CAVING

This is the best caving area in the country and most caves are Maya ceremonial sites, so you will often come across the remains of a body or an artifact. The **Chiquibul Caves** (see page 271, the Cristo Rey Road beyond Caracol) are the longest in Central America and they have rooms that are second to none for beauty. Some require that you rappel down on ropes or visit by boat. If a dry cave is your preference, head to nearby **Chechem Hah Cave** (see page 302), which can be visited independently. **Actun Chapat** and **Actun Halal** (see below) are also nearby. The architectural work inside Actun Chapat makes the exploration more interesting than at some other caves.

At least one cave trip is a must when in Belize, and San Ignacio is the best place from which to do it. It matters not whether you hire a guide for a customized trip or join a tour and share the excitement with others. See below for recommended guides.

Actun Chapat, which translates as "Cave of the Centipede," is presently being researched by archeologists. It is about 20 miles south of San Ignacio, and you must have a guide to show you inside. The trip requires travel along old logging roads and a walk in the jungle.

First discovered in 1982, the cave has been mapped. There are two entrances with a chamber that is about a quarter-mile long in between. A torch and the back of a pyrite mirror were found here, and items made from stone and animal bones were discovered in the cave proper. But the most interesting objects are the terraced platforms, stairways and shelves. There is even a bench carved into the cave wall in one room. One tiny room has resident ghost-faced bats, an endangered species (so leave them alone).

Actun Halal, in the Macal River Valley, is a small cave with two entrances. It's more of a rock shelter than a cave. The entrances are connected by a passage that measures about 75 feet (26 meters) long. The petroglyphs inside are what make Actun Halal interesting. In one room is a wall that has a calcium carbonate waterfall flowing down it. Shine your light and you'll see it sparkle. There are five petroglyphs carved on this wall and more in the smaller room nearby.

GOLF

Golf at Clarissa Falls is at Mile 71.2, ☎ 824-3916, along the Western Highway. This special "Clarissa" game uses only five holes. Each player receives one ball and one club. It takes skill to get a hole in one. The fee is US $5 per person.

SWIMMING

Cool off in the pool and then relax on the deck and enjoy some home-cooked meals at **Crystal Paradise Lodge**, Cristo Rey Village, ☎ 824-2014 or 824-2772. The cost for swimming is US $2.50.

TOUR COMPANIES

Like snorkeling or diving on the cayes, cave touring is the thing to do while in Cayo. There are dry and wet caves (with rivers), some with exceptional formations, others with exceptional Maya artifacts. The most appealing aspect of exploring in the Cayo region is that guides and tour operators will cater to what you want, rather than vice-versa. Regardless of what you choose, expect to pay US $50-$80 for the day.

Easy Rider, 24 Burns Avenue, San Ignacio, ☎ 824-3734, www. belizex.com/easy_rider.htm, runs horse trips in the Mountain Pine Ridge area. The owner, Charlie Collins, offers half-day excursions for US $25 and full-day excursions for US $40. The horses are gentle, so children can be accommodated. He will also arrange visits to caves, ruins and waterfalls.

Western Auto Rental, 29 Burns Ave, ☎ 628-8987 or 620-6640, below the Venus Hotel, offers great half- or full-day trips on horseback. The horses are in good shape and the guides can take you to see things you would not see on most other tours.

Belizean Sun Travel and Tours, Box 180, San Ignacio, ☎ 601-2630, belizeansun@btl.net, specialize in cave tubing and visiting dry caves. They also run jungle night walks with overnight camping, which allows you to see nocturnal animals and try to sleep as the howlers sing their lullaby. BST also likes to do bike tours, especially with small groups. They have now expanded and can arrange all-inclusive adventure trips. This is a very good company.

Mayawalk, 19 Burns Avenue, ☎ 824-3070, www.mayawalk.com, is a one-stop shop. Aaron Juan offers tours that are high adventure, involving activities like spelunking in a cave after rappelling down the canyon wall. Or mountain biking to a jungle river and camping overnight to the music of the howler monkey. The trips are not for the out-of-shape adventurer. If whitewater is your desire, this is also a good company to arrange kayaking/rafting trips on the Macal River. Mayawalk has an impeccable reputation.

International Archaeological Tours, West Street, ☎ 824-3991, 606-3115, www.belizeweb.com/iat/index.html, has licensed guides who specialize in local archeological sites. IA Tours can take you to Maya ceremonial caves not yet mentioned in guidebooks. These caves have been found by guides that work for IA tours. If you would like something different, contact these people. IA also offers canoe rentals. I suggest that you take a knowledgeable guide on your trip, especially if you are not very experienced. During high water, some of these rivers can be dangerous.

Belize Close Encounters, Box 1320, Detroit Lakes, MN 56502, ☎ 888-875-1822 or 218-847-4441, www.belizecloseencounters. com, has been operating in Belize for over 13 years and knows the country well. They represent over 60 resorts and can combine a number of activities with suitable accommodations. Their best skill is creating custom trips, whether it be caving or diving, museums or horseback riding. The San Ignacio area is their specialty.

EQUIPMENT RENTALS

Black Rock, ☎ 824-2341, rents canoes for US $30 a day. If staying at Black Rock Lodge, you get the advantage of a vehicle pickup after the run out from the resort to San Ignacio.

Belizean Sun, ☎ 824-4853, offers kayaks for US $30 a day, plus pickup and delivery. Tube rentals are US $5 for 2.5 hours on the river. Bike rentals are US $7.50 per day. A valid ID or credit card must be left as security. This is a really good deal. They also offer tours with guides (to Xunantunich and elsewhere) for US $50 per day.

David's Adventure Tours, 8 Hudson St., (in Rest. Pollito Dorado), ☎ 824-3674, offers overnight camping, hiking, birding and canoe caving trips. I have had complaints about the conduct of the guides used by this company. Unless you hear along the trail that things have improved, I suggest using another company.

The Trek Stop, ☎ 823-2265, www.sanignacio.com, offers a shuttle service to the airport for $30 per person.

■ NIGHTLIFE

 Brown Sugar Plaza has a **movie theater** so you can take in the local latest. No matter how many small bars open and close, **Eva's** remains the one place where you can always find locals (and tourists) repeating themselves non stop all day and all night. For a classier jazz night or quiet drink, walk over to **Aguada's**, ☎ 804-3609, in Santa Elena and be served an excellent drink while enjoying the jungle sounds. Or try **Caesar's Place,** ☎ 824-2341, about 10 miles out on the highway going east. For the most part, unless going to the two places mentioned below, nightlife in San Ignacio consists of dinner after sunset followed by a beer at **Chingos** or any other bar along the streets and early to bed.

Roomba Room, Buena Vista and Benque Viejo, opens after six and is the best place to dance and party. The music is loud, the drinks strong, and the crowd young. Plus, if staying in town, the walk home is downhill.

The **Stork Club**, 18 Buena Vista Drive, ☎ 822-2034, at the San Ignacio Hotel, is the place for a drink before you have your steak in the restaurant. The club has a happy hour every evening, but it is especially popular on Friday.

> **ODD FACT:** *In 1806 a law was passed that required all heads of families to have six fire buckets, one ladder and one hook with a rope attached in their homes. This law is still on the books.*

Cahal Pech Tavern, at Cahal Pech, ☎ 824-3380, features a wide variety of local bands. The drinks are not costly and the place is popular with travelers.

The **Casino** is in the San Ignacio Hotel on Buena Vista Drive, although it's not part of the hotel (it rents space there). It's a good spot to lose a couple of dollars. If boredom is a problem, this can be a lively place.

■ SHOPPING

This is your last chance to shop in Belize if you are headed to Guatemala and your first chance if you are coming from there.

The Indita Maya Gift Shop, West Street, ☎ 824-4346, is a small shop well stocked with local artwork.

Lisa's Boutique, West Street, ☎ 824-3366, has high quality items. If you need something really nice to wear to dinner, have a look at the blouses and dresses here.

The Belize Gift Shop, West Street, ☎ 824-4159, has a wide selection of gifts and souvenirs in all price brackets. The people are friendly – that's the biggest draw.

Amber Mystic, Far West St. and Eve St., are open from 9 am to 6 pm daily. The owner has a fairly good supply of English books that she will either sell or trade two for one. The shop also carries jewelry, CDs of local music and numerous pieces of art done by emerging Belizean artists.

■ PLACES TO STAY

The San Ignacio Hotel, 18 Buena Vista Drive, ☎ 824-2034, www.sanignaciobelize.com, $$$$, was first opened in 1976 by Escandar Bedran and has since become a family operation, taken over by his daughters. The 25-room hotel sits

HOTEL PRICES	
$	$20 to $50
$$	$51 to $75
$$$	$76 to $100
$$$$	$101 to $150
$$$$$	over $150

on 14 acres of land that overlook the Macal River. Each newly renovated room has private bath with hot water, fan or air conditioning, and cable TV. There is also a gift shop, a pool, a basketball court and a very good steak house.

The hotel also has Petie, an expat from the United States. Petie, a green iguana, had never lived in the jungle before arriving at the hotel. Petie's original owner realized that living in Los Angeles was not good for him, so she shipped him to Belize. Since his arrival, he has become the inspiration for the Green Iguana Project, designed to protect the green iguana, an endangered species.

The project is located on the hotel grounds. You can watch as the collected eggs are incubated and hatched, then see how the little iguanas grow until they are big enough to be left on their own in the jungle. There is a fund set up that allows you to adopt an iguana for US $20. See www.sanignaciobelize.com for more details.

The Casa Blanca Guest House, 10 Burns Avenue, ☎ 824-2080, $$, is new, clean and comfortable – the best bet in town. Each tastefully decorated room has private bath with hot water, tile floors and fans. The owners are friendly and helpful and guests can use a kitchenette to make a cup of tea or a sandwich. This hotel is probably the most secure in downtown San Ignacio.

The New Belmoral, 17 Burns Avenue, ☎ 824-2024, $$, has 11 clean, comfortable rooms, all on the second floor. Some have private baths. If you can, pick a room not overlooking the street, as those are a bit noisy. There is a common sitting area and a balcony that overlooks the action below. The operators of this hotel will do everything they can to make your stay pleasant.

The Hi-Et Hotel, West Street, ☎ 824-2828, $, is a family-run budget hotel. Rooms have a balcony and shared bath, but there is no hot water. Despite that, this quiet hotel is popular.

Martha's Guest House, 10 West Street, ☎ 834-3647, $$, has been around for a long time and some of the rooms are reported to be nice. However, the owner was far too busy balancing her books to show me a room. It seems that the eight rooms have fans and some have private baths.

The Pacz Hotel, 4 Far West Street, ☎ 824-4538, www.paczguesthouse.com, $$, has large clean rooms with private bathrooms. This is a tiny place with only five rooms. You get complimentary coffee in the morning and they are located above Erva's Restaurant, one of the town's best places to eat. The street is very quiet, so noise at night is not a problem.

The Piache Hotel, 18 Buena Vista, ☎ 824-2032, $$, is not on the same property as the San Ignacio Hotel, even though they share an address. The Piache is on the opposite side of the street. It's a comfortable establishment, with a beautiful garden. Rooms are tiny but clean, and come with fans and private baths with hot water.

Tropicool Hotel and Bike Rentals, 30 Burns Street, ☎ 824-3052, $$, is clean and bright. There are shared bathrooms, ceiling fans in each room, a common room with TV, and a laundry facility.

The Venus Hotel, Burns Avenue, ☎ 824-3203, $$, is central and has been totally redone so the clean rooms all have tiled bathrooms, air conditioning and cable TV. The balcony, overlooking the market, is a great place to sit and drink a beer while enjoying the action. The owners are friendly and willing to help.

Hotel Mallorca, 12 Burns Ave., ☎ 824-2960, $$, has large rooms with private baths and large beds. You can have either air conditioning or fan and they also have single rates. The hotel has been remodeled; everything is spanking clean. The staff is friendly and helpful. They take credit cards. This is a good place to stay.

Cahal Pech Village Resort, ☎ 824-3740, www.cahalpech.com, $$$, is on Cahal Pech Hill above San Ignacio and just beyond the ruins. On a clear day, those sitting on the porch can see the Castillo of Xunantunich plus the valley all the way to Guatemala. There are rooms in the main building and cabins interspersed around the property. The thatch-roofed wooden cabins are large and have screened in porches from where you can enjoy the views. The jungle vegetation houses exotic birds like toucans. Everything is clean here. A restaurant serves excellent food (loved the fry jacks) and the swimming pool features a waterfall as a backdrop. There is a gift shop and Internet available. The resort can arrange trips to the caves, Guatemala, Mountain Pine Ridge and Caracol. Some trips can be done by horseback. At one time, there was a disco next door that often disturbed the guests. To rectify the problem, the de Silvas, owners of Cahal Pech, purchased the disco and closed it. They will eventually develop the property into rentals.

El Chiclero Camp Resort, #2 West Ford Young Drive, Cahal Pech Hill, ☎ 824-3132, www.chiclerocampresort.com, $$/$$$, has both rooms in the main building and five native-styled cabins made from bamboo and thatch. The cabins have fans, private baths, two beds, hot water and cable TV. The rooms have the same, plus air conditioning. There is private parking, a gift shop, laundry service and bar and restaurant where the meals are cooked in a clay oven or on a barbeque grill in the Maya fashion. The place is spotless and located within 15 minutes walk of the center of town. They also offer horse riding, bird watching or canoeing trips.

© Chiclero Camp Resort

The West

■ PLACES TO EAT

Nefrys Restaurant, Main St., ☎ 601-5838, offers Mediterranean dishes chosen from the best of Greek, Moroccan, and Lebanese recipes. They are served in stomach-filling quantities at affordable prices, averaging around $14. I hear the pork ribs with plum sauce are excellent. The

RESTAURANT PRICES	
$	$5 to $10
$$	$11 to $25
$$$	$26 to $50
$$$$	$51 to $75
$$$$$	over $75

only drawback is that it takes time for the cook to prepare the dish, so you need to budget a pre-dinner drink into the experience.

Café del Sol, ☎ 822-4899, $$, serves coffee in a garden. Their yogurt smoothies are a must and the French toast is served with lemon cream-cheese in the center. Wow! This is the place to eat fresh-baked muffins, drink coffee, write postcards and hang out. There is also a **book exchange** at the café. The gift shop here has some artistically designed crafts that are worth a look.

Erva's Restaurant, Far West Street below Pacz Hotel, ☎ 824-2821, $. The food is gourmet, and this place remains a favorite for its seafood and pizzas. The coffee is good and the hash browns served with breakfast are second to none in all of Belize. The chicken Cordon Bleu, with mushrooms and a cream sauce, is highly recommended, as are the shrimp cooked in butter and tons of garlic. There are also many vegetarian dishes from which to choose.

Prior to opening in 1997, Erva's was a small Deli patronized by locals and tourists. But Erva is a professional chef and her talents weren't being fully realized, so she opened the restaurant. For me, the smoked pork chops with mushrooms and salad is best.

Eva's Restaurant & Bar, 22 Burns Avenue, ☎ 804-2267, $, is the best place to make connections, collect information, find someone to share a trip. However, it can be a bit noisy and and often you have to listen to a drunk repeating himself while you try to enjoy a beer. It's often hot, too, so sitting outside at the tables on the street is a good option. Stewed chicken with rice is the most popular dish. There is a book exchange and a gift shop.

Hannah's, 5 Burns Street, ☎ 822-3647, $$, across from the Casa Blanca, has good Indian curry. It is all freshly made and served in the best of Indian style. Foods with sauces are the best, as you get far more spice for the price.

Martha's Kitchen, 10 West Street, ☎ 822-2283, $$, has a very nice porch covered in vines. The service is slow and the food unremarkable. I also found the proprietor anything but pleasant. I think maybe Martha has had too many tourists and she no longer appreciates their business. For good coffee and a nice atmosphere, go to Erva's instead.

Maxims Chinese Restaurant, 23 Far West Street, ☎ 822-2283, $$, serves fast and consistently good food. Although the décor is not the fanciest in Belize, the portions are large and the service is good. There is often a long line up of people waiting to take out meals, which is a good sign.

Pop's on West Street, $, is a tiny spot that doesn't have fancy décor, but Pop is a legend so the faithful continue to patronize the place. The breakfasts are okay, but occasionally the food is cold.

The Running West Steak House, 18 Buena Vista (at the San Ignacio Hotel), ☎ 824-2034, $$$, has just been remodeled but the delicious steaks haven't changed. They also have imported wines and serve some delightful dinner drinks. There is also one vegetarian meal on the menu. Have a drink at the Stork Club bar (downstairs), go to the restaurant for a steak and then sleep in one of their rooms.

The Serendip Restaurant, 27 Burns Street, ☎ 822-2302, $$, has south Indian foods. They specialize in seafood, Indian-style. Meals are reasonable and the portions good. The Indian food served here is giving Hannah's a challenge and justifiably so. The only thing that I could criticize is that it doesn't open until 6 pm and often people want to start looking at the menu before then.

The Aguada Hotel, ☎ 804-3609, www.aguadahotel.com, $$, in Santa Elena, offers one of the best meals available in the two towns. Everyone I spoke with constantly reminded me that this was the place to go. Although it is located in Santa Elena, it is not far to walk for those staying in San Ignacio. The food is good, the portions ample and the prices reasonable. Plus, your meal is enjoyed in a pleasant and comfortable atmosphere. I mention it in the San Ignacio section because it is worth the walk up.

Green Dragon Internet Coffee Shop, #8 Hudson Street, ☎ 824-4782, is an Internet Café that used to serve the best cappuccino in town. They also have ice cream that kids believe comes from the Magic Dragon. They sell health foods, books, gifts and arrange

The West

tours. Green Dragon is open from 8 am to 8 pm every day but Sunday. The café was sold shortly after the 5th edition came out and is again for sale (in negotiations) at time of writing. One interested buyer is the owner of the Belize Jungle Dome at Banana Bank. If he takes this over, I can guarantee that it will again become one of the best places in town to hang out and drink coffee.

Chingo's Bar and Grill, Burns Ave, ☎ 804-0142, is fairly new in town and has a pleasant atmosphere, although the prices are a bit high and the quantities a bit low. It is a great place to have a beer.

SAN IGNACIO TO BULLET TREE FALLS

Bullet Tree Falls is northwest of San Ignacio. From the wooden bridge between Santa Elena and San Ignacio, follow the road and keep traveling west. Pass the sports grounds and, instead of turning to go into downtown San Ignacio, keep going straight.

If you do not have your own car, take a taxi (US $7.50) or a *collectivo* (50¢) from the bus station in San Ignacio.

> **SAFETY ALERT**
>
> The road to Bullet Tree Falls is not recommended for cycling or hiking. There have been some hostages taken and some tourists have been robbed by gun-wielding thugs. Women have also been raped. Although it seems that the crimes are targeted toward the higher-end traveler, I think everyone should take care. But things change and robbers get caught. Check in town for the latest information before heading this way by bicycle.

Bullet Tree is a tiny Spanish-speaking village of 2,000 people. It is five miles from San Ignacio. Just beyond the village is where you will find the Maya ruins of El Pilar.

■ THINGS TO DO

Be Pukte Cultural Center, in Bullet Tree on the San Ignacio side of the Mopan River Bridge, is open Friday to Monday, 9 am to 3 pm. The center's name, Be Pukte, means Bullet Tree. Inside, it has a model of El Pilar done to scale. The center also sells handicrafts made by locals. There are wood and slate carvings, but my favorite are the corn-husk dolls. These make a great gift.

The **Fiesta of El Pilar** is a fairly new event that starts around 10 am on the last Saturday of April. The attraction of this party is the exhibition of traditional Maya dances, like the Hog Head, the Moro or La Chatona. Live music from local artists is part of the celebration.

El Pilar ruins are seven miles north of the Mopan River Bridge. There are numerous signs indicating where to go along an all-weather road. The drive or cycle uphill is steep, a total of 900 feet (300 meters) of elevation gain to the ruins. Once at the site you will see a building with a green roof, the caretaker's house. Stop here to pay the US $5 entry fee that includes a map of the trails. There is a picnic area and washroom facilities at the entrance.

The longest trail in the property is less than two miles and goes to Chorro Waterfall along El Pilar Creek. The trails have resting benches. El Pilar Creek starts at the east end of the site and El Manantial Creek is at the west end. What is interesting about this is that neither Tikal nor Caracol had water sources on their properties; they had reservoirs.

El Pilar is on 100 acres of land and the ruins are divided into four sections, with the western section set within Guatemala and thus not accessible from Belize. A huge causeway links the eastern and western sections of the city. It measures 100 feet (30 meters) across in places and is walled on both sides. The purpose of the wall hasn't been established and the final destination of the causeway has not been found. Some suspect that it linked Tikal with El Pilar, since the two centers are only 28 miles apart.

The practice in Belize is to preserve, rather than restore, old sites and when you visit El Pilar you will find much of the city under jungle vegetation. As you walk the trails – there are five in all – you may spot a bit of a building's corner or a staircase leading into a tunnel. A snake may slither from under a shrub or an orchid may be seen blooming on a branch. These things give the site a sense of wildness.

The site, believed to have been occupied from 500 BC to AD 1000, has 25 plazas and numerous temples that stand 50 to 70 feet (15-20 meters) above the plaza floors. The **Wing Temple** in Plaza Copal had eight plaza floors beneath it, indicating about 3,000 years of occupation. Some plazas are up to 1.5 acres in size and the north plaza, called **Nohal Pilar**, has four pyramids and a ball court around it. There is a huge staircase on the north side leading to the plaza and a ramp on the south side.

North of Nohal is **Xaman Pilar**, with palaces that feature underground tunnels and stairways. There is only one door to Xaman

Pilar. This, too, is unusual as numerous exits are always present in Maya buildings, especially in places where the elite resided.

El Pilar has several corbel vaults where each layer of stone juts out over the one below until the two sections of wall meet at the top. This creates a cramped space. Many of the stairways were made with quarried limestone.

In the middle class residential section there are about 540 houses per square mile and the entire site is believed to be about three or four times the size of Tikal.

Currently, Dr. Anabel Ford from the University of California has been excavating at the site. She mapped the area in the 1980s and started excavating in 1993. Dr. Ford has been working consistently at making the site attractive for tourists and at promoting the Be Pukte Cultural Center in the village.

Masewal Forest Garden, www.marc.ucsb.edu/elpilar/education/forest_garden/masewal.html, 1.5 miles down the Paslow Falls Road, belongs to Don Betto, a Maya. Don is knowledgeable in medicinal plants, a skill he learned from his father, who was a famous snake doctor in the area. Betto's 15-acre garden has more than 500 plants. You can go on a guided tour with him and ask all the questions you like, for US $5.

■ PLACES TO STAY

Hummingbird Hills, Paslow Falls Road, ☎ 614-4699 or 413-527-4363, www.hummingbirdhills.com, $$, is located on 12 acres of replanted ranch land. They have three cabins, made of hardwood and thatch. Two cabins sleep four people and have private baths and hot water, fans and mosquito netting. One cabin sleeps only two and has a shared bath. There is also a tenting site and restaurant on the property. The owners have a unique craft; they make jewelry out of recycled copper.

> **AUTHOR NOTE:** *The Maya weave fibers from the agave plant to make hammocks.*

The Parrot Nest, ☎ 820-4058 or 614-6083, www.parrot-nest.com, $$, is on the way into Bullet Tree from San Ignacio. Take a *collectivo* to the village and walk 10 minutes to the lodge. This unique place has two treehouses built in the tips of guanacaste trees. There are also four cabins on stilts and two bathhouses. Cabins have fans and all but one has shared bath facilities. Three sides of the property are bordered by the Mopan River and, since the water is calm, it is a good place for swimming. The on-site **restaurant** serves breakfast (US $4) and/or dinner (US $8) on the verandah, which overlooks the jungle. The owners will cater to dietary needs if you let them know ahead of time.

SAN IGNACIO TO SAN JOSE SUCCOOTZ

▸▸ *Return to the Western Highway and continue from Mile 70 at San Ignacio to the border. The road is good, the resorts first class and the rolling hills a pleasure to watch.*

■ PLACES TO STAY

As you continue along the Western Highway, the road on the right (north) at Mile 71.2 leads to a resort on the Mopan River. **Clarissa Falls Resort**, Box 44, San Ignacio, ☎ 824-3916, $$$, www. belizereport.com/lodging/clarissa. The lodge has 11 thatched-roof cabañas, all

HOTEL PRICES	
$	$20 to $50
$$	$51 to $75
$$$	$76 to $100
$$$$	$101 to $150
$$$$$	over $150

tastefully decorated with Maya weavings. Each cabaña has a fridge, stove, private bath, hot water, fan and electricity. There is also a bunkhouse that is less expensive, a campsite for tenting and an RV park for motor homes. Barbeque pits and picnic tables are interspersed throughout the property.

The resort is neat and tidy, the lawn well kept, and the animals that cross the lawn are fun to watch. Nearby, on the Mopan River, tubing is the sport of choice, and many people choose to visit the ruins up the river and then float down to the lodge. The falls are not huge, but they are pretty. The lodge has tubes for rent at US $5 per

day and transportation to the ruins, where your float trip starts, can be arranged.

There is a very small **golf course** on the property where you can rent a club and ball and play the "where it lands" style of golf. Although there are only five holes, it takes skill to get yourself a hole in one.

The food at Clarissa Falls comes recommended by Belizeans. The most popular dinner is a spaghetti dish cooked with a good dash of garlic, and the *relleno negro* soup is a meal in itself. Each bowl holds a huge piece of chicken, some vegetables and an egg. For dessert, try the rum-soaked fruit cake.

Returning to the Western Highway, take the next road on the right, just a few hundred meters past Clarissa Falls turnoff. It goes to **Nabitunich Lodge**, ☎ 824-2096, www.nabitunich.com, $$$. Nabitunich means "Little Stone Cottage" in Mayan. The lodge and its five stone cottages are located near the banks of the Mopan River. From the garden you can see el Castillo at the Xunantunich ruins; it's a mere 10-minute walk away.

The lodge sits on 400 acres of land that has been owned by the Juan family for several generations. It has an organic vegetable garden as well as a coffee plantation. You can enjoy a meal at the on-site restaurant (meals can be included in the price of your room).

▶▶ *Back on the Western Highway, just after Nabitunich Lodge turnoff, is a secondary road to the left (south) at Mile 72 called the Hydro Dam Road.*

THE HYDRO DAM ROAD

Green Haven Lodge, Box 155, San Ignacio, ☎ 800-889-1512 or 820-4034, www.ghlodgebelize.com, $$$. The owners of the lodge are French, and these well-kept cabins have a taste of France in their décor and their cleanliness. The larger rooms have hardwood floors, tiled bathrooms and Belizean-made furniture. There is a swimming pool or you can play volleyball, badminton or petanque (a game from southern France). If you need to wind down, you can take advantage of the masseuse services.

The **restaurant** offers real French cooking – dishes such as *boeuf bourguignon* or filet mignon – and vegetarian dishes. The desserts are exceptional. The restaurant has the only wine cellar in Belize, as far as I know. The service matches the quality of the food and the setting is romantic. You can eat inside or on the spacious deck, where there is always a breeze.

▶▶ *There is a fork in the road, the right goes to Black Rock, the left to the rest of the resorts.*

Follow signs for the **Black Rock Lodge**, Box 48, San Ignacio, ☎ 824-2341 or 824-3296, www.blackrocklodge.com, $$$. The lodge, nestled into 250 acres of jungle, was previously inaccessible by road, but can now be reached at any time of year. Set on a hill above the Macal River, this first-class hideaway overlooks Black Rock canyon and cliffs. The view is stunning. Each of the slate and thatch cabins has screened, louvered windows, double beds, fans and Belizean art. Some cabins have shared bath. This resort is remote – a good place to visit for an authentic jungle experience.

Visitors often take a **canoe** from the resort and run a few of the smaller rapids on the way into San Ignacio for a beer. The staff at the lodge will pick you and the canoe up once you are done. Or you can go to Vaca Falls for a day of swimming and cave exploring.

One of the things you may see near Black Rock is an oropendola's nest hanging from the trees. Julian Sherrard, the lodge owner (along with his dad), identified this nest for me.

GOLDEN PENDULUM

Oropendola means golden pendulum. The bird is so named because of its long, bright-yellow (*oro*) tail feathers and its hanging nest. These nests, ranging in size from three to six feet (.9-1.8 meters) long, take nine to 11 days to build and there are  often up to 40 nests on one tree. The bird uses palm frond fibers and grass to make the nest. These essentially black birds are polygamous and often the males will fight while protecting their harem. The female lays one or two eggs, which are incubated for 15 days. It takes one month of care before the young ones leave home. They eat insects, grain and seeds and are very gregarious.

Chaa Creek Resort is along the left fork a short way, ☎ 824-2037 or 820-4010, www.chaacreek.com, $$$$$. It sits on 330 acres at the edge of the Macal River and boasts numerous unexcavated Maya ruins. The 19 thatched-roof, Hansel and Gretel-style cabins are exquisite in design and comfort. They are screened, and have porches with sun decks, private baths, mahogany beds, tile floors and original art pieces.

An international reputation speaks for Chaa Creek. In 2002 they won the Condé Nast Ecotourism Award. In 2001 they won the America Society of Travel Agents Environmental Award and the Caribbean Sustainable Tourism Award. In 1998, they won the Green Hotel of the Year Award from American Express and the Caribbean Hotel Association. This year the resort was chosen by the readers of *Travel + Leisure* magazine as one of the 25 best hotels in Mexico, Central and South America. They have also been praised by numerous prestigious magazines (all articles are available at the lodge) and there isn't a local in Belize who won't tell you how superb the resort is. They are often featured on TV travelogues. Chaa Creek, in 2007, received the prestigious Green Globe Award, the first company in Belize to be awarded the world's highest environmental standard certificate. Chaa Creek has been recognized for the work they have done in implementing environmental and social policies.

Chaa Creek has miles of maintained trails for guests to walk, as well as a **Natural History Museum** (open daily, 8 am to 5 pm, US $6 entrance), ☎ 824-2037. The museum displays flora and fauna and has a model of the Macal Valley. You can also peruse the museum's archives and topographic maps of the area.

HOWLING SUCCESS

Chaa Creek's Natural History Center, Yerkes Regional Primate Research Center and the Belize Zoo have worked together to relocate some howler monkeys along the lower Macal River. Yellow fever killed most of the population in Cayo around 40 years ago. Loss of habitation and low diversity resulted in the animals disappearing totally. However, now they are back. The relocation project started with 16 animals being placed in the area. They have flourished and have spread as far as the village of Cristo Rey.

The **Blue Morpho Butterfly Farm** is included in the museum's entry fee. The farm was built so that guests could learn about the four stages the butterfly goes through during its lifecycle.

THE LIFE OF A MORPHO BUTTERLY

The blue morpho, with its iridescent blue wings, is found in rainforests in Central and South America. With a wing span of 13-17 cm (five-seven inches), this king of the butterfly world can fold his wings at night and hang onto the bottom of a leaf or branch so his enemies can't see him.

Morphos eat flowers, leaves, rotting logs, sap and juices. They love the sun and live from a few days up to eight months.

When in the caterpillar stage the morpho is red-brown in color, with patches of lime green. It is cannibalistic. The hairs on the caterpillar are irritating to the skin of humans.

The morpho's enemies are birds, fish, larger insects and people. We use the wings, because of their multi-layered flat fibers, to make clothing. The wings are also used to make jewelry.

The resort has Trek-950 **mountain bikes**, **horses** and **canoes** available to rent. There have been more than 250 different birds spotted on the property, making it a big draw for birders.

Ix Chel Tropical Reserve, which houses a medicine trail (see below), came into being because of the dedicated work of Rosita Arvigo and her husband Greg Shropshire. After moving to Belize in 1981, Rosita worked with Dr. Elijio Panti, the Maya healer from San Antonio who lived to the age of 103. Rosita learned both healing practices and spiritual traditions from Panti.

Ix Chel is the name of the Maya Goddess of medicine.

Besides working with scientific organizations that are researching the uses of medicinal plants for diseases like cancer and AIDS, Rosita and Greg go into areas that are going to be developed or logged to salvage any plants that they don't already have at Ix Chel. The plants are taken to the Terra Nova Medicinal Plant Reserve, located adjacent to Ix Chel. This is a government-sanctioned area, encompassing 6,000 acres. The transplants are done just in case there is danger of the plants going extinct.

Rainforest remedies, herbs and tonics can be purchased at the reserve. For example, the "female tonic" contains, among other things, the man vine, (the "male tonic" does not contain the girl vine, just the man vine). A cold remedy uses black-ass bitters (I don't know what this is, but it sounds interesting) and garlic, while the bark from the gumbo limbo tree is used as a diuretic, and for sores, fever and venereal disease. The use of chinchona for quinine and foxglove for digitalis has been known for a long time. The hope of the reserve is to find other cures from common plants.

Panti Rainforest Medicinal Trail, ☎ 824-3870, www.rainforest-remedies.com, is open daily from 8 am to 4 pm and costs US $5.75 per person. Located above the Macal River and next to the Chaa

Creek Lodge, it can be accessed on foot or by canoe. To canoe is easier, although more complicated to orchestrate.

There is a shelter at the trailhead, where you register and listen to a talk before going on a self-guided tour. You can also hire a guide for an extra US $7.50 to tell you about the plants. However, all the plants are labeled with common and scientific names and their uses are explained.

du Plooy's Resort, Big Eddy, San Ignacio, ☎ 824-3101, www.duplooys.com, $$$$. This is a small place with cottages dotted along the Macal River. There are four room choices. The first is a luxury duplex that has a wraparound porch, large rooms, whirlpool bathtub, coffee maker and fridge. Rooms on the lower level of the duplex have two beds and a couch. The second choice is one of the detached cottages that have private baths and spacious rooms. The third option is a room in the lodge. Finally, there's a seven-bedroom Pink House designed for large families or small groups. Most prices include meals.

This is an ecologically minded resort, so they have tiled roofs instead of cutting palm thatch (to preserve trees), they have no beef on the menu because they don't want more rainforest destroyed for cattle grazing, they use no throw-away containers, and all their vegetable garbage is composted.

The property is lush in vegetation and the late Ken du Plooy had such a green thumb that the family had to start the **Belize Botanical Garden**, www.belizebotanic.org, on the next piece of property in order to get some of the plants out of the hallways of the hotel. Today, the gardens hold over 120 species of orchids. There is also a nursery and two ponds where fish, birds and plants live together. The gardens are often visited by foxes, armadillos, gibnuts and a very shy tapir. One of the projects started here is the growing of xate (shahtay), a plant used by American florists to decorate their arrangements. It will stay alive for up to 45 days after cutting. Plant poachers from

Orchids are the specialty of the Belize Botanical Garden.

Guatemala and Belize have picked it almost to extinction. For more information on this, go to the website.

This is one of the best places to stay if you want to enjoy a lot of wild life, plant life and human comforts. There is so much to explore that leaving the resort would not be necessary for days and days. I also found the owners (daughters of Ken) have taken over and offer the high quality service first started by their father. He would be proud.

Ek Tun, ☎ 303-442-6150 or 824-2002, www.ektunbelize.com, $$$$, is almost at the end of the Hydro Dam Road. This remote little spot has two thatched-roof, hardwood cabins tucked into the jungle. There are private bathrooms with hot water, fans, lots of windows and oil lamps. Each cabin will sleep up to five people. Chosen by *Belize First Magazine* as one of the top 10 most romantic places to stay, and number four in the top 10 jungle lodges, Ek Tun will certainly give you a restful vacation. Meals are included in the price of the rooms.

Martz Farms is 7.9 miles in on the Hydro Dam Road, ☎ 824-3742, www.martzfarm.com, $$. This is the most remote place to stay near San Ignacio and has been recommended by many travelers. Commonly called the Water Hole by ex *chiclero* farmers, the 200 acres are dotted with fish ponds, pasture land and jungle plants. There's also a spring-fed creek that has a 90-foot (27-meter) waterfall that drops into a natural bathing pool (see *Vaca Falls, below)*. The two thatched-roof cabins overlook the Macal River. Both have porches, private bath and fans, but the most popular place now is the tree house set above the waterfall. This wooden structure, perched in a tree, is open all around. If you would like to stay in it, you must reserve early as it is the most popular spot along the road for adventurers. I love it!

Windy Hill Resort, Graceland Ranch, ☎ 824-2017, www.windyhillresort.com, $$$$$, is just two miles (three km) past San Ignacio along the Western Highway. Follow the signs. This is the classy place you can see perched on the hill above San Ignacio. They offer either standard room

rentals or all-inclusive packages. The cabins have private baths and air conditioning or fans, cable TV, and soft beds. On the premises are a bar and restaurant, fitness center, pool, Internet access, gift shop, and tour office. There are also horses for rent and nature trails that you can walk. The food in the restaurant is good and the meals a fair size. Check their website for seasonal specials. This is an excellent establishment and the owners go out of their way to accommodate your needs.

■ THINGS TO DO

 The Trek Stop and Tropical Wings Nature Center is on your left, ☎ 823-2265, www.thetrekstop.com, $. This is a small place with comfortable cabins and tenting pads interspersed throughout a 40-year-old orchard that has mango, avocado and coconut trees. Trails run throughout the 22-acre property, and signs identify plants.

The cabins are small but clean, and each bed has a mosquito net. Those who are tenting can rent a luxury-sized tent and pad or, if you have a tent, you can rent a place to pitch it. The center is close to the border and Xunantunich ruins, so it is an excellent spot for budget travelers. Grocery stores are within walking distance, and you have access to kitchen facilities, laundry and the Internet. Water here is heated by solar panels and there is a composting toilet. The library and friendliness of the owners made me want to stay for weeks.

The Trek Stop has two-person inflatable **kayaks** for rent for US $17.50, **mountain bikes** for US $10 and **inner tubes** for US $6 per day. The interpretive center and butterfly house cost US $2.50 to enter and are worth every penny. The center is collecting more information every year from the scientists (botanist and ethnobiologist) who own the place. They are knowledgeable, liberal minded and fun to be with.

The **restaurant** is one of the most reasonably priced in the area and offers French toast and fry jacks, hamburgers or vegetarian spaghetti, stir-fried vegetables or club sandwiches. If you crave calories, the cheesecake is a must. If that isn't to your liking, how about a hot banana in rum sauce? You can also get a packed lunch to take with you on a day trip.

■ CHECHEM HAH CAVE

 This cave is one of the few with inside architectural work done by the Maya. If you have a car or bike, you can go on your own. Otherwise, you may need to hire a guide in San Ignacio (see page 312 for a list of guides).

To get here, go eight miles on the Hydro Dam Road or the Arenal Road (they are the same) until you see a small sign to the right. The road should not be driven without four-wheel-drive, especially in rainy season. You can walk down to the farm of the Moraleses and they will take you into the cave. There is a US $10 charge for the tour. A steep, 20-minute climb will take you to the cave opening. You should carry water with you.

The Moraleses discovered the cave in 1989 after watching their dogs disappear and then reappear a while later from somewhere in the bush. The family followed the dogs and found the opening to the cave.

The entrance is small and has been secured by stones. There is a locked gate to prohibit looting. The cave is about a quarter-mile long, with ladders and ropes placed to help you climb around. Inside the rooms you will find storage vessels, plates and a stele. It is believed that the cave dates back to 600 BC and was used for storage and as a ceremonial center. Although some things have been removed to the Archeological Center in Belmopan (and the museum in BC) many objects have been left in the cave.

■ VACA FALLS

Vaca Falls are spectacular. They drop about 200 feet (70 meters) from the tiny creek (the one you crossed to get to the Chechem Hah cave) down into the Mopan River. There is a swimming pool near the bottom. The walk down is about 25 minutes and the walk up is only twice as long. Remember to carry drinking water. Also, dampen a scarf to place over your head for your climb back up. It will help keep you cool.

▶▶ *Back on the Western Highway, go to Mile 72.8 and turn left (south) onto a secondary road.*

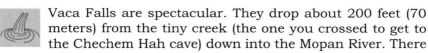

SAN JOSE SUCCOTZ

San Jose Succotz is at Mile 73.1 on the Western Highway. This town of about 1,200 people (most of them Maya) lines the banks of the Mopan River and many of the residents work at the Xunantunich ruins as laborers, caretakers or guides. The town's liveliest times are during fiestas, when traditional Maya dances, food, music and games are enjoyed. The most famous of these fiestas is held in April, when the town celebrates the feast day of St. Joseph. Contact the Trek Stop, ☎ 823-2265, for info.

Historically, the area was occupied by the Maya who, wanting to get along with the Spaniards, had signed a treaty with the Mexican government. This treaty gave the Maya autonomy in return for recognition of the Mexican government. The British, however, wanted

The West

to log mahogany in the area and so they dealt directly with the Maya of San Jose Succotz. This angered other groups loyal to Mexico and they destroyed the village. But the village was soon rebuilt and logging resumed.

Along the road across from the ferry crossing is **Benny's Kitchen** offering Mexican food and fresh juice served on a nice deck. Near Benny's is **La Plaza Café**. **Rolson's** is also along this strip. This is where the famous *minchalta* drink can be purchased. It consists of beer, tomato juice, lime juice and all the hot peppers that can be held in one person's fist. Yikes!

■ XUNANTUNICH RUINS

 These are the most accessible ruins in all of Belize, reachable by bus, car, bike or on foot. Whichever mode of transportation you choose, you'll have to take the little hand-operated ferry across the Mopan River (it carries cars). There is no charge for the ferry, but your entry ticket to the ruins must be turned over to the ferry operators on your trip back.

The ruins are open daily from 8 am to 5 pm and the cost is US $5 per person. The ferry quits for an hour every day during lunchtime. If your bags are getting heavy to lug around, leave them with the ferry operators.

There are numerous licensed guides at the ferry dock. If you are even remotely interested in archeology, hire one. The charge is US $15 an hour for two people.

After driving or walking the .6 miles uphill, you will be greeted by the imposing tower of El Castillo. At the entrance to the site are toilets, a picnic spot and a museum. Inside the museum is an impressive scale reproduction of the ruins. There are also some stelae that were found at the site and a replica of the frieze found on El Castillo. The replica makes it much easier to identify what archeologists tell us is on the frieze.

HISTORY

Located on a limestone ridge, Xunantunich was originally investigated in 1895 by **Thomas Gann**, the British Medical Officer who was the first to visit many of the Maya sites in Belize. The next one to stomp around the ruins was **Teobert Mahler**, who photographed El Castillo and turned the pictures over to the Peabody Museum at Harvard University. He also mapped the main plaza.

Gann returned in 1924 and unearthed some burial sites. Some suspect that he removed the treasures from inside the tombs and some of the glyphs found around the main plaza. Whether he did or not, those treasures are gone.

Eric Thompson was the next to poke around Xunantunich. He uncovered a few ceramics from the late classic period that were buried in the area west of the main plaza. This is where the middle class Maya resided.

Linton Satterthwaite from the University of Pennsylvania, was the next to work at the site and he uncovered most of El Castillo's very well-preserved frieze that incorporates the carving of Venus shifting from morning to evening star.

From the early 1950s until 1979, a plethora of archeologists came and went. They uncovered bits and pieces, but it wasn't until **Dr. Prendergast** and **Elizabeth Graham** of the Royal Ontario Museum arrived in 1979 that serious work was done.

Xunantunich means "Maiden of the Rock" in Mayan, but in the early part of this century the ruin was often referred to as **Benque Viejo**. The name Xunantunich comes from one of the carved monuments showing a ruler with a headdress.

MAYA DAY NAMES & THEIR MEANINGS

Imix . . sea dragon/water/wine
Ik . . . . air/life
Akbal . . . . night
Kan . . . . corn
Chicchan . . . . serpent
Cimi . . . . death
Manik . . . . deer/grasp
Lamat . . . . rabbit
Muluc . . . . rain
Oc. . . . . dog
Chuen . . . . monkey
Eb . . . . broom
Ben . . . . reed
Ix . . . . jaguar
Men. . . . . bird/eagle/wise one
Cib. . . . . owl/vulture
Caban. . . . . force/earth
Eznab. . . . . flint/knife
Cauac . . . . storm
Ahau . . . . lord

*These names were taken from the book, **Mayan Calendar Made Easy**, by Sandy Huff (self published). Most names are in agreement with other references, but the odd one is totally different. For an example, Chuen means monkey according to Huff, but frog according to other sources.*

Sunset at Xunantunich.

EXPLORING THE RUINS

The largest pyramid and the main attraction is **El Castillo**. It stands at 130 feet (40 meters) above the plaza floor. You can climb to the top for a look at the surrounding countryside (well worth the climb). This is the second-highest structure in Belize; the highest is at Caracol.

It was on El Castillo that the famous **frieze** was found. Looking at the frieze, the man with the big ears and earrings is the Sun God, Kinich Ahua. Beside him is the moon and then the signs that stand for Venus. The frieze also incorporates signs for the different days in the Maya calendar. The carved stone, which went all the way round the pyramid, was covered in plaster and then painted.

There are six major **plazas** and more than 25 **temples**. A **ball court** behind (south of) El Castillo is believed to have been abandoned early, maybe at the same time as Tikal fell. The ball court was about 30 by 60 feet (10 by 20 meters) in size – it was not an extremely big one.

The family lines of Maya rulers were unable to keep power for very long. Two hundred years seems to be longest ruling period, after which the family was overthrown and another line crowned. The main plaza was elevated and partitioned off from the rest of the

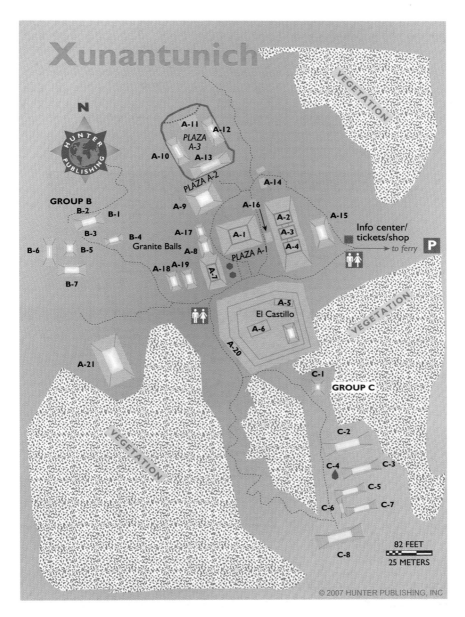

site, indicating that during the last years of Xunantunich's existence, the ruling class was in conflict.

Eight **stelae** and two **altars** have been found in the central group. Most are plain, probably because they were originally covered in plaster and painted with glyphs. Of the carved ones, two fell down. One landed face up and was weather-worn over the years, render-

The West

ing the glyphs unreadable. However, carvings on the altar that landed face-down are still visible. They focus on fertility and warlords (apparently, warlords were a sign of fertility).

The group of buildings to the west of the main plaza is in disrepair. A small grave was found in one of the platforms. It was that of a female who had extensive dental work done, indicating that she may have been upper class. Her upper incisors were notched and her lowers were notched and then resurfaced. She had a ceramic whistle to accompany her to heaven.

MY MY MAYA TIME

According to the Maya calendar, each day of the 20-day month had a name and number and each month had a name and number. This resulted in each day having four titles; one for the number and one for the name of the day and then one for the number and one for the name of the month.

About 1.6 miles north of the main plaza is the city of **Actuncan**, which has a 27-meter (88.5-foot) pyramid. A stele found there indicates that the city was the predecessor of Xunantunich.

It was around AD 890-900 that Xunantunich was abandoned. Some believe this was due to an earthquake.

■ PLACE TO STAY

Across the highway from the ruins is the first-class **Royal Mayan Resort and Spa**, ☎ 823-2497 or 888-271-3483, www.royalmayan.com, $$$$, located on a hill that truly makes it royal. Well-kept rooms come complete with TV, private bath, hot water and air conditioning. The spa offers a pool, gym, sauna, Jacuzzi (overlooking the ruins) and a massage parlor. If you need to be pampered, this may be the place. There is also a **restaurant** and bar on site.

The resort will pick you up at the airport and arrange any type of tour you want, from horseback riding to caving to shopping. Special rates are offered for long stays and all-inclusive packages are possible.

BENQUE VIEJO DEL CARMEN

Benque Viejo del Carmen, Mile 74.5 of the Western Highway, is almost at the end of the road/country. The village of Benque has about 5,000 people and most are Spanish-speaking.

■ HISTORY

The Maya living here are from the **Chan Maya**, the last to be subdued by the Spanish. This didn't happen until 1697. After the British came along, logging became the major industry of the area. The name remained Spanish and it means "Old Bank," with bank referring to a logging settlement.

Today, the town has a hospital, town hall, a number of government offices, a post office, church and cemetery. There are a few places to eat and stay, although most people go on to The Trek Stop (see page 302) in San Jose Succotz or into San Ignacio. The town's most exuberant festival occurs on July 16th in honor of the patron saint, Our Lady of Mount Carmel. As with all Maya festivals, there is dancing, music, food and fun.

■ THINGS TO DO

The **El Ba'lum Art Gallery**, 43 Churchill Drive, is more of an art museum than gallery. It has many artifacts related to the art world that are of interest, from musical instruments to photographs.

The **Chechem Hah Cave** and **Vaca Falls** are also just south of Benque along the Hydro Dam Road (see pages 302 and 303).

Poustinia Earth Art Park is three miles out of Benque. Contact Luis Alberto or Deborah Ruiz, ☎ 822-3532, www.poustiniaonline.org, for more details. Located on 270 acres of land, this is where artists come to express themselves in the new medium called earth art. Earth art occurs when an artist creates a piece of work and lets the natural world, in this case the jungle, re-work the piece. This is when artist and nature unite in creation.

Established in 1997 by Luis Alberto Ruiz with the help of his London-based teacher, Adrian Barron, Poustinia was registered as a not-for-profit entity. Poustinia has had artists and writers come from around the world to design and create. Some use man-made items in combination with natural elements to create their works, while others use only rock and soil. Artists wanting to contribute to the park must produce sculptures that are three-dimensional and use stones, wood, living trees, seedlings, concrete, metals and plastics from dump sites. The final expression should project how human art and nature can co-exist.

Sixty acres of the land is in traditional garden with an arboretum that has some rare and endangered hardwoods of Central America. There are also Maya mounds, ponds and trails throughout the area. Originally a cattle farm, the land has gone back to its natural vegetation with the remains of things like a sugar grinder, Maya mounds and ponds where cattle once drank being transformed into pleasing items rather than discarded objects. Artists have come from England, Wales, Norway, Brazil, Guyana, Barbados, Venezuela and the United States to blend culture and art into this new environmentally sensitive park. Artists Manuel Piney from Venezuela, Ian Steadman from England and David Stewart from the US have been working on their projects this year. Stewart has completed his. If you need a letter of invitation to apply for funding, the Board of Directors is happy to review your project.

The two **Eldorado cabins** at Poustinia are fully equipped with stove, kitchen utensils, bed linen and towels. There is running water and generated electricity. A cabin will hold up to six people and the cost is US $80 for a double and US $20 for each additional person. Transportation to and from the center can be arranged, as can transportation for shopping. There is a charge for this. Call ahead to make arrangements.

SHOPPING

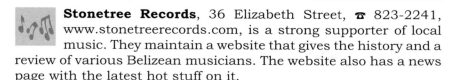

Stonetree Records, 36 Elizabeth Street, ☎ 823-2241, www.stonetreerecords.com, is a strong supporter of local music. They maintain a website that gives the history and a review of various Belizean musicians. The website also has a news page with the latest hot stuff on it.

PLACES TO STAY

The Mopan River Resort, Riverside North, ☎ 823-2074, www.mopanriverresort.com, $$$$$, is owned by Pam and Jay Picon, who worked for *Belize Report* (published by Belize Tourism). They have a good insight on what tourists want. This is an all-inclusive resort, meaning that the room, the food, the drinks and the tours are included in the price.

All 12 cabins are hardwood and thatch with large sitting areas, cable TV, fans, mini-bars, in-room safes and double sinks in the bathrooms. The verandahs are pleasant for bird watching or just sitting. The main lodge has a huge open-air deck, where you can enjoy either Thai, Italian, Mediterranean or Mexican dinners. Hors d'oeuvres are served before every dinner, along with your evening cocktail. And homemade cinnamon buns are offered to help sweeten your coffee in the mornings.

There's a swimming pool, a 20-foot birding tower and live entertainment twice a week. You can canoe, kayak, raft or hike independently. One of the excursions included in the price is a day at Tikal, but it is offered only on Tuesdays and Fridays. If you want to participate, plan to be here on either of those days.

The **Maya Hotel** on George Street has rooms that could be used in a pinch, but I would much rather go the extra mile and stay at the Mopan or in San Ignacio.

PLACES TO EAT

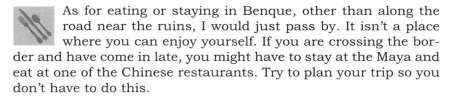

As for eating or staying in Benque, other than along the road near the ruins, I would just pass by. It isn't a place where you can enjoy yourself. If you are crossing the border and have come in late, you might have to stay at the Maya and eat at one of the Chinese restaurants. Try to plan your trip so you don't have to do this.

The West

DIRECTORIES

■ GENERAL DIRECTORY

THE WEST – GENERAL DIRECTORY		
■ OUTFITTERS, GUIDES & TOUR OPERATORS		
Belizean Sun Travel	☎ 601-2630	belizeansun@btl.net
Easy Rider	☎ 824-3734	www.belizex.com/easy_rider.htm
Intl Archaeological Tours	☎ 824-3991	
Mayawalk	☎ 824-3070	www.mayawalk.com
Mountain Rider	☎ 820-4036	
■ ATTRACTIONS		
Belize Zoo	☎ 820-2004	www.belizezoo.org
Caracol Ruins		www.caracol.org
Green Hills Butterfly Ranch	☎ 820-4017	www.belizex.com/green_hills.htm
Monkey Bay Wildlife Sanctuary	☎ 820-3032	www.monkeybaybelize.org
Old Belize Historical Center	☎ 222-4286	www.oldbelize.com
Panti Rainforest Medicinal Trail	☎ 824-3870	www.rainforestremedies.com
Poustinia Earth Art	☎ 823-2084	www.angelfire.com/pe/poustinia
Tanah Maya Art Museum		www.awrem.com/tanah/experience.html
■ TRANSPORTATION		
Safe Tours Car Rental	☎ 824-3731	dcpil@yahoo.com
Western Auto	☎ 628-8987	
■ GROUP RESOURCES		
Dept. of Archeology	☎ 822-2106 or 822-2227	
Habitat for Humanity	☎ 227-6818	habelize@btl.net
LABRN Scholarship Foundation	☎ 323-732-0200	
■ SERVICES		
Techno Hub (Internet service)	☎ 822-0061	
■ USEFUL WEBSITE		
Belize Tourism		www.belizetourism.org
■ SHOPPING		
Art Box, The	☎ 822-2233	www.artboxbz.com
Belize Gift Shop	☎ 824-4159	
Caesar's Palace	☎ 824-2341	www.belizegifts.com
Indita Maya Gift Shop	☎ 824-4346	
Lisa's Boutique	☎ 824-3366	

■ ACCOMMODATIONS DIRECTORY

THE WEST – PLACES TO STAY	
Aguada Hotel ($$)	☎ 804-3609; www.aguadahotel.com
Almond Hill Motel ($$)	☎ 225-1088; obsession@btl.net
Banana Bank Lodge ($$$$)	☎ 820-2020; www.bananabank.com
Belize Jungle Dome ($$$$)	☎ 822-2124; www.belizejungledome.com
Belmopan Hotel ($$$)	☎ 822-2130
Black Rock Lodge ($$$)	☎ 824-2341; www.blackrocklodge.com
Blancaneaux Lodge ($$$$$)	☎ 820-3878; www.blancaneaux.com
Bull Frog Inn ($$$)	☎ 822-2111; bullfrog@btl.net
Caesar's Place $$)	☎ 824-2341; www.belizegifts.com
Cahal Pech Village Resort ($$$)	☎ 824-3740; www.cahalpech.com
Casa Blanca Guest House ($$)	☎ 824-2080
Chaa Creek Resort ($$$$$)	☎ 824-2037; www.chaacreek.com
Clarissa Falls Resort ($$$)	☎ 824-3916; www.belizereport.com/lodging/clarissa
Crystal Paradise ($$$)	☎ 824-2014; www.crystalparadise.com
DuPlooy's Resort ($$$$)	☎ 824-3101; www.duplooys.com
Ek Tun ($$$$)	☎ 824-2002 or 303-442-6150; www.ektunbelize.com
El Chicleroi Camp Resort ($$-$$$)	☎ 824-3132; www.elchicleroicampresort.com
El Rey Inn ($)	☎ 822-2841
Five Sisters Lodge ($$$)	☎ 820-4005; www.fivesisterlodge.com
Green Haven Lodge ($$$)	☎ 820-4034; www.ghlodgebelize.com
Hibiscus Hotel ($$)	☎ 722-1418; www.hibiscus@btl.net
Hidden Valley Inn ($$$$$)	☎ 822-3320; www.hiddenvalleyinn.com
Hi-Et Hotel ($)	☎ 824-2828
Hummingbird Hills ($$)	☎ 614-4699; www.hummingbirdhills.com
Jaguar Paw Jungle Resort ($$$$$)	☎ 820-2032
Log Cabins ($$-$$$)	☎ 824-3367; www.logcabins-belize.com
Martha's Guest House ($$)	☎ 834-3647
Martz Farms ($$)	☎ 824-3742; www.martzfarms.com
Maya Mountain Lodge ($$$)	☎ 824-2164; www.mayamountain.com
Mopan River Resort ($$$$$)	☎ 823-2074; www.mopanriverresort.com
Mountain Equestrian Trails ($$$$$)	☎ 820-4041; www.metbelize.com
Nabitunich Lodge ($$$)	☎ 824-2096; www.nabitunich.com
New Belmoral ($$)	☎ 824-2024
Pacz Hotel ($$)	☎ 824-4538
Parrot Nest ($$)	☎ 820-4058; www.parrot-nest.com
Piache Hotel ($$)	☎ 804-2032
Pine Ridge Lodge ($$$$)	☎ 606-4557; www.pineridgelodge.com

THE WEST – PLACES TO STAY	
Pook's Hill Lodge ($$$)	☎ 820-2017; www.pookshillbelize.com
Royal Mayan Resort ($$$$)	☎ 823-2497; www.royalmayan.com
San Ignacio Hotel ($$$$)	☎ 822-2034
Touch of Class Comfort Inn ($$)	☎ 824-4006; www.touchofclasscomfortinn.com
Trek Stop ($)	☎ 823-2265; www.thetrekstop.com
Tropicool Hotel ($$)	☎ 824-3062
Tropical Education Center ($$)	☎ 220-8003
Venus Hotel ($$)	☎ 824-3203
Warrie Head Lodge ($$$$)	☎ 227-7185; www.warriehead.com
Windy Hill Resort ($)	☎ 824-2017; www.windyhillresort.com

■ RESTAURANT DIRECTORY

THE WEST – PLACES TO EAT	
Aguada Hotel Restaurant ($$)	☎ 806-3609
Braun's Family Restaurant (n/k)	☎ 823-0196
Bullforg Inn ($$)	☎ 822-2111
Café del Sol ($$)	☎ 822-4899
Caldium Restaurant ($$)	☎ 822-2754
Cheers Restaurant ($)	☎ 614-9311
Chingo's Bar & Grill ($)	☎ 804-0142
Erva's Restaurant ($$)	☎ 824-2821
Eva's Restaurant ($)	☎ 804-2267
Golden Choice Buffet (n/k)	☎ 823-0421
Green Dragon ($)	☎ 824-4782
Hannah's Restaurant ($$)	☎ 822-3647
JB's Watering Hole(n/a)	☎ 820-2071
Martha's Kitchen ($$)	☎ 822-2283
Maxims Chinese Restaurant ($$)	☎ 822-2283
Nefry's Restaurant ($$)	☎ 601-5838
Rong Feng Restaurant (n/k)	☎ 823-2688
San Ignacio Hotel facilities ($$$)	☎ 822-2034
Serendip Restaurant ($$)	☎ 822-2302

Guatemala

The Belize-Guatemala border is at Mile 76, 1.2 miles from Benque, and you can either take a taxi or walk, but be warned that this is a country road and the journey seems far longer than a mile because of the excruciating heat. There is not a blade of grass to offer shade along this stretch. Go out St. Josephs Street one block past the cemetery, turn left (south) and follow the road. Most people who cross here make the side-trip to Tikal.

GETTING HERE

BY AIR

If it is rainy season, flying is better than traveling overland. You can fly to Flores, Guatemala by **Maya Air** (☎ 800-225-6732, 226-2435, www.ambergrisecaye.com/islandair) or **Tropic Air** (☎ 800-422-3435, 226-2012 in Belize, www.tropicair.com). Both have two flights daily leaving from Belize City. From Flores, the airlines will arrange ground transportation to Tikal.

ORGANIZED TOURS

All tour companies offer trips to Tikal. Most are by van and most go only for one day. This option allows you a fairly knowledgeable tour guide but cuts your time at the ruins to a minimum. The price of these tours has gone up drastically because the border

Stepped pyramids.

© George Bailey

now charges US $20 per person to leave the country, whether you leave for three minutes or the rest of your life.

■ BY CAR

Driving a rental vehicle requires special insurance. Be certain that you have this before leaving Belize. See page 100 for a full list of vehicle rental agencies.

If driving your own vehicle, you will be issued a permit to drive in Guatemala. You must have a valid International, Canadian or American drivers license and registration papers for your vehicle. The Guatemala driving permit is valid for 30 days and may be renewed in major centers (there are no places where you can renew between Tikal and Belize). You can purchase liability insurance in the major centers in Guatemala, but all other coverage must be bought in your home country.

■ BY BICYCLE

Cycling should be done during daylight hours only. The roads are now paved all the way to Tikal and south to Guatemala City. Plan the stages of your trip and pace yourself so that you are in a village before dark. It is 37 miles from Melchor on the border to Los Cruces junction (also called Ixlu Junction) and another 1.2 miles to El Remate. Tikal is an additional 20 miles past Remate. From the border, it is a long cycle in the heat on black pavement, although there are places to stay in Melchor, Los Cruces, El Remate and Tikal.

MONEY

Once at the border you can obtain currency with **money changers** or you can go to an **ATM** in Flores. The exchange rate is seven quetzales for one US dollar. Dealing with money changers, you may get a bit less than the going rate at the bank, but the more you exchange, the better the rate. Using US cash for exchange will also result in a better rate than changing Belize dollars. Money changers will now accept traveler's checks and give you the same rate as cash.

There is a **bank** on the Guatemala side of the border that is open from 8:30 am to 6 pm on weekdays, but it doesn't have an ATM. There is also a service charge for changing traveler's checks. But why bother with the bank when the money changers will exchange the checks for you with no service charge?

If going to Tikal, you should have enough quetzales to last until you get to a bigger center, such as Flores, or you return to Belize. There are no money changers or banks at Tikal itself and, although the big hotels take charge cards, they will not give you a cash advance. If you plan to visit Flores, you will need money for transportation, food and a room.

Once across the border, you will find everything is cheaper than in Belize, sometimes 50% less. However, there is far more bartering for goods and services. Being a foreigner, you will usually be expected to pay more.

CUSTOMS & VISAS

Everyone needs a visa (10 quetzals, less than $2) to enter Guatemala. Travelers from developed countries like America, Canada and Europe should have no problem getting one at the border. You simply pay your shekels and away you go. People from developing nations such as Botswana, Yeman, Moldova or Bangladesh must apply to the Guatemalan Immigration Department for a pre-approved visa. I've always got mine at the border with no problem, but I have heard of others who were turned away. Since this procedure changes periodically, check with the consulate on Church Street in Benque, ☎ 823-2531.

You will be charged an exit fee and a Conservation Fee when leaving Belize, a total of almost US $20. This fee is charged every time you leave Belize. Also be aware that the border guards will sometimes refuse to give you a full 30-day visa when entering Belize. The only way to get extra days is to apply for an extension at the cost of $25.

While in Belize this last time I heard over and over that corruption was seeping into the government. This to me seems like exploitation of the visitor and it will do nothing to help Belize.

IN GUATEMALA

■ OVER THE BORDER

Once over the border, **Spanish** is the language so you'd better pull out your dictionary. Buses will be waiting at the border or at the market in Melchor, a short walk away. They go when full or almost full. Also, minivans and taxis go to Los Cruses, Flores, El Remate and Tikal on a regular basis. The cost is US $10 per person. This is the easiest way to go.

Food is always offered in or near markets. Women have plates of tortillas, sandwiches, fruits, eggs and empanadas. Pop is safe to drink, as is mineral water. Drink as much as you want. The bus driver will stop for bathroom breaks anytime you wish. Usually.

■ DESTINATIONS

Decide where you want to go. **Santa Elena** is on the shore of **Lake Petén Itza** and **Flores** is on an island connected to the mainland by a causeway. Flores is the more popular destination. There is every possible class of hotel in Flores and numerous cafés in which to eat and hang out. Tour agencies can provide almost any service you may want.

If you're going directly to **Tikal**, then you have the option of staying in **El Remate**, just 1.2 miles north of Los Cruces (if it is light enough you can walk to El Remate from Los Cruces) and 20 miles south of Tikal. Or you can go all the way into Tikal and stay there. There are also places to stay in Los Cruces, but El Remate is far more interesting and just two km up the road.

A good taxi driver is **Otto Hernandez**, ☎ 5-875-3369, who will take you all the way to Flores or over to El Remate/Tikal. He is not a speed demon nor is he a snail, and he is willing to speak English so he can tell you what you are passing as you head down the road.

A ROUND-UP OF ACCESSIBLE MAYA RUINS

The Maya ruins in this area are numerous and, unless you are a true archeologist looking for a new project, you may not want to visit them all. Some have been partially excavated and others are under thick jungle growth. Some would take days to reach and are no more than a mound in the jungle. There are 23 named sites within 24.5 square miles. A few of these are accessible by ground transportation (walking/cycling/mule/bus) or by air. Here's a brief description of some sites, most of which have been looted to a degree.

Manantiel is just across the border. The name means "spring water." There has been some excavation by American University students.

Topoxte is on Lake Yaxja and is best reached by boat from the village of El Sombrero. Restoration is in progress. The site is small and it was not of political importance during the height of the Maya kingdoms.

Nakum is 12 miles north of Yaxja and to get there you will need to take a trail through the jungle.

Holmul is located on a ridge about 24 miles north of Manantiel. To reach it, follow the road from Melchor going north. It can be walked or cycled. There has been a lot of exploration, excavation and looting at this site. The ceramics found here are similar to those of Xultun. The city sits on about 35 acres of land on top of a hill. It's not a big city, but already looters have devastated some of the buildings. However, the vaulted rooms are in good condition. A causeway joins one section to another. The highest pyramid is about 41 feet (12.5 meters) above the plaza floor.

Xultun is on the Rio Azul, north of Yaxje. Xultun was a vassel state of Tikal. Although much has been looted at Xultun, there was an unusual pot with a screw top lid found here by archeologist REW Adams.

El Mirador was discovered in 1926 and it predates Tikal. This site is accessible from the north shore of Lake Petén Itza. It is about 61 miles from the lake and the last 24 miles are mostly on a trail and very bad road. Spectacular artifacts have been taken from Mirador. It has the highest structure of all the Maya pyramids, Dante Pyramid, which rises 216 feet (65 meters) above the plaza floor. Mirador was abandoned in about AD 100.

Xachun is 15 miles north of Tikal and accessible during dry season by bike or four-wheel-drive vehicle. The oldest building ever found in the Petén is located at this site. It dates back to 2000 BC. The archeologists who first came to excavate did some damage to the temples when they were looking for grave sites. This damage has been partially rectified by plastering with mortar to keep the buildings together.

Ceibal, Aguateca and **Tamarindito** are all reached by boat from Sayaxche, on the opposite side of the river from the road. (The ferry that runs across the river takes cars.) There are basic places to stay in Sayaxche and food is never a problem as long as you are not fussy. Ceibal is 11 miles from Sayaxche up the Rio de la Pasion. Although the ruins aren't big, the stele found here is intricately carved and shows a warrior with spear.

■ EL REMATE

El Remate is a small village about three km after Los Cruses and 20 miles/33 km south of Tikal on the east end of Lake Peten Itza. It is home to 200 families and offers many types of accommodations and places to eat, from the five-plus star hotel belonging to Francis Ford Coppola to the little Guatemalan *hospadaje*. Prices range from US $7 per person in a dorm up to a couple of hundred for luxury accommodations.

GETTING HERE

Buses/minivans go to Las Cruces every hour and cost 20 quetzals per person. There is also a van that goes from Las Cruces to El Remate for 5 quetzals per person. If you miss this one, walk – it's just three kilometers. A taxi from the border into El Remate runs 200 quetzals and can be shared with up to four people. If there are five people, you will be charged 250 quetzals.

THINGS TO DO

Most travelers stay in Remate and then take a **minivan** to the ruins between 4:30 and 5:30 am so they can capture the ambiance of the rising sun. Vans return at around 2 pm and cost $6 per person. Tickets can be purchased at your hotel, where you will be picked up and delivered after your visit to Tikal. The vehicles are in good shape and reliable. Take a lunch with you as the expensive food at the ruins is not very good and the portions are tiny.

Yaxja Nakum National Park, located on Lake Yaxja, is a popular place to visit even though there is only one temple. This is because an episode of *Survivor* was filmed here, thus making the site known. You can hire a van to take you to the site or you can go to Los Cruses and then take a van going to the border, getting off at the road going to the park. Or, you can hire a guide and van in El Remate to take you. Ask at your hotel.

Cerro Cahui Park is one kilometer down the road, past Don David's. The park is open from 8 am to 4 pm and costs 20 quetzals to enter. There are two groomed trails that you can follow; one is shorter than the other. The longer one takes about three hours to walk and has some elevation gain so the lookouts reveal both Lake Peten Itza and Lake Yaxja and their surrounding valleys. However, the biggest draw is to see and hear the howler monkeys. I saw about a dozen. There are also spider monkeys to be seen.

Camino Real is a trail along the lake that goes toward Las Cruces. This is an excellent area to look for birds. **La Lancha** will take you onto the lake and up the river nearby for less than $20 a day. See Don David for the boat excursion.

Study Spanish at Ixmucane, liotucomar@yahoo.com, located just off the main road (follow signs), charges just over $100 for 20 hours of lessons plus home stay. This is a deal! They also offer horses for rent that can be taken on the Camino Real.

PLACES TO STAY & EAT

Casa de Don David, on the lake about 200 feet after the turn off the main road, ☎ 5-306-2190 or 7-928-8469, www.lacasadedon

david.com, $$, is the most popular place. If you really want to stay here, make reservations before you arrive. It is popular for a reason. The well-tended gardens around which the rooms are situated go down to the lake. There are many birds hiding in the vegetation, sipping on the nectar of the flowers. You can watch them from the gazebo that is to one side of the lawn. Each room is nicely decorated and has a private bath, hot water and air conditioning. Internet is complementary for guests and the hotel accepts both Visa and MasterCard. Don David can change money if you are in dire straights, but it is best that you bring enough money with you. There is a nice gift shop on site that sells a lot of local carvings. Don David has lived in Peten since the 1970s. Before moving to the present site he owned a hotel at Las Cruces. David works hard with locals helping them establish services for tourists. He has married a local lady and has dedicated his life to the region. If you have any questions, David will probably be able to help you.

The **restaurant** at Don David's serves the kind of food tourists want, like hamburgers along with cold Guatemalan beer (way better than Belikin). Sit in his open-air dining room and enjoy the gardens with all its wildlife. The service is as first class as the food.

Mon Ami, $/$$, about .6 miles (one km) down the road along the lake, has lovely dorms with four beds to a loft. There is tons of room for each dweller and the rooms are bright. They also have cabins with private baths tucked into the jungle. The restaurant, set under a palapa, serves very good food.

Posada Ixchel, $, on the main road just before it splits, has comfortable cabins that are large, clean and have porches. There are no private bathrooms but the communal ones are very clean and there are enough that you don't have to wait. The owners are helpful and accommodating. This is a good place to stay.

Las Gardinias, $$, on the main road just at the split, has rooms with private bath and hot water. The rooms are clean and comfortable and the restaurant is always full of foreigners so you know the food is good. The Internet, however, is slow and expensive.

Other places along the road are constantly being built in both traditional Maya style and modern North American style. The places I have named are just samples of what is available. The farther along the lake you go, the more surprised at the quality you will be. Have a look around. Take your time. Enjoy El Remate - it is a good place to be.

TIKAL NATIONAL PARK

Tikal National Park occupies 226 square miles of ruins and jungle in the northern Petén region of Guatemala. For me, Tikal is the most mystical place on the planet. Although I haven't been to every interesting site on earth, I found Tikal more special than the Great Wall of China, the Pyramids of Egypt, the temples of Thailand, the monasteries of Tibet, or Machu Picchu in Peru. If you are able to visit early in the morning, just at sunset or during a full moon, you too will come away with a feeling of splendor. I am not the only one who believes that Tikal is splendid – about 25,000 tourists a year come to the park.

Tikal not only has impressive restored pyramid temples in the main plaza, but also some wild jungle that clutches onto parts of the city. Birds and animals hide in these jungles, as do snakes. And the site is huge – it takes hours to walk around the main plazas. If you want to really explore, it takes days.

■ RECENT HISTORY

 It was in 1848 that **Modesto Mendez** and **Ambrosio Tut** came to Tikal with an artist by the name of **Eusebio Lara**. Lara drew while the others wrote a brief description of the city and their work was published in the Berlin Academy of Science Magazine in 1853.

The next to visit Tikal was **Dr. Gustav Bernoulli** of Switzerland, who instigated the removal of carved wooden lintels from Temples I and IV. These ended up at the museum in Basel.

Percival Maudslay, an Englishman, came in 1881 and mapped the major archeological features. A German named **Teobet Mahler** came representing the Peabody Museum of Harvard University, photographing everything he could. Many came after Mahler, including **Sylvanus Morley** for whom the museum is named. Morley excavated the site and tried to prevent looting.

The ruins of Tikal were first declared a national monument in 1931, shortly after S. Morley stopped excavating in Guatemala. It wasn't made into a park until 1955 and was the first such park in Central America. In 1979 it became a World Heritage Site and, finally in 1990, the reserve was added to encompass more of the ruins and wild jungle area around them.

■ EXPLORING THE PARK

The park covers 142,328 acres and the central city fills 10 square miles. There are 344 people employed in Tikal in positions of administration, resource management, education, research and research assistance. There are also grounds keepers and trail clearers, guards and caretakers.

A daily entrance fee of US $10 is collected as you come into the area. If you arrive after 3 pm you will be given a ticket for the next day. Dogs and firearms are not allowed in the park. Parking of a vehicle is US $4 a day.

Inside the park you will find three hotels, all of which have restaurants. Besides these eateries there are three *comedores* that offer meals at inflated prices. Tenting is permitted near the restaurants, and hammocks are available to rent.

> **AUTHOR NOTE:** *Carry water at all times. The atmosphere can be dehydrating.*

The **Sylvanus Morley Museum** is open Tuesday to Sunday, 9 am to 5 pm. Admission is US $2 per person. Morley was an archeologist who worked in the Petén between 1914 and 1928. He was interested in the inscriptions of the Maya and, under the Carnegie Institute of Washington, managed to record many of the works at Piedras Negras and Uaxactun. He wrote two books, *Ancient Maya* (1946) and *Inscriptions of Petén* (1938).

The museum displays artifacts from tombs, such as ceramics and jade, bone and stone carvings. It also has replicas of stelae and friezes from Tikal. But the best exhibit is a reproduction of Temple I, where King **Jasaw Chan K'awiil** was laid to rest upon jaguar and ocelot pelts. There were over 16 pounds (seven kg) of jade jewelry on his body and he wore a cape covered in pink and orange seashells. Although he was a tall man for his time (about 5' 5", 1.7 meters), the heavy ornaments he was buried in must have been made specifically for death as they would be too heavy to wear during life. We know from the information found in Tikal that his mother's name was Lady Jaguar Cushion and that he built the first great pyramid in honor of his wife. He defeated and killed rival Calakmul, so that K'awiil's control of the trade was secure. One stele says that he lived beyond 40 years of age, and archeologists believe he was around 60 when he died. Because of his importance, his burial temple had nine terraces and three ceremonial rooms at the top.

The original museum was built in 1965 and was called the Tikal Museum. It has since been restored and renamed.

The **visitor center** is at the entrance to the ruins. It has a coffee shop and a gift shop that sells high-end Guatemalan crafts as well as William R. Coe's book *Tikal*, published by the University Museum, University of Pennsylvania, first printed in 1967. I purchased my copy in its 12th printing and that was in 1985. It is still the best guide to the ruins and the one from which I learned the most.

Next to the visitor center is the scale model of Tikal. This is well done. There is also a center holding some of the stone works found at the site.

MAYA TIME	
600 BC	Pre-Classic Period starts
AD 250	Early Classic Period starts
AD 550	Late Classic Period starts
AD 900	Post-Classic Period starts

■ THE ANCIENT CITY OF TIKAL

 Tikal is the modern name for the city, but a glyph deciphered by Schele and Matthews gives the original Maya name as **Mutul**. They translated this from what they believed to be the city's emblem, the back of a head with hair hanging straight down. The hair is knotted in place with a band of hair that comes from the front and sides of the head.

Tikal was a ceremonial and bureaucratic center. It controlled trade between those living in the Yucatán peninsula and those in the Caribbean. To show their power, the kings of Tikal built monumental temples and great plazas. They had their priests and elite adorned in elaborately designed robes and rich jewelry.

Ball games and human sacrifice were common. Slaves taken in battle and utilized by the kings were considered signs of wealth. Scribes were honored members of the educated classes.

As you enter the ruins of Tikal, a path leads left to the central acropolis, the sweat house and the Mendez Causeway. Veer to the right and you'll pass complexes O, Q and R sitting on each side of the path. The two pyramids (Q & R) were built by Hasaw Chan K'awil to mark the passing of a katun (close to 20 years). Unlike Belize, Guatemala reconstructs its ruins so these two pyramids have, in front of them, reproductions of the stelae and altars that were there centuries ago.

Tikal

To El Cruce & Flores

Tikal Inn

P

Comedor Tikal
Comedor Corazón de Jesús
Comedor Imperio Maya

Jaguar Inn

Restaurant

Inspectoria

i

Park Staff Quarters

Sylvanus Morley Museum

Jungle Lodge

Tikal Reservoir

To Temple of the Inscriptions

N

HUNTER PUBLISHING

© 2007 HUNTER PUBLISHING, INC

JUNGLE

GROUP H

1000 FEET
300 METERS

COMPLEX Q

COMPLEX R

GROUP I

GROUP F

Sweat House

Central Acropolis

MENDEZ CAUSEWAY

GROUP G

East Plaza Temple

MALER CAUSEWAY

COMPLEX P

COMPLEX M

COMPLEX O

Causeway Reservoir

Palace Reservoir

Temple I

Great Plaza

Temple V

Temple Reservoir

South Acropolis

Plaza of Seven Temples

MAUDSLAY CAUSEWAY

West Plaza
Temple II
Temple III

Bat Palace

El Mundo Perdido

TOZZER CSWY

COMPLEX N

Temple IV

JUNGLE

At the end of the path, turn left and walk along the Mailer Causeway to the North Acropolis, where the Great Plaza and Temples I and II are located. Since this site is huge, I will cover only the main temples and a tiny bit of history. If you need more detailed information or want to explore farther, purchase William Coe's book, *Tikal*, sold at the visitor center. There are signs indicating where each path leads and getting lost in Tikal is no longer a great problem.

There are over 3,000 buildings in Tikal, some dating to 600 BC and others as recent as AD 900. During its height of power, Tikal had over 100,000 citizens.

The **Great Plaza** has **Temple I** on the east side facing Temple II on the west side. Temple I towers majestically at 170 feet (52 meters) above the plaza floor. It was called the Temple of the Giant Jaguar, so named because of the jaguar carved on one of the lintels and because of the crouching jade jaguar ornament found much later inside the tomb. The temple was built around AD 700, during the late classic period, with nine terraces (nine was a sacred number for the Maya) supporting the building platform and a three-room temple on top. The stairway features high steps that must have been a horrid climb for the short Maya kings and priests, especially when they were dressed in heavy robes.

The temple chambers at the top are corbel-vaulted. Interior wooden beams and the lintels are made of zapote, a rot-resistant wood. Inside, there are handprints on the wall, probably made by a bunch of kids fooling around after the city was abandoned (this is my opinion, not that of archeologists). Below the temple was a grave, and above the grave a pit filled with broken pottery, incense burners and animal bones left by those living in the area after the collapse of Tikal.

In the temple's tomb was Jasaw Chan Kawiil (see S. Morley Museum, page 323), who was placed at ground level and had the temple built over him. Some of the human bones found here have dates carved on them, the last date being 731. This is close to when archeologists suspect he died.

The ceremonial rooms were also corbel-vaulted. At one time, Temple I had Jasaw Chan Kawiil's face inscribed on the surface. That would be a daunting view to look at every time you came to worship. Jasaw Chan Kawiil's son succeeded him and ruled for a number of years.

The tomb was found by a Harvard student working on his thesis. His name was N.M. Hellmuth and, with the luck of a beginner, he found the richest tomb in Tikal. Inside was the jade jaguar, plus 180 other pieces, some jade, some bone. The bone fragments were

Guatemala

carved with inscriptions and pictographs of gods in canoes paddling to Maya heaven. The lines of these carvings were filled with cinnabar, a mineral found in the presence of mercury.

Once you climb the stairs of the temple you will see Temple II across the plaza to the west with the Central Acropolis beside it. The North Acropolis, built about AD 200, is to the right and the Eastern Plaza is behind you.

Temple II is on the west side of the plaza and stands at only 125 feet (42 meters) above the plaza floor. It is believed that this temple was built before Temple I, because the base is lower than that of Temple I, and that it originally stood at 140 feet (42 meters) above the plaza floor. Temple II is commonly called the Temple of the Masks because of the two masks carved on each side of the third terrace. Of the three lintels on the top, only the center one is carved. Inside there is graffiti. One scene from the graffiti is of a bound victim being impaled by a spear. At the base of this pyramid was the largest stele ever found in Tikal, standing at nearly 12 feet (3.6 meters). Its

Temple II.

accompanying altar was also found; both were smashed but have since been restored. To date, no tomb has been found under Temple II.

> **AUTHOR NOTE:** *Although graffiti is usually destructive, that found at the temple is considered historical data.*

The Great Plaza also had two rows of stelae and altars placed along the south boundary. Some of these stones were used to record historical information. Others were plain and were probably covered in plaster and paint. The second stele from the left (Stele P21) on the Great Plaza came from the West Plaza, 330 feet away (99 meters). It was transported without the use of wheels. All told, there were 70 stelae and accompanying altars in this plaza during the late classic period.

Carved stelae were always laid side-by-side with carved altars while plain stelae were always with plain altars. It is believed that when a line of priests and kings declined, the following rulers would destroy the stelae and altars, along with the stories inscribed upon them. Beneath all the stelae and altars were sacrificial items, such as nine pieces of chipped flint, nine pieces of obsidian or nine sea shells.

The **North Acropolis** is the biggest so far found in the Maya world, with a base covering about 2.5 acres. Started about AD 200, most of the acropolis was used as funeral structures for the elite. Some of these were Jaguar Paw, Curl Nose and Stormy Sky.

Stele 8 (found in group G) is gruesome, showing men lying on an altar waiting for the dagger to be plunged into their hearts. Archeologists assume that the sacrificed men were captured warriors.

The Northern Acropolis has up to 12 other acropolises buried underneath, dating as far back as 200 BC. By AD 1 there were four structures in the acropolis, and 800 years later there were 16 looming many feet above the previous buildings. Each building had huge masks between the wide staircases that led to the ritual platforms.

In structure **5D-34,** found at the corner of the acropolis, a priest was buried with nine attendants in a tomb carved into the bedrock. The attendants were alive at time of burial. There was also a crocodile and turtles buried with this priest. Looters in later years desecrated this temple. The stele, commonly called the Red Stele because of the stone's color, was broken apart and taken up to the altar.

Structure **5D-33** is in the center of the acropolis, near the front. It consists of three layers, each layer belonging to a different era. This structure eventually reached a height of over 60 feet (20 meters). Its most striking features are the fearsome masks flanking the stairs. One is over 10 feet high (three meters) and has a big hooked nose.

One of the caches found in the acropolis contained numerous decapitated heads, probably belonging to captured enemies.

Stele 5 was found in front of 5D-32 and has the most detailed carvings of all those found at Tikal. The carvings are long vertical lines of hieroglyphics.

Burial chamber 116, in front of structure 5D-73, had the largest pyrite mosaic mirror to be discovered. The treasures of carved jade make this the third-richest tomb ever opened. Also found was a pearl necklace, richly decorated alabaster, wooden vases and a diviner's kit containing shaman's tools. The name on one of the vases was Batab of the Sky family.

Temple IV stands alone beyond the west plaza and is being consumed by the jungle. It is the job of the grounds keepers to hack away at the foliage. It's the highest temple in the city, standing at 212 feet (65 meters) above the plaza floor. It is also the one least excavated. Archeologists have estimated that 250,000 cubic yards of material was used to build this temple and its platform. Some of the interior walls are 40 feet thick (12 meters). The hieroglyphs on the lintels say that the building was built around AD 741 and give a record of dynastic successions. There is also a portrait of Jasaw Chan Kawiil with his son Yik Chan Kawiil.

You must climb up steep ladders to the top of Temple IV, but the view is like nothing else you have seen. If you are fortunate enough to be in the area when no one else is around, this is the place to sit and read a book while the monkeys come to entertain you.

Temple V is presently being excavated and restored at the cost of 7.2 million quetzales, a price shared between Guatemala and Spain. The temple stands at 190 feet (58 meters) and has a tiny room at the top measuring 2.5 feet wide (one meter). The rear wall of this room is 15 feet thick (five meters). Another interesting feature of this building is that it has rounded corners.

The Temple of Inscriptions requires a walk through the jungle along the Mendez Causeway. As you walk, use all of your senses to feel what it is really like in the jungle. This temple was found by the original owner of the Jungle Lodge (see *Places to Stay*, below), who is now retired.

Built around AD 736, the temple is topped by a 40-foot (12-meter) comb covered in hieroglyphs. It is suspected that Yik Chan K'awiil is entombed here. Although the temple is not high, the inscriptions are interesting. The stele in front has a carving of a ruler with blood dripping from his incised penis. With these types of practices, it is no wonder the population dropped.

Lost World (Perdido Mundo) is south of Temple IV. This very high pyramid at one time had four staircases with the stones in-between decorated with huge masks. It is worth the climb to look at the rest of the city rising above the green vegetation.

The Plazas were often market places. East plaza, flanking the back of Temple I, is one such place. The **Central Plaza** covers an area of four acres and was built over a 500-year period. The structures around this plaza were used for administrative purposes. To date, five reservoirs have been found. (Proximity to a water source was never an attraction for the Maya when they chose building sites; they probably collected rain water, much the same way people in the area do today.) The two main causeways connecting the plazas and temples of the city are now used as walkways.

A **Sweat House** (found near complexes O, Q and R) was used by the Maya for ritualistic purposes. Priests went there before performing special rites and ball players went there before a game. The **ball court** at Tikal is not very impressive. You need to go to Copan in Honduras to see a really good one. Located between Temple I and the Central Acropolis, Tikal's ball court has been partially excavated and restored.

Group G is along the Mendez Causeway that is about 200 feet wide and goes into the jungle for a mile. The group is easily reached from the causeway and is one of the site's best palaces in Tikal. There is an inner and outer courtyard with a vaulted passageway in-between. This is a very different example of residences found in the old city.

Near Complex N stands **stela 16**, an impressive carving of the costume worn during the late classic period. This stela is carved on all sides, something not usually done during that time. Near it is **altar 5**, which has excellent hieroglyphs around the outer edge and two priests standing over a sacrificed head. This altar was on Guatemala's 10 quetzal note.

The Museum costs 10 quetzals to enter, well worth the visit. It is well laid out, not crowded, and everything is labeled. If you have the time, be certain to see it.

There are rumors that the cost of visiting Tikal will soon double. This would be a pity, as I would hate people to miss it because of the expense. The site is well organized and strongly controlled without losing any of its magnificent splendor. There are places where tree roots are holding the ruins together, while most of the temples now have wooden staircases so visitors can climb to the top without destroying any of the stonework. The animals, birds and insects are still in the jungle, singing away or running across your path, but the guards are inconspicuous, standing quietly in the shade of a huge cieba tree or under a guanacaste.

THE STORY

Everywhere you walk in Tikal you will find a stele or an altar, a carved lintel or a stone mask. All these items, along with the pottery and stone carvings found in the tombs, tell the story of the Maya in general and Tikal in particular.

We know that the ruler Yax Chaktel Xok, also known as the First Scaffold Shark, died about AD 200. Chak Toh Ichak, Jaguar Claw the 1st, was the ninth ruler of Tikal and he died in 378. He led the city to victory over Uaxactun and died on the day of victory.

We know that Lord First Crocodile, also known as Curl Nose, ruled until 420. He is buried in the North Acropolis. His son Siyal Cahn Kawiil became the 11th ruler.

Tikal suffered under 137 years of war with Calaknul. Of the city's 11 rulers, we know the names of eight. In 554, Lord Water from Caracol and Double Bird of Tikal had a battle and Caracol won. In 562, Tikal was ruled by Lord Lizard Head and he also lost a battle to Caracol.

Tikal went to war in 672 against Dos Pilos under the leadership of Shield Skull, the 25th ruler of the city. Finally, Jasaw Chan Kawiil came to power and won over Jaguar Paw 2nd, the leader of Calaknul. During Jasaw's rule, and his son's rule, Tikal saw the building surge that resulted in Temples I and IV being built. There is an inscription in Temple II that suggests Lady Twelve Macaw, wife of Jasaw, was the ruler.

But then Tikal declined. Wars between cities ended. It could have been due to drought, loss of men at war, pestilence or overpopulation. Whatever the reason, form your own stories as you walk through this mystical place gathering the snippets of information that most interest you.

■ PLACES TO STAY

Jungle Lodge, ☎ 502-926-1519, $$-$$$, is the most popular place to stay and eat. The bungalows are duplex style, with tile roofs and plaster walls. Outside are decks and a swimming pool. The grounds are well kept, with pathways that lead between the buildings. The restaurant serves the tastiest meals and the largest portions in the area. It does this at the lowest price. Service is slow in the morning.

Hotel Tikal, ☎ 502-926-0065, $$-$$$, has both rooms in the hotel building and bungalows around the grounds. Hot water and electricity is available from 6 to 11 pm, but this isn't guaranteed as electricity throughout the Petén is sporadic. The restaurant is expensive and the portions are small.

Jaguar Inn, no phone, $-$$, www.lacasadedondavid.com, has cabins, dorms and tenting. If tenting or in dorms, you can rent lockers for your gear. Cabins have large windows, decks, fans, cable TV and hot water in private bathrooms. This hotel has been around for a long time. The **restaurant** here also sells snacks.

■ PLACES TO EAT

Places to eat are as numerous as places to stay and offer every type of food possible. Ask around and see where others are going. I like Don David's and Las Gardinias but I also ate at Mon Ami (all in El Remate) and at a few of the restaurants along the main highway. I was not disappointed once in the food, the portion size or the price.

DIRECTORY

GUATEMALA DIRECTORY	
■ PLACES TO STAY	
Casa de Don David	☎ 502-306-2190
Hotel Tikal	☎ 502-926-0065
Jaguar Inn	no phone; www.lacasadedondavid.com
Jungle Lodge	☎ 502-926-1519
■ INFORMATION	
Guatemalan Consulate	☎ 823-2531

The South

You will be using three highways to go south.

The **Manatee Highway**, or **Coastal Highway**, starts at Mile 30 of the Western Highway just west of Belize Zoo. It leads to Gales Point and continues south to Dangriga. It has a rough gravel surface, though I have heard talk of paving it in the near future.

The **Hummingbird Highway** starts at Mile 47.7 of the Western Highway. The route runs past the city of Belmopan and down to Dangriga (also known as Stann Creek) on the coast. The Hummingbird Highway is a paved route.

The **Southern Highway** starts at Mile 48.7 of the Hummingbird Highway and goes south to Punta Gorda on the coast. At Mile 21.3 of the Southern Highway, a road goes off to Placencia, located at the end of a long peninsula. Placencia is approximately halfway along the coast between Dangriga and Punta Gorda. The Southern Highway is paved beyond the Placencia turnoff, but not all the way to Punta Gorda.

Each of the highways has its own set of attractions, from small coastal towns to large cities and nature preserves. Most destinations can be reached by bus, although many travelers enjoy the flexibility of hiring a car and heading out independently to explore.

ALONG THE HIGHWAYS

■ COASTAL (MANATEE) HIGHWAY

MILEAGE ALONG THE COASTAL HIGHWAY	
Mile Zero	The turnoff at La Democracia on the Western Highway, where the Coastal (Manatee) Highway starts.
Mile 2.3	**Sibun River Bridge**
Mile 12.8	**Corn House Creek**
Mile 19.6	**Big Creek**
Mile 28.7	**Mullins River Bridge**
Mile 36.1	**Gales Point**

■ HUMMINGBIRD HIGHWAY

The mileage is measured from the turnoff on the Western Highway where the Hummingbird Highway starts. Some road signs along the highway are confusing as they start from Belize City. I have started Mile Zero at the beginning of the highway.

MILEAGE ALONG THE HUMMINGBIRD HIGHWAY	
Mile Zero	The turnoff at Guanacaste National Park on the Western Highway, where the Hummingbird Highway starts.
Mile 5	**Roaring River Estate**
Mile 11.4	**Jungle Lodge Caves Branch & Jaguar Creek**
Mile 12.4	**St. Herman's Cave**
Mile 13.6	**Blue Hole National Park**
Mile 14	**Premitus B&B**
Mile 32	**St. Maragaret's Village & Five Blue Lakes National Park**
Mile 46.2	Gales Point turnoff
Mile 48.7	Southern Highway splits from the Hummingbird Highway
Mile 54.7	**Dangriga**

■ SOUTHERN HIGHWAY

 The mileage is measured from the turnoff on the Hummingbird Highway where the Southern Highway starts. I have started Mile Zero at the beginning of the highway.

MILEAGE ALONG THE SOUTHERN HIGHWAY	
Mile Zero	The turnoff on the Hummingbird Highway where the Southern Highway starts.
Mile 6	**Mayflower Ruins**
Mile 8	**Silk Grass**
Mile 10	**Hopkins Junction to Sittee River**
Mile 12.5	**Sittee River to Hopkins**
Mile 15	**Maya Center/Cockscomb Basin**
Mile 21.3	**Placencia Peninsula**
Mile 42	**Monkey River Town**
Mile 73	**Indian Creek & Nim Li Punit Ruins**
Mile 83.2	**Maya Villages, Lubaantum Ruins, Rio Blanco, Blue Creek**
Mile 100	**Punta Gorda**

THE COASTAL HIGHWAY

Follow the Western Highway from Belize City as far as La Democracia at Mile 29.9 just west of the Belize Zoo. The road crosses many creeks – Corn House Creek, Mahogany Creek, Soldier Creek, Big Creek – on its way to the Caribbean. Citrus fruit trees grow in the fields along the way and rocky limestone cliffs hide unexplored caves.

At Mile 36, you can make a right turn (south) or a sharp left (north) to Gales Point. This is a very rough road and it takes a long time to get anywhere.

■ GALES POINT

Gales Point is a tiny Creole village of about 500 people. It is located on a spit that flows into Southern Lagoon. Staying in Gales Point will give you a unique experience that mixes culture with wildlife. The area has the best turtle nesting grounds in the western world, the best large-bird breeding areas in Belize's south and the purest Garifuna culture in Central America. You have access to both freshwater lagoons and the Caribbean Sea. There are caves in the Peccary Hills and unexcavated Maya ruins close by.

HISTORY

 In the mid-1700s Jamaican refugees, called **maroons**, settled at Gales Point and other isolated places in Belize. They lived quietly, fishing in the ocean and lagoons and gathering food from the nearby jungles. They wanted a peaceful life.

The **Maroon Wars** started in Jamaica in 1720, when some African slaves refused to be oppressed by their owners. The slaves escaped to the hills of Jamaica where they lived independently, much to the chagrin of their old masters. They often chose inaccessible and inhospitable places to live, which ensured their safety.

"MAROON"

The word "maroon" comes from the Spanish/Arawak word "cimarron," which describes domestic cows that escaped their owners and took to the hills. The word was soon transferred to the escaped slaves and took on the connotation of being fierce, wild and unbroken.

The wars in Jamaica didn't end until 1739. During that time some slaves escaped to other countries.

The **Baymen** came to cut the trees. They employed (virtually enslaved) the blacks living in the Belize River, Sibun River area and some of the Maroons of Gales Point. In 1820, a revolt was led by two slaves named Will and Sharper. They managed to stave off their oppressors for over a month. Eventually, the maroons negotiated peace for freedom. Those who came from Gales Point returned to their dwellings and lived quietly, integrating their African culture with that of the Baymen. Today, those people with maroon background are fiercely proud and practice their customs with confidence.

GETTING HERE

 Driving to Gales Point from Belize City is no problem; you can get there in a few hours. However, the road is rough and there are not many services along the Coastal Highway until you reach its end, Gales Point.

Cyclists will find it is a long way, especially in the heat. If you decide to do it, be certain to have sustenance and lots of water.

Some **buses** use the Coastal Highway to go directly from Belize City to Gales Point. **Richie Bus**, ☎ 522-2130, located at the main terminal in Belize City, runs two buses daily that stop in Gales Point. Other buses take the Coastal Highway to Dangriga without stopping at Gales Point. If you jump on one of these and get off at the turnoff, you must walk the last 2.5 miles to the village.

Still other buses take the Hummingbird Highway to Dangriga. From there, you can catch a second bus to Gales Point. Buses leave regularly from 6 am to 5 pm for Dangriga from Belize City. The cost is US $5. Three buses go from Dangriga to Gales Point each day.

Boats in Belize City can be hired to take you to Gales Point. The three-hour trip is spectacular. You travel up the Belize River to the Burdon Canal (see *The West*, page 222) and then into a small creek that flows into Northern Lagoon. You can then either go through another small creek and into Southern Lagoon and float down the lagoon to Gales Point, or go halfway down the lagoon and out to the ocean at Manatee Bar River. You would then follow the coast to the village. Although I never made this trip, I understand it is one of the nicest in Belize. If you would like to do it, book with a tour operator in Belize City (see page 136).

Swimming hole at Guanacaste National Park.

THINGS TO DO

Gales Point Manatee Community Sanctuary covers 170,000 acres around Gales Point that includes cayes, ocean, beaches, mangrove swamps, tropical and pine forests, lagoons and karst hills. The main purpose of this sanctuary is to protect the manatee. The Northern and Southern Lagoons provide a safe environment. There is freshwater coming in from the Manatee River, Soldiers Creek and Corn House Creek and salt water through the Bar River. The salt water carries fresh food for the manatee.

The Southern Lagoon has a depression, fed by an underground spring, that is believed to be the home of about 50 manatees. It is here that you have the best chance of seeing one, but patience is needed. A manatee can stay underwater for 25-30 minutes before coming up for a breath of air. Manatees exchange 98% of their lung capacity in one breath, which allows them long periods of time between breaths.

Manatees weigh around 1,000 pounds (450 kg) and can be as heavy as 3,000 pounds. They eat about 150 pounds (67 kg) of vegetation a day, most of it sea grass. They hear well. While watching for manatees, listen for the sound of a snorkeler – it could be a manatee breathing. They sound the same.

There are two cayes on Northern Lagoon that are prime nesting places for birds and crocodiles. **Bird Caye** consists mostly of red mangrove and is home to egrets, herons, cormorants and white ibis. The unnamed caye just south of Bird Caye is also a nesting place for these birds, plus the caye hosts the king vulture and the brown booby. Nesting takes place from March to July.

Once nesting is over for the birds, the Morelet's crocodiles move in and nest from December to February. After the eggs hatch, young crocodiles can often be seen sunning themselves along the shores.

The hawksbill turtle has prime nesting grounds along the deserted shores of the Caribbean just north of Gales Point. There are about eight miles of uninhabited sandy beach where 200 hawksbill nests have been found. This is very rare. The largest community found before this was 16 nests. The nesting period for the hawksbill is between June and August, but turtles have come ashore as early as April and as late as October.

Richard Slusher of Gales Point worked as a researcher with American Biologist Greg Smith and together they established the **Turtle Protection Program**, www.communityconservation.org (click on Belize), for this nesting area. They made Leroy Andrewin of Gales Point a Turtle Guard, whose job it is to look for tracks along the beach made by the nesting females. When he finds a nest, he puts cages or sticks and old fishnets over the area so predators can't get

to the developing eggs. During the hatching period, he cleans the beach so the little ones don't have any problem reaching the water. Obstructions, like a piece of Styrofoam, could make the difference of life or death for the new turtles. After they reach the water, the life of the turtle is in the hands of fate. It is believed that only one in every 1,000 turtles lives long enough to reproduce.

The conservation status of the hawksbill turtle is listed as Critical.

To view turtles nesting or hatching you must go to the **Gales Point Tour Guides Cooperative** (no telephone number, ask in town) and hire someone to show you where they are. It is against the law to harass these creatures in any way. If caught doing so, you will be jailed. Remember that Belize jails are very crowded and have no TV.

Ben Loman Cave is a multi-roomed limestone cave with an underground stream running through. It has many interesting stalagmites and stalactites, as well as Maya artifacts. The trip up the lagoon and through the jungle takes three to four hours. The cave is found between the two lagoons and two hills, on the north arm of Jenkins Creek. Be sure to hire a guide for this trip – getting lost in the cave could be fatal. Besides, the guide will take you directly to the cave, whereas you could tromp around the jungle for hours looking for it.

Fishing in the Manatee River is excellent (the maroons have been doing it for about 250 years). Tarpon is the best catch but, since you have access to both the freshwater lagoons and the ocean, you can pretty much choose your catch.

PLACES TO STAY

Gales Point Cooperative (contact the community phone, ☎ 209-8031, and ask what you wish to know or ask in town once you arrive), $$, has five rooms in a large house on the lagoon. The rooms are all on the second floor so they catch the breeze, and each has two beds and a

HOTEL PRICES	
$	$20 to $50
$$	$51 to $75
$$$	$76 to $100
$$$$	$101 to $150
$$$$$	over $150

private bathroom. Food is made by the villagers and eaten in the communal dining room.

There are also rooms in private houses. Miss Alice has two rooms and a large backyard in which to sit. Miss Elain has four rooms and a meeting place for small groups. Miss Iona has four rooms upstairs and Miss Bridget has three rooms on the second floor. All Miss Bridget's rooms have a nice view. Miss Hortense has two rooms with fans. All ladies offer meals with the family.

Gentle's Cool Spot, no phone, on the main road in town where the buses turn around, has basic accommodations that cost less than the private houses. It also has a nice little bar where you can sit and drink while gathering information and making connections.

Manatee Lodge, Box 1242, Belize City, ☎ 877-462-6283 or 220-8040, www.manatee lodge.com, $$$, has nine rooms in a large colonial building situated at the very tip of the peninsula. The spacious rooms have hardwood floors and private baths with hot water. The

property is huge and encompasses mangrove swamp, savanna and jungle. Canoes are available for guests to use on the lagoons. The **restaurant**, $$$, serves American and Belizean foods and the bar serves great rum punch.

You have a choice of booking your stay as an all-inclusive or just renting a room. The lodge will arrange any type of tour or trip around the area for a reasonable price. See their website – it will convince you to visit.

PLACE TO EAT

 Orchids Café, ☎ 220-5621, $$, the best place to eat in town, serves good international, Belizean and vegetarian meals. A comfortable deck overlooks the lagoon. Like Gentle's Cool Spot, Orchids is also an information center.

THE HUMMINGBIRD HIGHWAY

To reach the Hummingbird Highway going to Dangriga (as well as the Southern Highway to Punta Gorda) follow the Western Highway from Belize City to Mile 47.7. Mile Zero is at the junction where Guanacaste Park is located.

> **AUTHOR NOTE:** *I have covered* **Belmopan** *in The West chapter (see page 233) because it is near the junction, at Mile 1.3 of the Hummingbird Highway.*

The Hummingbird Highway, in the heart of the limestone cave country, goes up and down and around curves, beyond which lie rich farmland and citrus groves. There are karst outcrops riddled with caves and numerous wildlife sanctuaries to visit along the way. The road is seal coated as far as Dangriga and is in excellent condition for driving. Travel is relatively fast and traffic is low. However, if cycling, your elbows (not to mention your bottom) would get a bit sore. Seal coating makes for good driving, but is very bumpy for cycling.

■ ARMENIA & VICINITY

At Mile 8 is the village of Armenia, where **Garcia's Bunkrooms and Cabañas** has one very basic cabin that sleeps three and costs US $25 and a dorm next door that sleeps up to eight people for $7. 50 per person. There is an outside toilet and shower. Stay here only if shelter is needed at that moment. Although friendly, it is very basic. Garcia's has a sign by the highway and is beside a vegetable stand and a speed bump. Ask at the vegetable stand to see the accommodations.

THINGS TO DO

 Jungle Lodge and Adventure Center, Box 356, ☎ 822-2800, www.cavesbranch.com, $$$$, is at Mile 11.4 of the Hummingbird Highway and .6 miles on a secondary road. On the secondary road, take the left fork part way in. Tucked into 58,000 acres of jungle setting, part of it on the Caves Branch River, this is an adventurer's destination. There are cabañas, dorms or tenting spaces (US $5) for rent. Tours offered at this rustic spot are spectacular. You can take just a place to stay or opt for an all-inclusive package. Buffet-style meals are available: breakfast is US $12 per person and dinner is US $17.

I found the guides working for owner, Ian Anderson, pleasant; I found Ian himself unapproachable. Ian has taken some Canadian mountaineering rescue techniques and adapted them for jungle rescue. He has started the Belize Search and Rescue Organization and trained his guides in both first aid and the skills of rescue.

Their most spectacular trip, called the **Black Hole Drop**, is just as it suggests – a rappel into a sinkhole that drops 300 feet (90 meters). You will spend the night in the sinkhole. First-rate equipment is included in the cost of the trip. Anderson offers easier cave trips, but he is interested mostly in hard-core adventurers.

Jaguar Creek, ☎ 820-2034, jagcreek@btl.net, is on the right-hand fork of this same secondary road that goes to the Jungle Lodge. It's a Christian-based ecological site attached to Target Earth and the Eden Conservation Program. Located on 10 acres of subtropical forest, Jaguar Creek offers lessons in conservation, and a strong religious tone is part of the philosophy. They can accommodate up to 40 people in the eight dorms and wooden cabañas.

You can learn about solar power, flourescent lighting, energy-efficient cooling systems, water-saving techniques, compost toilets, tank-less water heaters and gray-water leach fields. Most of the students come from American and Canadian Christian Universities. Individual travelers can visit for a tour and receive information about this type of living environment. There is no charge, but a small donation would be appreciated and put to good use.

You should call or e-mail ahead so someone will be there to help you. It should also be noted that they can rent cabins to the general public, but this is a Christian project and religion is part of the package.

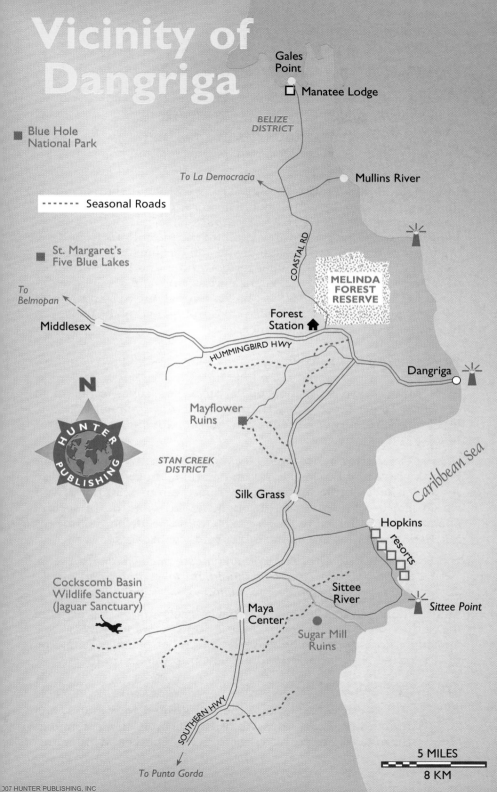

Vicinity of Dangriga

Gales Point

□ Manatee Lodge

BELIZE DISTRICT

■ Blue Hole National Park

To La Democracia

○ Mullins River

- - - - - - Seasonal Roads

COASTAL RD.

MELINDA FOREST RESERVE

■ St. Margaret's Five Blue Lakes

To Belmopan

Middlesex

Forest Station 🏠

HUMMINGBIRD HWY

Dangriga ○

Mayflower Ruins ■

STAN CREEK DISTRICT

HUNTER PUBLISHING

N

Silk Grass ○

Caribbean Sea

Hopkins

resorts

Cockscomb Basin Wildlife Sanctuary (Jaguar Sanctuary)

Maya Center

Sittee River

Sittee Point

Sugar Mill Ruins

SOUTHERN HWY

To Punta Gorda

5 MILES

8 KM

▸▸ *Return to the Hummingbird Highway. At Mile 12.4 is St. Herman's Cave on the right (west). From the cave you can walk the 1.8-mile trail over to the Blue Hole National Park, where you can swim in a cenote. You can also drive the highway to the Blue Hole.*

 MYSTERIOUS MAYA: *The Maya believed* cenotes *were openings to the underworld.*

Blue Hole Horse Trails, ☎ 820-2020, www.bananabank.com, is just past the Cave Branch Bridge. The horse camp is affiliated with Banana Bank Lodge. There are 11 horses here, plus some guides. You can take a half- or full-day trip into the mountains from here. There are two trails; one goes high and can be done only during dry weather. The lower trail is safer for both rider and horse when it's wet. They cross a river, pass rock walls and slip through rainforests. The cost is US $60 for half a day, about 3½ hours, and $100 for a full day. They will also take you on overnight trips, but this must be arranged in advance.

■ ST. HERMAN'S CAVE

St. Herman's Cave is probably one of the easiest caves to visit in all of Belize. To get there (other than by driving or cycling), take any bus from Belize City or Belmopan heading south and ask the driver to let you off at the cave.

Stop at the **visitor center** and pay your US $4 entry fee – good for both the cave and Blue Hole National Park. Managed by the Belize Audubon Society, the area is open from 8 am to 4:30 pm. If you would like to go all the way through the cave and out a second opening, you will need to hire a guide, available at the visitor center. Near the center are picnic tables and washrooms.

▌ **AUTHOR NOTE:** *You will need good walking shoes or boots and a flashlight. Bring a bathing suit too, if you would like to swim.*

First established in 1965 as a tourist attraction, the 575 acres of jungle has seen, at last count, over 7,500 visitors each year. The limestone karst topography features a number of caves joined by underground rivers that eventually flow into the Sibun River.

HIKING TRAILS

 The visitor center, where the **self-guided tour** starts, has numerous displays describing the life cycle of bats found in the area. There are also descriptions of birds and other animals that haunt the forests nearby. If you go only 1,000 feet (300 meters) into the cave, a guide is not required. The honor system is practiced here.

A 10-minute walk along a maintained trail brings you to the small entrance of the high-ceilinged cave. A stairway that was first carved by the Maya leads down into the cave. The entrance is about 60 feet wide (18 meters), but it gets bigger as you walk and the cave's center measures 120 feet across (36 meters).

Inside, use a flashlight to follow the trail markers. The gigantic stalactites and stalagmites have taken eons to form; they grow about one inch in 800 years. Tiny cracks in the ceiling of the cave occasionally add an eerie light. With a guide, you can go into the cave and come out at a second opening, where a trail leads back to the start.

When the cave was first discovered in modern times, vessels were scattered around. Archeologists say that the Maya collected the water dripping off the rocks and called it "Zuh uy ha," meaning virgin water. The vessels, along with some spears and torches also found in the cave, were removed by the Department of Archeology.

From the cave, follow the trail to the hilltop observation tower, where you can spot some of the 256 bird species found in the area. The tower gives you a great view of the surrounding landscape. This is a one-hour walk from the cave. If you want a longer jungle hike, follow the trail to the rear entrance of the cave and back to the visitor center. This will take about three hours, total.

The park has over five miles of trails. If you follow the **Nature Trail** beyond the park border, you will come to Mountain Cow Cave, which can be entered for a few feet (more with a guide). **Crystal Cave**, also along this stretch, is one of 10 in the world that has such a high quality of crystals, which are classified higher than those

Stalactites at Crystal Cave.

at Actun, a popular tourist destination. There are also lots of Maya artifacts in this cave. The only qualified guide to take you into this cave is Marcos Cucul, www.mayaguide.bz. Contact him ahead of time to be certain that he is available when you wish to go. Marcos is one of the most skilled guides in Belize. Visit his site.

Two trails lead from the cave to the Blue Hole. The **Hummingbird Trail** goes up a steep hill, through lush jungle and over to the change room at the hole. The second trail follows the highway just inside the cover of the forest. On either trail, it is just under two miles to the Blue Hole and takes about 45 minutes to get there. You will be able to see lots of birds along this walk.

THE BLUE HOLE

 The Blue Hole was green when I was there. This sinkhole (a cave with its roof caved in) measures 300 feet across and 100 feet down (90 x 30 meters) from the top of the rocks to the pool's bottom. The pool itself is 24 feet deep (seven meters).

The water in the sinkhole comes from an underground stream that flows into an underground cavern, the opening of which forms an odd echo chamber. A swim in the hole is a lovely way to cool off. However, if it is during the rainy season the pool may be muddy.

PLACES TO STAY

 Those with their own tent can camp near the visitor center. You must ask permission, pay BZ $5, and be shown where you can pitch your tent. The campground has not been kept up and is no longer a good place to stay.

Ringtale Village, just south of the Blue Hole, has the **Primitas Farm Bed and Breakfast**, Box 80, Belmopan, ☎ 220-8259, pascott@btl.net, $. This is a working farm where agronomist Patrick Scott grows produce such as cashew, cocoa, bread fruit, guava, mango and avocado, as well as many different citrus fruits.

The farmhouse has four rooms for rent, each with two twin beds. Two rooms have private baths with hot water. The morning breakfast holds the promise of fry jacks and/or Johnny cake, along with freshly squeezed fruit juice. Staying at this B & B gives you easy access to the Blue Hole and St. Herman's Cave, as well as the **Sleeping Giant** and **Five Blue Lakes Park**. The Sleeping Giant is a couple of peaks rising above a small waterfall that, from a distance, look like a sleeping person. The same hills are shown as part of the watermarks on Belize dollars. This area is just 10 minutes from the farmhouse.

▶▶ *Following the Hummingbird Highway south, at Mile 29 you will cross the Hummingbird Gap, the pass leading from the mountains down to the ocean. There was once a restaurant on the top of the hill, but it is now closed. Turn east at Mile 32 of the highway to St Margaret's Village and Five Blue Lakes National Park. If you are cycling or walking, this place is a must.*

Kropf's Bakery, Mile 33 (33 miles north of Dangriga), ☎ 614-9553, is a Mennonite farm that is worth stopping at for some fresh bread or cakes and cookies. There's a small sign at the driveway. A loaf of bread or a large slice of banana bread costs BZ $2.50. The food is fresh and it goes quickly. The kitchen is spotless.

Over the Top Restaurant, Mile 32, has a great entrance and exit. It sits across from the entrance to Blue Lakes. The restaurant is owned by Francis Read and he offers some tasty food, like tamales or Belizean chicken and beans (BZ $7). His beer is cold and the ice cream is especially recommended.

Davis Falls, Mile 15, close to the village of Alta Vista (there is a sign at the turn-off), are eight miles off the highway along a pretty rough road that winds through citrus farms. You need a good 4X4 to get through. The falls are the second-largest in the country and drop more than 300 feet over granite rocks into a pool that is good for swimming. It's a two-hour walk from the road to the falls, after you have driven the eight miles in.

■ FIVE BLUE LAKES NATIONAL PARK

St. Margaret's Village is the gateway to the national park. The village has grown a tremendous amount in the last 20 years. In 1980 it had a population of 60 people, but refugees from El Salvador and Guatemala increased that number to 415 by 1991. Today, the population is over 800.

To get there by bus, take any southbound bus from Belmopan and ask them to let you off at St. Margaret's. The cost is US $1.50 per person. You can also catch a bus going north from Dangriga (US $2). Driving or cycling from Belmopan can easily be done in a day.

The **visitor center**, ☎ 822-5575, swa@btl.net, for the park is in the village. It's open from 8 am to 4 pm. Since the work in the park is mostly voluntary, the park fees (US $2.50 per day) go totally to maintenance.

Five Blue Lakes National Park was established on Earth Day in 1991. The 4,200 acres of broadleaf forest features a collapsed cave or cenote that covers an area of 7.4 acres and reaches a depth of about 200 feet (70 meters). In ancient times, the Maya are believed to have used these waters as sacrificial wells (not for humans).

The lake gets its name from the different depths of water that cause the different colors, rather than the number of lakes there are. Surrounding three sides of the lake are hills and limestone rock faces riddled with caves. Maintained trails can be followed from near the visitor center in the village to and around the lake.

In summer 2006, the waters receded considerably. This is possibly due to the collapse of an underground wall or cave that previously dammed the water. Ask locally for the lake's current condition.

THINGS TO DO

One favorite place to visit in the park is an **orchid-rich is-land**. To reach it, you must walk along a sunken limestone ridge. There is a lookout tower and a changing room near the lake should you wish to swim. The picnic area has a covered shelter and the tenting area has an outhouse.

An egret, one of many birds found in Five Blue Lakes National Park.

The **River Trail** crosses and follows the river for a bit and then goes to the **Duende Caves**, where you will find the uncommon lesser dog-like bat hanging near the entrance. They always roost where there is light.

At the very back of the lake are numerous **sinkholes** with walls up to 100 feet (30 meters) high that are decorated in clinging plants. Many caves can be seen with connecting tunnels that run for miles. The possibility of getting lost is very real. Unless you have a guide, do not go far inside. But even a short walk into some of the rooms will be a feast for your eyes.

To date, 167 species of **birds** and over 20 species of **bats** have been spotted here. **Fishers** can try their luck for bay snook and tuba, which hang out near the drainage point of the lake at Indian Creek.

When I was here, the howlers made me nervous with their serenade.

Guides

Guides who are knowledgeable in cave exploration, herbal medicine healing methods and local folklore are available at the visitor center. The cost of hiring a guide and equipment runs anywhere from US $50 to $100 per day. If you want to do some very difficult climbing and cave exploration in this region with a skilled guide, contact Marcos Cucul, www.mayaguide.bz. Get in touch with him ahead of time to be certain that he is available. Marcos is one of the most knowledgeable guides in Belize and, because of this, has access to places other guides do not.

WHERE TO STAY & EAT

 At the park's visitor center in the village you can book a room, rent a tent space (US $2.50 per night) or **rent bicycles**, so you need not walk the six miles to the lake. You can also opt for a home stay, $$, at the village. The **Hummingbird Tourist Connection**, ☎ 822-2005, handles some of the bookings. The **Hummingbird Cabañas Women's B & B** has over 20 places for visitors to stay. The meals offered by these families are reasonably priced and are authentic dishes belonging to the culture of the host family. You can request a stay with a Maya, Creole, Hispanic or Garifuna family.

▶▶ *Back on the Hummingbird Highway, past St. Margaret's Village (Mile 46.2) and to the left/north, is the turnoff to Gales Point. Another 2.5 miles to the right (south) is the turnoff to Placencia and Punta Gorda. The road straight ahead goes for six miles to Dangriga. This section of the road is surrounded mostly by citrus fruit farms that were established by the end of World War II. They now account for almost 15% of the nation's total citrus production.*

AUTHOR NOTE: *The sacks you see covering bananas hanging on the trees are to prevent the fruit from insect damage.*

■ DANGRIGA

Dangriga, with a population of about 10,000, is at the end of the Hummingbird Highway and on the ocean. It's bordered by Stann Creek to the north and Havanna Creek to the south. Populated mostly by Creole and Garifuna, Dangriga becomes nicer the farther into the town you go.

AVERAGE TEMPERATURES & RAINFALL		
	Daily temp.	Monthly rainfall
JAN	75.6°F/24.2°C	11 inches/27.9 cm
FEB	78.4°F/25.3°C	8 inches/20.3 cm
MAR	79.3°F/26.3°C	6 inches/15.2 cm
APR	81.5°F/27.5°C	4 inches/10.2 cm
MAY	83.5°F/28.6°C	7 inches/17.8 cm
JUN	83.8°F/28.8°C	14 inches/35.6 cm
JULY	83.3°F/28.5°C	16 inches/40.6 cm
AUG	83.5°F/28.6°C	16 inches/40.6 cm
SEPT	83.3°F/28.5°C	18 inches/45.7 cm
OCT	80.0°F/26.7°C	15 inches/38.1 cm
NOV	78.1°F/25.6°C	14 inches/35.6 cm
DEC	80.1°F/27.2°C	12 inches/30.5 mm

Source of above data: Historical and current records at the Melinda Forest Station situated nine miles from Dangriga Town in the Stann Creek District.

HISTORY

Alejo Benni was an escaped slave living in Cristales Village, Honduras in 1823 when he and others sided with the Spaniards during an uprising. Fearing for reprisals, he and 27 other adults and 12 kids hopped into a couple of dugout canoes and headed across the Bay of Honduras toward Belize. Two days later, while paddling along the shore, they saw some clear creek water flowing into the ocean. They stopped and drank.

Benni called the water **Dangreugeu Grigeu**, or "Standing Creek." The name was shortened to Stann Creek by the British and it was not until Independence that it was changed to Dangriga.

When Benni's group landed they built one large home where they could live together and protect each other from possible harm. There were other Garifuna living in the Sibun River area who, because they were believed to be so dangerous, were not allowed near Belize City after dark. Some thought that the Garifuna could incite hatred and cause a rebellion just by their presence. Benni's group was welcomed by these people. Within a year more Honduran escapees had joined the community and over 100 huts had been erected at Stann Creek.

Benni remained in Stann Creek as the leader with a man called **Bartholemew Yurumei Cacho** as second-in-command. Benni lived with his mother and two wives until age 40, when a tree hit and killed him while it was being cut down. It is believed that there are still descendants of Benni living in Stann Creek today.

Prior to the arrival of the Benni clan, there were a few English settlers living in the area, trading with the native Indians and growing vegetable gardens. They neither resisted nor welcomed the arrival of the Garifuna.

Shores of Stann Creek, Dangriga.

GETTING HERE

Traveling by car or bicycle, take the Hummingbird Highway. By bus, you can travel by the Hummingbird or the Coastal Highways. A Southern Bus Company bus leaves from Belmopan at 8:30 am daily and costs US $3. From Belize City, a bus leaves every hour from 6 am until 5 pm from the main terminal and costs US $5. These buses stop at Belmopan to pick up passengers.

The two local airlines (**Tropic Air**, ☎ 800-422-3435, and **Maya Air**, ☎ 522-2659) offer five flights a day. Flights cost US $46.50 one way.

If going to the cayes from Dangriga, go to the southern bank of Stann Creek across from Riverside Restaurant and talk to the men who have boats for hire. I did not negotiate my trip to the cayes from here so I have no recommendations.

> **AUTHOR NOTE:** *The grass seen along the road that looks like sugar cane is actually elephant grass.*

THINGS TO DO

Gielisi Garifuna Museum, George Prince Road, (on the way into town), is open Monday to Friday, 10 am to 5 pm and Saturday from 8 am to noon. The cost to enter is US $5 per foreign person. This museum was opened in 2004 and already the bronze statue at the entrance has been vandalized, as has the monument in the front yard. I'd say skip it until someone gets interested in keeping the place up.

Garifuna Settlement Day is November 19th, but is celebrated on the weekend closest to the 19th. It is the biggest party in all of Belize. If you are in the area on this date, book a hotel ahead of time and join the festivities. Starting the night before the celebration is the Garifuna drum and "jump up" (dance), which lasts until just before dawn. Every barbeque barrel in the district is hot and cooking something authentic. Everyone in town is "dragging the gut" (drinking beer), eating and dancing to the beat of the Punta drum.

It is said that the women, when dancing, can do up to 200 hip rolls a minute. Some call this provocative, some call it back-breaking. It is supposed to be a re-enactment of the cock-and-hen mating dance, where the one dancer tries to outdo the other. It should also be noted that there are about 20 women to each man doing this dance.

Traditionally, the music was composed by women who sang about cheating husbands, sick kids, oppressive landowners and any other social commentary that came to mind. The music has a repetitious double-metered beat and the singers

Garifuna drummer.

do a call-and-answer type of song.

At dawn dugout canoes are loaded with food, drink, drums and masked people dressed in brightly colored traditional clothes. They paddle to the shores of Dangriga, climb out of the boat and ask officials if they can settle on the land. Permission is given and they go to the church where they celebrate their arrival in exuberant

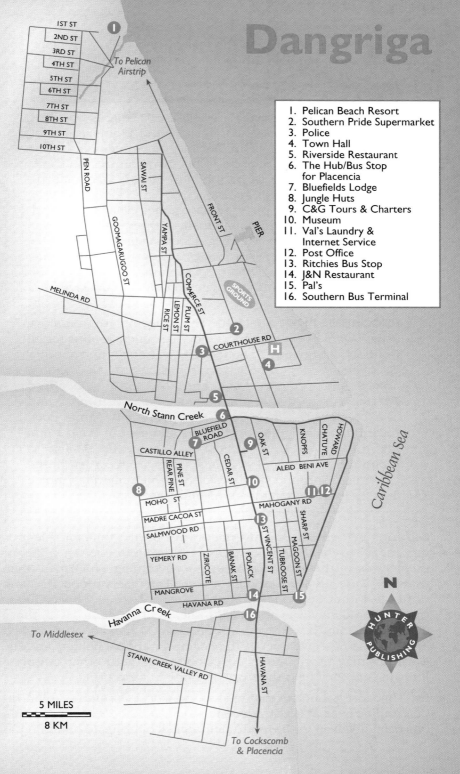

Dangriga

1. Pelican Beach Resort
2. Southern Pride Supermarket
3. Police
4. Town Hall
5. Riverside Restaurant
6. The Hub/Bus Stop for Placencia
7. Bluefields Lodge
8. Jungle Huts
9. C&G Tours & Charters
10. Museum
11. Val's Laundry & Internet Service
12. Post Office
13. Ritchies Bus Stop
14. J&N Restaurant
15. Pal's
16. Southern Bus Terminal

© 2007 HUNTER PUBLISHING, INC

chants and music. After that, the real party begins, with more food and drink and a parade with bands and flower-decked floats.

PUNTA ROCK

Punta Rock was started in 1980 in Dangriga by Pen Cayetanno, a self-taught musician and painter born in 1954. He played music in Mexico and Guatemala before he realized the uniqueness of his own culture. He came home, and together with Mohobub Florez, Myme Martinez, Bernard Higinio, Peter Jeep Lewis, Faltas Nolberto and Calypso Lopez, put a band together. They quickened the sound of the traditional music they remembered from childhood, added an electric guitar and some turtle shells and three years later were recognized at the International Jazz Festival in New Orleans. Cayetano's studio is at 74 St. Vincent Street and he invites music and art lovers to visit.

RECORDED PUNTA MUSIC: The following are just a few artists whose CDs you may enjoy. The most famous for all Punta Music is **Andy Palacio's** *Til Da Mawnin*, and another is *Keimoun*. **Cayetano's** recordings are *In Mi Country, Sweet Africa, Punta Rock* and *The Beginning*. **Brad Pattico's** recordings are, *Ethnic Boom n Chime* and *Belizean Boom n Chime Band*. Another famous Punta Rock recording artist is **Nelson Gil**. His albums are *Baila Punta* and *Giving My Love*. Almost as famous as Palacio is **Mohobub**. Traditional women's songs are recorded in the CD called *Garifuna Women Voices*, which includes music from Belize, Guatemala and Honduras.

Garifuna Settlement Day has not always been a time for celebrating. In 1857 when the Garafuna were trying to eke out a life for themselves in the Dangriga area, the government informed them that they were squatters and put them all on reservations. It wasn't until 1941 that Settlement Day was recognized as a special day, though no holiday was attached to the event. Then in 1943, those living in the south were permitted to have a holiday on that day. Finally in 1977, November 19th became a national holiday and the Garifuna may now share their celebrations with other cultures. Prior to that they held their celebrations in secret.

Dr. Theodore Aranda is the head of the World Garafuna Organization and he lives at 28 St. Vincent Street, ☎ 522-2933. Dr. Aranda has been involved in the monumental task of trying to obtain reparation for the Garifuna people for wrongs suffered under the British during the 1700s. This task was started in the mid-1990s when it was first established that the Garifuna were entitled to reparation. The organization, then national, had to become international before it could continue its pursuit. This happened at a convention in New York in 1998. The movement has grown and now the organization has solid plans for the Garifuna people. If you wish to offer support or learn what has happened in the recent past, please stop in to Dr. Aranda's office.

If you're interested in going birding in the area, contact **Birding Pals**, www.birdingpal.org, the birders' networking group. There is a Birding Pal in Dangriga. You can read more about the group and its history on page 166.

Gra Gra Lagoon is just two miles south of Dangriga and is good for birding. Go to the beach in town and head right (south) until you come to a fairly decent-sized creek flowing into the ocean. Yemeri Creek borders private property. Do not cross it, but head upstream to the lagoon. Gra Gra is a small lagoon and estuary that is the nesting site of numerous birds. The lagoon is under protection for both birds and crocodiles. The walk will take about an hour and, even if you are not a birder, you may want to stretch your legs on this quiet outing.

These rafters get a close-up view of an iguana.

You can cycle to **Mayflower ruins**, a total of 15 miles each way. See *The South*, page 360, for a description of the ruins. The ruins themselves are not spectacular but the jungle is and bird sightings are good.

Kayak rentals are available from **Island Expedition's** local Dangriga office from December to the end of April. Single kayaks run $35/day; doubles are $55/day. Or you can rent by the week for $210/single, $350/double. Contact them at ☎ 522-3328, or visit www.belizekayaking.com.

Tour Agencies

C & G Tours and Charters, 29 Oak Street, ☎ 522-3641, cgtours@ btl.net, $$, has tours to the reef and the ruins. The owner, Mr Godfrey Young, offers prices that are reasonable to places where other companies may not be able to take you. One such place is Dangriga itself, a city tour that includes a visit to a drum crafting shop, a Garifuna Temple, a cassava farm, a hot sauce factory and the Green Bottle Winery. You may also get to meet a Bouyei (High Priest) at the temple. This is a full day's tour for US $50.

C & G also specializes in a **Mayflower Bocawina National Park** trip. Go with them if you don't want to do it yourself. They will point out birds and plants, animal prints and animals that may not be spotted by the untrained eye. They offer two hikes; one goes along Silk Grass Creek to a waterfall and takes only half an hour. The second, the **Antelope Falls Trail**, is a moderately strenuous climb with an elevation change of 300 feet (100 meters). Once at the falls, those with energy to spare can climb to the top of the mountain. The best feature of this tour company is their cultural knowledge.

SHOPPING

 Garifuna culture is represented in the **Gallery of Benjamin Nicholas**. Nicholas is one of Belize's most famous artists. Born in 1930 in Barranco to farming parents, Nicholas studied art in Guatemala. His brilliance was quickly recognized and he received a fellowship to study at the University of Minnesota for three years. He has since received many awards and commissions to do paintings in public buildings.

Besides Nicholas's works, drums made by **Austin Rodriguez** are on display. The gallery is located at 32 Tubroose Street, ☎ 502-3752, and is open from 8:30 am to 4:30 pm every day, except Sunday. For authentic Garifuna foods, **Mrs. Felicia Nunez**, 5 Southern Foreshore, ☎ 522-2385, has been recommended. **Mrs. Williams**, another famous artist in Dangriga sells hand-made baskets and hats. **Sabal's Farm** (just out of town) makes cassava bread for purchase. Eating cassava bread at least once is a must while in the south.

PLACES TO STAY

Chaleanor Hotel, 35 Magoon Street, ☎ 522-2587, chaleanor @btl.net, $$, is one block west of the main post office. This is a great place, clean and comfortable with friendly hosts. A new section has spacious rooms with private baths, hot water and tiled floors. There is free coffee

HOTEL PRICES	
$	$20 to $50
$$	$51 to $75
$$$	$76 to $100
$$$$	$101 to $150
$$$$$	over $150

and water offered in the main lobby, where you can sit and enjoy your drink. The rooftop **restaurant** and bar serves good food, both international and Belizean, at reasonable prices. During high season Garifuna drummers perform at the hotel.

The owner of the Chaleanor Hotel, Chad, is a bucket of knowledge about the area and is never too busy to give you a piece of useful advice. His son is a guide.

Jungle Huts, 4 Ecumenical Drive, ☎ 522-3166, $$, has 10 rooms, all with private baths and hot water. Located some distance from the beach, this is a good place to stay if you need a touch of quiet, especially during the Settlement Day celebrations.

Bonefish Hotel, 15 Mahogany Street, ☎ 522-2243 or 800-798-1558, www.bluemarlinlodge.com, $$$, is just up from the waterfront. The rooms have fans and private baths with hot water. They are very clean (Ihave been told this by fellow travelers). When I came to look at the rooms, I woke up the desk clerk and in his drowsiness he was unable to show me a room. This is also the office for Blue Marlin Lodge on South Water Caye.

Pelican Beach Resort at the north end of Dangriga, ☎ 522-2044, www.pelicanbeachbelize.com, $$$$, was first a dance hall bought by Mr. Bowman Sr. in 1969. It was his son and daughter-in-law who saw the potential of it becoming a resort, so they moved to Stann Creek (as the

town was then called) and started renovations. In 1971, the doors were opened at this first-class hotel. All rooms are on the second floor of the main building and have private baths with hot water, telephones, cable TV and air conditioning or fans. A second building, also of colonial design like the main one, has eight additional rooms.

There is a beachfront **restaurant** and bar, a gift shop and an interesting aquarium in the lobby. The restaurant offers numerous seafood and vegetarian dishes. In the morning, complimentary coffee is usually ready by 5:30 am. A sister hotel is located on South Water Caye, just 14 miles from Dangriga.

Bluefield Lodge, 6 Bluefield,, bluefield@btl.net, ☎ 522-2742, $$, comes highly recommended by more than one traveler I met. The lodge's owner, Louise Belisle, is a pleasant lady who runs a tight ship. Her rooms are clean and most have private bathrooms with hot water. Some rooms have TVs. There is also a nice balcony on which to sit. You should book ahead of time as this place is always full. Check at the up-to-date bulletin board near the front desk for news and travel contacts.

Pal's Guest House, 868 A Magoon Street, ☎ 522-2095 or 522-2365, $$, palbze@btl.net, has rooms set right on the beach. All have private baths and hot water, as well as fans and TVs. There are also rooms in the older building suitable for budget travelers. Only some of these have private bathrooms. I think the place is overpriced and the rooms in the older building are a bit tattered. However, the newer ones are facing the water and all have a little balcony.

Ruthie's Cabañas, 31 Southern Foreshore, ☎ 502-3184, $, has four cute little cabins with private bath, TV, and fan. The yard is nice. The cabins are small but the people are so very friendly that it makes staying here a pleasure.

Seaclift B & B, Magoon St., ☎ 522-3540, $$, is on the beach behind a fence and protected by a couple of large guard dogs. There is air conditioning and private bathrooms with hot water in the two available rooms. The big draw is the lovely balcony overlooking the ocean.

Vicky's Hostel, 1 Sharp St., ☎ 502-3324, has a unisex dorm for BZ $12 per person. It is so crowded that you must leave the room to change your mind.

PLACES TO EAT

The Riverside Restaurant on Stann Creek near the bridge is open every day except Sunday. It offers a plate of Creole foods for less than US $5.

Sunshine Restaurant, Havana St, has a good wonton soup for US $4. Anything else is barely okay. A far better place is the **Rainbow Restaurant**, north of the river bridge on Main Street, ☎ 522-2620. It is open daily from 10 am to midnight. They are the best in Dangriga for all meals. The egg foo yong and the fried rice are excellent. Large meals cost US $5.

J & N Restaurant, 18 Havana St, ☎ 522-2649, is a new place just opposite the bus station. It has great meals and, judging from what I heard, is the best eatery in Dangriga.

OTHER SERVICES

Vicki's Laundry & Internet Café, 1 Sharp St, ☎ 502-3324, was a great concept when it first opened. However, now, you can drop your laundry off and they will do it, charging US $2 per pound (expensive). It takes a few hours for them to do a load but the work is good and the clothes come back neatly folded. The Internet works well and there are quite a few machines at the back of the building.

Drums of Our Fathers Monument, Dangriga.

THE SOUTHERN HIGHWAY

To follow the Southern Highway that goes from the Hummingbird Highway to the southern tip of Belize, join the road that is six miles west of Dangriga. There is a service station on the corner. The junction will be considered Mile Zero. It's not paved all the way to Punta Gorda, but the unpaved part, when I was there, was only about 18 miles. The road should be completed by the time this book is published.

This is the road that will take you to the Jaguar Preserve, Sittee River, Hopkins and numerous wildlife preserves. You can also catch a ferry to either Guatemala or Honduras from Punta Gorda.

Follow the Southern Highway for six miles and turn right (west) to the Mayflower ruins. After 4.5 miles on the secondary road you will come to the Mayflower. The ruins and surrounding 7,100 acres have recently been made into a national park called the **Mayflower Bocawina National Park**. Bocawina is the mountain seen beyond the ruins.

■ MAYFLOWER RUINS

Mayflower is a small site that has been partially excavated. It has two **pyramids**. One had a large amount of sand and boulders brought in to make the base for numerous platforms. This was topped with a thatched-roof ceremonial building. In front of this pyramid, known as Maintzunun (meaning small hummingbird), was a pit where offerings to the gods were burned. During one of the later phases of occupation, the buildings at this pyramid were destroyed by fire. The second pyramid is much smaller and has just one level. It is called T'au Witz, which means Place of the Local God of the Hill. A small stele and altar were found here, along with some pottery shards.

PACT invested BZ $37,500 (US $18,000) for an ecological assessment of the area. As a result of the study, the area became a park.

To get here, turn off the main highway at the sign and follow the secondary road for 4.5 miles. It passes through acres and acres of orange groves before hitting the 7,000 acres of low-land broadleaf forest. The cost to enter the park is US $5 per person. From the gate, you can walk to Bocawina Falls, one of the prettiest in the country. Antelope Falls is the second set,which are worth a visit. Both can be reached in one day by taking a loop through the jungle back to the visitor center. The hike to Antelope Falls requires some up and down walking, while the other route is fairly easy. You can also go to David Falls and walk the four miles along a trail to the visitor center. However, at time of writing, this trail was not completed. Check before you head out.

Along the trails you may see peccary, howler monkeys and all three types of toucans, plus a very old jaguar who uses the road at night to hunt. There are also deer. To date, 242 species of birds have been spotted, including the rare keel-billed motmot.

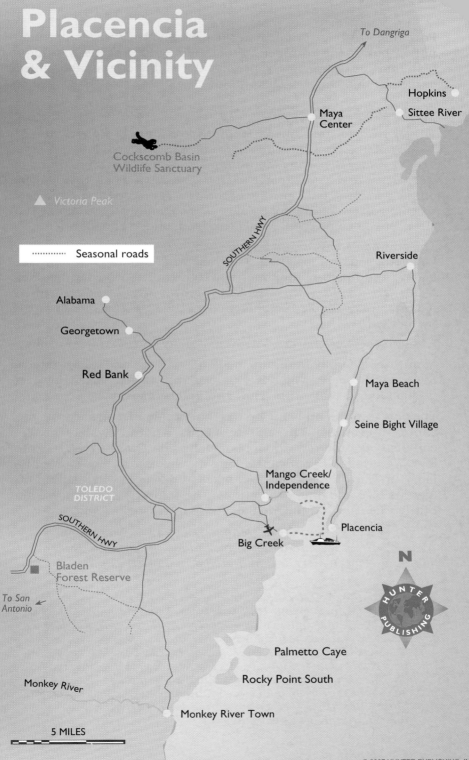

Placencia
& Vicinity

To Dangriga

Hopkins
Sittee River

Maya
Center

Cockscomb Basin
Wildlife Sanctuary

▲ *Victoria Peak*

Riverside

SOUTHERN HWY

············ Seasonal roads

Alabama

Georgetown

Red Bank

Maya Beach

Seine Bight Village

Mango Creek/
Independence

*TOLEDO
DISTRICT*

Placencia

Big Creek

SOUTHERN HWY

*Bladen
Forest Reserve*

*To San
Antonio*

N

HUNTER
PUBLISHING

Palmetto Caye

Rocky Point South

Monkey River

Monkey River Town

5 MILES

aching is a huge problem in the park and the warden has a do-
.ation box at the entrance to the building for anyone wanting to
help him get equipment to prevent the killing of animals. All fees
earned at this park go back into it.

A PLACE TO STAY

 Next to the ruins is **Mama Noots Jungle Resort**, ☎ 422-
3666, www.mamanoots.com, $$$, tucked into 50 acres
under Bocawina Mountain. This is the only private land on
the reserve and a great place to stay. The cabañas all have screens
on the windows, fans, private baths with hot water and, from each
balcony, a view of Antelope Falls. One cabaña has two rooms that
sleep three people each. Meals can be included or separate.

The grounds are well kept and the cabins are far from each other so
you get a sense of isolation. They use wind or sun power for elec-
tricity, and micro-hydropower when the other two can't be used.
Meals are made with organically grown foods and vegetarian
options are available. Breakfast costs US $10, and dinner is $18
per person.

A guiding service charges $50 for half a day and $70 for a full day.

Mama Noots family were rum distillers in Belize and they produced
the Royal Reserve, which is still available at her place. However,
they no longer make rum, they run hotels instead.

The best thing about being here is that **jungle hiking** starts at your
cabin. You can visit **Three Sisters Falls**, a natural waterslide. You
can also take the rewarding hike along Silk Grass Creek to Ante-
lope Waterfalls. If you want a long day hike, a trail goes from the
lodge up Back Ridge Creek. All hikes in this area will result in nu-
merous bird and animal sightings. The resort also runs horse and
buggy rides around the area for those interested.

> **AUTHOR NOTE:** *Mama Noots was Nan Noots
> great grandmother's nickname. It became Nan
> Noots when she was growing up. I love the name.*

▶▶ *Return to the Southern Highway and drive/cycle to the village of Silk
Grass. This is at Mile 8.* **Silk Grass** *is a small community of fewer
than 500 people. It has a medical center, church, school and some
houses. Silk grass is what people once used to make rope.*
*Continue along the Southern Highway to Mile 10 and a secondary
road called Hopkin's Junction. This is the turnoff to Hopkins. The sec-
ondary road heads east, makes a half circle through Hopkins four
miles from the turnoff, and turns south past a strip of luxury hotels to
Sittee River. It then goes west to join the Southern Highway, again just
2.5 miles south of Hopkin's Junction.*

■ HOPKINS

Hopkins has a population of about 1,000 people. It was rebuilt in 1961 after Hurricane Hattie demolished the original town. For a restful time, a good introduction to the Garifuna culture and finally the possibility of trying some Garifuna food, plan a stop at Hopkins. If your time there is during a festival or on a Saturday night, you will be especially lucky as the local people are receptive to strangers joining them while they drum and dance to Punta Rock.

Hopkins has one main street that goes north and south along the coast. The secondary road leading from the Southern Highway comes into the village at the center of this road. If you would like to learn more about the town, visit www.hopkinsbelize.com.

HISTORY

Originally, a community called Newtown, settled in the 1800s, was located a few miles to the north of present-day Hopkins. But a hurricane hit in 1942 and demolished that town, so the residents moved a bit south and renamed the town after a bishop who had drowned in the area 20 years before. Since the town was built, little has changed; the people are still fishers and farmers who work all week, socialize on the weekends, and go to church on Sundays.

In 1961, Hattie decided to do devastation similar to that inflicted by the 1942 hurricane. This time, however, the people rebuilt their village rather than moving.

In 1997 the power station burned and residents went back to using generators that were supplied after the 1961 hurricane.

GETTING HERE

Three **Southern Bus Line** buses go into Hopkins from the junction on the Southern Highway. They pass through Hopkins and Sittee River each day at 12, 3 pm and 5 pm. You can also catch any bus going south and get off at Hopkin's Junction; anyone with a vehicle will give you a ride into town. **Cycling** is safe and easy.

GRACIOUS GREETINGS

When greeting anyone after 2 pm in Belize, you should say, "good evening." If greeting anyone after dark, you should say, "good night." North Americans find it hard to use "good night" as a greeting, and find 2 pm a bit early to be saying "good evening."

THINGS TO DO

There is not much to do in Hopkins except hang out at the beach, eat, drink, rest and enjoy the Garifuna culture. However, the **bamboo** stands around the area are worth taking a look at, especially if you have not been to the Orient. It will make you appreciate the reverence the Chinese have for this plant. Walk along any stretch of road and you will see them. You can also rent a **kayak** and paddle up or down the coast and up Boom Creek to spot some birds. The **jungle trips** are always spectacular. You can also cycle to **Mayflower ruins** or take a taxi for US $12.50 to the Jaguar Preserve and hike their trails (see page 376 for a full description of this unique preserve).

Just across from Tipple Tree Beya at the south end of the village is **Hopkins Laundry**, with a variety store next door.

You may see black and white t-shirts for sale in town. They cost US $10 and the profits go toward the **School Book Awards**. These awards are given to students with the best essay. The title of the essay must start with "Why I deserve." Besides winning the essay contest, a student must have a year of high marks in all subjects to win the prize, which is US $100.

> **AUTHOR NOTE:** *The water supply in Hopkins can be disrupted at any time, so it is advisable to always keep a full bottle. The water, when running, is chlorinated and safe to drink from the tap.*

EQUIPMENT RENTALS

Many places offer bikes and kayaks to their guests, but **Tipple Tree** (see below) actually rents bicycles to one and all for US $15 a day and kayaks for US $20 a day. **Jungle Jeanies** (☎ 523-7047) also offers kayaks for US $20 a day.

NIGHTLIFE

It is best to be in Hopkins during the weekend, when you are more likely to run across a fund-raising party that could feature a local band. If some sort of sports game has ended, there's usually a party. All nightlife includes Punta Rock.

The Watering Hole Bar and Tropical Inn, in the center of town (no phone), has pool tables to help wile away the hours. Although these are popular bars with the locals, they don't rock late except on Saturday night.

Lebeha, at the north end of the village (follow the signs), was the first bar in town and it is still running because of the drumming that is practiced here by professionals and amateurs alike. Bato, one of the more skilled drummers, is usually there on Friday nights to play with anyone who is interested. There is a cover fee of US $5 per person. They also give drumming lessons on Saturday afternoons, starting at 2 pm. The owners promote local drumming and have a CD for sale.

Home made *hoodoot*, a popular Garafuna dish, is offered on weekends. It consists of fresh fish boiled in coconut milk and eaten with mashed plantain. It may be popular, but it certainly isn't my favorite. The cost is US $7 per serving.

PLACES TO STAY

In Hopkins

 Tipple Tree Beya, ☎ 520-7006, www.tippletree.net, $$, is near the south end of the village on the beach. The comfortable cabins have private bathrooms with hot water, fans and hardwood floors. Each cabin has a coffee maker, a fridge to keep the beer cold and a verandah from which to watch the ocean.

© Patricia Sturman

There are also two adjoining rooms for larger families (sleeps four) and a brand new cabin at the back that has a sitting area, sink, microwave and kitchen table. This cabin is a very good deal. All cabins are solid wood tastefully decorated with local art. Owner Trish Sturman is a strong supporter of local culture.

TIPPLE TREE WHAT?

Tipple Tree Warri is an African/Caribbean pit and pebble game. Boards are available at Tipple Tree Beya and Trish will help you learn the game. The board has two rows of six warri (houses) that are actually indentations in a hardwood board. Each player has 24 pebbles or seeds; four are placed in each warri. The players take turns moving in a counterclockwise direction. No dice are used. Each player may move only the seeds on his side of the board. A player starts by moving four of his seeds. The idea is to keep the warris with more than two or three seeds. If the seeds are moved and there are three or fewer seeds in the warrie, then the seeds are captured. When all six warries are empty on a player's side, his opponent must move so as to give up seeds. If a player captures all his opponent's seeds, he wins the game.

The game is so complicated that I don't quite understand my own and Trish Sturman's instructions. However, it is fun to play. Be sure to try it while in Hopkins.

Tania's, ☎ 523-7058, $, west of the beach, in a motel-style building. It's very hot here, although the rooms do have ceiling fans and some offer private baths. I thought it was a bit grotty. There are five rooms; one has a kitchen.

HOTEL PRICES	
$	$20 to $50
$$	$51 to $75
$$$	$76 to $100
$$$$	$101 to $150
$$$$$	over $150

The Hopkin's Inn, ☎ 523-7013, www.hopkinsinn.com, $$, sits on the beach. These two cabins can hold eight people and a new cabin (in process) will hold four more people. The white stucco cabins with red tile roofs are exceptionally clean and comfortable. They feature hardwood floors, fridges, coffee makers, private baths and fans, as well as screened windows. Breakfast of coffee, fruit and

homemade bread is included in your room rate. German is also spoken and Greg Duke, one of the owners, is a certified guide who can take you on many trips. His favorite is to the headwaters of the Sittee River. I must agree with his choice – the river is one of the most spectacular in Belize.

Ransoms Seaside Garden Cabins, ransoms@belizemail.net, www.members.tripod.com/cabanabelize, $, has been owned by Barry Spawn since 1984. He has made the property very attractive so his place is often full, but I understand reserving can be a problem so I'd say use this as a hit or miss place. If he has a cabin, great; if not, move on. The two cabins are tucked into a garden just a few feet from the beach. Each has a hot plate, small fridge, bath

and TV. There is also a fan and daily maid service. Kayaks and bikes are available and Barry has a book trade. For the lazy, there is a hammock on the porch. To get here, follow the road into Hopkins. At the end of the road, turn right, south, and at the forth lane turn left. There is a sign. Follow the road to the ocean. If no one is there, enter an unoccupied cabin and follow the instructions left on the table.

Windschief, ☎ 523-7249, www.windschief.com, $$, was once Jungle Jeanies but has been purchased by a high energy European, Oliver Guthoff, who is adding a lot of fine touches. The wooden cabins on stilts can sleep up to four people and are spotless and comfortable. Each has two beds with kitchen, satellite TV, radio and cold-water shower. Both cabins have porches with hammocks and are close to the beach. There is Internet service run off satellite for $5 per hour or you can plug your own in for no charge. Oliver also has 21 windsurfing boards and 30 sails so you can enjoy the wind under almost all conditions. At the end of the day, you can sit at his surf-side bar and exchange stories with other surfers.

Yugadah Inn, ☎ 503-7089, $, nunezjoy@hotmail.com, has four clean, but basic, rooms with fans. The bathroom is shared. The name of the hotel means village. Recently, Yugadah's has had a face lift so the place is much more appealing.

Lauruni Cabins, $$, on the north side of the road, are also basic, but they are a good deal. The clean rooms come with a double and a three-quarter-sized bed, good for three people (four if two kids share the three-quarter-sized bed), private baths with hot water, fans and cable TV. If no one is there when you arrive, go to Innies Restaurant and ask for Marva.

Caribbean View, ☎ 523-7050 $/$$, just north of the police station, has eight rooms at different levels of comfort. There are basic rooms with shared bath, spacious rooms with private baths and hot water, and beachfront cabins. All have fans and sitting areas (some just a small table with chair). Rates can be negotiated for long-term stays.

Heartland Inn, ☎ 523-7153, $$, on the beach, has two cabins with private baths, hot water, fridges and screened windows.

Lebeha, no phone, $, has two basic thatch and palmetto cabins with shared bath. This is a really funky place bordering on the primitive. Drumming sessions take place here on Friday nights, so if you are an early bedder, this would not be a good place to stay. However, if you are into Garafuna culture, you'll love it.

Jungle Jeanies, ☎ 523-7074, www.junglejeanie.com, $$/$$$, has moved to a larger place just a bit south along the road. There are signs. When they moved, they brought two of their cabins with

them so the budget crowd won't be disappointed. The rest of the seven wooden cabins are interspersed around the well-groomed gardens so they are non-intrusive to others. The cabins are spacious and well designed – one even has a loft. All have porches, private baths with hot water, fridges and coffee makers. The showers are all molded plastic so no leaks or mold. There are fans, writing desks and lamps in the cabins. The well-run restaurant offers special dishes like crêpes for breakfast. Bicycles are available for rent, and there's a volleyball court, horseshoe pits and a new entertainment center where you can take yoga or dancercise instructions or even have your own private party. For those camping, you can also pitch your tent here.

Whistling Seas, ☎ 503-7203, $$/$$$, run by Marcello and Obita Williams, is a lovely new place near the beach. Each cabin has private bath, coffee maker, painted floors and color TV. The property is exceptionally clean and the yard is well groomed. For larger groups, there is one big cabin with three double beds. All cabins have a nice porch and lawn chairs. The restaurant serves excellent meals.

Wabien Guest House, ☎ 523-7010, $$, has singles or doubles with private bathrooms and fans. The owners are eager to make you feel welcome and will prepare authentic Garifuna food for you if you contact them ahead of time.

South of Hopkins

Hamanasi, Box 256, Dangriga, ☎ 520-7073 or 877-552-3483, www.hamanasi.com, $$$$, is set on 17 acres with 400 feet (125 meters) of groomed beachfront. The name means almond tree in Garifuna. There are eight beachfront rooms, four beachfront family suites and four tree house cabañas in the forest. The rooms are spacious, the smallest measuring 17 x 26 feet. All have eight-foot porches, fans, screened windows, air conditioning, hardwood furnishings, local folk art and tiled bathrooms with hot water.

A 50-foot freshwater pool sits in front of the colonial-style restaurant and reception center. This is where all activity takes place; people team up to go diving or discuss their trip to the ruins. There is a wrap-around porch and a patio on the roof. Included in the price is a breakfast of fresh fruit, juice, tea/coffee and a basket of fresh bread. The bar serves everything, including imported wines. Dinners, $$$, are served on tables decked out with crisp linen and fresh flowers.

Two-tank daytime dives are available for US $70, and there's also a PADI certified instructor, diving courses and a dive shop. Dive trips usually head north of Tobacco Caye and include such sites as The Cathedral, South Cut, Carrie Bow Ridges, South Water Wall and The Abyss. Night dives are also offered and bikes and kayaks are available for guests.

Jaguar Reef Lodge, ☎ 800-289-5756, www.jaguarreef.com, $$$$$, has exquisite white stucco and thatched cabins (14 in all) tucked inside a garden abundant with plants. Each spacious room has tile floors, mahogany furniture, a mini-bar and fridge and hot water in the private bathroom. There are three styles of accommodations, each unique and exquisite in décor. The bathrooms especially have had great care given to them, with double sinks, ceramic tiles and huge hot tubs, some which are larger than rooms available in other areas of Belize. There is rattan furniture, open beamed ceilings and personal safes in the rooms.

There are two pools on site, one with a swim-up bar. The hotel is close to the water where you can use complimentary kayaks to paddle around. Those who take an all-inclusive package get things like private kayak lessons or free sailing. The most popular package for families is the Adventure Package that includes cave tubing, snorkeling, jungle walks and some boating. The restaurant, $$$, serves both local and international dishes. The thing that impressed me most about this hotel was the quiet.

Iguana Lodge is close to Sittee River and is run by Jaguar Reef. It's a nice kayak trip from Jaguar Reef to Iguana Lodge, where you can lounge on the hammock and have a drink.

Pleasure Cove Lodge, ☎ 520-7089, www.pleasurecovelodge.com, $$$, is a tiny place with only five rooms placed around a pool. Each room has a TV and VCR, private bath, tiled showers, air conditioning and fans. The owners offer bikes, kayaks and golf carts for guest use. There's an on-site bar and restaurant,

$$$, which features international or Belizean cuisine (it was the crêpes that caught my attention).

Pleasure Cove can arrange many types of tours, but they specialize in fishing – fly, spin or trolling. They know the location of the best permit flats in the world (not far from the lodge).

Beaches and Dreams, $$, ☎ 523-7078, www.beachesanddreams. com, $$$, is two miles south of Hopkins, right on the beach. It has four luxury rooms with hardwood floors and walls, 14-foot ceilings, rattan furniture, fans, verandahs and private bathrooms with hot water. Guests have complimentary use of kayaks and bicycles.

It is the Canadian hospitality and the food, $$$, that is the draw to this place. I heard about the meals long before I came to the resort. When I arrived, a couple was wolfing down a waffle with real maple syrup. They couldn't speak until they had finished. The shrimp on a stick is a favorite while sipping on a happy-hour drink. There are numerous kabobs from which to choose; the seafood dinner is also popular. Dessert is a must – fried bananas. Even if you are not staying here, try to stop in for a meal.

PLACES TO EAT

You can eat in someone's home as long as you order ahead. Meals seldom cost more than US $10. **Wabien Guest House** will also take special requests. Hopkins is one of the best places to get typical Garifuna food, such as areba, bundiga, tapau or sere. What are they? You'll have to try them and let me know what you think.

RESTAURANT PRICES	
$	$5 to $10
$$	$11 to $25
$$$	$26 to $50
$$$$	$51 to $75
$$$$$	over $75

Another option is to take a stroll or cycle down the beach to one of the bigger hotels, like **Beaches and Dreams**, where the food is legendary.

Sarita the Sweet Bun Lady supports herself and her children with her backyard baking. Be certain to buy one of her pastries. Ask in town which is her place.

Wine made by residents from local fruits and berries is worth seeking. A bottle from grape concentrate is about US $5 and one made from local fruits and berries is about US $9. My problem is an unquenchable taste for "real" wine made from grapes. But some of the local fruit wines softened that prejudice.

Iris's Place, north of town on the main drag, serves the best breakfast, lunch and supper, all of which can be enjoyed on a nice porch. The hamburgers are small and require two to satisfy some appetites. The fries are delicious.

Innie's Place is farther north than Iris's, but offers similar food and service. Getting special dishes is possible as long as you let them know ahead of time. It is best to go either the day before or in the morning of the day you would like a meal and let them know what you want and when you will want it. Ask a local to point out her house.

Marva's, close to the center of town, is the other good place to eat. If you get tired of Iris's or Innie's then switch to Marva's. Innie's, Iris's and Marva's are establishments owned and operated by local people. They are all good, and I recommend them.

Cho-Chi-Bo Restaurant is on the main road just south of Tipple Tree. It has been recommended to me although I never ate here. Let me know if you do. Other places of interest in town are the **Internet Café, So Much Hemp** and **Joya Art Center**. However, you hardly need a guidebook to explore Hopkins.

■ SITTEE RIVER

Continue past the resorts south of Hopkins for about four miles to Sittee River, a tiny Creole community located on the deepest river in Belize. The Sittee estuary heads inland for 10 miles from the Caribbean Sea. Here, you'll see freshwater fish and plants near the surface and manatees, stingrays and saltwater fish in the deeper water.

Many people use Sittee River as a stopping-off point en route to Glover's Reef. However, I urge you to stay at least a day or two so you can enjoy the culture and wildlife. The Sittee, host to so many interesting birds and animals in its green waters, is my favorite river in Belize.

GETTING HERE

Three **buses** (Southern Bus Lines) go from Hopkins Junction through Hopkins and past Sittee River each day. They come by the junction at noon, 3 and 5 pm. The road is rough gravel dotted frequently with potholes.

THINGS TO DO

 Paddle up the Sittee River and look for manatees, toucans, crocodiles, stingrays, frogs and green or orange iguana. The river is wide and slow and should be paddled early in the mornings when there are more birds and animals around. There are also the **Betsy Snowdon** and **Sapodilla lagoons** to visit. Paddling downriver, past the gas station, you will see a small channel on the right (south). This leads to the Betsy Snowdon Lagoon, where numerous birds nest. Since this is not an often-visited lagoon, your chances of spotting wildlife are better than they are in many other places. You can continue through the lagoon to the mangrove swamps near the ocean and then up the ocean to Sapodilla Lagoon. As

Keep your eyes peeled for wildlife as you paddle.

you paddle these lagoons, the highest mountain to the south is Victoria Peak, now recognized as the second-highest mountain in Belize (Doyle's Delight is the highest).

To return, paddle into the ocean and then back up the river to your starting point. Visiting both lagoons would be an all-day excursion. Be certain to take water and food.

Canoes can be rented from Glover's Guest House (☎ 520-7099, beside the dock) and at Toucan Sittee (☎ 523-7039, birdcity@btl.net).

Miss Minn (Minerva McKenzie), ☎ 523-7072, an herbal specialist and snake doctor, lives next door to Glover's Guest House owned by the Lamont family. You can order meals from Miss Minn if staying in Lamont's dorm. The food is Creole, spicy and good. You need to order a few hours ahead of time. Miss Minn is also an admirable woman worth talking to. Her husband was a logger who had a load of logs accidentally fall on him while at work. While he lay in agony, the rescue crew came with a crane to lift the logs so they could get him out and off to hospital. This they did, but before the paramedics could get him out, the logs fell again and this time killed him. Miss Minn was left fending for herself and her children. She did very well.

Possum Point Biological Station is on the opposite side of the river from Glover's Guest House, so you need a boat for access. The station is on 23 acres of land and is used mostly by scientists and educational groups. However, you are more than welcome to paddle across and walk along the one mile of **trails** they have going through the jungle.

Serpon Sugar Mill is now a park with a cut trail that leads to the mill. The path starts 1.8 miles east of the Southern Highway and .6 miles west of Sittee River. A strangler fig near the mill has a 100-foot circumference. The mill was functioning in the 1860s and the main piece of machinery to see from that era is a steam-powered cane crusher made in Richmond, Virginia. The mill, which was originally operated by an ancestor of Belikin Beer's Bowan family, is the oldest in the country.

You can **sail to Glover's Reef** on the Lamont family's sailboat, which was built in the 1850s by Jones Dock & Co. in Belize City. Constructed out of sapodilla and pine wood, the vessel was made to carry sand to construction sites along the coast. The Lamonts booked it to bring sand to them, but the boat arrived three days late operated by four drunk sailors with a dead chicken tied to the mast. The captain, with a serious hangover, sold the boat and all that went with it to the Lamonts. They got rid of the sailors and chicken before unloading the sand. The captain later wanted the boat back but the Lamonts refused. Now they use it during calm weather to sail to Glover's Reef. It carries up to 50 people and the trip can take anywhere from four to six hours one way, depending on the weather. The cost is US $50-75 per person.

Second Nature Divers, Box 91, Dangriga, ☎ 523-7038, www.belizenet. com/divers.html, is based on the Sittee River close to its mouth. The people here specialize in diving trips to South Water Caye Marine Reserve, but they also like the  Grand Channel, Hole in the Wall, The Crack and Elkhorn Crossing. For more experienced divers, they offer a run to Sharks' Cave, where black tip and grey reef sharks can be found.

Second Nature has equipment for rent, offers lessons and can arrange for any land tours you may want. It will also make reservations for you at different cayes.

PLACES TO STAY

Glover's Guest House, ☎ 520-7099, $, owned by the Lamont family, is beside the dock and next door to Miss Minn's. The house offers dormitory-style accommodations and can sleep 13 people. Each bed has a mosquito net. The property is hospital-clean and there is a shower house next to the dorm. You can also camp on the grounds if you have a tent. There are canoes for use. Again, in my opinion, exploration of the river is a must.

HOTEL PRICES	
$ . . . . $20 to $50
$$ . . . . $51 to $75
$$$ . . . . . . $76 to $100
$$$$ . . . . $101 to $150
$$$$$ . . . . . . over $150

If a dorm is not what you want, stop at the **Toucan Sittee**, ☎ 523-7039, www.toucansittee.info, $/$$, just up the road from Glover's and by far one of the best places to stay in all of Belize. The cabins are set in a manicured yard dotted with fruit and palm trees and edged by the Sittee River. There are so many different birds on the grounds that some of the bigger hotels bring their guests here to birdwatch. The wooden cabins have accommodations for every budget, from a five-bed bunkhouse that shares a bath with a two-bedroom pad to a riverside apartment with a small kitchen. One of the apartments near the river has two double beds, a fully

© Toucan Sittee

equipped kitchen and a private barbeque pit. Those who don't want to cook can order meals from the owners – what a treat that is! When I was there, I had shrimp with sweet corn done in a cream sauce that made me lick the plate. Meals can be served in an outdoor palapa hut or your screened-in porch. At night, the place is so quiet only your heartbeat can be heard.

You can use one of their bicycles or canoes. Artists will find Yolita (the owner's daughter) an interesting cartoon artist. Her work, displayed throughout the property, reveal her great sense of humor, not to mention artistic skill. There are discounts for long stays or off season rentals and they take both Visa and Master Card. I would highly recommend staying here for at least three days. If rest is what you want, stay longer

Lillpat Sittee River Resort, ☎ 520-7019, www.lillpat.com, $$$$, is half a mile from the sugar mill on 50 acres of groomed yard surrounded by jungle. They have only four double rooms, all of which are luxurious. There is air conditioning, private bathrooms, wicker furniture, satellite TV and a swimming pool. The price of the room includes breakfast. The restaurant, $$$, offers European, Italian and American foods.

Kanantik Reef & Jungle Resort, ☎ 520-8048, www.kanantik.com, $$$$$, is nestled at the mouth of the Sittee River. This luxury hotel offers private cabañas with thatched roofs, double sinks in bathrooms, air conditioning and front porches. This lodge is exquisite, with an onsite restaurant, patio barbeque area and bar. All tours and meals are included in the room price. Tours can be arranged to ruins, upriver or out fishing.

PLACES TO EAT

A truck comes to Sittee River every Saturday evening or early Sunday morning to sell in-season **produce** that you can take out to the cayes or to eat while in town. The truck is old and carries a weight so heavy the back bumper almost scrapes along the ground. The produce is fresh and reasonably priced.

Your first choice for meals should be at Toucan Sittee, but you must stay there first (highly recommended). Baring that, **Miss Minn's and Glover's Guest House**, $, offer family-style meals – both places are recommended. If staying more than a day or so, be certain to have a meal at **Toucan Sittee** up the road (see above).

The **grocery store** up the road has some basic products and lots of cold pop. Sir Kalvert Renolds, the man who runs the place, has worked as a judge and a policeman, and is generally considered a good citizen. The interesting thing about this non-assuming person is that he was knighted by the Queen. If, like me, you've never spoken to a knight before, now is your chance.

▶▶ *Return to the Southern Highway at Mile 10 and continue south. The Sittee River turnoff is at Mile 12.5 of the highway. The next landmark is the Kendall Bridge that goes over the Sittee. At Mile 15 is the Maya Center and turnoff to the right (west) for the Cockscomb Basin Wildlife Sanctuary and Jaguar Reserve, Belize's showcase reserve.*

■ COCKSCOMB BASIN WILDLIFE SANCTUARY & JAGUAR RESERVE

Maya Center Village will likely be your home base when you visit the reserve. It has a total of 138 residents. Nine families who live in the village were relocated from their milpa farms in what is now the Cockscomb Basin Wildlife Sanctuary. One of the complaints of the relocated families is that they were not given new land after they were moved, but had to purchase or rent it from the government. And now, when they enter the park, they have to pay.

You must stop at the village and purchase a ticket (US $5 for foreigners) before entering the park. The ticket booth is in the gift shop at the entrance to the village. The shop is a co-op with a large selection of items from here and Guatemala. However, I do think the items were a tad overpriced.

Across the road is a trail that leads to a butterfly farm. Follow the trail across the creek and up the hill. The butterfly house is straight ahead once you emerge from the jungle. There is a $5 entry fee. When I was there I couldn't find anyone around so I don't know how well the farm is being managed. I did see a few butterflies through the window.

Cockscomb Basin Wildlife Sanctuary and Jaguar Reserve is six miles up the hill past the village. Since most of the way is steep, walking would take all day and cycling would take at least a couple of hours.

A **taxi** from the village to the sanctuary/reserve for one to five people will cost US $12.50 and $2.50 per person extra over five. To Dangria, the fare will be US $125, and to Hopkins, US $40.

Call **Hermalino Saqui**, ☎ 520-3034, or **Julio Saqui**, ☎ 520-2042, for taxi service. **Julio and Ernesto Saqui**, ☎ 520-2021, are also certified guides, who can take you to Victoria Peak, as can **William Sho**, ☎ 520-2042, another certified guide. These men are the best, but if you are not able to get hold of them, go to the grocery store/bar and talk to the proprietor. He will be able to rustle up a guide with whom you will be happy.

> **AUTHOR NOTE:** *The word yaguar in Mayan means "he who kills in one leap." The Spanish pronounce a "y" like a "j" so it is easy to see from where the word came.*

HISTORY

 Wildlife research scientist **Alan Rabinowitz** conducted a study in 1982 that two years later resulted in 3,000 acres being declared a "No Hunting" zone. It took another two years of hard work to have the area declared a reserve. This was the first land on the planet ever dedicated to the preservation of the jaguar and it got the attention of the world. The government in 1990 relocated nine Maya families living in the area and expanded the land to its present size. At that time, it was recorded that the reserve encompassed 102,400 acres of land, but with new electronic measuring devices, the recent GIS calculation indicates that there are only 86,929 acres.

It is believed that the reserve is habitat for 30 jaguars and that there are as many as 200 in the adjacent reserves (Chiquibul National Park to the west and the Maya Mountain Forest Reserve to the south). To keep these animals company (and well fed), 15 howler monkeys were  relocated from the baboon sanctuary up north (see page 148) in 1992 and another 23 added in 1993.

From the 1940s until 1983 (prior to the lands becoming a reserve), logging firms used the area. They took the wood, but they also paid rent and a per-stump fee to the government. The last company in there was the Belize Exotic Woods and Veneer Co. Old maps of the area show timber camps with names like Sale Si Puede (Leave if you can) and Vas a Fierno (Go to Hell).

TERRAIN

This moist tropical forest contains the headwaters of three important waterways: the **Swasey River, South Stann Creek** and the **Sittee River**. The Swasey is a tributary of the Monkey River. This is a lush environment for the numerous plants that grow here. On one trip the drive in took me past a field of bird of paradise and blooming wild bananas. The odor and the view was intoxicating. Nature is the main attraction.

A red-footed Booby.

The jaguar, a nocturnal creature, is the third-largest member of the feline family. An adult male can grow to 6.5 feet (two meters) long and weigh up to 220 pounds (100 kg). Females are about two-thirds as large as males. Jaguars are territorial and each male keeps about 16 square miles of territory. When walking on the trails, you will see lots of jaguar tracks, even if you never see the animal. The park also has 55 mammals, including pumas, margays, ocelots, jaguarundi, brocket deer, peccaries, and pacas.

There are armadillos, the jaguar's favorite meal, and otters, coati, kinkajous, anteaters and tapirs. There have been 300 birds recorded in the area and one small Maya ruin hides in the jungle.

The **visitor center** at the entrance to the park marks the site of a vanished logging village called Quam Bank. Outside the center is a mahogany tree planted by Prince Philip of England in 1988. Close to that is an "earth art" truck (now being taken over by the jungle) that once belonged to Alan Rabinowitz, the founder of the park. Inside the center are displays of the region's geology, flowers and animals. There are some butterflies and a single jaguar skin, donated by a man who no longer wanted it on display in his bar. In a jar, where all good snakes should be, is a fer-de-lance. I hope this is the closest you will ever come to one. There is also a relief of the Cockscomb Basin so you can figure out where you were after you take your planned hike.

Cockscomb Basin Wildlife Sanctuary

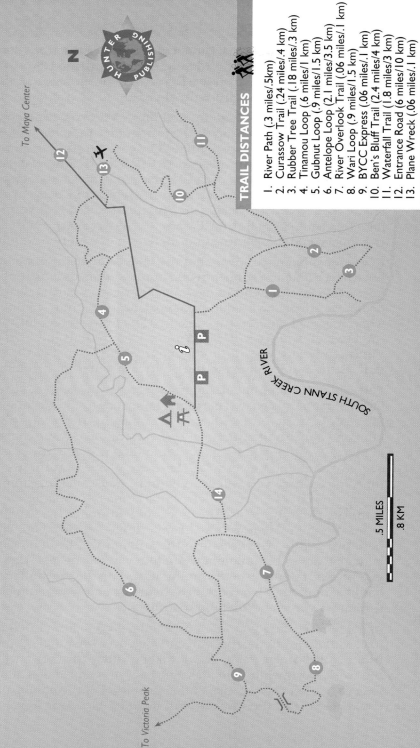

N

To Maya Center

To Victoria Peak

SOUTH STANN CREEK RIVER

TRAIL DISTANCES

1. River Path (.3 miles/.5km)
2. Curassow Trail (.24 miles/.4 km)
3. Rubber Tree Trail (.18 miles/.3 km)
4. Tinamou Loop (.6 miles/1 km)
5. Gubnut Loop (.9 miles/1.5 km)
6. Antelope Loop (2.1 miles/3.5 km)
7. River Overlook Trail (.06 miles/.1 km)
8. Wari Loop (.9 miles/1.5 km)
9. BYCC Express (.06 miles/.1 km)
10. Ben's Bluff Trail (2.4 miles/4 km)
11. Waterfall Trail (1.8 miles/3 km)
12. Entrance Road (6 miles/10 km)
13. Plane Wreck (.06 miles/.1 km)

.5 MILES
.8 KM

HIKING

 Just beyond the visitor center numerous trails lead into the jungle. The short **Plane Wreck Trail** leads to a wrecked plane that crashed during a wind storm because the pilot never saw one of the high trees. He lived.

To make the four-day hike up and down **Victoria Peak** you must have a permit (US $5) from the Forestry office in Belmopan, ☎ 822-3412. You must also hire a guide. The cost of camping on the trail is US $5 per day and a guide is US $12.50 a day. Pay your fee at the Department of Forestry. First climbed in 1888 by Goldsworthy, Victoria Peak was then considered the highest in Belize. Now that credit goes to Doyles Delight in Chiquibul Reserve. If you wish to hike this trail, do so during dry season. In wet season the climb up is slippery and dangerous, and there are also more mosquitoes.

It was recommended to me that the hike be done in rubber boots. I have never hiked in rubber boots, but it sounds as if blisters would develop before the end of day one. However, wearing wet leather boots for three days sounds almost as bad. Start hiking early, when it is cool, and be sure to carry lots of water. A tent will keep the bugs off while you sleep. You can rent a tent in Maya Center Village to take with you up the mountain. The cost is US $10 per tent. Bring water tablets to purify stream water for drinking.

The trail to the summit of Victoria was recently cleared, so walking for the first part is easy. There isn't much change in elevation to the first camp at the Sittee River, eight miles in. Here you will find a kitchen shelter and outhouse. Day two will take you to base camp at Mile 12. Although much shorter in distance, day two is grueling as you go up and down hills. There are no views until just before the camp, where you will see Victoria's Peak sticking up over the green. You must cross a rocky knoll prior to dropping down into campsite two. Jump into the creek and sit under the waterfall before settling in. Make yourself comfortable because you will sleep here two nights. The ascent to the summit will be done with only enough food and equipment to sustain you for the day. Day three's ascent will take five hours, minimum. Part of the walk requires boulder-hopping up a creek bed. Near the end, you must crawl up through a gorge and then onto a ridge.

In these three days you will have climbed 3,543 feet (1,080 meters) in elevation. From the top, you can look over the jungle to a second peak, called Molar Peak. As all hikers know, the views will make the work worthwhile. The descent back to camp takes almost as long as the ascent because of the steepness of the climb. Day four could get you all the way out, but it would be a long day.

If Victoria Peak does not fit into your plans, a shorter, one-day hike takes you to **Outlier Peak** only four miles one way with an elevation change of 1,800 feet (600 meters). It will take you six hours to get to the top, which translates into an average of .6 miles an hour – that's pretty slow walking. The first part of the hike isn't too bad, but the last 45 minutes requires quite a bit of vine and root climbing. Near the top you will see both Victoria and Molar Peaks. It takes about three hours to return. Water must be carried and a guide is recommended, although not essential.

There are other trails available, named so you can guess what you will see – Tiger Fern Trail, Ben's Bluff Trail, Antelope Trail, Gibnut Trail and the Wari Loop. Some have waterfalls in which to cool off, while others seem only to have tons of leaf-cutter ants. Some trails take as little as 10 minutes to complete.

The park director is Ernesto Saqui, ☎ 520-3033. Call him for any details you may need that the warden at the visitor center can't help you with.

PLACES TO STAY

You can stay at the park if you wish. **Dorm-style beds** (US $20) sleep six to a room and there are also private **cabins** (US $50 a night). All guests have use of a well-equipped kitchen. **Tenting** sites are also available for US $5 per person. Halfway up the road to the park is a white house that offers rooms for US $55 per person. This is luxury. Call Ernesto Saqui, ☎ 520-3033, to make arrangements for staying in the white house. If staying in the park, see the warden at the visitor center.

HOTEL PRICES	
$	$20 to $50
$$	$51 to $75
$$$	$76 to $100
$$$$	$101 to $150
$$$$$	over $150

The village runs a **home stay program**, which is also organized by Ernesto Saqui, ☎ 615-2091, nuukcheil@btl.net. The cost is US $20 per person and it includes one dinner and one breakfast. Meals only are available for US $5 per person if you are not staying in a home but need to eat. Staying in the home of a Maya will give you a lot of insight into the ways they live in harmony with the jungle.

All of the places listed below are in the Maya Center Village.

Nu'uk Che'il Cottages, ☎ 615-2091, $$, features a group of cottages at the end of town closest to the reserve. The name means "middle of the forest," and it perfectly describes the setting. Each cottage is a white plaster, thatched-roofed building with two rooms. They are basic, but clean, and the rooms have fans and electricity. There are separate bathroom facilities. The owner is Aurora Saqui, wife of the park director and sister of the famed Garcia Sisters from San Antonio, Cayo District (see page 231 for more about the sisters).

Mejen Tzil Lodge, ☎ 520-3032, isaqui@btl.net, $, has a row of rooms with a shared porch. The rooms are basic but, again, clean and comfortable. None offers a private bathroom; the toilet is an outhouse. You can get meals here even if you're not a paying guest. The **H'men Herbal Center and Medicine Trail** is on Nu'uk Che'l Cottages grounds and you can walk it for US $2. The lodge supplies a handout so you can guide yourself. Alternate attractions include Maya spiritual healing prayers, acupuncture, a snake doctor, chiropractor, midwife and herbal doctor. You can learn a lot by speaking with these people. There is also a gift shop at the center.

Nu'uk Che'il Restaurant, $, ☎ 615-2091, provides local dishes like corn tortillas, tamales, corn porridge and corn biscuits. Maya tea is also offered. They have a delivery service up to the sanctuary and reserve. You must order in town and they will deliver the meal when you want it.

▶▶ *Return to the Southern Highway at Mile 15. Continue south for 6.3 miles, over the South Stann Creek River Bridge, until you come to the road to Placencia at Mile 22.2.*

■ PLACENCIA PENINSULA

Placencia Peninsula is a 16-mile strip of sandy beach that has resorts all the way to the tip. Seine Bight is the only village. Placencia has replaced Caye Caulker and Ambergris Caye as the most popular beach destination in Belize. For the most part, places along the coast here are less expensive and the services are better than they are at any other beach locale in Belize. Close proximity to the ocean gives you the opportunity to enjoy all water activities. Plus, you are closer to land destinations you may wish to visit, like caves and ruins.

Placencia itself went through hell on October 8th, 2001, when Hurricane Iris hit and destroyed almost everything. But, like the phoenix, Placencia rose out of her ashes to reign again.

Most of the action is on the left (east) side of the road going to Placencia, because the ocean and beaches are the main attraction. The water to the right (west) is referred to as "the lagoon" and is popular with birders.

Since the last edition of this book, the lagoon side of the peninsula has developed with swamp land being filled with sand so huge houses can be built on top.

I have tried to list the hotels as they occur along the strip. Most places offer something unique and I am certain there is something for everyone. For information on Placencia, the absolute best website is www.placencia.com. It offers objective information about services on the peninsula and there is almost nothing that can't be answered.

We'll follow the peninsula from Riversdale to Placencia town.

GETTING HERE & GETTING AWAY

▸▸ *Turn left at Mile 22.2 off the Southern Highway. Drive/cycle for 1.5 miles and stay right at the curve. It is another 10 miles to Riversdale and the start of the strip. Turn right (south). The Placencia Lagoon will be on your right (west), visible for part of the drive down, and the Caribbean is on your left (east), visible for the other part.*

If you would like to get to the mainland and continue south, hop on the **ferry** that goes from Placencia over to Independence or Mango Creek (the same town split by a creek). From there, it is only five miles to the Southern Highway. The ferry goes twice a day; once mid-morning and once mid-afternoon and it meets the buses traveling north and south along the Southern Highway. If going south, it's a waste to travel all the way up the peninsula and then back down again. All buses along the Southern Highway stop at Mango Creek.

Gulf Cruise Boats leave from the dock in Placencia for La Ceibe, Honduras every Friday and return every Monday (US $25). There are also private boats that will take you. For further information, go to the dock and enquire.

THINGS TO DO

Besides lying on the beach and tanning, **swimming**, drinking beer and eating, you can try **snorkeling**, **diving** or **fishing**. You can play coconut **bowling** or go for a **booze cruise**. You can write postcards or go sailing. For diving or snorkeling, explore the more than 20 miles of underwater canyons and mountains dotted with fish of every size and color imaginable. All these activities are just off shore. Twenty dive sites close by cater to all skill levels. You can also visit some of the cayes – Laughing Bird, Pumpkin, Ranguana and Silk cayes are all close.

There is **windsurfing**, **sea kayaking** and **bird watching** on the lagoon along with grand slam **fishing** opportunities. Most hotels along the strip have tour offices and some have equipment rentals or dive shops.

See *Tour Operators*, below, for tours, equipment rentals and prices.

Besides lying in the sun and drinking rum, you can attend the **Lobster Fest**, which celebrates the opening of lobster season and is usually held on the weekend following June 15th. Check with the tourist office, located at the most southeast end of the town, or go to their website, www.placencia.com, for the latest information. This fun-filled weekend is a must if you are anywhere near here. The festival features a fishing tournament, races, a parade, dancing, food and concerts. Although I have never been around for the festival itself, judging from the photos I have seen, hundreds of people attend. Proceeds from the festival are used for community improvements. I also recommend that you enter in the draw, which offers prizes such as airline tickets to the US and all-expenses-paid weekends at luxury resorts in Belize.

The **Booze Cruise** is for those who are tired of moving or just want to lie back and spend a day on the deck of a boat sightseeing. On

the way up the peninsula, you will stop for refreshments (cost extra) at some of the more famous lodges like Jay Birds, Rum Point Inn and Robert's Grove. The trip ends at Mango's in Maya Beach, at which time you return to Sugar

Placencia

To Seine Bight & Dangriga

□ Robert's Grove
□ Miller's Landing

□ Rum Point Inn

□ Mariposa Resort

□ Sak's Place
□ Turtle Inn

MANGO CREEK

MAIN ST

□ Toucan Lulu
□ Manatee Inn
□ Lydia's Guest House

□ BJ's Restaurant

● Laundromat

Caribbean Sea

□ Sea Spray Hotel

Donna's Rooms □
Kingfisher
Adventures

Sugar Reef
Sunset Lodge
Debi & Dave's Last Resort □

□ Ranguana Lodge

□ Daisy's

□ Cozy Corner Restaurant

● Purple Space
Monkey Internet

□ Secret Garden House
□ Dianni's Guest House

Placencia Lagoon

● Saddle Caye South

☎ BTL (phone) office
□ Coconut Cottage
□ Omar's Guesthouse & Restaurant

Cayescape Tours ●

SIDEWALK

Bakery ●
Pickled Parrot
□

● Wallen's Mkt

□ Sugar Reef Sunset Lodge
● POLICE

The Galley □

GAS

● Nite Wind Guiding Service

Tourist Office ℹ

POST
OFFICE ●

Ocean Motion Guide Service ●

Guatemala boat dock

Placencia
Caye

To airport

□ Paradise Vacation Hotel

Soulshine Resort □

□ Tipsy Tuna Sports Bar

N

BIG CREEK

GAS

HUNTER
PUBLISHING

NOT TO SCALE

Reef for a complimentary cocktail on their deck overlooking Placencia Lagoon. This tour is offered by Cayescape Tours, ☎ 523-3285 (see below).

Anyone with a boat will likely be willing to take you on a **river trip** – the Monkey River is a popular choice (see *Monkey River Town*, below).

Cool Running Bike Rentals, on Placencia Road beside the lagoon (no phone) offers rental bicycles at reasonable rates.

Laughing Bird Caye Marine Park Visitor Center is open from 9 am to 4:30 pm. In order to visit the caye you must get a permit from the center first. It's located at the harbor end of town east of the town dock. See *The Cayes* chapter for more details.

Seine Bight is a tiny Garifuna village of about 800 people four miles north of Placencia. It's nestled between the sandy beaches of the Caribbean on the east and the Placencia Lagoon on the west, with the highway running through the center. Besides luxurious resorts, Seine Bight offers a unique cultural experience with the Garifuna people. Whether walking around with friends or taking a four-hour historical/cultural walking tour, you will enjoy this quiet little place.

In the center of Seine Bight, **Veras** offers traditional Belizean dishes of chicken, rice and beans. There is also the **Kulcha Shack** and **Lola Delgado's** if you'd like to listen to music as you eat.

The **Hungry Gecko** on the main street has a restaurant upstairs and a local grocery store down. The restaurant's meal of the day is excellent. Otherwise, it takes time for the staff to cook what you order. The meals are large. The grocery store is a good place to purchase things like hot sauce or spices to take home as they charge you the same prices as they do Belizeans.

Seine Bight has a church, a police station and a community center, as well as two **Dugu temples** where the Garifuna worship. Priests from the temples can rid members of things like bad luck or illnesses by singing, dancing, drumming, eating and drinking. Visitors are welcome.

The Placencia Airstrip is the next landmark on your way south along the peninsula, en route to Placencia (town).

Placencia has a population of about 10,000. It's known for its famous sidewalk that runs for 4,071 feet (1,221 meters). Named in the Guiness Book, it was originally built so that fishers could haul their day's catch up in wheeled barrels. The sidewalk was almost totally destroyed by Hurricane Iris, but residents are finding creative ways of raising money to rebuild the walkway and the town.

Besides being the latest sea and sun hotspot in Belize, Placencia is a friendly village where you will feel welcome. The tourist office has been operating since 1998 and is not just an information center. It publishes a community newspaper that sells for BZ $1 (or you can read it on-line at www.placenciabreeze.com). The staff also coordinates fund-raising events like the Lobster Fest. In the past, they raised enough money with these events to rejuvenate the famous sidewalk. They organize tour-guide training sessions and are the main information center during a hurricane. The office is open Tuesday to Saturday, 9 am to 5 pm and is located at the most southeast end of the town. They can give you an indication of what a room or tour will cost.

TOUR GUIDES/COMPANIES

You can fish with world-famous angler Charles Leslie of **Kingfisher Adventures**, ☎ 523-3323 or 523-3322, www. belizekingfisher.com. His 30 years of experience allows him to take you to places where you have the chance to earn the Grand Slam prize for catching permits, bonefish and tarpon all in one day. He owns Tarpon Caye, complete with a fishing camp, cabañas for rent, plus a clubhouse and fly-tying shop. Lessons are offered. The cost is US $275 a day for fly-fishing and troll lessons, $450 for blue water, and $275 a day for light tackle.

RECOMMENDED FLIES

Charles Leslie suggests using the following flies:

- Tarpon – Clouser Minnow, Cockroach Deceivers
- Permit – MacCrab del Mecken, Moe Fly
- Bonefish – Crazy Charlie, Bemini Bone, Snook Fly
- Barracuda – Cudo Fly, Fish Hair and Nylon Middlefish Balad.

UnBelizeable Adventures Ltd., ☎ 523-3179, www.unbelizeable-adventures.com, specializes in arranging weddings, honeymoons and educational tours. These can be all-inclusive. For weddings, the company will take care of all wedding plans and also organize trips to caves, ruins or cayes. I should have asked if they would marry you in a Maya temple, send you into a cave on a honeymoon and then provide Garifuna fertility treatment.

Destinations Belize, ☎ 523-4018, www.destinationsbelize.com. Mary Toy offers the usual trips to anywhere in the southern part of Belize, whether it be a hike to a Maya cave or a canoe journey up a jungle river. However, her specialty is in customized tours of the more rugged type. If you have camping equipment and would like to camp on the cayes, Mary can get you there. You may camp only on Silk Caye, North East Caye on Glover's Reef and in the Punta Ycacos area near the Punta Ycacos Lagoon. Rates vary depending on the type and length of your trip, but all details are provided on their website.

Guides must be used for many of the trips you take in Belize. You can hire one through a company or, on some occasions, you can request a special one. In Placencia, **Captain Bobo**, ☎ 603-0342, is a favorite. He does runs up the Monkey River (see *Monkey River Town*, page 402). This tour ends with a search for the ever-elusive manatee. Because Captain Bobo is so experienced, he often has success in finding the animals. An all-day tour for four people is US $250, including a cooked lunch.

If you are looking for something just a bit different, **Cayescape Tours**, ☎ 523-3285, offers a trip on the Sennis River. Lunch is included in the US $50-$75 fee. You begin this trip by taking a motorboat (laden with kayaks) up the river that flows through mangroves and jungle. At one point there is lush jungle on one bank and grassland on the other. This is prime birding country. As you continue, the banks close in and eventually you must switch to the kayaks. The water has also become clear at this point. Stop for a swim – the water is cool on top but warm near your feet, due to the undercurrents. On the way back the tour stops at a mangrove caye, where you can watch for manatee.

The same company offers a Booze Cruise (US $50), which starts at 10 am and goes up the coast, stopping at Sugar Reef, Jay Birds, Rum Point Inn, Roberts Grove, Wamasa Bar and Mango's at Maya Beach. The tour ends at the Sugar Reef Bar with a complimentary drink (if you can take any more) and a glimpse at the setting sun.

Ocean Motion Guide Service, ☎ 523-3363 or 523-3162, www. ocean-motion.com, has been offering tours from Placencia since 1995. Most of their tours revolve around the water, and cost between US $50 and $75. Whale shark snorkeling is a favorite. They also have snorkel equipment for rent at reasonable prices. Ocean Motion works with the University of Calgary studying the howler monkey on the Monkey River.

Toadal Adventure, ☎ 523-3207, www.toadaladventure.com, offers sea kayaking trips for small groups (no more than 10) who have not booked from home for an all-inclusive trip. If you decide, on the spur of the moment, that you want to kayak on the ocean and camp in a tent, talk to these people. They want an active crowd and have all equipment, including North Face tents, Wilderness

Systems Sealution kayaks, Seatwo closed-cockpit kayaks and Wilderness System open-cockpit kayaks. Life jackets are included with the rental. Chosen in year 2000 as the Tour Operator of the Year, they also won the National Tourism Award for Tour Guide that same year. A six-day, five-night island kayak trip costs US $965 per person, while a four-day, three-night jungle river journey costs US $538.

Nite Wind Guiding Service, ☎ 523-3176, is located along the sidewalk close to the town dock. Local Calbert Gardiner has been guiding for 15 years and knows every good fishing spot close to Placencia. You can also charter a boat for any trip of any duration. The cost for a guide and boat is US $275 a day. Boats for hire must be negotiated.

Saddle Caye South, ☎ 523-0251, www.kayakbelize.com, has tents, snorkeling gear, kayaks, and dry and wet bags for rent. Discounts are available to those renting for longer than a day. To get to the office, walk along the path behind the basketball court near Wallen's Market. Turn left (south) on Rocky Road and continue to a small channel. Turn right onto a lane south of the channel. The SCS lodge and office is just at the end of the lane at the lagoon pond. Overnight kayak trips run US $200 per person, and day kayak rentals are US $30.

Sea Horse Dive Shop, ☎ 523-3356 or 523-3166, www. belizescuba.com, has three boats to take out divers for day or night trips. With over 20 years experience, the owner knows where to go, especially during whale shark season. PADI and NAUI qualified divers offer instruction. A night dive costs US $75 per person; wall dives are US $75 and shark dives are US $100.

PLACES TO STAY

Plantation Beach

The first beach at the north end of the peninsula is called the Plantation. The first resort along the peninsula is the **Lost Reef Resort**, ☎ 606-7262, www.lostreefresort.com, $$$. It has individual cabins around a pool that overlooks

HOTEL PRICES	
$	$20 to $50
$$	$51 to $75
$$$	$76 to $100
$$$$	$101 to $150
$$$$$	over $150

their 120 feet of beach. The five cabins have private baths, queen-sized beds, and porches. Guests may use snorkeling gear, kayaks, on-shore fishing gear and bicycles. The resort can arrange day-trips or a day's fishing. There is a restaurant that serves fairly good meals.

Calico Jacks, ☎ 520-8103, www.calicojacksvillage.com, $$$, is the only hotel along this beach. A pirate-themed resort named after the 18th-century pirate, it has a rustic elegance. The hotel has seven thatched-roof cabañas on the beach with private baths, air conditioning and fans and every bed has a mosquito net. The floors are hardwood and the showers are wheelchair accessible. Interspersed along the beach, each spacious cabin has a splendid view of the ocean and the upper ones have a private balcony. The two-bedroom family cabins are popular, so you should book ahead. There is no TV, Internet or telephone, so seclusion is guaranteed. There is a swimming pool, restaurant and gift shop; all facilities are

© Calico Jacks Village

wheelchair-accessible. The owner is from the US and he knows that many of us like coffee in bed in the mornings. The coffee bar has a real cappuccino machine that is constantly in use (always a good sign), and the restaurant always has fresh seafood on the grill. **One-eyed Jack's beachfront bar** is a favorite hangout for those wanting to visit or meet new people. If sailing is your thing, you can rent a kayak or the resort's 52-foot ketch for a stay on the water. If land touring is your thing, bicycles and cars are also available for rent.

Maya Beach

Maya Beach is next along the peninsula. If staying along these beaches without transportation, local taxis cost $10 one way to Placencia. There are no buses, but hitching is not a problem. **Mango's Bar** is the favorite watering hole in this area. It is a high thatch roofed, beachfront building that is always full of foreigners. Although I haven't eaten here, I have received lots of recommendations for it.

Maya Beach Hotel, ☎ 520-8040, www.mayabeach.com, $$, has five theme rooms – Angelfish, Hibiscus, Iguana, Toucan and Jaguar – each with paintings from local artists. They have ceiling fans, private baths and hot water. The **Calypso Café** offers tropical drinks to go with your Belizean cuisine meal.

Joyce & Franks Bed and Breakfast, ☎ 561-683-3899, www.belizebandb.com, $$$$, is a grand two-level house on the beach. Each air-conditioned room has a fridge, microwave, double bed and private bath with hot water. The dock has a thatch hut, a sun deck and a diving board. Inside, the dining room features a great sitting area overlooking the Caribbean where you can enjoy all your meals or just the breakfast, which is included in the cost of the room. The owners are liberal-minded and love to sit and tell tales of the latest hot spot for birders or cyclists.

Maya Breeze, ☎ 523-8012, www.mayabreezeinn.com, $$$/$$$$, has cabins on the beach with nice-sized porches for lounging. There are four units in all, two with two bedrooms and the other two with one. All have air conditioning, and the kitchen has a fridge. Kayaks are available for rent and, on the side of the resort facing the lagoon, there is a café.

© Maya Breeze Inn

Green Parrot Beach Resort, ☎ 523-2488, www.greenparrotbelize.com, $$$$$, has two-storey, thatched-roof, wooden beach houses. The main floor has a living room and kitchen, while upstairs is a loft with one queen-sized and one single bed. The houses can hold four people and the kitchen is fully equipped. There is a beach-side patio and bar.

Diving Pelican Seaside Suites (vertical caption)

Diving Pelican Seaside Suites, ☎ 243-4591, www.thedivingpelican.com, $$$, have three suites with ceramic tile floors, French doors opening onto the beach, private bath, fully supplied kitchens with fridge and stove, and cable TV with DVD players. This is a very well kept and clean establishment. There is a palapa on the beach for guests and the place is within walking distance of the Hungry Gecko for great local cuisine. Snorkeling off the beach is recommended as the fish are numerous and exotic. Since there are just three suites, it feels like you've landed on a deserted island. They take Visa and MasterCard.

Barnacle Bill's Beach Bungalows, 23 Maya Beach Way, ☎ 523-8010, www.gotobelize.com/barnacle, $$$$, has two secluded bungalows with full kitchens. Actually, these are little houses, complete with everything except food and booze. Run by Bill and Adrian Taylor, these cabins can be rented for no fewer than three nights. They are good for honeymoon seclusion.

Singing Sands Resort, ☎ 523-2243 or 800-649-3007, www.singingsands.com, $$$$, is nestled in a lush garden with a 40-foot pool in the center. Six thatched-roof cabins have fans and fridges inside. There's also a **restaurant** (dinner runs about $20), gift shop and equipment rentals on site. Birders staying at the resort may use canoes to go to the lagoon. There is a nice dock leading from the beach to a hut where you can get some shade.

Maya Playa, ☎ 523-8020, www.gotobelize.com/mayaplaya, $$/$$$, has three cabins that are available by the day, week or month. The thatched-roof cabins sleep four, with two in the loft. There are shared cooking facilities. The owners rent equipment and can also arrange for a trip to Laughing Bird Caye.

Seine Bight

The only problem with staying at Seine Bight is that a taxi into Placencia costs $10 one way.

If you are in the area or just passing through, stop at the **Hungry Gecko**. Located just south of Mango's Bar, the Gecko serves huge portions of local cuisine for very reasonable prices. If you take the meal of the day, you will be served instantly, but if you want something à la carte, it will take time to prepare. Below is a grocery store that sells hot sauces and spices for far less than you'll pay in the tourist centers.

Blue Crab Resort, ☎ 520-4104, www.bluecrabbeach .com, $$$, has four air-conditioned rooms and two cabañas dispersed around five acres of land. The rooms feature hardwood floors, private baths, and each has a porch overlooking the water. The fan-cooled, thatch-roof cabins also have hardwood floors. Children under 16, traveling with parents, stay free. The gardens and jungle at the Blue Crab Resort are harmonious, housing many birds, lizards, fox, possum, coati and raccoons. There is even a pet coati named Bubbles, who occasionally comes to visit, and a jaguar with two cubs has been sighted. There are bikes available for rent and tours to other places can be arranged. The **restaurant**, $$, right on the ocean, offers special Asian cuisine. Linn, the chef, was born in Taiwan and loves to prepare her specialties. She also cooks American dishes.

Nautical Inn Adventure Resort is owned by Americans-turned-Belizeans Ben and Janie Ruoti; ☎ 520-3595, www.

nauticalinnbelize.com, $$$$. The hotel was one of the first on the peninsula and is still one of the biggest. There are 22 rooms, all with patio doors opening onto a pool. This is a very attractive place to stay. In addition to the nice rooms and pool, there is a gift shop, bar, and **restaurant**.

IGUANA MAMAS

The Ruotis (of the Nautical Inn, ☎ 520-3595) are involved in the iguana-raising project. They collect eggs that are vulnerable to predators and place them in an incubator, where the eggs are kept under controlled temperatures until they hatch. The baby iguanas are fed twice a day for four months after birth, during which time they are never touched by humans. Once they reach maturity, the iguanas are sent to nature preserves around the country.

North of Placencia Airstrip

When receiving directions, you will be told that the following resorts are "north of Placencia Airstrip." After Seine Bight, the locals refer to the resorts along the road as either north or south of the airstrip.

Robert's Grove, ☎ 523-3565, in the US 800-565-9757, www. robertsgrove.com, $$$$$. Classified as a five-star resort, Robert's offers it all, from qualified diving experts to a luxurious swimming pool in the front yard. Although five years ago the lodge had only four rooms, today it offers 32 in all, 12 of them luxury suites. The resort has added a new 50-foot Newton dive boat to its fleet and expanded the marina on the lagoon. The fly-fishing center has also been enlarged to accommodate the growing number of fishers who are drawn to the area. The location is perfect for fly fishers, who are able to catch a permit, a bonefish and a tarpon all on the same day. Robert's Grove also has a massage parlor, steam room, whirlpool and a salon offering manicures, pedicures and facials. It has a fitness room, kayaks, canoes, windsurfing boards, sailboats and bicycles for guest use. In the restaurant, $$$, a professional chef offers a different type of pasta each night. Wednesdays are reserved for poolside barbecues that feature dishes like lobster kabobs and shrimp scampi. The meal is accompanied by Garifuna drummers and dancers or reggae bands.

> **AUTHOR NOTE:** *Many kitchens advertised as "fully supplied," have microwaves but no stoves.*

Rum Point Inn, ☎ 523-3239 or 888-235-4031, www.rumpoint. com, $$$$$, has been around since 1974 so they must know what people want. Rum Point is fairly large, with 12 rooms in the main lodge and 10 cabañas. Each room has air conditioning, fridge and a personal safe for valuables. A fish-shaped pool may tempt you, but if sea water is your preference, the beach has a private dock and thatched huts for guests. The use of bikes, kayaks and snorkeling gear is complimentary. After a day of touring, you can book a massage to get rid of the aches or visit the library and bury your nose in a book. The owner is a librarian, so reading supplies are extensive and include magazines, newspapers, reference and history books and some good classics.

> **LOCAL LINGO:** *The Creole word "backra" means a white person and comes from "raw back" or sunburn.*

Miller's Landing, ☎ 523-3010, www.millerslanding. net, $$$/$$$$, has three rooms in one building and another two buildings with upper and lower rooms. The upper rooms are the most luxurious and come complete with waterbeds – just in case you don't get enough ocean during the day. There is a pool, gift

© Miller's Landing

shop and **restaurant**, $$, which serves the best pizza on the entire peninsula. The bar often has live entertainment. This resort is the furthest from the road and presents a good deal.

South of the Airstrip

Because jets don't land at the airstrip, the noise is of no consequence.

Mariposa Resort, ☎ 523-4069, www.mariposabelize. com, $$$$, has two cabins on the beach. Mariposa means butterfly in Spanish and, to me, this place is appropriately named. The cabins are decorated with Maya glyphs and statues, Italian tiles, fans and queen-sized beds. There are private baths with hot water,

and fully equipped kitchens with fridges, stoves (with four burners), microwaves, toasters and coffee makers. There are dishes and cookware so all you need is your food and drinks. Each cabin has its thatched-roof hut on the beach and there is a beach shower. The cabins are within walking distance of the village.

Sak's Place, ☎ 523-3227, www.saksatplacencia.com, $$$$/ $$$$$, has every combination you could wish for, from a cabin with kitchenette that sleeps four to six people, to regular rooms, Colonial suites, Colonial Rooms, Garden Rooms or Belize Studio Apartments with full kitchens. There are even two budget rooms that share a bath for US $30 (double). Most rooms have tile floors, fans, private baths with hot water, verandahs and kitchenettes. The luxury side of the hotel offers a spa, reflexology treatments, massage therapy and yoga lessons.

This is a prominent establishment and the owner has been involved in many tourism/environmental projects in Placencia. He offers a 12-mile sea kayaking trip to French Louis Caye and a fully catered overnight campout. Part of French Louis Caye is mangrove forest. Snorkeling off the shore is possible, as is paddling over to another uninhabited, unnamed caye close by.

Turtle Inn, ☎ 523-3244 or 800-746-3743, www.blancaneaux. com, $$$$$, was totally destroyed by Hurricane Iris. This gave the owner, film producer Francis Ford Coppola, an excuse to rebuild the inn according to his own idea of luxury, which gravitates toward Asian design. Tucked into the natural jungle are 11 cabins with private baths, queen-sized beds, living rooms with pullout sofas, decks and outdoor beach showers. The beach runs along 650 feet (195 meters) of the coast. There is a pool, restaurant, dive shop and tour company. The **Gauguin Beach Grill**, $$$$, offers fresh seafood cooked over coconut husk coals.

Placencia

Toucan Lulu, ☎ 760-433-5451, www.toucanlulu.com, $$$$, has one cabin located on the sidewalk available for rent by the week. This is almost home, with fans, a full kitchen and full bath with hot water. It's clean and comfortable, good for a small family.

Manatee Inn, ☎ 523-4083, www.manateeinn.com, $$, has six clean rooms off a common porch. Each has a private bath, fan and fridge. The building is made partly of local hardwoods and is situated right in town, close to everything.

Lydia's Guest House, ☎ 523-3117, see the accommodations page at www.placencia.com, $, has eight rooms in a nice house with a verandah. Each room has a fan and shared bath. There are limited kitchen facilities available, but breakfast can be ordered ahead of time.

Sea Spray Hotel, ☎ 523-3148, www.belizenet.com/seaspray, $$/ $$$, has 19 rooms newly built after the hurricane and two more on the way. This is a good example of the Phoenix rising out of the ashes. There are a variety of accommodations, and every option has a private bathroom with hot water and fan. Some rooms accommodate two people only, with either a double bed or two singles. Some have fridges and open porches or beach decks. As you get more elaborate, the rooms have coffee makers and kitchenettes and are closer to the beach.

Ranguana Lodge, ☎ 523-3112, www.ranguana belize.com, $$$, offers five little cabins on the beach, right in town. They are clean and comfortable and have porches. Each one features a private bath with hot water, fans and a fridge.

Deb and Dave's Last Resort, ☎ 523-3207, see the accommodations page at www.placencia.com, $, has four basic rooms with fans and shared bathrooms. Although not on the beach, Deb & Dave's is very clean and the bus passes right by here. This is another really good deal.

Serenade Guest House, ☎ 523-3380, www.belizecayes.com, $$$, is a colonial-style house a block off the beach, behind Cosy's restaurant. The white plaster and bright tiles make it look clean at all times. All rooms have air conditioning and private baths. The owners of this guest house also own Frank's Island in the Sapodilla Cayes. If you are looking for a secluded paradise, ask them about it. Equipment rentals are available here.

Westwind Hotel, ☎ 523-3255, see the accommodations page at www.placencia.com, $$, has eight rooms with private baths, fans and fridges. On the beach there is a comfortable thatched-roof hut with hammocks. There are also two vehicles available for rent.

Carol's Cabañas, ☎ 523-3132, accommodations page at www. placencia.com, $$, has six individual units with or without baths, and/or kitchenettes with fridges. The owner, Egbert Cabral, would rather fish than work. If you would like to go with him, he may be able to get you a Grand Slam.

Secret Garden House, ☎ 523-3420, www.secretgardenplacencia. netfirms.com, $$, is a two-bedroom house on stilts. It's fully furnished and can sleep four comfortably.

Dianni's Guest House, ☎ 523-3159, $$, has four rooms with fans, fridges and private baths. A large balcony is adjacent to the rooms. Kayaks are offered for rent and Internet service is available. The staff will also do laundry for you. A gift shop is attached to the house. This is a clean and comfortable place to stay.

Coconut Cottage, ☎ 523-3155, www.placencia.com/members/coconut.html, $$$$$, is on the beach toward the north end of town and near the airstrip. These two spotlessly clean cabins have private bathrooms with hot water, fans and minimal kitchen facilities. **Harry's Cabañas** are also part of this operation. There are three cottages at Harry's for US $50 per night.

Omar's Guest House, ☎ 609-3135 or 609-2326, $, is along the sidewalk across from the school. The beach can be seen from the deck and so can the stars. After the hurricane, Omar rebuilt his hotel using recycled wood from Sonny's Resort, one of the first places built in Placencia. Some rooms have private baths, and all rooms are clean and large with ceiling fans. There is a laundry service and a restaurant downstairs.

Paradise Vacation Hotel, ☎ 523-3179, paradiseplacencia@hotmail.com, $/$$, was built in 1984 and sits on the shore overlooking the town dock. It has 16 rooms with fans, some have private baths and hot water. Kitchen facilities are limited, but there is a lovely deck on the second floor that is good for watching the action. This is a good deal.

Be Back Cabins, ☎ 523-3285, $$, are near the football field crossroads and are high in the air so they catch every little bit of breeze. If two are sharing a bed, these immaculate cabins are a good deal as the owners charge for the cabin, not per person. Cabins are totally equipped for comfortable living. Reasonable weekly and monthly rates offered.

Sea Side Hotel, no phone number available, $, has four basic rooms located just off the sidewalk. It is quite secure; the front door locks. Rooms have much-needed fans and private baths. However, the bathrooms need some bleach and if the fellows looking after the rooms decide to play music after midnight, you can't get away from the sound.

Soulshine Resort and Spa, 1 Placencia Point, ☎ 877-700-7685, 523-3347, www.soulshine.com, $$$$$. If it is pampering and body repair you need, this is the place. It is truly a spa in the old Roman style. There are the usual amenities like a **restaurant**, bar, swimming pool and secluded beach. Your package can be with or without meals. But above and beyond those amenities, there is the spa aspect. Sunshine offers reflexology, aromatherapy, yoga or Japanese Reiki. You can have a Maya facial treatment that uses red clay and herb-scented towels or a scalp massage with herb-drenched oils. Their best treatment is the ancient Maya bath. This takes 45-60 minutes and starts with a soak in herb-scented water, followed by a shower and a warm pool soak. You then graduate to a hot pool soak, a cold shower, a massage, another cold shower and a rest on the porch with a glass of water. If this doesn't suit you, there are also moor-mud wraps and seaweed wraps. For the salt rub, they combine salt, cornmeal and almond oil and rub it on your skin. You can be certain at the end of this one there will be no unwanted marks or calluses anywhere on your body. To reach Soulshine, walk behind the soccer field on the lagoon side of the peninsula (past south waters). There is a path from the soccer field to the

point, where you will see the island. Across from the little island is a doorbell mounted on a pole. Ring the bell and the little ferry will come across the 75 feet (22 meters) of water to get you. According to some, the quality of service has dropped recently and the place is now for sale.

© Soulshine Resort

South Waters Resort, ☎ 523-3308, www.southwatersresort.com,. $$$$$, is the elegant yellow and white colonial house right on the beach on the lagoon side of the peninsula where numerous catamarans dock. There are rooms in the main building as well as condos with air conditioning, full kitchens, dining rooms, living rooms with sofa-beds, walk-in closets, full bathrooms and porches. Each condo can sleep up to four people comfortably. They also have beach cabins that sleep two, with private baths, ceiling fans, coffee makers and microwave ovens. They can arrange tours and have kayak rentals, laundry service, maid service and cable TV with DVD players.

PLACES TO EAT

All of the bigger resorts offer dinner to non-guests. Most serve good food. Check out the hotel listings above for additional places to eat.

Omar's Restaurant, ☎ 609-3135 or 609-2326, $, on the sidewalk in Placencia, is well known and highly recommended for spicy Creole food. Rarely is this place not crowded. The food is good and there is lots of it. Prices are reasonable.

Tutti Frutti Italian Ice Cream Shop, $, in Placencia, has 24 flavors of homemade ice cream. Some of the more delectable flavors are vanilla chocolate chip, strawberry and mango delight. This is a must.

Purple Space Monkey Internet Café, $$, offers cappuccinos, lattés and espressos to help you get through the frustration of deleting all your unwanted hotmail messages.

Cozy Corner Restaurant on the beach was adamant that I not include his place in this book. In revenge, I am including him, but I can make no recommendations. He was far more interested in the women's body-building show blaring from a TV in the corner.

Crows Nest Café, ☎ 523-3308, is open 6:30 am to 10 pm daily and is located in the huge palapa in front of South Waters Resort and beside the dock. This is a great place to have a drink and watch the fishers/divers come and go. I especially like the look on men's faces as they pay for their gas that was used in the catamarans. I cannot attest to the food served here as I was so entertained by the fishers that I forgot I was hungry.

SHOPPING

Art N Soul Gallery, on the sidewalk, ☎ 503-3088, has some very nice painting done by Greta Leslie and other local painters. It is worth a stop if you are looking for art.

NIGHTLIFE

Placencia offers most of the nightlife on the peninsula. **Sugar Reef Sunset Lounge**, 13 Sunset Drive, ☎ 523-3289, $$, has a 36-meter (120-foot) deck overlooking the lagoon. This is one of the best places in Placencia. Besides the daily happy hour there are other fun forms of entertainment, like a horseshoe competition (winner gets a bottle of rum). The owners are fun and their enthusiasm for their town spills over into the drinks.

Pickled Parrot, ☎ 523-3102, www.pickledparrotbelize.com, $$, with Wendy Bryan formerly of Canada's CBC, is still serving her eminent tropical blended drinks. Examples of this are the Blue Hole, the Yellow Bird, the Belizean Hurricane or the always popular Parrot Piss. This place is famous – I can suggest only that you try it. After you've had enough Parrot Piss, try their pizza – it's a great combination.

Tipsy Tuna Sports Bar, ☎ 523-3179, is on the beach in Plancencia. It has a ladies night and karaoke every Thursday. There's a big-screen TV and pool tables for you to enjoy while sipping a rum or a Belikin.

> **LOCAL FLAVOR:** *A favorite drink is* **rum bitters,** *a concoction of special herbs and bark soaked in rum for days before you drink it.*

In Seine Bight, **The Wamasa** is a nightclub and **Sam's Disco** is for the Reggae crowd.

LEAVING THE PENINSULA

To leave Placencia, you can cross over to Mango Creek/Independence by a ferry, which runs twice a day; once mid-morning and once mid-afternoon. It meets the buses traveling along the Southern Highway and takes only foot passengers, no vehicles. If going south, it seems senseless to me to travel all the way up the peninsula and then back down again. All buses along the southern highway stop at Mango Creek.

> ▶▶ *If you rejoin the Southern Highway at the turnoff to Placencia, continue south. The road to Red Bank is at Mile 32; turn right (west).*

Red Bank has a population of 700, most of them of Maya descent. The community is often referred to as the Holy Grail by birders because, from January to March, it is home to the scarlet macaw. Within 15 minutes walking time, you are guaranteed to see at least two and as many as 92 of these endangered birds. Villagers, trained as guides, admit that long ago they used to eat the birds because they were so plentiful.

If you wish to stay in the village you should phone in advance. There is a village phone, ☎ 503-2233. Whoever hears the phone will answer, but it may take a little while so give it a few minutes before you hang up. A four-room guest cabin is available, $. It stands on stilts and is tucked into the jungle with a freshwater creek running beside. Rooms all have double beds and window screens. You must share a bathroom. There is no electricity; kerosene lamps are used in the evenings. Meals can be ordered ahead and are minimal in cost. However, if you want any extras, like a beer or snacks, bring them with you. You can also book a room through the **Belize Audubon Society**, ☎ 223-4533, or the **Programme for Belize**, ☎ 227-5616, in Belize City.

> ▶▶ *Continue along the Southern Highway. If going into Mango Creek or Big Creek, take the turnoff at Mile 38.6. You'll be turning left (east).*

Mango Creek and **Independence** are the same town, divided by Mango Creek. It has a shrimp processing plant and shrimp from here are sent all over the world via Belize's deep-water port, Big

Creek. The area also has a lot of citrus farms that ship their produce from Big Creek. The road into Big Creek is mostly for transport trucks.

At one time there was a proposal to have a bridge built between Mango Creek and Placencia but, to date, there is no funding. For the traveler, there is little in Mango Creek or Big Creek.

▸▸ *Continue south along the Southern Highway to Mile 42 and turn left (east) to Monkey River Town. (The road signs may not correspond with this guide as they measure the distance from Belize City, while I measure the distance from Belmopan.)*

■ MONKEY RIVER TOWN

Monkey River Town is an isolated Garifuna community with a population of about 270 people. It offers just two places to stay, two bars to visit after the sun goes down, two places to eat and two ways to get there. This really is a "two-can" town.

HISTORY

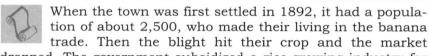

When the town was first settled in 1892, it had a population of about 2,500, who made their living in the banana trade. Then the blight hit their crop and the market dropped. The government subsidized a rice-growing industry for awhile, but when the subsidies fell, so did the population. Then Hurricane Hattie hit in 1961 and devastated the village. The people rebuilt and in 2001 Hurricane Iris again demolished the place. The monkeys of the area died from yellow fever and some local hunters resorted to killing crocodiles, selling their hides for a profit. As a result of all this hard luck, many businesses moved to a different port and the town, in 1981, was demoted to village status.

This has left Monkey River Town a wonderful little village that has simplicity as an asset. There is a large green sign near the harbor that says "Welcome to Monkey River," and somehow the greeting feels genuine. Today there is a police station, a community center, a school and a church linked by sand streets. Wood houses built on stilts dot the public places and there are no neon lights. If you want something, you ask. To find anyone you must go to the dock, where most people who aren't fishing or making meals are playing dominos. This is a serious game; get involved in it while gathering information.

GETTING HERE

To reach Monkey River by **bus** is difficult. You could get off at the Southern Highway turnoff, but from there it is another 14 miles, too long for most to walk in one day. Avid walkers might manage it, though, as the road is level.

If you **drive** or **cycle**, continue straight along the Southern Highway to Mile 42 and turn left (east). Follow the secondary road for 14 miles to the Monkey River, where you will leave your car. At the river, holler for someone to bring you across in a boat. Just holler at the men playing dominos. You'll probably be the excitement of the day.

The other option is to hire a **boat** and come down the coast or rent a **kayak** for a few days and paddle down from Placencia. It is about 20 miles, a long day's paddle even under good conditions.

THINGS TO DO

A **Monkey River boat trip** can be done independently or with a tour from Placencia (see page 406 for list of operators). Dugout canoes are available for rent in Monkey River Town. Just ask. Prices will have to be negotiated, budget for US $7-10 an hour.

As you enter the river, you leave the coastal breezes and mangroves at the mouth and move on green waters that slice through

Bird of Paradise are found growing wild at the sides of the roads.

the jungle. Orchids and bromeliads cling to the trees that overhang the banks. If you look carefully, you may find a bat or two hanging on the undersides of the branches. Iguanas are plentiful, munching away at the leaves of the trees. Occasionally you will hear the frightening howl of the monkey. The birds are phenomenal. Watch for oropendula, with their bright gold tail feathers as they look around and then fall with a plop into their nests.

The Monkey River originates at Richarson Peak in the Maya Mountains and drains the Swasey and Bladen watersheds. Paynes Creek National Park and the Punta Ycacos Reserve stretch to the south from Monkey River Town. This diverse area includes five different systems; upland forest, coastal plain, fresh water, estuaries and coral reef. The people of Monkey River have been working hard to include some of the lands north of the river into the Paynes Creek National Park. They are hoping that the money from increased tourism will be a strong enough argument for the government to agree.

Paynes Creek National Park was established as a preserve in 1994 and a national park in 1999. It covers 11,600 square miles of wetland bordered by the Monkey River on the north, Ycacos Lagoon on the south, the Caribbean on the east and savanna on the west. There were many plans for this park area, including one by an American developer who wanted to put a cruise ship facility and resort at the lagoon.

To get there you must paddle from Monkey River Town south along the coast to Punta Negra, a jut of land sticking out into the Caribbean with a tiny village on it. The distance from Monkey River is about 14 miles and then an additional hour from Punta Negra to Ycacos Lagoon. After going around Punta Negra, paddle down the coast to Punta Ycacos. It is less than six miles. **Punta Ycacos** is a distinct peninsula pointing south. Once there, look for a trail on the beach that leads to a boardwalk. Follow the walk that is lying over a marsh till you get to the lagoon. There is a ranger station beside the lagoon. It is about a one-hour walk on maintained trails from the station to the broad-leafed forests. Trail descriptions are posted at the ranger station.

Jabiru Pond, near the ranger station, is best walked around from January to March, when the birds are nesting. The other option is to walk to Crocodile Pond, a wide section of the creek where crocodiles breed and feed. Camping is available near the ranger station, but you must bring your own food.

Ycacos Lagoon is between four and nine feet deep (one and three meters), with mangroves surrounding most of it. You can often see lily pads and reeds growing on the water and crocs sunning themselves close by. Because this is such an isolated lagoon, the chance of spotting manatee or lagoon-nesting birds is good. About 300 birds have been sighted in the park. Hawksbill turtles also come to nest here, although the best place to see them is around Gales Point north of Dangriga. The lagoon also has some huge fish, including some tarpon and permit. You can fish from the dock or from a canoe, but it's catch-and-release only.

MAYA MEMENTOS

The Maya knew that if people didn't have salt in their diets they would become tired, feel aches in their joints and dehydrate. At Ycacos Lagoon, archeologists have found signs of Maya salt plants, where they would boil the brine from the lagoon to form salt cakes. These they traded for mountain products at Lubaantun, Nim Li Punit and Uxbenka.

The **Punta Honduras Marine Reserve** borders Paynes Creek National Park on the ocean side. This 327-square-mile reserve became a protected area in 2000. An estuary within the reserve was created by the outflow of seven rivers. On the water, there are about 135 mangrove islands and only 10% of them have dry land. One of them, Abalone Caye, is closest to the most sensitive area and will have a ranger's station built on it in the near future to help protect the mangrove and fish populations.

Underground Maya storage sites have been found on Wild Cane Caye, within the reserve. It is unknown if the water has risen since the early days of the Maya or if the land has sunk. Archeologists have also found some animal bones here. The bones are from fish, turtles and manatees, suggesting that the Maya ate these creatures.

Since the last hurricane, the area has been denuded of vegetation, but regrowth is quick. Within another couple of years, trees will start to reach the 100-foot (30-meter) mark again.

TOUR GUIDES

 Clive (of Clive's Place, ☎ 709-2028, see below) has brothers and cousins who have lived in the area all their lives and can take you almost anywhere you wish to go. They will probably be successful in showing you what you want to see.

Elroy's Tour Guide Service, ☎ 523-2014, is a good place to start looking if you don't want to see all the tourist money going to Clive.

Percivil Gordon, ☎ 520-3033, is another long-time outdoorsman who knows the Monkey River area well. Both Elroy and Percivil are quiet, non-assuming people who know their stuff.

PLACES TO STAY

 Clive's Place, ☎ 709-2028 or 720-2025, www.monkeyriver-belize.com, $$, is operated by the family of Clive Garbutt. The family includes his mom, dad, wife, sisters, brothers, cousins, nephews and anyone else who would like to attach themselves to this gregarious man.

HOTEL PRICES	
$	$20 to $50
$$	$51 to $75
$$$	$76 to $100
$$$$	$101 to $150
$$$$$	over $150

Clive's is officially called the Sunset Inn, but everyone calls it Clive's Place. It has eight rooms situated off a porch on the second floor of a wooden building. Each has a fan and private bathroom with hot water. You can take all your meals at Clive's for another US $15 a day. The downstairs bar and restaurant often feature drummers and dancers. Clive and the men in his family would rather fish than play dominos, so if you're an angler, consider hiring one of the family members to take you.

Bob's Paradise Hotel, ☎ 429-8763, $$$$/$$$$$, is a three-star hotel asking a five-star price. Bob's is also a mile out of town. It has six thatched-roof huts with private baths, hot water and fans. There's also a bar and **restaurant** attached. Bob's seems to cater mainly to people going fishing.

PLACES TO EAT

 Alice's Restaurant, ☎ 520-3033, $, offers food for all the travelers who arrive on boat tours coming up the river. Ask for directions to Alice's. She will invite you in, offer you a seat and go off to prepare and, shortly after, serve your meal. You will be offered the same as she gives her family.

Of course, you can go around back of the village and eat at Clive's Place too. He will make you welcome.

Punta Negra, a tiny fishing village of under 100 people down the coast about 20 miles from Monkey River Town, is accessible only by boat or private plane. It has one high-end hotel called the **Black Point Retreat**, ☎ 722-0166, www.blackpointretreat.com, $$$$$. This is a fishers' resort located within sight of three reserves – Payne's Creek National Park, Punta Honduras Preserve and Sapodilla Cayes Reserve. Rooms are individual Mongolian yurts scattered on 30 acres of isolated jungle terrain. They are tastefully decorated and have two bedrooms each, private baths with hot water, two double beds, desks and fans. On-site is a **restaurant** and bar, tackle shop, pool table, fly-fish station and e-mail service. The price to stay includes all meals, booze and transportation to the fishing sites. If you're craving extra isolation, the owners will take you out to Seal Caye, a private island. It's more rugged and offers secluded wilderness. Black Point Retreat is currently offered for sale, so check first before planning to stay here.

▶▶ *Return to the Southern Highway at Mile 42 and drive or cycle south. The road meanders south through milpa farms and citrus groves with the Maya Mountains to the west.*

TERMITE TERRAIN: *The big gobs of amorphous dirt you see on the sides of trees, fenceposts and elsewhere are termite nests.*

There are numerous rivers to cross – the Swasey, the Bladen, Deep River and Golden Stream – before you reach Indian Creek Village at Mile 73.

■ NIM LI PUNIT RUINS

Indian Creek is a tiny Maya village with only one guest house (beyond the village), a gas station and a small grocery store. It serves as the gateway to Nim Li Punit ruins. The ruins and guest house are 1.25 miles west of the village along a hilly road. If coming by bus, ask the driver to let you off at the road to the village and walk the rest of the way in. The walk will take about an hour.

EXPLORING THE RUINS

Nim Li Punit ruins is a small site known mainly for its **stelae**. Named after the longest stele found at the site, Nim Li Punit means Big Hat. That stele, which measures over 31 feet high (nine meters), had a carving on the front of a figure with a huge headdress. This stele is the tallest ever found in Belize and the second-tallest found at any Maya ruin.

Mapping of the ruin was completed in 1976 by **Norman Hammond**. **Barbara McLeod** conducted a survey of the stelae found and the information lay dormant for six years until **Richard Leventhal** started excavations in 1983. He discovered that the buildings of Num Li Punit were of unique construction, of a sort that was done only in southern Belize. The buildings were put together with dry masonry sandstone rather than with mortar. It is believed that this site maintained religious alliances with Lubaantun and Uxbenka.

There is a small **visitor center** at the ruins with some artifacts and a map of the site.

This ruin has three divisions, the west, east and south. The west has two **temples** with plazas at each. The eastern area has an **observatory**, where the Maya studied the stars. Between the southern and eastern sections is a small but well-defined **ball court**.

It is the southern section that is the most impressive. Here, archeologists found most of the stelae and three **royal tombs**. Inside the tombs were 36 pottery vessels, some of which are in the visitor center.

Twenty-six **stelae** have been found, eight of them carved. One carving is of a ruler with some copal incense being thrown into a flame. Resin from the Copal tree, found in abundance throughout southern Belize, was burned as incense by the Maya. There are two other human figures on this stele, plus a mythical creature holding the pot with the flame.

 MYSTERIOUS MAYA: *The Maya carved on the front of stelae. Although glyphs appeared around the pictures, it is on the sides and backs that the text, the dates and stories were usually inscribed.*

PLACE TO STAY

 Indian Creek Guest House, ☎ 709-6324, info@belize lodge.com, $$, is situated across from the ruins (1.25 miles from the highway). It has eight rooms that can accommodate three or four people each. Two rooms share a bath. For a bit more privacy, consider renting one of 12 cabins located behind the guest house, on a hill. They have air conditioning, tiled bathrooms with hot water, fans and hardwood floors and walls. The beds are covered with mosquito nets. The sitting area is comfortable, with a couch, chairs and tables. If you want to enjoy real jungle atmosphere, this place is highly recommended. Remote, wild, and comfortable is the description.

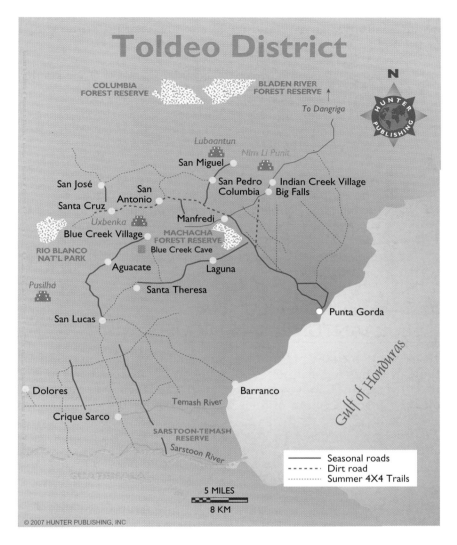

Toldeo District

COLUMBIA FOREST RESERVE

BLADEN RIVER FOREST RESERVE

To Dangriga

N

Lubaantun

Nim Li Punit

San Miguel

San José

San Antonio

San Pedro Columbia

Indian Creek Village

Santa Cruz

Big Falls

Uxbenka

Manfredi

Blue Creek Village

MACHACHA FOREST RESERVE

RIO BLANCO NAT'L PARK

Blue Creek Cave

Aguacate

Laguna

Pusilhá

Santa Theresa

San Lucas

Punta Gorda

Dolores

Barranco

Temash River

Crique Sarco

Gulf of Honduras

SARSTOON-TEMASH RESERVE

Sarstoon River

GUATEMALA

Seasonal roads
Dirt road
Summer 4X4 Trails

5 MILES

8 KM

© 2007 HUNTER PUBLISHING, INC

Two miles down from the main lodge is the **House of the Jaguar**, another luxury lodge situated in the jungle. The rooms are every bit as beautiful as those at Indian Creek. Here, two jaguars were born in captivity and were destined for a Mexican zoo. The owners rescued them and set them free. They now live on the property, freely, and you as a guest may get a chance to spot them from the fourth-floor observation deck. There is a restaurant and bar with a gourmet chef. The jungle has many paths to explore.

Five miles farther down stream is the rugged jungle camp that can be reached only by canoe. There is a screened eating room at this site. Arrangements for this can be made at the guest house. The owners will arrange overland trips, such as visiting Xunantunich or the Belize Zoo.

▶▶ *Continue along the Southern Highway from Mile 73 to Mile 83.2. At the gas station, turn right (west) for the Maya villages of San Miguel, San Pedro Columbia, San Antonio, Santa Cruz, Santa Elena and Blue Creek Village. There are also the ruins of Lubaantun, Uxbenka, and the Rio Blanco Forest Reserve and Blue Creek Cave, the Bladen Nature Reserve and the Columbia Forest Reserve.*

AUTHOR NOTE: *The road (I will refer to it as the San Antonio Road) that goes to the above places is rough. Most people go to Punta Gorda and then take a bus, which runs four times a week – on Tuesday, Thursday, Saturday and Sunday – to the village they wish to visit. Others take a bicycle, a taxi or a private vehicle.*

■ SAN PEDRO COLUMBIA, LUBAANTUM & SAN MIGUEL

There are home stay programs in some of the villages, and San Antonio even has a guest house. But, generally, there are few amenities. If you want to have your meals with the Maya, you must order ahead. They will go out of their way to accommodate you.

▶▶ *For San Pedro Columbia, Lubaantun and San Miguel, turn off at Mile 83.2 of the Southern Highway. Go west for two miles along the San Antonio Road until you come to the sign that indicates San Pedro Columbia and Lubaantun ruins. Turn right (north) and follow the road.*

San Pedro Columbia is a Maya community with about 700 residents. The community has seven churches, a police station, a school and a small shop in town. The village is known for its hand embroidery.

People came to San Pedro from the Petén area of Guatemala, escaping from the oppression. They carried with them the statues of Santo Domingo, San Pedro and Santa Concepcion and settled in two locations before finding the clear waters of the Columbia River.

THINGS TO DO

March 19th is the **Feast of St. Peter**. The festival includes harp music, eating and dancing. To attend this celebration is a unique experience as the village is isolated and the festival is traditional. March is also a good time of year to visit the Columbia River Forest Reserve.

The **Golden Stream Watershed Corridor Preserve** covers 35,000 acres of land that links the Bladen, Chiquibul and Puente Honduras Marine Reserve. In this area are numerous jaguars and the river has natural pools that are good for swimming.

Bladen River Nature Reserve is 97,000 acres of rainforest near the Bladen Branch of the Monkey River in the karst foothills of the Maya Mountains. It is very difficult to reach; travel is along old logging roads and you'd need the services of a guide, available in San Pedro Columbia. Guides with horses can be hired in Santa Cruz, just past San Antonio (see page 418). Speak with the alcade (leader of the village) in San Pedro. You should also have hiking gear, food and determination.

The reserve has a lot to offer, including sinkholes and caves, waterfalls and wildlife. It was originally opened in 1990 for scientific research. Among the 194 birds identified here, the great curassow is the most rare. Around 300 species of animals have been noted and the crested iguana is often seen. An ancient Maya site in the Quebrada de Oro Valley has unexcavated tombs and courts, and a stone-paved avenue.

Adjacent to the Bladen Reserve is the **Columbia River Forest Reserve**. This is best visited between January and March. You can reach it by walking north from the village. Again, you must follow old logging roads. Although I have heard that this reserve can be reached from San Jose or Cirque Jute, I have no solid information about guides from those villages and they do not have home stay programs in place.

The reserve was mainly set up to protect the mahogany tree and was first made into a nature reserve in 1968. However, the mahogany project was abandoned in 1978 and the forest was left for logging until 1994, when the boundary was redefined and the area again made into an official reserve. Of the 400 plant species identified here, the common wood nymph was spotted for the first time ever. Also, two new frog species were discovered in late in 1993. More than 200 birds have been identified, 35 of which are rare for this area.

The reserve also has the **Little Quartz Ridge**, quartz standing 3,412 feet high (1,040 meters). It slopes along a creek in which shelves have formed, making good ledges for nesting animals and birds. The ridge, it is believed, was formed from a fault cut. There are also limestone karst caves, sinkholes and waterfalls. One of the sinkholes is about 800 feet deep (330 meters) and a quarter-mile wide.

> **AUTHOR NOTE:** *Numerous logging roads inter-connect within this reserve and taking a guide will insure that you do not get lost. Even if you have an adventuresome spirit and a good sense of direction, I still recommend hiring a guide.*

The **Lubaantun ruins** are located at the top of a hill on manicured lawns. The parking lot is at the bottom of the hill and it doesn't take more than three minutes to reach the entrance. Stop at the new visitor center and pay the US $5 entrance fee (the caretaker is not always there so you may get lucky and not have to pay). There is also a bathroom and picnic table at the site. Santiago Che, the caretaker at Lubaantum, protected the ruins for years from vandalism and robbery. He now replicates many of the artifacts found here. Ask him about them. If you are interested, he will sell you one.

First discovered by locals, the ruins were not investigated until 1903 when **Thomas Gann** went in and mapped the structures around plaza IV. **Harvard University** then became interested and sent **R.E. Merwin** to check things out in 1915. He took photographs, mapped more than Gann did, and discovered a ball court that had three carved stone markers depicting men playing the famous Maya ball game. The markers were taken to Peabody Museum at Harvard.

In 1926 the **British Museum** sent in Joyce and Thompson to do some investigating, but there was nothing conclusive reported and Thompson got called out to investigate stelae found in Guatemala. Nothing happened for almost half a century. Finally, in 1970 **Norman Hammond** mapped out the ceremonial center and the surrounding areas. He decided that the main period of occupation was around AD 730 to 890. Presently, Richard Leventhal from New York has been doing work on the site.

"Lubaantun" means Place of the Fallen Stones. When looking at the construction – cut stones held together without mortar – it is simple to see why the stones have fallen. The roots of trees and the growth of plants have pushed and toppled the walls.

Lubaantun was built in three sections. The central core is the religious area where 11 **temples** have been found around five **plazas**. The middle ceremonial section consists of three **ball courts**. Three ball court markers and numerous pieces of pottery were also found. This has led archeologists to believe that Lubaantun was a popular sports center. Around the outer rim of the city were the residential homes.

The site ruled an area of 327 square miles that covered diverse landscapes, including mountains, ocean and farmland. The Maya from this city could get stones from the mountains for building and they could hunt and grow agricultural products in the foothills. The ocean offered them seafoods and medicinal plants. The avail-ability of these products made Lubaantun fairly self sufficient.

THE CRYSTAL SKULL

The most interesting story attached to Lubaantun is the tale of the Crystal Skull. Dr. Mitchell-Hedges and his daughter Anna were supposed to have been at Lubaantun in 1926 doing some research. On her 17th birthday, Anna spotted a glitter in the ruins that had not been excavated. It took six weeks to uncover the glitter, which turned out to be a crystal skull.

The skull was carved from one piece of clear quartz crys-tal and stood 5 3/16 inches wide by 4 7/8 inches deep and 7 7/8 inches high. It weighed 11 pounds, 13 ounces. When found, there was not a scratch on it. After another three months, they uncovered a jaw, which fit perfectly into the skull.

Supposedly, Anna was permitted by the native people liv-ing near Lubaantun to take the skull in trade for food and medicines. Around that time, a similar skull was obtained by the British Museum and put on display in England. The Mitchell-Hedges team claimed that their skull took 150 years to carve and that it was 3,600 years old. They also claimed that it was used by high priests in ceremo-nies that caused death to certain people.

Nick Nacerino, a researcher, became interested in the skull and its story in the 1980s. It didn't take him long to find inconsistencies in the tale. Crystal scratches easily, so it was highly unlikely that the skull had been lying in the ruins for centuries. He also found that the Maya peo-ple would never trade one of their icons for a few pieces of food or medicine. No elders remembered an American (Canadian actually) girl at Lubaantun during that period. Nacerino found that there was no record of the skull be-fore 1943, an oddity for an archeologist to keep such a significant find a secret for that many years. Nacerino also found that in 1943 there was a bill of sale for the skull from Sotheby's to Dr. Mitchell-Hedges in the amount of £400. The skull was sold to Sotheby's by Eugene Babon, a known antiquities dealer and producer of fake items.

Finally, in 1996 a firm in Germany proved that the skull had been made within the last hundred years. Since this revelation, Anna Mitchell-Hedges has been unavailable for comment and the British Museum has removed their skull from exhibition.

San Miguel, a village of 380 people, is just beyond Lubaantun along the same road. It has a library, a school, a church and a small store. Visitors are welcome.

Tiger Cave is about a half-hour walk from San Miguel. The story goes that a dog chased a jaguar cub into the cave and so it got its name. If you have a local guide, he will be able to show you the Blue Hole hot spring en route to the cave.

Tiger Cave requires a creek crossing; a canoe is left at the spot. The interior of the cave has ceiling holes so light seeps down to allow visibility inside. There is pottery on some of the ledges and a stream farther inside.

PLACE TO STAY

San Pedro Columbia (or just Columbia as it is locally known) has a **home stay program**. Check with the village alcade in San Pedro or call ☎ 722-2470 to make advance arrangements.

There is a new guesthouse opening that will have a few rooms. Ask for Don and Zoe's place and locals will direct you.

▶▶ *Return to the San Antonio Road and continue west for another 1.5 miles just past Manfredi, an odd little community that has a sampling of just about every culture in Belize. Turn left (south) and go along the road for nine miles until you arrive at Blue Creek. You will pass a Mennonite farm that has tons of machinery. Obviously, they are not the fundamentalist Mennonites. Pass through the village of San Pedro and on to Blue Creek.*

■ BLUE CREEK VILLAGE & BLUE CREEK CAVE

Blue Creek Village is a Maya community of about 40 families situated on 500 acres of land. It has one hotel.

HISTORY

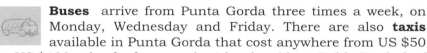

Originally the Kekchi and Mopan Maya escaped from the oppression in Guatemala and settled on the creek. They called the village Rio Bravo and, to supplement their basic living, they traded salt for cocoa beans with the Maya living in the caves just up river. In 1961 Hurricane Hattie destroyed the village and many families left. But slowly, over the years, other families moved in. The village was re-named Blue Creek. Mennonites moved into the area. They tried to integrate some of the Maya into the Mennonite religion but were unsuccessful. Today, there is a productive Mennonite farm adjacent to the village property and the two groups live in tolerance of each other.

GETTING HERE

Buses arrive from Punta Gorda three times a week, on Monday, Wednesday and Friday. There are also **taxis** available in Punta Gorda that cost anywhere from US $50 to US $100 a day for four people. A local resident, **Pablo Bochub** of Roots & Herbs in Blue Creek, ☎ 722-2834 or 608-2879, herbs@btl.net, can be hired to drive you to the caves.

THINGS TO DO

Blue Creek Cave, called "Hokeb Ha" in Mayan, is a short walk from the lodge (see below), up slippery rocks along the creek. A walking stick should be used and good shoes are essential. If coming from the village, walk along the creek but do not cross the bridge. Instead, stay on the trail going up the creek. You will pass the lodge on the way.

The cave is big and the creek actually flows from it, causing water to run over the rocks at the entrance. In rainy season, there is a waterfall that washes some of the stalagmites and stalactites near the mouth. You will need lights to go into the cave any distance, but you can easily get to the pool, just a few feet inside. It's a great place for swimming. A ceremonial altar and some ceramics were found inside the cave.

PLACE TO STAY

 Blue Creek Rainforest Lodge, ☎ 722-0013, ize2belize@ aol.com, was almost completely destroyed by Hurricane Iris. When I was there they were rebuilding. However, the walkway over the jungle canopy that was such a tourist draw in the past will not be reconstructed for a few years. Four wood cabins sleep two people each and have screened windows and fans. Bathrooms and showers are in the main lodge. Tucked into the jungle and beside the creek, the cabins are within five minutes of the cave entrance. A **restaurant** at the site serves mostly typical Maya food. The cost is US $85 per person, including meals, jungle hikes, caving and river walks in the area.

▶▶ *To reach San Antonio, Santa Cruz Waterfall, Uxbenka ruins, Santa Cruz, Santa Elena and Rio Blanco National Park, you'll need to return to the San Antonio Road. Continue for about three miles west of Manfredi to San Antonio.*

■ SAN ANTONIO

San Antonio is the largest Maya village in Toledo District with a population of about 1,000. It has a grocery store, two churches, a community center, a mission house, a health center and a hotel.

HISTORY

The **Mopan Maya** living in San Antonio came from San Luis in the Petén of Guatemala in 1883, escaping oppression and starvation. They called their new village St. Luis in honor of the statue of the saint they had carried, but later renamed the village San Antonio, after the younger brother of St. Luis. They kept Luis as their patron saint.

The town's stone church sits fairly high on the hill and was built with stones obtained from nearby archeological sites. The church has eight stained glass windows that came from St. Louis, Missouri. An old church was being torn down in St. Louis and the windows were going to be destroyed. A priest walking by noticed this and salvaged the windows. He then had them shipped to Belize, where they were installed in this church.

GETTING HERE

Cycling to San Antonio is difficult as the road is rough, the way is long, and the hills become steep once past Manfredi. Also, there are few amenities. A **bus** arrives from Punta Gorda on Tuesday, Thursday, Saturday and Sunday.

THINGS TO DO

If you are here in mid-August, you may be able to catch the **Festival of San Luis**, the patron saint of the town. This is a nine-day event that is not only fun but has a story attached to it. There are nine religious/administrative leaders in the village and one leader each day is responsible for making a feast for the entire village. Friends of the leader help butcher pigs and the friends of the wife of the leader help prepare the food. They make Maya bread and boil corn in lime that is taken from the shells of snails. They make tortillas and prepare sweetened cacao to drink.

Each day, in the morning, the masks and costumes to be used in the festival are blessed at the church, drums beat and then a procession goes to the home of the leader responsible for that day's feast. The procession is led by a person who wears the mask of the deer. Marimba music is played and accompanied by drums, harps, violins and mandolins. Once at the host home, the music continues and feasting starts. A dance, like a ballet, is performed by 12 people. The dancers represent Maya hunters, Maya women or hunted animals. The one representing the jaguar is a humorous character who teases the hunters. The deer is a solemn character, for good reason. The deer is caught and symbolically killed. Its skin is given to the women in the dance.

The feasting and dancing goes on for most of the day. This is repeated every day for the nine days until the last day when an 18-meter (60-foot) greased pole is erected and competitors try to scramble up to get the prize of food, drink and money that has been placed on the top. When the winner reaches the prize, the church bells ring and the person in the jaguar mask is caught. The revelers eat and drink for the last time and then the festival is officially over.

The **Uxbenka ruins** are also called the Santa Rita ruins. They are situated across from the water tower just outside San Antonio. It is a short climb up the hill to the unexcavated ruins.

First located in 1984, the site had 20 stelae, seven of which were carved. Today, there are 13 still at the site, lying in the ground eroded by weather and covered by moss and jungle. A tomb lies partially open – it looks like a hole in the ground with stones supporting the sides. There are plazas and temple walls at this tiny site, but not much excavation has been done. In the late 1980s a team of archeologists salvaged some artifacts and opened the tomb. There is no charge to visit this site and it takes less than 15 minutes to poke around.

PLACES TO STAY

Bol's Hilltop Hotel, ☎ 702-2124, $$, is across from the stone church. It offers seven basic rooms with shared bathrooms. Meals can be arranged at the hotel or through the locals. One of the typical Maya meals that should be tried here is picary caldo. A picary is an animal that lives in the hills and his meat tastes like pork. The Maya fix it with herbs and spices – a real treat.

HOTEL PRICES	
$	$20 to $50
$$	$51 to $75
$$$	$76 to $100
$$$$	$101 to $150
$$$$$	over $150

The TEA Guest House, ☎ 722-2096, $$, allows you to stay in a cabin shared with five other people. During the day, Maya guides lead excursions and teach you about the jungle. Your stay includes three traditional meals with a Maya family and, in the evenings, you can listen to their stories and music and watch some dancing. The TEA Guest House is similar to a home stay, only you – and the Maya family – have more privacy.

Home stay allows you to stay in a Maya home, to sleep in a hammock in the same room as the family, to wash in the river and to use an outhouse. You will work during the day with the family, whether it be chopping wood, harvesting coffee or making tortillas. For this program you can either check with the village alcade or call in Punta Gorda, ☎ 722-2470, for arrangements. The cost of this program is about US $5 per day, plus $2 per meal. This is a true immersion program.

■ SANTA CRUZ

Santa Cruz village has a population of about 400 people and is just 1.25 miles past San Antonio along the same road. There are two **home stay** houses in Santa Cruz. One is with Marcus Sho and the other is with Santiago Ash. If you would like to stay with them, ask in the village or go to Rio Blanco National Park Visitor Center and inquire there.

Everisto Shoe and Venancio Canti have **horses** for rent. They are sanctioned by the Rio Blanco National Park to take visitors through on horseback. The men also offer birding tours and visits to ruins. To find these men, ask at the Rio Blanco Visitor Center or in the village of Santa Cruz. They need only one day's notice to prepare for a trip and can accommodate quite a few riders. This is a good place to rent horses and for trips into the Columbia Forest Reserve (see page 374).

Santa Cruz Waterfall is about .3 miles out of Santa Cruz going west. This pretty waterfall is 30 feet wide (10 meters) and just as deep. There is a picnic area and a place to swim, making it a popular destination for the locals.

▸▸ *Santa Elena is at the end of the San Antonio Road about another1.8 miles beyond Santa Cruz.*

■ SANTA ELENA & RIO BLANCO NATIONAL PARK

Santa Elena has a population of about 200 and is now part of the TEA home stay program (above).

Rio Blanco National Park is five miles past San Antonio. The cost to enter the park is US $2.50 or 50¢ for locals. If hitching here, plan to return to town between 4 and 5:30 pm, when most traffic is on the road.

First established in 1994, the 105 acres of park are maintained by the people living in the area. This is a fairly new concept in Belize and it is called an Indigenous Peoples Park. With the help of the Peace Corps in general and Steve Roberts in particular, a park plan has been established and the group is working to fix a boundary and develop some walking trails.

The **visitor center** was constructed by volunteers of the Trek Force Expeditions and has some charts on display. There is also an arts and crafts room and two dorms that can accommodate six people in all. Outhouses and a picnic table are nearby. There's also a tenting place that I believe to be the best wilderness-tenting spot in the country.

The **trail** down to the river is well maintained and does not take long to walk. The river, even at the end of dry season, has plenty of water – enough, in fact, to allow one to dive from an outcrop of rock 20 feet (six meters) above a deep pool. I wouldn't do it, but the kids I was with sure had fun jumping in. I have been told that no one has succeeded in hitting the bottom of the pool.

Jaguar prints have been seen in the park and there are toucans, peccaries, gibnuts, iguanas and other such animals. This is not a highly visited area and it allows for the sighting of many more creatures than in more populated places.

Hiking trails are located on the far side of the river. A guide (you can rent a horse too) will be able to show you different medicinal plants that are used by the Maya.

 MYSTERIOUS MAYA: *The Maya believe that parrot bones carry rabies and if a dog eats the bones, he will die.*

▶▶ *Return to the Southern Highway at Mile 83.2 and continue south for another three miles. Turn west (right). In another three miles you'll reach the village of Laguna.*

■ LAGUNA VILLAGE

Laguna Village has about 300 people, almost all Maya. There are two schools, two churches and one health post. The village has a home stay program in place, as well as a TEA Guest House. Nearby attractions include a cave and a lagoon. Staying in this village will give you a good Maya-life experience. One of the things I noticed was that the little girls are not at home helping mom make tortillas, as is traditional. Instead, they are scrambling around the soccer field giving the boys a lot of competition for dominance of the ball.

If you want to learn to **weave**, enquire at Miss Rosa's house in the village or at the office of the organizers of the home stay program in Punta Gorda, ☎ 722-2470. This is the only place in the entire country where I found someone willing to teach this skill.

THINGS TO DO

Guides are available in the village. If staying at the TEA Guest House, guides for these hikes can be included in the cost of your stay.

Agua Caliente Lagoon, set on 6,000 acres of reserved land, is a two-hour walk from the village. Your walk there leads through pasture and milpas, across creeks and then enters a marshland. There's a ranger station at the marsh, but no services, only an outhouse.

This is known as a dirty hike – you will quite often be in mud up to your knees after you enter the marsh. Near the lagoon, the wildlife increases and the landscape has a backdrop of limestone hills. Wood storks, herons, egrets, ducks, cormorants and kingfishers are often seen here. The trip should be done with a guide because the trail disappears quite often and you could get lost.

Laguna Cave is a 1.5-hour hike from the village. You must cross a stream and go to the limestone mountain looming over the village. Once there, you will be faced with a 12-foot climb up a rustic ladder to the cave's entrance. This is a dry cave and cracks in the ceiling allow some light inside. As you enter, the cave slopes downward and you may notice some bats hanging around. At one time, the Maya used the cave, but artifacts have been taken out to the archeological holding pen in Belmopan. This cave was used to make offerings before planting started. It is a 20-minute walk through the cave to a second opening. This trip should be done with a guide.

PLACES TO STAY

TEA Guest House, ☎ 722-2096, has been rebuilt since the hurricane and now sleeps about eight people on bunks in two rooms. It is basic. It runs on the same basis as the one in San Antonio (see above).

There's also a home stay program. Check with the village alcade or call ☎ 722-2470 for arrangements. The cost of this program is about US $5 per day plus $2 per meal.

▶▶ *Return to the Southern Highway at Mile 86 and continue south to Mile 100 and the entrance to Punta Gorda.*

■ PUNTA GORDA

Punta Gorda has a multicultural population of about 4,000 people. It has three streets that parallel the bay and it takes very little time to walk from one end of town to the other. This is the outback of Belize. If you want to hike or bike in the backcountry, then make Punta Gorda your base. You can immerse yourself totally in a culture by living a few days with the Maya or the Garifuna. Punta Gorda is also close to the sea, so snorkeling, diving and fishing are all possible.

HISTORY

 After the Maya civilization declined, the Toledo District was sparsely populated by the **Manche Chol Maya**. They remained unconquered by the Spanish until the end of the 1600s. Then disease hit and their numbers decreased. Those who survived were soon subdued by the British and sent to live in the highlands of Guatemala.

The next wave of people who came to the area were the **Garifuna**. They settled in Punta Gorda, Punta Negra and Barranco and their descendents are still there today, living mostly by fishing.

Finally, in 1868 some **Confederate soldiers**, looking for a safe place to live after the Civil War in the States, settled in Cattle Landing, just north of Punta Gorda. Within two years 12 sugar mills were erected to process the hundreds of acres of sugar that were planted. The area flourished. But when sugar prices dropped, the mills closed and those who remained were forced to live subsistence lives.

In the late 1800s and all through the 1900s the Maya living in Guatemala often escaped to Belize from the oppression and demand for more taxes. Today, the Maya make up 64% of the entire population of Toledo District.

AVERAGE TEMPERATURES & RAINFALL			
	Daily temp.	Monthly rainfall	Rain Days
JAN	75.0°F/23.9°C	.5 inches/1.3 cm	13
FEB	77.4°F/25.2°C	.2 inches/.6 cm	9
MAR	79.2°F/26.2°C	.2 inches/.6 cm	6
APR	82.6°F/28.1°C	.3 inches/.84 cm	6
MAY	83.7°F/28.7°C	.5 inches/1.3 cm	9
JUN	83.7°F/28.8°C	1.9 inches/4.9 cm	20
JULY	82.4°F/28.0°C	2.3 inches/5.9 cm	25
AUG	82.6°F/28.1°C	1.9 inches/4.9 cm	23
SEPT	83.1°F/28.4°C	1.4 inches/3.7 cm	23
OCT	81.5°F/27.5°C	1.1 inches/2.6 cm	16
NOV	79.5°F/26.4°C	.8 inches/2.2 cm	16
DEC	77.2°F/25.1°C	.6 inches/1.6 cm	13

Source of above data: Historical and current records at the Belize College of Agriculture (Central Farm) situated five miles from San Ignacio Town in the Toledo District.

GETTING HERE

The Southern Highway is now paved all the way to Punta Gorda, which makes travel time shorter and safer.

Two **bus** lines, Southern and James, have service from the main bus terminal in Belize City to Punta Gorda. Between them, they run buses every two hours from 6 am to 2 pm. There is one additional bus at 3 pm. The ride is scheduled to be six to eight hours, but it could take up to 12 hours, depending on the road and weather conditions.

Buses leaving Punta Gorda for Belize City start at 3 am and continue every hour until 6 am, then one leaves every two hours until noon. The cost is US $11 to Belize City and less for every destination before that.

Boats arrive in Punta Gorda from Puerto Barrios, Guatemala, every day and smaller motor boats often arrive from Livingston in Guatemala. Boats leave the harbor at Punta Gorda for Guatemala at least once a day for the one-hour run to Puerto Barrios.

Motorboats also go to Livingston periodically. Check at the bulletin board on the dock to see if there is one scheduled when you want to make the trip. The cost depends on who you travel with and how full the boat is. Bartering is the name of the game.

> **AUTHOR NOTE:** *Be aware that many people climb into small dories and cross the Caribbean to Guatemala, but this is unsafe. If a sudden squall or storm breaks out, you could end up in the water forever.*

At least five **flights** a day to and from Belize City and Punta Gorda are offered by **Tropic Air** (☎ 800-422-3435, 226-2012 in Belize, www.tropicair.com) and **Maya Air** (☎ 422-2333). The price is less than US $100.

THINGS TO DO

Fajina Craft Center, ☎ 722-2167. Market days are Monday, Wednesday, Friday and Saturday. Although not as colorful as the markets in Guatemala, Fajina has some interesting crafts.

Internet service is available at the **Cyber Café** on Front Street. Alternately, go to **Dennis Bruce's** place (also on Front Street, close to the entrance of town). He has an eclectic business that includes renting one computer.

TOURS/EQUIPMENT RENTALS

Bike rentals are available at the Wahema Hotel, ☎ 702-2542, on Front Street near the entrance to town. The owner has numerous single-gear bikes for US $15 a day. He expects to have multi-geared bikes in the near future. You can usually negotiate a better price for longer usage.

Punta Gorda

To Waluca

Arvin's Landing

Joe Taylor Creek

Caribbean Sea

To Dangriga

AIRSTRIP

KING ST

QUEEN ST

PRINCE ST

FRONT ST

Roots & Herbs
Taxi Station

GAS

POLICE
POST OFFICE

$

Punta Gorda
Bike Rentals

WEST ST

CHURCH ST

BACK ST

SCHOOL

MAIN ST

FRONT ST

Bus
Station

Cemetery

1. Erie Camping
2. Tranquility Lodge, Veranda
   Restaurant
3. Waluscos & Gommier's
   Restaurants
4. Sea Front Inn
5. Wahlma Hotel
6. El Café
7. Charlton's Inn
8. Spice Café
9. Emory's Café
10. St. Charles Inn
11. Pallavi Hotel & Grace's
    Restaurant
12. Dem Dats Doin Office
    Guatemala Ferry
13. Customs & Crafts Center
14. Earthrunnins
15. Ice Cream Parlor
16. Fish Market
17. Nature's Way
18. Punta Caliente
19. Traveller's Inn

NOT TO SCALE

Punta Gorda Bike Rentals is on Main Street across from the ice cream parlor and just up from the school. They have one-gear bikes, too. If Wahema is rented out, try here.

There are no car rentals in town, but you can hire a **taxi** to get you around, or ask anyone with a vehicle. The cost, including gas, is between US $50 and $100 a day. A taxi can hold four people, plus driver. The owner of the Charlton can and often will find you a vehicle with driver.

Roots and Herbs on Back Street, ☎ 722-2834, will take you to caves, villages and ruins for US $75 for the day. Their vehicles are good for the backroads.

Tide Tours, ☎ 722-2129, specializes in tours of southern Belize. They are happy to run custom excursions too; for example, you can ask for a guide, a cook, etc.

PLACES TO STAY

Toledo Eco Tourism Association, 65 Front Street, ☎ 702-2096 (Nature's Way Guest House) is involved in promoting an elaborate home stay program for tourists. You can stay in a dorm that is shared with other visitors interested in a new cultural experience. The theory behind the separate cabin (as opposed to the home stay where you live with a family) is that the dorm gives privacy to both you and the family. Sleeping with other strangers of my own culture isn't privacy in my eye, but being away from the family does give them a break.

Your TEA cabin will have a private outhouse and some cabins have a shower house next door. In the day, you can go on a hike, a canoe trip, or a guided visit to a ruin, waterfall or cave. Your guide knows the plants and animals, the trails and the extra things that make a visit to a ruin special.

The final advantage to this program is that the participating villagers have been trained in story telling, dance demonstrations and music so when they perform for you, it is interesting and professional.

TEA in 1996 earned an award for outstanding achievement in eco tourism from the International Tourism Exchange. Originally founded in 1990 with the help of Chet Schmidt of Nature's Way Guest House (see below), TEA helps the outlying communities earn a little money from tourism. The downside is that those living in the villages who do not have the same philosophy or standard of commitment as TEA do not get to participate.

Other **home stay programs** can be arranged at the tourist office in Punta Gorda, ☎ 702-2029. The cost is US $5 per night and $2 for

The South

each meal. You can also arrange this stay with the local alcade (leader) of the village. Those programs are much less expensive than the TEA, but the focus is also different. With them, you get to sleep in the house with a Maya family. If a child is sick during the night, you get to experience that too. You help make meals, wash clothes or pick coffee beans. Whatever is in progress for that day becomes part of your day.

Nature's Way Guest House, 67 Front Street, ☎ 702-2119, $, is at the end of the road, almost on the water. This large wooden structure offers rooms with bunk beds, tables, chairs and fans. The bathrooms are shared. There's also a common room and a dining room, where you can order meals.

HOTEL PRICES	
$	$20 to $50
$$	$51 to $75
$$$	$76 to $100
$$$$	$101 to $150
$$$$$	over $150

St Charles Inn, King Street, ☎ 702-2149, $$, has 13 rooms with private bathrooms. It's a funky little place, clean and comfortable. The grocery store downstairs is open until 9 pm. Go there to enquire about your room.

Charlton's Inn, 9 Main Street, ☎ 722-2197 or 702-2440, dwagner@btl.net, $/$$, is across from El Café. The rooms are clean and spacious, with private baths, cable TVs, air conditioning or fans and hot water. This is a good deal and the owners are cooperative when working out a trip, making airline reservations and arranging trips to caves.

Wahima Hotel, ☎ 702-2542, $, is on the water near the entrance to town. The rooms are basic, but clean, and have private bathrooms and fans. This is a very good deal. The owner is reasonable and will negotiate better prices for longer stays.

Pallavi Hotel, 19 Main Street, ☎ 702-2414, $$, has rooms with fans and private bathrooms. This is a newly renovated place and everything is hospital-clean. The on-site restaurant, **Grace's**, is popular with locals. The food is good, but the dining room can be hot. Try to sit under a fan.

Sea Front Inn, Front Street, ☎ 702-2300, seafront@btl.net, $$$, is at the north end of town. It is a large three-storey building with a blue tin roof and some stone siding, which looks pretty hurricane-proof to me. The quiet hotel has 10 spacious rooms with private baths, air conditioning and cable TVs. The restaurant serves breakfast only.

AUTHOR NOTE: *In Belize electricity is called current and many houses are without it.*

Punta Caliente, Back Street, ☎ 702-2561, $$, puntacal@btl.net, has eight rooms with cable TVs, hot water and ceiling fans. Two rooms have air conditioning, and all have private bathrooms. A roof-top cabaña overlooks the countryside. The hotel is 100 feet (30 meters) from the bus station and is directly across from a branch of the University. The owner is a non-assuming man who makes you feel comfortable right away.

Tate's Guest House, 34 Jose Maria Nunez St, ☎ 722-0147, $, has five rooms that are sparkling clean, especially the bathrooms. Each room has a bedside table, private bath and fan.

Mahong's Guest House, 11 Corner North and Main, ☎ 722-2044, $$, has eight clean and comfortable rooms. The big draw here are the stories you can get from Mr. Mahong.

Circle C Hotel, 117 West St, ☎ 722-2726, $$, is owned by Aurora Coe, the local herbalist who has learned from generations past. Aurora uses plants and herbs grown in her garden to cure minor ailments. She has seven rooms for rent that have private bathrooms with hot water, TVs, fans, and laundry service. English is spoken and camping is available. Her garden is the draw.

Traveller's Inn, Back Street, ☎ 702-2568, $$$, is next door to the Punta Caliente. It is a clean, pleasant hotel, with a restaurant on site that serves breakfast only. The entire hotel is decorated with ceramic tile, which makes sounds echo.

© Tranquility Lodge

Tranquility Lodge, ☎ 606-3572, www.tranquility-lodge.com, misspenny@starchefs.com, $$/$$$, is at Jacintoville, about two miles north of town, next to the camping site. It offers luxurious accommodations, tastefully decorated and spotlessly clean, for reasonable prices. The rooms are large, with ceramic tile on the floors and original art on the walls. Private bathrooms have hot water and rooms have air conditioning (one room even has remote-controlled air conditioning). Pickup from the Punta Gorda airport is complimentary.

The lodge is situated on 20 acres of cared-for jungle. Jacinto Creek runs through the back section. As many as 250 different bird species have been sighted here within one week. The owners are interesting and will do almost anything to make you feel comfortable. This is truly a treasure. The **Veranda Restaurant** on site is the most elegant place to eat in Punta Gorda (see below).

IRIE Camping, $, Cattle Landing, is next door to Tranquility Lodge. It offers outside toilets and a shower house. The owners serve some vegetarian snacks and locally picked herb teas.

El Pescador, ☎ 722-0050, www.elpescadorpg.com, is an exclusive fishing resort that costs US $500 a day, per person. It sits on 470 acres of jungle with 1.5 miles facing the Rio Grande. The spacious rooms are on property that is secluded. There is a pool, restaurant, bar and wraparound deck. Fishing (included for the price), goes on for eight hours a day.

PLACES TO EAT

Walucos Restaurant and **Gomiers** are both along the stretch between the north end of town and behind the Seafront Inn. Gomiers is highly recommended by people living and working in Punta Gorda as volunteers. He offers exotic vegetarian foods and specializes in organic and soy meals. A daily special is always available, but the vegan sausage or the fish sandwich are not to be missed.

Veranda Restaurant, ☎ 606-3572, $$$, is on the premises of Tranquility Lodge at Jacintoville. It's tastefully decorated, with fresh flowers on each table, non-intrusive candle lighting and crisply ironed linens. These things make it romantic. The wine list is one of the best in the country. I had the shrimp and cheese pie that was like eating a seafood cheesecake. My mouth waters every time I think of it. The cooks use just-plucked veggies for their salads and seafood caught fresh daily for their entrées. The cheesecake dessert (I like rich foods) is worth coming back for.

El Café, on North Street, $, is a no-nonsense place that is almost too clean. The owner offers great breakfasts. I had a banana shake that was so thick I had to spoon it up. The specialty is Creole food. If spice is what you want, this is the place. Prices are reasonable. If you need a quiet place to read or think while sipping the best coffee in town, you won't be bothered here.

Grace's Restaurant, 19 Main Street, $$, has the best Belizean dinners in the center of town. It's popular with local businessmen, so arrive before or after "rush hour" if you don't want to wait for a seat.

Earthrunnins, 11 Main street, ☎ 722-2007, $$, is popular with foreigners. The owner offers a variety of tasty American and seafood dishes. This is popular with an after-dinner crowd.

Ice Cream Parlor, Main Street by the school, $, has the best (and only) ice cream and their hamburgers are good too. It's closer to the south end of town, attracting guests from Nature's Way or Punta Caliente. If you arrive on a late bus in the dark, have your supper here.

Spice Café, 6 Front Street, $$, is run by Pat O'Neill, an expat trying to promote local art. Her burritos and tacos are reported to be tasty and the coffee is always good. When her musicians get going in the evenings they too can be worth listening to. Originally, the restaurant was a Creole Culture museum and many of the artifacts are still there, making the atmosphere interesting.

Emery's Café, North Street, $$, at the north end of town, is run by Carl Barona, a fly-fisher who has many fisher friends, so his dishes always feature the fresh catch of the day.

Mary's Café, one block south of the clock tower, offers homemade Belizean food and is frequently patronized by most of the ex-pats living in the area. There is no best dish – they are all good.

NIGHTLIFE

 Nightlife in Punta Gorda is almost an oxymoron. Besides a romantic dinner at the Verandah, you can go to the Spice Café and see if they have live entertainment. The huge deck at the **Cabin Creek Bar and Restaurant**, just north of the bridge, is the hangout spot in town, but even it was pretty quiet when I was there.

■ BARRANCO

Barranco is a Garifuna village with about 150 citizens. It has electricity, plus one community phone, a store, a bar, a police office, a school and two churches. Barranco is part of the TEA and home stay programs. Besides enjoying the lifestyle of the residents, you can participate in their evening drumming sessions or visit the Temash Sarstoon National Park with a guide. You can hire a guide in Punta Gorda or in Barranco. If taking a boat down to Barranco, it is easier to hire the same boatman for the park rather than negotiate a second trip.

The place becomes almost eerie when you listen to the locals drumming in the evenings while sitting on the beach by a fire.

GETTING HERE

 There is a rough, dry-season road for **4X4 vehicles**. Cycling is not advised. The distance is too long and there are no amenities along the way, not even a little village. The best way to get here is by **boat** – these can be hired at the dock in Punta Gorda.

THINGS TO DO

Temash Sarstoon National Park, established in 1992, is 41,000 acres of remote land preserved between the two rivers. The Sarstoon River borders Guatemala and the Temash borders the northern boundary of the park. In-between is a sandy marsh with white and red mangroves growing up to 100 feet high (30 meters). Orchids and bromeliads grow abundantly in this moist climate and the white-faced capuchin monkey has also been spotted, making this seldom-disturbed area its home. You must have a boat to visit the park. The easiest way to get there would be to hire a boat at the dock in Punta Gorda. Prices are negotiable, but US $75-$100 a day is reasonable.

DIRECTORIES

▪ GENERAL DIRECTORY

THE SOUTH – GENERAL DIRECTORY

▪ OUTFITTERS, GUIDES & TOUR OPERATORS

Blue Hole Horse Trails	☎ 820-2020	www.bananabank.com
C & G Tours	☎ 522-3641	cgtours@btl.net
Captain Bobo	☎ 603-0342	
Cayescape Tours	☎ 523-3285	
Destinations Belize	☎ 523-4018	www.destinationsbelize.com
Elroy's Tour Guide Service	☎ 523-2014	
Jungle Jeanies	☎ 523-7047	jungle@btl.net
Kingfisher Adventure	☎ 523-3323	www.belizekingfisher.com
Manfred Lohr	☎ 824-2276	
Nite Wind Guiding	☎ 523-3176	
Ocean Motion Guide Service	☎ 523-3363	www.oceanmotion.com
Percivil Gordon	☎ 520-3033	
Roots & Herbs Taxi	☎ 722-2834	
Saddle Caye South	☎ 523-0251	www.kayakbelize.com
Sea Horse Dive Shop	☎ 523-3356	www.belizescuba.com
Second Nature Divers	☎ 523-7038	www.belizenet.com/divers/html
Tide Tours	☎ 722-2129	
Toadal Adventure	☎ 523-3207	www.toadaladventure.com
UnBelizeable Adventures	☎ 523-3179	www.unbelizeableAdventures.com

▪ SHOPPING

Art N Soul Gallery	☎ 503-3088	
Fajina Craft Center	☎ 722-2167	
Gallery of Benjamin Nicholas	☎ 502-3752	

▪ ATTRACTIONS

Five Blue Lakes Visitor Center	☎ 822-5575	swa@btl.net
Jaguar Creek Ecological Site	☎ 820-2034	jagcreek@btl.net

▪ GROUPS/ORGANIZATIONS

Belize Audubon Society	☎ 223-4533	
Programme for Belize	☎ 227-5616	

■ ACCOMMODATIONS DIRECTORY

THE SOUTH – PLACES TO STAY	
Barnacle Bill's Beach Bungalows ($$$$)	☎ 523-8010; gotobelize.com/barnacle
Beaches and Dreams ($$)	☎ 523-7078; www.beachesanddreams,com
Be Back Cabins($$)	☎ 523-3285
Black Point Retreat ($$$$$)	☎ 722-0166; www.blackpointretreat.com
Blue Crab Resort ($$$)	☎ 520-4104; www.bluecrabbeach.com
Blue Creek Rainforest Lodge ($$$$$)	☎ 722-0013; ize2belize@aol.com
Bluefield Lodge ($$)	☎ 522-2742
Bob's Paradise Hotel ($$$$-$$$$$)	☎ 429-8763
Bol's Hilltop Hotel ($$)	☎ 702-2124
Bonefish Hotel ($$$)	☎ 522-2243; www.bluemarlinlodge.com
Calico Jacks ($$$$)	☎ 520-8103; www.calicojacksresort.com
Caribbean View ($-$$)	☎ 523-7050
Carol's Cabañas ($$)	☎ 523-3132; www.permitpow.com
Chaleanor Hotel ($$)	☎ 522-2587; chaleanor@btl.net
Charlton's Inn ($-$$)	☎ 722-2197; dwagner@btl.net
Circle C Hotel ($$)	☎ 722-2726
Clive's Place ($$)	☎ 709-2028
Coconut Cottage ($$$$$)	☎ 523-3155
Deb & Dave's Last Resort ($)	☎ 523-3207; www.placencia.com
Dianni's Guest House ($$)	☎ 523-3159
Diving Pelican Seaside Suites ($$$)	☎ 243-4591; www.thedivingpelican.com
El Pescador ($$$$-$$$$$)	☎ 722-0050; www.elpescadorpg.com
Glover's Guest House ($)	☎ 520-7099
Green Parrot Beach Resort ($$$$)	☎ 523-2488; www.greenparrot-belize.com
Hamanasi ($$$$)	☎ 520-7073; www.hamanasi.com
Heartland Inn ($$)	☎ 523-7153
Hopkin's Inn ($$)	☎ 523-7013; www.hopkinsinn.com
Indian Creek Guest House ($$)	☎ 709-6324; info@belizelodge.com
Jaguar Reef Lodge ($$$$$)	☎ 800-289-5756; www.jaguarreef.com
Joyce & Frank's B & B ($$$$)	☎ 561-683-3899; www.belizebandb.com
Jungle Huts ($$)	☎ 522-3166
Jungle Jeanies ($$-$$$)	☎ 523-7074;
Jungle Lodge & Adventure Ctr ($$$$)	☎ 822-2800; www.cavesbranch.com
Kanantik Reef & Jungle Resort ($$$$$)	☎ 520-8048; www.kanantik.com
Lillpat Sittee River Resort ($$$$)	☎ 520-7019; www.lillpat.com
Lydia's Guest House ($)	☎ 523-3117; www.placencia.com
Mahong's Guest House ($$)	☎ 722-2044

THE SOUTH – PLACES TO STAY

Mama Noots Jungle Resort ($$$)	☎ 422-3666; www.mamanoots.com
Manatee Inn ($$)	☎ 523-4083; www.manateeinn.com
Manatee Lodge ($$)	☎ 877-462-6283; www.manateelodge.com
Mariposa Resort ($$$$)	☎ 523-4069; ww.mariposabelize.com
Maya Beach Hotel ($$)	☎ 520-8040; www.mayabeach.com
Maya Breeze ($$$-$$$$)	☎ 523-8012; www.mayabreeze.com
Maya Playa ($$-$$$)	☎ 523-8020; www.gotobelize.com/mayaplaya
Maya Village Home Stay ($)	☎ 520-2021; nuukcheil@btl.net
Mejen Tzil Lodge ($)	☎ 520-3032; isaquire@btl.net
Miller's Landing ($$$-$$$$)	☎ 523-3010; www.millerslanding.net
Nature's Way Guest House ($)	☎ 702-2119
Nautical Inn Adventure Resort ($$$$)	☎ 520-3595; www.nauticalinnbelize.com
Nu'uk Che'il Cottages ($$)	☎ 615-2091
Omar's Guest House ($)	☎ 609-3135
Pallavi Hotel ($$)	☎ 702-2414
Pal's Guest House ($$)	☎ 522-2095; palbze@btl.net
Paradise Vacation Hotel ($-$$)	☎ 523-3179; paradiseplacencia@hotmail.com
Pelican Beach Resort ($$$$)	☎ 522-2044; www.pelicanbeachbelize.com
Pleasure Cove Lodge ($$$)	☎ 520-7089; www.pleasurecovelodge.com
Primitas Farm B & B ($)	☎ 220-8259; pascott@btl.net
Punta Caliente ($$)	☎ 702-2561; puntacal@btl.net
Red Bank Guest Cabin ($)	☎ 503-2233
Ranguana Lodge ($$$)	☎ 523-3112; www.ranguanabelize.com
Ransom's Seaside Garden Cabins ($)	ransoms@belizemail.net
Robert's Grove ($$$$)	☎ 523-3565; www.robertsgrove.com
Rum Point Inn ($$$$$)	☎ 523-3239; www.rumpoint.com
Ruthie's Cabanas ($)	☎ 502-3184
St. Charles Inn ($$)	☎ 702-2149
Sak's Place ($$$$-$$$$$)	☎ 523-3227; www.saksatplacenica.com
Seaclift B&B ($$)	☎ 522-3540
Sea Front Inn ($$$)	☎ 702-2300; seafront@btl.net
Sea Spray Hotel ($$-$$$)	☎ 523-3148; www.belizenet.com/seaspray
Secret Garden House ($$)	☎ 523-3420; www.secretgardnplacencia.netfirms.com
Serenade Guest House ($$$)	☎ 523-3380; www.belizecayes.com
Singing Sands Resort ($$$$)	☎ 523-2243; www.singingsands.com
Soulshine Resort ($$$$$)	☎ 877-700-7685; www.soulshine.com
South Waters Resort ($$$$$)	☎ 523-3308; www.southwatersresort.com
Tania's ($)	☎ 523-7058
Tate's Guest House ($)	☎ 722-0147

THE SOUTH – PLACES TO STAY	
TEA Guest Houses/Home Stay ($$)	☎ 702-2096
Tipple Tree Beya ($$)	☎ 520-7006; www.tippletree.net
Toucan Lulu ($$$$)	☎ 760-433-5451; www.toucanlulu.com
Toucan Sittee ($)	☎ 523-7039; www.toucansittee.info
Tranquility Lodge ($$-$$$)	☎ 606-3572; misspenny@starchefs.com
Traveller's Inn ($$$)	☎ 702-2568
Turtle Inn ($$$$$)	☎ 523-3244; www.blancaneaux.com
Vickie's Hostel ($)	☎ 502-3324
Wabien Guest House ($$)	☎ 523-7010
Wahmia Hotel ($)	☎ 702-2542; www.placencia.com
Westwind Hotel ($$)	☎ 523-3255
Whistling Seas ($$-$$$)	☎ 503-7203
Windscheif ($$)	☎ 523-7149; www.windscheif.com
Yugadah Inn ($)	☎ 503-7089; nunezjoy@hotmail.com

■ RESTAURANT DIRECTORY

THE SOUTH – PLACES TO EAT	
Alice's Restaurant ($)	☎ 520-3033
Crow's Nest Café ($)	☎ 523-3308
Earthrunnins ($$)	☎ 722-2007
J & N Restaurant (n/k)	☎ 522-2649
Nu-uk Che'il Restaurant ($)	☎ 615-2091
Omar's Restaurant ($)	☎ 609-3135
Orchids Café ($$)	☎ 220-5621
Pickled Parrot ($$)	☎ 523-3102
Rainbow Restaurant ($$)	☎ 522-2620
Sugar Reef Sunset Lounge ($$)	☎ 523-3289
Tipsy Tuna Sports Bar (n/k)	☎ 523-3179
Veranda Restaurant ($$$)	☎ 606-3572

The Cayes

Turquoise water under clear skies, white sand dotted with green palms, colorful fish of every size and coral swaying in the waves. These are common images of Belize. Diving, snorkeling, sailing, fishing, windsurfing and sea kayaking are what most people do in Belize. Other travelers may read, tan, drink and eat seafood. For all this we head for the cayes.

The cayes of Belize have the second-largest **coral reef** on the planet and their two atolls include some of the most challenging dive sites in the world. The area is huge, with only three cayes being densely populated. Many are uninhabited and others are uninhabitable.

The Cayes

Because of their fragility and unique natural contribution to the planet, parts of the region were set aside as preserves and parks. Then, in 1996, the seven sites were made into a UNESCO World Heritage Site. They are **Bacalar Chico National Park, Blue Hole Natural Monument, Half Moon Caye Natural Monument, South Water Caye Marine Reserve, Glover's Reef Marine Reserve, Laughing Bird Caye National Park** and **Sapodilla Cayes Marine Reserve**.

Fishing is always good here, whether you are a sports fisher, an underwater photographer, or a diver/snorkeler trying to spot a rare ocean inhabitant. The cayes of Belize are for the active and the sedate, the old and the young, the dreamer and the realist, the rich and the middle class.

WHAT'S IN A WORD?

Is the word Cays, Cayes, Quays or Keys? Cayo in Spanish means shoal, rock or barrier reef. Cay or Caye in old French means sandbank or bar and that word originated from the medieval Latin word Caium. The Oxford Etymological Dictionary states that in 1707, in his book *Jamaica*, the author Sloane claimed that the Spaniards used Cayos, whence by corruption comes the English word Cayes. Falconer in the Dictionary Marine (1789) claims the word Caies means a ridge of rods or sandbanks, commonly called in the West Indies Keys.

If you want a **party scene** after a day playing on or in the water, then Ambergris Caye, Caye Caulker or Tobacco Caye are the places to go. If **seclusion** and quiet is what you seek, head to Glover's Reef or a resort on one of the privately-owned cayes. If you need **adventure** in the sun, go kayaking in the south.

THE CAYES IN A NUTSHELL

About 450 islands are bordered by 150 miles of reef that runs between 10 and 40 miles from the shoreline. The islands are of four types. There are the **wet cayes** that are mainly mangrove and are often partially under water. There are **coral islands** that are solid clumps of dead coral. The **sand cayes** are the most habitable. They are a combination of sand, coral and mangrove. Finally, there are three **atolls** – Glover's Reef, Lighthouse Reef and the Turneffe islands.

The corals that eventually form the reefs and, in turn, the coral and sand islands, are constantly producing more mass through a process that also helps clear the water. Except when a hurricane has just gone through, you can always see 50 feet or more (15 meters) down in the water and between March and May you can often see up to 200 feet (60 meters).

Opposite: Aerial view of Belize's coral reef.

Because of this natural beauty some of the areas have become preserves. On Glover's Reef, for example, there is an experiment in progress that has part of the atoll as preserve, while the other part is used for commercial and sport fishing. The success of this project is shown in the increased number of fish that are spilling over into the fishing area from the protected section.

■ NATURAL HISTORY

 It doesn't matter whether you are diving, snorkeling or walking along the beach, you will come in contact with coral and water creatures while on the cayes. **Corals** are alive. They are without backbones or vertebrae and are made up of moving polyps. These polyps have tentacles that reach out and trap small creatures floating by; they do this only at night. As a byproduct, they generate calcium carbonate that, after the coral dies, forms the reef structure.

In the waters of Belize there are 36 species of soft coral and 74 species of hard coral. Only hard corals make up coral reefs. Living with the coral is algae, which grows in the tissue of the polyps. The algae is what gives coral its different shades of green, brown and pink. Algae produces oxygen and other byproducts of photosynthesis that the coral consumes. Algae also rids the coral of its waste materials.

There is coral everywhere in the ocean, but the hard corals you are likely to see in Belize include the brain, short and long star, finger, elkhorn, staghorn and plate corals.

CORALS

HARD CORALS

- **Pillar corals** form cylinders or spirals up to 10 feet long (three meters).

- **Boulder**, knob or mound corals are the bases for the reef structures in Belize. While growing, they resemble mountains, domes or knobs.

- **Brain corals** are usually cylindrical in shape with fissures like a brain. They are abundant in the waters of Belize.

- **Staghorn and elkhorn corals** look like their namesakes. They can be seen on the reef crests, the parts of the reef that are occasionally exposed. The back of the reef is the landward side and the fore reef is the side facing the ocean. Staghorn coral in Belize usually grows behind the reef, while the elkhorn, which grows on the other side, takes some of the wave action from the ocean.

■ **Leaf and plate corals** look likes leaves or trees. Some are quite fleshy and the polyps become hidden in the flesh.

BLACK CORAL ALERT

Black Coral is not one you will see in the waters of Belize. It takes about 100 years for a piece of black coral to grow one inch. The **Sustainable Sea Project**, partially funded by National Geographic, found that deep in the waters of the Caribbean, the black coral was "sparsely distributed, small and in marginal health." It is better not to purchase black coral jewelry and create a market for this rare coral.

SOFT CORALS

Soft corals include the hydro and octo-corals.

■ One species of **hydro** coral is **fire coral**, which has a poison in its cells that causes burning on your skin when touched. These corals are tree-shaped.

■ **Octo-corals** are soft corals that look like plants and are hard to tell from seaweed. Octo-corals include the **feather plume**, which can grow up to six feet long (1.8 meters); **sea fans**, delicate lace-like formations; and **sea whips**, which look like whips.

▨ DIVING & SNORKELING

Because Belize is not overly crowded by locals or tourists, you may find yourself the only diver in the water at one of the walls or caves. The coral gardens and turtle grass beds often lie inside the reef and are seen just before the walls, caves and tunnels. Because of the complex cave systems throughout Belize, some of these caves extend under the ocean while others, like the Blue Hole, have actually caved in.

The coral is host for the rest of the marine life that can be seen around the cayes. Spotting a hawksbill turtle or a queen angelfish, a pork fish or a fairy basslet is as much a thrill as seeing the whale shark or barracuda. Jellyfish and sea urchins can often be seen from the shore. The fish trapped in tide pools formed by solid chunks of coral are numerous along the shores of some islands.

CAYE ETIQUETTE

If going anywhere around the cayes and atolls, be certain to follow some basic rules.

- **Anchor** in the sand only.
- Don't collect **coral** or purchase products made from coral.
- **Don't move** or touch any of the corals or plants, as this may damage the coral and disturb the living creatures hidden within.
- Leave underwater caves and ledges within a short period of time as the **air bubbles** can become abrasive to delicate organisms. Have only one person enter the cave at a time to avoid crowding and coming in contact with some of the plants or corals.
- Be **conscious** of what you are doing. If you feel something touch you, don't panic and kick as this could possibly cause more damage. Move away carefully.
- **Do not feed** or "ride" with marine animals like rays or dolphins.
- Observe **fishing laws** and respect closed seasons. This includes avoiding lobster or conch during the closed season.
- **Do not disturb** in any way the nesting and hatching grounds of the sea turtles.

> **AUTHOR NOTE:** *Diving after flying is quite safe. However, you should stop diving at least 24 hours before flying to prevent decompression problems.*

DIVE BOATS

 Check the boats before hiring one. If the price sounds too good, it probably is. The cost of a dive is around US $50 and may decrease if you do more than one dive in a day. A higher number of participants may also decrease the costs.

A good boat should have radio communication in the event of an accident or problem. Legally, boats must have life jackets, compass, fire extinguisher and a spare motor. The boat should carry oxygen, a recall device and a first-aid kit. For strong-current dives, the crew should have a special descent line and for deep dives an extra tank should be hung at about 15 feet (five meters).

> **AUTHOR NOTE:** *If going in a large group, make certain everyone's name is on the captain's list and that everyone is back on board before leaving the dive location.*

A **recompression chamber** is available only on Ambergris Caye. If diving at the more remote sites, be extremely cautious as it could take far too long to reach the chamber should you be in need. To help pay for the chamber and its support staff, dive operators donate US $1 from the cost of every tank that is filled.

CERTIFICATION

 Bring your **certification card** with you. No captain can give you a tank unless you have a card. If you are not certified, you can take lessons in Belize. There are as many qualified instructors as there are course options.

Divers are classified as **novice** if they have fewer than 25 dives under their belt (tank) and don't dive deeper than 60 feet (20 meters). **Intermediate** divers have anywhere from 25 to 100 dives under their tanks and dive up to 120 feet (40 meters). **Advanced** divers have logged over 100 dives. Your skill level will determine where you can dive while in Belize. A good dive master will not let a diver go down alone on her/his first dive. He will join you and assess your skill.

If **snorkeling**, you will probably not go out beyond the reef, as the clearest and calmest water is within the reef or the lagoons of the atolls. The one danger for snorkelers is that the sun's rays may not be felt until it is far too late to prevent second-degree burns. Wear a t-shirt and put on waterproof sunblock.

GETTING HERE

There are only two ways to reach any of the cayes: by plane or boat. At each main city (or in the vicinity) along the coast, boats leave regularly for the cayes. You can also book special charters and live-aboard boats can be hired.

Both **TropicAir** (☎ 800-422-3435, 226-2012 in Belize, www.tropicair.com) and **Maya Air** (☎ 422-2333) offer numerous flights every day to Caye Caulker, Amergris Caye and Chapel Caye, and the prices are less than US $50 each way.

The cost of a **boat trip** to any of the cayes depends on how many share the expense and how far you need to travel. Regular **water taxis** go to the most popular islands near Belize City. Some resorts include the cost of getting to their island in the total cost of staying there. Other resort operators or private boat owners offer trips on scheduled days to reach an island. For example, Glover's Reef can be reached by taking their boat from Sittee River and the cost is US $40 each way, but the service is available only on certain days. If you want to go out on a non-scheduled day, the cost is about US $350 for the boat. Reaching some of the islands can be quite costly – a boat to Blackbird Caye is US $400 each way.

Once on the islands you can usually walk or rent bikes and golf carts to get around. Electrically-powered carts are popular on Ambergris Caye.

NORTHERN CAYES

■ AMBERGRIS CAYE

Ambergris Caye is the largest and most densely populated island in Belize. It has hotels, restaurants, bars, discos, tour agencies, gift shops and tourists. The snorkeling and diving sites are numerous and spectacular, with most sites situated just half an hour's boat ride from San Pedro. The reef is only half a mile off the sandy beaches of the island. Although not widely done, windsurfing is excellent around Ambergris. The song *La Isla Bonita* by Madonna is about this island.

> **AUTHOR NOTE:** *The motto of Ambergris Caye is "No shoes, no shirt, no problem."*

It is believed that the island was named by British whalers, after the sperm whale's waxy gray secretions (called ambergris) found floating on the water. The secretions come from the sperm whale's intestine, and are used in making perfume. Read *Moby Dick* for an elaborate description.

The two main ocean sites to see on Ambergris are **Bacalar Chico** and the **Hol Chan Marine Reserve**. The most popular dive and snorkeling sites include the famous **Mexican Tunnel, Mexican**

Rocks and Mexican Cuts, Hol Chan Cut, Shark-Ray Alley and **Bacalar Chico**.

Non-water people should visit the lagoons on Ambergris, where the wildlife hangs out. Because the island was once an extension of the mainland, many animals not normally seen on islands are found on Ambergris.

HISTORY

 The **Maya** used the entire island They fished and traded with the Yucatán Maya. Long after the downfall of the cities like Xunantunich, Tikal and Caracol, the outlying villages such as the one on Basil Jones Plateau continued to thrive.

In the early 1500s the **Spanish** tried to infiltrate the island, but the Maya drove them off – for a time anyway. By the mid 1600s it is believed that some of the **pirates** needing safe refuge used Ambergris. They left bottles, coins and treasures behind.

There is a document in the Belize archives that describes the indignation of the **British** after the Spanish raided some of their settlements at Ambergris. That was in 1828 and is the first record of British settlers being on the island.

The island was originally deeded to the Belize Agricultural Company that eventually went broke. The land was then purchased by two Belize City businessmen named Welsh and Gough.

The Caste Wars in Mexico forced many of the Maya to flee the Yucatán and in 1848 the first of these people arrived in San Pedro. They received protection from British authorities and soon the community grew to 50 families.

These families paid rent to the Bibbins Brothers, who the Maya believed owned the island, although the Bibbins were only managers for Welsh and Gough. However, the two were good landlords, often taking eggs or fish in exchange for rent so the Maya continued to live and flourish without complaints to any authorities.

In 1850 the village was named San Pedro after the Christian guardian of fishers. The Spanish wanted control of Ambergris because they felt it was part of the Yucatán. There were a few skirmishes between them and the British until, in 1893, a treaty was signed giving the British in Belize authority over Ambergris. After that, the island was passed on to numerous other owners until **James Hume Blake** purchased it in 1873 for his stepdaughters, Romana and Maria. Blake earned a lot of his wealth as a gunrunner during the Caste Wars. But he was a respected runner because he occasionally came to the rescue of captured Maya prisoners. Blake purchased the island for BZ $625 (US $315) which, even in those days, was a low sum. By 1886 the family was living on the island and selling parcels of land to other interested investors. There was intermarriage between the investors and the Blake family and the resulting dynasty became powerful. They demanded high rents from the peasants and often booted Maya families off the plots they had worked for years.

Once **logging** and **chicle** became major industries in Belize, the peasants living in the area of San Pedro worked for these industries. Between the 1880s and the depression, the **coconut** business became important for the economy and many Maya worked on the plantations. One of the biggest markets for coconut was the United States. A byproduct of the nut is **cocal**, an incense used by the Maya. Although difficult to produce, it brought some money to the workers. In 1942 and again in 1953 hurricanes destroyed not only the homes but most of the coconut trees. The coconut industry on Ambergris never recovered. The people turned to lobster fishing.

Lobster was sold either live or cooked. However, it didn't take long for someone to realize that it could be canned for export. A bit later, it was frozen and by 1934 the first freezer boats were carrying the delicacy to Florida. The price of the tails in those days was anywhere from 1¢ to 1.5¢ a pound. However, as lobster became a popular delicacy, the price went up to around 5¢ to 7¢ a pound. Small planes were then used to transport the meat and the industry dominated the island.

Lobster was abundant and fishing it was lucrative. Some of the men could catch up to 1,000 lobster in a week, with the tails weighing up to six pounds (2.7 kg). But fishing was hard, as it was all done without the help of machinery. There were no lobster traps. The men dove without masks or fins. Once lobster traps were introduced, lobster fishing became a bit easier and it didn't take long for the numbers of lobster to decline. By 1955 the fishing close to San Pedro was non-existent. However, the lobster traps allowed fishing in deeper water. The men realized that they weren't getting their fair share of the profits so they formed a cooperative that resulted in decent prices being collected for their catch. Today, because of the over-fished waters, there is a minimum size limit on lobster that can be brought in.

The Blake family continued to live through the economic ups and downs until the 1960s, when the government expropriated (at fair market value for the land) and resold the property as city lots.

Shortly after the lots were sold, **tourists** arrived and, in 1965, the Holiday Hotel was opened to accommodate them. Tropic Air began flying commercial planes onto the island. The Paradise Hotel was the next to be opened and that was soon followed by Coral Beach Hotel. Soon there were hotels cheek-to-jowl along the beach.

GETTING HERE & GETTING AROUND

 The most convenient way to reach Ambergris Caye is to catch the **water taxi** from Belize City. They leave from the Marine Building and from the Tourist Village in Belize City. Just show up. Two companies run a total of 10 boats a day. Another company runs water taxis from Corozal. Their boats leave from the town dock in Corozal. In San Pedro, some boats arrive at the pier by Shark's Bar in the center of town, while others arrive at the back of the island just north of the airport.

There are 22 **flights** a day offered by Maya Air and Tropic Air. Planes depart from both the international and the municipal airports.

Returning to Belize City from San Pedro, you have the same options.

The caye is not so big that you need a car. However, there is no public transportation either. You can rent a **golf cart** or a **bicycle** (see *Equipment Rentals & Tour Agencies*, below). **Water taxis**, available at the town docks, will also take you up or down the island. San Pedro is the only village on the island.

> **AUTHOR NOTE:** *If you take a taxi from the airport or the dock, and you ask the driver to take you to a hotel, he will take you to one where he gets 10% commission. That money will be hidden in the price of your room. If you went to the same hotel on your own, the cost would be 10% less.*

At one time, a reaction ferry crossed the San Pedro River, but it sunk during high water, causing a lot of headaches for the local government so they decided to build a bridge. The ferry is no more and the bridge is high over the water so if flooding does occur again, the bridge will not be affected.

SIGHTSEEING

Hol Chan Marine Reserve Office, Caribena Street, San Pedro, ☎ 226-2247, hcmr@btl.net, has numerous maps and charts to read. One that is really good is a side view of the cut at Hol Chan. The same chart shows how the water levels have changed in the past 7,000 years, which explains why some of the Maya ruins in the area are underwater today. Open daily from 9 am to 5 pm, this is a great place to spend an hour at midday, away from the sun.

Ambergris Library, at the south end of Front Street in San Pedro, is open daily from 8 am to 4 pm. The library is small and could use additional books for both children and adults. If you have extras (or would like to bring them), donations would be appreciated. It has some local poetry books and a limited selection of history books. I did some historical research in the library while I was there and the librarian was very helpful. This is a nice place to spend an afternoon.

Rosie's Massage, ☎ 226-3879, is across from Ramon's and south of Steve and Becky's. Rosie will give you a combination massage and aromatherapy or deep-tissue massage, Swedish therapy, reflexology, shiatsu or a facial for US $25 an hour. She will come to your room to do these services. Rosie speaks little English; Spanish is her first language.

The Football Stadium, in the center of San Pedro, is used as an outdoor theater when entertainment comes to town. Otherwise, it is pleasant to sit at the stadium and watch the locals play their much-loved football (soccer). Near the stadium is the church with San Pedro standing watch over the fishers. He is a bit ghoulish looking.

Go to see the **carving** at the San Pedro Holiday Hotel. The head was carved by the famous Belizean carver **George Gabb**, and depicts the ethnic groups in Belize – Maya, Creole and Mestizo. It is carved from zericote wood, the hardest wood known, and is so dense that it sinks in water. Gabb also has carvings at the Radisson Fort George in Belize City. This piece of art is worth going to see.

THINGS TO DO

Costa Maya Festival, www.ambergriscaye.com/festival, is the biggest celebration in San Pedro. It's held in August, but check the website for exact dates. If you plan on attending you will need to have a room booked well in advance. Literally thousands of people from every corner of the country arrive on Ambergris for the celebrations.

Each of the participating countries – Belize (the host), El Salvador, Guatemala, Honduras and Mexico – has a day when their cultural specialties are featured. This includes dress, food, music, dancing and story telling. The beauty pageant is held on Thursday and big name musicians (people like Andy Palacio, the Iligales and Santino's Messengers) come to entertain on Saturday. The parades feature exquisite floats, clowns and every noise-maker imaginable. There is also a greased-pole climb, fishing derbies, volleyball tournaments and, for the kids, foot races.

Each year the festival gets bigger. If you would like to taste Belize at its party best, this is a must.

The San Pedro Carnival is held the Friday to Tuesday before Ash Wednesday at the beginning of lent. It's the last binge before the 40-day fast that Catholics perform before Easter. Although not a food fest, they must give up something they love for that time period. Many give up cigarettes or beer and all must give up meat.

The carnival is fun and is the last true Mardi Gras-style festival in Belize. People dress in outrageous costumes, men often dress as women and fun is the requisite. What San Pedro-ans enjoy the most is the painting and splashing of each other in the streets. The party-goers use water colors and eggs to shmuck anyone going past.

St. Peter, the patron saint of fishers, has his own festival on June 27th (St. Peter's day). It starts with a blessing at the church for all the fishers, followed by concerts, work shops, parades, lectures and dances. This event is much milder than the Carnival or the Costa Maya celebrations.

Township Day is November 27th. In 1984 San Pedro was raised in status from village to town. They celebrate with boat races, fishing derbies and parades.

The Cayes

Natural Attractions

Bacalar Chico Marine Preserve can be visited only by boat. The most interesting way to do this trip is to include a circumnavigation of the island and stop at Hol Chan and Shark Ray Alley near the southern end of the caye. You can also have the pleasure of doing a bit of bird watching as you pass between the island's western side and Little Guana Caye Bird Sanctuary, a prime location for the blue heron and roseate spoonbills.

Boats can be hired from Belize City, San Pedro or Sarteneja in Orange Walk District (see *Equipment Rentals & Tour Agencies*, below).

Bacalar Chico is classified as a Zone A area, which means there is no fishing or collecting permitted at any time. Flora are not to be picked or removed and buoy moorings should be used whenever possible. All these restrictions mean that snorkeling is excellent.

Bacalar Chico became a preserve in 1996. It encompasses 15,000 acres of marine land and 12,000 acres of coastal land at the north end of Ambrigris Caye. Included are Maya ruins, turtle nesting sites, a historical channel and walking trails.

Bacalar Chico is a channel cut through the mangroves that reminds me of the Everglades in Florida. This narrow channel was dug by the Maya 1,500 years ago so that they could take their canoes up to Chetumal Bay to trade without going all the way around the island. At Rocky Point, on the east side of the island, they would have had to enter the open sea and possibly dangerous or rough water.

The visitor center, open daily from 8 am to 5 pm (closed from noon to 1 pm), is on the old Pinkerton Estate at the very north end of Ambergris. The charge to enter the park is US $5 per person. There is a 12-foot (seven-meter) observation tower above the visitor center. From its top, you can see almost all the way to Tulum.

The concrete jetty and walkway here are remnants of the Pinkerton Estate, as are the concrete pillars that support the new visitor center. As you approach the jetty, you will notice a rocky circle about 100 feet from shore. This is a breakwater made with old stones from the abandoned Maya site of San Juan. The breakwater was made by Pinkerton to protect his land from the ocean when the winds blew in from the north and the water was rough.

Hol Chan Marine Reserve is four miles south of San Pedro and hosts 30,000 visitors a year. It is one of the most popular marine sites in Belize. Hol Chan means "little channel" in Maya. The channel is about 10 meters wide (30 feet) and just about as deep. It is known for the moray eels that live in small caves along the walls, but it is also rich in other wildlife, making it a popular dive and snorkeling site.

With the dedication of Jacques Carter and the New York Zoological Society, Hol Chan became the first marine reserve ever recognized in Central America. Established in 1987, it covers about five square miles and encompasses three different marine zones – reef, mangrove and sea grass beds. Since its inception the number of fish in and around the reserve has increased noticeably. Touching or disturbing any of the fish or plants is strictly forbidden. There is a park warden at Hol Chan watching what you do and collecting the US $3 fee required to visit.

Although you'll see a lot of coral growth on the cut at Hol Chan, there's also evidence of damage due to visitors' carelessness. But even with all the traffic in the area, there are still lots of fish to watch.

Maya Ruins

I describe these sites going down the island from the north. You will probably visit in a boat and the cost usually includes a stop at the ruins. Check with your tour operator before you pay.

Near the visitor center of **Bacalar Chico Preserve** you will see a few mounds where the **San Juan** trading site was originally located. Parts of it jut into the water. There are pottery shards, tools, spearheads, obsidian, bones and bottles lying on the ground. It is illegal to collect or remove any of these pieces, but you may look. Some of the items found here (and taken to the museum) came from as far away as the Pacific coast of Guatemala and central Mexico.

In one of the graves, two dishes had been placed lip to lip. Inside were some bones, thought to be fish bones. However it was later discovered that they were the remains of a fetus. Another grave had many vessels and jade pieces, along with deer bones and antlers. From these grave pieces, it is deduced that the man buried here may have been a stone worker. There have also been bottles and coins found near San Juan that come from the pirates who hid in the place while waiting for their next galleon to come by or while hiding from the Spanish navy.

Just through the mangroves is a trail that will take you up a hill to the **Santa Cruz** trading site. It has some wells that are secured around the rim by stones. There is also a plaza and some burial mounds.

After you leave Santa Cruz the Bacalar Chico Cut through the mangroves leads you to another site. On the way, keep an eye out for fish in the underwater caves. You may even spot one of the 200-pound groupers that are reported to hang around under ledges in the area.

The **Chac Balam ruin** is not far from the cut. Originally, the Maya had to dig this harbor by hand. Today the harbor has again been cleared, although the trail to the ruin can be difficult and wet. There are deep holes just under the surface, so take a pole to check the ground before stepping. Once at the entrance to the ruin, you will see signs posted by the park officials indicating the names of trees.

Although Chac Balam is believed to have been a trading center, there are many shallow graves in the area, including burial mounds at the entrance. Some archeologists think that this was a place where the Maya came to bury their dead. One site had the remains of a man with blood-letting tools and receptacles, indicating that he was of the elite, since only the rich did such things.

Ek Luum, on the windward side of the island and just south of the cut, is about 820 feet (250 meters) up from the beach. There are two mounds here, one that had ceremonial pottery shards and one with residential debris. But this was a small village, as were others, like the one on the north side of San Pedro Lagoon. There is little to see.

Yalamha ruins is at the entrance to Laguna Francos on the western side of the island. These ruins were named appropriately. Yalamha means under water and, due to rising water levels, that's where the ruins are. This tiny, early classic residence may be a major clue as to why there aren't more early classic ruins in Belize; the sea has swallowed the sites. When on your circumnavigation of the island, have your captain point out this site.

All the ruins on the north end of Ambergris have harbors that allow boat access. They also feature small plazas between residential mounds. Because they were trade centers, the towns often had the highest-quality goods from far away places.

The area of **Rocky Point** and **Robles Point**, just south of the Bacalar Chico Cut on the east side, are nesting grounds for the green and loggerhead turtles. Rocky Point is the only spot in Belize where the mainland touches the coral reef; you can see parts of the reef sticking up out of the water as you approach. If in a boat at Rocky Point, you must go out onto open sea and then cut back in again at Punta Azul. If going the other way, cut out at Punta Azul and in at Rocky Point and continue your circumnavigation.

Basil Jones ruins are on the Basil Jones Plateau, just south and inland of Rocky Point. There is little left of the ruin today, but some of the stone walls are thought to have marked private property boundaries. Some archeologists believe that the people living here were farmers. Some shell heaps were found, but looters have taken any treasures that may have been left. The rock outcrops that you can see in the area contain the oldest rocks in Central America.

Today, the plateau's south end is home to the Nova Shrimp Company and its restored Gulf Oil airstrip. Also here is the timeshare resort of Cabaña Reef, whose manager, Adam Chandler, was found murdered in Honduras in 2002. Just beyond Cabaña Reef is the Basil Jones Beach Resort, also a timeshare.

The **Marco Gonzalez ruins** are probably the largest of the sites on Ambergris. They are just 1.8 miles south of San Pedro. The city had a central plaza with several small courtyards. It is believed that the people from here traded with those at Lamanai. The most interesting thing about this site is that it is believed to have been occupied well into the 1200s, long after many other cities were abandoned.

ADVENTURES ON WATER

Dive & Snorkeling Sites

It is impossible in the scope of this book to describe the 50 or so different sites that I know of along the reef near Ambergris. The most popular snorkeling/dive sites are Boca Ciega (for very advanced divers) and Bacalar Chico, Corral Gardens and Mexico Rocks, Mexico Tunnel and Mexico Cut for intermediate divers. But there are places like Buena Vista Canyon, Victoria Canyons, Palmero Canyon, Tres Cocos, Cypress Tunnels that are attractive and suitable for all skill levels.

The cost of a single dive is US $25-$40; if you book two or three dives for the same day, the cost decreases. Night dives are popular; snorkelers enjoy this sport also. The cost is US $10-$20 more per person for night dives.

In the sea grass beds at Hol Chan is the **Boca Ciega sinkhole**, or cave without a roof. The blue sponge fans and sea fans are abundant here. You must have permission from the warden to enter this area. Those diving along the cut should be aware that outgoing tides can create a strong current. All care should be taken not to drift with the tide into open water. This area should not be confused with Boca Ciega, just offshore from San Pedro, where you go about 100 feet (30 meters) deep. The sinkhole dive is for intermediate levels.

Shark Ray Alley is a snorkeling site in shallow water just north of Hol Chan Cut. Fishers long ago used to clean their catch along this strip, thus attracting nurse sharks and stingrays, who came for the easy feed. Today, tour operators feed the fish so tourists can watch Caribbean sharks and eagle rays.

> **AUTHOR NOTE:** *It will be your decision whether you approve of feeding animals. Ask the tour operators about their habits before paying to go. Personally, I believe that feeding any wild creature takes it away from its natural way of life and creates problems the animals can't cope with once the human has disappeared.*

Mexico Rocks, with its shallow waters, was named after the coconut plantation that sat on shore above the site. Brain coral and sea fans are numerous, as are small caves. The sea grass area is a good hiding spot for stingrays and batfish. Since the water is protected by the reef and the depth is only about 25 feet (eight meters), visibility (usually to the bottom) is almost always good. Close by is the spectacular pinnacle (near a canyon exit) called the **Mexico Rocks Pinnacle**. There is also a wall drop-off with tube sponges near the pinnacle and nearby are the **Mexico Tunnels**, suitable only for experienced divers. A light is needed and you must go with a dive master.

The Pescador Cavern and Tunnels are only for the advanced diver. The dive is about 100 feet (30 meters) through a long tunnel, at the end of which is a 200-foot (60-meter) drop. This is a popular site. If there are too many people when you arrive, go over to **Punta Arena** just north of Pescador and you will find similar formations.

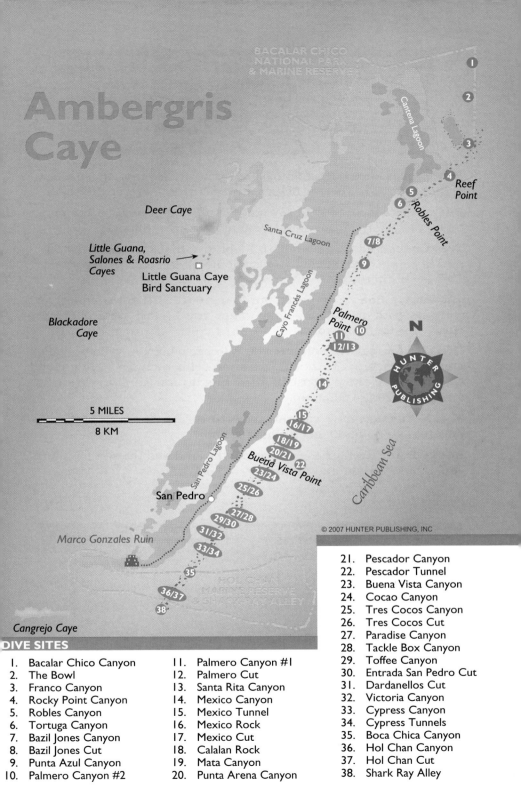

Ambergris Caye

BACALAR CHICO NATIONAL PARK & MARINE RESERVE

Cantena Lagoon

1
2
3
4 — Reef Point
5
6
Robles Point
7/8
9

Santa Cruz Lagoon

Deer Caye

Little Guana, Salones & Roasrio Cayes →
Little Guana Caye Bird Sanctuary

Cayo Francés Lagoon

Blackadore Caye

Palmero Point
10
11
12/13

14

N
HUNTER PUBLISHING

5 MILES
8 KM

15
16/17
18/19
20/21
22
Buena Vista Point
23/24

San Pedro Lagoon

San Pedro ○

25/26
27/28
29/30
31/32
33/34
35
36/37
38

Caribbean Sea

Marco Gonzales Ruin

HOL CHAN MARINE RESERVE & SHARK RAY ALLEY

© 2007 HUNTER PUBLISHING, INC

Cangrejo Caye

DIVE SITES

1. Bacalar Chico Canyon
2. The Bowl
3. Franco Canyon
4. Rocky Point Canyon
5. Robles Canyon
6. Tortuga Canyon
7. Bazil Jones Canyon
8. Bazil Jones Cut
9. Punta Azul Canyon
10. Palmero Canyon #2

11. Palmero Canyon #1
12. Palmero Cut
13. Santa Rita Canyon
14. Mexico Canyon
15. Mexico Tunnel
16. Mexico Rock
17. Mexico Cut
18. Calalan Rock
19. Mata Canyon
20. Punta Arena Canyon

21. Pescador Canyon
22. Pescador Tunnel
23. Buena Vista Canyon
24. Cocao Canyon
25. Tres Cocos Canyon
26. Tres Cocos Cut
27. Paradise Canyon
28. Tackle Box Canyon
29. Toffee Canyon
30. Entrada San Pedro Cut
31. Dardanellos Cut
32. Victoria Canyon
33. Cypress Canyon
34. Cypress Tunnels
35. Boca Chica Canyon
36. Hol Chan Canyon
37. Hol Chan Cut
38. Shark Ray Alley

> ### ECOLOGY
>
> Scientists have found warning signs of ecological problems, including a lack of plankton and plankton-eating fish. Living conch are scarce, although there are a lot of empty conch shells in the waters, indicating that the waters were rich in marine life in the past.

Palmeros is known for its huge limestone arches that house many of the larger fish. There is often a strong current here, so take care.

Buena Vista is an 80-foot (24-meter) dive that is good for the photographer. Many finger canyons here hide big groupers.

Tres Cocos and Cut is a 50-100-foot dive that has a healthy display of corals. The narrow gorges should be explored with caution. This is an intermediate dive.

The **Tackle Box** has typical spur and groove structures and huge canyons with parrotfish. Some walls are almost vertical. Look closely for the tube worms.

Don't let **Amigo's Wreck** lure you into believing you will see some great pirate's boat. This boat was sunk deliberately in 1996 (albeit by pirates) for the purpose of attracting divers. Stingrays, sharks and groupers are common.

M & M Caverns have vibrantly colored coral mountains and tunnels that go 60 to 90 feet down (20-30 meters).

Rocky Point is where the reef meets the land and the shallow canyons house tarpon and groupers.

Fishing

SEASONAL FISHING CHART	
The following information was provided by Journey's End Hotel.	
BONEFISH	A year-round catch. Peak months are March-August, but other months offer good opportunity too.
PERMIT	March through to the end of November offers excellent catches.
TARPON	The possibility of catching tarpon is fair for December, January and February, good for March and April and excellent for the rest of the year.
BARRACUDA	Prime months for barracuda are December through March, although catches are taken all year.
SNAPPER	Snapper catches are good in December, January and May to September, excellent from February to the end of April, and then fair for October and November.

Journey's End Hotel also provided the following equipment information. Bonefish rods should be between 5.5 and 6.5 feet long (1.6 and 1.9 meters) with reels holding 200 yards of six- to eight-pound test mono lines. The best lure is a 1/8 ounce jig with the hook pointing up in pink or brown/white.

For fly gear, fishers should use #6 on a calm day and #8 or #10 in stronger winds. Reels should have 200 yards of 20-pound test Dacron backing plus floating fly line, neutral in color with a nine-foot leader. Tippets should be eight- to 10-pound test and clear. Flies should not be weighted and should be on a #6 hook. They should be orange or patterns of white, brown and pink.

Tarpon and permit like spinning or plug casting outfits that have lures from 1/2 ounce to one ounce. Line should be 12- to 14-pound mono or Dacron. For smaller tarpon, use two feet (60 cm) of 40-pound mono shock leaders. Fly rods for #8 or #9 lines are perfect. Tippets plus shock leaders of 50- to 100-pound mono are best. Flies should be Stu Apte in black/red/grizzly, black/red, white/red or yellow/red or Lefty's Deceivers in white or white topped with green. 1/0's are best.

Reef fishing is best done with stiff casting or spinning rods and reels with 17- to 20-pound test. White jigs are winners, tipped with plastic worms. Size should be 3/4 to 2 ounces for all depths.

Parasailing

Parasailing is offered by **Fido's Fun Sports** in the center of San Pedro. The cost is US $50 if you go alone, $90 if you go tandem. I have never parasailed, but it looks like a blast. So far, Fido's is the only business offering this sport on Ambergris Caye.

Windsurfing

For some reason, this sport has not really caught on in Belize, though the conditions are excellent. From January to March the winds are constantly 15 mph and the water is never below 80°F. Wet suits are not needed, but sunscreen is. From April until June the waters are calmer so the conditions are better for beginners. From September to December (hurricane season) the weather can be a bit touchy.

Lessons for windsurfing run about US $225 for eight hours. This includes equipment. The eight hours are spread out for two or three days. Day one for beginners starts with 15 minutes of dry-land practice and then 45 minutes of water practice with the instructor in a boat beside you. Straight board rentals cost about US $20 an hour for the long boards or $80 for five hours and US $25 an hour for short boards or $100 for five hours. See *Equipment Rentals & Tour Agencies*, below.

Sailing

Sailing, unlike surfing, is pretty popular in Belize. For those learn-

ing, the conditions are optimum. Easy-to-operate sailboats like the Laser Pico, with or without jib, cost about US $20 an hour to rent. Catamarans, which require a bit more skill, cost about US $75 for half a day. See *Equipment Rentals & Tour Agencies*, below.

ADVENTURES ON LAND

Cycling

A trip up to either end of the island is highly recommended. The sand is soft in places, so peddling can be difficult, but I loved cycling through the residential part of town away from tourists and then on through the **Basil Jones Plateau**.

Cycling south will take you to the **Marco Gonzalez ruins**.

Across the street from the Island Super Store at the south end of San Pedro is **Barry Bowen's** place. The Bowens are Belize's most influential (and maybe richest) family. They own the Belikin Beer Company. The school on the property is a private, upscale place. The grounds are manicured to a golf course finish. This is a nice place to cycle past while gawking.

Birding

Just west of Ambergris Caye is the **Little Guana Caye Bird Sanctuary**, which includes Little Guana Caye and Los Salones Caye. These cayes were turned over to the management of the Green Reef Society (see below) in 1998. A non-profit, non-governmental organization formed in San Pedro in 1996 by concerned citizens, the organization has been working to preserve the nesting grounds inside the cayes of Belize. Recently, it has been lobbying (unsuccessfully) to include **Rosario Caye** in the protected area. From what I understand, Rosario Caye is privately owned and development is planned.

On Little Guana you'll see blue herons, white ibis, tricolored herons and reddish egrets, of which the island has the largest colony in the Caribbean. Roseate spoonbills are no longer found here. An unnamed caye that sits between Sand Point and Mosquito Caye is a nesting site for many wading birds.

Reddish egret.

The entire western side of Ambergris Caye between **Laguna de Cayo Frances** and **San Pedro Lagoon** harbors a large population of birds that come to feed, nest and roost. It's a diverse group that includes the huge wood stork, the tiny hummingbird, reddish egret, brown booby and the tri-colored heron. Because the area between the two lagoons is not under protection, it is under threat and poaching of the juvenile wood stork has drastically decreased this bird's numbers. Fishing and unregulated tourism are other threats.

The **Green Reef Society**, 100 Coconut Drive, San Pedro, ☎ 226-2833, www.greenreefbelize.com, welcomes visitors interested in the conservation of the birds. Please stop in to give support and maybe learn the latest news about nesting birds in the area.

Butterfly Migrations

The **sulfur butterfly** usually migrates at the end of June or early July from Central Mexico over the Yucatán and down to Central America. As the food becomes scarce in Mexico, the numbers migrating south increase. One year at Caribbean Villas (see *Places to Stay*), Wil and Susan Lala estimated that there were 1,600 butterflies per hour passing their place.

The sulfur butterfly is a daytime flying species that is black with metallic green bands and long tails on its hind wings. Because the larvae feed on food not presently available in Belize it is believed that they migrate rather than make the area their home. Although it is common to see them at Lala's place in July, there have been sightings as late as August in other parts of Belize like Cayo District and Monkey River Town.

According to lepidopterist Matthew Barnes, www.tropicalmoths. org, a specialist on the topic of moths and butterflies, there are many migrations through the country and much-needed studies are just beginning. It is believed by some scientists that the numbers of insects in tropical forests indicate the health of that forest. A study to prove this was conducted in the Rio Bravo area in the 1990s.

Jan Meerman did a study in Belize during that same period (along with numerous other people) and he concluded that some migrations have had up to one or two million butterflies/moths passing through Belize in a day. It is estimated that up to 1,500 species of moths and butterflies pass through or live in Belize at any one time. As conditions change and studies increase, so do the numbers sighted.

The biggest problem I found in watching butterflies is that there are not enough good reference books on the topic.

 The **Atlas of Neotropical Lepidoptera**, Volume 3, edited by J.B. Heppner, costs £49.

 If you can find it in a used bookstore, Bernard d'Abrera's **Introduction to the Butterflies of the Neotropics**, Hill House, UK, 1984, (now out of print) is about the best source of information.

Golfing

Island Mini Golf and Ice Cream, Sea Grape Drive, one block west of the Barefoot Iguana, south of the airport, ☎ 226-3061, is open weekdays from noon to 9 pm and weekends until 10 pm. I'm not certain about the mini golf, but the ice cream is well worth the walk over there. They also make tropical smoothies, milk shakes and sundaes.

EQUIPMENT RENTALS & TOUR AGENCIES

 Joe's Bikes, ☎ 226-4371, corner of Pescador Dr and Carabeña St., has bicycles for rent at a rate of US $10 a day. I rented a bike from Joe and when he saw me he got the shiniest pink bike in the shop. He was so proud to let me have it. These are all one-gear bikes with wide tires, so traveling in the sand is okay but difficult, especially in the heat. Be certain to carry lots of water. You should also be aware that one-gear bikes do not have handlebar brake controls. To stop you must peddle backwards.

The Sail Sports, in front of the Holiday Hotel, ☎ 226-4488, www.sailsports.net, offers boards and small sailboats. The cost of a windsurf board is US $20 an hour; longer rentals receive a discount. They have a variety of boards to accommodate different ability levels. Sailboats rent for US $20-$45 an hour; lessons are US $60 per person. Sail Sports offers lessons (both windsurfing and sailing) that teach safety first and technique second.

> AUTHOR TIP: *Everyone carrying this book who deals with Sail Sports gets a* **10% discount**. *If you do enough with Sail Sports, you'll get back the cost of this book!*

Fido's Fun Sports, ☎ 226-3513, www.ambergirscaye.com/water sports, is on the beach just north of the football field and below Fido's Sports Bar. It rents kayaks for US $10 an hour or $50 a day. Sailboats cost US $20 an hour or $100 a day. Windsurfing boards cost US $70 a day. Fido's now offers the popular parasailing sport. Their sail is able to carry up to three people and costs $70/one person, $120/two people and $165/three.

Monchos Golf Cart Rentals, Middle Street, ☎ 226-3262, www.monchosrentals.com, charge about US $12.50 an hour, $60 for 24 hours and $245 for a week. These battery-powered vehicles are the way to go when on Ambergris, and you can rent either six- or four-seat carts. A full day's rental is eight hours and costs $60 for the bigger one and $45 for the smaller. For 24 hours, a large cart is $91 and the smaller one $61 (including a $1 overnight parking fee). An additional US $6/$4 per day provides a damage waiver for the cart. **Polo's** on Front Street, ☎ 226-3542, is another rental company. Their carts were in good condition.

There are numerous companies that rent carts on Ambergris and they all charge about the same. Some carts now are gas-operated, rather than electric. The gas ones make more noise and pollute the air. **Island Adventures**, Coconut Drive, ☎ 226-4343, not only have carts but they have scooters as well. One hour costs $15 and four costs $35. You must have a valid driver's license to rent and no children are permitted to drive.

> **AUTHOR NOTE:** *No vehicles are to be parked on Front Street on Friday, Saturday or Sundays, 6 pm to 6 am.*

Ramon's Village, ☎ 226-2071, at the south end of San Pedro, has rental bicycles for US $25 a day and golf carts at $75 a day. Kayaks cost US $75 and windsurf boards are $75 a day.

Amigos del Mar, ☎ 226-2706, www.amigosdive.com, is a dive shop along the beach that offers excellent excursions. They follow the "safety first" rules. This dive shop group has also been instrumental in putting buoys on the reefs to guide boats and divers. **Alfonse** is a local guide who knows where the fish are hanging out. He can be booked through a few agencies in town, including Amigos.

Blue Hole Dive Center, ☎ 226-2982, www.bluedive.com, is on Front Street in the center of town. They offer numerous dive and snorkel trips, but they specialize in an overnight trip to the Turneffe Islands, Lighthouse Reef and the Blue Hole. The two days include five dives, some deep-sea fishing and all meals. The dives at Lighthouse and Turneffe are less than 70 feet (21 meters), except for the Blue Hole, which is a deep dive. You will be supervised by a dive master during this dive. Your night out will be spent on Half Moon Caye, where you will probably see some red-footed boobies, iguanas and hermit crabs. All camping and sleeping gear is provided. You have a choice of sleeping on the boat, on the sun deck or in a tent. Park entry fees are not included in the price of this trip. Blue Hole Dive Center also has underwater camera gear for rent.

Ambergris Divers, Barrier Reef Drive & Black Coral St., ☎ 226-2634, www.ambergrisdivers.com, is operated by Karen and Robert Canul. They offer day-trips to the Blue Hole and Turneffe Atoll, and diving or snorkeling trips around the area. Excursions to the atoll and blue hole are great because they leave early in the morning (6 am), just as daylight is approaching, and don't return until almost dark.

Tanisha Tours, on Pescador Drive and Middle Street, ☎ 226-2314, www.tanishatours.com, offer many trips, but they specialize in mainland tours. I recommend the boat ride up the Belize River to

Altun Ha, a well-excavated site. For US $115, everything is included – breakfast, lunch, beer, rum punch, soda, water and park entrance fees.

Seaduced by Belize, ☎ 226-2254 or 226-3221, www.ambergris caye.com/seaduced, is on Middle Street. Look for the purple picket fence. Seaduced offers a wonderful trip cave tubing on the mainland. The trip starts by going up the Belize River, where there are crocs and iguanas. A river trip in Belize is a must. Once you have seen the Belize Zoo and had lunch at a resort in the jungle, you go for a half-hour walk. At the cave entrance, lights will be provided before you start to float through the caves where Maya once worshipped. The cost for this trip is US $140 for the entire day, which includes all park fees, breakfast, lunch, some rum punch or beer, and transportation. The food, served by Rebecca, comes recommended.

Larry Parker's Reef Divers, on Front Street across from the Spindrift, ☎ 226-3134, offers a glass-bottom boat trip that includes a stop to snorkel at Hol Chan Marine Reserve and Shark Ray Alley. The cost of the trip is US $25 for half a day, plus US $5 park entrance fee. Your gear is included in the price. The boat leaves at 9 am and 2 pm daily.

Aqua Dives, Sunbreeze Hotel, ☎ 226-3415, www.aquadives.com, offers half- and full-day diving and snorkeling trips in the area, plus they go out to Turneffe Atoll or the Blue Hole and Lighthouse Reef for a reasonable price. They also do fishing charters and night snorkeling. If you want a PADI course, they offer this too. Visit their website for current prices.

SERVICES

 Today, there are more Internet sites than there are diving possibilities. The usual charge is between $5 and $7.50 per hour. The best bet is to find a shop with air conditioning.

Asian Garden Day Spa, Coconut Drive across from Ramons, ☎ 622-5788, www.asiangardendayspa.com, is for those who need a bit of kneading. They do reflexology, facials, body scrubs, waxing, and Thai massages using holistic oils. Services cost anywhere between US $45 and $125.

Dr. Teresa Damera, Manta Ray St., next to Tropic Air hanger, ☎ 226-2686, is a specialist in family medicine should you need some special attention while on the caye.

SHOPPING

 There are many, many souvenir shops and kiosks on Ambergris Caye. Famous ones, like Toucan Too, will automatically attract you. I visited many and have chosen only a few to mention. These to me, are exceptional.

Stores are usually open by 9 am and close at night by 9 pm.

Island Super Market, Coconut Drive at the south end of the village, ☎ 226-2972, sells vanilla for US $1.50 a liter, a great price. There is nothing like vanilla from Central America. The store also sells alcohol and non-expired Kodak film.

There are two very large markets at the north end of the island before the bridge. Both have ATMs and a large selection of foods, although their liquor sections are a bit less elaborate.

Mario's Fruit and Veggies, on Middle Street, has the motto, "bueno, bonito y barrato" (good, beautiful and cheap). This is where you will find the highest quality produce at the lowest prices. Fido's (see below) purchases produce from here. Mario's also has seasonal fruit juices for US $2.50 a half-gallon.

La Popular Bakery, Middle Street and Buccaneer, ☎ 226-3242, serves freshly baked goods (and they are really good) daily. They open at 8 am and close around 6 pm, at which time they are usually sold out of everything. The very best purchase here is the vanilla yogurt. Do not miss tasting this homemade gem.

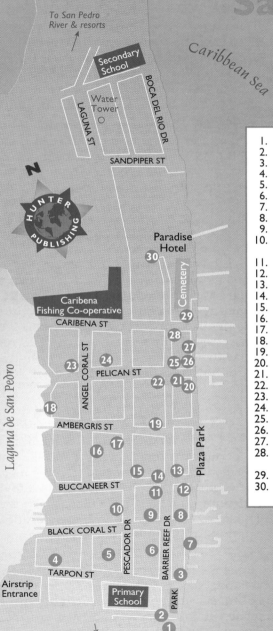

Downtown San Pedro

Caribbean Sea

To San Pedro
River & resorts

Secondary
School

Water
Tower

BOCA DEL RIO DR

LAGUNA ST

SANDPIPER ST

Paradise
Hotel

30

Cemetery

Caribena
Fishing Co-operative

CARIBENA ST

29

28

27

ANGEL CORAL ST

23   24   25 26

PELICAN ST

22   21
            20

18

AMBERGRIS ST   19

16   17

Laguna de San Pedro

15   14   13

BUCCANEER ST   11   12

10   9   8

BLACK CORAL ST

PESCADOR DR

BARRIER REEF DR

4   5   6   7

TARPON ST   3

Airstrip
Entrance

Primary
School

PARK

PLAZA PARK

2

1

To Marco Goinzales
Ruins & resorts

1. Sun Breeze Motel
2. Café Olé
3. Ruby's Hotel/Library
4. Mickey's Restaurant
5. Moncho's Golf Cart Rentals
6. Sail Sports
7. Holiday Hotel, Celi's
8. Cannibal Café
9. Coral Beach Hotel
10. Joe's Bike & Little Pete's
    Bike Rental
11. Belize Bank
12. Spindrift Hotel/Western Union
13. Police Station
14. Toucan Too
15. Post Office
16. Ambergris Art Gallery
17. Elvi's Restaurant
18. La Popular Bakery
19. Barrier Reef Hotel
20. Jambel Jerk Pit
21. Fido's Courtyard & Funsports
22. Artesano
23. Reef Restaurant
24. Mario's Fruit & Veggies
25. Cyber Café (Internet)
26. Mayan Princess
27. Lilly's Caribbean Lodge
28. San Pedrano, Tomas Hotel/
    Marta's
29. Blue Tang Inn
30. Paradise Villas/Tradewinds
    Paradise

HUNTER PUBLISHING

NOT TO SCALE

© 2007 HUNTER PUBLISHING, INC

Barefoot Books, South end of Pescador Drive (Middle St.,) across from Mickey's, ☎ 206-2577, www.barefootbooks-belize.com, carries both new and used books, maps and travel guides. They have over 10,000 books in all from which to choose. Excellent addition to the city!

Beauty of Nature Gift Shop is in the same shop as Tanisha Tours on Middle Street near Pescador Drive, ☎ 226-3310. Their brightly colored furniture, handmade by Rene Gerreo, breaks down for easy shipping. Rene also does custom orders. If you want an exceptional conversation piece to take home, look at this furniture.

Ambergris Art Gallery, ☎ 226-2695, ambergrisart@btl.net, at the Sun Breeze Hotel, carries works from the best painters in Belize. Large paintings sell for US $2,500 or more. If you are an art connoisseur, this is a good place. I spent more than an hour here and could have stayed much longer. They carry paintings by **Eduardo Papo Alamilla**, an exceptional painter who does realistic images of Belize. Papo has been painting since he was 16 and has developed an international reputation. Another painter featured at the gallery is **Marcos Larios**, originally from Guatemala. An admirer of Papo, Larios uses far more vivid colors than Papo and his scenes are busy. He has had exhibitions in California, New York, Chicago, Arkansas, Colorado, Guatemala and Puerto Rico. **Walter Castillo** is from Nicaragua and his paintings are a bit more interpretive than those of the other two. Castillo likes to paint scenes about Maya, Creole and Garifuna people. He taught himself to paint, to read and write English and to play the guitar and drum. He has had exhibitions throughout Central America, the United States, Europe and Asia.

Artesano, ☎ 226-2370, opposite Fido's Courtyard on Front Street, has some exquisite ceramics painted by local artists. Artesano allows you to have your own art embedded into another medium so that you can keep it as a permanent image. They can take your photo, painting or computer-generated graphic and transfer it onto a ceramic tile. As their special glaze heats, the image melts into the glaze and becomes embedded into the tile. These tiles can be used as decorations in a frame (like a picture) or as wall art. For ideas, look at the murals in the bathrooms at Fido's. The original piece in the ladies' room is four by three feet (1.2 by .9 meters).

Artesanos can also put images onto mugs, polyester fabric (like mouse pads), shirts, key chains, clocks and trinket boxes with inlaid ceramic tiles. Some of their t-shirts, calendars and mugs are sold in support of the local animal humane society. Tiles made here can be shipped to Canada and the US for no extra cost and to other places for a minimal charge. I was impressed with the work they do.

Toucan Too, Front Street, ☎ 226-2445, sells Belize hot sauces, coffee and calabash art. Calabash is a gourd that is cleaned, dried and then painted. Coconut utensils and wine glasses are unique at Toucan Too. They also sell black coral jewelry, which I think should be avoided, even though these people have a license to sell it.

NIGHTLIFE

All nightlife takes place in San Pedro.

Crazy Canuck's Bar, ☎ 226-2870, is just toward the beach from Estel's and is the most famous and hospitable bar in town. Of course – it's run by a Canuck. Everywhere along the road, I'd hear from travelers to be certain to stop and have a drink/some food at this bar. It's popular for a reason. It starts serving by 11 am and stays open until 11 pm.

Bare Foot Iguanas, ☎ 226-4220, is a hopping bar that features exotic and erotic dancing girls with names like the "Energizer." There is a US $5 cover charge. This bar is open only on weekends and does not follow the "low noise" bylaw voted in a few years ago. Often they don't open until all other bars are closed and then they hop until dawn. This is not my favorite place and it is obviously for the really young and strong.

Jaguar's Temple (no phone number available), a disco across from the football stadium, is moderate for noise. It attracts a young crowd who like to party longer and louder, but a bylaw forbids bars to make so much noise that it disturbs those wanting to sleep. The owners of discos like Jag's have had special sound-proofing put into their premises.

Fido's Sport's Bar and Courtyard, ☎ 226-3176, is undoubtedly the place to hang out from mid-afternoon to late evening. Live music – often local bands – is offered every night, starting at 8:30 pm. The bar overlooks the ocean and, with traditional art displayed, is inviting. If you need company, you will find people here. I loved Fido's.

Wet Willy's, on the waterfront, ☎ 226-4054, has a beer-chugging contest every Friday night. It requires a team of five persons to enter the contest. Wednesday night is ladies' night, when each lady gets a complimentary shot of booze. You can also have breakfast from 7 am until 2 pm. If you happen to fall asleep on the beach after the beer-chugging contest, it is good to know that coffee will be ready by seven.

Pier Lounge, on the beach at the Spindrift Hotel, ☎ 226-2002, has the famous chicken drop every Wednesday night. At the event, up to 100 bets can be laid on the number that you think the chicken will drop his doodoo upon. Winner takes all. Happy hour is from 4 to 6 pm daily and Friday night is ladies' night – that means a free kamakazee shot for us girls.

Palace Casino, ☎ 226-3570, is at Pescador Drive and Caribena, south of the airport. The casino is open from 7 pm to midnight every night except Wednesdays. It has 30 gaming machines and four tables. Not a big place, but big enough to take some of your extra cash.

Shark's Bar, ☎ 226-4313, $$, is on the water where taxis dock. It's open from 7 am until 11 pm for meals and the bar stays open until 2 am. Bar stools sit around a fish tank that is in the ocean. This spot has live music and reasonable prices.

PLACES TO STAY

In Town

Ruby's, ☎ 226-2063, $$, at the south end of Front Street close to the library, is a popular place with the backpackers, but I thought it horridly overpriced. The cost is US $25 for a basic single room without bath. Other inexpensive places in

San Pedranos.

town are **San Pedranos**, ☎ 226-2054, $$, **Marta's**, ☎ 226-2053, $$, and **Tomas's**, ☎ 226-2061, $$, all north from the wharf along Front Street. They have private baths and fans and cost US $25 per person (still overpriced). In low season, you may be able to get a better rate. During high season, though, I'd suggest you go to Caye Caulker instead. Of them all, Tomas's and San Pedranos are the best. Tomas's is clean and run by a local family. San Pedranos is run by an American.

Spindrift Resort, ☎ 226-2174 or 800-688-0161, www.ambergris caye.com/spindrift, $$$, is in the center of town, on the beach. The friendly owners have been in business for 15 years. The 30 rooms are clean and simple with private baths and fans. They are cleaned daily and laundry service is available. In addition to standard rooms, they have larger suits with kitchen facilities. There are reduced rates for longer stays. The hotel opens onto the beach and has Caliente's Restaurant on site. The best part of this hotel is how far the owners will go out of their way to make your stay a good one. For an inexpensive choice, right in the center of town, this is a very good deal. I would suggest during high season that you reserve your room in advance.

Lily's Caribbean Lodge, ☎ 226-2059, $$$, is on the beach just north of Tomas's. It's clean and the rooms are okay, but small. There are 10 rooms from which to choose and all have private bathrooms and air conditioning. The porch is a popular place to sit and watch the ocean.

San Pedro Holiday Hotel, ☎ 226-2014, www.sanpedroholiday. com, $$$$, is an historical icon as well as a hotel. It opened on June 15, 1965 and was the first hotel to be built in San Pedro. At that time there was no phone, no power, no refrigeration and only one vehicle on the island. The hotel was started by Celi McCorkle, a full-blooded Maya born in San Pedro. She opened five rooms at first and can remember having to hand-pump the water up to the rooms when the guests wanted a shower. She especially remembers how long some of those showers were. She got a break when a travel writer came to write a story. Not knowing what to tell the writer, she said that for ten bucks a day the visitor could get the room, three meals and laundry done. The rush was on.

What also helped was that she married a pilot who would bring people and supplies onto the island, thus eliminating transportation problems. As part of the deal, Celi had to mow the lawn so the planes could land.

Celi started renovating in 1973 and by 1978 had the present building with 14 rooms and two apartments. There is also a restaurant, a lounge, a deli, a dive shop and an air station. The hotel is the three-storey, pink and white building you see when you first come onto the island.

The Cayes

Coral Beach Hotel, ☎ 226-2013, www.coralbeachhotel.com, $$, on the main street, across from the San Pedro and close to everything in town.The hotel has been remodeled to include up-to-date conveniences while maintaining its old charm. The 18 rooms all have private bathrooms and double beds and the option of having air conditioning or the less expensive fan. Also part of the hotel is the Jambel Jerk Pit that is open by 7 am for those wanting an early coffee.

Mayan Princess Resort, ☎ 226-2778, www.mayan princesshotel.com, $$$, is a large hotel on the beach and in the center of town. All rooms have cable TV, phones, air conditioning and kitchenettes. There is a dive shop and gift shop on the premises, and bicycles and golf carts are available for rent.

Paradise Villas, ☎ 226-2087, www.belizevilla.com, $$$$, is in a quiet location at the north end of town just before the residential area. This white stucco resort is well maintained. There's a bar and a dive shop on the premises. You can choose a fan or air conditioning, and all rooms have private bathrooms with hot water. The deluxe rooms have king-sized beds, cable TVs and kitchenettes.

Blue Tang Inn, ☎ 226-2326, www.bluetanginn.com, $$$, has 14 newly renovated units, all with tiled floors, hardwood finishing and fully supplied kitchens. Fruit and coffee is served to guests every morning. There is no bar or restaurant on the premises, which makes it pleasantly quiet. If you need some action, head next door to Wet Willy's Cantina and Grill.

South of the Airport

Sun Breeze Beach Hotel, ☎ 226-2191 or 800-688-0191, www.sunbreeze.net, $$$$/$$$$$, is across from the airport. It has 38 standard rooms in a two-storey structure built around the pool.

There is a patio, bar and restaurant. Lush vegetation keeps the grounds quite cool. Each room has air conditioning, private baths with hot water, tile floors and television. The five deluxe rooms also have Jacuzzis. There is a gift shop, dive shop and dock at the hotel. **Caruso's Restaurant**, on site, serves the best Italian cuisine on the island.

© Casado Internet Group

> AUTHOR NOTE: *Places located near the airport do not have a noise problem because planes stop flying by dark and there are no jets, only prop planes.*

Ramon's Village, ☎ 226-2071 or 800-magic-15, www.ramons. com, $$$$/$$$$$, is just beyond the airport on the water side of the road. The village has an immaculate garden setting with rustic thatched-hut cabins whose outside appearance hides the luxury. The spacious garden attracts numerous birds. The managers are friendly and went out of their way to help me, so I assume this is normal procedure. Ramon's was the fifth hotel to be built in San Pedro. Its dive shop is well equipped and the dive masters offer triple-tank and night dives at locations as far away as the Turneffe Islands.

© Casado Internet Group

Steve & Becky's Cute Little Hotel, ☎ 800-magic-15, $$$$, is across from Ramon's and is run by the same crew. These are tiny cabins like the kind Robert Service would have in the Yukon. All the services available at Ramon's are also available to those staying in the cabins. Each cabin has private bath and air conditioning. There is a tiny garden on the property, but it is nothing when compared to the one at Ramon's.

Mata Rocks Resort, ☎ 226-2336 or 888-628-2757, www. matarocks.com, $$$$, is a clean, comfortable place a mile south of town. The 11 rooms (two suites) are on the beach and have hardwood and tile finishings inside and stucco on the outside. There is a beachfront bar, complimentary use of bicycles and a pool. Breakfast is included. The owners are liberal-minded.

Changes in Latitudes B & B, ☎ 226-2986, www.ambergriscaye.com/latitudes, $$$, is a neat little house surrounded by a picket fence. It has six rooms with private entrances, private baths with hot water, air conditioning and fans, and tasteful décor. This is a very homey place. A full breakfast is included in the price; I found the hot muffins offered every morning by Canadian, Lori Reed were reason enough to stay. You can also use the kitchen facilities to make snacks or small meals.

Belize Yacht Club, ☎ 226-2777 or 800-688-0402, www.belizeyachtclub.com, $$$$$, is elegant and expensive. Purchased by Austrians in 1995, the resort is Austrian style, clean and efficient. This is where the prime minister and delegates from seven Central American countries chose to stay when they were on Ambergris for a special event.

The suites have one to three bedrooms and come with air conditioning, telephone, cable TV, kitchenette and private, furnished balcony. Most have an ocean view. Within walking distance of the village center, the club has 40 suites, two **restaurants**, a full marina, a tour desk, a dive shop and a gift shop. There is also a fresh water pool. The tour desk can arrange for almost any trip you could want, both on the water and on the mainland. There is a little patio restaurant with a few tables and comfortable atmosphere where you could enjoy a coffee even if not staying at the club.

San Pedro Inn, Princess Drive, ☎ 226-3825, www.backpackersbelize.com, $, has 20 small rooms with two beds to a

room, and a fan. A shared bath is located in a large house on stilts. The owner Peter Lawrence, offers a deal including bed with dinner and beer for around $20 per person, per day. There is a nice porch where guests like to hang out when not doing tours in the vicinity.

Exotic Caye Beach Resort, ☎ 226-2870 or 800-201-9389, www. belizeisfun.com, $$$$$, is truly exotic. These rustic thatched-roof cabins are professionally decorated and interspersed around a large pool. Each bright cabin has a fully supplied kitchen, air conditioning and a living room couch that opens to accommodate any extra member of your party. Those with an upstairs bedroom are very comfortable. If you are with a group or sharing the cost, this is a good deal. This beach-side resort has a pool, dive shop, massage parlor, boat dock and volleyball court. They offer several packages. A special seven-night package costs $150 per person, per day and includes the condo, and four two-tank diving days and one three-tank day.

Corona del Mar, Woody's Wharf, ☎ 226-2055, www.belizeone. com/corona delmar, $$$/$$$$, is a quiet place with no public bar or restaurant. The rooms have high ceilings, carved wooden doors, cable TV, telephones, living rooms, dining nooks, kitchens, combination bathtubs and showers, air conditioning, fans and balconies. The resort faces the ocean. Breakfast (included) consists of eggs with potatoes and toast, juice and coffee.

© Casado Internet Group

Coral Bay Villas, ☎ 226-3003, www.coralbaybelize.com, $$$$, has six condos, each with air conditioning in the bedrooms and fans in all other rooms, private verandas and fully equipped kitchens and dining rooms. They have cable TV, daily maid service, laundry service, a private beach, and complimentary use of bicycles and kayaks. This is the lovely white colonial house you can see on the beach with relaxed tourists on the lounge chairs in front. Good place.

© Casado Internet Group

Coconuts Caribbean Hotel, ☎ 226-3500 or 226-3677, www. coconutshotel.com, $$$/$$$$, is not elaborate, but it is certainly

© Coconuts Caribbean Hotel

comfortable. It's located right on the beach. All cabins can sleep up to four people and come with private bathrooms and air conditioning. A breakfast of fresh muffins, juice and coffee is included in the price. For dinner, head up the beach to the pool-side barbeque at Toucan's, ☎ 226-2148.

Caribbean Villas, ☎ 226-2715, www.caribbeanvillashotel.com, $$$-$$$$$, are located on 4.5 acres on the beach surrounded by jungle vegetation that makes this a private bird sanctuary. You may spot as many as 200 species here. As you walk to the viewing platform through the shore-line forest, you will pass unfamiliar plants that have been labeled for your convenience. Littoral forests are located on the second dune or natural rise of a caye, and the trees that grow there must be salt-tolerant. Most of the trees are fruit-bearing and you are welcome to pick any fruit that's ripe. Off the pier there are up to 60 species of fish, and some people have even seen seahorses.

The rooms have some efficient features like a spot to hide your suitcase under the counter. All rooms have air conditioning, mahogany wood trim and slatted windows, non-intrusive security systems, hideaway beds, fully furnished kitchens and ocean views.

Xanadu Island Resort, ☎ 226-2814, www.xanaduresort-belize. com, $$$$/$$$$$, features a variety of accommodations, from a loft suite to a three-bedroom apartment. The buildings are de-

© Xanadu

signed to be energy efficient. Inside, the kitchens are completely furnished, and there is central air conditioning, cable TV, telephones, tiled bathrooms and hardwood finishings. Loft rooms are exceptionally attractive. There is a freshwater pool, a dock, as well as complimentary use of bicycles and kayaks. There is no bar or restaurant.

Banyan Bay Resort, ☎ 226-3739, $$$$$, www.banyanbay.com, has 36 units with full views of the ocean. They all have two bedrooms (one with Jacuzzi), two bathrooms, full kitchens, cable TV and air conditioning. Suites are tastefully decorated and most are over 1,000 square feet. The hotel has a pool, restaurant, dive shop, gift shop and 24-hour security. The beach is exceptional and considered the best on the island. Because there is a break in the reef in front of the hotel, they get some wave action which makes swimming more fun. There are discount rates for off-season.

© Villas at Banyan Bay

Victoria House, ☎ 226-2067 or 800-247-5159, $$$$/$$$$$, is at the southernmost end of Coconut Drive and is the exquisite mansion seen from the water when approaching Ambergris Caye. The plantation-style rooms have mosquito nets, air conditioning, floor-to-ceiling windows, private baths, hardwood floors and mini-bars. Rooms open onto a wrap-around balcony. There is a freshwater pool, bar and restaurant on site. This is truly an elegant place to stay and, during low season, prices are not all that bad.

Banana Beach Resort, ☎ 226-3890, www.banana beach.com, $$$$, has 35 units, each capable of sleeping four. There are three standards of rooms, but all have fully furnished kitchenettes with stove, fridge and microwaves, as well as cable TV, air conditioning, in-room safes and telephones. All are decorated with ceramic art and woven tapestries. There is a garden pool, beach bar, dive shop and rental unit for kayaks and windsurf boards. The beach, called Mar de Tumbo, is the best around San Pedro with deep water and little seaweed.

© Casado Internet Group

North of the River

Captain Morgan's, ☎ 226-2567 or 888-653-9090, www.belizevaca tion.com, $$$$$, is considered a retreat rather than a hotel. It is located 3.5 miles from town, with a private beach, no telephones, no TV, but lots of activities to keep you busy. The 35 palmetto and thatched huts have air conditioning, private baths, mahogany finishings, window seats and balconies.

© Captain Morgan's Retreat

Captain Morgan specializes in weddings on the beach. For special effect, conch shells line the walkway and flower petals are used instead of paper confetti. The hotel has an activities director who will make all the arrangements. However, if you are planning on a marriage here, you should book ahead. When I was here in mid-April (low season), the hotel had performed eight marriages already that month.

AUTHOR NOTE: *To follow true* **Belizean marriage custom**, *you must walk up and down the beach after the ceremony. Whenever you meet or see someone you must stop and kiss your new spouse while the onlookers clap and cheer.*

The on-site restaurant is expensive but high in quality. The dinner specialty is shrimp, snapper or lobster cooked in cream, parmesan and mozzarella cheese with basil, garlic and tomato.

MARRIAGE IN BELIZE

Marriage in Belize requires a license costing US $100 for foreigners. You must be in the country for three days before applying for the license and those under 18 years of age need parental consent. Anyone previously married must have documents proving divorce or widowhood. For more detailed information and valuable cautions, go to www.travelbelize.org/honeym.html.

Journey's End Hotel, ☎ 226-2173 or 800-460-5665, www.journeysend-resort.com, $$$$$, is another luxury resort that focuses on relaxing getaways, rather than activity-laden vacations. Guests have complimentary use of tennis courts, kayaks, sailboats, wind-

© Journey's End Resort

surf boards and canoes. All units have air conditioning, mini-refrigerators, hair dryers and coffee makers. The 50-acre site also has a fully equipped dive shop and a tour office that can arrange trips to any of the caves or ruins. They also offer fishing trips for anyone interested in bagging a grand slam.

There is an excellent restaurant that will cook your catch. The resort also caters to the romantic tropical wedding. I found this place peaceful and especially relaxing.

Capricorn Resort, ☎ 226-2809, www.ambergriscaye.com/capricorn, $$$$, is three miles north of San Pedro. It has three air-conditioned beach cabins with hardwood ceilings, two double beds, balconies and private bathrooms with hot water. You also get the luxury of having priority for reservations at their world-class res-

taurant. Breakfasts are complimentary, as is use of kayaks and bicycles. You can cycle into town, visit a few of the sites and return by dark. There is a well-supplied library if you run out of reading material. Any tour diving expedition or mainland tour can be arranged (pick up at the hotel).

© Capricorn Resort

Essene Way, ☎ 226-3258 or 888-297-8950, is an oddity that has been closed since the last hurricane. The church/owners are now trying to sell each individual unit. It is worth a poke-around. The place was bought from the Belizean Hotel by a non-denominational Christian church group and transformed into a retreat. The church group believes in both the old and new testaments of the Christian bible. They claim to be direct descendants of those who wrote the Dead Sea Scrolls. I found Jonah and the Whale quite an interesting addition to the grounds (you'll see).

Salamander Cabañas, offshore by 10 miles, ☎ 602-1713, www.salamanderbelize.com, $$$-$$$$, is just the place to escape to if San Pedro, with its tourist entertainment, is too busy for you. Salamander is a private island that has eight cabins, five facing the ocean and three tucked into the jungle. Each cabin has a private bath with hot water, porch, hardwood floors, louvered windows and fans. The comfortable beds are covered with mosquito nets. The restaurant offers both local cuisine and gourmet delights. There is also a bar where you can get a cold beer or one of the best panty rippers in the country. Since this is an environmentally sensitive resort, they combine with other family-run tour companies to take their visitors to different locations in the country.

PLACES TO EAT

In Town

 Celi's in the Holiday Inn Hotel, ☎ 226-2014, $$$, is reported to have good grouper cooked with three cheeses and covered in a white sauce. However, when I ate there, I found the prices far too high and the portions far too small. There were only a few items available on the menu and

RESTAURANT PRICES	
$	$5 to $10
$$	$11 to $25
$$$	$26 to $50
$$$$	$51 to $75
$$$$$	over $75

a large (but weak) rum drink cost US $5. This was the first hotel in town and has been open since the mid-'60s.

Lilly's Restaurant, ☎ 206-2059, $$$, is on the beach at the north end of town. The meals are good, but scanty, unless you order one of the specials of the day, but this ends up being expensive.

Elvi's Kitchen, ☎ 226-2176, $$$, is on Middle Street and has been overrated for a long time. The high prices are not warranted (by either food quality or service). The portions are also small.

El Patio, Black Coral Street, between Front and Middle Sreets (not to be confused Middle Street on Coconut Drive at the south end of town) is an excellent place to have a dinner. The atmosphere is pleasant, the waiters are attentive and the large meals are very well cooked. I would recommend the shrimp pasta for less than $10. Their beer is cold too. I found they got many repeat visitors.

Estel's Dine by the Sea, ☎ 226-2019, is past the airport but before Caribbean Villas. It's a tiny place, neat as a pin, with breakfast offered all day. They open at 6 am for the early coffee drinkers and close at 5 pm. The food is excellent and Estella will make orders to go. I recommend some of her muffins, which are made North American style, even though she is an Aussie.

Caramba, Pescador Drive, ☎ 226-4321, www.ambergriscaye.com/caramba, open 11 am to 2 pm and 5 pm to 10 pm daily except Wednesdays. They offer fresh seafood ($10-$15) and good old burgers ($4.50-$6). Their seafood selection is commendable and well prepared.

Early-risers will like the **Dockside Bar & Grill**, $$, at the Hustler Pier, which opens at 6 am. It closes at 2 pm. Their morning fresh fruit platters are tasty.

Jambel Jerk Pit, ☎ 206-2594, $$$, has jerk chicken that has the spice of true Jamaican cooking. Once you start eating, it is hard to stop, as evidenced by the restaurant's popularity. It also makes vegetarian dishes.

Cannibal Café, $$$, is between the Holiday Inn and the Coral Beach Hotel. Their motto is that they want you for lunch, but none of my friends went missing when we ate there. Meat and seafood are the specialties. The atmosphere is pleasant and prices aren't high.

Reef Restaurant, $$, at the north end of Middle Street, is a Belizean eatery that serves large portions for reasonable prices. The average cost is under US $6 for a meal, very low for Ambergris. The food is good.

Caliente, ☎ 226-2170, $$, at the Spindrift Hotel in the center of town, has good ceviche, a wide variety of seafood and the best coconut chicken in town. You'll find Maya, Mexican and Jamaican foods on the menu. This is a popular place. From Caliente, go over to **Esteles** for some key lime pie.

Mickey's, ☎ 226-2223, $$, is on the backside of the island, just north of the airport. Its burritos are so big they overflow the plate. The cost is US $3.50. Go for lunch, but get there early as Mickey's is very popular.

> **AUTHOR NOTE:** *Lobster cannot be caught from Valentine's Day until mid-June.*

Lion's Club, on Front Street near the church and statue of San Pedro, has a chicken barbeque every Friday night. The proceeds go toward development of social amenities like the new clinic. The cost is US $2 for a plate of chicken and some salad.

Manelly's Ice Cream Shop, on Front Street, ☎ 226-2285, is open from 10 am to 8 pm. Manelly's has homemade ice cream and frozen yogurt. Especially good is the rum and raisin ice cream. I keep pushing the ice cream in Belize. I couldn't seem to get enough.

Blue Water Grill, ☎ 226-3347, $$, in front of the Sun Breeze Hotel, offers sushi on Tuesdays and has happy hour every day from 4 pm to 6 pm.

Ruby's Café, ☎ 226-2063, $, beside the library on Front Street, has homemade pastries. It gets so swamped early in the morning that you must have patience in order to get served. The line is a good indication of the quality of food.

South of the Airport

Purple Parrot, ☎ 226-2071, $$$, at Ramon's, has poolside dining with live music from 6 to 10 pm on Tuesday and Friday nights. The atmosphere is quiet, the food is good and the views are romantic.

Victoria House Restaurant, ☎ 226-2067, $$$$, is at the south end of the island and overlooks the water. It has plantation-style décor and elegance. Reservations are a must. The menu is fairly extensive and the service refined to an art. You can order things like pork tenderloin served over vegetable stir fry with shrimp and peanut saté for US $16.50 (not an exorbitant price for food of this quality). At lunch, stop by the juice bar, which serves sandwiches.

Jade Garden, ☎ 226-2506, $$$, at the south end of town, has a huge menu and serves the cheapest lobster in town. The Chinese food has been consistently good for years. The restaurant is now up for sale so I don't know how long you will be able to get food from this old classic.

Pauly's Pizza, Tarpon St., ☎ 226-2651, is open Monday to Saturday, 11 am to 10 pm, and Sunday, 5 to 10 pm. They offer the famous cinnamon sticks that cost $7.50 for a 12-inch (small) stick. You can purchase pizza by the piece to snack on while walking around. Sitting in the restaurant means you have to listen to the ever-playing television.

Blue Grill, $$, on the beach next to the Sun Breeze, has excellent breakfasts, good service and strong coffee. The portions and prices are decent.

> **AUTHOR TIP:** **Rick** *is a blind man who walks around the streets of Ambergris pushing a cart and selling hot tamales. It is amazing how well he can manage on his own. Be certain to try at least a few of his homemade goodies.*

Ali Baba's Restaurant (no telephone), $$, at the south end of town, serves Lebanese foods that include stewed lamb, hummus, falafels and couscous salad. This is a real treat in Latin America. Prices are reasonable; you can purchase a whole chicken for $7.50. Better still, they have falafel and kufta. The food is such a treat.

Toucan's Pool-side BBQ is in front of the Coconut Beach Hotel, ☎ 226-2148, $$. The barbeque is offered from 6 to 10 pm every Tuesday evening and is popular with both tourists and locals. It features such dishes as Caribbean fish, pork ribs and shrimp kebobs, all for around US $10. Reservations are necessary in peak season. Open every day.

El Patio Restaurant, Coconut Drive, ☎ 226-3063, www.amber griscaye.com/elpatio, $$, has tables both inside and out, interspersed between white Doric columns that make you feel as though you are in Rome or Athens. There is even a roving musician to play a romantic tune while you eat. The most notable dish is a tropical chicken cooked in pineapple.

George's Country Kitchen, Coconut Drive, ☎ 226-4252, $$, is open from 6:30 am to 3 pm and again from 6 to 9 pm. This is a sparkling clean eatery that concentrates on quality of food rather than atmosphere.

Jerry's Crab Shack, Coconut Drive, across from Ramons, ☎ 206-2552, is a funky place serving pizza with a thin crust and tons of mozzarella cheese. They also have a famous crab cake dinner for about $12. This is a popular stopping spot.

Yumil's Crab and Steak House, Coconut Drive, next to the Yacht Club, open 6:30 am to 9:30 pm (no phone), is the latest high-quality cuisine center on Ambergris. Whether it is breakfast, lunch, dinner or a snack, the quality and selection here are exceptional. Breakfast could start with blueberry pancakes, followed at lunch with pasta salad, snacks of shrimp cocktail or fried conch strips. Dinner should be either steak and lobster or steak and shrimp followed by a key-lime pie or some other less decadent sweet. The restaurant is new and overlooks the ocean.

North of the River

Capricorn Restaurant, ☎ 226-2809, $$$$, is by far the most romantic place to eat on the island, and the quality of food cannot be met by any other restaurant on Ambergris. The only drawback is that they can take only 50 guests per night for dinner. This means that, during high season, you should book up to three days in advance. If staying on Ambergris for a while, be certain to make this one of your destinations. It is such a special place; make sure you have time to eat like the French (taking hours). This is not only my opinion. *Condé Naste's* Dine Out Section voted Capricorn one of three "must" places to visit in Belize.

Eating at the Capricorn is not simply appreciating a meal, it is an experience. While sipping wine, you can enjoy sun-dried tomato pesto drizzled over cream cheese and scooped up with spiced baguettes, or stone crab claws and roasted garlic. Take your time with a filet mignon marinated in red wine and portabello mushroom sauce with seafood served on the side. Finish it all with some boozy cake (rum chocolate) and a liqueur. You may need to waddle out, but it will be worth it. The bill, excluding alcohol, will run about US $35-$40 per person.

Capricorn is three miles north of San Pedro so you'll need to arrive by water taxi or via the Capricorn's boat service. Going home in the moonlight after a splendid meal is a romantic way to end your evening.

The restaurant is closed to the public on Wednesdays.

◼ CAYE CAULKER

Once a quiet backpackers' haven, Caye Caulker has changed a lot since I first saw it in the early 1980s. A few places (like Tom's and Edith's or Emma's) have survived unchanged through the transformation, while other businesses (like Chocolate's boat service) have grown into large enterprises.

Caye Caulker is five miles long and only 1.2 miles at its widest point. This tiny island has 800 permanent citizens and 33 hotels that can sleep around 320 people, which means that at any one time there can be no more than 1,200 people on the island. That translates into a fairly peaceful environment even when it's busy.

There are two drawbacks to Caulker. The first is the sand fleas and mosquitoes. If there is no breeze, you need to use tons of repellent. It seems that these bugs are worse in the south end of the island than the north. The second drawback is that there are almost no places offering rooms to single travelers unless they pay the price of a double. This was a problem 20 years ago and it hasn't been rectified. If you are a woman alone, you are not wanted in many places.

And if Ambergris Caye is a color brochure, then Caye Caulker is a business card. Ambergris Caye lays on fancy restaurants and large resorts, while Caulker sticks with the basics.

HISTORY

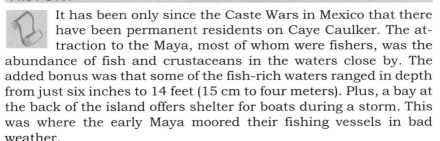

It has been only since the Caste Wars in Mexico that there have been permanent residents on Caye Caulker. The attraction to the Maya, most of whom were fishers, was the abundance of fish and crustaceans in the waters close by. The added bonus was that some of the fish-rich waters ranged in depth from just six inches to 14 feet (15 cm to four meters). Plus, a bay at the back of the island offers shelter for boats during a storm. This was where the early Maya moored their fishing vessels in bad weather.

In the late 1800s a man by the name of Luciano Reyes purchased the island. He had wanted Ambergris Caye before, but was outbid (by just $50) by James Blake. Reyes purchased Caye Caulker for the grand sum of US $300 and soon started selling parcels of land to his relatives. One of his descendants is the owner of the Paradise Hotel.

How the island got its name isn't known. It is believed that pirates came and *caulked* their boats, thus the name. Others say that the first boat-building families on the island were known for their caulking skills. However, cartographers still use "Corker" on maps made in England.

Most people, since the first families arrived, earned their living by fishing. In 1961, Hurricane Hattie hit and caused the famous "split" at the north end of the residential area. During that storm, Hattie destroyed 82 of the 90 homes on the island. She also picked up and threw the schoolhouse that had 13 students inside hiding from the storm. All were killed.

Then in 1969 a Dr. Hildebrant from the University of Corpus Christi came with students to study marine biology. They camped in tents and cooked their own meals. Word must have spread because it was shortly after that the hippies and backpackers on the Gringo Trail from Mexico to Guatemala began stopping on the island to rest.

By the 1980s Caulker was discovered and tourism became an important part of the economy.

GETTING HERE

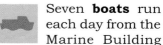 Seven **boats** run each day from the Marine Building and six arrive each day from the Tourist Village in Belize City. **Caye Caulker Water Taxi**, ☎ 203-1969 or 209-4992, www.gocayecaulker.com, offers the following service:

■ Belize City to Caye Caulker – 9 am, 10:30 am, 12, 1:30 pm, 3 pm, 5 pm

■ Caye Caulker to San Pedro – 7 am, 8:30 am, 10 am, 1 pm, 4 pm

■ San Pedro to Caye Caulker – 8 am, 9:30 am, 11:30 am, 2:30 am, 4:30 am

■ Caye Caulker to Belize City – all taxis leave Caye Caulker half an hour after they leave San Pedro. It takes 45 minutes to reach Caye Caulker from BC and an additional 30 minutes to go from Caulker to San Pedro. The cost is $7.50 one way.

There are also a dozen **flights** a day from the two local airlines – **TropicAir** (☎ 800-422-3435, 226-2012 in Belize, www.tropicair.com) and **Maya Air** (☎ 422-2333).

If coming by boat, you can be met at the dock by a "helper" who will offer to find you a hotel room. Be aware that this person will be paid a commission for taking you to the hotel and you will be paying that commission in the cost of the room, making it more pricey than if you came to the hotel on your own. Hotel owners know who their touts are, but you won't.

When leaving Caye Caulker, boats go from both the front and back docks. The last water taxi to Belize City leaves around 3 pm from the back dock and around 5 pm from the front. They will stop at Caye Chapel and St. Georges Caye on request.

ADVENTURES ON WATER

Windsurfing

 There are usually 20 days a month where the wind conditions are at level 6 on the Beauford Scale. Most days average between 4.5 and 6.8, which means conditions are great for bumping and jumping (windsurfing terms).

On Caye Caulker, an area known as the **Swash** offers runs of about a mile. It sits outside the reef, so big swells and waves are common. To the north of this area is the **Washing Machine**, where tidal currents, waves and rocks can present even the experienced with a challenge. Those with less experience can go inside the reef where there are runs of up to two miles on flat water.

You can even surf out to some nearby **islands**. This should only be done with a guide (the rule is never sail in unknown waters without a guide).

See *Equipment Rental & Tour Guides*, below.

THE BEAUFORT WINDSCALE		
The Beauford Windscale was first defined in 1805 by Admiral Beauford for sailors. This system of measuring wind velocity is still used by sailors, windsurfers and boaters.		
BEGINNER	Level 0	0 mph – calm
	Level 1	1-3 mph – light air
	Level 2	4-7 mph – slight breeze
INTERMEDIATE Your technique needs to be very good if you are out in level 5 winds.	Level 3	8-11 mph – gentle breeze
	Level 4	12-18 mph – moderate breeze
	Level 5	19-24 mph – fresh breeze
SKILLED	Level 6 breeze	25-31 mph – strong
EXPERT Anything stronger than level 8 is suicide.	Level 7	32-38 mph – moderate gale
	Level 8	39-46 mph – fresh gale

Safety for Windsurfers

- If you fall off your board, stay with it. Your board floats.
- Never sail alone.
- Know the national distress call.
- Know your wind directions. Only very skilled surfers can go against the wind to get back to shore. The idea is to travel sideways against the wind.
- Watch for boat traffic and avoid heavily used areas.

Diving & Snorkeling

I tried out a couple of excellent guides, but also kept my ears open and heard about others. When you look for a dive operator, be certain that they are licensed by the Belize Tourist Association. Non-licensed guides will give you a deal, but often they do not have safety training or equipment like jackets or radios. Saving some money could cost you your life.

Ask to see guides' official government identification cards, which guides should carry at all times. If they have the necessary documentation and their boats have all the safety equipment, they are probably okay. Often, guides will approach you privately rather than through a tour company. This is free enterprise. If you feel okay about dealing directly with a guide, then do so.

Dive Sites

Stingray Village is similar to Stingray Alley off Ambergris Caye. It became popular with the rays when fishers cleaned their daily catch and threw the unwanted parts into the water. The rays soon learned to stick around. The site is not visited by as many tourists as the one on Ambergris Caye. Snorkelers get a chance to see big fish at Stingray Village.

The Split on the north end of the island before the mangrove swamps is a great place to take your own snorkeling gear and just poke around. Swimming is okay also. The split was caused by a hurricane and it separates the sandy beach area from the mangrove swamps. On the mangrove side, the island is seething with bird life. To visit, you should rent a **kayak or canoe** and paddle around. See *Equipment Rental & Tour Guides*, below.

The mangled cement sidewalk just before the split is an example of the powerful force a hurricane can produce. The beach south of the sidewalk was blown away but the community got together and brought in sand. The Lazy Lizard on the south end of the split is a great place to have a drink and howl at the birds across the way.

The **North Cut** and **Wreck** are at the same place. Because of the fast currents, these coral canyons are popular with drift divers. The dive goes down to 130 feet (40 meters) and people often see groupers, yellowtail snappers, moray eels and nurse sharks. The Wreck is a 50-foot (15-meter) boat that sits at 70 feet (20 meters).

Sponge Avenue slopes down 40 feet (12 meters) and has deep cracks and crevices to the edge of the wall along the reef across from Caye Caulker.

The Pyramid Flats and **The Tunnel**, east of the caye, often have stingrays, eaglerays and loggerhead turtles tucked between the star and brain corals. There are a fair number of spur and groove formations close by. The tunnel offers divers the possibility of seeing copper sweepers and horse-eyed jacks. Visibility is good, going down to 200 feet (60 meters) on clear days.

Brain coral.

Many dive shops will take you to **Sergeants Caye** and **Goff's Caye**, about 35 miles south of Caye Caulker. See *Cayes Near Belize City*, page 500.

Canoeing

Around da Caye is the canoe race to enter in July if you happen to be on the island. The race is in conjunction with the Lobster Festival. This race takes paddlers around the entire island of Caye Caulker. Women and/or men are welcome.

Allie Ifield of **Toucan Canoe**, ☎ 226-0022, toucancanoe@yahoo.com, has canoes for rent at US $25 a day. Allie advises serious racers to bring their own paddles, which are easy to store while traveling.

An avid canoeist from northern Canada, Allie is working in Belize to promote women canoers. She is trying to establish equality for women who want to race. For more about canoeing in Belize, see page 280-283, or go to www.blackrocklodge.com.

PLACES TO STAY

1. Anchorage Resort
2. Auxillou Beach Suites
3. Blue Wave Guest House
4. Chateau Giselle
5. Costa Maya Cabañas
6. Daisy's Hotel
7. De Real Macaw
8. Ignacio's Beach Cabins
9. Iguana Reef Inn & Bar
10. Lazy Iguana B&B
11. Lena's Guest House
12. Loraine's Guest House
13. Guest House Marin
14. M&N Apartments
15. Mara's Place
16. Mira Mar Hotel
17. Morning Star Guest House
18. Motel 1788
19. Popeye's Beach Resort, Restaurant & Bar
20. Rainbow Hotel
21. Rommie & Jim's Inn & Sidewalk Café
22. Sandy Lane
23. Sea Beezzz Hotel
24. Seaside Cabañas
25. Seaview Hotel
26. Shirley's Guest House
27. The Tropics Hotel
28. Tina's Backpacking Hostel
29. Tom's Hotel
30. Trends Beachfront Hotel
31. Tropical Paradise Hotel
32. Vega Apartments
33. Vega Houses
34. Vega Inn & Gardens

PLACES TO EAT & DRINK

35. Lazy Lizard Bar & Grill
36. Barefoot Caribe
37. China Restaurant
38. CocoPlum Gardens
39. Glenda's Restaurant
40. Habañeros Restuarant
41. Happy Lobster Restaurant & Bar
42. Marin's Restaurant & Wish Willy's Restuarant
43. Oceanside Bar & Restaurant
44. Rainbow Grill & Bar
45. Rasta Pasta Rainforest Café
46. Sand Box Restaurant
47. Syd's Restaurant
48. Tropical Paradise Restaurant
49. Lighthouse Ice Cream Parlour

TOUR OPERATORS

50. Big Fish Dive Center & Snorkel Shop
51. Frenchie's Diving
52. Paradise Down Scuba
53. Anwar Tours
54. Carlos Guided Eco Tours
55. Caye Caulker Tour Guide Association
56. Driftwood Tours & Dive Connections
57. E-Z Boy Tours
58. Hicaco Tours
59. Juni's Sailing Trips
60. Raggamuffin Tours
61. Sea Hawk Sailing
62. Star Tours
63. Tsunami Adventures

SERVICES

64. Library, Village Council Office, Health Center, Post Office
65. Caye Caulker Cyber Café
66. Cayeboard Connection (phone, Internet)
67. Laundry
68. Water Taxi Association
69. Meteoride Water Taxi

SHOPPING

70. Caribbean Colors Art Gallery
71. Chocolate's Gift Shop
72. Herbal Tribe
73. Miriany's Gift Shop
74. Toucan Gift Shop
75. Albert's Mini-Mart
76. Friendship Shopping Center
77. Madeline's Hardware

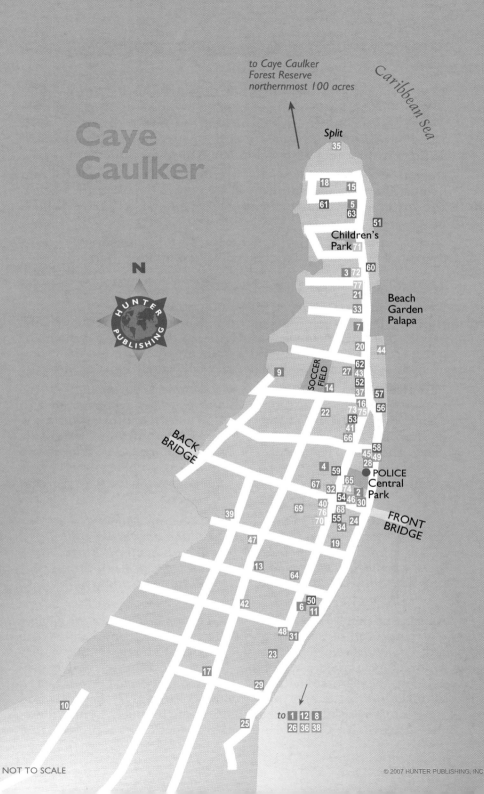

Caye Caulker

to Caye Caulker
Forest Reserve
northernmost 100 acres

Caribbean Sea

Split
35

N

18   15
61   5
63
51
Children's
Park   71
3 72   60
77
21
33
7   Beach
Garden
Palapa
20   44
62
27 43
52
9   37   57
14   16   56
22   73 75
53
41
66
58
45 49
4   28
59   POLICE   Central
Park
67   65
32 74 2
54 46 30
69   40   FRONT
76   BRIDGE
70   55   68
34   24
19

BACK
BRIDGE

SOCCER
FIELD

39
47
13
64
42   6
50
11
48 31
23
17
29
10   to 1 12 8
25   26 36 38

NOT TO SCALE   © 2007 HUNTER PUBLISHING, INC.

ADVENTURES ON LAND

Hiking

 Hike the 1.5-acre **CCBTIA Forest Preserve**, at the south end of the island (no phone). The preserve is named after the black catbird that actually meows rather than trills. There have been 150 species of birds spotted in this littoral forest, so an early morning walk would be justified for birders.

On an island in the preserve you'll see plenty of salt-tolerant plants. Along the maintained trails, many of the trees are labeled. The visitor center is manned by volunteers and hours are a bit erratic.

Just beyond the preserve is a graveyard with Spanish-style graves that sit above ground. Past the graveyard is the airport.

EQUIPMENT RENTAL & TOUR GUIDES

 Toucan Canoe, ☎ 226-0022, toucancanoe@yahoo.com, has canoes/kayaks for US $25 a day or $10 an hour. This is a great deal – either paddle up to and around the mangrove area of the island to bird watch, or paddle around the island as fast as you can to prepare for the local canoe race in June.

Paradise Down, ☎ 226-0437, www.paradisedown.com, at the north end of the island on Front Street, was recommended in *Sports Diver Magazine* in May, 2002 as a PADI approved company. It was the enthusiasm of the dive master that drew me to this place. They hire Piggy Guesman as their fishing guide, a local who knows the spots. Depending on the trip you choose, the cost is about US $50 for half a day. They offer an overnight trip to the Blue Hole for US $145 per person.

> **AUTHOR NOTE:** *Although it is not recommended, the thrill of diving under water and having a shark come close enough for you to grab his fin, let him pull you along and feel his muscles wiggle is a sensation never to be forgotten. Many companies offer this trip.*

Anwar Snorkel Tours, ☎ 226-0327, at the north end of the village, offers many tours, almost all of them involving snorkeling. Rico and Javier Novelo are part of a family that knows the waters around Caye Caulker. When they take you to a site, as a safety precaution, they snorkel with you. Their most successful tour is to a manatee-protected area on Swallow Caye, where they can find these elusive animals in their natural environment. From there, they go to Goff's Caye, where you can snorkel as a prelude to a

Shark Ray Alley visit. The tour goes from 9:30 am to around 5 pm and costs less than US $100 per person.

Star Tours, ☎ 226-0374, www.startours.bz, is a snorkel and dive shop located at the Tropics Hotel. Like all tour operators here, Star can take you anywhere, but they specialize in mainland tours to places like the Belize Zoo and on jungle river trips. As I've said before, at least one river trip should be done while in Belize. The cayes are great, but the jungle is spectacular. The cost is about US $100 per person per full day.

Frenchie's Diving Services, ☎ 226-0234, www.belizenet.com/frenchies.html. When I was at Frenchie's, everyone was busy taking out a very full boat of divers. They have a lot of equipment for rent. Depending on the dive you choose, prices run between US $100 and $ 150 per person, per day.

Tsunami, ☎ 226-0462, www.tsunamiadventures.com, has a good boat that can take you out fishing or island hopping. Their snorkeling trips go to popular sites, and their guides were able to point out and identify various kinds of marine life that were new to me. Tsunami is also open to charters should you want to get a group together and customize a trip. This is a good outfit. Costs vary according to the type of trip, but prices are competitive.

Winnie Estelle Charter Cruises, ☎ 226-0394, are great for those who can get a group together and hire the boat for longer periods of time. For example, an eight-hour trip to Hol Chan Marine Reserve, the Coral Gardens, Shark Ray Alley and the Manatee Reef costs about $660 for 12 people. That is cheaper than individual bookings and, during low season, these prices can be haggled over.

Chocolate's Tours, Front St., ☎ 226-0151, chocolate@btl.com, has been heavily involved in promoting conservation to the area with a special interest in the protection of the manatee. Chocolate has been around for a long time; he was first made popular with tourists by Lonely Planet way back in the late 1970s. Chocolate offers trips to other islands and to see manatee but he doesn't go every day. If you are intent on traveling with him, make your reservations early.

SERVICES

Caye Caulker Internet Service, on Middle Street north of the Sandbox, charges US $2.25 for half an hour and $4.25 for an hour – a lot cheaper than many I found in Belize. When I was there, the machines were all occupied, and they seemed quite fast. The **Caye Board** on Middle Street offers Internet service for US $2 for 20 minutes, $6 for an hour and $10 for two hours. The best place I found was in the drug store next door to Marine's Guest House. There are just two machines, but they are fast and the prices are the lowest in town.

The **laundry** is behind Habaneros, going toward the back dock. It offers coin-operated machines for US $2 a load, which includes wash and dry. The second laundromat, behind Wish Willies, is cleaner.

SHOPPING

Shopping is not the big thing at Caye Caulker but there are craft and art shops along the main streets. During high tourist season the shops are open from around 9 am and close around 9 pm every day.

Chocolate's, near the north end of town, has more imported goods than local art. There are batik sarongs and silver jewelry imported from Bali and woven bags and place mats from Guatemala. If you need an outfit suited for the tropics, this is a good place to look.

Galeria Hicaco, at the south end of town, has more Belizean products.

The bigger hotels often carry a few choice items. There is a new gift shop next to the ice cream parlor (it should be visited before the gift shop) that sells some unique items.

NIGHTLIFE

Caye Caulker has good nightlife, but there's no special gathering spot. Many establishments offer live music. Since the noise bylaws have been introduced, loud entertainment must be confined behind specially sealed doors and windows so the neighbors are not disturbed.

Lazy Lizard, located on the south side of the split, is a great place to have a drink and howl at the birds across the way. It is the last wooden building in the village. The bar is open from midday to 11 pm.

I and I Bar is just off the south end of Middle Street. This neat three-storey thatched-roof building bounces at night. Of course, always be careful if partying at night as you are a mark for those needing money. And if your senses have been dulled by alcohol, your chances of being robbed are even greater.

Bamboo Sports Bar, Front Street has cold beer on tap. What a treat. The downside is that it costs more than at home.

PLACES TO STAY

Tom's Place, ☎ 226-0102, $$, is along the beach, south of the water taxi dock. This hotel has been here a long time. The rooms, which you must pay for in advance in, are clean and spacious for a budget hotel, but they are hotter than Hades. My fan barely turned. Every time someone

HOTEL PRICES	
$	$20 to $50
$$	$51 to $75
$$$	$76 to $100
$$$$	$101 to $150
$$$$$	over $150

along the hall opened or closed a door, the echo was nerve shattering. The shared bath had only cold water, which was appropriate. I also got the feeling that a woman alone wasn't too welcome.

Sea View Guest House, ☎ 226-0205, www.belizenet. com/seaview/ , $$, has six rooms facing onto a verandah. Each has a double bed, ceiling fan, table and chairs, dresser and private bath with hot water. The hotel is very clean. English, German and Spanish are spoken. They also offer windsurfing lessons and equipment rentals.

Loraine's Guest House, ☎ 206-0162, $, has seven tiny yellow cabins on stilts. The cabins are available for doubles only. Each cabin has a private bath, a double bed and a chair. It is certainly clean enough, but the cabins are also very hot. The owner is friendly.

Ignacio's Beach Cabins (☎ 610-2200), $$, has 19 private cabins that are better painted than Loraine's (these are purple) but the owner will not take reservations. The cabins are close to the airstrip, there is no hot water and the grey water drains into the sand below. Towels and toilet paper are not included. However, the screens on the louvered windows are good and the fans work.

Shirley's Cabins, ☎ 226-0145, www.shirleysguesthouse.com, $$/$$$, has nine cabins in a fenced yard on the beach beside the new forest preserve. Each cabin has a fan, fridge, stove, coffee pot and private bath with hot water. This place is clean and comfortable.

Lazy Iguana, ☎ 226-0350, www.lazyiguana.net, $$$, has four tastefully decorated rooms that splay off a common sitting room. The two-storey building, near the back of the island close to the airport, is immaculate. If you want fine décor, a quiet room and isolation from the action, this is a good place. Breakfast is included in the price.

Anchorage Resort, ☎ 226-0304, anchorage@btl.net, $$$, has 18 double rooms with private baths and hot water, fans, two double beds, fridges, cable TVs and private balconies. I'm not sure what to say about this place except that it was alright.

Tropics Hotel, ☎ 226-0374, www.startoursbelize.com, $$, is across from the beach. It has clean rooms with air conditioning, private baths and hot water. Overall, it is neat and tidy.

Rainbow Hotel, ☎ 226-0123, $$, has been renovated, painted and generally spruced up. The rooms face the ocean and have air conditioning, cable TV and private bathrooms with hot water. There is a small **restaurant** and bar on site.

De Real Macaw Guest House, ☎ 226-0459, www.derealmacaw. com, $$, has four clean and tastefully decorated rooms with private bathrooms and hot water. This facility is on the beach at the north end of town. The rooms have tiled floors, fridges, and air conditioning or fans. There is a wraparound porch with hammocks for guest use. De Real Macaw is a real find. The owners will go out of their way to make you comfortable and, for the price, you won't get better in Caulker.

Sobre Las Olas ("On the Wave" in English), ☎ 226-0243, $, has four basic units with private bathrooms and fans. The rooms are spacious and very clean. Located on the north end of the village, this little hotel is a good deal.

La Costa Maya, ☎ 226-0122, $$, is a fairly new building of blinding-white stucco (good for keeping things cool) just off the street near the split. It's clean and each room has a fridge, stove and private bathroom with hot water. There is tile on the floor and a balcony accessible from each room. The owners are friendly and the prices are reasonable, although there is no deal for singles.

Tina's Backpacker's Hostel, ☎ 226-0351, www.staycayecaulker. com/hostel.html, $, has moved and is now facing the water and near the central park. There are five dorm-style rooms that sleep six to a room. She also has two rooms that have a double bed in each. There are kitchen facilities and a pleasant sitting room. Lockers are available. The gardens are a real draw where chairs are interspersed among the vegetation. Like all hostels, this is a great place to meet other travelers and socialize. Great place for the young!

Diane's Beach House, ☎ 226-0083, www.staycayecaulker.com/beach house.html, has two condo-type houses that have two bedrooms each and easily sleep five. There is a fully supplied kitchen in every house. Each is newly painted with bold colors and decorated inside with soft colors.

Mara's ☎, ☎ 226-0056, $, just before the split, has six individual cabins that are tiny, but clean. Each has cable TV, double beds and private bathrooms with hot water. The front porch of each cabin also has a hammock. The owner at Mara's was very accommodating on my visit. The only drawback is that the wood walls are a bit drab. There are no prices for single occupation.

Trends, ☎ 226-0094 or 226-0097, www.gocayecaulker.com/members/trends.html, $, across from Dewey's, is a wooden two-storey structure that is clean and neat. However, the yard has no trees, making it seem a bit exposed. There is a good book trade library and the hotel will ac-commodate visitors in wheelchairs. Rooms are for two, but even for a single person this is a good deal. Each room has private bath and some have air conditioning. Trends has been so popular that they now have a second place a few hundred feet south of the dock. These rooms are in a two-story house and are of the same quality as those in the bigger place by the dock.

Popeye's, ☎ 226-0032, www.popeyesbeachresort.com, is a new hotel just south of the dock, along the beach. There are deluxe cabins, standard rooms and suits. All have air conditioning, private baths with hot and cold water, cable TV, double beds and re-frigerators. They offer 24-hour electricity and palapa huts on the beach. There is complimentary coffee for hotel guests. I am really glad that Popeye found Olive-oil and has opened his hotel.

Marine's Guest House, ☎ 226-0110, $, on Middle Street, was once Lucy's (Lucy retired to the States). But the place hasn't changed in 20 years – it's still clean and inexpensive. The wooden building has been kept up and you have a choice of either private or shared bathrooms. This is one of the best bargain places on the island, complete with a flourishing flower garden.

Tree Tops, ☎ 226-0240, www.treetopsbelize.com/misc.html, $$, is a cosy place, only 50 yards from the water, with clean and tastefully decorated rooms. This wooden building is bright. Two rooms have a shared bath and two have private baths. There are fans, cable TV, fridge and tiled floors. This is a good deal for two people.

Iguana Reef Hotel, ☎ 226-0213, www.iguanareefinn.com, $$$, has 18 rooms with fans, fridges, private baths, hot water and air conditioning. There is a bar and good restaurant on the premises. Long-stay rates are especially good. The price for a double (singles are the same price) is US $100 per night, but the discounted rate for a week is just over US $70 for a double.

Barefoot Caribe Hotel and Restaurant, ☎ 226-0161, www.barefootcariberesorts.com, $$, is brand new and sparkling clean. I rave about the restaurant; the hotel is directly across the street and is every bit as clean. The rooms are in a U-shaped building with a large open court in the front. There are numerous standards of rooms available, with the regular having a double bed, fan, cable TV, hot and cold water in the private bathroom and tiled floors. The suites have a queen and double bed, air conditioning and fan, a small fridge, spacious closet, and a private balcony. They also offer complimentary purified water. The owners are pleasant and the staff is happy working for them. I loved this place. I'd suggest booking ahead to guarantee a room.

Tropical Paradise, south end of town, ☎ 226-0124, www.tropicalparadise.bz, $$/$$$, has lovely rooms and cabins right on the beach at the quiet end of the island. This hotel is managed by

the same company as Tropics Hotel, next door. All rooms have private bathrooms and hot water, and the luxury suites have two double beds, fan and air conditioning, fridge and cable TV. The staff is pleasant and the restaurant is open early enough to give you coffee before you head off on a tour.

Chocolate's Guest House, ☎ 226-2151, $$$, at the north end of the island, has one room with private bathroom and hot water, tile floors, fan and a coffee maker. The property features a porch with a hammock. Chocolate is famous from the early 1980s when he was recommended by Lonely Planet as the boat man to hire. He's still around, but is now more interested in preservation of the environment. Even if you are not interested in renting his place, you may want to drop in and get some stories from the "old days" while checking out his tours. He is one of the best boatmen around.

PLACES TO EAT

There is a lot to choose from on this island, but be careful. Often, a popular restaurant goes on reputation rather than being consistent in quality. I found many places that were charging far too much for what they offered. Although I've tried to be brutally honest with my recommendations, things do change. Ask other travelers for their opinions.

RESTAURANT PRICES	
$	$5 to $10
$$	$11 to $25
$$$	$26 to $50
$$$$	$51 to $75
$$$$$	over $75

The kids selling coconut breads, Creole bread, Johnny cakes and brownies are safe and highly recommended. **Snake** (real name is Erral) drives around on his golf cart every day selling meat pies, empañadas, tamales and key lime pie. **Bones** comes to town every afternoon and sells brownies with a coconut topping. Both sell food that is tasty and safe to eat.

Habañeros Herbs and Spice, on Middle Street up from the front dock, is popular. The cost for a large dinner is US $25. They specialize in hot peppers and have even painted their entire building in hot pepper colors. However, they also serve homemade pastas and island-famous fajitas with tortillas. You have a choice of sitting on the wraparound porch or inside. Habañeros opens at 6 pm and not a minute before. Although the food is really good and second only to Don Corleone, Habañeros has almost priced itself out of my market. I noticed that it isn't nearly as busy as it was in the past.

Glenda's Bakery, $, located in the blue house on Middle Street just before the airport, is the best place to get fresh baked goods. Think cinnamon buns, but think early as they are usually gone by 9 am. Glenda's place reminds me of the old days when we went to someone's house and got the specialty for a reasonable price. The little area where Glenda serves her meals is spotless. The bakery opens at 7 am during the week and is closed on Sunday.

Rasta Pasta, ☎ 206-0356, $$, relocated from Placencia, Rasta serves vegetarian foods, chicken fish, seafood, turkey bacon, ham and sausage. Breakfast is served till noon. Maralyn Gill is known throughout Belize for her homemade granola, breads, cheese-cakes, coconut chocolate chip macaroons, and brownies. For main courses she serves things like conch fritters, huge burritos and Thai curries. Maralyn takes great pride in the fact that she has never used animal fats in her cooking. Rasta Pasta is next door to the police station (this keeps you in line). It opens at 7 am and serves food until 9:30 pm. However, the bar serves things like homemade ginger beer and piña coladas until midnight. Happy hour, from 4 to 7 pm, includes free appetizers. Often, there is reggae music at night.

Full Moon Restaurant (no telephone), $$, previously Il Biscaro next to the Blue Wave at the north end of the island, serves small portions that are not exceptional. The omelets are eatable, but the food is better at Glenda's.

Chan's Fast Food is between Front and Middle Streets up from the dock. The meals are reasonably priced (chow mein for US $3) served in Styrofoam and eaten on the go. If you are in a hurry, the snack will sustain you until you get across to BC or Ambergris.

Chinese Restaurant, no phone, $$, at the north end of town just before the Municipal Park, is very popular, with good food and large portions. This is right on the main street near the split. The downside is that you must sit inside.

Syd's, ☎ 226-0994, is the supper version of Glenda's. It's located on Middle Street and is nicely decorated with Maya masks. Syd offers burgers (spiced with his own sauces) and fries for US $3 and huge burritos for US $1. The lobster here is the best-tasting and least expensive on the entire island. The only downside to this restaurant is that it can be hot. They never open before 6 pm (that is Belizean 6 pm).

Tropical Paradise Restaurant, ☎ 226-0124, is one of the oldest restaurants on the island and one of the better places to go for breakfast. They open at 7 am. The French toast or pancakes are good and the cost is about US $3 a meal. I also enjoyed snacks midday here – the portions are big and prices low. This is a good deal.

Don Corleone, Front Street, ☎ 226-0025, should be patronized at least once while on the island. The atmosphere is elegant, the service excellent and the food unforgettable. The pastas and sauces are freshly made by a professional chef and the spices and herbs are freshly picked. There is a large wine selection and the Italian ice creams are a welcome treat. The restaurant is also open for breakfast and comes highly recommended. Once people found this place, they usually returned. The prices are reasonable: a dinner for one, with wine and appetizer, is about $25. I can't say enough about the food served here.

Wish Willey's is at the back and north end of the island. He now serves meals from his kitchen into a sitting area that is best when you bring your own chair. The waiter likes to have a cigarette hanging out of his mouth when he serves. The lobster I had was so tough I couldn't cut it with the knife I was given so I had to use my own sharp Swiss army knife. The final touch was that Willey charged more than anyone else on the island for the meal. Stay away.

Herbal Tribe, on front street near the north of the island, serves the most horrid food I have ever had on this planet except for Tibetan Tsampa (ground barley, rancid yak-butter and salted black tea). The ribs that my husband ordered were thin slices of shoe leather sitting on a pile of pork fat. You'd be better off going across the street to the Barefoot Restaurant, to enjoy a good meal overlooking the bay.

Sand Box, ☎ 226-0200, $$, in the center of town, is open from 7 am until 10 pm and is one of the more popular places on the island for meals and drinks. They offer dishes like curried fish and conch ceviche or seafood salad for reasonable prices. Vegetarians can munch on things like stuffed eggplant with mushrooms. Happy hour is from 3 pm to 6 pm daily.

CoCo Plum Cage, near the airport at the south end of the island, is tucked away in the trees and well worth looking for, especially when you are in need of a cappuccino. The omelets are notorious around the island, so breakfast is a must, at least once. They also serve vegetarian foods.

Amor y Cafe, on the main street near the south end of town, is very popular for breakfast and you often have to wait in line to get a table. Their granola with yogurt and fruit is excellent, as are the fresh juices. They are open from 7 am until noon, but I think pressure for longer hours from patrons may force them to stay open later.

Barefoot Caribe Restaurant, Front St., ☎ 226-0161, www.bare footcariberesort.com, is new, clean, and has a great balcony where you can enjoy fresh shrimp (my recommendation) while looking at the ocean. The strawberry slushies are another draw – freshly made and huge for the price. Service is good.

CAYES NEAR BELIZE CITY

Almost all tours, dive trips and boat excursions are offered by the resorts themselves. Most of these are quite expensive, but travelers with just two weeks for vacation seem to like this option. There are also some all-inclusive operators (see *Outfitters Who Do All the Work,* page 88).

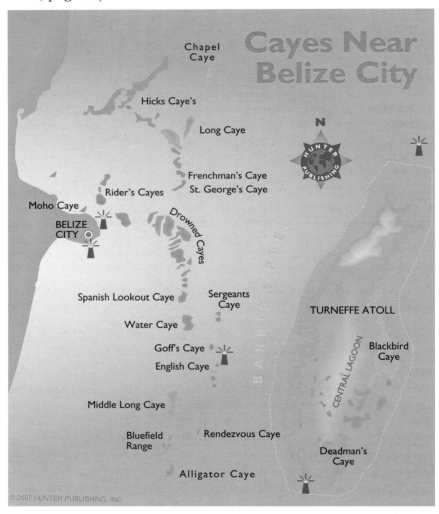

Chapel Caye

Cayes Near Belize City

Hicks Caye's

Long Caye

N

Frenchman's Caye
St. George's Caye

Rider's Cayes

Moho Caye

BELIZE
CITY

Drowned Cayes

Spanish Lookout Caye

Sergeants Caye

TURNEFFE ATOLL

Water Caye

Goff's Caye

CENTRAL LAGOON

Blackbird Caye

English Caye

Middle Long Caye

Bluefield Range

Rendezvous Caye

Deadman's Caye

Alligator Caye

© 2007 HUNTER PUBLISHING, INC

■ MOHO CAYE

Moho Caye is a great spot to hang out with the university crowd from Belize City. Take the little ferry from The Landing, located two blocks from the university. Just walk down University Drive until you hit the water. The ferry ride takes five minutes and costs US $2.50 for a round-trip ticket. It leaves once every hour.

> **AUTHOR NOTE:** *Don't confuse this one with a second Moho Caye just out of Placencia.*

At Moho, you can sit on the deck of the restaurant, ☎ 223-5350 (the name and owners keep changing but the phone number stays the same), overlooking the ocean with the trade winds fluffing your hair while you schmooze (and drink) with the up-coming elite of Belizean society.

■ CHAPEL CAYE

© Caye Chapel Resort

This caye is privately owned by businessman Larry Addington from Kentucky. He developed the island to accommodate corporate meetings. If you are curious about this very high-end spot (US $1,500 per person, per night, without food or drinks), put on your best running shoes or hiking boots and go have a look. The island is open to the public when the resort is not booked by large corporations. At one time, raucous British soldiers would come here for R & R. Island Resort, where they once partied, has been demolished.

Twelve daily flights go to the island from Belize City (US $46.50 each way) and the airstrip is big enough to accommodate small jets. Both Maya Air and Tropic will stop en route to Caye Caulker or San Pedro.

Besides poking around the resort or playing a game of golf (see below), look for old **graves** of some of the Spanish who were killed at St. George's Caye during the famous battle of 1798.

The resort is now called **Caye Chapel Island Resort**, ☎ 226-8250, www.cayechapel.com, and is very exclusive, with 3,800 square feet of living space per villa. This includes two private master suites, large bath and dressing areas that have hydro spas, private sun terrace accessible from each master bedroom, formal living room

and dining room, cable TV and climate control (AC). Those are the luxury suites, but if that is a bit too much for you, try the smaller 700-square-foot casitas, which have about the same amenities but only one bedroom and less than 1/5 the size. Besides staying in these luxurious accommodations, you have the use of the pool, and the best golf course in Belize (not hard to beat) along with a great restaurant. During low and mid season, the casitas are quite affordable, but during high season the villas are a bit much, running at $1,500 per day. I have heard that these villas also include a butler, but was unable to get confirmation.

GOLF

An 18-hole golf course undulates for 7,000 yards across Caye Chapel. The front nine holes are tight and there is a water trap on every one. The back nine holes have more variety and one is a 600-yard par 5. Sand is a hazard on all holes. The course is a good test of target golf, where your shots have to be accurate.

Should you want to just play golf, their day-fee is a mere $200, which includes as much golf as you can play from 9 am to 4 pm plus the use of a cart and clubs. As a bonus they include a lunch at the pool. They excuse the high cost of being on the island to assure privacy not found elsewhere.

> **ENVIRONMENTAL NOTE:** *There was some controversy about the pollution damage a resort like this creates, but apparently the grass is a variety called paspalum, which uses 50% less fertilizer and pesticides than does ordinary grass.*

■ SERGEANT'S CAYE & GOFF'S CAYE

Sergeant's Caye and Goff's Caye are just south of St. George's Caye, near Belize City. These two islands sit on top of the reef. There are three others that are similar in the Turneffe Island area.

Sergeant's Caye covers about 1,000 square yards and has exactly three coconut trees on it. The water around this island is shallow, with 20-35-foot drop-offs. This is a good place for beginning snorkelers to see big vase sponges. The royal gramma (fairy basslet), a rarely seen fish, has been spotted in these waters. You may also spot an old bathtub that was left by previous inhabitants after a hurricane went through.

Goff's Caye is close to Sergeant's. In contrast, it receives over 500 tourists a week that arrive in about 40 boats. National Geographic Society sponsored a study near the caye in 2001 for their sustainable seas program. They were studying the slow-growing but quickly disappearing black coral.

On the island, barely 200 feet across (60 meters), is an open-sided, thatched-roof hut that can be used for shade. There is also a bit of vegetation above the water line. This is where your tour company will provide you with a lunch if it is included in your trip.

When the manatees are caring for their young, they often come to this island to feed on sea grasses. Most of the water around Goff's Caye is shallow and a good place for snorkelers to see fans and coral. Inexperienced snorkelers should not head to the outer side of the reef, which offers deep water and good visibility, but large swells and strong currents. There are both spur and grooves and solid drops near this island.

■ RENDEZVOUS & PAUNCH CAYES

Rendezvous and Paunch Cayes are tiny islands barely 1,100 feet across (330 meters), but the snorkeling available here make them a popular destination. If things are too busy at Goff's or Sergeant's Caye, then these are a good second choice. The islands also sit on top of the reef.

■ ST. GEORGE'S CAYE

St. George's Caye is nine miles from Belize City, 20 minutes by boat. The U-shaped island has only 20 permanent residents, so a wild time is not what you will find here.

Originally the capital of Belize from 1650 until 1784, this tiny island still exudes an ambiance of colonial life. There are old houses with manicured lawns, some dotted with cannons and many enclosed in picket fences. The island is only 1.5 miles long and less than a mile wide. It has a **historical cemetery** at the south end and **Fishermen's Town**, to the north, where the fishers live.

The Cayes

HISTORY

Many times during the 1700s, the Spanish invaded St. George's Caye and took residents as prisoners. Some were sent to a prison in Havana and kept there for over 40 years, while others were taken to Honduras. Then after some saber rattling, on September 10th, 1798, the Spanish decided to invade St. George's Caye once and for all. They had 32 ships loaded with cannons, ammunition and 2,000 men. The British had 117 sailors on HMS *Merlin*, 50 men on two sloops and 112 men on seven gun flats. The residents lay in wait to defend their little island. The Spanish fired their cannons, inspiring 200 Baymen on the mainland to jump into anything that floated and join those defending the island. The battle was successful for the British; they didn't lose one man and the Spanish fled, never to return to the island again. Some of the Spanish who died in the battle are buried on Caye Chapel.

THINGS TO DO

Besides enjoying life, you can **sail**, **windsurf**, **snorkel** or **dive**. If you're here on September 10th, you'll be able to enjoy the fun of **St. George's Day**, when people dress in red, white and blue to show their patriotism.

Blue-spotted grouper.

Diving

For divers, the caye offers a coral wall decorated with sea fans and whips. The depth is anywhere from 45 to 130 feet (15 to 40 meters). Groupers, moray eels, blue tangs, horse-eyed jacks and sergeant majors frequently hang around the coral. This is considered a good/intermediate diving spot.

PLACES TO STAY

Pleasure Island Resort, ☎ 223-0744, www.stgeorgescaye pleasure.bz, $$$/$$$$, is a family oriented resort that specializes in relaxation. There are 11 rooms designed to hold up to four people, in colonial-style buildings surrounding a central courtyard. Each accommodation has a private bathroom with hot and cold water and private balcony with hammocks. There are wooden floors, pleasant décor, air conditioning and comfortable beds. The resort has recently been renovated by new owners, so everything is spit-polished clean. The restaurant, in the main building, offers both local and international dishes. They will also cook up your catch for you if you are lucky with the rod. The bar has two now-famous drinks that should be tried during their happy hour special that starts each night at 7:30 pm. They are the CocoNuts Blower and the Nice 'n Nauti. Activities such as fishing, diving and snorkeling can be arranged. Pick up from the airport is optional and costs $75.

St. George's Lodge, ☎ 220-4444, www.gooddiving.com, $$$$, had the first dive shop in Belize. Since its inception in 1977 the resort has had numerous repeat guests. One of the draws for divers is the practice of using Nitrox (a mixture of oxygen and nitrogen) for diving. This is believed by some to  be less dangerous than the traditional method. The lodge has 10 rooms and six cottages with thatched roofs, hardwood floors, private baths and an endless amount of quiet. It uses solar and wind power and collects rainwater for washing. The big thing to do here is get married, have a reception and then stand at the dock and wave goodbye to your guests before entering your wedding chamber. All reports are that this is a great place to get married.

SWALLOW CAYE

This mangrove caye is close to Belize City, and increased boat traffic from there in recent years has left places like Swallow Caye or the **Northern Drowned Cayes** inundated with traffic. Their manatee populations were being reduced as many animals were being cut and sometimes killed by the passing boats. Chocolate Heredia and his wife Annie from Caye Caulker, along with a group of concerned citizens, formed the **Friends of Swallow Caye**. They were instrumental in having these islands and their surrounding waters made into a sanctuary in July 2002. It took 17 years of hard work and lobbying before they realized success. For more information, contact Annie and Chocolate Heredia on Caye Caulker, ☎ 226-2151, www.swallowcayemanatees.org. Chocolate and Annie are now busy promoting conservation in the schools and getting more protection for the manatee.

The 9,000 acres of water that include Swallow Caye and some areas of the Northern Drowned Cayes now have signs around them to warn the boaters that animals may be around. There is a resting hole where the manatees can often be found and a narrow creek in the mangrove where they swim.

Many bottlenose dolphins, American crocodiles, upside-down jellyfish and other marine life live in or near the sanctuary.

One of the things you can do as a visitor to the area is make certain your boat operator does not race near the islands or harass or grab one of the animals. Anchors should be carefully placed. Even swimming in the area is prohibited. Make a deal with your boat driver. If he breaks the rules (make them clear before leaving port) that protect the marine life, you don't pay.

GALLOWS POINT & ENGLISH CAYES

Tiny Gallows Point Caye is seven miles from Belize City. I'm convinced it has the ghosts of some who were hanged here for crimes that today would barely warrant a wink. There is one place to stay, **Gallows Point Resort**, ☎ 227-3054, $$, www.belcove.com/gallows.html (contact is through the Belcove Hotel, 9 Regent Street, Belize City). While here, you can sleep, snorkel, sleep, read and

drink. Maybe for variety you could fish from a dugout and, if you're a skilled fisher, save yourself some food money.

English Caye is a tiny island about 10 miles east of Belize City. It has sandy beaches and a few coconut trees and is of no interest to the local diver/snorkeler or tourist. At one time it had a lighthouse designed to alert ships to the reef. Once a ship got close enough, a smaller boat would come out from English Caye and guide the larger vessel through the reef.

SPANISH LOOKOUT

Ten miles east of Belize City, this is 186 acres of mangrove and buttonwood forest, sea grass bed and coral sand. Other than watching birds fly and manatees swim, there isn't much to do except dive, fish, eat and drink.

Spanish Bay Resort, ☎ 220-4024, www.spanishbaybelize.com, $$, has housed many divers, fishers, shellers and marine scientists. Its 10 cabins have fans, hardwood paneling and private bathrooms. You can also rent an apartment with a kitchen for US $40 per day. You can cook for yourself or arrange to have food included in the price.

The dining room, decorated with charts and maps, has a wraparound deck but no electricity. If you dine here, the vegetables that are served are mostly grown on the island. The resort uses solar panels for some power and generators for compressing the tanks.

Diving and **fishing** trips can be included in the price of your accommodation or paid for separately. Transportation from Belize City is US $25 per person, with a minimum of two people in the boat. Visiting Spanish Lookout is a good deal, especially if you want to be able to return to Belize City quickly and inexpensively, yet avoid the crowds of the bigger islands that are closer to the city.

BLUEFIELDS RANGE

This cluster of tiny islands, only one of which is inhabited, sits inside the reef about 20 miles south of Belize City. The one occupied island has a few cabins, a commercial fish camp, mangrove and palm trees and a tiny beach. The beach was at one time bigger, but the last hurricane took out a lot of it.

Ricardo's Beach Huts, contact at #4 Banak St, Belize City, ☎ 227-8469, to make reservations and arrangements for transportation to the island. There are nine little huts on stilts that sit over the water. These are basic with no plumbing. The outhouses are okay. The minimum stay is two nights and three days. Besides having a rest from civilization, you can watch birds, snorkel from shore and fish from a dugout.

> **AUTHOR NOTE:** *There are 160 miles of walls along the reefs in Belize for divers and snorkelers to explore.*

■ TURNEFFE ISLANDS ATOLL

The Turneffe Islands is an atoll 25 miles east of Belize City. The central lagoon, dotted with about 200 mangrove cayes, is eight miles wide and 30 miles long. The mangroves have created a rich environment for marine life and this is where every level of diver can find rare species of fish and corals. The visibility level is always between 100 and 150 feet (30-45 meters).

The lagoon is inundated with flats and the mangrove nutrients attract so many fish that anglers are almost guaranteed a grand slam if they come at the right time of year. The winds and tide currents move the nutrients from the islands around the central lagoon area and to the flats.

There are four cuts for boats to enter into the lagoon. The first is the eight-foot-deep North Cut located about 400 yards from Coco Tree Cayes. The South Cut is about 150 yards from Big Caye Bokel and is also about eight feet deep (2.4 meters). The southwest entrance is at Pirates Creek, just above Caye Bokel and the last one is at Blue Creek, two miles north of Big Caye Bokel. The last two cuts are about five feet wide and eight to 13 feet deep.

DIVING

Because of this healthy environment, the schools of fish are huge. It is normal for a diver to brag about seeing over 30 rays swimming together. Turtles and dolphins are also common. White-spotted toad fish, eagle rays, jewfish, morays, groupers and horse-eye jacks are often seen here.

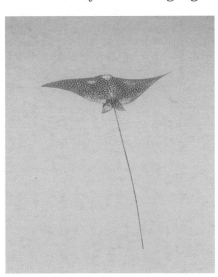

Spotted eagle ray.

Although the north is not very good for diving and the west side of the atoll has too many wide grooves and very few coral spurs, there are other sites that do offer interesting challenges. The eastern reefs are a varied terrain with abundant sea life; the south is for the experienced, offering walls and currents that challenge even the best divers.

The most famous site is **The Elbow** at the southern tip. Here, dog and cubera snappers, Ber-

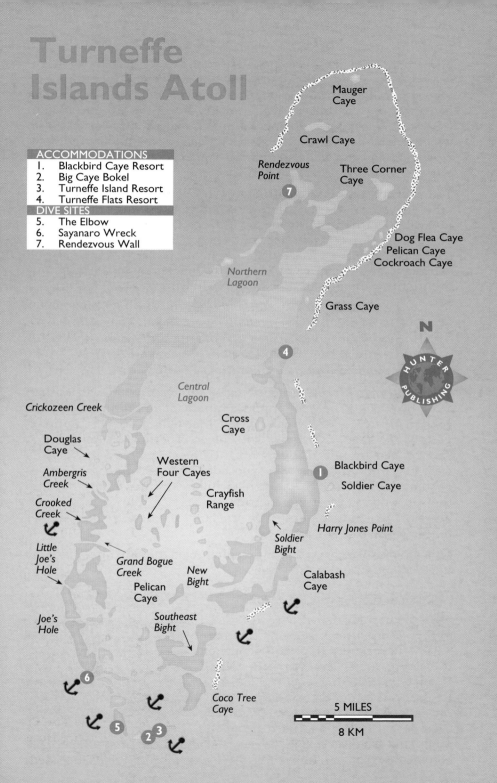

Turneffe Islands Atoll

ACCOMMODATIONS
1. Blackbird Caye Resort
2. Big Caye Bokel
3. Turneffe Island Resort
4. Turneffe Flats Resort

DIVE SITES
5. The Elbow
6. Sayanaro Wreck
7. Rendezvous Wall

Mauger Caye

Crawl Caye

Rendezvous Point

Three Corner Caye

Dog Flea Caye
Pelican Caye
Cockroach Caye

Grass Caye

Northern Lagoon

Central Lagoon

Cross Caye

Crickozeen Creek

Douglas Caye

Ambergris Creek

Crooked Creek

Western Four Cayes

Crayfish Range

Blackbird Caye

Soldier Caye

Harry Jones Point

Soldier Bight

Little Joe's Hole

Grand Bogue Creek

New Bight

Calabash Caye

Pelican Caye

Joe's Hole

Southeast Bight

Coco Tree Caye

N

HUNTER PUBLISHING

5 MILES

8 KM

muda chup and horse-eye jacks are common. The reef reverses direction here, creating spurs that average 60 feet (18 meters) and groove formations 100 feet deep (30 meters). Seas at this spot can be rough and the current often sweeps divers toward open water. Control of buoyancy and air consumption is essential for this dive, which is best done as a drift. As this area is home to the predators, on a good day you will see up to 50 eagle rays swimming together. Yikes!

The **eastern reef** is a continuous vertical reef that measures 35 miles long. Parts of this wall slope out about 100 yards and then, at about 50 feet down (15 meters), it drops. There is also a ridge at about 250 feet (75 meters) that shows the wave pattern. This causes some of the reef's erosion. At about 80 feet (24 meters) you will likely see some huge tuna and king mackerel, and occasionally an Atlantic blue marlin or a sailfish will whiz by.

> **AUTHOR NOTE:** *Many sites at the Turneffe atoll are good for intermediate divers. Some are really good for snorkelers too. The best website I found describing the various sites was* **www.ambergris-caye.com/pages/town/diveturneffe.html**.

The ***Sayanaro* Wreck** is a passenger/cargo ship that was sunk in 1985 by a local. The wood frame is rapidly deteriorating, but it is a good place to practice wreck dives. Other places, like the **Rendezvous Wall,** have overhangs with holes. The hole at Rendezvous was caused by rain dripping on the limestone when the oceans were lower and the rock was exposed. The hole connects to the lagoon in the center of the atoll, allowing freshwater to flow out into the salt water. Unfortunately, this causes death to the surrounding coral, which turns white. Divers, being creative creatures, refer to this white coral as icebergs.

This atoll is also covered in little patch reefs that are often like tiny tide pools just under the water.

PLACES TO STAY

There are three resorts and even at peak seasons there are never more than 300 people on the entire atoll. The **Turneffe Island Resort**, ☎ 220-4011, 800-628-1447, http://angleradventures.com/TurneffeIsland/TurnefIs.htm, is on Big Caye Bokel at the southern tip of the

HOTEL PRICES	
$ . . . . $20 to $50
$$ . . . . $51 to $75
$$$ . . . . . . $76 to $100
$$$$ . . . . . $101 to $150
$$$$$ . . . . . . over $150

atoll. This is a diver's/fisher's resort at which, for US $300 per person per day, you can have three dives plus all your meals included.

Fishers can be out on the water for about six hours a day, but their package costs more than the diving package. Anyone wanting single occupancy in a cottage must pay almost the same as for a double. If you don't want to dive or fish, other less-expensive packages are available. The dive shop offers Nitrox (mix of oxygen and nitrogen) tanks for US $7 each. The week-long package also includes a day at the Blue Hole and one night dive.

The resort has cabins that were built in the 1960s and have since been remodeled to offer first-class comfort. Each cottage has a private bathroom, screened porch, fan and air conditioning. The food includes things like fresh-baked bread and freshly caught fish. The resort also has a library, kayaks and windsurfers for your use.

Blackbird Caye Resort on the east side of the atoll, ☎ 223-2772, 888-271-3483, www.worlddive.com (click on "Destinations," then "Belize," then "Blackbird Caye Resort"), $$$$$, is an hour and a half from Belize City. The resort offers a choice of 10 cabins on 166 acres of island. Each cabin has a nice sitting area, two beds and private baths with showers. The cabins are made of coco palm and thatch and all have porches. There is a choice of dive/fish packages and the cost is less than at Turneffe Island Resort. Fishers are asked to bring their own equipment as there is none for rent. Dive packages include three dives a day and fish packages include two trips a day with a guide. There are also sailboats, windsurfers, kayaks and canoes for the guests to use at no extra cost.

The island has cabins that belong to the **Oceanic Society**. In conjunction with Texas A & M University, National Geographic Society and the Fort Motor Foundation, the society has been studying the behavior patterns of the bottlenose dolphin. You can join the researchers at the field station for around US $200 a day.

Turneffe Flats, ☎ 220-4046, 800-815-1304, www.tflats.com, on a secluded island on the northeast side of the atoll, caters to fishers, divers and snorkelers. Their packages include pick-up and delivery to and from Belize City, one week on the island, and three dives every day or, if fishing, a 16-foot fishing boat with a guide (there must be at least two anglers in the boat to avoid an additional charge). All meals are included in the packages. For one week fishing, the cost can be up to US $3,700; one week's diving costs about $1,550; and a non-activity package costs $1,425 per person.

The remodeled cottages all have air conditioning, private baths and showers. The food is either Belizean or American. There is a gift shop that sells flies and tackle, among other things.

■ LIGHTHOUSE REEF ATOLL

Lighthouse Reef atoll lies 40 miles southeast of Belize City. The lagoon inside this reef is probably the most famous of the three atolls in Belize. It is home to the famous **Blue Hole**. The southern end hosts the **Half Moon Caye Natural Monument**. Jacques Cousteau, in 1972, took his ship *Calypso* to the hole and started investigating its depths. He filmed what he found and had it exposed over television worldwide. The area immediately became popular with tourists in general and divers in particular. However, Lighthouse Reef is also famous for its fishing opportunities, both on the flats and in the deeper waters outside the reef.

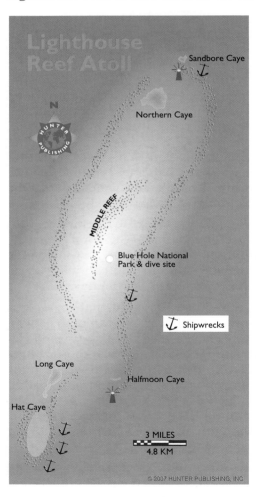

Of the five islands in the lagoon, **Hat Caye** has no permanent residents, but the diving close to the cayes is popular among those who have intermediate skills. **Sandbore Caye** is an easy paddle by kayak from Lighthouse Reef Resort on Northern Caye. Just a few fishers and a lighthouse keeper live on the island. Mr. Pete, the lighthouse keeper for over 75 years, was still there last I heard. The lighthouse is an 80-foot structure that can be climbed to get an overview of the atoll.

Long Caye is a mature mangrove swamp with three internal lagoons that house saltwater crocodiles and a huge population of nesting egrets. However, Long Caye is mostly a diver's spot.

PLACES TO STAY

Calypso Beach Retreat, Long Caye, ☎ 303-523-8165 or 303-814-0789, www.calypsobeach retreat.com, is a new bed and breakfast and the only accommodation available on this lovely little island. The inn is built of Belizean hardwoods and each of the four guest rooms has poster beds with mosquito nets and local artwork that adds charm. There are tiled bathrooms and ocean views.

HOTEL PRICES	
$ . . . . $20 to $50
$$ . . . . $51 to $75
$$$ . . . . $76 to $100
$$$$ . . . . $101 to $150
$$$$$ . . . . . . over $150

The kitchen and dining room are a common area for guests, plus there are diving and fishing lockers, a gift shop and kayaks. Being so isolated, it is recommended that you include meals in your package. This is a good deal as it works to just a bit over $100 a day. There are other options, such as a fishing package that in-

© Calypso Beach Retreat

cludes guide, boat and gear, or a snorkeling package that includes a trip to the Blue Hole. But the owners are flexible. If you have a specific idea in mind, run it past them and they will try to accommodate you. This is an excellent place to go if you need a rest in one of the most romantic spots in the Caribbean.

Lighthouse Reef Resort, ☎ 800-423-3114, www.scubabelize. com, is currently closed, but should have reopened by the time this book is off press. It has a private airstrip so you can arrive by plane. There are 11 units on the water – five cabins with fans and private baths plus six luxury villas (that rent for a little more than the cabins) with two double beds, tiled floors, fans, fridges, air conditioning, mini-bars, porches and private baths. The price for accommodations includes transportation from Belize City to and from the island, all meals and up to 17 dives (the goal) for the week. The cost for this is around US $300 a day.

The dining room is in a central building with a wrap-around porch and you can eat either inside or outside. Occasionally, the resort puts on barbeques, to which guests are invited. Although the meals are not gourmet, they are well prepared and substantial in size. The central building has a TV, stereo, VCR and library.

The Cayes

Island Expeditions, ☎ 800-667-1630, www.islandexpeditions.com, operates a luxury base camp in the park on Half Moon Caye. From there, its guests scuba dive, snorkel and explore the reefs by kayak. Guides share their knowledge about the reef ecosystem.

Base camp accommodations are tent-walled cabañas, safari-style tents raised on wooden floors. Rates (which run $1,499 for seven days and eight nights) include all meals, transfer from the airport and a last night's stay at the Biltmore Hotel in Belize City to complete your vacation.

DIVING

Lighthouse is not just a diver's paradise; fishers too love it here. The flats are great for bonefish and the unofficial re-cord for a catch is held by an American woman; the fish was 12 pounds (5.4 kg). If you just want to rest, the resort has 500 feet (150 meters) of beach and 15 acres in which to wander.

In addition to the Blue Hole and Half Moon Caye dive sites (profiled below), over a dozen well-known sites run along the eastern wall of the atoll. Some popular ones are **Captains Choice, Black Coral Forest, The Abyss** (that has a two-lipped wall), **Quebrada, Pete's Palace, Tres Cocos** and **The Aquarium**. They are all intermediate dives that go to 130 feet (39 meters).

HALF MOON CAYE

This natural monument is a 45-acre island that stands a maximum of eight feet (2.4 meters) above sea level. It's made from crushed coral, some of which has cemented to-gether to form tide pools around the shore. The island's east end has coconut palms and the west end is thickly vegetated, mostly with the orange-blossomed ziricote tree, the gumbo limbo with its peeling skin, and the spider lily. The island is host to many birds whose droppings enhance the growth of these plants.

As your tour operator pulls up to the dock, you will see a welcome sign and the visitor center. There is no water on the island so you should have some with you. Pets are not allowed and fishing and hunting is strictly forbidden. Register at the center and pay your US $5 to enter the preserve. The center is open from 8 am to 4:30 pm.

Half Moon Caye, established in 1982, was the first marine preserve in the country. At one time, it had a **lighthouse** station, built in 1820, but it collapsed and a second was built in 1848 using the foundation stones from the first. This one didn't collapse, but it was eventually de-activated until, in 1931, the station was again put to use and a steel tower added. Today, the lighthouse is solar powered. It is not climbable because it is falling to pieces. The lighthouse is located at the southeast corner of the island.

Half Moon Caye.

The island was first made a reserve in 1928 and then a national monument in 1982. The reserve status was necessary to protect the **red-footed booby**. This is one of only two places in the world (Tobago is the other) where boobies have white plumage, rather than the common dull brown. The birds nest in the ziricote thickets at the west end of the island. To view the boobies, take the **walking trail** that leads from the visitor center to a viewing platform. The island gets an average of 120 visitors a week so staying on the trails is essential. Boobies nest in mid-December, the eggs hatch in March and the chicks are grown within two months. The birds leave the island by mid-August. The boobie population has fluctuated since the late 1950s. In 1958 there were 1,389 boobies; by 1988/89 that figure had dropped to 889. The last count I could find was done in 1991/2 when the population was again up to 1,325 birds. However, some reports say there are up to 4,000 that frequent the island now. Boobies are constantly harassed by the ubiquitous **frigate bird**.

According to one source, another 98 species of birds have been seen on the island and 77 of those are migrants. Seventeen of those migratory species are seen often enough to indicate that they are spending the winter on nearby islands.

Half Moon Caye is also host to **iguanas**. One species is known as the "bamboo chicken" because of its good meat. It is red, with black bars on its back. Wish Willy, another common species, grows to three or four feet long (1-1.2 meters) and is yellow with black bars. The green iguana has been spotted here too. It is only the male who is green; females are orange.

The **giant anole**, a lizard, is found on all the cayes around Lighthouse Reef. The male is colorful, with a white throat, blue forehead, pink dewlaps and green body. Anoles are real chameleons who can change to a gray/black within minutes.

But the big draw is the **Belizean atoll gecko**, found nowhere else on the planet. Like many geckos, this one is nocturnal. **Loggerhead** and **hawksbill turtles** also nest on this island.

Diving near this caye offers a coral ridge at about 25 feet (7.5 meters), after which the wall drops for thousands of feet and is dotted with caves, bridges, canyons and tunnels.

BLUE HOLE

 The Blue Hole, another national monument, is about a quarter-mile across and 480 feet deep (144 meters). Two narrow channels in the walls allow boats to reach the hole's center.

Although Cousteau is the one credited with making the Blue Hole famous, he wasn't the first to film it. In the early 1960s Al Giddings, an underwater cinematographer, went into the hole and produced the film called *Painted Reefs of British Honduras*. The Canadian Film Board then financed another production about the hole in 1965 or 1966. This piqued the curiosity of Cousteau, who came in the late 1960s and explored. Although there are rumors that Cousteau blasted the two channels in the reef so he could get his boat through, this is incorrect. Nor did Cousteau's son die in the hole.

The Blue Hole is an eroded sinkhole that was a land-cave around 10,000 years ago. As the sea levels rose and covered the cave, the roof crashed in and the corals grew around the rim. It is believed that an earthquake caused the reef to tilt about 12 degrees, causing overhangs with stalactites and stalagmites to sit at precarious angles. Snorkeling at the rim is spectacular, but it is divers who really enjoy this site.

Divers will see the first stalactites and stalagmites at about 25-50 feet (7.5-15 meters). The water at this level is a bit murky and a light is needed. However, once you hit lower depths, visibility improves. The water temperature stays around 76°F (24°C). The first ledge is at about 150-165 feet (45-49 meters) and some of the cuts go back about 15 to 20 feet (4.5 to 6 meters). Some ledges form V-shaped tunnels that narrow toward the back. The farther down one goes, the better the formations.

This is for the skilled diver only. Your dive master should be with you at all times. Because decompression time is around 10 to 15 minutes, the operator should leave a spare tank at the 20-foot depth. Buoyancy control is essential.

On the west side of the hole at 150-200 feet (45-60-meters), a tunnel leads to a cave that goes on to a second tunnel and cave. This, in turn, leads to a third cave. Some believe that this cave system works its way back to the mainland. However, no one has gone through. Exploration of these caves is dangerous as the silt on the bottom is easily disturbed which causes visibility to drop.

There are no whirlpools in the Blue Hole. In fact, because water movement is almost non-existent, there is little marine life – one must stay near the rim to see anything alive. There you will see anemones, shrimp, angel and butterfly fish, elkhorn coral and purple sea fans. One diver reported lobsters up to four feet long (1.2 meters). I find that almost as difficult to believe as Cousteau blasting a hole in the reef.

THICK LIPS, HARD-MINDED

During one study in 1970 a strange phenomenon was observed. A huge number of conch migrated in a southwest direction. They were all adults with thick shell lips. If one was taken out of the water and sent in a different direction, it soon turned itself and continued in the southwest direction. The studies could give no reason for this.

CAYES NEAR DANGRIGA

TOBACCO CAYE

Tobacco Caye is 9.7 miles east of Dangriga and it takes about 45 minutes by boat to get there. This five-acre island is similar to what Caye Caulker was in the early 80s, a laid-back tourist party spot. If you want good diving or fishing, plus a bit of nightlife, this is the place.

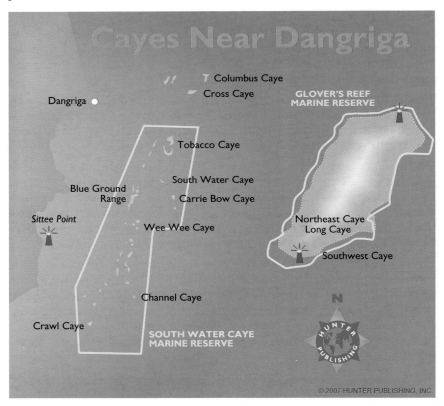

Tobacco Caye can be reached from Riverside in Dangriga. Two boats go to the caye on a regular basis. Captain Buck (pronounced "book") leaves from the dock in front of the Riverside Café every day at noon and leaves Tobacco Caye every day at 9 am. He is also available for fishing trips or touring of the cayes. Elwood Fairweather is the other person who comes to Tobacco Caye on a regular basis. He leaves Riverside Tuesday and Friday and charges US $15 each way. Mr. Fairweather also rents rooms on Tobacco Caye for US $25. This price includes meals.

> **AUTHOR WARNING:** *There have been unscrupulous "helpers" who offer boat rides. After they have your money, the boat never appears. Be certain to book your boat at the Riverside Café with a recommended guide.*

Snorkeling is good right from shore on Tobacco Caye. However, stay out of the channel where boats pass. One woman was killed in early 2002 when a motor boat passed over her. Locals have now put up buoys, but you must also be careful. The dive site closest to the caye is **Shark's Cave** and is for advanced divers only (a cave full of sharks sounds like suicide to me). There's a shore dive at **Tarpon Channel**, at the south end, where the reef curls around the island. Between March and November, this cut is full of tarpon that can weigh up to 300 pounds (135 kg) and measure up to eight feet (2.5 meters) in length.

Tobacco Channel is just a mile or so off the east side of the caye. If you stay close to the reef, you may see large nurse sharks hovering in a few sand gullies. Stingrays and eagle rays are common.

Two popular **birdwatching** spots are **Bird Caye** and **Manawa Caye**.

PLACES TO STAY

Tobacco Caye Lodge, ☎ 520-5033 or 227-6247, www.tclodge belize.com, was originally called Island Camps. It features six single- , double- or triple-occupancy cabins on the beach along the west side of the island. Each has a fan, private bath, electricity from solar panels and a

HOTEL PRICES		
$. . . . . $20 to $50		
$$. . . . . $51 to $75		
$$$. . . . . . . $76 to $100		
$$$$. . . . . $101 to $150		
$$$$$ . . . . . . over $150		

rain-water shower. During high season, the cost is US $80 for a single, US $120 for doubles and US $180 for triples. This includes all your meals and transportation from and to Dangriga. During low season the prices are about 75% lower.

Ocean's Edge, ☎ 614-9633, oceansedge@btl.net, has seven cabins with private baths and hot water for US $45 per person, including meals.

Reef's End Lodge, ☎ 522-2419 or 520-2037, www.reefsendlodge.com, is run by Saint Malo (the bad Saint). The rooms are large, with three beds in each, two doubles and a single. The cost is US $60 a day, which includes all meals and use of canoes. There is also a catering service should you wish to eat in your room.

Gaviota Coral Reef Resort, ☎ 509-5032, has rooms for US $50 a day, including all meals. It sits in the middle of the island and looks well run. There are shared baths only, and a bar. Gaviota has a homier feel than some other party places closer to the landing dock.

Tobacco Caye Diving, ☎ 520-5101, info@tobaccocayediving.com, has rooms with fans, private baths and electricity. It offers packages for US $1,000 per week that include two dives each day, two night dives, all meals and transportation from Dangriga.

Coco Plum Island Resort, ☎ 520-2041, www.cocplumcay.com, sits on a tiny island eight miles from Dangriga. It is the island's only resort. There are five cabins, each near the water and facing the rising sun. The cabins have queen-sized beds, kitchenettes, private bathrooms with hot water, air conditioning and fans, private verandas and tiled floors. The resort offers tour packages and many special discounts. Wedding in mind? What a romantic place to start a marriage; the resort will do all the preparations. Their website is informative.

■ COCKNEY ISLAND

There is a tiny lagoon at one end of the island. If seclusion is what you are looking for, this is definitely a quiet place. **Cockney Island**, ☎ 522-0334, www.belizeseaclub.com, is a new resort on a freshly cleared mangrove island. The owners were still bringing in and rearranging the sand when I was there. The round thatched-roof huts are spacious and well decorated. Each has a private bathroom and electricity generated from solar panels. The price is US $50 a day ($85 for double occupancy), including three meals. Although Cockney Island has a bar and restaurant, there is no dive shop. Additionally, arrangements for transportation must be made independently. I think this policy is likely to change once they have settled in and are able to sort out all the services people want.

SOUTH WATER CAYE

South Water Caye is a 15-acre island 14 miles east of Dangriga that is a part of the South Water Caye Marine Reserve (see below). There are three main hotels on South Water and the reef is close enough that you can easily swim to its edge.

A beautiful caye, South Water is inundated with pelicans who perch on almost every post or pole on the island. I spoke with some people staying at Pelican Beach Resort and they couldn't say enough about how good it was – the food, the sea, the snorkeling, everything.

SOUTH WATER CAYE MARINE RESERVE

This 62-square-mile reserve includes numerous islands, 10 mangrove cayes, two mangrove ranges and a twin caye. A ridge of reef runs the length of the park and is the longest reef ridge in Belize.

The eastern border of the reserve is just east of the drop-off along the reef. The northern border includes the **Man-O-War Caye**, a red mangrove island that houses over 350 nesting frigate birds every year, one of the largest colonies in the Caribbean. Other South Water Caye residents

Male Magnificent frigatebird, its throat inflated in breeding season.

include brown boobies, yellow-crowned night herons and tons of pelicans.

Just south of the Man-O-War is the **Carrie Bow Caye** where, since 1972, the Smithsonian Research Station has been located. The Smithsonian has conducted huge studies on sponges and medicines derived from the ocean. Between Carrie Bow and **Wee Wee Caye** is a sand bore rise, where areas of exposed rock are occupied by nesting sooty terns. Beneath these exposed rocks are huge barracudas and rays.

Twin Cayes has a seaweed farm, the first in Belize and the second in the Caribbean. Run by the Dangriga Development Initiative, the farm was established to replace the fishing business lost when the area was made into a reserve. The seaweed that is being used is actually an algae that looks a bit like tumble weed. It grows well on patch reefs. A hundred pounds (45 kg) of harvested weed dries to about 10 pounds (4.5 kg) of sellable product. It is used mainly as an aphrodisiac, but is also supposed to cure colds, headaches and fatigue. It alleviates problems with glaucoma, arthritis and TB and can be consumed (hidden) in ice cream, cakes, breads and drinks – especially those with alcohol. This last, they claim, really brings out the aphrodisiac's power.

Wippari and **Rendezvous Cayes** form the southern boundary of the marine reserve.

PLACES TO STAY

Blue Marlin Lodge, ☎ 520-2243 or 800-798-1558, www. bluemarlinlodge.com, offers all-inclusive packages for either eight days or five days. You can opt to stay in one of three unique dome-shaped igloos, painted a cool ice blue. There are also nine standard rooms and three upscale cottages. But it

© Blue Marlin Lodge

was the dining room that impressed me the most about this place. The settings were exceptional, everything was spotless and the food was tempting. The drink list included some very nice wines. The cost, US $225 per person, per day, includes meals and two or three dives.

Pelican Pouch Beach Resort, ☎ 520-3044, www.southwatercaye. com/home.html, is at the southern end of the island and is an inviting place, even if it isn't the most luxurious. The grounds are spacious and well kept in traditional colonial style. The dining room is in a wooden building that was formerly a convent belonging to the Sisters of Mercy. Five rooms are on the second floor, above the dining room. All rooms have fans and partial bathrooms; the showers are in a separate building. The price, including all meals and transportation to and from Dangriga, is US $100 a day based on double occupancy. If staying in a cottage, it's another $27

per person. Any activities like diving or snorkeling are extra. This is my choice of places to stay on the island.

International Zoological Expeditions, Leslie Cottages, ☎ 520-5030 or 523-7076, www.ize2belize.com, was one of the first ecological/educational

HOTEL PRICES	
$	$20 to $50
$$	$51 to $75
$$$	$76 to $100
$$$$	$101 to $150
$$$$$	over $150

destinations in Belize. The majority of guests who come to IZE are zoological students and their instructors, who come to study the living museum in the surrounding waters. There is a classroom with videos and reference books. Five cabins are available at a cost of US $135 per person, per day, meals included. Each has a fan, a private bath and hot water. Two of the wooden cabins sit over the mangroves. If you stay in one of these, you can watch the wildlife from the comfort of your room.

© IZE, Inc.

Satellite **Internet** service is available to anyone at IZE for US $5 for 30 minutes.

At the southern end of the South Water Caye Marine Reserve is **Wippari Caye,** ☎ 522-3130, which has four cabins available for US $175 each, meals included. This is mostly a fisher's haunt.

> **AUTHOR NOTE:** *All the tiny skiffs you see floating in calm waters belong to conch divers. Wait a moment and you will see a diver surface, usually with a conch in hand.*

■ GLOVER'S REEF ATOLL

This remote atoll is protected as a UNESCO World Heritage Site. Being from northern Canada, I like the isolation. The atoll sits about 30 miles east of Dangriga and can be reached from Dangriga, Hopkins, Sittee River or Placencia.

Glover's is the smallest of the atolls in Belize. It is about 20 miles long and seven miles wide. In addition to remoteness, it offers some of the best walls in the world for divers and over 700 patch reefs for snorkelers. Because it is a marine reserve, fishing is restricted. The deepest point of the lagoon is about 50 feet (15 meters) and the clarity of the water is exceptional.

Underwater, the reef has more than 60 species of stony coral, over 200 species of fish and uncountable numbers of invertebrates. The 50 miles of walls start at around 25 feet (7.5 meters) and drop to 2,600 feet (780 meters).

The eastern side of the atoll is a wall with a sheer drop of 2,600 feet (780 meters). The western side has a sloping reef. The entire area is on the Bartlett Trough, a fault line.

WHAT'S IN A NAME?

Glover's was named after pirate John Glover who hid among the islands while waiting for Spanish ships, laden with treasures taken from the New World. There are rumors of sunken treasure hidden on the atoll but so far no one has admitted to actually finding anything. With hurricanes adjusting the landscape so often, it is hard to say where the treasures would be today.

The biological diversity of Glover's is another draw for wildlife enthusiasts. The reef has nesting sites for turtles and rare birds, such as the white-capped noddy, white ibis or boat-billed heron. From March to May, whale sharks are frequently seen and, due to the marine reserve status, the numbers of fish and crustaceans have drastically increased.

There are four islands on this atoll. One has a marine biological station and the others have resorts that offer accommodations ranging from a Robinson Crusoe experience to a lush hotel. I personally prefer the Robinson Crusoe experience.

Glover's Marine Reserve includes the entire atoll, as well as all the surrounding waters to a depth of 600 feet (180 meters). There is a no-fishing zone over the southern 20% of the atoll. The rest of the reserve is closely monitored by rangers to ensure that restrictions are adhered to.

Northeast Caye is one of my favorite places in Belize. This is where you can play at being Robinson Crusoe, children are safe, and where the marine life is exceptional. I am from northern Canada and I love this type of environment, but it is not for everyone.

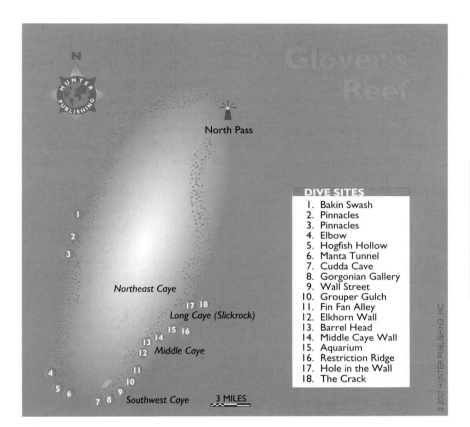

North Pass

DIVE SITES
1. Bakin Swash
2. Pinnacles
3. Pinnacles
4. Elbow
5. Hogfish Hollow
6. Manta Tunnel
7. Cudda Cave
8. Gorgonian Gallery
9. Wall Street
10. Grouper Gulch
11. Fin Fan Alley
12. Elkhorn Wall
13. Barrel Head
14. Middle Caye Wall
15. Aquarium
16. Restriction Ridge
17. Hole in the Wall
18. The Crack

Northeast Caye
Long Caye (Slickrock)
Middle Caye
Southwest Caye

3 MILES

The nine-acre island is owned by the Lomont family, who came to Belize in the 1960s and made it their home. The family purchased the caye in 1978 from Nel Morgan, a descendent of the famous Captain Morgan. Nel's grandfather (not Captain Morgan) is buried on the island beside the big gumbo limbo tree.

From Sittee River or Dangriga, boats to Northeast Caye cost US $350 for up to six people or US $40 per person if taking the scheduled run. If coming from Placencia, the cost is US $400 and from Belize City the cost is US $600 for up to six people. Contact Glover's Atoll Resort, ☎ 520-5016 or 614-8351, www.belizemall.com/gloversatoll.

Accommodations offered at **Glover's Atoll Resort** on Northeast Caye, ☎ 520-5016 or 614-8351, www.glovers.com.bz, are varied. The palmetto huts on the beach have thatched roofs and kitchen facilities. For a homey touch, stairs leading to the sleeping quarters are lined with conch shells. On the porch are hammocks and inside are two beds, a table and mosquito nets. The cost is US $199 per week, per person. The thatch on the roofs lasts about 20 years (unless a hurricane wipes it out completely). The kitchen is below the sleeping area and is basic. There are kerosene stoves and tarps around the upper half that can be lowered if it gets windy. All kitchen utensils are supplied. Night lighting is from kerosene lamps and toilets are the composting kind. Showers use well water, which can be a bit murky, as it is salt water that has filtered through sand. On its journey from the ocean to the well, the water loses its salt but it gains some of the alkaline products from the roots of the palm trees. The Lomonts come in on Saturday and return to the mainland on the following Sunday.

Dorm beds are available. They come with a fully equipped kitchen and cost US $149 a week, including transportation to and from Sittee River. The Lomonts also have camp sites for a mere US $99 a week, including the boat trip.

One advantage of staying on this island is that you can make your own meals. You must bring your own alcohol as there is no bar on the island.

BEWARE: Recently, I have heard complaints about the owners of the island having too much of their own alcohol and making things more than a bit unpleasant for visitors. My advice is to cook your own meals and bring everything you need, including snorkeling gear, and thus be away from the family or be prepared to pay the $350 to get off the island earlier than scheduled. If you are a group, the cost would not be prohibitive, but if you are alone this would be expensive. If you are alone, do not come to this resort.

There are **kayaks** and **canoes** for rent that can be used for getting around the atoll. Or you can sit on one of the many lawn chairs and watch the resident iguanas and scorpions sun themselves.

Snorkeling is good right from shore and can especially be enjoyed by children. While I was there, we went to the wall and in a very short time I saw wahoo, king mackerel, dolphin, barracuda, grouper, Spanish mackerel and tuna. We also saw spotted and southern stingrays, parrotfish, gray angelfish, sergeant majors, banded butterfly and barrel sponge. Plus, there were the fish I can't name.

Divers can go out twice a day and take one night dive. According to recent reports, the dive equipment used at this resort is not maintained properly and can be dangerous.

> **WARNING:** The most recent reports from travelers is that the services here have deteriorated to the point where guests are no longer safe. Please consider other options.

Long Caye Wall dive site was once rated by Jacques Cousteau as one of the three best dives in the world. It has giant elephant ear sponges, Atlantic spadefish, tons of rays, spiny lobster and much more. Other famous sites around Glover's Reef are **The Abyss, Middle Caye Wall, The Crack** and **The Pinnacle**s. The water is so clear that you may be tempted to go deeper than you should. Be aware that the nearest decompression chamber is at Ambergris Caye, a few hours away by fast boat.

Fishers love the flats here, which are seething with permit and bonefish just waiting to give you the fight of your fishing life. Tarpon have been recorded to grow up to eight feet long (2.4 meters). Note that marlin are fished on a catch-and-release basis only.

FISHY FACTS

Parrotfish swim as a harem with only one male. When he dies, the strongest female changes color and her sexual orientation. She becomes the ruler of the harem.

Long Caye is close to Northeast Caye and can be reached by kayak or canoe for a day's activity. This is the island where Slickrock Adventures takes their kayaking groups for a few days' camping. Long Caye and Northeast Caye are the types of islands you see on postcards. Long Caye has the **Off the Wall Dive and Gift Shop**, ☎ 614-6348, www.offthewallbelize.com, where you can purchase some unique tie-died garments. The shop also offers diving courses for all levels. Although I didn't dive with them, I understood that safety was a major concern. This may be because they are not far from Slickrock's camp and Slickrock is very safety-conscious.

Dive prices are reasonable. One dive costs US $40, six dives cost $195 and 12 dives cost $385. Their courses run from US $210 for the "adventure diver" (it takes 1½ days) to $385 for full open water (four days). Rental gear is also inexpensive.

The rustic accommodations at the other end of the island belong to Slickrock. There are thatched-roof cabins and palapas for tenting.

Although they are not available to the general public, by all means poke around to get a feel for what Slickrock offers on guided adventures.

Middle Caye is owned by the Wildlife Conservation Society. Founded in 1895, this group was originally called the New York Zoological Society. The WCS is dedicated to research and conservation and has actively been researching marine life in Belize for more than 20 years. They purchased this 15-acre island in 1994 to establish the Marine Research Station and to provide a Park Headquarters base for the Belize Fisheries Dept.

The station's research is interesting. One of their studies has been on the bleaching of corals. It is believed that coral begin to die in temperatures over 88°F (31°C) and then turn white. Summer 2001 temperatures were slightly higher, but there was no evidence of bleaching. That same year, warm seas off the coast of Australia saw significant bleaching of the coral. There is no explanation.

The WCS has also started looking at the brown seaweed that's starting to cover a lot of the patch reefs in the atoll. The seaweed is thriving due to the reduced numbers of parrotfish and sea urchins, both vegetarians who eat copious amounts of seaweed.

The station's fish preservation program, under the leadership of Belizean scientist Dr. Charles Acosta, has been (in my opinion) hugely successful. The theory to begin with was that if an area was left to its own devices with no fishing/harvesting permitted, fish numbers would increase. Within a short period of time, the no-touch area's conch and lobster increased in number. So did the fish. When the area got crowded, some fish moved over to the unprotected area. This in turn resulted in increased catches for fishers and made tourists happy because they started seeing more marine life.

The scientists working at Glover's are also studying the declining shark and Nassau grouper populations, once so abundant in the Caribbean. One of their goals is to manage these populations.

During daylight hours you are welcome to visit Middle Caye and learn about their latest studies and conservation beliefs. You will be made more than welcome. If you feel that you would like to support this organization and their work, buy one of their fund-raising items (a t-shirt or a hat).

Southwest Caye has two resorts and an adventure base camp run by **Island Expeditions**, ☎ 800-667-1630, www.islandexpeditions. com, $$$$. Guests stay between two and five nights, either as a

Island Expedition's base camp at Glover's Reef.

weekend jaunt or as part of a longer package that includes land excursions. At Glover's Reef, they learn about the reef, using sea kayaks to explore. Facilities include a lodge building and tent-walled cabañas, safari-style tents raised on wooden floors.

Isla Marisol Resort, ☎ 520-2056 or 520-0319, www.islamarisol. com, \$\$\$\$, is owned by the Usher family who have owned the island since the 1940s. This small, intimate resort has five cabins, all wood, all new and designed for couples. Each has fans, louvered windows and private bathrooms with hot water. The restaurant serves excellent foods, often featuring conch, lobster or spicy chicken. The vegetables are brought in fresh from the family's farms on the mainland. A bar sits over the water, away from the cabins.

© Isla Marisol Resort

Manta Resort, ☎ 206-463-0833, 800-326-1724, www.mantaresort. com, \$\$\$\$, has rooms with air conditioning, fans and private bathrooms with hot water. This is a diving/fishing resort where package deals are the best option. The cost is US \$240 per person for a room, three dives a day, all food and locally produced alcohol, as well as transportation from Belize City to the caye and back. Manta also has sailboats, kayaks, canoes and sailboards for guests. There is a gift shop, volleyball court, horseshoe pit and a restaurant. Close to Southwest Caye are numerous dive sites, including **Hole in the Wall, the Barrel Head, Fin Fan Alley** and **Wall Street**. If those names aren't creative enough, how about **Hogfish Hollow**? You can also take diving lessons from dive masters here. The owner, Mike Finstien, owns Manta Resort, Black Bird Caye and the Royal Mayan Spa near San Ignacio. He's also involved with the Tourist Village in Belize City.

CAYES NEAR PLACENCIA

LAUGHING BIRD CAYE

This national park is the southernmost island of the Central Lagoon and measures 1,400 feet long and 120 feet wide (420 x 36 meters). It sits 11 miles east of Placencia on a coral shelf called a faro or shelf atoll. It is made up of 1.8 acres of palm, littoral thicket and mangrove swamp. It drops steeply on the side walls like an atoll. There are only a few like it in the world.

The island once was home to laughing gulls. However, with increased human traffic, the gulls have moved to another island. Laughing Bird Caye was designated a protected area in 1981 and a national park in 1991 in the hope that the birds would return. Since the park has been established, camping has been abolished and mooring buoys have been secured to avoid boat damage to coral. There is a charge of $4 to enter the park.

> **LAUGH A LOT BIRD**
>
> The laughing gull is white with gray wings and a black head. The bird is about 15 inches long (42 cm) and has a distinct hahaha call. A beggar, the laughing gull will crash a picnic party or scoop up garbage that is thrown off fishing boats. It also eats shellfish, crabs and shrimp. Female gulls nest in colonies in tall grasses or on open ground. Every year they lay one to three green/brown eggs that take about 20 days to hatch. The young leave the nest by the time they are five or six weeks old.

Although the laughing birds aren't plentiful at present, there are still tons of frigates and boobies here, and the area around the island offers excellent snorkeling for beginners. Close to the island the reef has been damaged by El Niño, hurricanes and humans, so visibility drops to 100 feet (30 meters). However, farther out the staghorn and elkhorn corals are good. There are also patch reefs and coral ridges close to the island.

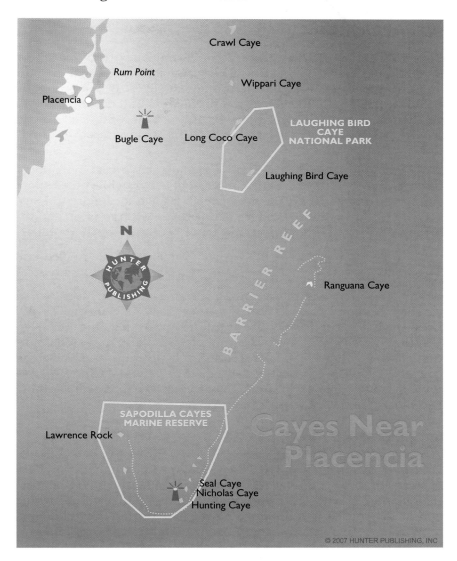

■ RANGUANA CAYE

Ranguana Caye is 18 miles from Placencia, just outside the barrier reef. It is rumored that the Ranguana area has the best bonefish flats in Belize, but I've heard that rumor about other areas. The island has three rustic cabins that stand on stilts along the shore.

Each cabin has two beds, bedding and a stove. Hot showers and toilets are in the central building. Tenting is also available and kayaks are on hand for use by guests.

SAPODILLA CAYES

Sapodilla Cayes Marine Reserve is 28 miles south of Placencia and 40 miles east of Punta Gorda. The reserve was formed in 1996 and encompasses 14 sand and mangrove cayes. It is a one-hour boat ride (US $150) to reach any of the islands that dot the reserve. Of the 76 square miles of reserve, only 2% is land. The rest is mostly patch reefs, sea grass beds, and spur and groove formations.

The outer rim of the reserve has a shallow-water reef, some sections with less than 16 feet (five meters) of water, while other spots emerge during low tide. The area is best known for its pristine lettuce coral that grows on ridges. **Tom Owen's Caye** is on the reserve's northern border and **Lime Caye** is on the southern edge.

LIME CAYE

Lime Caye often has many tourists from Livingston, Guatemala visiting. As many as 9,000 come to these islands each year. Tiny Lime Caye is exceptionally beautiful. It's only a few minutes from Hunting Caye, where there is a military base and a customs station. This is where people traveling by boat enter and leave the country. Lime Caye is part of the Sapodilla Cayes Marine Reserve. If you wish to stay on the island, bring your own food and camping equipment as there are no amenities.

HUNTING CAYE

Hunting Caye has a wonderful beach shaped in a half moon on its eastern shore. This is a favorite nesting place for the hawksbill turtle. Offshore, manta rays and dolphins are often seen and whale sharks are reported to congregate near here during the full moons in March, April and May. There is also a lighthouse, an immigration post and a BDF station.

TURTLE TRIVIA

Hawksbill turtles nest for six months, from July to October. Each female will nest about four or five times during the season and each nesting will be about 14 days apart. She lays around 140 eggs each time, each one measuring about 1.5 inches (4 cm) in diameter. They hatch within 60 days. This means that you could either see a turtle lay her eggs or see the little ones hatch for eight months of the year.

Serenade Island Resort, ☎ 523-3380, www.belizecayes.com/island.htm, has three cabins dotted over four acres of privately owned island, secluded from civilization yet with amenities like electricity, running water, a restaurant and a bar. Although they are not the most luxurious cabins, they are comfortable and clean. Different packages are available. A four-night stay with all meals and a complimentary one-hour massage is US $800. Camping is also available. You can eat in the restaurant or bring your own food and cooking utensils. The resort runs **fishing** trips for US $250 a day, $125 for half a day or $35 an hour. There are jackfish and spadefish, and the great fighting bonefish on the flats near the cayes.

The restaurant sits over the water so you can watch sea life while eating dinner.

The resort has a well-supplied **dive shop** that also carries fishing gear. There must be at least two persons per fishing or diving trip and the cost is US $65 per person. Snorkeling costs $25 per trip; gear is included. You can also rent a canoe or snorkel to get close to other islands and snorkel from there. Canoeing to the other islands, some that are less than 1.2 miles away, is good for bird-watchers, especially around the mangrove islands. Canoes cost $10 per day.

Hunting Caye's dive spots offer the chance to see Atlantic mantas and spotted eagle rays. The predominant corals are staghorn, elkhorn, finger and brain coral.

> **AUTHOR NOTE:** *A fishing license is required for non-nationals and costs US $25. It can be purchased at most tackle shops.*

The Cayes

CAYES NEAR PUNTA GORDA

WILD CANE CAYE

Wild Cane Caye, north of the Puerto Honduras Reserve, was at one time a trading site for the Maya who traveled up and down the coast exchanging products as they went. However, it is believed that 1,200 years ago travelers from the Inca settlements of Tihuanaco in present day Bolivia and Sacsahuaman in Peru would sail across and spend a night on Wild Cane Caye before going inland to trade with the Maya living there.

SNAKE CAYES

Snake Cayes are four islands just 17 miles northeast of Punta Gorda. Under calm seas, you can reach them in 45 minutes. The cayes got their name because they once had lots of boa constrictors living there. These have since disappeared.

Snake Cayes are not part of the barrier reef but are part of an isolated coral ridge growing on a limestone ledge. Most of the islands have mangrove only, but a few coconut trees are starting to grow. Manatees have been spotted near these islands and sea birds abound.

It is on **Middle Snake Caye** that the brown noddy and drilled terns nest. The caye was put into the preservation zone because of this.

East Snake Caye at one time had a lighthouse and was called Lighthouse Caye, but now there are two lighthouses on it. Instead of calling it Two Lighthouse Caye, they changed the name to East Snake Caye.

South Snake Caye has no beach but it is a favorite spot for fishers to pull up lobster and barracuda.

West Snake Caye has an attractive coral beach on its west side. Inland, there is a lagoon where birders stalk. There is a thatched hut just up from the beach where you can get some shade.

PORT HONDURAS MARINE RESERVE

This reserve was established in 2000 and covers 519 square miles of water just off the coast north of Punta Gorda. It begins at a point where seven rivers flow together into an area that has conditions similar to an estuary. This, of course, is prime birdwatching habitat.

The 135 mangrove islands in the reserve house hundreds of species of fish, but the islands are not hospitable to humans, with only 10% of their area in dry land. Gill nets have been abolished in the reserve.

There was a lodge on Mojo Caye, but at time of writing it was up for sale and not being used as a lodge. This could change soon.

DIRECTORIES

■ GENERAL DIRECTORY

THE CAYES – GENERAL DIRECTORY		
■ OUTFITTERS, GUIDES & TOUR OPERATORS		
Amigos del Mar	☎ 226-2706	
Anwar Snorkel Tours	☎ 226-0327	
Aqua Dives	☎ 226-3415	
Blue Hole Dive Center	☎ 226-2634	www.ambergrisdivers.com
Chocolate Tours	☎ 226-0151	chocolate@btl.net
Fido's Fun Sports	☎ 226-3513	
Frenchie's Diving Services	☎ 226-0234	www.belizenet.com/frenchies.html
Island Adventures	☎ 226-4343	
Joe's Bikes	☎ 226-4371	
Larry Parker's Reef Divers	☎ 226-3134	
Off the Wall Dive Shop	☎ 614-6348	www.offthewallbelize.com
Paradise Down Scuba Diving	☎ 226-0437	www.paradisedown.com
Ramon's Village dive shop	☎ 226-2071	www.ramons.com
Sail Sports	☎ 226-4488	www.sailsports.net
Seaduced by Belize	☎ 226-2254	www.ambergriscaye.com/seaduced,
Star Tours	☎ 226-0374	www.startours.bz
Tanisha Tours	☎ 226-2314	www.tanishatours.com
Toucan Canoe	☎ 226-0022	toucancanoe@yahoo.com
Tsunami	☎ 226-0462	www.tsunamiadventures.com
Winnie Estelle Charter	☎ 226-0394	
■ SHOPPING		
Ambergris Art Gallery	☎ 226-2695	
Artesano	☎ 226-2370	
Barefoot Books	☎ 206-2577	www.barefootbooks-belize.com
Beauty of Nature Gift Shop	☎ 226-3310	
Island Super Market	☎ 226-2972	
Toucan Too	☎ 226-2445	

THE CAYES - GENERAL DIRECTORY		
■ SIGHTS/ATTRACTIONS		
Hol Chan Marine Reserve	☎ 226-2247	
■ GROUPS/ORGANIZATIONS		
Green Reef Society	☎ 226-2833	
■ GOLF		
Chapel Caye Golf	☎ 226-8250	
■ TRANSPORT		
Caye Caulker Water Taxi	☎ 203-1969	
■ SERVICES		
Asian Garden Day Spa	☎ 622-5788	www.asiangardendayspa.com
Monchos Golf Cart Rentals	☎ 226-3262	
Polo's Golf Cart Rentals	☎ 226-3542	
Rosie's Massage	☎ 226-3879	
■ USEFUL WEBSITES		
www.ambergriscaye.com		
www.placenciabreeze.com		

■ ACCOMMODATIONS DIRECTORY

THE CAYES - PLACES TO STAY	
Anchorage Resort ($$$)	☎ 226-0304; anchorage@btl.net
Banana Beach Resort ($$$$)	☎ 226-3890; www.bananabeach.com
Banyan Bay Resort ($$$$$)	☎ 226-3739; www.banyanbay.com
Barefoot Caribe Hotel ($$)	☎ 226-0161; www.barefootcariberesorts.com
Belize Yacht Club ($$$$$)	☎ 226-2777; www.belizeyachtclub.com
Blackbird Caye Resort ($$$$$)	☎ 888-271-3483 or 223-2772 www.worlddive.com/destin/land/belize/blackbird.htm
Blue Marlin Lodge ($$$-$$$$)	☎ 520-2243; www.bluemarlinlodge.com
Blue Tang Inn ($$$)	☎ 226-2326; www.bluetanginn.com
Calypso Beach Retreat (n/k)	☎ 303-523-8165; www.calypsobeachretreat.com
Capricorn Resort ($$$$)	☎ 226-2151; www.ambergriscaye.com/capricorn
Captain Morgan's ($$$$$)	☎ 226-2567; www.belizevacation.com
Caribbean Villas (n/k)	☎ 226-2715; www.caribbeanvillashotel.com
Caye Chapel Island Resort ($$$$$)	☎ 226-8250; www.cayechapel.com
Coral Beach Hotel ($$)	☎ 226-2013; www.coralbeach.com
Corona del Mar ($$$-$$$$)	☎ 226-2055; www.belizeone.com/coronadelmar
Changes in Latitudes B & B ($$$)	☎ 226-2986; www.ambergriscaye.com/latitudes
Chocolate's Guest House ($$$)	☎ 226-2151
Cockney Island ($$)	☎ 522-0334; www.belizeseaclub.com

THE CAYES – PLACES TO STAY

Coco Plum Island Resort (n/k)	☎ 520-2041; www.cocoplumcay.com
Coconuts Caribbean Hotel ($$$-$$$$)	☎ 226-3500; www.coconutshotel.com
Coral Bay Villas ($$$$)	☎ 226-3003; www.coralbaybelize.com
De Real Macaw Guest House ($$)	☎ 226-0459; www.derealmacaw.com
Diane's Beach House (n/k)	☎ 226-0083; www.staycayecaulker.com/beachhouse.html
Essene Way	☎ 226-3258
Exotic Caye Beach Resort ($$$$$)	☎ 226-2870; www.belizeisfun.com
Gallows Point Resort ($$$)	☎ 227-3054
Gaviota Coral Reef Resort ($$$)	☎ 509-5032
Glover's Atoll Resort ($$-$$$$)	☎ 520-5016; www.glovers.com.bz
Ignacio's ($$)	☎ 610-2200
Iguana Reef Hotel ($$$)	☎ 226-0213; www.iguanareefinn.com
International Zoological Expeditions	☎ 520-5030; www.ize2belize.com
Isla Marisol Resort (n/k)	☎ 520-2056; www.islamarisol.com
Journey's End Hotel ($$$$$)	☎ 226-2173; www.journeysendresort.com
La Costa Maya ($$)	☎ 226-0122
Lazy Iguana ($$$)	☎ 226-0350; www.lazyiguana.net
Lighthouse Reef Resort ($$$)	☎ 800-423-3114; www.scubabelize.com
Lily's Caribbean Lodge ($$$)	☎ 226-2059
Loraine's Guest House ($)	☎ 206-0163
Manta Resort ($$$$)	☎ 888-271-3483; www.mantaresort.com
Mara's Place ($)	☎ 226-0056
Marin's Guest House ($)	☎ 226-0110
Marta's Place ($$)	☎ 226-2053
Mata Rocks Resort ($$$$)	☎ 226-2336; www.matarocks.com
Mayan Princess Resort ($$$)	☎ 226-2778; www.mayanprincesshotel.com
Ocean's Edge ($$)	☎ 614-9633; oceansedge@btl.net
Paradise Villas ($$$$)	☎ 226-2087; www.belizevilla.com
Pelican's Pouch Beach Resort ($$-$$$)	☎ 520-3044 www.southwatercaye.com/home.html
Pleasure Island Resort ($$$)	☎ 209-4020; www.stgeorgescaypleasure.bz
Popeye's (n/k)	☎ 226-0032
Rainbow Hotel ($$)	☎ 226-0123
Ramon's Village ($$$$-$$$$$)	☎ 226-2071; www.ramons.com
Reef's End Lodge	☎ 522-2419; www.reefsendlodge.com
Ricardo's Beach Huts ($$$$$)	☎ 227-8469
Ruby's ($$)	☎ 226-2063
St. George's Lodge ($$$$)	☎ 220-4444; www.gooddiving.com
Salamander Cabañas ($$$$)	☎ 602-1713; www.salamanderbelize.com

The Cayes

THE CAYES – PLACES TO STAY	
San Pedranos ($$)	☎ 226-2054
San Pedro Holiday Hotel ($$$$)	☎ 226-2014; www.sanpedroholiday.com
San Pedro Inn ($)	☎ 226-3825; www.backpackersbelize.com
Sea View Guest House ($$)	☎ 226-0205; www.belizenet.com/seaview
Serenade Island Resort	☎ 523-3380; www.belizecayes.com/island.htm
Shirley's Cabins ($$-$$$)	☎ 226-0145; www.shirleysguesthouse.com
Spanish Bay Resort ($$)	☎ 220-4024; www.spanishbaybelize.com
Spindrift Resort ($$$)	☎ 226-2174
Steve & Becky's Little ($$$$)	☎ 800-magic-15
Sun Breeze Beach Hotel ($$$$-$$$$$)	☎ 226-2191; www.sunbreeze.net
Tina's Backpacker's Hostel ($)	☎ 226-0351; www.staycayecaulker.com/hostel.html
Tobacco Caye Diving ($$$)	☎ 520-2101; info@tobaccocayediving.com
Tobacco Caye Lodge ($$$$)	☎ 520-5033; www.tclodgebelize.com
Tomas ($$)	☎ 226-2061
Tom's Place ($$)	☎ 226-0102
Tree Tops ($$)	☎ 226-0240; www.treetopsbelize.com/misc.html
Trends ($$)	☎ 226-0097; www.gocayecaulker.com/members/trends.html
Tropical Paradise ($$-$$$)	☎ 226-0124; www.tropicalparadise.bz
Tropics Hotel ($$)	☎ 226-0374; www.startoursbelize.com
Turneffe Flats ($$$$$)	☎ 800-815-1304 or 220-4046; www.tflats.com
Turneffe Island Resort ($$$$$)	☎ 800-628-1447 or 220-4011 http://angleradventures.com/TurneffeIsland/Turnefls.htm
Victoria House ($$$$)	☎ 226-2067
Xanadu Island Resort ($$$$-$$$$$)	☎ 226-2814; www.xanaduresort-belize.com

■ RESTAURANT DIRECTORY

THE CAYES – PLACES TO EAT	
Bare Foot Iguanas	☎ 226-4220
Barefoot Caribe Resort ($$$)	☎ 226-0161
Blue Water Grill ($$)	☎ 226-3347
Caliente ($$)	☎ 226-2170
Capricorn Restaurant ($$$$)	☎ 226-2809; www.ambergriscaye.com/capricorn
Carumba (n/k)	☎ 226-4321; www.ambergriscaye.com/carumba
Celi's ($$$)	☎ 226-2014
Crazy Canucks Bar	☎ 226-2870
Don Corleone ($$$$)	☎ 226-0025
El Patio Restaurant ($$)	☎ 226-3063
Elvi's Kitchen ($$$)	☎ 226-2176

THE CAYES – PLACES TO EAT

Estel's Dine by the Sea	☎ 226-2019
Fido's Sport's Bar	☎ 226-3176
George's Country Kitchen ($$)	☎ 226-4252
Hideaway Sports Lodge ($$$)	☎ 226-2269; www.hideawaysportslodge.com
Jade Garden ($$$)	☎ 226-2506
Jambel Jerk Pit ($$$)	☎ 206-2594
Jerry's Crab Shack ($$)	☎ 206-2552
Lilly's Restaurant ($$$)	☎ 206-2059
Manelly's Ice Cream Shop	☎ 226-2285
Marino's Bar	☎ 206-2389
Mickey's ($$)	☎ 226-2223
Moho Caye Restaurant (n/k)	☎ 223-5350
Palace Casino	☎ 226-3570
Pauly's Pizza Place ($)	☎ 226-2651
Pier Lounge	☎ 226-2002
Purple Parrot ($$$)	☎ 226-2071
Rasta Pasta ($$)	☎ 206-0356
Ruby's Café ($)	☎ 226-2063
Sand Box ($$)	☎ 226-0200
Shark's Bar ($$)	☎ 226-4313
Syd's ($)	☎ 226-0994
Toucan's Pool-side BBQ ($$)	☎ 226-2148
Tropical Paradise Restaurant ($)	☎ 226-0124
Victoria House Restaurant ($$$$)	☎ 226-2067
Wet Willy's bar	☎ 226-4054

Appendix

EMERGENCY CONTACTS

■ EMBASSIES

EMBASSIES	
CHINA, 20 North Park Street, Belize City	☎ 223-1862 or 227-8744
COLUMBIA, 12 St. Matthew Street, Belize City	☎ 223-5623 or 223-3025
COSTA RICA, 11A Handyside Street, Belize City	☎ 223-6525
CUBA, Urban Ave./Manatee Drive, Belize City	☎ 223-5345
EL SALVADOR, 49 Nanche Street, Belmopan	☎ 822-3404
GUATEMALA, 8A Street, Belize City	☎ 223-3150 or 223-3314
HONDURAS, 22 Gabourel Lane, Belize City	☎ 224-5889
MEXICO, 18 North Park Street, Belize City Embassy Square, Belmopan	☎ 223-0194 or 223-0193 ☎ 822-0497 or 822-3837
UNITED KINGDOM, Belmopan	☎ 822-2146 or 822-2717
UNITED STATES, 29 Gabourel Lane, Belize City	☎ 227-7161
VENEZUELA, 19 Orchid Garden, Belmopan	☎ 822-2384 or 822-2789
EUROPEAN COMMISSION, Eyre & Hudson Streets, Belize City	☎ 223-2070

■ CONSULATES

CONSULATES	
AUSTRIA, 16 Regent Street, Belize City	☎ 227-7070
BELGIUM, 126 Freetown Road, Belize City	☎ 223-0748
BRAZIL, 8 Miles Northern Highway, Ladyville	☎ 225-2178
CANADA, 80 Princess Margaret Street, Belize City	☎ 223-1060
CZECH REPUBLIC, 6 Westby Alley, Orange Walk	☎ 322-3373 or 322-2225
CHILE, 109 Hummingbird Highway, Belmopan	☎ 822-2134
COSTA RICA, 7 Shopping Center, Belmopan	☎ 822-3901
DENMARK, 13 Southern Foreshore, Belize City	☎ 227-2172
DOMINICAN REPUBLIC, 10 Roseapple Street, Belmopan	☎ 822-3781
ECUADOR, Mile 1.5 Arenal Road, Benque Viejo	☎ 823-2295
FRANCE, 109 New Road, Belize City	☎ 223-2708
GERMANY, Mile 3.5 Western Highway, Belize City	☎ 222-4371 or 222-4369
GUATEMALA, Church Street, Benque Viejo	☎ 823-2531

CONSULATES	
GUYANA, 7 Barrack Road, Belize City	☎ 223-2469
INDIA, 5789 Goldson Avenue, Belize City	☎ 227-3991
ISRAEL, 4 Albert/Bishop Streets, Belize City	☎ 227-3991 or 223-1432
ITALY, 18 Albert Street, Belize City	☎ 227-8449
JAMAICA, 4 Eve Street, Belize City	☎ 223-5672/5619/5621
Ambergris Avenue, Belmopan	☎ 822-2183
KOREA, 120A New Road, Belize City	☎ 223-5924
LEBANON, Mile 2 Western Highway, Belize City	☎ 224-4146
MOROCCO, Mile 2 Western Highway, Belize City	☎ 224-4154
NETHERLANDS, 14CA Blvd/Banak Street, Belize City	☎ 227-3612
NICARAGUA, 49 North Front Street, Belize City	☎ 224-4488
NORWAY, 1 King Street, Belize City	☎ 227-7031
PANAMA, CA Blvd/Mahogany Street, Belize City	☎ 222-4551
PERU, 33 Freetown Road, Belize City	☎ 223-4487
RUSSIA, 18 A Street/Princess Margaret Drive, Belize City	☎ 223-1151
SURINAME, 5789 Goldson Avenue, Belize City	☎ 223-4487
SWEDEN, 2 Daly Street, Belize City	☎ 224-5176
SWITZERLAND, 41 Albert Street, Belize City	☎ 227-7363 or 227-7185
TRINIDAD & TOBAGO, 56 Regent Street, Belize City	☎ 227-1679
TURKEY, 42 Cleghorn Street, Belize City	☎ 224-4158

BIRDING CHECKLIST

BIRD	DATE	LOCATION
❏ American bittern		
❏ American coot		
❏ American golden plover		
❏ American kestrel		
❏ Amazon kingfisher		
❏ American pygmy kingfisher		
❏ American red start		
❏ American white pelican		
❏ American wigeon		
❏ Anhinga		
❏ Aztec parakeet		
❏ Baird's sandpiper		
❏ Bananaquit		
❏ Bank swallow		
❏ Bare-throated tiger heron		
❏ Barn swallow		
❏ Bay-breasted warbler		
❏ Belted kingfisher		
❏ Black catbird		
❏ Black vulture		
❏ Black-and-white hawk eagle		
❏ Black-and-white warbler		
❏ Black-bellied plover		
❏ Black-bellied whistling duck		
❏ Black-collared hawk		
❏ Black-crowned night heron		
❏ Black-headed saltator		
❏ Black-necked stilt		
❏ Black-shouldered hawk		
❏ Black-throated blue warbler		
❏ Black-throated green warbler		
❏ Blue grosbeak		
❏ Blue-gray gnatcatcher		
❏ Blue-gray tanager		
❏ Blue-winged teal		
❏ Blue-winged warbler		
❏ Boat-billed heron		
❏ Boat-billed flycatcher		
❏ Brown jay		
❏ Brown pelican		
❏ Brown-crested cormorant		
❏ Buff-throated saltator		
❏ Canadian warbler		
❏ Cape May warbler		
❏ Caribbean dove		
❏ Caspian tern		
❏ Cattle egret		
❏ Cave swallow		
❏ Chachalaca		

Appendix

BIRD	DATE	LOCATION
❑ Chestnut-sided warbler		
❑ Clapper rail		
❑ Cliff swallow		
❑ Collared plover		
❑ Common black hawk		
❑ Common ground dove		
❑ Common moorhen		
❑ Common night hawk		
❑ Common pauraque		
❑ Common snipe		
❑ Common yellowthroat		
❑ Crimson-colored tanager		
❑ Dickcissel		
❑ Gray catbird		
❑ Gray hawk		
❑ Gray saltator		
❑ Gray-breasted martin		
❑ Gray-fronted dove		
❑ Gray-headed dove		
❑ Gray-headed kite		
❑ Gray-necked rail		
❑ Great black hawk		
❑ Great blue heron		
❑ Great egret		
❑ Great heron		
❑ Great kiskadee		
❑ Greater yellowlegs		
❑ Green kingfisher		
❑ Green-backed heron		
❑ Green-winged teal		
❑ Gull-billed tern		
❑ Herring gull		
❑ Indigo bunting		
❑ Jabiru stork		
❑ Killdeer		
❑ Laughing gull		
❑ Laughing falcon		
❑ Least bittern		
❑ Least grebe		
❑ Least sandpiper		
❑ Least tern		
❑ Lesser night hawk		
❑ Lesser scaup		
❑ Lesser yellow-headed vulture		
❑ Lesser yellowlegs		
❑ Limpkin		
❑ Little blue heron		
❑ Louisiana's water thrush		
❑ Magnificent frigatebird		
❑ Magnolia warbler		
❑ Mangrove swallow		

BIRD	DATE	LOCATION
❏ Mangrove warbler		
❏ Merlin		
❏ Muscovy duck		
❏ Northern boat-billed heron		
❏ Northern jacana		
❏ Northern parula		
❏ Northern rough-winged swallow		
❏ Northern shoveler		
❏ Northern water thrush		
❏ Olivaceous cormorant		
❏ Osprey		
❏ Pale-vented pigeon		
❏ Pectoral sandpiper		
❏ Peregrine falcon		
❏ Pied-billed grebe		
❏ Potoo		
❏ Prarie warbler		
❏ Prothonotary warbler		
❏ Purple gallinule		
❏ Reddish egret		
❏ Red-winged blackbird		
❏ Ring-billed gull		
❏ Ringed kingfisher		
❏ Roadside hawk		
❏ Roseate spoonbill		
❏ Rose-breasted grosbeak		
❏ Rough-winged swallow		
❏ Royal tern		
❏ Ruddy crake		
❏ Ruddy ground dove		
❏ Ruddy turnstone		
❏ Rufous-necked wood rail		
❏ Sanderling		
❏ Sandhill crane		
❏ Sandwich tern		
❏ Scarlet tanager		
❏ Semipalmated plover		
❏ Short-billed dowitcher		
❏ Snail kite		
❏ Snowy egret		
❏ Snowy plover		
❏ Social flycatcher		
❏ Solitary sandpiper		
❏ Sora		
❏ Summer tanager		
❏ Spotted sandpiper		
❏ Stilt sandpiper		
❏ Sungrebe		
❏ Swainson's thrush		
❏ Swainson's warbler		
❏ Tennessee warbler		

Appendix

BIRD	DATE	LOCATION
☐ Tree swallow		
☐ Tri-colored heron		
☐ Tropical mockingbird		
☐ Turkey vulture		
☐ Upland sandpiper		
☐ Vermilion flycatcher		
☐ Western sandpiper		
☐ Whimbrel		
☐ White ibis		
☐ White-crowned pigeon		
☐ White-rumped sandpiper		
☐ White-tailed hawk		
☐ White-tailed kite		
☐ White-winged dove		
☐ Willet		
☐ Wilson's plover		
☐ Wood stork		
☐ Worm-eating warbler		
☐ Yellow-breasted chat		
☐ Yellow warbler		
☐ Yellow-crowned night heron		
☐ Yellow-throated warbler		
☐ Yucatán jay		

Index